THE STAIR SOCIETY

SELECTED JUSTICIARY CASES

1624-1650

EDITED WITH AN INTRODUCTION

by

J. IRVINE SMITH, M.A., LL.B., Advocate

SHERIFF OF LANARKSHIRE AT GLASGOW

Vol. II.

EDINBURGH

THE STAIR SOCIETY

1972

ISBN 0 90229202 1

PRINTED IN GREAT BRITAIN BY WILLIAM HODGE AND CO., LTD., GLASGOW

CONTENTS

PREFACE

With the appearance of the present volume the Stair Society resumes after a long interval its publication of cases selected from the Books of Adjournal of the Justice Court. This project was begun by the late Sheriff Stair A. Gillon, who in 1953, with the assistance of several collaborators, brought out for the Society a volume of annotated cases drawn from the years 1624 to 1639. In so doing he was following in the steps of Robert Pitcairn who in his *Criminal Trials,* published in the early nineteenth century by the Bannatyne Club at the suggestion of Sir Walter Scott, its President, had extracted trials and other cases occurring in the period from 1488 to 1624. Pitcairn's somewhat subjective principle of selection was adopted by Gillon, namely cases conceived by the Editor to be in content of importance as 'elucidating some historical point or illustrating some features of national character, customs and manners, hitherto but imperfectly known'. The extensive use made of these records by Hume in composing his *Commentaries on the Law of Scotland Respecting Crimes* seemed to Gillon to preclude a selection based on purely legal criteria. The various procedural stages of each case were gathered together by Pitcairn and Gillon to facilitate the reader's understanding.

This enterprise, resumed by Sheriff Gillon, was carried forward for the Stair Society by Sheriff Hector McKechnie on the same basis of selection and editing as before, until illness obliged him to withdraw. The Society then secured the services of another Sheriff, J. Irvine Smith, who is also Honorary Lecturer in the History of Scots Law at Glasgow University, and who was associated with Sheriff McKechnie in the work before he withdrew, to edit and annotate the cases. He has been ably assisted by Miss D. M. Hunter, M.A., Edinburgh who has checked the references and the locations of the geographical names. It is the intention of the Society that this volume will shortly be followed by another bringing the period covered up to the establishment of the Commonwealth in 1650. This will contain an index to all three volumes of Justiciary Cases published by the Stair Society.

I.D.W.

INTRODUCTION

THESE notes do not presume to supersede the introduction, written with such authority, wit and style, with which the late Sheriff Stair Gillon prefaced the first volume of this collection. That introduction indeed was intended to serve for the whole collection from 1624 to 1650 which he had intended to edit, and in it he dealt with the constitution and personnel of the court, with its procedure and its location. What I have attempted instead is to supplement that introduction by drawing attention to certain aspects of the reports which bear particularly upon the history of Scots Criminal Law and Procedure and the administration of justice generally in the country in the first half of the seventeenth century.

At the outset I may perhaps be permitted a word on the circumstances in which I have attempted to edit these cases, and to prepare these notes. I have, I fear, been unable to work on them other than in such leisure time as I have had. I have, therefore, been unable to work on them consistently for any lengthy period, even of days, and I am conscious of how frustrating in the experience, and how unsatisfactory in the result, such sporadic application is likely to be. This may help to explain and to mitigate—though I appreciate it cannot condone—errors and omissions which have escaped myself and those who have been good enough to read a manuscript, which must at times bear the hallmarks of haste. It will also go some way to explain the long delay which has elapsed between my taking over the sole responsibility for the work from the late Sheriff Hector McKechnie and its present publication. Successive literary directors of the Stair Society have borne—with seeming patience at least—the many excuses for the delays I was obliged to offer. The late Sheriff McKechnie invited me to co-operate with him here a year or so before his death. That short co-operation was for me a revealing, instructive and rewarding experience. He had already collected materials which I have found invaluable and, but for these, I fear the delays would have been even greater and the result much the poorer. I would, therefore, acknowledge as fully and as warmly as I can, my personal debt to him, in this, as in so many other aspects of the History of Scots Law, on which he was always ready to give, with humour and charm, of his unrivalled knowledge and judgment. Many friends and colleagues have given me the benefit of their comments. From the present literary director I have had not only indulgence, but practical assistance in preparation of the manuscript for publication, which go far beyond the scope of his official duties. Miss D. M. Hunter, M.A., Edinburgh, undertook the immense labour of checking the references and geographical locations for me. She discussed the notes with me and gave freely of her time and knowledge of seventeenth century Scotland. Without her assistance I would not have been able to keep to the time-tables that were eventually set me. The generous assistance, however, that I have received from all these quarters in no way renders me the less personally responsible for the text, notes and introduction as they now appear. For these the responsibility is mine.

Sheriff Gillon's first volume covered the period 1624 to 1639. There were omitted from it, however, a number of cases for the period 1630 to 1639 which appear in the present collection. The pagination of the present volume follows that of volume 1, and page references to cases in that first volume contained in this introduction and notes are preceded by the figure '1'. The introductory notes in this volume refer to cases printed in volume 1, to the cases printed in the present volume, and to those to be printed in the third projected volume, which is presently with the printers. No page references to that third volume are presently available and cases in it are referred to here by their name and date. In the present text the figures in brackets and heavy type refer to the pages in the original manuscript. In an attempt to make what is frequently an involved and obscure text the more comprehensible I have been liberal of punctuation—non-existent in the original—and of capital letters—in the original used arbitrarily. Where arguments are long and numerous with sub-headings, as for example in the case of *Mr. John Stewart of Ladywell* (p. 424 at 429) and *John Gordon of Haddow* (p. 487) the liberty has been taken of numbering the submissions in brackets in an attempt to introduce some order, which the original clerk found unnecessary. The statutory references are to the Glendook edition of the Laws and Acts of Parliament of Scotland, 3 volumes.

Finally on the mechanics of the matter, I have attempted to divide the introductory notes into sections dealing with particular topics. This has, I fear, led to some overlapping of subject matter and of citation of cases. With such a scheme, however, I have found this fault to be inevitable, and it may be that what has been sacrificed by way of brevity is somewhat redeemed at least—particularly in the absence, as yet, of an index—by having most, if not all, the case references from the manuscript on a particular topic listed in the appropriate section.

The Background.—The cases reported here cover a period of twenty years—a period which witnessed some of the most revolutionary and dramatic incidents in the history of a country not unfamiliar with revolutionary and dramatic incidents. At its start only an occasional ripple stirs the waters of the Carolingian peace. State and Church were apparently at one. The Crown having succeeded to the wealth and security of England is comparatively immune from the rivalries of the great Scottish houses, and, in the phrase of James VI, it is still able to govern Scotland with the pen where its forebears could hardly do so with the sword; and if some might doubt, none were prepared actively to question, the Crown's claims to its ancient prerogatives. The pretensions of the Kirk of John Knox and Andrew Melville having been curbed by His late Majesty—and its once devout son, James VI—though still lingering under the surface, had neither the strength nor the influence to trouble the body politic. At the end of the period all this is changed. The ancient constitution has been destroyed. A revolutionary government is in control. The Crown, though surviving, is bereft of its prerogatives—'The real greatest change at one blow that ever happened to this Kirk and State these 600 years bypast' (Balfour: *Annals II* p. 379). The extreme Presbyterian party is in control of the Kirk, and the reign of the Zealots—attempting to produce a theocracy as rigid as ever Calvin could have envisaged—substituted for what had been, on the whole, a moderate and a benevolent episcopacy.

Through it all—the years of peace and the years of what were known as 'the Troubles'—the Justice's Court sits, and from the nature of the cases coming before it, whatever changes the Covenanters may have wrought in Kirk and State their activities little influenced the criminal activities of the lieges of Scotland. Statute enjoined the holding of Justice ayres twice a year over all the shires of the Realm (1587 c.82), and while some such ayres were held (I. p. 6) their records have disappeared, and from the nature, number and origins of the cases heard in the Justice's Court in Edinburgh, and reported in this collection, it may be concluded that the regular holding of Justice ayres in the localities was unpractical and ignored. The Justice's Court indeed had neither the personnel nor the resources to enable it to conduct the business at Edinburgh as well as in the localities, and if a Privy Council commissioner and his company, sent to apprehend suspects in the North, could be attacked and fired upon by those they were seeking, and the commissioner himself be murdered, it is unlikely that the Justice Court would have fared much better. (*John Grant and Ors.* p. 343). There were arguments, then, equally strong on the grounds of expediency, convenience and safety—at least from the point of view of the court—for its remaining in Edinburgh, and, in the comparative security of the Capital—though even that, on occasion, could be fraught with risk—hearing cases from all parts of Scotland.

But if justice found difficulty in going to the localities, it is hardly surprising that the localities sometimes found even more difficulty in going to the seat of Justice. To have accused, complainers and witnesses, all available at the proper time and place is frequently the despair of a modern public prosecutor. To the seventeenth century prosecutor, public or more often private, is added the responsibility of having not only complainers, pursuers, witnesses and accused, but assisors as well, most of them from parts of the country far removed from Edinburgh, and that at a time when tenuous or non-existent communications made the country geographically and linguistically divided. There are many adjournments because of non-attendance of parties, witnesses or assisors, for which the reports only occasionally give explanations, but these are sufficient to show that geography, the elements and the plague all played their parts, as well as personal reluctance on the part of the individuals concerned. In *Frendraught* v. *Glenkindie and Ors.* (p. 354), 'the stormie season of the year' is the explanation for absent accused. In *Malcolm Durward* (p. 363) neither pursuers, accused, witnesses nor assisors can travel from Aboyne to Edinburgh 'without haizard and perell of all thair lyves in respect of the violent storme and tempest and snaw in the north pairtis' (p. 364). While a court might be able to convene in Edinburgh, trial might be impossible because of plague in other parts of the country. In *Andrew Rattray, McCoule and Ors.* (23rd June 1647), the Messenger-at-Arms responsible for executing the criminal letters, by reason of the plague 'wes incloset and keepit incloset as ane suspect person of the plague' and so could not return the criminal letters, a prerequisite to further procedure. The opposite also could apply. In *Robert Adie* (18th June 1645) the accused gave as excuse for his non-appearance in Edinburgh 'the danger for my compearance in Edinburgh be the infectioun now present thair . . . and for sundry other causes'. To add to these natural difficulties, trouble might arise because of collusion between the Messengers-at-Arms and the accused, resulting in the non-appearance of jurors. In *William Anderson and Ors.* (p. 374), the pursuer explains the non-attendance of jurors on the ground that the Messenger has 'been seduced' from executing the citations because of the defenders or 'utherwais has played the knave'.

The permanent obstacles then were the hazards of bad roads, of tempest, snow and plague and the risks always inherent in travelling through a country in which violence was endemic. Early in the sixteenth century Sir David Lindsay could speak of how 'nane durst ride but into feir of weir' i.e. unless in warlike array, and the picture here has not greatly changed. The fact indeed that one was riding to court rather than for any other business might increase rather than diminish the risk (*Mr. James Mowat* p. 463). In the years after 1638 and particularly in the course of the 1640's, to these hazards, and to the reluctance of men to leave their homes in times of such uncertainty, there were added the very real and aggravated dangers of travelling through a country experiencing the horrors and vicissitudes of war. At the start of the Troubles it is impossible to say whether the occasional delays were due to the new situation or were merely due to a recurrence of the old. From the formation of an active King's party in Scotland, however, and particularly after the advent of Montrose, the situation profoundly changes and during the year of his victories the record of the Justice's Court repeatedly attributes the failure of cases to proceed to the effects of the war in the districts where the charge originates. In *Leslie* v. *Stewart of Ryland* (12th June 1644) it is the jurors who are absent, an absence explained as 'in respect of grit troubles within the north partis . . . the said assisours nawayis durst compear'. Accordingly in respect of 'the grit trubles with in the north pairtis' the Justice-Depute deserts the case. In the same month—it was the month of much military activity in the north-east on the part of the Gordons on one side and the Covenanters on the other,—the Justice-Depute again deserted because of troubles in the country (*George Gledstone*, 5th June 1644). Five months later—the time of Montrose's victory at Tippermuir and his capture of Aberdeen—it was the accused who could not compear 'in respect of the great troubles of the North pairtes of this Kingdom raisit be the Earl of Montrois and utheris Ireish rebels his followers,' and because the accused himself was assisting Argyll against these various rebels (*Thomas Nicolson and Ors.*, 13th November 1644). Again the case was deserted. In March 1645 (*Sir Alexander Irvine of Drum and Ors.*) it was pursuers and assisors who failed to appear and again, 'in respect of the troubles in the North partis so that naither perseweris nor assysours micht peaceablie travel,' the court deserts. On 17th February 1647 neither witnesses nor assisors could be summoned 'be reasoun of the trubilles, outbreks, and insolent miscareiges in the northe pairtes of this kingdom be the malignant persons and thair associateis' and an adjournment was granted in order that at a later date all might 'repair safelie' to court.

Besides affecting the pace of court business 'the Troubles' are occasionally reflected in the subject matter of cases coming before it. Thus in *John Gordon of Haddow* (p. 484) an aftermath of the skirmish known as the Trot of Turriff, became the subject of a charge of murder, and counsel had not only the opportunity of regaling the Bench with an elaborate citation of the Auld Laws but with the novel experience of making submissions on the Law of Arms. A case which anticipates the direction to the jury in *HMA* v. *Sheppard*,

1941 J.C. 67 is *Francis Edmonston and Anor.* (p. 502 and 504) where a charge of mutilation and theft against a serving soldier was deserted when the accused produced an act of the Privy Council narrating that the complainer was a deserter, that the accused was charged to apprehend him, and that any wound the complainer received was in opposing the said commission 'and so he procured the same deservedlie'. In one case, *James Freisch* (13th August 1644), the Justice-Depute sat with two Edinburgh Bailies appointed by Parliamentary Commission, with the Procurator Fiscal prosecuting a case of desertion on the part of a Scottish soldier. Even the foreign wars of the period affected the Scots courts—and that not just in the penalties of banishment to serve in foreign wars, imposed on certain accused. Scots serving abroad could still find themselves subject to the jurisdiction of the Justice's Court, as where Lieutenant John Biggar found himself charged with a slaughter alleged to have occurred 'within the Countie Doun in Ireland' (12th July 1648). Parliament was mindful of the services of the Justice-Deputes in the course of the war. On 18th March 1647 it awarded Robertoun, Justice-Depute, £100 sterling in respect of his services on the Committee of Process and in respect of the references by Parliament to the Justice's Court during the time of the troubles (*APS* VI (1) 761).

Title to Prosecute: Landlords' Responsibility.—The Act 1587 c.77 conferred title on the Lord Advocate and the Treasurer to pursue all slaughters or 'utheris odious crimes although the parties be silent or wald utherwayis privilie agree'. Neither official, however, construed the statute as conferring an undoubted title, and in practice private prosecution remained the normal way of initiating criminal proceedings where a private injury was involved. The King's Advocate is found pursuing alone, principally in cases, like Treason, which concern 'the welfare of the state'. One object of the 1587 Act had been to limit the abuses to which private prosecutions were subject, and the present record, as regards private crimes, demonstrates that while the King's Advocate was not prepared, unless in exceptional circumstances, to supersede the private prosecutor, he could, by granting or withholding his concurrence to private prosecutions, exercise some control over the private prosecutor and, in exceptional circumstances, where the private prosecutor, for whatever reason, failed to act, he could by himself pursue private crimes. The necessity for his concurrence may have been in doubt at the start of the period. Neither in *Alexander Mowbray* (p. 349) nor in *James Haliburton* (p. 389) is there challenge of the pursuer's title, though the King's Advocate does not concur (for other examples see I. p. 34, and 86). By 1648, however, his concurrence is regarded as essential. In *Lyon* v. *George Gordon and Ors.* (12th November 1647 and 1st March 1648) in charges of theft and stouthrief, the pursuer was ready to proceed but in respect that His Majesty's Advocate could not compear to concur with the pursuer, the case was continued.

His Lordship's concurrence however was not always conditional on the existence of *probabilis causa*. It would appear that it was not difficult to obtain, and, on occasions, was certainly given on inadequate investigation. In *James Haliburton* (24th November 1647)—a charge of rape—the prosecution was with the concurrence of the Lord Advocate, but, after a short continuation, the pursuer passed from the charge on the ground that the accused is 'innocent thereof'. In *Adam Brown* (25th January 1643) again the King's Advocate concurred, but the informers eventually declared the panel 'frie and innocent' of charges and passed from the pursuit, because the information they had obtained was 'sinisterouslie maid'. (See also *Donald Foullar*, p. 505). Any proper investigation of such cases would surely have revealed their lack of substance before his Lordship's consent was granted.

The period sees a final attempt made to restrict his title to prosecute where the private party refused to do so. It had long been decided that in cases of homicide the King's Advocate could insist without the concurrence of the kindred of the deceased. His position as regards 'a private crime', involving patrimonial loss was, however, less clear. In the case of *Patrick Bald* (8th February 1649) it was argued that where the private party refused to act all other interest ceases. The Advocate's reply was that he might pursue for crimes without the concurrence of the complainer, and albeit that the complainer desist or collude. However confident his assertion sounded, it may be that the Advocate still had some doubt as to his position, since in that case he took the opportunity of a continuation to obtain a special warrant from the Committee of Estates to prosecute the charges. Whether this move was from necessity, or merely to confirm his title, that title was not again to be open to serious challenge in such a situation. It is, however, impossible at this period to lay down hard and fast rules on this matter. There are a number of cases where the King's Advocate cites a special authority from the Privy Council to prosecute, where such might have been deemed unnecessary. (See e.g. *Charles Goldman* I. p. 65). Where the accused were men of influence and of substance, it was the practice for the Advocate to obtain the authority of the Privy Council to proceed, and in all cases of treason a special warrant from the Crown or Privy Council remained the practice. See *HMA* v. *the Earl of Nithsdale and Viscount Aboyne*, 12th July 1643, and Mackenzie, *Criminals* II. XX.2.)

Alongside acceptance of the Crown's pre-eminence as prosecutor there lingered throughout the period—and that in circumstances never clearly defined—traces of the Roman principle that a member of the public might pursue a crime which did not affect him personally either in kin or property. This is surprising in view of the decision in *Crosbie*, 1616 (Hume II.218)—where, in a charge of theft, the court found 'nae process at thir (i.e. the pursuers) instance for any crime *committed and done others*, except the persons owners of the goods stowin or the King's Advocate were present and insisted on the pursuit of the panels therefor,'—surprising, but nonetheless a fact. Parliament recognised the right by inference at least in cases of Kirk disturbance (1587 c.27), defined by Mackenzie (*Observations* p. 226) as a *crimen publicum* that may be punished at the instance of the minister or any other that will pursue—though in the two cases of it reported here (*Young and Ors. and Menzies and Ors.* 24th July 1649), the Lord Advocate pursues with the procurator of the Church and a minister of Aberdeen respectively, joined with him as 'informers'. Latterly a restricted interpretation may have been placed on the word 'informer', but at this period it can be, and often was, synonymous with 'pursuer'. It is certainly not restricted to prosecutions in cases where the informer has suffered personal bereavement or patrimonial loss. Thus in *John Kirko and*

Herbert Maxwell (p. 507) the Lord Advocate *and the minister* 'pursue' for incest and adultery, and from the record it appears that whatever the reverend pursuer may have lacked in evidence, he made up for it in enthusiasm, and suffered from no misgivings as to his title to pursue. He had already pursued Kirko for incest before parliament and, while passing from the pursuit against him and his co-accused in the Justice Court, he expressly reserved his right to pursue him before the Privy Council. In *Adam Brown* (25th January 1643) the charge is one of opening lockfast places and masterful theft, and the pursuers are initially the Lord Advocate and two private individuals, named Rome. At an adjourned diet the King's Advocate fails to appear but the two informers, designed 'persewaris', formally abandon the pursuit and declare the panel innocent, a formal step they could not have taken had their interest not been accepted as involved, and the court record of the abandonment deemed equivalent to *res judicata.* (See also *Donald Foullar,* p. 505).

Apart from some 32 cases on indictment, the other some 110 prosecutions reported in this and the next volume are initiated by private prosecutors or informers, usually with the concurrence of the Lord Advocate. The 1587 c.77 Act was concerned with situations where parties might 'be silent' i.e. fail to complain or pursue, or where they might 'privilie agree' i.e. settle for payment of a sum of money. Whatever the justification at this period for the former fear—and there was some—there is little doubt that before many of their prosecutions had progressed far, some were prepared 'to privilie agree' (i.e. settle). It is indeed difficult to resist the suspicion that some such prosecutions were but a means used to promote or accelerate what would now be regarded as a reparation claim. This point was expressly made in the case of *James Hart* (p. 332)—though it was hardly appropriate at the stage of relevancy at which it was raised. The defence there complained that the charge was made 'to get ane composition of geir of the puir timorous man'. The jury here acquitted in the teeth of the evidence, but suggested that the Justice deal with the accused to give satisfaction to the deceased's relatives—a suggestion the accused rejected. In theory the King's Advocate in such cases as settled, could and should have continued the prosecutions, but there is a degree of elasticity as to his Lordship's approach, and clearly, where parties were at one, and the crime was not heinous, he was prepared to allow theory to take second place to expediency.

Kirk disturbance and the uncertain position of informer excepted, the title of private prosecutor was restricted to cases in which the individual had a private and peculiar interest, as where he had been wronged personally or wronged in the person of those near to him. As in the imposition of penalties, the law was concerned to vindicate wronged feelings and restrict the desire for revenge by the nature of the penalty it exacted, so in recognising title to prosecute in cases of homicide it accepted that the criminal act, particularly in a country where ties of kin were strong, affected a wider range of the victim's relatives than was subsequently recognised. Mackenzie's claim that title to prosecute, apart from the victim, did not go beyond the degrees wherein marriage was forbidden, has no support in the present period. Besides the relict (i.e. widow or widower) the parents, children, collaterals and 'remanent kin' or next-of-kin of the deceased, are regularly found pursuing for homicides. In *Walter Jameson* (I. p. 84) the private prosecutor who pursues with the consent of the King's Advocate in a charge of murder and slaughter, is a grand nephew of a deceased who died 38 years before. In *John Anderson and Ors.* (p. 409) a child in his mother's arms is named as one of the pursuers. 'Peculiar interest' moreover was not restricted to ties of blood. In cases of homicide a master was recognised as having interest in the loss of his servant and was accordingly entitled to prosecute (*Donald McAngus* I. p. 46). A similar case in the present record is *John MacDonald of Invergarry* (p. 460). The tutor of a child might prosecute, as in the case of Lieutenant Mark Kerr, where the uncle and tutor of a 14 year old boy, allegedly abducted, was admitted as pursuer (2nd November 1649).

Moreover the title of private prosecutor was not restricted as it later became to cases of homicide of a relative. Such title was sustained where a servant was the victim or the crime was of a patrimonial nature. Servants and tenants might of course prosecute on their own (*James Haliburton and Anor.* p. 389), but it generally required the means, courage and determination of a master or landlord if a victim in humble circumstances was to have criminal remedy. Accordingly masters are regularly found prosecuting for injury and loss to their servants as individuals, or along with themselves. In *Walwood* v. *James Gray and James Reid* (p. 387) the master pursues on his own behalf and on behalf of his servant alleging him to have been the victim of assault. Lord Couper (17th February 1647) pursues a similar action in a case of masterful theft and stouthrief of the 'hale guids, gear, plenishing and bestial' against *Andrew Rattray*, and does so as heritable proprietor of the towns and lands specified, and as master to his said tenants. In *Cuthbert* v. *Lachlan McKintosh and Ors.* (28th January 1648) the private pursuer pursues for himself, his daughter and his tenant in charges of assault, abduction, hamesucken and theft. A refinement is introduced in *Alexander Strachan of Glenkindy* (p. 350). The laird of Frendraught—than whom no one in the period can have had greater experience of title to prosecute and its limitations—pursues for himself and 'as maister to his wrakit and oppressit tenants', and as their assignee to 'the reiffis hearschips and depredatiouns lybellyt'. Towards the end of the collection an attempt is made to restrict this principle. In *Innes* v. *James Gordon* (7th July 1648), where the charge was one of theft of victual from the pursuer and his tenants, the defence argued that a master of ground cannot pursue for anything stolen from his tenant if the property belongs to the tenant. The prosecutor answered this by claiming that both he and his tenants were in possession of the victual stolen, and that he pursued for himself and as assignee to the tenants. As happens so often in the present record, the Justice-Depute evaded the opportunity to pronounce on this nice question of title to prosecute, by the convenient device of holding that the libel and the facts were not criminal, and that accordingly the matter should be remitted to the civil judge.

The problem facing a prosecutor, however just, resourceful and determined, where witnesses are terrified, or a community united in its desire to protect the wrongdoer, is one of the perennial problems in the administration of justice. The theory on which the modern system is based, that witnesses will come forward, and having come forward, will testify frankly and honestly in cases of serious crime, in terms of the oath they have taken, is one which anyone familiar with the criminal courts knows falls very far short of reality. In circumstances where political, sectarian or economic interests are at the root of crimes, or relatives are involved, the modern theory usually ceases to bear any relation to reality. It was a predicament, if possible, even more familiar to 16th and 17th century Scotland, where loyalties to clan and kin, as well as self interest and fear, united in certain districts and for certain crimes to produce not only a conspiracy of silence on the facts—and that even where an inquisitorial system was as here in operation—but a protection for the alleged culprit which enabled him to escape any arrest and all questioning.[1] Where such a situation exists today it can only be penetrated—and there but occasionally—by a professional criminal investigation department. It was a situation which was then commonplace, and one for which, in the disturbed state of the country, and in the absence of any police forces, no effective remedy was possible.

One aspect however was recognised, namely, that the only persons amenable to the coercion of the central authorities who could know of and control the activities of professional thieves, often because they were themselves participants, were the chiefs and the landlords among whose men and clansmen the more daring and startling crimes of violence and dishonesty originated. Raiding the cattle of the Lowlands was a way of life for the clans on its borders, a way of life which itself invited and frequently got, personal retaliation. War between the various noble houses and their followers was a characteristic of Scottish history for centuries.[2] In an attempt—and it must be conceded frequently a vain one—to curb this endemic violence, Parliament in 1528 c.6 and 1594 c.227 attempted to make landlords responsible for the activities of in-dwellers on their lands. By the latter Act landlords and bailies were required to find surety to make their men tenants and servants, suspect of crimes, answerable to justice and to produce them to the courts, and provision was made for payment of redress to wronged parties. Practice and precepts did not always go together as far as these statutes were concerned (see *H.M.A.* v. *Alexander McEan and Ors.* 25th November 1647 and *Lachlan McKintosh of Daviot and Ors.* 28th January 1648), but the Acts could occasionally be invoked and enforced. For example in *Alexander Strachan of Glenkindy and Ors.* (p. 350) the pursuit was against a number of noblemen and lairds as landlords and masters to rebels specified in the criminal letters, charging them to enter and present these their tenants before the Justice-Depute. This charge was regarded as no mere formality. The Laird of Glenkindy produced three of his tenants, and excused himself as regards another on the ground that that other was not one of his tenants and so he could not be answerable for him. Another Laird appeared and offered himself ready to defend any of his tenants. The Marquis of Huntly was sufficiently concerned to purchase a suspension of the charge from the Privy Council. The Laird of Innermarkie failed to appear and the court ap-

[1] In the murder of Gordon of Dunkyntie and his son by 'certaine Hieland limmers' in August 1633, the victims' relative, the Marquis of Huntly, tried unsuccessfully to detect offenders. Spalding's comment (*Trubles* I.43) is that 'in all his lyf do his best, he (i.e. Huntly) could never get tryell of this murder, who extendit his moyan to the full thairanent, so he deit but (without) revenge. Sum thocht this strange, that the gryt Marquess of Huntly sould see his blood destroyit without tryell or reparatioun.'

[2] 'If two nobles of equal rank happened to be very near neighbours quarrels and even shedding of blood is a common thing between them and their very retainers cannot meet without strife.' John Major, *History*, Scottish History Society p. 48.

pointed a diet of proof at which the pursuer by his own oath and the evidence of two witnesses might prove against that party, 'the quantities, as pryces' of the items stolen (p. 357). Such a case, however, does no more than demonstrate that the statutes in question were not in desuetude; their contribution to producing law and order, so far as the present record is concerned, was negligible.

Where these statutes were not invoked, the prosecutor on occasions prosecuted the landlord for harbouring or resetting those who, it was alleged had committed crimes, or as being art and part of them. (See *John Grant and Ors.* p. 343; *Lady Rothiemay* p. 359.)

Inquisitorial Procedure.—What could have been the disastrous effects of the system of sporadic and arbitrary private prosecution was somewhat mitigated by the form taken by criminal procedure once a charge was intended or proferred. What is in operation in Scotland in the period of these reports—and, with some important qualifications, it was indeed to survive until 1908—is an Inquisitorial system bearing most of the hallmarks of the mature inquisitorial systems of Europe. Seventeenth century Scots law had a profound and, what some might consider as a proper regard for the ascertainment of the facts of a case, as the principal object of criminal procedure. It had indeed little alternative but to adopt such an approach when around it was a situation often bordering on anarchy, and at certain times and places crossing that border. It is a dangerous predicament in which communities from time to time find themselves. Some appreciate the danger and react more quickly than others. Seventeenth century Scottish reaction was to place in the hands of a number of tribunals and individuals, powers to investigate in a judicial or *quasi* judicial manner the origin of crimes attaining notoriety in the community, and allegations against persons suspected of crimes. The tribunals were concerned with ascertaining facts, not with providing rules whereby two sides might, more or less decorously, sublimate a trial by combat in words, and they would have regarded as unrealistic and dangerous, if not perverse, any system in which an accused person could not be examined, confronted with the evidence against him, and asked for his explanation, and in which the verdict might turn on considerations which bore little or no relation to the facts.

They did not believe that a witness's recollection was likely to be improved by the passage of time, and acted upon that conclusion. In this context they considered that value and weight should attach to depositions of witnesses taken by a judicial tribunal, in particular, shortly after the event. A statement made on deposition in the course of an inquisition was, in the majority of cases, the evidence which was adduced to the trial either by production of that deposition alone, or by the witness formally adhering to it. There was, therefore, little opportunity for the witness to have, what he so frequently has today, namely second thoughts on the matter, and the right to appear in the witness box and to say, with comparative immunity, that what, a few days after the event, he claimed he saw, was never seen, never said, or never meant.

Such depositions were taken with care and with patience (see for example, *James Mowat and Ors.* p. 463) and in circumstances which, in the main, went a long way to justify the weight that was placed upon them. The local or lower tribunals which took them were judicial in character. They usually consisted of several individuals, and these, from their designations at least, were men responsible and experienced in life. They frequently came from the locality of the crime and so could be expected to be in a position to direct their questions along relevant lines. Before the Church courts and in the Justice's Court there is evidence of the accused being represented at such investigations and of his being permitted to put what in effect were cross-interrogatories. The procedure also meant that witnesses could be examined in their own locality and so saved the trouble and time of a journey to Edinburgh (John Littil I. p. 174).

This inquisitorial system at this period can be observed operating at four different levels, and some cases can involve more than one of these levels.

1. In cases which produced local notoriety, as by the gravity and nature of the crime, or the scandal it attracted, local Kirk sessions or magistrates, or a combination of both might carry out investigation of witnesses and of suspects.

2. In cases of serious crime or offences which peculiarly concerned the state, as leasing-making, false-coining or riot, pre-trial investigation by Parliament, the Privy Council or its commissioners, or by one or more Lords of Session, or by a combination of these was common. Here also, the accused or suspect was liable for examination as well as witnesses.

3. The Lord Advocate or his Deputes and/or the Justice-Depute or Deputes could examine suspect and witnesses in cases where a suspect was apprehended, but criminal charges had not yet been preferred.

4. Where a criminal charge had been preferred by indictment or criminal letters the examination of witnesses as a stage in the criminal proceedings, was normally undertaken by one or more of the Justice-Deputes, usually with the Crown represented, and on occasions the defence also. The evidence so taken lay *in retentis* to be produced at the trial.

There was no reason why investigations should not be made by two, more, or all of such bodies or individuals from them. In *William McCrae* (20th February 1650) it took five years for a particularly savage and aggravated charge of rape—the victim was an 18-year-old, bed-ridden girl—to reach the Justice's Court. The circumstances of the case were such, however, as to attract widespread attention and concern and the resulting investigation illustrates how the inquisitorial system could operate in the period. In a case so notorious there is no question of investigation being confined to one tribunal or individual. First of all the complainer was examined at her home on 15th March 1645, a few days after the alleged event, by the minister of North Berwick, the Session Clerk and certain Elders. Eight days later the complainer, her parents and four neighbours were examined by the Kirk Session of North Berwick and depositions taken. On 9th April three of the witnesses were examined in Edinburgh by Lord Tofts, a Lord of Session, and the Justice-Depute Robertoun, who also examined the complainer and took a further deposition from her. Two months later the Justice-Depute Colville and a committee consisting of the Minister of North Berwick, a notary public, who was also Session Clerk, and another man, re-examined the complainer's father. Both the examining Justice-Deputes presided at the trial. No doubt the fact that the accused was on active service as a soldier explains the delay in bringing the case to court, but when he was eventually put to the knowledge of an Assize, the majority of whose members were from

North Berwick, it was on the depositions alone, so frequently and so carefully taken, that the prosecution successfully relied for a conviction.

Investigation by the Kirk Session or Magistrates.—There are many examples of local investigations by Kirk Sessions or Magistrates or representatives of both. The immediate object of such investigations, especially where the scandal related to witchcraft, incest, adultery or some other of the 'sin' crimes of the day, was to ascertain if proceedings before the Kirk Session were necessary. The result of many such investigations was, in the first instance, proceedings before the Session or other Church court which might end in ex-communication, a sentence of itself attended by grave civil consequences. Thereafter, however, what had been cognosced upon by the Church courts was taken up by the private pursuer and by the Crown. 'Sin crimes' were their main concern but they could and did competently investigate and decide, often with the accused represented, such matters as 'the quality of the murder'—whether a homicide is done of wilful intent or whether it was accidental. Having decided it was the former, they could initiate proceedings which resulted in the accused being ex-communicated, and finally could make the whole evidence, decision and sentence in the Church courts available to pursuers or prosecutor to found on in the criminal courts. (See *William Fraser* p. 443.) Where they considered there was a breach of the law, inappropriate for action by themselves, they could bring the matter before the proper authority. When Thomas McKie, a former Sheriff Clerk of Wigton, banished for forgery, illegally returned to Scotland, it was the Presbytery of Wigton who reported the matter to the General Assembly, who in their turn brought it before Parliament, who ordered his arrest (p. 538). Depositions taken before Church courts were accorded great weight. In the eyes of the Lord Advocate at this period—though not by Mackenzie's time (*Criminals II. XXIV.5*)—a deposition taken before and certified by the Presbytery 'is judicial albeit nocht civil and sua man mak faith,' (*Isobel Young* I. p. 114). The Kirk Session inquiry was not always favourable to the prosecution. It could favour the defence and its results be made available to the defence, in a subsequent trial in the Justice Court as in *John Young* p. 313 at 314. (On this matter of Kirk Session investigation see the section on Sexual Crimes, below.)

Investigation by Privy Council and Parliament.—Parliament, the supreme judicatorie (Mackenzie, *Criminals II. III. I.*), initiates enquiries particularly, but not exclusively, into cases involving political considerations. Thus in *John Stewart of Ladywell* (p. 423) a committee of the Estates of Parliament investigated the whole matter (p. 431), took what the minute describes as 'all lawful tryell, both be writt and witnesses,' examined the accused on oath, held that what was not confessed by the accused, was proven by witnesses, found the accused guilty and remitted to the Justice's Court for punishment. Where Parliament or Privy Council made preliminary investigation it was common for it to appoint certain of its members to sit in the Justice's Court at subsequent proceedings before him. Parliament might investigate charges of lesser crimes, as it did in the case of *Christian Pringle and Ors.* (3rd July 1649). There, Parliament appointed a Committee of Investigation under the Justice-Depute, who examined *inter alios* the panels on a charge of theft by housebreaking, and, on consideration of its report, the accused were acquitted.

The practice of the Privy Council investigating accusations by means of letters of precognition or *super inquirendis*, described in the note to *James Johnston* (p. 324 at 326) were exceptional procedures, the effect of which was generally to supersede process before the Justice's Court. Parliament and Privy Council could lend the majesty of their name and the intimidation of their methods, however, to the preliminary investigation of crimes eventually disposed of by the ordinary criminal courts. The Privy Council was particularly concerned with keeping the public peace and with offences concerning public welfare. Accordingly, in a charge of devising and counterfeiting of 'fals and adulterat money,' John Galloway and Bartilimo Gilmour are almost certainly the prisoners examined by a committee of the Privy Council on the 8th December, 1636 (*RPC*[2] VI. 34). The Committee consisted of Lord Lorn, the Bishop of Moray, the Depute Treasurer, the Lord Advocate, the Justice-Clerk and the Justice-Depute, or any three of them and their commission gave them power 'as they shall find cause' to put the accused to torture for discovery of their accomplices. If there were accomplices these were not disclosed, but in the circumstances, the confession by the two suspects is not surprising (p. 330).

Investigation by the Justice-Deputes.—Having no control over the evidence on which the jury proceeded, and no duty to charge them on the law or on the facts of a case, the effective and significant functions of the Justice-Depute were to investigate the facts either before or after the service of the indictment or criminal letters or both before and after, to determine questions of relevancy, to supervise procedure in court, and, on an admission or verdict of guilty, to impose sentence, either on his own initiative or after consultation with the Privy Council. In practice the exercise of the first of these functions tended to lighten his Lordship's labours as regards the others—with the exception of the last.

In some cases preliminary enquiries before any libel has been raised are carried out by the Justice-Depute acting alone, with one or other of his colleagues, with the Kirk Sessions or their members, or with inferior or superior judges. In *Alexander Milne* 4th July 1649, he examined with a Baron Bailie. The officials who joined him in *William McCrae* have already been noted. In *Thomas Nicolson and Ors.* (13th November 1664) he was ordered by Parliament to precognosce the case and to report to them before allowing the case to go to a jury.

Where a case is in court the normal procedure, after relevancy has been determined, and before the jury is empanelled, is for the Justice-Depute to appoint a time for the examination of the prosecution witnesses. This is carried out in the presence of representatives of the Crown and often in the presence of the panel and/or his representatives (see *John Husband* 11th November 1647) and both sides could submit interrogatories—which, on occasions at least, were numbered—that they wished put to the witnesses (p. 472). This procedure is followed even where jurors are available in court (*John Husband*

11th November 1647). A variation was for the Justice-Depute to take the evidence of a witness in the presence of the accused and of the unempanelled jurors (*Alexander Milne*, 4th July 1649). In one case (1. p. 280) where the panel was unrepresented at the examination of witnesses, the court ordered that the depositions be made available to the defence for their consideration. Where the defence objected to the evidence of a witness being received, the witness was examined and the defence objection noted. The objection, however, appears academic since, in such a situation, the controversial deposition went to the jury. The inference from this, and from the submission noted, is that the question of the competency of the witness was left to the jury (*James Mowat*, p. 463). Where it was suspected that witnesses might fail to appear for examination, as where they had been outlawed for failure to answer their citation, the court, before examining them, might give them the opportunity of relaxing themselves from the horning and in the meantime 'commit thame to ward to remaine thairin unto the tym they war examinat upon the facts and deidis containit' in the criminal letters (*Alexander Strachan of Glenkindy* p. 351 at 356). The evidence so taken could then lie *in retentis*, and as regards the witness it became a matter of indifference whether he again disappeared or not.

Statements so taken were in the majority of cases read or produced to the jury. On occasions a witness might be adduced formally to adhere to his deposition; on rarer occasions he might testify before the jury (*David Howison*, 28th July 1643), but neither was deemed necessary. There is one example in the present record of witnesses who had been examined by the Justice-Depute being ordained to be present at the trial, not only to 'verifie and make good thair depositiouns' but also to declare 'what farder shall be interrogat of them aither be the pursuers or the panel anent thair knowledge of the slauchter,' (*Gavin and Lues Marshall*, 20th December 1643).

The apparent contradiction between the practices of taking, adducing and founding on such depositions, and the terms of the Act of 1587 c.91, requiring that the whole proof be adduced in the presence of accused and assize gave the defence occasional misgivings, but none, it would appear, to the Crown, to the Court, to the Privy Council or to Parliament, who alone might have remedied the situation. The Lord Advocate's view of the practice was that 'it is an very ordinar and allowable custom that the witnesses be ressavit and examinat before the mater pass to ane assyse, and their depositiouns to be keepit *in retentis*, and thaireftir producet to the assyze for thair informatioun, quhilk the pursuer refers to the Justice' (*Mungo Rose and Ors*. 31st July 1646).

It would be perhaps be crediting the Justice-Depute with unprecedented restraint to expect him when examining accused and witnesses to confine himself to questions submitted to him by the parties. The Justice-Depute moreover was apparently not even expected to remain impartial. He was not faulted if, on a plea of Not Guilty, he heard the witnesses, came to his own conclusions and put these conclusions to the accused with the suggestion that he admit the charge. In *John Morrison and Ors*. (p. 524 at 527), where there was not only a plea of Not Guilty but a Special Defence of Impeachment, the Justice-Depute examined the Crown witnesses and was evidently convinced by them. Next day when the trial was due to start he clearly regarded the plea of Not Guilty as perverse and notwithstanding the presence of two experienced advocates—Nisbett and Baird—

for the defence, he proceeded to demand of the panel 'Gif he had come to ane remorse of conscience for the slauchter committit (the word will be noted) in the manner specifeit in his dittay, and earnestly desyrit (him) to cum to ane cleir confessioun thairof' (the word 'confession' will also be observed). It may be that his Lordship had been advised that a plea of guilty would be forthcoming before he so disclosed his mind in the matter. If he had not, however, the panel was unusually accommodating since, to his Lordship, the report reads, he, 'with great repentance, confessit'.

Whatever the personnel and status of the investigating tribunal, the evidence of the suspect and accused himself was regarded as of critical importance and herein the truly inquisitorial nature of the procedure is apparent. The idea that the suspect should be immune from questioning by the body charged with investigating the facts would have been scorned by contemporaries as irrelevant and unrealistic. The criminal law was then conducting an unceasing rear-guard action against lawlessness in all its forms and it was impossible in such a situation for it to ignore a weapon so effective to the proof of guilt and therefor to its object, as compelling the accused to answer questions. No doubt, in the hands of the later Stuarts, the inquisitorial system pursued by the use of torture produced a violent reaction against it whose effects are still felt. In the period of the present record, however, the system was accepted without question. It would be attributing to the investigating tribunals a degree of impartiality to which they would have laid no claim, nor indeed wished to have laid any claim, to suggest that their questioning of a suspect was directed primarily to obtaining his version of the events, though this they would obtain. That someone had become suspect or accused, presumes the existence of depositions or 'bruit' (rumour) against him. The investigating tribunal examined him knowing what the evidence or 'bruit' was against him. No doubt in the majority of cases they were convinced of his guilt beforehand, were untrammelled by the concepts of fairness to the accused, and directed their questioning to obtaining what they regarded as that 'most secure' of all forms of proof, namely, a confession. With this and with this by itself the prosecution could ask for a verdict of guilty from a jury. Repeatedly in the present collection the prosecutor relies on the confessions of the panel emitted before Ministers, Kirk Session, Magistrates, Justice-Depute, Privy Council or Parliament. The confession is either simply produced or, if taken before other officials than the Justice-Depute, it may be ratified and approved by one or more of that body to whom it was originally made (*Duncan McGregor* 15th July 1643). The accused himself might ratify a confession as did *Margaret Cunningham* (p. 534) and *Margaret Chalmers* (19th January 1648). Such an accommodating attitude was hardly to be expected from more hardened accused but, so far as the court was concerned, such an attitude was unnecessary. The original confessing deposition sufficed, even where the panel—and it happened but rarely—having confessed on examination, then denied the charge at the trial diet. Where a confession had been obtained, further to dispute the charge was but to delay the inevitable. In the case of *Alexander Hamilton*, a 'Warlock,' (I. p. 143) having obtained a confession from him in examination, at the trial diet the court asked him if he would abide by his confession or resile in any way from it. It is difficult to resist the view that this was a mere matter of formality. His fate, even before his formal plea of guilty, was sealed. The option is narrated as given him 'as he sould ansuer befoir the tribunall sait of Christ before quhome he is schoirtlie to compear'. That last phrase must have given him clear indication of what was expected of him and what was to be his fate.

The competency of statements obtained from an accused in such an examination was not restricted to the trial of that accused. There is no rule that statements made outwith the presence of an accused are inadmissible against him. A statement obtained from one accused incriminating another could be competently used against that other as and when he was brought to trial. Thus in *Margaret Cunningham* (p. 534) a confession made before the Kirk by one adulterer was subsequently used at the trial of the other, and in the trial of *Catherine Oswald* for Witchcraft, the Crown relied for proof on one charge, upon a deposition made by another witch before her conviction in an entirely separate prosecution and renewed by her at the stake (I. p. 139. For another example see *John Burgh*, 24th November 1643).

Another aspect of the inquisitorial system that is encountered is the 'confrontation' of accused by complainers, and of witnesses by counter-witnesses, not only in the course of preliminary investigations but at the trial itself. Thus in November 1629, in a charge of witchcraft, the Privy Council (*RPC*[2] III. p. 345) in granting commission to the Bishop of Dunblane, the King's Advocate and the Justice-Depute to examine two alleged witches, conferred also power to confront them with others who can give best evidence, and in the case of *John Burgh* (24th November 1643)—again a charge of witchcraft —one of the adminicles of evidence against him was the incriminating statement of another witch, since executed, who adhered to her statement at her trial and who, before her execution, had been confronted with Burgh. When being examined before the Privy Council on her knowledge of the burning of Frendraught Tower, *Margaret Wood* (I. p. 161) made certain incriminating statements against another person. That person was then in custody and was brought forth of his ward 'in presence of the Counsall and confrontit with the panel'. An example of confrontation in the course of a trial occurred in that of *William Fraser* (p. 443). There the panel's father gave a disputed account as to what had happened in proceedings before the Church courts. Two Ministers who had given evidence earlier in the case were thereupon recalled, 'confronted' with the witness, and given the opportunity of deponing on their version of what he claimed had happened (p. 451). If a prosecutor in the inquisitorial system wanted argument in support of the effectiveness of the process of confrontation, he could cite it from the case of Margaret Wood, because there, when she was confronted with the witness, 'the panel being convict in conscience granted her former deposition to be false' (I. p. 161).

Testimony obtained in such preliminary investigations was equivalent to evidence given on oath before a court. Thus a witness could be prosecuted for committing perjury before a Privy Council investigation. The Lord Advocate in one case took what could be regarded as a somewhat exaggerated view of such an incident. He claimed that an accused had 'made fals depositioun . . . made in the presence of the Lords of His Majesty's Counsall, quhairin she can nae mair be excusat nor gif she had committed murder with her ain hands'—but however extreme the simile, his Lordship's meaning is clear. (*Margaret Wood* I. p. 161.) There is only one case which is an exception to the binding nature of the pre-trial deposition, namely, *John McKathie and Ors.* (20th November 1646). Here, a first accused, in a civil process arising out of the same facts as subsequently formed the basis of a criminal charge, was alleged to have made a deposition before the Bailies of the Canongate incriminating one of his co-accused. The deposition was produced. In the Justice Court, however, that first accused denied the deposition and 'past from it'. The court gave no decision on what *prima facie* was an incompetent step by the accused. Perhaps because the deposition had been made in a civil process, or because the case was ultimately dealt with by referring it to an arbiter, and so treated as raising a civil question, the normal rule was ignored.

Torture was competent only to the Privy Council and Parliament but there is little evidence of its use in the present record. In only three cases—cases of witchcraft excepted—is it mentioned, and there only as threatened. In one case the Privy Council (*RPC*2 VI. 347) threaten it in the case of two accused suspected of coining offences and that for the purpose of discovering their accomplices. If in that case it was in fact used, it failed in its object (*John Galloway and Anor.* p. 330). Another case refers to circumstances in which torture might have been appropriate. There, on a narrative that the accused had made contradictory statements in his depositions, the private prosecutor petitioned the Privy Council asking them to order the accused to prove an alibi for the night of the crime and to terrify him by torture because of his inconsistent depositions. That the panel had made such contradictory statements apparently gave rise to a presumption of guilt, where torture would have been competent to the Privy Council. They did not, however, accede to the petition, but remitted the case to the Justice-Depute (*John Littil* I. p. 174-5). Parliament authorised torture by the Magistrates of Montrose in *Robert Walker and Ors.* (p. 536), a particularly deliberate and aggravated murder, but again there is no record of that torture being carried out.

When it came to witchcraft, however, torture in all but name, and frequently in name also, was applied to all victims. They were examined for the devil's mark, at which investigation the Justice-Depute is on occasion recorded as presiding (I. p. 140). They were deprived of sleep. The English Commissioners in 1652 heard how confessions were forced from certain alleged witches by the Kirk. The accused claimed they were forced into confessions by 'exceeding torture'. Their thumbs were tied behind them and they were then hung up by them. They were then whipped, after which lighted candles were set to the soles of their feet and between their toes. Lighted candles were put in their mouths and their heads were burned. Four of six accused died of this torture. Another who was suspected of witchcraft was kept twenty-eight days on bread and water, being stripped naked and laid on a cold stone with only a hair-cloth over her. Others had hair shirts dipped in vinegar put on them to remove the skin (*Spottiswoode Miscellany* ii.91). By the stage they emitted their confessions, the sanity and responsibility of such victims are in doubt, and only a mind insane or *in extremis* can explain the circumstantial confessions to sexual intercourse with the devil, the bewitching of animals, the murdering of others by spells and all the other extravagancies which make up the charges and confessions of witchcraft in the present collection. (See for example *Jean Craig* 27th April 1649.)

If torture, however, does not much figure, pressure is the only word that can be used to describe certain of the methods used by, or accompanying the enquiries, of some at least of these inquisitorial tribunals. No limits were apparently set on the Justice-Depute's power to remand in custody pending enquiry or trial. A panel aged 12 at the time of the crime was warded for two and a quarter years before being brought before the criminal court (13th December 1646 *Margaret Lambert*). *Patrick Meldrum of Iden* (20th November 1646) was detained in custody from August 1646 until July 1647. *Margaret Cunningham* (p. 534) charged with adultery and murder of the resulting child, confessed to the murder in circumstances, where the desire for a confession clearly outweighed all sense of humanity on the part of the investigators. She confessed to a committee consisting of two Edinburgh Ministers, a Bailie, a Reader, and a Merchant Burgess who assembled to examine her when she was bedridden after she had been 'brocht up to the Tolbooth of Edinburgh in ane wand (wicker bed').

Where the accused refused to emit the desired confession and could not be brought to see the error of his ways at a first examination, repeated interrogation was tried. *John Rylay* (21st July 1643) was imprisoned for some ten weeks before trial on a charge of rape and when the trial finally commenced he had been 'dyverse tymes examinat'. He remained obdurate however, and with justification. The pursuers eventually preferred a compromise to a conviction and agreed to his voluntary banishment. Pause, however, should be given to any temptation to condemn out of hand such repeated interrogation. Today repeated questioning of a witness or suspect outwith the actual trial is condemned. Repeated, protracted and often abusive questioning of a witness or accused in the process of cross-examination in the witness box is not only permitted, it is sometimes commended as a valuable forensic skill. In the seventeenth century the situations were simply reversed.

The Charge, Criminal Letters and Indictment.—Long practice required that the libel, be it by criminal letters at the instance of a private prosecutor, or by indictment at the instance of the Crown, must specify certain matters; names of parties, day, year, place, cause of complaint and damage (*Quoniam Attachiamenta* c.80; Mackenzie, *Criminals* II.XXI.2). In the present collection it is the exception for the libel to enter the record, but where it does, 'the cause of complaint and damage,' the circumstances of the crime, are given in great and circumstantial detail (I. p. 254; Hume, II. p. 285). In the majority of cases no accused duly served could complain that he did not have detailed notice of the circumstances which the prosecutor claimed established the charge and distinguished the accused's act from others of the same class. After the Restoration when the Not Proven verdict as a special verdict was introduced, it is claimed that the prosecutor came to specify the facts in the libel on which the jury was to be invited to pronounce, with greater detail than formerly (*Introduction to Scottish Legal History,* Stair Society Vol. 20 p. 442). Having regard to the occasional libel reproduced here, however, it is difficult to see how more detail could have been included. The elaboration with which the facts are set forth explains the frequency and the prolixity of the defence pleas to the relevancy. The greater the detail given, the greater is the opportunity for argument that some or all of the facts libelled do not support the conclusion of the crime charged having been committed, or, if committed, having been committed by the panel.

The exception to this is where an accused is charged with acting art and part. Here, the circumstances of the crime are specified but the precise part played by the panel, so accused, is not. The tradition that he should have such notice died hard in the hands of defence counsel, and is still invoked in the present collection. Parliament, however, wearied of the diverse exceptions and objections, had enacted that it was sufficient for relevancy that such an accused be simply charged as art and part of the crime libelled (1592 c.153). The circumstances from which accession was inferred, however, were wider than today. The test of accession was still *inter alia* those by whose counsel, direction or assistance the crime is committed (Mackenzie II.XXXV.I.) but it also involved acts subsequent to the crime, 'as by ratihabiting or resetting' (Mackenzie, *Criminals* II.XXXV. 7 and 8), particularly where there had been some accession prior to the deed. To establish accession, however, it was unnecessary for the prosecutor to either libel or prove what precisely the panel had done by way of counsel or assistance. His mere presence could be enough. In modern law only in charges of mobbing and rioting and certain charges of forming part of a disorderly crowd is it sufficient for the prosecutor to prove presence in the mob or crowd to secure a conviction (per Lord Cockburn in *Cairns and Others* 18th Dec. 1837, 1 Swinton p. 605). In such cases a common purpose is attributed to all those present in the mob (Hume, *Commentaries*, I. p. 422-3), because such presence of itself may render substantial assistance. In other crimes, however, mere presence with persons accused does not now, in the absence of evidence inferring counsel or assistance, establish accession (*HMA* v. *Kerr and Ors.*, 1872 2 Couper 334). Where crimes of violence against a person and crimes against property were committed by groups in the seventeenth century, however, the law applied a test similar to that presently applied in charges of mobbing and rioting. It inferred participation from mere presence. In this, in the circumstances of the time, it was being realistic. One did not consort with such a group of rievers as the 'oppin and notorious rebellis callit the licht horsemen,' (p. 319) or ride with John Dow McGregor and his band of broken men (p. 343), without knowing what one was doing. Thus, throughout the collection, 'being in company' with a principal accused, or being found with a group which had committed criminal acts, was of itself deemed sufficient to infer concert. Thus in *Patrick Gilroy and Ors.* (I. p. 268), two are charged with being art and part and being in company with the principal accused, in charges of housebreaking, theft and stouthrief. The Crown's view of accession in theft was that those who 'resseves, makis use of, and disponis upon thois stowin (stolen) goodis, and keepis up cumpenie with the steillaris thairof without reveilling and delyvering the one or the other unto the judge or the pairtie' were partakers of the theft (*James Hay of Muiryfauld* 20th November 1646). In *Callum McKerracher* (I. p. 288), the charge is 'reset of theft and keeping company with thieves and broken men in thair deeds thir money years bygain'. There is a similar libel in charges of abduction, housebreaking and theft in *Duncan McGregor*: 'art and part and for being in company of John Dow McGregor and others, their complices, all broken men' (15th July 1643). In *Duncan Watson and Ors.* (p. 319) the libel is keeping company with the others and so 'art and part with them of the haill heirschipis'. Such an approach necessarily made matters much easier for the prosecution. Such association itself could, of course, amount to a substantive crime, as where in *Duncan Watson and Ors.* (p. 319) one charge relates to being in company with the 'licht horsemen' after the Royal Proclamation prohibiting inter-communing with them, or in *John Grant and Ors.* (p. 343) where one of the charges is reset of rebels. The high-water mark of the principle is *Gray and Reid* (p. 387), a charge of treasonable wounding. The non-compearing accused, Gray, is alleged to have struck the blow. The only allegation against Reid is that he was in company with his co-accused. (For an elaborate discussion of the law of art and part in relation to theft and reset see the report in the case of *James Hay of Muiryfauld*, 20th November 1646).

In three respects, however, at least by the standards of even the late seventeenth century and subsequently, the accused at this time found himself at a disadvantage in relation to the terms of the libel: First, specification of the date of the crime was not regarded as critical unless where the defence asked for its specification with a view to pleading alibi, and even then there was no onus on the prosecution to prove the date (Mackenzie, *Criminals* II.XXI.2).

Secondly, long passage of time, even of decades, conferred no immunity to prosecution either in law or in fact. There is no law of prescription of crimes. Its existence indeed is not even considered as a valid argument on the relevancy of long delayed indictments. Libels are raised many years after the event when precise specification is impossible, and the type of evidence available, by any standard, unreliable.

Thirdly, while circumstantial specification of the principal charge or charges was given, the prosecutor who had been careless in his drafting, or unlucky in his witnesses, had the unusual advantage of being able to conclude his libel with some vague charge, unspecific as to time and place, which might succeed if all else failed.

The latitude as to time claimed by and accorded to prosecutors proceeded on the principle that the fact of the crime was critical, its date largely irrelevant. They thereby escaped the bane of many a modern pleader, namely, the inability of the average witness to condescend upon date. Thus in *John Gordon* (12th March 1645) charges of bigamy and adultery are undated. In *Alexander Mowbray* (p. 349) theft or reset is charged over a period of eight consecutive months or 'at leist in ane or uther of the saidis monethis'. In *James Haliburton* (p. 389) a charge of assault is libelled as 'in ane or other of the days of October last' 1639. Such latitude as this is perhaps unexceptionable. Not so, however, those libels where such is the latitude claimed that specification of the locality as well as of time becomes impossible. In *James Neilson and Ors.* (I. p. 29) a libel of using false measures reads that between January 1600 and August 1625 at leist in ane or uther of the said monethis and years of God respective' the panels had so acted in various unspecified markets and fairs within the Kingdom. In *Callum McKerrocher* (I. p. 288) unspecific charges of theft and reset are libelled as having occurred 'thir mony zeiris bygane'.

Stale Prosecutions.—Passage of time, even of decades, conferred no immunity upon a suspect either in law or in practice, and he could never know when some past criminal act might be resurrected at the instigation of a vindictive or covetous private prosecutor, bent on obtaining assythment, who may have known nothing of the deed or of the victim, or at the instigation of a public prosecutor anxious to lend colour and weight to a more recent charge by invoking one from the past, or ready to use such a stale charge for political ends. The latitude allowed as to time not only negatives any suggestion that prescription of crime applied but, in practice, resulted in prosecutions so stale that many could only be brought home to an accused by his own confession or by invoking hearsay, and the remainder were inevitably liable to put an accused in a position of grave danger and embarrassment if he were minded to attempt to resist them. There are many instances in the present collection of such stale prosecutions. Thus, in *John Gordon* (I. p. 61) an alleged slaughter in February 1613 is brought to court in January 1627. In July 1630 the court is concerned with a slaughter allegedly occurring 35 years earlier when the accused was 13 (*Duncan Campbell* I. p. 149). At the end of the day this charge was submitted to arbitration, but neither the competency nor the injustice of it or of arbitration after such a time, was challenged. *James Wilson*, on 20th December 1649, faced a charge of incest alleged to have taken place 'a threttie fyve zeir since or thairby'. In *William Dalgarnock* (p. 551) a charge of theft by housebreaking and opening lockfast places is alleged to have occurred thirteen and a half years earlier. Where witchcraft was involved there was no limit to either the vagueness of the charges or the antiquity of their date. Thus, for example, in *John Dick and his spouse* (21st March 1649), two charges of murder by casting spells came to trial twelve and twenty-two years respectively after the alleged events. To prove murder by human agencies after such delays would have been difficult enough; to prove murder by supernatural powers might have been thought impossible. The panel here, however, did not put her prosecutors to such trouble since she 'confessit all' in the presence of the Minister of Tranent and 'divers famous witnesses'.

It seems probable that such stale crimes were resurrected only where the panel found himself on another more up-to-date charge, and the prosecutor wished to invoke the earlier charge simply to lend the latter weight and credibility. Thus in *James Wilson* (20th December 1649) a charge of incest thirty-five years earlier, is linked with what is a more recent, but still unspecified, charge of adultery. Again, however, proof of the earlier charge would surely have been impossible, but the panel pled to both.

Even those engaged on the administration of justice were not immune from stale charges arising from allegedly incompetent and illegal discharge of their office. Thus, in *Maxwell of Broomholme* (p. 401), 'a Judge and Baillie-depute of the Lordship of Eskdale,' is charged in 1641 with the murder of two thieves, convicted by a jury in his court some eighteen years earlier, in that he sentenced them to death by drowning. The issue in the case was whether the panels had been taken 'with the fang,' that is with the stolen property, in their possession. If they had been, the execution was competent, if they had not, the prosecution contention, to which the Lord Advocate lent his name and presence in court, was that the execution would have amounted to murder. The panel here stood in some danger since the Baron court minute did not specify that in fact the original accused had been taken with the fang, and the matter only ended by the King himself intervening to stop the proceedings. The case well illustrates the possible dangers in which such stale prosecutions might place a party. There is, moreover, the suggestion here that the prosecution arose not from the belated malice of private prosecutor, who after all could have acted much earlier, and who did not appear at the Bar (p. 402), but from political motives (see p. 409 note 6). Either situation demonstrates the predicament in which an accused might find himself in such a case.

Vague Unspecified Charges.—Where there are a series of charges it is common for the libel to conclude with some vague general allegation of violent or criminal conduct, incapable of proof in the modern sense. Thus, a schoolmaster charged with incest, had also to face a charge that he was a 'vyle and filthy lievir and abuser of his body at diverse tymes' with his scholars (I. 95-6). An even vaguer charge was that which concluded the libel against *George Weir and Anor.* in 1638, namely 'of common thift and pykrie in steilling and cutting of pursis in dyverse mercatis and faires within this Kingdom thir dyverse zeirs bygane' (p. 366). A similar charge—'and for commoun thyft and commoun resset of thyft etc.'—had been sustained in *George Wright* (I. p. 222). In *James Neilson and Ors.* (I. p. 29), the charge libels *inter alia* that between 1600 and 1625 the panels 'in dyverse faires and mercatis' within the Kingdom, bought clothes with false yardsticks, without other specifications. The case of *Callum McKerracher* (I. p. 288), which libels unspecific charges of common theft, common reset of theft and keeping company with thieves and broken men 'thir mony zeirs bygane,' has already been noted. Similar charges were libelled in the lower courts. The last charge against the deceased in the case of *Maxwell of Broomholme* (p. 401 at 404) was of 'common thift, resset of thift, in-fang and out-fang and pykrie etc.'. (See also Croft Dickinson: *Court Book of Carnwath* p. 56, 61.)

In such situations if proof was thin or doubts remained on any of the specific charges, such an appeal to the accused's previous bad character could hardly fail to make good such deficiencies. Alternatively, if the prosecutor failed on the specific charges, with such a vague charge, and relying on the local knowledge of the jurors, he could at least hope to secure a conviction on something.

Representation.—The Crown is represented by the Lord Advocate himself, or, where he produces a mandate, by an Advocate-Depute. The Advocate appears personally in a high proportion of the cases, especially when the office is held by Sir Thomas Hope, and his deep involvement in the political issues of the day never wholly isolates him from his primary function of representing the Crown in the criminal courts. Private prosecutors are usually represented by Advocates but these have no exclusive right of audience in the Justice's Court, and Writers and Solicitors frequently appear (e.g. *George Currour* I. p. 209, *William Anderson and Ors.* p. 374, *George Anderson of Braco and Ors.* p. 385). An Advocate's 'servitor' or 'devil' can appear, particularly on formal matters (*Stewarts* v. *Mercer and Others* 30th June 1643; *Fraser* v. *Irving of Drum*, 14th March 1645). Occasionally the private pursuer is represented by a layman. In one case

(*William Anderson and Ors.* 374 at p. 376) where the Lord Advocate appears for the Crown interest, Alexander Kycht, writer, appears producing his mandate as procurator for the private prosecutor. While there is nothing apparently to preclude a Writer from conducting the whole case, in practice, he generally only appears alone where proceedings are of a formal nature.

Where an accused has confessed in the preliminary investigations, and where he admits guilt at the diet of trial, he is not usually legally represented. Where, however, he disputes the charge, legal representation is common, and where he is a person of substance—here with but one exception (namely *Mr. John Stewart,* p. 423)—such representation is not only common, it is invariable, and it is often multiple. One, two or three Advocates are regularly found appearing for one accused, and on occasions each is found making submissions on particular aspects of the case, or acting much as junior and senior might do at the present day (see *James Hay of Muiryfauld,* 20th November 1646). There was no reason why all accused persons should not have been legally represented. The Act 1587 c.38 entitled them to be represented by Advocates and prelocutors, and a later Act of the same year (c.91) empowered the court to compel Advocates and Procurators to appear for those 'accused of treason or for quhatsumevir crime'. Practice confirms that the court was prepared to use this power, and to use it regardless of the status of the accused. The Court of Session appointed counsel for the Countess of Errol in 1597 (Pitcairn I (11) 367) and in a case where some accused were apparently able to instruct counsel on their own behalf, a remaining co-accused, apparently of humble origin has two counsel to act for him, 'conform to ain command of the Lords given to them' (*John Littil and Ors.* I. p. 172). While the court was prepared to use this power, it had, however, to be asked to use it. The availability of free legal advice then, as now, does not mean that an accused will necessarily avail himself of it. The attitude of some accused in this respect does not change from the 17th to 20th centuries. By indifference, by choice, by design, by the hope of further delaying trial, or by the hope of evoking jury or judicial sympathy by appearing unrepresented on the day, then, as now, accused are found appearing for themselves. The attitude of the courts then, and now, was similar. If he delayed taking steps to secure legal representation then the fact that he appeared alone was his own responsibility. In *James Ramsay* (p. 315) a plea from the accused that he was unrepresented was met by the reply that he could have had counsel appointed for him had he applied to the Privy Council or Court of Session. The Lord Advocate Hope's comment in that case in 1635, that it was not the practice of the Justice's Court to delay criminal prosecution 'in default of procuratouris to defend, specially qhair the pairtie defenderis uses na diligence thameselffis to haif procuratouris for thair lauchfull defence'—is the same argument as commended itself to Lord Justice-Clerk Thomson in 1959 (*Thomson* v. *H.M. Advocate* 1959 J.C. p. 15 at p. 18). Last minute instructions were not unknown, even where the panel should have known better. Sir John Stewart of Methven (I. 92) is represented by two counsel whose first motion to the court—in the result successful—is that the diet be continued 'that in the meanetyme the prelocutouris mycht haif tyme to advyse and prepair thameselffis seeing they had nocht as zit red the summondis' (I. p. 93).

Advocates in criminal causes, says Mackenzie, 'are called prolocutours',

(*Criminals* II.XX.2). The term prolocutor here includes all members of the legal profession, Advocates, Writers, Solicitors, but in addition it includes persons who can lay no claim to the possession of legal qualifications. The idea that one was better with one's friends at court than with a lawyer died hard. The pursuer's prolocutors in the case against *Thomas Crombie* were four lairds (I. 19). In *David Rattray, McCoule and Ors.*, the 'servitor' to a laird appeared for three of the panels (23rd June 1647). When Francis Edmonston was tried for acts done in the course of military service, his prolocutors were an Advocate, a Writer and his Commanding Officer (p. 502). In *James Ramsay and Anor.* (p. 315) the accused's prolocutor was Lord Spynie, whose principal qualification for appearing—and none could gainsay its relevance—was that he himself had been convicted by the Regality court of St. Andrews of 'invading and bluding' the pursuer, i.e. he had himself been convicted of the offences for which the panel was now being prosecuted. *Ludovic Stewart* (28th February 1648) in a case arising from a feud between Sir George Maxwell, his Laird and superior, and Sir James Maxwell, is represented by the former. Even where a laird or superior did not act as prolocutor, he might lend his support to his follower by attendance at court. When *James Hart,* burgess of Stirling, came up for trial on a charge of slaughter on the High Street of Stirling, the defence complained that the Lords Mar and Stirling 'sitting in the heighest roume' compeared with the pursuers—the daughters of the deceased and the Crown—and were 'assisters of the perseweris in this persuite'. The prosecution however claimed that they only were there as spectators (p. 332 at 333). Such lay representation might be for only part of the process, as where James Muir nominated a merchant to represent him at the examination of the witnesses by the Justice-Depute (p. 523).

Some accused considered that forensic effort should be supplemented by more primitive, extra-judicial, and what are and have always been more proven, methods. *Thomas Crombie* and his co-accused, already referred to (I. p. 18), charged with slaughter, were represented by no less than four advocates. Steps, however, had been taken to supplement this legal assistance by ways only hinted at in the official record. There, the only mention of supporters for the accused is a reference at the conclusion of the report, when the prosecution abandons, and the accused protests at the great charges and expenses 'that their friends and well-wishers has sestenit in cuming sae far frome thair ane hooses to the Burgh of Edinburgh' for the trial. The friends and well-wishers, however, were not a small group of anxious relatives, intent on following the accused's fortunes at court. The panel was accompanied from Perth to Edinburgh by 80 burgesses, 5 earls, 6 lords and 26 barons 'on the burgh of Perth's desire to back him' in his defence. (*Chronicles of Perth*, Maitland Club). It would perhaps be too much to expect that the pursuers' having eventually received 'certain and sure informations of the panel's innocency' of the charge, and their abandonment of it, was entirely unconnected with his being attended by such a noble, numerous and distinguished concourse.

Lay representation in court, however, is the exception. Where a charge is to be disputed the panel generally has the benefit of legal representation, generally by an advocate, on occasions, especially where the proceedings are formal, by a writer or solicitor; sometimes where there are more than one accused, both advocate and writer are found acting together (*Andrew*

Wilson and Anor. p. 458). A criminal bar is emerging or has emerged. Certain counsel appear again and again for the defence. Thomas Nicolson, James Baird, John Gilmour, John Nisbett, David Heriot, Roger Mowat are among the more popular names who found the criminal bar a fertile source of business.

Their reputations must have been based on different considerations than those of their modern successors. There was little room for the eloquence and the emotion, the personal involvement and the indignation, frequently regarded as the hallmark of the modern successful Scottish Criminal Jury pleader. Evidence was generally in the form of written depositions and the jury included some of the witnesses, and it is impossible to effectively cross-examine on written depositions, and difficult to demonstrate that a critical witness is unreliable or a downright liar when the witness himself is a member of the jury and likely to be its foreman. (*George Norie*, p. 514, 518, note 2.) Where the principal question was whether the facts libelled in the indictment were proved, where the jury might be expected to know these facts from their own knowledge, and where evidence 'contrair the libel' was incompetent or discouraged—though in the present period that rule is becoming relaxed—the main efforts of defence counsel were devoted to learned and laborious debates on the facts narrated in the criminal letters and indictments, with the object of having these dismissed, in whole or in part, on the ground of irrelevancy. In pursuit of this object there was no limit to the ingenuity, enthusiasm, patience, courage, time, and often, it is to be feared, indiscretion of the pleaders. Their arguments tended to be without end, and with Replies, Duplies, Triplies, Quadruplies, Quintuplies and so on, the submissions moved further and further away from the brutal, sordid or bloody circumstances of the crime. It would be difficult to blame the bench if it, as a matter of course, shared the exasperation expressed openly on one occasion at least by the Lord Advocate, when (*Margaret Woode*, I. p. 154 at 163) he protested that 'seeing the panel and her prolocutouris has beene hard at grit length, that thairfoir the judges wald declair the process to be closet, and the parties be no farder hard; desyreing the Justice to anser thairupon'. It is difficult to know whether to admire more the patience of bench or that of bar; that of bench because of the prolixity, and, it is to be feared, insubstantial nature of many of the defence submissions, to which, it appears from the record, it was obliged to listen and see recorded; or that of the bar, because the apparent indifferences of the bench to their industry and learning, never appears to have dismayed or deterred them. If results are the test of a successful debate on relevancy, rarely is any part of their plea sustained, and the learned Justice-Depute does not even do them the courtesy of offering them his reasons for rejecting their pleas. (For an example see *James Hay of Muiryfauld*, 20th November 1646, where a lengthy and substantive argument on relevancy provokes no opinion from the justice-depute notwithstanding numerous continuations). It seems doubtful indeed if the Bench sometimes even heard these elaborate submissions. Where the clerk of court could fail to note the court's disposal of a defence motion because of 'the tumult quhilk was in the house or tolbuith that day' (p. 470), it can be assumed that on such occasions counsel had more to contend with than judicial indifference. Limits of neither time nor subject appear to have been placed on their submissions. In the course of such debates questions of pure relevancy were mixed with matters of fact and arguments on probabilities. (See *James Hart* p. 332.) The only excuse for some such submissions must be that, while they may not have penetrated the ears or mind of the justice-depute, they might be calculated to influence some of the potential assisors who were listening to them from the body of the court. No doubt, also, the panels on whose behalf they were advanced, derived from them some encouragement and satisfaction, if not comprehension.

When it came to the evidence by which the facts libelled were to be proved the defence was virtually powerless. All evidence was relevant, and all relevant evidence was competent, and a plea to the competency of a particular witness was rare. There is evidence here that, when the Justice-Depute examined witnesses, defence counsel were entitled to put 'cross-interrogatories' but, it seems probable that these were not put arising out of testimony given in chief, but were written interrogatories. (See *James Mowat* p. 463.)

On rare occasions counsel are reported as making submissions after the evidence is led. The report of the trial of *William Fraser* (p. 443) records the evidence at unusual length and thereafter the submissions of prosecution and defence counsel. Each spoke twice, the defence having the last word. It seems probable, however, that these submissions were directed to the Justice-Depute rather than to the jury. Certain of them were directed to the competency of witnesses which ought to, but may not, have been a matter for the Justice-Depute rather than the jury, and the Latin maxims with which counsel liberally studded his submissions were unlikely to have much persuasive effect upon the jurors. In *James Mowat* (p. 463) where again the evidence is given at length, defence counsel criticised the witnesses and their testimony in detail, and, whether this was directed at the jury or the bench, it was undoubtedly expressed in the jury's presence. Here, in addition, counsel did address the jury desiring them to note the uncertainty of the oaths of the pursuers and criticising certain of the witnesses. If counsel habitually failed to make much impression upon the Justice-Depute the fact does not appear to have deterred them from continuing to try. Where counsel appeared, few accused here can claim that he had not prepared his brief. Even where the most hopeless case was disputed, counsel spared no efforts. There is only one case in which there is suspicion that counsel were afraid to do their duty, namely the case of *Mr. John Stewart of Ladywell,* (423) prosecuted for leasing-making, a sinister and a disturbing prosecution even for that age. He alone of these many accused, claimed he was unable to find counsel to act for him.

The Court.—Of the four Justice-Deputes, Colville of Blair, Robertoun, Heriot and Henderson, who preside in the court during the period, by far the greater part of the work is carried out by Colville and Robertoun. The former, appointed in 1607, sat continuously until 1650, and was to survive the Commonwealth to preside again until 1664 (see I. p. 5-6). They sit singly or in pairs and, in cases of importance, could be joined by the Justice-General. The Privy Council and Parliament might also appoint assessors to sit with them, particularly where either body had conducted preliminary investigations (see *Mr. John Stewart of Ladywell*, p. 423). This practice of appointing assessors was followed, at least until the early eighteenth century, and the presence on the trial court of members of the tribunal which had already carried out preliminary investigations into the charge, afforded a cogent disincentive to any witness wishing to depart from any deposition he had earlier given (see the Trial of Captain Green, 1705 State Trials XIV. No. 438) but, while Parliament and Privy Council might appoint assessors to assist the Justice-Depute in the conduct of a trial, and no doubt also to ensure that such trial was brought to what they deemed its proper conclusion, and while both might be consulted by the Justice-Depute on matters of sentence, neither is found exercising any effective control over what were at times apparently arbitrary and unjudicial actings on the part of the Justice-Depute. If the panel at this period was on occasions liable to be put at a disadvantage by the latitude of time claimed and the antiquity of certain of the charges made in the indictment and criminal letters, he was invariably subject to what at times appear to come perilously close to the whims and caprices of the Justice-Deputes in matters of procedure. It is perhaps too much to hope that their Lordships would be prevailed upon to give reasons for their almost invariable rejection of the pleas to the relevancy so frequently and so protractedly argued before them. Not only did many of the arguments hardly merit a reasoned decision, but, where there is no appeal court on such matters, his Lordship might have been forgiven for taking the view that a reasoned decision was hardly necessary. More difficult to understand is the refusal of the bench again and again to face up to and to resolve what were undoubtedly questions of substance argued before it on relevancy. An example is *Innes* v. *James Gordon* (7th July 1648), where a master pursued a charge of theft from himself and his tenants. The defence raised the question of his title to sue on behalf of his tenants where the property belonged to them, even where the master pursued as the assignee. This was a pure question of relevancy, and one raising, what at that period, was undoubtedly a question of importance. There remained, moreover, the question of fact, namely, the allegation of theft from the pursuer himself. The refusal of the Justice-Depute either to deal with the question of relevancy or to permit the trial to proceed on the charge of theft from the pursuer, was and remains, incomprehensible. No reason other than that he found the libel and facts to be not criminal is given for his remitting the matter to the civil judge. A similar course was taken in *Kennedy* v. *Thomas Donan* (p. 367) where, on criminal letters libelling opening lockfast places and theft of documents, the Justice-Depute held the facts to be 'naways capital or criminal . . . but altogidder civil and so competent to the civil judge to be cognoscit civilie'. The Justice-Depute's procrastination in such matters of law earned the occasional rebuke of the Lord Advocate (see *Lady Rothiemay* I. p. 285) but it made little difference. Where, as in *James Baillie* (p. 400), when the case came before the court, parties were agreed the matter was civil, the Justice was content to let the matter drop.

Not only were decisions on novel questions of law rare, there is evidence for the view that the Justice-Depute was on certain matters in the fortunate position of not being obliged to take such decisions on his own responsibility. If the question was whether an Act of Parliament was in desuetude or the extent of its application, he could seek the advice of the Lords of Session (*Alexander Gourlay* I. p. 49). If the defence argument raised difficult questions on the interpretation of the Act of Oblivion, he could continue the case that in the meantime he might be advised by the Lords of the Privy Council 'anent the pronouncing of his interlocutor' (*John Gordon of Haddow* p. 484). If on granting an adjournment he was in doubt as to detaining the panel in custody he could ask the advice of Parliament (*Patrick Meldrum*, 20th November 1646). The nature and practice of such references indicate that the status of the Justice's Court on matters of law and procedure was very much subordinate to the Privy Council.

The Justice-Depute must bear responsibility for what, in practice, is one of the main characteristics of the seventeenth century system, namely, the absence of any comprehensive code of criminal procedure and the absence of any formal standards of court practice. Once the case was before him, the Justice-Depute in practice—and subject to such references to Parliament and Privy Council as he cared to make—enjoyed a complete control over its procedure, and convenience did not even dictate that he follow the procedural precedents which he himself had set in earlier cases. Where statute or practice had enjoined that certain procedures be followed—as for example the fundamental requirements of the Act 1587 c.91 requiring the whole proof to be adduced in the presence of assize and accused—these are frequently ignored, without comment from parties, and certainly without remedy to them. So far as the present record is concerned, moreover, in the main the Justice-Depute exercised his powers without attempt at consistency and without offering the pleaders any reasons for his often conflicting decisions. It required an extreme situation to produce an exception to this state of affairs, as in *Janet Corsar* (p. 414) where he refused to allow the Lord Advocate to pursue for a different crime than that libelled. He had indeed achieved a consummation devoutly to be wished by those exercising judicial function: he was entitled to order a particular course of action without having to offer any reasons for his decision and without having to justify his decision, since, for all practical purposes, it was unappealable. The power of the Privy Council to supervise lower courts was not a power that in practice was exercised in the circumstances or in the manner of an appellate tribunal. If indeed arguments were required to prove the necessity for an appeal court not only to ensure that the lower court was put right where it went wrong, but by the mere existence of the right to appeal, to ensure that the lower court exercised its powers with discretion and accordance with practice, they are to be found, and to be found in abundance, throughout the present record.

The instances are many and cover every stage and aspect of criminal procedure. The following are but some of the more extreme examples.

The accused was entitled to be served with a copy of the indictment or criminal letters. The fact that this had not been done, however, in some cases, did not prevent the court from insisting that the case proceed. *Lady Rothiemay* (I. p. 278) indeed had not even received an accurate or complete abridgement. The Justice-Depute nevertheless proceeded to hear the witnesses, and that apparently in the absence of the panel and her counsel. In *William Anderson and Ors.* (p. 374) the accused only received a 'tikit' (i.e. an abridgment of the charge) 'nawayis conteneing the circumstances of tyme, place and maner' of the slaughter charged. In *Margaret Wood* the indictment before the court was 'disconforme to the coppie delyverit to the pannell,' and the defence motion for an adjournment to consult with their client was refused (I. p. 154-5). *John Morrison* (p. 524) was only a little more fortunate when he protested that he had not received a copy of the charge and knew nothing of its details. He was allowed sight of the charge, but only on the condition that he agreed to the immediate examination of the prosecution witnesses (p. 527).

The court apparently took no exception to business being carried out in its absence. On such occasions when the Justice-Depute is not present his functions could be carried out by the Depute-Clerk of Justiciary (*John McDonald* p. 460) or the diet is simply deserted (*Henry Sunter of Magus,* 15th November 1644). On one occasion the court is minuted as consisting of the Justice-Clerk and two sergeants (*John Irving* v. *Ors.* p. 380). On all these occasions, however, the business was formal, and no doubt this had been known to the Justice-Depute beforehand and explains his absence.

It is in the course of the trial, however, that the court is able to indulge its unpredictable and arbitrary conduct to extremes. The commonest example is disregard of the provisions of the Act of 1587 c.91 requiring that the whole probation be led in the presence of assize and accused. The court's disregard for the express provisions of this statute is so regular and so flagrant that the Act might as well have been in desuetude. The usual procedure, as has been noted, was for the Justice-Depute to appoint a diet at which he took the evidence of the witnesses, and at the trial, the depositions so taken, were simply produced. Even this practice, however, could vary in detail. The Justice-Depute could examine the witnesses outwith the presence of the accused or his representatives. On other occasions he could hear them in the presence of the accused and of 'the persons to be admitted upon his assize standing at the bar' (*Alexander Milne,* 4th July 1649). At other times for no apparent reason, evidence was led *viva voce* to the assize.

Disregard of this statute apart, however, what would now be classified as serious irregularities on the part of the Justice-Depute in the conduct of a trial, which even in the context of seventeenth century practice could not have been justified, passed apparently without comment and certainly without redress. The pursuers in *Duff* v. *Lord Banff and Ors.* (14th February 1650) found themselves in the embarrassing situation of many a litigant whose counsel happened not to be present at the calling of the case. The pursuers here were obliged to ask leave to go out of court to search for him. This leave having been granted them, however, they must have been considerably surprised to discover, as and when they returned, that defence submissions *ad longam* had been heard, and that the Justice-Depute had deserted the case against the accused on the ground of the pursuer's non-compearance. Perhaps his Lordship had good ground for this course in that the defence were able to produce Letters of Slains, a Royal Remission and an order from the Privy Council to desert the diet on a charge that was 22 years old. According to the report, however, he deserted solely on the non-compearance of the pursuers. In *William Fraser* (p. 443) there appears to have been no justification for his high handed conduct. The panel, on a narrative that he 'naither hes spoken with friend nor procuratour in this matter, being keepit in close presone,' and had only forty-eight hours notice of the diet, made the modest request for a continuation. This was refused and that in terms which suggest that the court considered any continuation a waste of time. The panel was ordered there and then to state his defences 'gif ony he hes'.

The Justice-Depute gave no protection to accused against what, even for that period were sometimes highly prejudicial actings by the prosecution. A confession by an accused, short of a formal plea of guilty, in theory required corroboration, but it is not unusual for the Justice-Depute to permit juries to found a verdict of guilty on a confession alone, as they did in *John Grant and Ors.* (p. 343). Unconnected accused and charges are permitted to be heard together. In a multitude of charges against open and notorious rebels arising from troubles in the north-east, two charges of theft in Lanarkshire apparently quite unconnected with the other charges, are permitted (*Duncan Watson and Ors.* p. 319). In another case two unconnected accused, charged with adultery and incest, are arraigned before the same assize (*Margaret Thomson and Jean Knox*, 28th May 1649). *John Gordon* (12th March 1645) was charged with bigamy, adultery and two charges of theft. So far as the Justice-Depute was concerned, these were apparently connected with one another, though in what way is not clear. He is recorded as declaring to the jury that he 'conjoined' all four charges 'desiring the assize to tak cognitioun of the saidis crymes fund relevant *conjunctim*'.

Not even the verdict of the jury was immune from his Lordship's intervention. Even he did not possess the power to transform a verdict of acquittal into what he may have deemed the more appropriate verdict of a conviction. He is, however, found qualifying a verdict of guilty. *Agnes Finney* (18th December 1644) was tried on 20 charges of witchcraft and convicted on eight of them. Whether his Lordship disagreed with this or not, or whether the record is faulty, he is minuted as holding that there was a conviction on only three of these charges. For the accused the limitation was academic since on any one of the three verdicts she would have been liable to the death penalty. The incident is, however, of more than academic interest to those concerned with the history of trial by jury. Where, moreover, a jury convicted on certain charges, but failed to make any findings of either conviction or acquittal on others, the court did not regard it as part of its duty to have the omission rectified (*John Grant and Ors.* p. 343). Even the necessity for a formal verdict from a jury where the accused is admitting guilt is in question. In some cases where he confesses, the Justice-Depute empanells a jury, who retire and consider their verdict. In others, the Justice-Depute proceeds to sentence on the plea alone.

In the result, while the average accused could have little doubt of his fate in the event of his being convicted, he might, with confidence, expect in the procedures by which it was sought to procure that conviction, an infinite and bewildering variety.[1]

Defence Witnesses.—In but one—but that the highly significant—aspect of procedure, the Justice-Deputes here exercise their discretion to innovate, and to innovate in the interests of the accused. Mackenzie (II.XXII.I) believed that

[1] One of the few situations in which the Depute acts to prevent abusive procedure and to protect the accused is where, at the trial diet, the pursuers fail to appear or fail to have assisors available. In such a situation, in the absence of good excuse, the court usually orders that the libel be deserted and no further criminal letters issued without its consent (*Harry Brown*, 28th July 1648).

not until 1661 was the accused entitled to 'the Benefit of exculpation,' i.e. the right to lead evidence in support of the defence, and 'contraire the libel,' as against relying on the Crown witnesses for favourable defence evidence. In fact, however, where the panel advanced a special defence, as of self-defence, it had long been competent for him to proceed by way of Brieve or Precept of Exculpation (See *Adam the Miller*, Cooper, *Select Scots Cases of the 13th Century* p. 42; and MacKechnie, *Judicial Process upon Brieves*, p. 11-12), whereby the special defence was tried first, and, if it was sustained, that terminated the proceedings. There is a survival of the old exculpation procedure in *John Gordon and Ors.* (12th April 1648), a case where Parliament held a defence of alibi relevant to elide the charge and ordered the Justice's Court to grant commission to 'ony unsuspect judge . . . in the cuntry (i.e. locality) to hear the probation of the defence' that parties be not put to the trouble of coming to Edinburgh. Moreover, there is evidence here of the defence obtaining the authority of the Court of Session to cite witnesses, though in what circumstances and to what effect that power was exercised is obscure (*John Anderson and Ors.* p. 413). Where a special defence was not pled, the traditional attitude was that the defence could not be heard to maintain or to prove facts contrary to those libelled in the charge. A rough logic justified their approach. It was not just, as Sheriff MacKechnie suggests, that they believed Crown witnesses did not commit perjury. It was also an attempt to prevent the commission of perjury by any witnesses at all. The attitude was that if the prosecution witnesses proved the crime, to permit defence evidence was necessarily to permit perjured evidence. If the prosecution witnesses did not prove the crime, then defence witnesses—perjured or otherwise—were unnecessary. Similarly, if a special defence was established, further inquiry was unnecessary into the principal charge. The practice of the Justice-Depute permitting the defence to allege 'contrair the libel', and his permitting prosecution evidence and defence evidence in replication, to be heard in the one process, is the significant procedural development of the present period, and it is a process particularly associated with the name of one prominent defence counsel, viz. Mr. Thomas Nicholson, younger. It remains, as it was still to do after 1661, a matter for the discretion of the court whether defence witnesses could be cited and adduced, but this discretion comes to be increasingly used where the defence, and on occasions the assize, desire it. The attitude of the Crown (Sir Thomas Hope, Lord Advocate) and defence (Mr. Thomas Nicholson) to the innovation may be studied in the submissions made in the case of *Janet Corsar* (p. 414). Here, the respective contentions as to what the facts were, made evidence for the defence imperative, if justice was to be done. The Crown libelled slaughter of a boy of eight as a result of repeated—but weaponless—assaults, which confined him to the house until his death. The defence was that the child could not have died from such 'straiks', since he did not die until 6 months after the alleged assault, and that 3 months after it he 'walkit abrod' in good health, played with other children, survived an epidemic of the plague, and died of what is called 'the fluxes'. These allegations—fatal it would have been thought to the charge libelled—the defence wished to prove by persons present at the Bar. No decision came from the Justice-Depute on this proposal until the matter had gone to the jury, and they it was who asked that the defence witnesses be heard. The Crown's principal objection was that the proposed course was an innovation. The defence, in reply, resorted to first principles, claiming that equity demanded the witnesses be heard, that the absence of precedent did not make the motion incompetent, and that the Act 1587 c.91, entitling the accused to prolocutors to propone a defence, implied an entitlement to prove that defence. What the Justice-Depute would have made of these impressive arguments had the jury not again intervened is uncertain, but intervene they did, and 'cravet earnestly', this time of the Lord Advocate, that the witnesses be received. His Lordship then agreed to their being heard, provided it was not taken as a precedent (p. 420). It would seem, however, that his Lordship's reservation came too late. The precedent had already been set; and, surprisingly enough, in a case heard less than a week before this debate, in which the same counsel (the Lord Advocate and Mr. Thomas Nicholson) appeared and the same Justice-Depute (Robertoun) presided (*John Anderson and Ors.* p. 409). Nicholson indeed could have founded on other and earlier proceedings, since he had successfully made the same motion in 1639 (I. p. 305), and against this background it is remarkable that the debate in *Corsar* could have produced the arguments it did, and could have failed to produce precedents of which all involved were aware. The precedent having been set however, Mr. Nicholson exploited it to the full and pressed it to strange lengths. In 1641 he persuaded the court to hear three defence witnesses to the effect that his client, who was absent, was not art and part of the crime charged, and to hear them before any prosecution evidence was led. So impressive was their evidence that the prosecution abandoned the case (*Andrew Wilson and Spouse,* p. 458). Nicholson again appeared for the defence in *George Norrie* (p. 515). Here, in a charge of mutilation, he alleged that the wound was self-inflicted. The Lord Advocate objected to this as 'contrair the libel' and, though the Justice-Depute is not reported as ruling on the matter, by implication he held the defence relevant. It went to the assize, who upheld it (p. 517), though the defence led no evidence on it. This case marks the end of the doctrine that a defence 'contrair the libel' is incompetent. Hereafter the question of leading evidence remains one for the discretion of the Justice-Depute. It must, however, have predisposed him to exercise it, that, if he failed to do so, the panel could apply to the Lords of Session, who are described by Sir Thomas Hope as invariably granting it if 'supplicat therefor' (p. 419).

The Criminal Calendar.—The most characteristic, as it was the most common crime coming before the court, was the crime of violence,[1] in all its many variations in fact, and with some refinements in law no longer encountered. Violence is a common aggravation of a multitude of other crimes, and not least is associated with certain crimes of dishonesty. This association produced some characteristically Scottish and evocatively named crimes: stouthrief, masterful theft,

[1] Many attended with circumstances of extreme brutality, see e.g. *Lyon of Muiresk* v. *George Gordon and Ors.*, 12th November 1647, a charge of masterful theft, stouthrief of cattle, treasonable raising of fire, burning and destroying of corn within a barnyard standing stacked therein, invading and pursuing the complainer with hagbuts and carbines, shooting of him through the left arm and 'lameing him thereof'.

herschip, hamesucken, deforcement, plagium. A catalogue of the subject matter of the prosecutions here demonstrates, if demonstration were needed, that criminal activity does not greatly change with time and place. What may change is the incidence of particular crimes at particular times and the reaction of the law to them in the way of prosecution and disposal. Certainly if now the law is accused of lacking in imagination in its sentences and disposals, it cannot be denied the credit of abundant experience—and that at first hand—not over years but over centuries, of the infinite varieties of criminal conduct, and of disposals which, if they have not satisfied the social scientist, have been accepted, if not applauded, as realistic by succeeding generations, and for which, even today, no demonstratively effective or acceptable alternative has been found.

There is no more revealing insight into the social life of the period than the incidence, variety and location of the charges reported in this and the next volume. The commonest crime reported here is homicide (slaughter, 33, in addition to treasonable slaughter 1, and accidental slaughter 2), murder (13), including murder under trust (2), and child murder (2). The violence was usually affected by means of a weapon and, where death was avoided, it commonly resulted in injuries giving rise to prosecutions for mutilation (17) and demembration (3). These crimes are so common that it is remarkable that Sir George Mackenzie failed to deal with them in his work on the criminal law, an omission remedied by Sir Alexander Seton of Pitmedden's treatise on the subject appended to the second edition of Mackenzie's *Criminals*, published in 1699. Other crimes involving violence are, illegal imprisonment (5), bearing and using hagbuts (6), hamesucken (5), wounding, and treasonable wounding (4). Theft, including theft by landed men (2), theft under trust (2), and reset (1) account for 25 of the cases, and there are some twenty-seven examples of aggravated thefts in the form of stouthrief, robbery (14), housebreaking (11), shopbreaking and opening lockfast places. Theft and its aggravations, indeed, and particularly stouthrieff form the majority of cases in the original manuscript. Sexual crimes form a high proportion of the cases here reported, undoubtedly because the Kirk regarded it as its duty to investigate and initiate such prosecutions. There are some six prosecutions for rape, eight for adultery, three for incest, three for bigamy and one for bestiality. Witchcraft accounts for some nine prosecutions, 'falset' or forgery and uttering for some seven. There is in addition a long catalogue of miscellaneous offences, too numerous to list here or in the following notes, but all testifying to the unfailing propensity and originality of certain of the lieges to come into conflict with the law, however unusual that law may be. Some of the more unusual of these prosecutions are for leasing making (1), kirk disturbance (2), breaking of dovecots (1), ploughbreaking (1), illegal cutting of timber (1), and forestalling and regrating (2).

Crimes Against the State.—A number of cases which concern the state are pursued by the Lord Advocate. They form but a fraction of the complete collection and, in some of them, the Crown is joined by a private pursuer. It is proposed to note only the more significant of those here.

Owing to the prevalent practice of trying cases of high treason before Parliament (see Mackenzie I.VI.2), there is only one example reported here of rising in arms against the King, which included 'a design of raising arms', thus illustrating that, in contrast with English law, *nudus conatus* was sufficient in Scotland (Mackenzie I.VI.4). Here the *Earl of Nithsdale* and *Viscount Aboyne* were charged with plotting to invade Scotland with Irish troops (12th July 1643). It is odd that it was pursued by the Lord Advocate on Criminal Letters and not on indictment but this was probably because the panels were at large and not in custody. In these circumstances the proceedings were naturally abortive. The accused were fugitated, denounced by the heralds and their moveables escheat to the Crown. Their heritage was not forfeited because that was incompetent when there had been no trial (Mackenzie I.VI.25). (Curiously enough treason trials figure little in Thomas Thomson's Acts of Parliaments of Scotland in this period, but this is probably because they were taken by commissioners.)

There are four cases of leasing making in the collection, *Lord Ochiltree* (I. p. 176), *Lord Balmerino* (I. p. 230), *Mr. William Haig of Bemersyde* (I. p. 232), and *Mr. John Stewart of Ladywell* (p. 423), all of which go a long way to justify Hallam's description of the crime as the 'old mystery of iniquity in Scots Law'. In Ochiltree's case and that of Haig the proceedings were abortive. In Balmerino's case, while the prosecution and result were unpopular, they could at least be justified as being in the letter and spirit of the relevant statutes. In the case of *Mr. John Stewart*, however, the law was utilized to destroy a political opponent, not by the Crown, but by a mighty subject. The statutes defining the crime (1424 c.43; 1540 c.83; 1585 c.10; and 1594 c.209) had for their object the protection of the Crown from calumny, which in practice meant simply criticism. The prosecution against Stewart on the other hand was at the instance of a subject (Argyle) as well as the Lord Advocate, for reporting to the Crown actions by Argyle, which it was clearly in the interests of the Crown to know. Hume's comment (I. 350) is that the panel was done to death for 'having done his duty'. The panel indeed found himself in a dilemma. To have known of Argyle's alleged speeches and to have remained silent on them could have amounted to treason. To disclose them was held to amount to leasing making. But for the extraordinary political situation of the day the charge here would have been impossible, and there is little doubt that it was brought to intimidate Argyle's political opponents.

There are a number of cases where acts otherwise illegal are aggravated by being libelled as treasonably done or as usurping Royal authority. Thus in 1637 a number of highlanders were charged on indictment with treasonably killing the Privy Council's commissioner in the exercise of his duty in apprehending certain McGregors (*John Grant and Ors.* p. 343). In 1626 *Donald McAngus of Glengarry* (I. p. 45) was accused by Lord Gordon of the illegal execution of one of the latter's servants, but the proceedings were abortive. Again, in 1641, *John Maxwell of Broomholme* (p. 401) was charged on criminal letters at the instance of the Crown and the relatives of two persons, one a boy in pupillage, with illegally trying and sentencing them to be drowned for sheep stealing nearly 20 years before, on the ground that the rolment of the Baron Court did not bear that they were caught with the fang, i.e. with the goods in their possession, which was essential to a baron's right to execute (Mackenzie II.XII.33). The Lord

Advocate alone pressed the case, which was based on illegal usurpation of the Sovereign's judicial authority. The King intervened—the only instance of this—and on a narrative that though the offence, if established, would have been capital, ordered the Justice-Depute to desert the diet simpliciter on the ground that the charge was stale and the deceased probably had in fact been apprehended 'with the fang'.[1]

There are five charges of plagium, i.e. illegal captivity, which was regarded as a constructive treason and libelled as such. Few crimes indicate more vividly the anarchic condition of the country, and, where the King's law could not even protect the liberty of the subject, it is not surprising that so many were ready to take the law into their own hands in seeking redress. The charges against *Lachlan McIntosh* (28th January 1648) may serve as an illustration of both points. He is charged *inter alia* with putting violent hands on a girl of about 11 or 12 years, 'casting her upon ane horse' behind one of his men, 'binding her thairupon with cordes, about the waiste and mydle pairtis of her body upon the said horse, and violentlie carried her away with them to the hills and mountains and utheris partis thairabout, keepit and detenit her in strait firmance' for four days 'unto the tyme she was relevit be force be the gentilmen and cuntrie people thairabout, furth of thair handis'. What is surprising with a crime so fundamental is the failure of the Crown consistently to pursue such charges to a conclusion. There is some justification for the Privy Council's intervention in *James Johnston of Corehead* (p. 324), finding that the warding complained of had been the lawful act of a bailie in the course of his jurisdiction. *Duncan McGregor* (15th July 1643) paid the supreme penalty for taking persons captive, but in *Lachlan McIntosh* (28th January 1648) charged with bearing hagbuts, abduction and illegal imprisonment, the case terminated when the panels were fugitated for failing to appear. In *Ludovick Stewart* (25th February 1648) again the pursuit came to nothing. Lastly in *Cunningham* v. *Lieutenant Mark Kerr and Ors.* (23rd November 1649) three soldiers kidnapped a boy under 14 on his way back from school in Leith and confined him in Edinburgh Castle. The Justices took a serious view of the matter and remitted it for trial in Parliament (Hume I.83; II.123).

Statutory Treasons.—Of all the harsh penalties imposed at this period that for treason was the most protracted, humiliating and painful. It not only involved death, it involved death by hanging, drawing (disemboweling) while the victim was still alive, and quartering. If any penalty could be expected to deter this was it, and the Scottish Parliament, its faith in the deterrent theory of penalty as yet unshaken, sought to curb crimes, which, for the time being, were particularly prevalent, by making them subject to the penalties appropriate to treason. The best known examples of such statutory or constructive treasons are murder under trust and theft by landed men contrary to the Act 1587 c.50: There are

[1] Burnett (*Criminal Law of Scotland*) prints this case in full (p. 59) but Hume did not appreciate its importance. He says he found no instance of a death sentence on a pupil and dismisses this case in a footnote (Hume I.195). It deserves wider publicity than it has hitherto received and for that reason it has been reprinted here.

three examples of the former in the present reports. In *Andrew Rowan of Barrshill* (I. p. 71) the victim is the panel's wife. In *John Dick and Janet Alexander* (21st March 1649) the accused are husband and wife, and the victims, the husband's brother and sister. In *Walter Urquhart and Ors.* (p. 550), where the charge was murder under trust and friendship, the report unfortunately gives no specification. Examples of prosecutions for theft by landed men are *Adam Brown of Crochmore* (25th January 1643), *Andrew Rattray of Dalrunzian* (17th February 1647), and *John Gordon of Auchleuchries and Ors.* (12th April 1648). Treasonable fire raising is libelled in *George Gordon and Ors.*, 12th November 1647, and there is one example in the present collection, apparently unknown to McKenzie, of wounding during sitting of Parliament (*James Gray and James Reid* p. 387). By the Act 1593 c.177 this was punishable as treason if committed near the place where the court was sitting. Another prosecution under the statute was *John Young* (I. p. 74) prosecuted for an attack on the bailie of Broughton regality at the door of the council room in Holyroodhouse. These statutory treasons are not actually declared to be treason but only to be punishable as such, with the result that the prosecutor does not have the privileges open to him in a proper case of treason, such as the right to call witnesses not normally admissible (e.g. women) and of immunity from the rule that if he fails in the prosecution he is himself guilty of treason.

Crimes of Violence.—The cases in this collection were originally collected with a view to 'illustrating some features of national character, customs and manners'. So far as concerns character and manners, they illustrate a society in which violence is endemic, if not customary, in all classes, in all forms and at all times, and in which the fatal or mutilating consequences of carrying weapons are everyday occurrences. They illustrate the legal system attempting to curb or restrain this violence by what would now be regarded as the most arbitrary and harsh of procedures, and the most punitive of penalties. Not only had the courts of the period to contend with a long tradition of violence and self-help, they lacked, with one possible exception, anything of the nature of a local police or an investigating tribunal, able and willing to investigate an alleged crime. There is little in the present record to suggest that the Justices of Peace at this period played any part in the initial investigation of crime except where Justices of Peace and Kirk Sessions were synonymous. The system relied in the main on the wronged party or his kin setting in motion any prosecutions, and while the wronged individual or kin in Scotland were only too willing to set right by violent means the wrongs done them,[1] it would be strange indeed if they differed much from their successors in their reluctance to become involved in the processes and delays of the law, which, whatever the conclusion, might well of themselves be

[1] There is one revealing incident here which occurs after a prosecution has commenced and which suggests that the private prosecutor or his friends were not content to let the law take its course. When *James Mowatt* and *Ninian Niven* travelled to Edinburgh to answer charges of mutilation they were unable to appear at one diet because of 'the suddene inconvenience befalling them be haifeing thair bodies and faces brunt with powder' in Edinburgh, 'quhairthrow they are not of abilitie to cum out of thair ludgings for keeping of this court without haizart of thair lyves' (p. 466).

the pretexts for further violence. *George Norie* (p. 514) was acquitted of mutilating David Taylor but he did not regard the verdict as ending the matter. He gave his oath that he 'dreadis the said David Tailyeair bodilie herme' and craved and obtained caution from him that he should be safe in person and goods. In *James Mowat and Ors.* (p. 463) the panels were found guilty and here both sides were ordered to find caution to keep the peace with one another: the panels as part of their sentence; the pursuers on a motion by the panels, that they 'dred thaim bodilie harme' from the pursuers (p. 483). The court obviously thought there was substance in the panels' fear, an attitude which may have been coloured by the earlier pre-trial incident of 'the suddene inconvenience' of the panels having their bodies and faces 'brunt with powder'. The lawburrows they sought were comprehensive. They were against the pursuers troubling them in their 'landis, takis, possessiones, guides and gear, and that thai, thair wyfes, bairns, and servands sall be hairmless and skaithless of thame and naways trublit or molestit, (p. 483). In many of the cases reported here what is a *quasi* civil settlement between the parties, is recorded as ending the proceedings before a verdict, sometimes as a result of remitting the matter to arbitration on the *quantum* of such damages (*Duncan Campbell,* a case of slaughter I. p. 49; *James Baxter and Ors.*, 1st February 1650, a case of mutilation). Such is the high proportion of cases, however, which are not pressed to any conclusion, that though a settlement is not mentioned, it can be safely assumed that this has taken place, and explains the absence of pursuer, jurors and witnesses at the trial diet, or the pursuer's decision then intimated to 'pass fra' his pursuit. This aspect of damages apart, however, there is enough here to illustrate that the reluctance of complainers to complain and of witnesses to testify, is no new phenomenon. When contemporaries could think it strange that so great a magnate as the Marquis of Huntly, when certain of his relatives had been murdered by 'Hieland limmers', 'should see his blood destroyit without tryell or reparatioun' because he could not detect offenders (Spalding: *Trubles* I.43), it can be appreciated what little chance a lesser complainer might have against the combined forces of silence, indifference, intimidation or fear. If, as in the present collection, many prosecutions for violence are begun but not concluded, and, if recurring experience is any guide, it would be reasonable to conclude that many more such prosecutions were never begun at all.

The commonest crime recorded here is homicide, ranging from deliberate murder to accidental slaughter. If some of these cases reveal sordid incidents in sordid lives and the violent reactions of a people much given to violence, some others—at least for posterity—are redeemed by throwing a revealing and fascinating light into the intimate and personal lives of the participants, and into Scottish domestic life in the seventeenth century. The proposition can be readily illustrated. The history of domestic bickering and unhappiness and the disastrous results of the intervention of another woman, that must lie behind the prosecution of *Robert Walker* and *Margaret and David Graham* (p. 536) for the murder of Walker's wife, has its parallel in every age, and has often before and since led to a charge of murder. Rarely, however, can the details have been so amply established, and these details evidenced such domestic bitterness, as they did in this case. Neither parties nor public here could complain that the charge lacked circumstantial and vivid detail. Walker and Margaret Graham are charged with hounding out David Graham, the latter's brother, to do the killing, but the murder was well planned. The husband, Judas-like, sent his wife 'out of her awin hoose . . . under nycht, to ane nychtbouris for ane pynt of aill', and it was on this humble but charitable mission that she was 'crewallie strangled' by Graham. The husband's reaction when the news was brought to him, and his subsequent actions reveal the measure of his hate and the extent to which this particular marriage had broken down. When Graham 'declarit to him that the deid was done', this newly-made widower 'rejoyset, and immediatelie thereafter took forth the said Isobel (i.e. the deceased) her plid, her petticoat and aprone, and passed to the place quhair the said Isobel was lying dead, and pat her said petticoat over her heid and knat (knotted) samyn with her aprone about her, and wrappit her within her awin plaid and thairefter the said Robert with the said David Graham, careid her to the mylne lead (lade) of Kinaver'. Robert's conjugal vindictiveness, however, did not end there—and it can only be vindictiveness. He confessed that he then 'trailit' her body through the lade 'to ane salmond croive' (cruive) and—a final macabre incident—there 'tuik her up in his airmes, and laid the said dead corpse within the croive with her plaid over her'. All this the three accused confessed, and in that day and age, at least, there can have been few who deplored their subsequent execution. Another incident of malice domestic which, for that age at least, revealed some originality, is the case of *John Dick* and his spouse, *Janet Alexander* (21st March 1649). They were convicted of murdering the husband's brother and sister, who lived with them, 'be poyseoning thame under trust and freindship with arsenak or rottin possone, in comprising thairof in het meit and baking of ane bannok whilk was ministrat' to the victims. In earlier cases poisoning had often been linked with witchcraft. No such liaison is in question here, but, to another accused, *Jane Craig in Tranent* (27th April 1649) goes the distinction of a series of alleged murders by witchcraft alone, without the intervention of such human, traceable and effective agencies as 'arsenak'.

The generality of accused, however, preferred more elementary means of killing and wounding. The 'bearing of hagbuts' and firearms was common. It was itself a statutory offence and occasionally prosecuted, but hagbuts were the weapons commonly used where groups were involved—groups which were in effect bands of armed men—as where *John Grant and his sons* and others 'being bodin with swordis, tairdges and guns, . . . be schutting of their guns at him and his company', slew, in circumstances of extreme barbarity, the Privy Council commissioner sent to apprehend them (p. 343; see also *George Adamson and Ors.* p. 385). The favourite weapon was the sword or quhinger and from the circumstances of the cases in which they figure, and from the cases of mutilation and demembration, they appear not only to have been carried as a matter of course by the men but, as is usually the case where weapons are carried, were used, as a matter of course, on the slightest provocation. In *Gavin Marshall* (13th April 1644) the weapon is 'a sword brag or knife'. In *Robert Hairschaw*, (5th February 1648), it is a sword. In *William Fraser* (p. 443), *John Morrison* (p. 524) and *James Gray* (p. 387) the weapon is a quhinger. *James Hart*, a Stirling burgess, must have been one of the few who did not actually carry a weapon at the critical moment, else he would hardly have been obliged to utilise, in the High Street of Stirling, so primitive and clumsy a weapon as the 'bar of ane grit kist or girnall'—or so it was alleged (p. 333).

It is impossible to resist the comment that the genesis of certain of these killings has a familiar ring to anyone acquainted with a Sheriff and Jury or High Court sitting in twentieth century Scotland, and it is consoling to know that what is presently called 'one word borrowing another' or 'a row in a pub' which results in violence, a charge of assault, a plea of self defence, a jury trial and an acquittal, has a long history, and is not peculiar to any one age or locality. It has precedents in the present collection. In November 1643 the douce burgh of Clackmannan was the scene of just such an incident. It began, congenially, with the victim asking one of the accused (*Lues Marshall*) for 'a pynt of wyne'. The amity, however, as is customary in such situations, did not last. It is claimed that 'efter some discourses passed' another man 'gave to Lues some evil and reproachful words quhirwith Lues made some such shairp answer, at quilk far by (beyond) Lues expectation' the victim—again following the time honoured pattern—'tuik exception'. Sundry comings and goings follow, until the victim 'offerit to stryke' the accused, and in fact assaulted the accused's father. The inevitable 'fight' then followed in which the accused, labouring under such gross provocation, 'drew his sword only to defend himself and naways to offend or wrong the gentilman'. Besides having a sword, however, the accused happened also to be carrying a knife—it is still a familiar and easy oversight—which happened to be readily to hand, and it was with the latter weapon that the killing was allegedly effected. In *Robert Hairschaw* (5th February 1648) the parties were 'convenit in ane ostler house in the Hinschaw, Carluke', where again 'ane discord and controversie fell furthe' which resulted in a sword wound on the victim. It needs but to alter the spelling and location for these narratives to read like reports from many a recent sitting of a Sheriff and Jury and High Court in Glasgow—even to 'the pynt of wyne'.

All classes and ages, laird and cottar, notaries public, ministers of the kirk, burgesses, tradesmen, even women and children, are involved in charges of slaughter. It is a measure of the strength of the habit of violence when gentry, such as Lord Ogilvy of Banff, Sir George Ogilvy of Carnousie, Irvine of Drum, Gordon of Geicht, the Lady Rothiemay, Sir Gilbert Menzies of Pitfoddel, and the like, could find themselves before the Justice Court as allegedly involved in crimes of violence. Political events too might bring an accused before the Court on a charge of slaughter and sometimes such a charge might raise issues of wide significance. *Sir John Gordon of Haddow* (p. 484), ancestor of the Earls of Aberdeen, was charged in 1641 with the murder in cold blood of a prisoner of war. He had the means and determination to dispute the Crown case in all its aspects of relevancy and fact. The case was eventually abandoned but not before the Justice Court had the rare and edifying experience of hearing learned and unusual submissions on the rights of captives and the duties of captors, in relation to slaughter and the Laws of War, a subject which had exercised the continental jurists, but which neither had, nor was to have, much significance, in fact or law, in Scotland, in the Troubles that followed.

All killing at this period is treated as appropriate for a criminal prosecution however casual or unintended. The differences in the qualities of the acts causing the death were reflected in the penalty or disposal. Even demembration done negligently was regarded as criminal (p. 529). In killing, where the fault was trifling, amounting to no more than negligence, the charges were not usually pressed to a conclusion and a composition or assythment was wont to satisfy parties. Some of the instances of negligence which gave rise to a prosecution, however, indicate that however indifferent to human life the lieges might be in practice, in the criminal law it was regarded as of consequence. There is an extreme example in 1632 where a father and son are pursued for the slaughter and death of a boy. The *locus* and *modus* of killing here are unusual, and go a long way to suggest that the golfer's enthusiasm to play as, when and where the opportunity presents itself is no modern development. The *locus* is the kirkyard and the *modus* is 'be giving him (i.e. the victim) ane deidlie straik with ane golf ball, strucken out with ane golf club'. *Ex facie* the charge arose from pure accident, and no one appears to have regarded the *locus* as involving any sacriligeous aggravation. It was abandoned, not because it was non-criminal, but because the pursuer discovered that neither accused struck the ball, but that it came from 'some uther person wha thane was playing within the said kirkzaird' (I. p. 204). The case disposes of the view that in the seventeenth century, churchyards were used exclusively for burials or post worship conversation, and suggests that seventeenth century golfers, to obtain a game, were prepared to accept hazards more numerous and artificial than is now the case. Another case which appears to involve simple accident is *James Mathieson* (p. 395). He is charged with what the libel calls 'rash and accidental slaughter', where the accused, apparently accidentally, caused stones to roll down the brae of Edinburgh Castle, killing a boy who was playing at the foot. The fact that the accused consented to banishment suggests that he did not expect the court to treat the matter as trivial.

One significant crime of violence which does not appear by name in the present record is assault. There are an abundance of cases of mutilation and demembration, which are simply aggravated assaults but with an elaborate law of their own (see Pitmedden's *Treatise on Mutilation and Demembration*). Assaults, however, falling short of such consequences and aggravations were either too frequent to be considered proper to the Justice Court and were appropriate to the lower Baron and Sheriff Courts, or, if prolonged and aggravated, came within the category of Riot and so were appropriate to the Privy Council, the tribunal principally concerned with keeping the peace.[1] Where an assault was libelled as treasonable wounding under the Act 1593 c.177, because occurring near the Parliament House when Parliament was sitting, it was competent to the Justice Court (*James Gray and James Reid* p. 387), but such statutory aggravations excepted, at the start of the period of the present reports, at least, there was doubt as to the competency of the Justice-Depute trying cases of serious assault, and if there was any question of the matter being pursued civilly the Justice deserted the charge (*John Angus* I. p. 263). In *James Scrymgeour* (Pitcairn, III.467) the defence submitted that a charge of hacking another's head with a quhinger 'is na capitall cryme but ane ryot, the tryal quhairof pertenis to the Counsell'. One assault which does appear here under the name of 'ryot'—though slaughter would have been a more appropriate charge—involved two women

[1] Rioting *per se* as distinct from mobbing is the name applied to the outrageous behaviour of a single individual (Alison, *Principles*, p. 510).

'delestably' abusing, assaulting and indecently assaulting one Thomas Brown, as a result of which he died (p. 392). The two ladies, however, failed to appear and the depute was denied the opportunity of determining whether he could competently deal with such a matter. In two later cases, *David Howison* (28th July 1643) and *Patrick Martin and Ors.* (19th November 1647) counsel were prepared to argue that he had not. In the former it was contended that where a charge is neither slaughter, mutilation or demembration, and blood is not drawn, it cannot be pursued criminally at all. 'Percussion straiken' (i.e. assault), it was argued, has 'never been use to be pursuit criminally before this', and could not be punished. In *Patrick Martin and Ors.*, a case *inter alia* of wounding to the effusion of blood, counsel argued that a charge of assault by drawing blood was only competent in the Sheriff Court and there for payment of a fine, i.e. a blood wite. Drawing blood, it was submitted, is not a crime. In both cases the arguments, however, were unsuccessful and the court remitted the matters to the assize. Thereafter the jursidiction of the Justice's Court in such charges was established.

Thefts.—The view that only aggravated assaults gave rise to a criminal remedy, apparent at the beginning of the period of these reports, was paralleled by a similar attitude to crimes against property. Where these were accompanied by violence or menaces, as with stouthrief (robbery), herschip (theft of cattle by force), they are prosecuted in the Justice's Court as a matter of course and exemplary penalties inflicted. Where the charge is one of repeated theft, here also, the competency of the prosecution is not in doubt. Where, however, the charge relates to a single instance, even where aggravated as by being accompanied by house-breaking or opening lock-fast places, there is on the part of the prosecutor a reluctance to press a charge to its conclusion, and on the part of the court a decided encouragement to that approach. On occasions the attitude of the court is such that it appears to hold, as a matter of law, that single instances of theft are not criminal, and that parties should seek their remedy before the civil court. Examples of such an attitude on the part of the prosecutor are the cases of *James Baillie* (p. 400) and *Mungo Rose and Ors.* (31 July 1646). Baillie was charged with the theft or reset of a horse. In defence, he affirmed that he bought the horse openly, and brought it to Edinburgh, and was willing to restore it to the pursuer provided the latter would swear that it was his property, reserving always his action of warrandice against the person who sold the horse to him. The pursuer duly swore, agreed to take the horse back and to pass from the criminal pursuit. He, too, reserved his civil right by formally reserving his right of action against the accused for 'damnage, interes and profitts of his said horse daylie sen the away taking thereof'. In *Mungo Rose and Ors.*, where the charge was much more serious—one of house-breaking, masterful theft and stouthrief of goods, gear and plenishing—the case was concluded by the pursuers consenting to the Justice-Depute remitting the case 'to be discussit civilie before the civil judge'. Here, too, the accused formally reserved their position by intimating that they reserved the right to pursue the prosecutor for slander, in having been called 'common and notorious thieves'.

Besides this attitude on the part of the prosecution there are several examples of a surprisingly restrained approach to acts of theft on the part of the court. In *James Donan* (p. 367), where the charge is theft of 'evidents, bandis, writs and securities' by opening a lock-fast charter chest, the Justice *ex proprio motu* held that theft by abstracting of evidents is 'naw ways capital or criminal but the samyn is all togidder civil and sae competent to the civile judge to be cognoscet civilie' (p. 368). Again, in *James Gordon* (7 July 1648), a more extreme case involving masterful theft of 'vittle' from the prosecutor and his tenants, the Justice-Depute found the libel and the facts to be not criminal, and remitted to the civil judge.

The cases reported here, on homicide on the one hand and theft on the other, suggest at least that the familiar criticism that the criminal law was more concerned with the protection of property than the protection of life, did not apply to the criminal law of Scotland in the 17th century.

Sexual Crimes.—A high proporion of the reports relate to sexual crimes: adultery (7) and accompanying child murder (2), bigamy (3) which necessarily included adultery, and could be prosecuted as either (Mackenzie was prepared to regard adultery as including theft (I.XVII.4) but there is no authority for this in the present record), rape (6), incest (3), and one charge of bestiality. Neither in these reports, nor in the comments of contemporaries, is there encouragement for the belief that the rule of the Saints produced in Scotland a reformation in the sexual morality of its people. An enthusiast like Kirkton could speak at this period of how 'in many places the spirit seemed to be poured out with the word' and how he had 'lived many years in a Parish where I never heard an oath, and you might have ridden many miles before you heard any', but, if oaths had diminished, other practices, not only continued to abound but appeared to be on the increase. Evidence for this is not confined to the records of the criminal courts. These can be abundantly supplemented from other contemporary references. This was one subject on which the commentators appear to have had an obsessive and eloquent interest. A generation before, the Kirk had complained of 'ugly heaps of all kinds of sin lying in every nook and part of the country' and of a spate of 'incest, fornication, adultery, sacrilege, theft, oppression, with false witnesses and finally with all kinds of impiety and wrong'. (*Booke of the Universall Kirk.*) In the mid-seventeenth century the picture had not materially changed. After the Restoration Sir James Turner, a level headed professional soldier, remarked that he 'never saw either public or private sin more abound than in the years 1643 and 1644 when the Solemn League and Covenant was subscribed by many' (*Turner's Memoirs* p. 160). The position did not improve. In 1646 the Commissioners of the Kirk petitioned Parliament to renew the laws against adultery and incest—'these odious sins having grown to such a height of abomination as is horrid to express' (*APS* VI(i) 552), and in 1650 one of Cromwell's soldiers, writing of the Scots, commented that 'Whoredom and fornication is the common darling sin of the nation' (quoted Mathieson: *Politics and Religion in Scotland* II.156). He is confirmed by Nicoll, a Scot, but a less biased observer than Kirkton, who speaking of 1650 says that 'sexual offences never more abounded than now', and three years later the Kirk is complaining of the 'growth of sin of all sorts, particularly pride, uncleanness, contempt of ordinances, oppression, violence and fraudulent dealing'. (Chambers *Annals* ii. 198.) Sexual offenders came from all classes. In the present record *Margaret Thomson*, a minister's daughter, and the wife of a minister, was convicted and executed for adultery with another minister (28th May, 1646) and the *Rev. John Bannerman* (15th July 1646) was dealt with for bigamy. Adultery was one crime at least on which the deterrent theory of penalty—and for notour adultery the penalty was death—appeared to have little effect. When the English came to occupy the country they contemplated the situation with shocked surprise.[1]

Such a reaction, as well as the circumstances of the charges reported here, would suggest that only the more aggravated of such incidents found their way to the Justice's Court. Sexual offences indeed were the one class of crime for the prosecution of which there existed in each parish, not only enthusiasm and tenacity—a charge of rape allegedly committed in 1596 is prosecuted in 1626 (I. p. 35) and *James Wilson* is prosecuted on 20th December 1649 for incest 'committed a threty five year since or thereby'—but also machinery for investigation and prosecution independent of a private pursuer. Added to the prurient and curious eyes of a rural community was a powerful and sometimes oppressive system of ecclesiastical inquisition. It was concerned with all crimes. In the present record it is found investigating charges as diverse as murder, witchcraft and adultery, and in one case of homicide determined whether the killing was casual or deliberate (*William Fraser* p. 443 at p. 450). In the burghs, in particular, the lay magistrates and Kirk Sessions are regularly found working hand-in-hand in investigating and penalising all forms of petty crime (G. D. Henderson, *The Scottish Ruling Elder*, p. 114). The Kirk's special province, however—originally accorded it by Calvin in his belief that discipline constituted 'the ligaments by which the members of the body are joined together and kept each in its proper place'—and justified by its desire to make the lieges of Scotland conform as closely as possible, not only in profession but in practice, to Scripture, were sexual offences. Throughout the country many such charges, eventually heard in the lay courts, began with arraignment before, and inquisition by, the Kirk Sessions, who then remitted the matter to the civil power, it being the theory that the Church of Scotland never assumed the least degree of power to inflict the smallest penalty (Robert Baillie: *Historical Vindication*, quoted in G. D. Henderson: *The Scottish Ruling Elder*, p. 111). In the present reports there are many examples of initial investigation and institution of criminal proceedings by ministers acting alone or with their sessions. (See the notes on Inquisitorial System above.)

[1] A report to the speaker of the Commons in 1652 from an English visitor speaks of the English commissioners for the administration of justice spending 'three days in the trial and fining of several persons for adultery, incest and fornication for which there were about 60 persons brought before the judges in a day; and it is observable that such is the malice of these people that most of them were accused for facts done diverse years since, and the chief proof against them was their own confession before the Kirk, who are in this worse than the Roman religion who do not make so ill an use of their auricular confession. Some of the facts were committed 5, some 6, 10, 16, 18 and 21 years since' (Firth, *Scotland and the Commonwealth*, p. 367-8).

Their investigations and prosecutions did not always end in conviction. The minister of Dunscore is named along with the King's Advocate as pursuer in a charge of adultery and incest against *John Kirko and Anor.* (p. 507) before the Justice's Court. That reverend gentleman certainly did not lack persistence, since he had already unsuccessfully pursued the same charges against the same accused before the Estates of Parliament. Before the Justice's Court, however, he was finally persuaded of the inadequacy of his evidence and abandoned the charges. Even in so serious a matter as rape, ecclesiastical interest could not prevail over determination on the part of parties to settle the matter. A charge of rape against *Donald Stewart* (p. 510) was deserted on production of a ministerial certificate that the accused and complainer were now happily married. Such conclusions, however, were the exception. The case of *William McCrae* (20th May 1650) charged with rape, and already referred to, illustrates how the system could operate. The victim, her parents and other witnesses were examined on three separate days by the minister of the parish and certain of his elders. Later the minister in question joined the Justice-Depute and the two of them spent two other days taking depositions. The minister in question may well have been a Justice of the Peace but, initially, at least, here, he was acting with his session in his ecclesiastical capacity. Further depositions were taken by a Lord of Session, and all these were produced to the jury. No other evidence was led before them and on the conviction that followed the panel was beheaded. In July 1642 *Margaret Cunningham* (p. 534) was executed for adultery and child murder, the proof of the latter being her confessions to two ministers, a reader, a baillie, and a burgess, when she had been 'brocht up to the Tolbooth in ane wand (wickerbasket) and examinat'. Depositions so taken by the Kirk were accorded high authority. In one case, *Alexander Gourlay* (I. p. 48) the King's Advocate claimed that statements to the presbytery commissioners 'aucht to be respectit as ane depositioun tane be the ordiner judges' (p. 51).

The influence of the Kirk extended not only to the investigation of sexual crimes, it extended also to their legal definition. Incest had been defined by Parliament, 1567 c.14, in terms of Leviticus c.18. The definition having been adopted from Scriptures, however, it was no doubt appropriate that its interpretation should be accorded the divines rather than the judges, and by the divines, and by the judges acting at their instigation, the text was given such liberal interpretation as would have considerably startled the authors of Leviticus. Such liberal interpretation is not confined to the period of the present reports. It had a long history. The Regent Moray (June 1569) had been much concerned as to whether a man having intercourse with a woman, who had been paramour to his mother's brother, committed incest (*Booke of the Universall Kirk.*) The General Assembly to whom he applied for a ruling on this intriguing point had no difficulty in assuring him that it did, and so set on its way a principle in which hardly any limits were set to the crime of incest. *John Weir,* in 1629 at a time when marriage to first cousins was permitted, was convicted of incest in marrying the relict of his grand uncle (I. p. 221). *Henry Dick,* having connection with his wife's sister, is convicted of incest (quoted Chambers: *Domestic Annals of Scotland II*, p. 29, where there is reference to a number of such cases). In *Jean Knox* (28th May 1646) the crime was given a further extension. She was convicted of incest in that, having become pregnant to one brother in 1644, she married another brother five months later. The only possible justification for the conviction was on the ground that having become pregnant to one brother, albeit illegally, a relationship was thereby set up which precluded marriage to the other. Since the original relationship however, was one of fornication, and plainly condemned by the Kirk, the logic of the conviction is difficult to follow. The panel here did not have the advantages of legal advice and, having regard to the ingenuity and prolixity with which counsel were prepared to devote their talents to pleas to the relevancy which were forensic rather than real, it is unfortunate that she did not ask the court to provide her with legal advice to argue a plea to the relevancy, which, in law, had more than usual substance. The Justice-Depute apparently entertained no misgivings as to the charge or the confession to it. At the date of the conviction however even the Kirk had its doubts on the matter (*Records of the Commission of the General Assembly* 1648-9 Vol. 2, p. 241, 289) and it was not until 1649 that an Act of Parliament was passed providing that consanguinity and affinity impeding matrimony is contracted by unlawful company of man and woman as well as by marriage (*APS* VI.I.475-6). By that date, however, the unfortunate Jean Knox was not in a position to derive satisfaction from the fact that she might have been wrongly convicted. Confessing the 'crime' on 28th May, she was executed by being 'hangit upone ane gibbet' on the afternoon of 1st of June, on the castle hill at Edinburgh.

The only conclusion to be drawn from the incidence of immorality and the attitude of the law to it, is that while seventeenth century Scottish society cannot be described as permissive, it can certainly be described as irrepressible.

The Jury.—The jury in this period is in a state of transition. It has not entirely abandoned its original function of declaring facts within its own knowledge. It has not yet attained the stage where its members, in theory at least, know nothing of the facts or of the participants and are solely expected to adjudicate on evidence led before them. The prosecutor had responsibility for summoning the 45 men from among whom, prior to Mackenzie's time, the King's Advocated selected the assisors—by this period almost invariably 15 in number. The risks inherent in permitting the prosecutor to cite and select jurors was to some extent mitigated by the elaborate system of challenges, i.e. on the grounds of infamy, relationship or the like.[1] The letter of the law entitled an accused to the judgment of his peers. From Assize David I, the law had been that 'na man aw to thole judgment from a less person than fra his peer, that is to say, an erle be erle; baron be barons, vavasseur be vavasseur, burgess be burgess; a less person may be judget be a mair person and nocht a mair be a less,' but this principle was not strictly adhered to in practice, and in the present collection juries usually consist of lowland lairds and Edinburgh burgesses on the one hand, and men from the neighbourhood of the crime who knew something of the accused and the facts, on the other. Ideally all the jurors should come from the

[1] For an elaborate description of the grounds of challenge see Willock, *The Jury in Scotland*, p. 171, *et seq.*

locality of the crime, and very occasionally in fact, they did, but this must have been impracticable in the majority of cases where a crime committed in outlying parts of the country was to be tried at Edinburgh.

In practice the jury was neither so impartial, divorced from knowledge of the facts, nor so passive as it has since become. A trial in Edinburgh of an alleged crime in Aberdeenshire or the Hebrides dictated that some at least, if not most of the jurors come from the *locus fori*. The presence of some jurors, however, who were not only from the *locus delicti* but who also knew the circumstances of the accused and of the facts, albeit at secondhand, was regarded as essential.[1] Mackenzie (*Criminals* II.XXIII.2) declared that assizers are in effect either judges or witnesses. In the present record practically every jury required a fluctuating proportion of the latter. The whole assize might no longer be expected to know the facts but, without some at least who did, the trial could not proceed, and in practice the words of style, whereby the court referred the charge to the knowledge of the assize, frequently meant precisely what they said. The functions of juror and witness were not distinguished. In *John Rodgers and Ors.* (p. 505) two men, cited for jury service, recognised when the case was adjourned, that next time they might be called as witnesses, and adopted the not unreasonable attitude that before they were cited again they should have their expenses for attendances already made. In *George Norie* (p. 514) the shopkeeper where the incident occurred, and who was clearly the principal witness, found himself on the jury and emerged as its foreman. So necessary was it that the jury know the facts, that a prosecutor, as in *William Dalgarno of Garnieston and Ors.* (1st March 1643), might competently refuse to go to trial before an Edinburgh jury, and demand an assize from the *locus delicti* who knew the facts, 'he dar nocht, nor will nocht trust the tryall of this, his pursuit, to those quho are ignorant thairof'. The Justice-Depute himself could adopt such an attitude. In the case of *John Kennedy* (p. 373) the Depute himself deserted the cause 'in respect of the want of assizers of sic persons as best knows the verity in the said matter', and this notwithstanding the presence in Court a sufficient number of impartial and uninformed potential jurors. How the learned Justice-Depute determined the absence of knowledge on the part of the jurors present is not disclosed, but presumably it must have been either by perusal of their designations or by interrogation of them. In *Sir Alexander Irving of Drum* (14th March 1645) the court 'in respect of the present troubles in the north pairtis,' so that 'nather persewaris nor *assysouris* micht peaccablie traivel' deserts the diet. Only acceptance of the jury's right to proceed on their own information explains the defence leading evidence in a case where the prosecutor had led no evidence at all (*John Young*, p. 313). Reliance on local knowledge was not however exclusive to the prosecutor; the defence too could invoke it (see *Allan Gourlay*, I. p. 48), and such reliance was not necessarily regarded as prejudicial to the defence. *Peter Balmano and Ors.* protested against an assize that did not have local knowledge, declaring that 'gif it were nocht dangerous for thame, albeit innocent, . . . to

[1] *John McCrory and Ors.* (Vol. I., p. 26) were tried in Edinburgh on charges that included piracy on a Glasgow ship off Jura and the hurting and wounding of Robert Hamilton, burgess of Glasgow. No jurors from the *locus delicti* were apparently cited, but seven of the jurors came from Glasgow.

refer thameselffis to the tryell of fyftene ignorant and unknawin assyzours thay sould verie willinglie for cleiring of thair innocencie offer thameselffis to be tryit be ane honest and unsuspect number of assyzours, indwellers in Dundie and cuntrie thairabout' (I. p. 37-8). In *Janet Corsar* (p. 414)—a charge of slaughter—the jury includes one of the men named by the defence as a witness. He was a surgeon, and the other medical man referred to in the debate as having treated the deceased, was also a member of the jury.

This anxiety to have some jurors from the *locus delicti* inevitably led to delays, and it is indeed surprising that so many jurors from outlying parts of Scotland were prevailed upon to travel to Edinburgh. Not only had they to contend with the difficulties and expense of travel but, as 'the Trubles' increased and civil war became endemic, there was added to the perennial reluctance of the lieges to become involved in the processes of justice, a natural reluctance to leave the familiar sights of home, and undertake the risks to life and limb inherent in journeying through a countryside always violent and rendered the more violent because of a war,[1] and where their attendance at Edinburgh might be protracted. Their convenience was given little consideration. Adjournments were common and the potential jurors are ordained to attend at the adjourned diet (e.g. p. 521).

For the prosecutor the personal knowledge possessed by the assize might be, and frequently was, competently relied on—and rarely relied on in vain—to make good defects in, or the complete absence of, relevant prosecution evidence. One experienced advocate submitted to the Justice-Depute that 'in law and by custom of all judicatories in case of notoriety, there is no further inquisition, and the assize are the inquisitors' (*Patrick Martin and Ors.* 19th November 1647). What was meant by 'notoriety', and who determined its existence, was not stated, but in practice in these reports the jury is frequently left to determine the gravest charges from its own knowledge. In 1619 (*Andrew Wast*, Pitcairn III, 466-7) the Lord Advocate called no evidence and was content to leave the matter with the jury 'seeing thay ar all indwellers in Dundie, to quhome the treuth of this matter was best knawin'. Recourse to such procedure is perhaps understandable in cases of witchcraft since there 'the common bruit (rumour) of the country' that the charge was reported to be true, and 'the notoriety of her (the panel's) guiltiness' are about as much as the prosecutor could hope for by way of evidence in the absence of a confession (see *Isobel Young* I. p. 116, and *Alison Nisbet*, p. 212). There was, however, no question of the practice being restricted to this type of crime, and conviction by what at the end of the day is rumour and hearsay is not only competent but common. A charge of hamesucken, which resulted in the death sentence, was established on 'the knowledge of the assize' with no evidence led (I. p. 290-293). In *John Marshall* (2nd February 1648) the jury retired to consider the case on their own knowledge, the only witnesses, all women having been repelled as incompetent. In *George Wright* (I. p. 222-4) the Crown confidently relied for a conviction in a charge of theft, on the oath of the private prosecutors that their charge was true, and on the assertion that 'the assize knawis the pannell to be guiltie of crymes foirsaidis, be the common voce

[1] See *Thomas Stewart of Ryland*, 22nd March 1643.

of the cuntrie'. On 15th February 1648 when *Robert Hairschaw* was tried for slaughter and rape, no evidence at all was led, and according to the minute the jury retired and convicted him after merely 'reiding . . . the dittay'. Again on 13th December 1643 the verdict on *Thomas Scott* was reached as a result of declarations 'made by diverse persons of thair (i.e. the jury's) number . . . who saw the straik given be the pannell' (Hume II, p. 319). In *James Ramsay* (p. 315) medical evidence of injuries sustained and the pursuer's oath of calumny was the only evidence led in the modern sense, and on it the jury convicted. How prosecutor and court reconciled this practice with the terms of the Act 1587 c.91, requiring that the accusation, reasoning, writs and witnesses and other probation and instruction whatsoever, shall be alleged, reasoned and deduced to the assize in the presence of the party accused 'in face of judgment and na otherwayes' is not disclosed, but clearly the apparent contradiction between practice and precept occasioned no misgivings.

To allow jurors to rely on their own knowledge can only be justified in a system where rules as to relevancy and competency of evidence are at best elementary, and at worst non-existent. It is inevitable that where a jury is entitled to use its own knowledge it can, if so minded, invoke every factor it knows prejudicial to an accused, and can proceed on hearsay or on evidence of character generally. That it was expected to do both is clear from the present record. Condemnation by 'the commoun voce of the cuntrie', 'the voce of the haill cuntrie' was good enough for the Advocate Depute (I. p. 223-4). The pursuers in protesting for wilful error at the empanelling of an assize to try George Wright on a charge of theft, encouraged the assize to proceed on their knowledge of his character. They declared that 'the maist pairt of thame (i.e. the jury) are cuntrie men and knaws the pannel his viscious lyfe and conversatioun, and that his guiltines of the particular thiftis contenit in his ditty is sufficientlie knowin to thame'. Apart from the oaths of calumny from two of the pursuers this was the sum of the evidence relied on—though the jury at the end of the day returned a discriminating verdict (I. p. 222-4).

Much indeed was expected from these jurors from the *locus delicti.* Where they filled the jury box along with Edinburgh burgesses, ignorant of the local facts and talk, and where no evidence was led, they must have persuaded their colleagues of the facts and guided them to a majority or unanimous verdict. In those cases where they were asked to rely on their own knowledge of the facts, or on the 'bruit of the cuntrie', they were indeed credited with a length and detail of memory which no modern court would expect of a witness, much less of a juror. The jury which tried *Alexander Hervie* in 1627 for 'the breking and lameing' of a former servant, consisted of local men and another of his servants, whose recollections were expected to extend back 14 years, to the date of the alleged crime (I. p. 67). *Peter Balmano and Ors.* in 1626 (I. p. 37) rejected an assize of fifteen 'ignorant unknawin assysours' and wanted instead 'honest and unsuspect jurors' who were personally expected to retain their recollection of an incident allegedly occurring in 1603. Examples of reliance on the memories of jurors for old incidents can be multiplied from this present collection.

Even, however, where no evidence was led, juries are found acting with what may be discrimination. Charges against *Robert Hairschaw* of slaughter and rape went to a jury entirely composed of men from the locality of the crime, some of whom at least were prepared to act independently. The case resulted in a unanimous and a majority verdict of guilty respectively (15th February 1648). In *George Wright* (I. p. 222) the jury did not accept, or was not prepared to proceed upon, common rumour where a pursuer failed to take the oath of calumny on the general charge. When *William Bow and Ors.* (24th February 1648) were charged with forestalling and regrating in connection with poultry, no evidence was led and the Crown sought a verdict on 'the notorietie of the pannellis guiltiness'. They were tried by a jury on which were two cooks and four poulterers from Edinburgh, who decided the case on their own knowledge, and said so in a special verdict of acquittal. They unanimously acquitted the accused and declared they did so 'specially because they (i.e. the jury) on no wayis knawis the pannell to have bocht any of the vivers contenit in the dittay, how they bought them, or quhat prices was tane be thame in the selling out thair-of, the assyze (sic) being altogiddar innocent (?ignorant) of the samyn alsweill in thair bying of the saidis viveris as in the selling out thairof agane'.

The system was not without some advantages. It is the exception for witnesses to testify before the assize and the latter can rarely then have had the opportunity to form an impression of the credibility of witnesses. Generally the witnesses' depositions had been taken before the Justice-Depute or other tribunal and all that was produced at the trial were the depositions to be read to the jury or perused by them. Where the witnesses themselves were produced it was usually only formally to adhere to their deposition. On the rare occasions where the evidence of a witness was taken in the presence of unempanelled jurors or was adduced before the jury verbally, there is no testing of that evidence by examination-in-chief, cross-examination and re-examination. The procedure in *David Howieson* (28th July 1643) where one witness was re-examined after others had testified is novel.[1] The reliability and credibility of the witness then could be assessed, and only assessed, by the personal knowledge on the part of members of the assize of the matters on which the evidence was given, or of the character and general credibility and reliability of the witness as an individual. This was recognised by the defence. In *Alexander Gourlay* where the Crown relied *inter alia* on a deposition of the complainer on the charge of incest, the accused offered to prove 'by the assisours thameselffis, to quhais wisdome, knawlege and conscience the pannell refers him selff,' that the complainer had exonerated the panel, on oath, before 'the haill congregatioun,' in the Kirk of St. Andrew's (I. p. 48, 50). Where there were language difficulties a member of the jury might resolve these, as where confessions in Gaelic were interpreted by one of the assize to his brethren (I. p. 273). The fact that some of these jurors knew the circumstances of the charges, and no doubt in an effort to have the whole circumstances elaborated before their uninformed colleagues, probably explains the request that occasionally comes from jurors to have persons they know to be in possession of evidence, examined and their evidence made available. Thus, in *Janet Corsar* (p. 414),

[1] There is anticipation of the modern system in *Gavin Marshall* (20th November 1643) where witnesses are ordained to be present at the trial to 'verifie and make good their depositiouns, and to declare what farther shall be interrogat of them, ather be the pursuers or the panel, anent thair knawledge of the slaughter'.

members of the assize 'for cleiring to thame of the veritie of the factis and deidis lybellit and thair better informatioun thairintill, maist humblie desyres' the Justice-Depute to hear the four witnesses nominated by the panel and present at the bar. In *William Fraser* (p. 443) the jury again asked that a particular witness be heard. Even after their verdict had been reached they might still try to influence sentence as where a youth of 15 was convicted and they earnestly interceded for him 'in respect of his zoung zeiris' (I. p. 263). Their recommendation carried sufficient weight with the Justice-Depute to warrant his remanding the accused in custody—albeit in irons—until the Privy Council be consulted. on sentence.

Evidence.—While so much reliance was placed on the jurors' personal knowledge of the accused and the charge, it was impossible to frame or apply any precise rules on the relevancy and competency of evidence. The occasional and accidental glimpses from modern practice of what jurors consider to be relevant to their deliberations, suggest that there is nothing, however remote and however irrelevant, that may not appeal to certain of their number as significant. Modern rules of evidence have attempted, though with what success remains doubtful, to restrict the jurors' opportunities for such speculative indulgence. In the seventeenth century, however, so far as the present record bears, there was nothing to limit the uses to which jurors might put their personal knowledge in reaching a conclusion, and little or nothing to restrict the content of the evidence by which the prosecutor sought to supplement the jurors' own knowledge. Challenge there might be of the competency of a witness by whom a fact was to be proved, but it can be confidently asserted that there was nothing in the facts affecting a charge against an accused which was not considered relevant, and nothing which was considered relevant which was not also considered competent for the jury's consideration. Counsel were ingenious and industrious in taking pleas to the relevancy, but their attention was primarily directed to the relevancy of the terms of the libel, not to the nature of the evidence by which that libel was sought to be proved. This liberal approach to evidence was moreover encouraged by the practice, already noted, of adding some vague, general and wholly unspecific charge to follow one or more detailed charges and adducing no evidence on it: for example, a final charge of theft from various unspecified markets (*George Weir and Anor*. p. 365); a charge of 'commoun thift and commoun resset of thift, etc.' as in *George Wright* (I. p. 222), or, as in a libel for incest, a final charge that the accused 'was ane vyle and filthie liever and abuser of his body at dyverse tymes uith zoung virganes, his awin scollaris, nocht worthie to be hard be ony chaste Christian ear' (*George Sinclair* I. p. 96). The phrase is revealing!—that which could not be heard, was apparently to be made the substance of a verdict. This is perhaps an extreme, but not uncharacteristic, example of the allegation, suspicion, rumour on any matter prejudicial to the accused, which a jury were entitled to take into account, either as amounting to a separate charge or as tending to prove the principal charges, without the necessity of the prosecutor leading evidence upon them.

Modern rules of evidence shun evidence of an accused's previous general bad character unless in exceptional circumstances, and consider specific bad character, as for example, a multitude of previous convictions even for a particular type of crime, to be irrelevant even when a further identical charge is preferred. In the present collection, however, the reputation a man enjoyed generally, and his criminal record in particular, were not only regarded as relevant, they were regarded as among the most significant adminicles of evidence that a prosecutor could found upon. Clearly, though an accused might only occasionally put his good character in issue,[1] if he possessed a bad character among his neighbours—and in a Scottish rural community, reputations, good or ill, were readily acquired and once acquired tended to endure—he ran the risk that sooner or later in the criminal courts that reputation might not only catch up with him, but might, of itself, destroy him. In the case of *George Wright*, already noted (I. p. 222-4), the jury are reminded by the prosecutor that as 'the maist pairt of thame are cuntrie men' they 'knowis the panell his vicious lyf and conversatioun' and on that are invited to convict. Common bruit and open fame of being an ordinary thief was deemed a good ground for the death penalty even in Mackenzie's day (*Criminals* II.XIX.8).

Hearsay of the accused's responsibility for the crime was regarded as important as character. 'Common Bruit' or 'rumour', so often and so confidently invoked, was nothing more than hearsay. It was sufficient if witnesses 'depone of their credulity and that they were informed of others' of the panel's guilt (Mackenzie *Criminals* II.XIX.8), and a counsel as experienced as Mr. John Nisbet accepted—at least in debate—that where there was notoriety of the panel's guilt further evidence was unnecessary, and 'the assyze are inquisitores' (*Patrick Martin and Ors.* 18th November 1647).

Oaths of Parties.—Neither at this period nor indeed until 1723 (Hume II. p. 357) was a complainer unequivocally admitted as a competent witness to the facts (*Balfour* p. 379). In many of the cases tried here, moreover, the complainers were next of kin of a deceased and themselves could know nothing of the facts. In this situation the complainer's part was restricted to swearing the oath of calumny if called on by the panel to do so. This was no mere formality. Where a complainer failed so to swear that ended the case. In *James Ramsay* (p. 315) the pursuer, at the request of the panel, gave oath that the crime was committed as libelled. In *William Fraser* (p. 443) the widow swore to the truth of her accusation, though it is clear from the whole history of the cause that she could have known nothing of it at first hand. That the oath of calumny was coming to be a more elaborate matter, however, particularly where the pursuer himself is the victim, may be the significance of certain incidents in the case of *James Mowat and Ors.* (p. 463 at 479). There the pursuers gave their oath of calumny, which must have contained sufficient detail to warrant the defence commenting as they did on 'the uncertaintie thairof', and later the pursuers were recalled to elaborate on their oath and to clear up points of doubt in it (p. 479).

[1] Even then with attendant risks. When *James Hart* produced a testimonial of his good character, the Lord Advocate replied that he would attack the character of the panel as a turbulent man, fined some 20 times, a resetter and outlawed on a charge of theft (332). He could have done this without notice, and jurors from Stirling would be bound to know the record of a Stirling burgess.

Reference to the oath of an accused is rare and the instances reported here bear out Hume s contention that the practice was restricted to cases where the charge raised, in a great measnre, questions of a civil nature or of inferior delinquencies. e.g. *Robert Burnett* (15th November 1637, Hume II 336) charged with cutting down trees; or *William Black* (3rd July 1646), where the charge was again cutting growing timber. Here the pursuer's procurator, in place of any proof, referred the charge to the panel's oath of verity, who, being sworn, denied the charge and in respect of that denial was assoilzied from it. In one case, *Robert Angus and Ors.* (p. 396) the pursuer refused to give his oath on the truth of the libel. That should have ended the case but the panels by their great oath swore that they were innocent, and in this case the pursuer then passed simpliciter from the pursuit.

Sufficiency and Competency.—The earliest case on the necessity for corroboration referred to by Hume is in 1705 (II. 382) but the matter had been determined, according to Balfour, as early as 1549: 'Twa witnesses at the least maks lawful probation,' (Practicks p. 373). It was accepted at this period, in theory at least —though in practice it was ignored—that an extrajudicial confession required corroboration (*William Fraser*, p. 443), and the necessity for more than one witness is implicit in the custom of the Justice's Court and the Privy Council in allowing ten witnesses to be cited on every separate matter of fact and article of the libel and no more (see Mackenzie, *Criminals* II.XXVI.20). In *John Biggar* seven witnesses were cited to speak to the crime (12th July 1648). There is nothing in the present record, however, to suggest that the court considered it part of its function to determine whether there was sufficient evidence adduced by the pursuer to entitle the jury to convict. Indeed, where a prosecutor relied on the notoriety of the charge, or the personal knowledge of the assisors, no such limitation was possible. The Justice-Depute's principal function was to examine witnesses and determine questions of relevancy. He does not direct the jury on either the law relating to the charge, or the evidence. This practice had to await the trial of Katherine Nairn in 1765 when Lord Kames attempted to assist the jury by addressing them on the evidence—a course to which exception was promptly taken by the defence, and the innovation made a ground for attempting to arrest judgment, in that it deprived the defence of the last word (see Roughhead, *Trial of Katherine Nairn*, p. 44 and 161). The individual pursuer in the present cases might be sufficiently conscious of the weakness of his case to abandon it, as where George Scott (24th February 1643) passed from a pursuit for slaughter against *Archibald Stobbo and Ors.* on the ground that 'they have not gotten sufficient tryell and probatioun of their guiltiness'. But in the light of the slender or non-existent evidence—in the modern sense (e.g. *John Young* p. 313)—in many of the cases the Justice-Depute unhesitatingly remitted to the knowledge of an assize, it can only be concluded that Mr. Scott's evidence was very thin indeed. Juries themselves must however have decided on the sufficiency of the evidence, as where an assize acquitted *William Smaillie and Anor.* of a charge of slaughter where the only evidence against them was an uncorroborated deathbed statement of the deceased to her sons, who were pursuers (I. p. 153/4).

Similar passivity characterises the Justice-Depute's attitude to questions of competency. In 1587 c.91, Parliament had laid down what appear to be clear and unequivocal rules for the conduct of a criminal trial, namely, that the accusation, reasoning, writs, and witnesses and other probation and instruction whatsoever, be alleged, reasoned and deduced to the assize in the presence of the party accused in face of judgment and not otherwise. It was never contended that this Act was in desuetude, but, so far as the actings of the court are concerned—and that notwithstanding frequent reminders of the existence of the Act from counsel—it might well have been. The King's Advocate and the Justice-Depute were at one on this. In one case (*Mungo Rose and Ors.*, 31st July 1646) where the King's Advocate had moved that witnesses be examined outwith the presence of the assize, and the defence objected, his Lordship replied by saying that it is 'ane very ordinar and allowable custom that witnesses be receivit and examinet before the mater pass to ane assyze and their depositiouns to be keepit in retentis and thereafter produced to the assyze for their informatioun, quhilk the pursuer refers to the Justice.' The procedure followed in many of the cases reported here demonstrates that this practice was a 'very ordinar' one indeed, and as far as the Justice-Depute was concerned, wholly 'allowable'. It operated even where the deposition founded on had been taken in relation to another accused in an entirely separate trial. In prosecutions for witchcraft, confessions obtained in one case were used in another. In *Catherine Oswald* (I. 130) the King's Advocate used the deposition made by one Toppok, another witch, before her conviction and after her conviction 'renewit and ratified by her at the stake,' in a later trial against a different accused. A similar course was adopted in *John Burgh* (24th November 1643). In *Alexander Gourlay* (I. p. 48) in a charge of incest, the prosecutor was allowed to adduce as evidence 'twa writtis' containing a report of the trial of the alleged victim. In *Gordon of Haddow* (p. 484) a charge of slaughter, an even more extraordinary situation arose. The Justice-Depute apparently saw nothing questionable, contradictory or incompetent, in admitting the deceased's last will and testament as an adminicle of evidence on how he was murdered (p. 492. Another example of this is *Thomas Crombie* I. p. 21).

Circumstantial Evidence.—On what would now be described as circumstantial evidence and was then referred to as 'presumptions', no limits were set. The significance of possession of stolen property in charges of theft (*George Weir* p. 365-6), and of false keys, raising of floorboards, and using a ladder, in charges of theft by housebreaking and opening lockfast places (*Patrick Bald*, 8th February 1649) were well appreciated. Other less convincing factors, however, were also regarded as significant. Attempts to delay or pervert the course of justice were regarded as equivalent to confessions to, or as strong adminicles of circumstantial evidence in, the charges with which they were associated. The court minutes treat failure by an accused to appear for trial as equivalent to guilt, and no doubt it was a cogent encouragement to a panel to attend that he had become 'acted and obliged' to appear at his trial under 'pain to be repute and estimat guiltie and culpable of the said cryme' if he failed to do so (*John Littil*, I. p. 171). Where *Thomas Bryce and Robert Liddell* were charged art and part of slaughter, and the alleged principal did not appear and was outlawed, it was claimed that he 'sua takis the cryme upone him' (I. p. 300). In *Andrew Rattray and Ors* (17th

February 1647) where certain accused failed to appear, the court 'adjudget, decernit and declaret the forenamet persones and ilk ane of thame committeris of the crymes' to be fugitive. Again in *Archibald Stobo and Ors.* (24th February 1643)—a charge of slaughter—John Stobo was denounced rebel for non-appearance and declared to have 'thairby . . . tane the slauchter above written upone him', and as late as 1664 when one Crichton escaped from the Tolbooth, the minute reads that by that escape he had taken the guilt upon him: (Scott Moncrieff *Justiciary Records* I. p. 100).

The unlimited scope of what was accepted as circumstantial evidence is illustrated by the evidence led in the case of *William Fraser,* a pedlar, tried in July 1641 for the murder of one David Curraour on 23rd April 1639 (p. 443). The homicide was admitted and the sole question was whether it was murder or what would now be deemed culpable homicide. Before he reached the Justice Court the panel had been outlawed for non-appearance at an earlier diet in July 1639 (p. 452) and—what is more significant—had been ex-communicated by the Kirk (p. 450) when the presbytery 'after due trial and examination of witnesses' found the killing in question to be wilful murder. Not for *William Fraser* and his like was the presumption of innocence, or the absence of pre-trial publicity. The full charge is not related in the present record, but, from the submissions, as well as from practice, it can be assumed that it specified in detail the various facets of the evidence on which the prosecutor intended to rely. Scottish counsel of that day can never be accused of lacking either originality, enthusiasm or courage when it came to debating the relevancy of criminal letters or an indictment, and, while in this case they took unsuccessful objections to the competency of certain of the witnesses, it is significant that the relevancy of the presumptions libelled went virtually unchallenged. Some of them made a formidable case even for these days. The widow of the victim could say little, but she formally took the oath of calumny of the charge that the accused was the only man and none other that murdered her husband. The significant evidence related to the panel's actings. There was evidence from his own deposition before the Justice-Depute of previous ill feeling, namely that he and the deceased had quarrelled three days before the killing, and that in the course of that quarrel the deceased had struck the panel. Following on the killing the panel admitted changing his name and fleeing the country. The procedure and the evidence before the presbytery enquiry and its conclusions are founded upon, as is the panel's excommunication by the General Assembly. The report incidentally illustrates the close liaison between Kirk and State in the investigation of crime. Two of the ministers engaged in the presbytery enquiry gave evidence to the assize of their having considered the question of whether the slaughter was accidental or wilful, of their examination of four or five witnesses, of the panel being present and legally represented. When it was alleged in the Justice's Court that two of the witnesses before the presbytery were incompetent, the two minister witnesses were confronted with this evidence and denied it. The 'common bruit' of the country—which, following on the Kirk's procedure and decision, must have been loud and strong—is invoked as of like significance to the evidence of admissions against interest by the panel, and his demeanour when making these admissions.

All this may be unexceptional, but finally, as if the evidence of the natural world were not enough, the prosecution was in the unusual and fortunate position of being able to supplement it with evidence of the supernatural.[1] The court heard from Lord Sinclair and others how the ship on which the panel was fleeing the country when 'past two myles of (off) schore and under sail with ane fair wynd . . . stoppit and wald nocht goe forwardis,' i.e. it was supernaturally stopped. Lord Sinclair testified that—as was understandable—this miracle aroused his interest, as it did that of many others. When the panel landed at Aberdeen there was evidence that in the presence of Lord Sinclair, Captain Sutherland, two bailies and the Sheriff Depute of Aberdeen, and many others, the panel fell on his knees and craved mercy, admitted the deceased had provoked him 24 hours earlier—an admission that elicited from Captain Sutherland the apposite, but hardly encouraging, remark, that provocation 24 hours earlier was not sufficient—claimed that he did the wrong negligently, expressed regret for it and appeared to the onlookers to be penitent. On all this the King's Advocate submitted, and submitted successfully to the jury, that there were 'all the indices requyret of the law concurring to the probatioun of ane slaughter' (p. 453).

Proof by witnesses and circumstantial evidence, however, was regarded as very much a second best. As in the Middle Ages, proof by confession was preferred as 'the most secure of all others' (Mackenzie, *Criminals* II.XXIV.2). In theory an extra-judicial confession deserved much weight but required corroboration. In *William Fraser* (p. 443), the King's Advocate concedes that such a confession is not of itself enough but required 'uthir indices, presumptiones, conjectouris' concurring with it. A judicial confession, however, albeit departed from before the jury, was of itself sufficient to warrant a verdict of guilty, and a judicial confession included confessions emitted, not only before the Justice-Depute in the presence of the assize, but confessions taken by the Justice-Depute outwith the presence of the assize (*Margaret Chalmers*, 19th January 1648) and also pre-trial confessions made to inferior magistrates, Kirk Sessions, Presbyteries and General Assembies, even to individual clergymen and laymen or to a combination of these. Since the courts of the Church were part of the civil establishment, and their procedures judicial, depositions taken before them were accorded in the present record—though not by Mackenzie's time (*Criminals* II.XXIV.5)—the respect due to 'ane depositioun tane be the ordinar judges,' (I. p. 51), or as the Lord Advocate put it in *Isobel Young* (I. p. 96 at 114) 'depositions before the Presbytery are judicial, and sua man mak faith'. In the case of *Jean Craig* (27th April 1649) the prosecutor founds on the panel's confession to charges of witchcraft made to 'the minister of Tranent and dyverse famous witnesses'. *Duncan MacGregor* (15th July 1643) confessed before two ministers

[1] Reliance in evidence on the supernatural was unusual but not unknown. Touching the corpse was a practice in Strathearn in cases of slaughter. The report of the case of *Andrew Smeaton and Anor.* charged with slaughter (I. p. 264) records a testimonial from a minister and others, that following an ancient custom of the district, one of the accused had handled the corpse, and embraced her, and offered himself to be in the grave with her, and to do all things possible as he should be required for proof and evidence of his innocence of the crime. The accused's willingness to undergo this macabre experience and the absence of reaction from the corpse were deemed significant. In charges of witchcraft the existence of the devil's mark was regarded as conclusive evidence of guilt (see *Janet Baker* and *Margaret Lauder*, 29th December 1643).

and a notary public, the former ratifying the confession before the court. *Margaret Cunningham* (p. 534) judicially admitted adultery to a tribunal consisting of two ministers, a bailie, a reader and a merchant burgess of Edinburgh. There are many other examples. *William Fraser* (p. 443) according to Mackenzie (*Criminals* II.XXIV.3) was condemned on a confession before the General Assembly at Aberdeen, though subsequently retracted, and Parliament, he claims, refused their opinion on the propriety of founding on such a confession. (For the circumstances in which such pre-trial confessions could be obtained see the section on Inquisitorial Procedure.

In certain cases the leading of evidence was deemed unnecessary, not because the panel confessed, but because by the time the case reached the Justice Court the critical facts had been determined by another tribunal. In the sinister prosecution of *Mr. John Stewart,* Commissary of Argyll, on a charge of leasing-making (p. 423) his guilt was assumed in the Justice's Court. The indictment narrates that the accused was examined on oath by a Committee of the Estates of Parliament, had there confessed and subscribed his confession to the charges, and, that what was not confessed, was proven by witnesses. The Committee having, in their own words, 'tane all lawful trial both be writ and witnesses', Parliament found the panel guilty of the charges and remitted him to the Justice Court 'to be punished for the said crimes'. The accused might there deny these charges, and, unless he was entitled to plead not guilty, there seems no reason for the case being remitted to the Justice Court, since Parliament itself could have sentenced him, but his case was a forlorn one. In cases of forgery of deeds, a decree of the Lords of Session reducing the deed in question was conclusive. *Thomas Lawson* and *William Blair* had little alternative but to confess the charge of forgery and uttering where the Lords of Session found the deed in question, a discharge, to be 'forgit by William Blair and used by Thomas Lawson'. They remitted the two accused to the Justice's Court, not for trial but, 'to be punished' (27th February 1650). The principle was not however confined to decrees of superior courts. *James Freish,* charged with desertion from the army, confessed the charge but, for verification, the prosecutor founded on the statute giving rise to the charge and on 'a testificate' from the panel's commanding officer that he was in fact a deserter (13th August 1644). Certificates from ministers, Kirk Sessions and surgeons are accepted as a matter of course on such matters as the panel's indisposition or age or the extent and nature of injuries—matters which might otherwise have been regarded as vital matters for proof (see e.g. *Hugh Somerville* I. p. 299, *James Ramsay* p. 315, *George Norrie* p. 514).

Sentence.—The approach of the Justice's Court to sentence—as it was the approach of every other court then exercising criminal jurisdiction—was determined by their attitude to crime. For them, the criminal act was not some uncharacteristic, unlikely to be repeated, and temporary aberration from the social norm on the part of the accused, for which he ought not really to be greatly blamed. Theirs was a text-ridden age and the favourite texts tended to be selected from the Old Testament, where judgment was not so much tempered with mercy as synonymous with vengeance. For them, as for the lay-man, a criminal act was one of the more positive manifestations of innate human wickedness, and—if the words of contribion which accompanied many of the judicial confessions in the present record is any guide—so also was it for the accused. To regard crime as anything other than a fit subject for punishment, retribution and expiation would have been emotionally impossible. Moreover, to have adopted any other approach would not only have been impossible, it would also have been impracticable. The retributive and deterrent theories of punishment, if they had ever considered them as such, would have been forced on the courts by the nature of the social situation confronting them, without the necessity of any intervention from the theologians. If crime was one aspect of human wickedness, the desire for revenge on the part of the victim and his kin was one aspect of human nature, and at that period neither was, nor could be, disregarded. Everywhere in Scotland the lieges were more ready to put right the wrongs done them by means of their own strong right arm—and the right arms of their friends and relatives, and all who were linked to them by bands of manrent—than they were to invoke the assistance of the criminal law and the courts.[1] It is a situation which is still not unknown in certain parts of Scotland, though, unlike the seventeenth century, there are today some who prefer to treat the situation as if it does not exist. In the seventeenth century, however, the courts in effect tended to accept that if the complainer were prepared to undergo the delays, 'trouble, fascherie and expense', and if unsuccessful, a possible monetary penalty, of setting in motion a criminal pursuit, then at the end of the day, if successful, such pertinacity should be rewarded, either by such pecuniary impositions as would not only vindicate the law but also adequately assuage the sense of wrong of the victim or his kin,[2] or, if the circumstances of the crime were too aggravated for a quasi civil settlement, then by a sentence which would afford the victim and his kin a similar, if vicarious, sense of satisfaction to that they would assuredly have enjoyed had they pursued the natural, and it would seem more normal, and, it is to be feared still popular, course of 'dealing with the matter themselves'.

The desire to restrict the instinct for revenge, particularly by satisfying it in the nature of the penalty imposed, was a well recognised principle. The late Mr. Justice Oliver Wendell Holmes, from a prodigious knowledge of laws ancient and modern, appreciated and described the situation, when he wrote (*The Common Law;* McMillan, 1968 edn. p. 36) that 'the first requirement of a sound body of law is that it should correspond with the actual feelings and demands of the community whether right or wrong. If people would gratify the passion of revenge outside the law, if the law did not help them, the law has no choice but to satisfy the craving itself and thus avoid the greater evil of private retribution'. Such a comment might have been written with the Scottish courts of the seventeenth century in mind, and the Scottish courts of the seventeenth

[1] Following on the fire at Frendraught Tower, certain gentlemen 'taking the fire havillie to hairt, and seeing na redress thairof be law, brakis out, ilk man suorne to another to live and die with utheris, and vowit to revenge thamselfis upon the laird of Frendraught be way of deed.' (Spalding, *Trubles*, I. p. 48.)

[2] The disposal in cases of mutilation and demembration illustrates the practice here. In *Cheyne* v. *James Mowat and Ors.* (463) the parties were fined the sum of 300 merks, and in addition were required to pay the sum of £1,000 as damages to each of the complainers.

century would have concurred wholeheartedly in the proposition. Indeed they would have regarded the proposition as self-evident. It is a reflection of the attitude of the community that even where the circumstances of the crime merited a minor penalty and payment of damages the court was at pains to limit the opportunities for private retribution and the inception of feud. The case of *Margaret Lambert* (13th December 1646) illustrates the point. In 1 644 when she was 12 years of age she was accused of the murder of a six-year old boy in Tulliallan and was detained in custody in Edinburgh. She remained in custody for two years and three months notwithstanding that, in May 1645, assythement had been paid and letters of Slains granted by the father of the deceased. On 13th December 1646 she was prosecuted for the murder by the King's Advocate. The case concluded—the King's Advocate concurring—with an order by the Justice-Depute that the child accompany her father home, make public repentance before the Kirk Session of Tulliallan and thereafter—and the significance is clear—in eight days of the repentance, that she remove and be banished furth of the Parish, to a distance of 12 miles. Only anxiety to prevent local trouble can explain such a disposal in such a case. Similar considerations could arise even without guilt as where the prosecutor abandons a pursuit against some of a number of accused. In *Andrew Wilson and Anor*. (p. 458) the pursuer agrees to pass from the pursuit of the two accused on condition that they and 'thair haill familie . . . remove thameselffis af the bounds of Aldie and landes thairof' and not to return. Here the object of their removal is frankly stated to be in order that 'the father, brether and remanent kyn and friendis' of the deceased might not 'ony wayis be irritat or provoikit to offence heirafter' (p. 459). Moreover such was the prevailing spirit of violence that a court sentence might itself be the pretext for further trouble. Accused as well as complainers are sometimes perturbed at the prospect. In *James* v. *Mowat and Ors*. (p. 463) the proceedings end with the accused *inter alia* being required to find caution for their future good behaviour to the complainers, and the complainers—on the accused's oath that they 'dred thaim bodilie harme' from the complainers—being required to grant Lawburrows that they will 'nawayis truble' the accused, their kin, servants and possessions. Similarly in *James Gordon* (7th July 1648) the panel deponing that he feared bodily harm of the pursuer, obtained lawburrows to the effect that himself, his wife, bairns, tenants and servants should be harmless of the pursuer, his wife, bairns, men tenants and servants.

Concern as to the effect of penalty on the public no doubt explains the readiness of the Justice-Depute to invoke the guidance of the Privy Council—the tribunal particularly charged with responsibility for keeping the public peace—on questions of sentence. In numerous cases, where the facts were unusual, where the verdict was open to question—as where it was only a majority verdict,—or where the competency of penalty was in question, the Justice-Depute continues the case until the guidance of the Privy Council has been obtained. The recommendations received from that body on such occasions while not only disposing of the particular reference, can have left the Justice-Depute in no doubt as to the attitude towards sentence expected of him from that the 'supreme judicatorie'.[1]

1 Where consulted the Privy Council did not always regard itself as confined to the penalties imposed by an Act of Parliament. Where *John Jobb* (19th January 1650) pled guilty to a charge of bigamy under the Act of 1551 c.19 the Privy Council ordered scourging and banishment, a sentence incompetent under the Act.

Deterrence too was regarded as significant. If only a fraction of the crimes committed resulted in a prosecution—and the comparative paucity of these reports for the period concerned, contemporary references to the incidence of crimes, especially of violence, as well as general experience, make that inevitable—and if only a fraction of the crimes prosecuted resulted in a conviction,—as is demonstrated by the present record,—then it is hardly surprising that when a conviction was obtained the law should have indulged in exemplary penalties which might be expected to deter. It is an age-old expedient. In the concept of statutory treasons—common law crimes for which statute prescribed that the sanguine and protracted penalties appropriate to a conviction for treason should apply—the Scots Parliament gave official and recurring recognition to its enthusiasm for the deterrent theory of penalty. It is now much out of fashion, but Parliament, the Privy Council and the Justice-Depute appear to have been assailed with no misgivings as to the effect of their penalties upon the accused, potential emulators among lieges, and the executioners themselves.

If the penalty as well as deterring, could be made to fit the crime so much the better. In cases of perjury the penalty usually included boring the tongue—the member by which the crime had been committed. Nicoll (*Diary*, February 1650) refers to one John Lawson who was bound to the Tron with a paper on his head declaring his fault. Then 'his tongue was drawn out with ane turks (pincers) by the common hangman, laid on ane littil buird . . . and run through with ane het iron or bodkin'. Whatever the deterrent effect of such a sentence it unquestionably ensured that John Lawson did not again commit perjury!

Crimes which by their nature 'cannot be repaired' (Mackenzie I.XIX.6) invariably attracted the death penalty: murder, slaughter, witchcraft, mutilation, aggravated thefts, false coining, reset of rebels, treasonable slaughter, bestiality, notour adultery and incest to name some such. The method of execution was usually hanging or beheading or strangling preparatory to burning. The lieges were meant to be left in no doubt about the consequences of convictions and much publicity attended them. Of the two notaries *Thomas Lawson* and *William Blair* (22nd February 1650) charged respectively with uttering and forgery, the Justice-Depute, after consulting the Privy Council, dealt with Lawson and could not be said to have faltered in his duty. Besides declaring the panel infamous, he ordered that his ears be nailed to the Trone with a paper on his chest proclaiming his crime and that he be banished the Kingdom. He remitted the question of Blair's disposal first to the Privy Council, but later to the Estates of Parliament. Their disposal must have reassured the Justice-Depute that his sentence on the co-accused erred, if anything, on the side of leniency. Their Lordships ordered that the prisoner be hanged at the Mercat Cross of Edinburgh with 'ane paper one his heed contening the cause thairof'. The precise wording was left to the Depute who, for the edification of the lieges, ordered that he have two papers—one on his back, the other on his breast 'beiring thir wordis in grit letteris "For forgeing and counterfeitting of fals writtis".' If such a disposal seemed appropriate to a charge of forgery, it is no surprise that the Justice-Depute should seek the Council's advice on the sentence on panels so notorious as *John Grant* and his sons, convicted of reset of rebels and treasonable slaughter (p. 343). Here the council ordered that they be executed by hanging but, in order that their fate should be a more lasting reminder to any of the lieges tempted to emulate their activities, the doom required that thereafter their bodies 'be hung up in yrone cheinyeis within the said place of executioun quhill (until) thay rote and consume'. In *Alexander Wylie* (4th July 1649) the sentence on a conviction for theft and slaughter was hanging and thereafter his head and right hand be struck off. The former was then to be displayed on an iron pike above the Netherbow gate and his hand at the gate of Leith Wynd. In these two last cases any attendant risks to the public health were deemed secondary to attempting to ensure the public peace.

The picture, however, is not all sanguinary and in one significant field at least the law is becoming less severe. The death sentence for theft was accepted as competent by Mackenzie (I.XIX.6) though he inclined 'to think that for simple theft a thief should not die'. He instances the Justices sometime hanging, even for very small faults, and quotes a case of the death sentence in 1661 for theft of a horse (*Thomas Neilson*). In inferior courts it was considered that three convictions, or the panel taken with the goods in his possession, were required before a capital sentence (*John Maxwell* p. 401). Precedents in favour of non-capital disposals, however, are set in the period of the present reports. Where there was a multiplicity of charges of theft, the circumstances were particularly grave, or charges of theft were accompanied by aggravation such as heirschip or housebreaking, e.g. *Duncan Watson and Ors.* (p. 319) and *George Weir* (p. 365), the capital sentence was inevitable. The case of *Alexander Craig* in January 1639 (p. 368) however, involving theft of six sheep, marks a departure. To execute an able-bodied young man at a time when the wars in Europe were affording occupation and profit to the Dugald Dalgetty's of Scotland was necessarily something of a waste. The panel could not conveniently be imprisoned since prisons in the sense of institutions in which a convicted person was deprived of his liberty were few, and such as there were, mainly occupied by those awaiting disposal,[1] and in any event the idea of imprisonment commanded little enthusiasm among judges, legislators or practitioners. The only alternative to death was therefore banishment and if, in addition to ridding the country of a wrongdoer, his youth and energy—so much misplaced at home—could be 'made serviceable' in the wars in Germany, the ends of deterrence, vindication, expiation, mercy and utility and perhaps even reformation, might all be congenially served in the one disposal. It appears that the culprits offered the opportunity of foreign service accepted their fate with alacrity and even with enthusiasm. *Alexander Craig* (p. 368) who for the theft of six sheep might have expected a hanging—as a century later his successors not only expected but received—was content—the Privy Council having been consulted—to enact himself in the Books of Adjournal to be banished from the Realm and Kingdom of Scotland and be 'delyverit for that effect to Captane Walter Murray to serve in the weiris in forane partis, and nawayis to returne back agane within this Kingdome at any tyme after his . . . away passing' without Royal warrant, under pain of death. There were many who welcomed the opportunity of following his example. The same day that Alexander Craig was sent to join Captain Murray,

[1] There is a congenial picture of an accused in custody in Moffat: *James Johnstone* (p. 324-5). He is described as in good health during his abode in ward, where his friends had access to him, 'eit and drank with him and tuik tobacco' (p. 325).

one *Richard Lauder* (p. 371)—whose talents, to judge by his criminal record, would be of inestimable value to himself and his fellow mercenaries in the chaos of the Thirty Years War (beside his record, Alexander Craig's six sheep are trivialities)—also agreed to pass furth of Scotland in the company of Captain Murray 'to serve him in the waris in forane pairtis and not to return to Scotland under pain of death'. In March of the same year a servant admitting theft of six silver spoons from his master, agreed to pass with Colonel Erskine furth of this Kingdom and serve him in the wars as a soldier (*William Barr* p. 373). Eight years later another servant (*John McLean*, 31st March 1647) admitting theft from his master ('furth of his Chalmer at Worcester, England . . . his littil coffir quhairin war dyverse of his jowellis') offered himself willing to underly whatever punishment the Justice should pronounce, and, on the advice of the Lord Advocate, and in response to a plea for mercy from the complainer, he was ordained to be banished, and of his own motive and consent became acted and obliged to pass furth of Scotland with Captain Fouller 'ane of the commanders under Sir Robert Murray his regiment.' Such disposals were not confined to charges of theft. In one case of rape, where the girl's father agreed, the accused consented to such banishment after ten weeks in custody (*John Rylaw*, 21st July 1643) and *John McCarroll*, an Irishman, 'wairdet . . . this half-year bygane' for adulterie, cheating in 'fenzeing himself to be dumb . . . off his awin frie and volunter consent,' preferred service 'as ane souldiour in the weires in forayne pairtis' to the sentence he might otherwise have expected (p. 379). Despite their professions of willingness to undertake such military service, the court took no chances of these budding recruits changing their minds. As might have been expected, Richard Lauder had given an earlier, similar undertaking, to the bailies of Edinburgh to the one he gave the Justice-Depute, and had nevertheless contrived to remain in Scotland. In the Justice Court they were all warded in custody until such time as their nominated commanding officer could attend to collect them.

Not all sentences were harsh. A variety of factors might lead the courts to mitigate the normal sentence or the manner of its infliction, and there are examples of surprising leniency. Even the death sentence might be inflicted with what in their view was some mercy. It can have been scant comfort to the panels *John Dick* and *Janet Alexander* (21st March 1649) that for murder by poisoning they were sentenced to death by beheading. The Justice-Depute, however, regarded such a sentence as an act of leniency. The minute reads that he 'mitigatis' the penalty to beheading in respect of their voluntary confession to the minister before the crime was discovered, and their 'trew and unfeinzit repentance with abundance of tears' in the presence of judges and assize. In the present record there is little of the torturing punishments at death familiar to, and condemned by, McKenzie a generation later. The traditional fate of the witch or the sexual pervert namely burning, is generally preceded by 'worrying at the stake' which at least saved the panel from the excruciating experience of the flames (e.g. *James Fiddes,* bestiality, 31st May 1650; *John Burgh*, witchcraft, 24th November 1643; *Janet Barker* and *Margaret Lauder*, witchcraft, 29th December 1643). Not only a verdict of guilty but the evidence on which it was based, might mitigate sentence. *Andrew Gylour* (p. 518) found guilty of raping, or 'forcing' a girl of 10 years of age, escaped with scourging, branding on the cheek and banishment. Since the death sentence had been imposed in charges of rape much less aggravated than here, the only probable explanation of such leniency in the circumstances of the report is that the conviction proceeded on the barest of evidence. On a finding of guilty of theft by a bare majority ('in regarde my convictioun went upone one or two of the assysouris voces and the crime was not greit') the Privy Council ordered banishment (*George Wright* I. p. 224). Even prosecutions for religious and some sexual offences, both of which in the prevailing spirit of the times could have been expected to evoke all that was harsh and vindictive in penalties, resulted in some mild disposals. *Mr. John Robertson,* a Jesuit, after 30 weeks 'in close preasone, in great misery' petitioned the Privy Council on his condition. They immediately ordered that he be relieved of close prison, and have liberty 'of ane free prisoner' (29th December 1643). There is nothing vindictive in the circumstances of the time, in the subsequent sentence imposed on him, and, in the following month, on a fellow religionist (*James Con* 12th January 1644), which merely required them to act and oblige themselves to depart furth of Scotland and not return.

Perhaps the most remarkable example of leniency, though doubtless contemporaries applied some other description to it, was the disposal in the case of *Mr. James Bannerman* (15th July 1646). This sometime minister at Caputh, in the Presbytery of Dunkeld, first appears in the record as imprisoned in Edinburgh for the crime of bigamy. Whether he was ever tried therefor, whether he had admitted the offence or whether he was simply detained on suspicion, is not disclosed. The crime, however, was undoubtedly regarded as a serious one in these days. *John Job* was to be scourged and banished on a plea of guilty (19th January 1650), and at least one accused, *John Guthrie* (1617, Pitcairn III, 429) had paid the supreme penalty. In Mr. Bannerman's case, however, the court's surprising, if not unique disposal, was that he become obliged to remain within the confines of Edinburgh, and subscribe an act in the books of adjournal to that effect. To the reverend gentleman, hitherto a country minister, the sentence of remaining in Edinburgh must have been received, not only with relief, but with relish. It must have afforded contemporaries an early and rare opportunity for discussion on the vexed and recurring theme of disparity of sentences. The reason for the lenience, which indeed is contrary to the relevant Act of Parliament, is not disclosed. It can hardly be that Edinburgh offered fewer temperations to the reverend gentleman than did Dunkeld, though it may be that in Edinburgh there were more of his ex-brethren ready, willing and able to keep a weather-eye on his activities.

Conclusion.—The present record ends on 17th July 1650. On that date the Justice's Court, with a calendar of unfinished business, sat for the last time for some eleven years, until the King came into his own again. It was a court that had contrived throughout the violence and the vicissitudes of the Troubles, even during the year of the great Marquis, albeit with many difficulties, many delays and many adjournments, to sit that the lieges might be 'servit of the law'. The situation in July 1650, however, was more menacing than anything produced by the domestic discords of the previous twelve years. To a people now much divided against itself had come the threat of foreign invasion, and this time from an enemy well equipped, well trained and well led. Such were the times that the Court of Session ceased to sit on 28th February 1650. The Spring and Summer of that year saw the capture and execution of the Marquis of Montrose, the uneasy association between Crown and Kirk, each hoping to use the other to further its own ends, and the continuing conflict between Zealots and Moderates. To eliminate the threat of a Covenanted King, Cromwell came north. His army was approaching Scotland on that July day when the Justice adjourned his court for what was to be its longest adjournment. Two days later the enemy was at Berwick. By the end of the month at Musselburgh. Edinburgh and the populace preparing for war, had by then more pressing concerns than even the administration of criminal justice in Scotland. On 3rd September at Dunbar, thanks to the Zealots, their preparations went for naught. Scotland suffered one of the most overwhelming defeats in her history and in its aftermath found herself subjected to a degradation such as she had not known since Edward I.

Among the many consequences of that defeat and aftermath was the replacement of the Country's traditional system of justice by one devised by her conquerors. 'Religion and justice being the tua pillers of the land were haughed and near driven doon'. At first courts were in abeyance and it was left to a committee of English officers to administer a rough but expeditious civil and criminal justice. So far as the latter was concerned, their approach was the traditional one of army officers. They had 'great respect to justice in doing execution upon malefactors such as thieves, harlots and utheris of that kind by skurgeing, hanging, kicking, cutting off their ears and stigmating of thayme with het yrnes (Nicolls *Diary* p. 69, 89). By the Declaration of 31st January 1652 all jurisdictions other than those derived from Parliament were annulled and, by April 1652, with the appointment of English Commissioners for the administration of justice, who dealt with criminal as well as civil business, the new system was introduced (Firth: *Scotland and the Commonwealth*, xxviii; p. 367). The personnel of the new system congratulated themselves that they administered criminal justice more evenly and more efficiently than did their Scots predecessors. Justice, said one commentator, was 'wont to be open and free for none formerly but great men, but now it flows equally to all (Terry: *The Cromwellian Union*, p. 180, 181), and even some Scots were constrained to concede that 'thair justice exceedit the Scottis in mony things, as wes reportit' (Nicolls *Diary*, p. 104). Undoubtedly they acted with more expedition than did the old Justice's Court if the claim is true that in 1652 they spent three days 'in the trial and fining of several persons for adultery, incest and fornication, for which there were above 60 persons brought before the judges in a day' (*Scotland and the Commonwealth*, p. 367). Above 180 cases of adultery, incest and fornication in three days by any standard represents a high incidence of adultery, incest and fornication, and truly a phenomenal expedition on the part of the court. To be able to sentence, much less try, some 60 such cases a day suggests, however, that the Commissioners had devised a form of summary procedure which was more concerned with statistics than with justice.

Expedition and impartiality, 'justice that exceedit the Scottis in mony things,' the English appointed Commissioners might provide, but, when they disappeared at the Restoration and the Justice's Court was revived, there were few to lament their passing. Expedition and impartiality might be very well, but they are tainted if they are imposed from without. As regards the old Justice's Court its procedures may have been arbitrary, its adjournments protracted and even unnecessary, its judges unwilling to accept responsibility for determining questions of law, its processes only too often used to blackmail an accused into a payment of assythment, its sentences harsh, but it had been the one tribunal with any hope of bringing to justice the powerful subject or the many bands of broken men who plagued the country and who could flout with impunity lesser jurisdictions. It was the one central criminal court which sat with any continuity throughout the period and, for all its faults, it was undoubtedly Scottish. For that alone, after 'the Englishry,' in the eyes of the lieges, it could be forgiven much. When it resumed on 29th June 1661, after the Interregnum with the ageing Alexander Colville of Blair again presiding,[1] and ready to resume where he had been obliged to leave off in 1650, the administration of criminal justice in Scotland resumed—for a further eleven years, until the court itself was reformed—its ancient, uncertain, but traditionally Scottish course.

J. IRVINE SMITH.

[1] Scott Moncrieff: *Justiciary Records*, Scottish History Society, Vol I., p. 1.

(335) [30 July 1630: Colvile and Robertoun JJ.D]

Slauchter. Reid v *Young. Acquit.*

Intran.—Johnne Young in Cassiltoun.[1]

Dilaitit of airt and pairt of the slauchter of umquhile Archibald Reid in Cassiltoun, committit in the moneth of Junii 1629 yeiris, within the dwelling hous of Thomas Moir, smyth in Cassiltoun, be streking him with ane hedget quhinger [*hedge bill*] in his richt airme and schairkill [*wrist*] bane thairof and utheris pairtis of his body to the grit effusioun of his bluid, quhairof he deceissit in October thaireftir.

Persewaris.—Elspeth Reid, as dochter; Johnne Reid, as brother; Mr. Robert Burnet, substitute[2] to Sir Thomas Hope of Craighall knycht barronet, Advocat to our Soverane Lord, for his Hienes intreis, conforme to his Lordships procuratorie producet.

Prelocutouris in defence.—Mr. Laurence McGill, John Dunlope, advocatis.

The persewaris producet the letters deulie execute and indorsate and tuik instrumentis thairupoun.

The pannell takis instrumentis of his entrie and protestis for his cautioneris releif.

Thaireftir the dittay being red and the pannell accuset be vertew thairof of airt and pairt of the slauchter abonewrittin, it is allegit that the dittay is nowayis relevant to pas to the knawlege of ane assyse in respect of the woirdis set down thairin beirand that the straik lybellit was gevin upone his schaikill bane quhilk is na vitall pairt; speciallie in respect that lang eftir the allegit straik gevin to the said Archibald Reid (nocht grantand the samyn) to the tyme of his deceis he wrocht his ordiner wark of smyth craft be forgeing at his studie making of hors schone, scheiring of his coirnes, binding and stouking and staking thairof and all uther his ordiner effairis up and down the cuntrie and nevir lay bedfast all that tyme till a littill befoir his daith hee contractit ane fever quhairof he deceissit, and sa deit nocht of that allegit wound, under protestatioun alwayis that the lybell is nawayis affirmet be the pannell in ony poynt thairof.

To the quhilk it is answerit be the perseweris that the lybell standis relevant nochtwithstanding of the exceptioun, becaus it is speciallie condiscendit thair-intill quhair the hurt and wound was gevin be the pannell, viz. the schaikill

[1] The panel was a miller (see *RPC*[2] III.26, *RMS* IX.246. Castleton is by Castlemilk in the parish of Carmunnock, Lanarkshire.

[2] See legal note 1.

bane and that the wound was deidlie and that he deceissit thairof; And as to that pairt of the alledgeance that the schaikill bane is no vitall pairt it mereitis na answer, becaus gif vitall pairtis be thais pairtis quhairin the lyfe consistis all the pairtis of the body sa man [*must*] be estimat: And gif it be tane for ane pairt *a qua fluit vita* aucht to be repellit in respect that in all pairtis of the body of ane man it is fund be experience that he may be hurt and deidlie woundit, as in the thie, the schoulder blaid, the airme, the scahkill bane, etc.; And quhair it is allegit that he convalessit and wrocht thaireftir etc., and syne fell in ane fever and deit thairof, aucht to be repellit in respect of the lybell beirand that he nevir convalessit bot deceissit of the wound, and it is nawayis relevant becaus he wrocht quhilk is nocht grantit bot that he deceisit.

To the quhilk it is duplyit be the pannell, adheirand to the former defence, that is is nottour and manifest be all experience and reasone in phisik that ony man being hurt in ane pairt of his body, quhilk is nocht ane vitall or noble pairt, and survives fourtie dayis eftir the hurt that it can [not] or may ony wayis be presumet that he deit thairof, quhair it is confessit in the dittay that he levit be the space of foure or fyve monethis eftir the hurt inflicted. And the exceptioun being tane *conjunctim* is mair pregnant nor the lybell or reply, under protestatioun alwayis that the pannell nawayis grantis the verritie of the lybell, and **(336)** forder to testifie that the persone deceissit he did nowayis apprehend ony suche thing that his allegit hurt was deidlie or that the pannell had hurt him, it is offerrit to be provin that the pannell and the defunct levit togidder in grit love and freindschip to the day of his death, ye in gritter love than with this persewar his brother.

The persewaris opponis the lybell and reply to all that is alledgit in the contrair; and as to the fourtie dayis allegit it was nevir red of aither in phisick or in law.

The Justice be interloquitour repellis the haill alledgeances abonewrittin in respect of the dittay.[1]

Assisa.—John Thomesone in Gallowhill; John Auldcorne elder in Aikinheid; Andro Ramage in Cassiltoun; Thomas Moir smith thair; Alexander Thomesone in West Cassiltoun; John Thomesone in West Cassilton; William Mitchell in Wyndhill; John Craig in Curmonnok; Andro S in Overtoun thairof; Thomas Wilkie burgess of Rutherglen; Michael Broun at Kirk of Kilbryde; Robert Mure in Westoun of Curmonnok; John Thomesone bailie of Rutherglen; John Pinkertoun proveist of Rutherglen; John Scott bailie thair.

The Advocat takis instrumentis of the sweiring of the assyse and protestis for wilfull errour gif thay acquit.

The pannel eftir reiding of the dittay takis instrumentis that nathing is producet be the persewaris for verificatioun thairof to the assyse; and for cleiring of his innocencie of the allegit cryme abonewrittin producet to the assyse ane testimoniall subscryvit be minister of Curmonnoche,[2] for himselff and in

[1] See legal note 2.
[2] Mr. Matthew McKaill was minister of Carmunnock from 1640 to 1649 (*Fasti* III.378).

name of the elderis of the said kirk and sessioun thairof, testifeing that the said minister and elderis had tryit that thair was nevir malice or discord betwix the pannell and umquhile Archibald Reid, and that nochtwithstanding of ony hurt or supposet wound gevin to him be the pannell nor nevir be word or gesture did bewray or utter ony malice or mislyk aganis him for ony caus quhatsoevir ather befoir his daith or at his daith, bot leving from the moneth of Junii to November thaireftir, the fever being befoir in his house and long eftir his daith amongst his haill famelie, he deceissit to all menis knawlege of the fever as at lenth is set down in the said testimoniall producet.

It is allegit be the persewaris that the testimoniall producet can nocht be respectit nather can it mak ony fayth, becaus it is surreptitious and subscryvit be the minister only and being allegit to be gevin out be the sessioun is nocht subscryvit be ony of the elderis; *Secundo* it is null becaus it wantis witnessis; *Tertio* it is offerit to be improvin be thais that ar upone the sessioun heir present at the bar; *Quarto* it is only the assertioun of ane man quhilk nather can be for the pannell nor aganis him.

It is answerit the objectiones maid be the persewaris aganis the testimoniall producet aucht to be repellit in respect of the testimoniall itself beirand that he is ane minister that makis the testificatioun and ane honest famous man that subscryves the same.

Quhilkis persones of assyse . . . all in ane voce be the repoirt of the said chanceller fand pronuncet and declairit the said Johne Young to be clene, innocent and acquit of airt and pairt of the slauchter of the said umquhile Archibald Reid in Cassiltoun and of the said dittay and haill poyntis thairof. Quhairupone the said Johnne Young askit instrumentis.

LEGAL NOTES.

1. This is an early example of the Lord Advocate being represented by an Advocate Depute.

2. Hume (I.185) gives a misleading impression of this case by merely saying that the defence of death after a period of time was repelled. It was however only repelled—and properly so—as a preliminary plea. The testimonial of the minister of Carmunnock that the deceased notoriously died of fever and remained on good terms with the panel was put to the assize, who thereupon acquitted. This is the only example traced of such weight being given to a ministerial certificate though they were often accepted as evidence that a panel was unfit through illness to attend his trial (see above I.55,91,118).

No evidence was apparently led for the prosecution though witnesses were available. The charge alone was read to the jury. Only on the ground that the jurors may have had personal knowledge of the incident—which from their designations is certain—and were entitled to use it in reaching their verdict, was there any reason for the panel producing his testimonial to them. If he denied the charge and the prosecutor produced no evidence, then, by modern standards an acquittal should have been automatic.

(267) [24 July 1635: Colville J. D.]

Mutilatioun. Flescheour v *Ramsay. Convict and hangit.*

Intran.—James Ramsay in Brechyn; Andro Lyndsay at the auld mylne of Ferne.

Dilaitit of airt and pairt of the hurting wounding and mutilatioun of Robert Flescheour [*Fletcher*] of Benschoe[1] of the mid finger of his richt hand, and of

[1] Ballinschoe, SE of Kirriemuir. Auld Mill of Ferne was probably on Noran water, S of Fern.

the thombe fornest finger thrid and fourt fingeris of his left hand and in effect of his haill left hand, committit neir to the kirk of Aberlemno [*Forfar*] upone the fyft day of Junii 1634 yeiris at the buriall of umquhile Margaret Fynlasone in Woidwrae,[1] the said Robert his tennent of his landis thairof.

Persewaris.—Robert Flescheour of Benschoe; Sir Thomas Hope of Craighall, knycht barronet, his Majesteis Advocat, for his Hienes intreis.[2]

Prelocutouris in defence.—Alexander Lord of Spynie.[3]

The persewar producet the letters deulie execute and indorsate upone the persones enterit upone pannell, as also aganis John Spalding at the mylne of Phynheavin (*Finhaven*], John Ramsay of Balnabreich,[4] William Ramsay in the woid of Phynheavin, and James Ramsay at the mylne of Phinheavin,[5] quhairby thay and ilk ane of thame ar lauchfullie charget be David Yieman messinger to find cautioun for thair personall compeirance befoir his Majesteis Justice and his deputtis this day and place in the hour of caus to underly the law for the cryme foirsaid mentionet thairintill, upoun the productioun quhairof togidder with ane roll of ane assyse also summond to this day upone the saidis persones defenderis the persewaris askit instrumentis and protestit for the cautioneris releif.

The persones enterit upone pannell takis instrumentis of thair entrie and protestis for thair cautioneris releif.

The persewaris past *simpliciter* fra the persute of the said James Ramsay in Brechin for the crymes contenit in the letters, quhairupone the said James Ramsay askit instrumentis.

Compeirit Alexander, Lord of Spynie, quha declairit that he compeiris this day as prelocutour for the said Andro Lyndsay now upone pannell in respect he could get na uther advocat or procuratour to defend in this matter.

My Lord Advocat answerit that he is weill pleisit that the pannell or my Lord of Spynie as prelocutour for him compeir and propone for his defence in law quhat he can or pleissis to eleid the criminall letters producet and red, bot as to the want of uther procuratouris the persewar declairis that he is sure gif it had pleisit my Lord of Spynie or the pannell to haif supplicat and cravet ather from the Lordis of Secreit Counsall or Lords of Sessioun advocatis it wald nocht haif bene refuiset, bot advocatis wald haif bene compellit to haif compeirit and pleidit in law for the pannellis defence under the pane of hoirning,[6] and it is nocht nor hes nocht bene the custome of this judicatorie to defer the persute of criminall letters or pairteis criminallie persewit in default of procuratouris to defend, speciallie quhair the pairtie defenderis uses na dilligence thame selffis to haif procuratouris for thair lauchfull defence.

[1] Woodwrae, just N of Aberlemno Kirk.

[2] See legal note 1.

[3] Alexander (Lindsay), 2nd Lord Spynie took part in public affairs (*Scots Peerage* VIII.162-164) but is not in *Lyon's List* as a member of the Bar. On the 7th of this month Fletcher successfully appealed to the Privy Council to stop a prosecution against him for alleged illegal apprehension instigated by Spynie who, he alleged, had mutilated him in 1634 (*RPC*2. vi.44; above I.238).

[4] 3 miles W of Brechin.

[5] There are Finavon names 5 miles NE of Forfar, near Tannadice.

[6] See legal note 2.

It was thaireftir allegit be my Lord of Spynie as prelocutour for Andro Lyndsay now upone pannell that na mutilatioun can be qualifeit nor provin in this persute aganis the pannell becaus thair is na testificatioun of chirurganes producet for cleiring thairof, and, gif ony sic testificatioun be, my Lord of Spynie for the pannell declairis he hes the contrair testification;[1] and farder allegit that, my Lord of Spynie himself, now prelocutour, being callit and convenit befoir my Lord Lyndsay as bailyie of the regalitie of Sanctandrois and his bailyie deputis for invaiding and bluiding of this persewar, he is convict in the said bailyie court of the persute and hurting of the said persewar.[2]

To the quhilk it is answerit be the persewaris that, albeit the former allegeance war verifeit as it is nocht, yit it can nocht be respectit *hoc loco*, nocht the first pairt of the said allegeance anent the testificatioun of chirurganes, becaus it is nawayis competent aganis the relevancie of the lybell to stay the samyn to pas to the tryell of ane assyse, bot is only competent aganis the probatioun; and as to secund pairt, anent his lordschips [*Lord Spynie's*] convictioun befoir my Lord Lyndsay, that can nocht purge the pannell of being airt and pairt of the cryme lybellit in this judicatorie aganis him.

It is farder allegit be my Lord of Spynie for the pannell that the Justice is nocht judge competent in this matter becaus the samyn sould be judget be the lord of the regalitie and boundis quhair the deid was committit, and the proceiding of the Justice herein is nothing elis bot to tak away the privilege and power of regaliteis quhilkis ar lauchfullie establischet be the Kingis Majestie and Estaitis of Parliament.[3]

It is answerit be my Lord Advocat that na regalitie hes previlege of repledgeing bot only of the persones inhabitantis and dwelling within the boundis of that regalitie, quhilk the defender now upone pannell is nocht, quha dwellis within the schirefdome of Forfar and nocht within the regalitie; and farder gifand the pannell had his residence and dwelling in the regalitie, quhilk is nocht, the allegeance aucht to be repellit except the regalitie war verifeit and that the bailyie or lord of the regalitie compeirit to replege conforme to his infeftment thairof.

The Justice be interlocutour repellis the alledgeances and findis proces, quhairupone the persewaris askit instrumentis.

Assisa.—James Dempster in Brechyn; James Lyndsay at the mylne of Kiriemure; James Gordoun in Over Benscho; John Ogilvie in Braikie; Adame Symsone in Carsgownie; John Semple, proveist of Dumbartene; Malcolme Crawfurd of Catisburne; Capitane Peter Rollok, chanceller; John Rollok, brother to Rollok of Powis; Chairles Dikiesone, burges of Forfar; David Dickiesone, bailyie of Forfar; John Symsone in Carsgownie; John Dikiesone, maltman in Forfar; James Smyth in Breachin; Andro Lyndsay [in] Fitterrago.

The persewars takis instrumentis of the sweiring of the assyse, and producet the doctouris and chirurganes testimoniall verifeing the mutilatioun

[1] See legal note 3.
[2] See legal note 4.
[3] See legal note 5.

lybellit subscryvit be Doctour Sibbald and be thre chirurganes, viz. John Pringle, David Douglas and James Brown.

The persewar at the desyre of the pannell being urget to geve his ayth gif the cryme lybellit was committit be the pannell, the said Robert Fletscheour persewar accoirding thairto, being deiplie sworne, declairit that the lybell is of verritie as it is sett down, and that thairfoir he hes just caus to persew the pannell as airt and pairt of the mutilatioun lybellit,[1] quhairupone my Lord Advocat askit instrumentis.

It is allegit aganis James Gordoun in Over Benscho that he can nocht be admittit upone this assyse becaus he is nocht worth the Kingis unlaw.

To the quhilk it is answerit nocht *relevat*, becaus he is ane heritour of landis and yairdis in Kiriemure, haldin of the laird of Fintrie and of the knycht of Innerquharritie, quhilkis payis to him xx lib. be yeir of yeirlie rent quhilk was verifeit, in respect quhairof the Justice admittis him as assysour.[2]

[Verdict: guilty 'be pluralitie of voittis'.][3]

In respect of the quhilk convictioun the Justice ordanit the said Andro Lyndsay to be committit to waird within the tolbuth or wairdhous of Edinburgh thairin to remane upone his awin expenssis quhill the Counsallis will and declaratioun war signefeit thairupoun.[4]

[The same day Alexander Lord of Spynie, as cautioner[5] fined for the non-compearance of James Ramsay at the mill of Phyneavin, John Spalding there, William Ramsay in the wood of Phineavin, John Ramsay of Bannabreich and Harry Guthrie, brother of the laird of Memes,[6] and they were put to the horn.]

LEGAL NOTES.

1. The Lord Advocate was a joint prosecutor in these criminal letters, and not as in some other cases merely a consenter.

2. It was here asserted by the Crown that the panel could apply to the Privy Council or Court of Session to have counsel appointed for him (p. 316). This indeed seems the plain meaning of the Act 1587 cap. 91 and the editor respectfully disagrees with the contrary view taken by the Court in *Graham* v *Cuthbert* 1951 *J.C.* 25. That decision may be justified as regards Sheriff Courts, but not the reasoning as regards criminal courts in general. Counsel were appointed by the Court of Session for the Countess of Errol in 1597 (Pitcairn I(ii).367). Hume notes other examples of this in 1633-34 (II.29-30 n.2) which were overlooked by their Lordships in *Graham*. The clearest enunciation of the principle is in the Lord Advocate's remarks in the present case where the panels show no indication of having been persons of substance, and already had representation. Lord Spynie (b.1597, *Scots Peerage* VIII.102,162-4) however does not appear as a member of the bar in *Lyon's List* and his acting for the panel may be explained by the part he himself played in the incident giving rise to the prosecution. See note 4 below. Certainly his submissions do not suggest a legal training. (See notes 3, 4 and 5 below.) A careful examination of the Privy Council Register by Sheriff P. G. B. McNeill revealed no case where the Privy Council appointed counsel, but where Lord Ochiltree had chosen his own counsel in his trial for leasing making in 1631, the Privy Council ordained them to act (*RPC*[2] IV.345; see above I.191). The Lord Justice General (Cooper) in *Graham* brushed aside Alison's view that the Act meant what it said (II.370) and their Lordships' remarks there show that they could not bring themselves to realize that the old attitudes of extreme hostility to the panel

[1] See legal note 6.
[2] See legal note 7.
[3] See legal note 8.
[4] See legal note 9.
[5] Counsel acting as cautioner for his client is unusual.
[6] He is not among those mentioned as cited; Mems and Memus are both near Kirriemuir.

were beginning to be overcome by the late sixteenth century, though the pendulum may have swung back in the seventeenth.

There is a familiar ring about the Lord Advocate's remark that it was not the practice of the Justiciary Court to delay trials where the accused was not legally represented 'speciallie quhair the pairtie defenderis uses na dilligence thameselffis to haif procuratouris for thair lauchfull defence'. He would have found himself in agreement with the Lord Justice Clerk (Thomson) in *Thomson* v *H.M. Advocate* 1959 J.C. p.15 at page 18.

3. A complaint that a necessary production had not been lodged in advance was repelled as an objection to relevancy as it would be today.

4. Spynie's second submission on behalf of the panel was that he himself, i.e. Spynie, had been convicted by the Regality Court of St Andrews of 'invading and bluiding' the pursuer, i.e. presumably that he had been convicted of the offences for which the panel was now being prosecuted. As the pursuers very properly pointed out, his Lordship's conviction did not preclude the panel's being accessory of the crime. See Pitmeddan I.88.

5. The defence plea that the justice had no jurisdiction at all was without merit. It was for the Regality Court in question to act and for its baillie to appear to claim his privilege (see Pitmedden I.88).

6. The term Verity is here, as often, used with reference to the oath of calumny which is taken by a pursuer *in limine* to the effect that he has just cause to proceed. The proper oath of verity was taken by the defender when the cause was perilled upon his oath (see *RPC*[1] X.106; *RPC*[2] III.499), which was not appropriate to proper criminal proceedings (Mackenzie II.xxv i), though there are examples of it in these volumes (e.g., William Black 3rd July 1646).

7. Kings unlaw' = £10. The necessary financial standard of jurors is dealt with in Mackenzie—Criminals II.xxiii.6 and xvi.2.

8. This is one of the rare majority verdicts.

9. There is no reference in the *RPC* as to what happened to Lindsay. He presumably purchased a remission. The side note that he was "hangit" cannot be accurate.

(000) [4 August 1635: Colville J.D.]

Theft and Heirschip. Lord Advocate v *Duncane Watsone and others.*

hangit	[1]	Duncane Watsone in Auchmany;
hangit	[2]	Johnne Gordoun in Woidheid;
baneist	[3]	Johnne McInnes;
hangit	[4]	Williame Beg in Wastertoun besyde Strathbogie;
hangit	[5]	James Cowie } sones to Alexander Cowie in Rawis;
baneist	[6]	Alexander Cowie } sones to Alexander Cowie in Rawis;
baneist	[7]	Johnne Cassie, borne in Banff;
hangit	[8]	Robert Moir at the mylne of Glenconrie;
hangit	[9]	Allaster Forbes in Strathdone;
acquit	[10]	Johnne Greg, chopman *alias* Gregour;
hangit	[11]	Thomas Grant in Knokalie in Urquhart;
baneist	[12]	Robert Watsone within the parochin of Carnewath;
hangit	[13]	Johne Aitkyn in Payntland.[1]

Dilaitit of dyvers poyntis of thift and utheris crymes specifeit and contenit in thair dittayis.

[1] Two of the accused (Nos. 3 and 10) are not sufficiently designated for identification; Nos. 1 and 2, 4-6, 9 and 11 were from Aberdeenshire; No. 7 was born in Banff, No. 12 is from Lanarkshire, and Nos. 8 and 13 have not been identified. No. 13 may be from Pentland, S.E. of Edinburgh, but his crimes were then committed more than twenty miles away; (Item 13, below).

Persewar.—Sir Thomas Hope of Craighall knycht, his Majestis Advocat for his Hienes intreis.

Assisa.—Alexr. Irwing of Lenturk; George Dempster in Newtoun; James Seatoun, burgess of Aberdene; John Ogilvie of Glassache; Mr. James Leith in Bucharne; John Caddell servitor to Ballindalloch; Alexr. Abercrombie of Birkenboig; Hector Abercrombie of Fetterneir; Alexander Keith of Duffes; George Bruce burges of Abirdene; Charles Stevin litster in Abirdene; George Gordon of Tilliechardie; Mr. Mathow Lumisden burges of Ab[erdeen]; John Duff burgess thair; John Grant fiar of Ballindalloche; assysers for the haill panells except Thomas Grant. Alexander Bannerman of Elsich assysor only for the said Thomas Grant with the other 14 preceiding Ballindalloche.

The Advocat for verificatioun of the dittayis producet the pannellis depositiones and confessiones of the crymes thairin contenit, askit instrumentis thairupoun and of the sweiring of the assyse and protestit for wilfull errour aganis thame gif thay acquit.[1]

Quhilkis persones of assyse being chosein sworne and admittit, eftir accusatioun be dittay at the instance of his Majesteis Advocat of the haill threttene persones befoir nominat upone pannell of the severall and perticuler crymes underwrittin specifeit thairintill: viz. [1] the said Duncane Watsone in Auchmanie off airt and pairt and being in companie with Adame Gordoun callit of Park, and utheris oppin and notorious rebellis callit the licht horsemen, in the northe pairtis of this realme at the grit heirschipis committit be thame upone the laird of Frendraucht and his tennentis dwelland upone his landis of Cowbairdie, Monalie, Cornehauche, Conzie Auchintynder, Boigfowtoun, Tortreis, Auchairnie, Glenmailling and Bagownie[2] committit in the moneth of lastbypast; and for the thiftious ressetting of the said Adame Gordoun of Park his handis of xxviii of the stowin and reft guidis, sic as ky, stottis and stirkis, rest and stowin be way of maisterfull thift and stouthreif fra the said laird of Frendrauchtis tennentis of his saidis lands; *Item* for contravening of his Majesteis Actis of Parliament[3] in beiring and weiring of hagbutis and pistolettis, schiting and mutilating of Archibald Mair thairwith, and streking and schuiting out of his eie; *Item* for the thiftious steilling of thre oxin furth of Bocharne pertening to Andro Thomesone in the boigis of Nothe and John Leith his tennent, at the leist the samyn thre oxin war thiftiouslie resset be the said Duncane af the principall steillaris handis immediatlie eftir the steilling thairof of certane knawlege that thai war stowin oxin, for the quhilk he payit only sax dollouris to the steillar thairof, as is confessit be him in his depositioun; And last the said Duncane for being in company with the saidis licht horsemen speciallie with Adame of Park [*sic*], Alexander Leith, John Braibner, Duncane Cuming, and utheris rebellis thair complices since thair first breking out, expres aganis the Actis of Parliament and his Majesteis

[1] Some of the assyse were later pursued for error in acquitting James Gordon, son of George Gordon of Logiealton (Vol. I. p. 241).

[2] Frendraught, 6 miles E. of Huntly, Strathbogie, Aberdeenshire. Cowbairdie and Corniehaugh are in a bend of the Deveron N. of Huntly. Auchairnie is near Frendraught, Monalie W. of it, and Auchentinder, S. The rest have not been traced.

[3] 1567 cap. 18; 1597 cap. 252; 1600 cap. 6.

proclamationes publeist thairupoun dischargeing all intercommoning or keiping company with thame, or furneissing ony meit drink money or uther confortable suppoirt to thame or ony of thame under the pane of deid.

[2] The said John Gordoun of Woidheid for being in companie with the said Adame Gordoun of Park, and of airt and pairt with him and his complices, rebellis and fugitives, at the steilling reiveing and away taking of James Clerkis guidis furth of Pennyburne in *anno* 1631 yeiris, at quhilk tyme xxxvi heid of nolt war thiftiouslie stowin, reft and away tane be the said Adame and his complices, speciallie certane hieland men brocht down be the said Adame of Park for herrieing of the said laird of Frendraucht his landis, off the quhilk xxxvi heid of nolt ane pairt was gottin and resset be the said John Gordoun, lykas he hes confessit in his depositioun his ressait of ane of thame being ane quoy.

[3] *Item*, the said John McInnes for contravening his Majesteis proclamatioun in following and keiping company with the said Adame Gordoun of Park and his complices, rebellis callit the licht horsemen, be the space of fourtene dayis togidder, and thairthrow airt and pairt with thame of the haill heirschipis committit be thame upone the said laird of Frendraucht and his tennentis in that tyme, quhilk being in the said rebellis company be the space foirsaid is confessit be him in his depositioun.

[4] *Item*, the said Williame Beg in Wastertoun for contravening his Majesteis proclamatioun in following and keiping company with the saidis rebellis and being airt and pairt with thame of the grit hearschip tane and reft away be thame out of the said laird of Frendrauchtis landis of Cowbairdie and Layneshaw in the moneth of Merche lastbypast, and of airt and pairt with the saidis rebellis of the herrieing, steilling and reifing of George Gairdnes houssis in Brokin Fauld under nycht at the tyme foirsaid, and taking away of his haill guidis, geir, insicht and plenissing pertening to the said George Gairdin: and for airt and pairt of the steilling of ane meir fra Alexander Smyth in Monalie sauld be him thaireftir to Thomas Duff in Inchethomak, confessit in his depositioun.

[5:6] *Item*, the saidis James and Alexander Coweis for cuming togidder in Februar last 1635 yeiris to the place of Frendraucht and thair under nycht for steilling and away taking of the haill lokis, irne bandis aff the duris and houssis of the said place, togidder with ane new camnes [*canvas*] of fourtene elnes, threscoir sax heares of small lynning [*linen*] yarne, ane stane of butter, ane quarter of lynt, with sindrie uther guidis, with the quhilk thai war challanget be David Angus, servitour to the said laird of Frendraucht; *Item* for steilling of ane new gray plaid fra John Donald in Murefeild, and of twa pair of hoise fra Robert Patersone; *Item*, for being in company with the rebellis at the grit heirschip committit upone the laird of Frendrauchtis tennentis of the Layneschaw, breking up of the dwelling house of Andro Gallen, steilling and away taking of the haill insicht and plenissing being thairin.

[7] *Item*, the said John Cassie for being in companie with the saidis James and Alexander Coweis at the steilling of the said John Donald his new gray plaid, as also in company with thame at the breking up of the said Andro Gallenis house, and steilling and away taking of the haill insicht and plenissing being thairintill.

[8] *Item*, the said Robert More for airt and pairt of the thiftious steilling furth of Boddome of saxscoir foure scheip pertening to Alexander and Andro

Leslies thair, committit be him in companie of Alexander Scheirar, John Jafray, Thomas Kelleid, George Gairne, and utheris thair complices, commoun and notorious thevis, quhairof conforme to his depositioun the said Robert Moir gat twelf scheip for his skair [*share*].

[9] *Item*, the said Allaster Forbes for airt and pairt of the robbing of William Leslie at the mylne of Inche, steilling and away taking fra him of his horse, his cloik sword and purse with the moneyis being thairin; as also for airt and pairt of the thiftious resetting of fyve blak stowin scheip af the steilleris handis in the moneth of November last.

[10 see later.]

[11] *Item*, the said Thomas Grant for the tressonable ressett of the tratour James Grant callit of Carrone, and keiping of him in maist secreit and quyet maner within his killogie[1] of Knokalie, he haifing in companie with him John Grant, fiear of Ballindalloche as his prissoner, quhome he keipit in companie with him in the said killogie the space of sevintene dayis and 17 nychtis, the said tratour James Grant being all that tyme furneist be the said Thomas Grant in meit, drink, bedding and all uther necessar thingis, confessit be the said Thomas in his depositiones to be of verritie contrair to his Majesteis proclamationes.

[12] *Item*, the said Robert Watsoun in Carlandame [*Carlindean, Carnwath*] for the thiftious steilling of ten scheip fra John Lyddell upone the thrid day of Julii last, with the quhilk fang of the saidis ten scheip, stowin be you the tyme foirsaid, ye was challanget and apprehendit, quhilk he hes confessit to be of verritie be his depositioun.

[13] *Item*, the said John Aitkyn, servand to Charles Brown in Pantland, for the thiftious steilling under nycht about Michelmes last 1634 of sax Lambes furth of the parochin of Pittienane [*Pettinain*] and schirefdome of Lanerk, quhilkis sax lambes pertening to William Mar and David Johnstoun in Grange within the parochein of Pittienane and schirefdome of Lanerk, as is confessit be the said John in his depositioun: *Item*, for steiling of nyne auld scheip and fyve lambes, furth of the parochin of Libbertoun and schirefdome of Lanerk, committit upone the nyntene day of Maii lastbypast; And last for the thiftious steilling and away taking of twa oxin furth of the landis of Gledstanes [*Gladstone*] within the parochin of Carnewath committit be him upone the xxiiii day of Julii lastbypast, confessit all be the said John Aitkyn judiciallie to be of verritie.

[14] *Item*, the said John Greg *alias* Gregour chopman for being in companie with Adame Gordoun of Park, William McGillievorie, and utheris of the licht horsemen rebellis and fugitives be the space of fourtene dayis togidder, and for being airt and pairt with thame of taking away be way of maisterfull thift and stouth reiff of the grit hearschip laitlie rest and tane up of the laird of Frendraucht his landis of Cowbairdie fra his tennentis thairof, quhairof fourtie heid of nolt of the said hearschip war drevin be the said John Gregour to Bryak fair.

[Verdict ('all in ane voce'); all guilty except John Greg *alias* Gregour who was acquitted of the crimes in his dittay.]

[1] A space beside the fireplace in a kiln.

In respect quhairof the Justice ordanit the haill persones on pannell to be tane up to the tolbuth of Edinburgh, thairin to remane quhill he be adviset with the counsall anent thair dome.

(275) [17 August 1635: Colvile J.D.]

Dome pronuncet upone Duncane Watsone, Johnne Gordoun and utheris.

The whilk day the persones underwrittin viz.: Duncane Watsone in Auchmanie; John Gordoun in Woidheid; Williame Beg in Wastertoun; James Cowie, sone to Alexander Cowie in Rawis; Johnne Cassie, borne in Banff; Robert Moir, at the mylne of Glenconrie; Allaster Forbes in Strathdone; Thomas Grant in Knokalie in Urquhart; John McInnes; Alexander Cowie, brother to the said James Cowie; Robert Watsone; and John Aitkyn, being brocht furth of waird and presentit upone pannell to heir dome pronuncet aganis thame as thay that war deulie and ordourlie convict be ane assyse in ane Justice court haldin upone the fourt day of August instant off the severall crymes contenit in thair dittayis; . . . and siclyk James Gordoun, son to George Gordoun of Logyaltoun, Donald McAirthur and John Menzies and John Grant, being lykwayis brocht out of waird and presentit upone pannell to heir dome pronuncet aganis thame as thay that war convict of the crymes contenit in thair conviction in ane Justice Court haldin in the Tolbuth of Edinburgh be Mr. Alexander Colvile, Justice Depute, upone the fift day of August instant,[1] [And] the Justice, be the mouth of Andro McAirthour, dempster of court, decernit, adjudget and ordanit the saidis Duncane Watsone, Johnne Gordoun, William Beg, James Cowie, Robert Moir, Allaster Forbes, Thomas Grant, John Aitkyn, Donald McArchour and John Menzies and ilk ane of thame, to be tane to the burrow mure of Edinburgh and thair to be hangit upone the gibbet thairof quhill thay be deid, and all thair moveabill guidis to be escheit and inbrocht to his Majesteis use as convict of the thiftious crymes contenit in thair dittayis; And siclyk decernit and ordanit the saidis James Gordoun, sone to the said George Gordoun of Logyaltoun, Alexander Cowie, Johnne Cassie, Robert Watsone, John McInnes, togidder with George Wat, John Grant and William Knokwoid in Cumnok, also dilaitit of thift and wairdit for the samyn within the tolbuth or wairdhouse of Edinburgh, to be of thair awin consent baneist this realme and nevir to be fund within the samyn at ony tyme heireftir without his Majesteis licence under the pane of deid; lykas the saidis James Gordoun, Alexander Cowie, John Cassie, Robert Watsone, Johnne McInnes, George Watt, John Grant, and William Kirkwoid actit thameselffis of thair awin consentis to depairt and pas away af this kingdome in companie of Capitane Thomas Moffet, and to serve him in the weiris and nocht to returne within this kingdome without his Majesteis licence heireftir under the pane foirsaid; And the said Capitane Thomas Moffet being personallie present acceptit thame as his sojoures and obleist him to transpoirt thame furth of this kingdome with

[1] These are all accused from another case not printed in the present collection but summarized in Vol. I, p. 241.

himselff swa that thai sould nocht be sene on the publict streittis or hiewayis quhill thair schipping and putting aburde, under the pane of fyve hundred merkis money.

LEGAL NOTE

The designation of the third and tenth panels seems quite insufficient (see Hume II.157).

This is the first case in this printed volume of a prosecution on indictment and of their being no legal representation though the crimes charged were capital.

(288) [26 November 1635: Colvile J.D.]

James Johnstone of Corheid.

Slauchter and illegal imprisonment. Moffet v *Johnstone. Desertit.*

The samyn day anent the criminall letters direct at the instance of James Moffet as eldest sone, Williame, Thomas and Walter Moffettis, his brether, also as sones, Jonet and Margaret Moffettis, as dochteris, Johnne Moffet, spous to the said Jonet for his entreis, James Moffet of Hoilhouse, John Moffet of Mekill Holme, James and Robert Moffettis, indwelleris in the town of Moffet, as neir kynsmen, with the remanent kyn and freindis of umquhile Mungo Moffet, indweller in the said town of Moffet, aganis James Johnstoun of Corheid,[1] sone naturall to umquhile Capitane James Johnstoun of Lochhouse, chargeing him to have fund cautioun for his personall compeirance befoir his Majesteis Justice and his deputtis this day and place to haif underlyne the law for the crymes following, viz. for invaiding hurting and wounding of the said umquhile Mungo Moffet in the foirheid committit within the town of Moffet in the moneth of October lastbypast, in ane fencet court haldin be the said James Johnstoun within the dwelling hous of James Moffet indweller thair, quhilk straik hurt and wound was gevin be the said James Johnstoun to the said umquhile Mungo in the said fencet court with ane battone or pyket [*pointed*] stalff than being in the said James his hand, and thaireftir for committing of him to prissone as ane malefactour within the wairdhous of the said town of Moffet, quhairin he was keipit and detenit in strait firmance and captivitie fra ellevin houris befoir none all that day and nicht following quhill the morne thaireftir about nyne or ten houris befoir noone, he being his Majesteis frie subject, and the said James Johnstoun haveing na warrand, power nor commissioun swa to haif strukin, abuset and incarcerat the said umquhile Mungo in maner foirsaid, off the quhilk hurt and deidlie straik gevin to the said umquhile Mungo in the foirheid be the said James Johnstoun in forme and maner abonewrittin he deceissit schortlie thaireftir, and swa was nocht only crewallie and unmerciefullie slane be the said James Johnstoun in forme and maner abonewrittin, bot also the said James Johnstoun in casting the said umquhile Mungo in pressone without warrand, Mungo being his Majesteis frie subject for the tyme, hes thairthrow usurpet upone him his Majesteis royall power authoritie and committit thairby oppin and manifest treasone,[2] as at

[1] Holehouse and Meikleholm are 2 miles N. of Moffat and Carehead 5 miles, near the Devil's Beeftub, all in Dumfriesshire.

[2] See legal note 1.

length is contenit in the saidis criminall letters. The foirnamet persones, persewaris thairof, compeirand be Mr Alexander Johnstoun, advocat,[1] as **(289)** procuratour for thame, quha producet the saidis criminall letters deulie execute and indorsate upone the said James Johnstoun, askit instrumentis thairupoun and protestit for releif of the saidis persewar cautioneris fund be thame at the raiseing thairof on the uther pairt; And on the uther pairt the said James Johnstoun of Corheid, defender, compeirand personallie in judgement, and enterand himselff upone pannell with George Deanes, advocat,[2] his prelocutour, quha producet ane Act of the Lordis of his Majesteis Secreit Counsall of the dait tennour and contentis underwrittin, quhairof the tennour followis;

Edinburgh, 26 November 1635. James Johnstoun, natural son of deceased Captain Johnstoun, called of Lochhouse, complains that he has been wrongfully charged by the above parties to compear this day before the Justice and his deputes for alleged detaining and slaughter of deceased Mungo Moffet. After hearing the reasons and allegations of the parties together with the depositions of witnesses for James Johnstoun, and the depositions and declarations of the relict, bairns and friends of the deceased, the Lords of Secret Council find that the said Mungo was committed to ward by the bailie of the Regality of Moffett for misbehaviour against himself; that he was in good health during his abode in ward where his friends had access to him 'eit and drank with him and tuik tobacco;' that on the morn when freed from ward he passed to the harvest field, bound and stooked his corn after the shearers and followed a hare 'to have red it frome the doggis and that he kuist his bonnet befoir it and that he had nather mutche nor clothe on his heid, and that in the following of the hair he lap als frelie over the burne as gif he had bene ane young man'; and that having attended the shearers until night he came home, supped and went to bed in good health, 'and was nather seik nor sair and that a prinkling [*tingling*] haifing fallin in his leg, and his awin wyfe being in bed with him halding him up, he deit suddantlie in hir airmes, and that his heid being narowlie luikit be sum being in the house who come in upone the raiseing of the schoute for his deathe, thay fand no kynd of swelling nor no taikin nor appeirance of ony hurt or harme that he had ressavit'. The Lords therefore find the said James Johnestoun innocent of the slaughter of the said Mungo, and of his detention in ward and ordain the Justice, Justice Clerk and their deputes to desert the said diet and to desist from pursuing him for these crimes hereafter, because the said James Johnstoun exhibited an act and rolment of the barony court of Moffet bearing that the said deceased Mungo had been lawfully committed for his 'misbehaviour and opprobrious speiches utteret be him against the bailyie and officer,' and produced witnesses whose depositions all agreed 'in ane voce,' and also because the relict and friends of the deceased gave no clear evidence against the said Johnestoun and declared that they would not 'sweir his dittay'.[3]

Eftir the productioun and reiding of the quhilk act and declaratour of Counsall the said James Johnstoun with his prelocutour abonenominat desyret that

[1] Son of Robert Johnston of Raecluch. Admitted 30 Jan. 1634 (*Lyon's List*, p. 112).

[2] Designed as 'servitor to Robert Burnett of Cringletie', admitted advocate 19 Nov. 1633 (*Lyon's List* 52).

[3] See *RPC*2 VI.141.

conforme to the ordinance and command set down thairintill the said criminall dyet mycht be desertit, and that his Majesteis Justice sould desist and ceis frome all calling accuseing or persewing of the said James Johnstoun, defender, for the said cryme at ony tyme heireftir for the ressones and caussis contenit in the said Act of Counsall. The Justice conforme to the Act of Counsall abonewritten and for obedience of thair lordschips ordinance and command sett down thairintill desertis the saidis criminall letters and dyet abonewrittin affixt and appoynttit thairintill, quhairupone the said James Johnstoun of Corheid, defender, with the said George Deanes, advocate, his prelocutour, askit actis and instrumentis.[1]

LEGAL NOTES.

1. The charge here avers that by illegally imprisoning the deceased the panel thereby 'usurpet upone him his Majesteis royall power and authoritie and committed thereby oppin and manifest treasone'. By the Act 1567 cap. 21 thieves taking any Scotsman captive were made liable to the pains of treason and *lese Majeste* i.e. the crime was made statutory treason. The Act was interpreted as applying whether the captives were taken over the Border or not (Mackenzie, *Criminals*, I.vi.xvii), but it applied only to thieves taking men captive. No case has been traced before 1604 where it was neld to be *treason* for persons other than thieves to take another captive. In that year *George Meldrum Younger* was charged *inter alia* with seizing and holding captive a number of men—including a Clerk of Session! The libel concluded that the accused was 'usurpand thairby our Soverane Lordis auctoritie upone thame, in taking the saidis persones, thay being his Majesteis frie leigis; haifing na power nor commissioun to that effect; in manifest contempt of his Majestie, committand thairby manifest tressone' (Pitcairn II.428-9). No reference was made to the Act 1567 cap. 21 for this proposition, but the accused confessed and there was no challenge of the relevancy. The proposition however was accepted by the Court in an interlocutor appearing to lay down for the first time that these facts amounted in law to treason. According to the report in Pitcairn (p.429) sentence was passed by the Justice General, and his principal depute (Hart) 'be the advyse of John, Erle of Montrois, Chancellor of this Realme, and dyverse utheris Lordis of his Majesteis Secreit Counsall and Session than sitting in judgement as Assessouris (*finding the saidis crymes to be tressonable*)'. Hume (I.83) considered this approach 'a rather strained notion', and it is submitted that it was not warranted by the statutory law of treason as it stood at that date. In the case of *Cunningham* v *Lieut. Mark Kerr* 13 November 1649, below however, no objection to the relevancy was tabled on this point although there was a debate on preliminary pleas. In the present case the libel follows very closely that of *Meldrum*.

Robert Fletcher of Ballinshoe was prosecuted for illegal imprisonment on 17th June 1635 but the Privy Council intervened to save him (above I.238). Complaint could also be made to the Privy Council of this crime (*RPC*[2] 1633.V.168).

By Hume's time the crime had become obsolete (I.83). Illegal imprisonment was still a criminal offence (I.339), but was considered by Hume as an aspect of the law respecting prosecution and trial.

2. This is the first case in this volume where the Privy Council interfered with the functions of the Justice Court. They held a pretrial before themselves, apparently on letters of precognition, on the issues of whether the deceased's original imprisonment was justified, and whether any injury he sustained in fact caused his death. They answered both in favour of the present accused and directed the Justice to desert the diet *simpliciter*.

Intervention by the Privy Council became increasingly common in the seventeenth century and took various forms. Some instances were unexceptional, as where the Privy Council ordered criminal diets to be continued because of harvest, to ensure that an accused was served with an indictment and had access to legal representation, or, where desertion was ordered on a supplication narrating that the kin of a slaughtered man and his slayer had agreed to submit their differences to arbitration. They might also appoint or order counsel to act for an accused before the Justice Court (Lord Ochiltree above I.176, 191). It might also be useful where what was involved were alleged defects in the trial court (*RPC*[2] V.167). Their interventions in other ways however were open to criticism as being, or appearing to be, an interference with the normal administration of the criminal law and the functioning of the

[1] See legal note 2.

Justice Court. On occasions they appointed some of their members to sit as assessors in the Justice Court. Several examples are reported in Vol. 1 of the present collection, of the Privy Council ordering cessation of prosecutions for reasons undisclosed (Vol. 1, 25, 43, 92, 150). In 1626 Charles I on being applied to for a Remission asked the Council to investigate a plea of self defence, which they held established. Here no prosecution appears to have been commenced (*RPC*[2] I.317-8).

The principal method of Privy Council intervention however was by Letters of Precognition. This process was an enquiry into the circumstances of fact in a criminal charge initiated by the party accused and conducted with less formality than a trial (Hume II.28). In the earlier part of the seventeenth century there are numerous entries in the Council Register relating the granting of Letters of Precognition on which subsequent decrees are only occasionally recorded (e.g. *RPC*[1] IX.33). Later however the grant of Letters and their conclusion is more fully recorded. In theory this process was considered appropriate: (1) where 'considerable persons are interested in the crimes committed, as noblemen or clans,' and where to remit to the ordinary Justice court might aggravate feud; and (2) when the circumstances of the crime were such that mitigation of penalty was necessary (Mackenzie, *Criminals,* II.vi.5). In practice however the scope was much wider and numerous examples might be cited. In *McMorran* v *Hamilton* 1628 (above I.82, 90) a panel accused of mutilation was tried first by the Council on a charge of Riot and acquitted, and then succeeded in a plea of *autrefois acquit* before the Justice who was ordered by the Council to desert. In another case the Council appointed two commissioners to take precognition of a sheep stealing case, and ordered the Justice Court to continue the criminal diet. It does not appear that in this case there was any special defence, which might have been contrary to the libel (*RPC*[2] VI.266-7). The conclusion is not recorded. In *Oswald* v *Rutherford* 1636 (below p. 328) the Council investigated the matter and acquitted because the acts libelled were done in the exercise of magisterial duty. In *Stewart of Ardvorlich* v *St Andrews students* 1643 (30 June 1643; *RPC*[2] VII.430) the Council held that the injuries sustained did not cause the death. After the Restoration there was an inconclusive result of Council intervention in *Coltherd* v *Sir John Bannatyne yr. of Corehouse* 1662-6 (Scott Moncrieff I.53, 151). In *Gregory* v *James Crichton and others* (*ibid* I.94, 100) the King directed the Justice Court to sist all process until the Council at the instigation of the King enquired if the deceased died of the wounds inflicted or of some other cause, but one of the panels broke ward, and so was held to have accepted guilt 'after which the Council refused to proceed in the Precognition which they had begun for his Majesties information'. In *Graham* v *Henderson* 1666 (Scott Moncrieff I.139) the Council investigated an allegation of slaughter, found that it was 'accidentally committed in a Tumult' and discharged all criminal pursuits raised or to be raised.

On occasions doubts as to the competency of the process of Precognition were expressed by the Council itself, and they appear to have been unwilling to extend the grounds on which the process was granted. In *Hay and Another* v *Leslies* 1633 (*RPC*[2] V.167); where the panels accused of slaughter impeached a third party as the person inflicting the wound, the Council intervened but with obvious reluctance. It was maintained that justice could not be expected in the Justice Court because of 'the unconstant and ignorant voices of ane country assize, who ar commounlie chosin be the partie persewar and ar persons for the most part at his devotioun'. (Until 1672 the prosecutor could cite what jurymen he liked (see Acts 1579 c. 76, 1587 c. 89), Hume II.305-7). As the locus, however, was Old Rayne near Inverurie in Aberdeenshire, it is difficult to see why they should have been any more biased than in any other of the many cases originating in that county. Their Lordships 'considering that precognitions of this kind are not usuall, nor warrantable be law, and yitt being careful to be informed of the truth' ordained the Justice, after hearing parties, to continue the diet, if there was cause to do so, to a named date, and to report to the Council. In the meantime they granted protection to the panels from arrest. Again in *Dunbar and another* v *Dunbar* 1636 (*RPC*[2] VI.336, 374) the Council refused to proceed at a party's request and remitted to the Justice as the only competent judge; as they did also in *Bruce* v *Marshall* 1643 (20 December 1643).

The whole procedure by Precognition was contrary to the Act 1587 cap. 80 enacting that no precepts for continuations be admitted in the Justice Court. It was condemned as an abuse by McKenzie (*Criminals* II, vi.5) and Hume (II.28). The former claimed that so manifold were its abuses that of all the many persons who applied to the Council for precognitions he had never known one who was brought 'to condign punishment'. Contemporaries however accepted it and the procedure probably served a useful purpose in certain types of case. It enabled the Council to investigate circumstances where the issue was whether a homicide was justifiable, especially if there was an allegation that it had been committed in the cause of official duty or where there was *penuria testium* (*RPC*[3] IV.517). The Crown at this period strenuously resisted any attempt on the part of the defence to advance a special defence—such as accident, self defence, alibi, death from another cause than the alleged crime—and the Justice deputes were under no obligation to grant a warrant to cite defence witnesses. In such circumstances the only way in which the defence could be sure that its allegations could be investigated was by the Privy Council, and where the latter held that there was no case for a criminal trial it was without prejudice to the civil rights of the parties.

On this whole subject I am indebted to Sheriff P. G. B. McNeill's Ph.D. thesis, 'The Jurisdiction of the Scottish Privy Council,' Glasgow University (unpublished).

(000) [9 November 1636: Colville and Robertoun JJ.D.]

[Compeared Sir John Hamilton of Orbiston[1] and produced his appointment as Lord Justice Clerk and Master of Ceremonies. This is summarised in *RMS* IX.602 and is similar to that of his predecessor, for which see Vol. I above p. 229.]

Prefatory Note to Oswald v *John Rutherford and others.*

The history of this case is as follows: the panel first called was a former provost of Jedburgh, and an elderly man (*RPC*[2] VI.204). On 9th August 1636 the panels, purporting to act in an official capacity, laid hands on the deceased when she was in an advanced state of pregnancy, and incarcerated her in a dungeon, where they were alleged to have ill-treated her. The matter was brought before the Privy Council on 15th August by her husband and relatives (*RPC*[2] VI.609).

The proceedings of 3rd November 1636, hereinafter referred to, are narrated at great length in the Privy Council records (VI.635-640), where there are reproduced the Petition and Information of the prosecutors and the interrogatories which both parties wished to be put to the witnesses apparently by the Privy Council.

The defence advanced to their Lordships by the panels on that date (*ibid* VI.341-2) was that the first pursuer, the deceased's husband, had illegally taken possession of a brown nag, that the baillie sent the town officers to recover it, and that the deceased resisted them, whereupon Rutherford warded her. She was released two days later and walked home, where the pains of childbirth came upon her and she died from some unexplained cause though no violence had been used towards her.

As appears below, the proceedings in the Justice Court were sisted, and ultimately abandoned by order of the Privy Council (below p. 330).

(345) [10 November 1636: Colvile and Robertoun JJ.D.]

Slauchter. Oswall contra *Rutherfurd and utheris. Continewit to the secund of December nixtocum.*

Dilaitit: John Rutherford, John Rutherford notary, William Jarden and Archibald Kirkpatrick.

Compeirit George Oiswall, wryter, indweller in Jedbrughe, and producit the criminall letters deulie execute and indorsat purchest at the instance of the said George Oiswall, as spous to umquhill Jonet Henderstoune, William Oiswall, hir only sone, Jonet Strudgeone, the relict of umquhill William Hendersone, merchand, burges of the said brughe of Jedbrughe, hir mother, with the remanent kyn and freindis of the said umquhill Jonet Hendersoune, againes Johnne Rutherfurde, callit Nether, ane of the baillies of the said brughe of Jedbrught, John Rutherfurde, notter thair, William Jarden and Archibald Kirkpatrik, twa of the officeris of the said brughe, quhairby they and ilk ane of thame ar chargit be Andro Graiden, officer of airmes to find cautioun for thair compeirance befoir his Majesties Justice and his deputtis this day and place in

[1] His portrait in his spotted robes (the earliest known of any Lord Justice Clerk) was formerly hung in the Parliament Hall over the door leading to the Signet Library.

the hour of caus to underly the law for airt and pairt of the crewall slauchter of the said umquhill Jonet Hendersoune, as also of ane young infant bairne than being in hir bellie being quick and twentie four weikis gaine thairwith, committit upoun the nynt day of August lastbypast, in forme and maner specifeit in the saidis criminall letters, upoun the productioun quhairof the said George Oiswall, persewar, askit instrumentis and protestit for releife of Robert Hendersoune, flescheour, burges of Edinburgh thair cautioner.

Oswald contra *Rutherfuird and utheris Continewit to the said secund day of December nixtocum*

Compeirit lykwayis judiciallie Maister John Galloway, wryter, burges of Edinburgh, *procuratorio nomine* for John Rutherfurde ane of the baillies of Jedbrught, John Rutherfurde, notter thair, William Jarden, and Archbald Kirkpatrik, twa of the officeris of the said brughe, and producit ane Act of the Lordis of Secreit Counsall daittit the thrid day of November instant ordaning and comanding his Majesties Justice, Justice clerk and thair deputtis to continew the criminall dyet abonewrittin appoyntit for tryell of the said John Rutherfurd baillie and his complices for the slauchter of the said umquhill Jonet Hendersoune and remanent crymis contenit in the criminall letters direct thairanent, to the secund day of December nixtocum, off the quhilk Act of Counsall the tennour followes:

At Edinbrughe the thrid day of November the yeir of God jmvic threttie sax yeiris,[1] the Lordis of Secreit Counsall continewis the actioun and caus of precognitioun intentit and persewit befoir the saidis Lordis at the instance of Johnne Rutherfurde, ane of the baillies of Jedbrughe, Johnne Rutherfurde, notare thair, William Jarden and Archbald Kirkpatrik, twa of the officers of the said brughe, againes George Oiswall, wryter in Jedbrughe as spous, William Oiswall, only sone, Jonet Strudgeone, relict of umquhill William Hendersone, merchand burges of Jedbrught, as mother, with the kyn and freindis of umquhill Jonet Hendersone for trying of the forme maner and circumstances of the alledgit slauchter of the said umquhill Jonet Henersone in the same forme as it is presentlie, but prejudice of pairtie unto the sevintene day of November instant to the intent both the saidis pairties may that day produce befoir the saidis Lordis such verefication and probatioun as they will use for proveing of thair mutuall complaintis to wit the said John Rutherfurd, baillie John Rutherfurd, notare, William Jarden, and Archbald Kirkpatrik for proveing of the heidis and poyntis contenit in the letters of precognitioun[2] raised be thame and the said George Oswell and the utheris defenderis on his pairt for proveing of the pointis and heides contenit in the criminall letters raisit be thame; And for this effect ordanis letters to be direct chargeing such personis as the saidis pairties will use as witnessis in this matter to compeir personallie befoir the saidis Lordis the said sevintene day of November instant to beir witnessing thairin, under the paine of rebellioun and putting of thame to the horne, with certificatioun to thame and they failzie, letters salbe direct *simpliciter* to put thame thairto; And quhairas it hes bene proponit and affirmed be the said

[1] This is summarized in *RPC*[2] VI.329.
[2] See legal note.

George Oswell that the said John Rutherfurd, baillie, in respect of his office and credite within the said brughe, will stay and hinder the witnessis to be usit be the said George Oswell from compeiring to depone, thairfoir the saidis Lordis ordanis the said John Rutherfurde, baillie, to exhibite with him the personis quhome the said George will use for proveing of his saidis criminall letters quhais names salbe tymeuslie given to him in bill be the said George Oswell; And the saidis Lordis for the better cleiring of this matter ordanis and commandis his Majesties Justice, Justice clerk and thair deputtis to continew the criminall dyet appoyntit for tryell of the said John Rutherfurde baillie and his complices anent the said slauchter untill the secund day of December nixtocum dispensing with thair personall compeirance and takand new cautioun of thame conforme to the ordour, lykeas both the saidis pairties being personallie presentt ar wairnit heirof *apud acta. Extractum de libris actorum secreti consilii S.D.N. regis per me Jacobum Prymrois clericum eiusdem sub meis signo et subscriptione manualibus sic subscribitur Jacobus Prymrois.*

For obedience of the quhilk Act and ordinance set down thairintill the Justice continewis this dyet with the tryell of the crymis contenit in the saidis criminall letters to the said secund day of December nixtocum, and ordanit cautioun to be fund for the saidis defenderis entrie and compeirance befoir his Majesties Justice and his deputtis to underly the law for the saidis crymis in the tolbuith of Edinburgh the said secund day of December nixt, under the paines contenit in the Actis of Parliament, quhairupoun the said Mr. John Galloway *nominibus quibus supra* askit actis and instrumentis and protestit for releife of Maister George Douglas, fieare of Bonjedbrught, cautioner for the defenderis foirsaidis of his cautionrie; Lykeas the said Maister Johnne Galloway for satisfactioun of the said Justice ordinance of his awin consent become actit and obleist for the saidis John Rutherfurde, baillie, John Rutherfurde, notar, and the saidis twa officeris thair entrie and compeirance the said secund day of December nixt befoir his Majesties Justice to the effect and under the panes foirsaidis.

(356) [2 December 1636: Colvile and Robertoun JJ.D.]

Deserted by order of Privy Council; see RPC[2] VI.340-1

LEGAL NOTE.

Another example of the Privy Council staying proceedings in the Justice Court until the Council had investigated parties' contentions on precognitions. See prior case notes.

(361) [22 December 1636: Colvile J.D.]

Lord Advocate v *John Galloway and another.* *Convict and hangit for fals cunyie.*

Intran.—Johnne Galloway in Kilmarannoche;[1] Bartilmo Gilmour wobster [*weaver*].

Dilaitit of the treasonable forgeing, devyseing and counterfutting of certane fals and adulterat money, sic as fals dollouris [*silver coins*] and fals cardiecues

[1] Kilmaronock parish at foot of Loch Lomond.

[*French silver coins*], haifand course (viz. the trew dollouris and cardiecues as guid and lauchfull money) within this realme for the tyme, and for outputting and venting [*putting in circulation*] of the samyn fals and adulterat dollouris and cardiecues amangst his Majesteis leigis as guid and sufficient money, expres aganis the lawis and Actis of Parliament[1] of this kingdome in maner and forme and at the tymes specifeit in thair dittay.

Persewar.—Sir Thomas Hope of Craighall, knycht barronet, his Majesteis Advocat, for his Hienes intreis.

The persewar producet the dittay anent the crymes foirsaidis thairin contenit, quhilk the persones on pannell eftir publict reiding thairof confessit judiciallie to be of verritie, quhairupone the Kingis Majesteis Advocat askit instrumentis.

Assisa.—John Lennox of Branschogill; Andro Stewin, merchand in Edinburgh; Archibald Davidsone, merchand thair; Adame Fleming, merchand thair; John Stewart, merchand thair; Thomas Bonar, merchand thair; William Bowman, tailzor burges thair; Jas [Loc?]hie, tailyour burges of Edinburgh; John Sword, wricht burges thair; John Mertimar [?], burges thair; Andro Young, merchand thair; Mungo Hunter, stabler in Edinburgh; Henrie Stanehous, baxter thair; Andro Hunter, baxter thair; James Mure, skyner thair; John Meane, younger, merchand thair.

The Advocat takis instrumentis of the sweiring of the assyse, and producet the pannellis depositiones confessing the crymes contenit in thair dittay to be of verritie, and thairwith repeittit the pannellis judiciall confessioun of the saidis crymes and protestit for wilfull errour aganis the assysouris gif thay acquit.

Quhilkis persones of assyse being ressavit sworne and admittit, eftir accusatioun of the saids John Galloway and Bartill Gilmour of the crymes contenitt in thair dittay, following, viz. for airt and pairt of the treasonable forgeing devyseing and counterfutting of certane fals and adulterat money sic as fals dollouris and fals cardiecues and for outputting and venting the same amangis his Majesteis legis expres aganis the lawis and Actis of Parliament of this kingdome committit be thame in maner and at the severall tymes following: In swa far as the saidis Bartie Gilmour and John Galloway in the moneth of Julii the yeir of God jmvic threttie fyve yeiris past togidder to the Ile of Turinch [*Torrinch*] at the watter of Enrik besyde Loch Lowmond, and thair eftir ane fyre was kindlet be thame with flynt and flourich [*steel*] thair was ane tyn plait pertening to the said John Galloway meltit upone the said fyre, and haifing mixtit thairwith certane melted bras and melted glas ane number of fals dollouris about threttene war cassin [*cast*] be thame and maid up of the said tyn plait in ane pair of tymber calmes [*moulds*] quhilk calmes was maid be the said John Galloway be the instructioun and directioun of the said Bartie Gilmour; Lykas schortlie thaireftir thair was also cassin be ather of the saidis persones a thre or foure half dollouris of tyn within the said John Gallowayis brewhouse; and thaireftir the saidis fals dollouris swa cassin and counterfute be thame was

[1] See 1449 c.29; 1469 c.40; 1540 c.124; 1563 c.70. (Legal note 1.)

cullouret and waschin over be thame with quick silver; Quhilkis fals dollouris abonewritten togidder with ane grit number mae of that soirt with ane number of fals cardiecues forget and cassin be thame, alsweill befoir the said moneth of Julii 1635 as sensyne, war vented past and furth be thame amongst his Majesteis legis as trew and guid cunyie [*coins*] and lauchfull money falslie and schamefullie dissaveing and circumvening thairby his Majesteis loyall subjectis; Quhilkis crymes thay haif confessit be thair depositiones, maid be thame in presens of the Lordis of Secreit Counsall,[1] as at lenth is contenit in the said dittay.

[Verdict guilty.]

For the quhilk cause the Justice be the mouth of James Grant dempster of court decernit and adjudget the saidis John Galloway and Bartill Gilmour to be tane to the mercat croce of Edinburgh upone Mononday nixt the xxvi day of December instant, and thair to be hangit whill thay be deid, and all thair guidis, alsweill moveable as unmoveable, heritages and anuelrentis gif thai ony haif, to be forfaltit escheit and inbrocht to our Soverane Lordis use as convict and fund guiltie of the saidis tressonable crymes, whilk was pronuncet for dome.

LEGAL NOTES.

1. Minor currency offences could be dealt with by the Privy Council (see *RPC*[1] VI.352). This was obviously a serious case of counterfeiting as passing false currency, and proceedings were on indictment at the instance of the Lord Advocate alone. There was no legal representation of the accused (see also *Duncan Watson and others,* above p. 319).

2. Though the panels are not specifically named they must be the suspects referred to in the entry in the Privy Council Register for 8th December 1636 (*RPC*[2] VI.347). Their confession in the present case is hardly surprising in view of the formidable personnel and intimidating methods of the investigating tribunal. Archibald, Lord Lorne; John, Bishop of Moray; Sir James Carmichael, depute treasurer; Sir Thomas Hope, His Majesty's Advocate; John Hamilton of Orbieston, Justice Clerk, and the Justice Depute, or any three of them, were appointed by the Privy Council 'to examine the prisoners challenged for fals dollers, as they sall find cause, and for discovery of thair complices to put thame to the torture . . . and to report upon Tuesday'. No time was wasted. The suspects were examined by the Committee, and admitted the crimes, came before the Justice Court on 22nd December and were executed on 26th December 1636.

Before the Justice Court the panels pleaded guilty and a jury was then empanelled to whom the Lord Advocate produced the panels' depositions admitted the crimes, taken by the Committee, and 'repeated' the panels' judicial confession made before the jury was empanelled. The panel did not plead after the jury was empanelled.

(377) [15 March 1637: Colvile and Robertoun JJ.D]

James Hairt burges of Stirling. Acquit of the slauchter of umquhile John Crystie.

Intran.—James Heart, burges of Stirling.

Dilaittit of airt and pairt of the slauchter of umquhile John Chrystie in Cambus[2] be geveing him ane deadlie straik upone the vayne organe [*ear*] of

[1] See *RPC*[2] VI.347 and see legal note 2.

[2] Village 2 miles NW of Alloa, Clackmannanshire.

his head with the bar of ane grit kist or girnell [*meal chest*] quhairwith he fell deid [?*unconscious*] to the ground, possing and punching him with his kneys and feit upone the breist, bellie, schoulderis, and sydis and uthers pairtis of his bodie, breking and bruiseing thairby his haill intrallis and noble pairtis within him, committit upone the twentie ane day of Januare lastbypast upone the hie streit of the brughe of Stirling, being Setterday and the ordiner mercate day thairof, with the quhilkis straikis hurtis and woundis he deceissit upon the last day of the said monethe of Januare thaireftir.[1]

Persewers.—Jonet Chrystie, Katharene Chrystie, dochters to the defunct; John Chrystie, brother sone; Sir Thomas Hope of Craighall, knycht barronet, his Majesteis Advocat for his Hienes intreis.

Prelocutour.—Mr. Thomas Nicolsone, younger.[2]

The pannell takis instrumentis of his entrie and compeirance and protestis for his cautioneris releiff.

The persewers producet the criminall letters deulie execute and indorsat upone the said James Heart, defender, together with ane roll of assyse, askit instrumentis thairupone, and protestit for thair cautioneris releiff.

The Justice with consent of ather pairtie alsweill persewer as defender contenowis this dyet to the moirne, the saxtene of Mairche instant, and ordanit the pannell to find cautioun for his re-entrie that day under the panes contenit in Acts of Parliament, for obedience quhairof compeirit Robert Erskene indweller in the Cannongait and become cautioun for the said James Heart his re-entrie the said day to the effect and under the pane abonespecifeit, quhairupone the persewer askit instrumentis.

(379) [16 March 1637: Colvile J.D.]

Mr Thomas Nicolsone as prelocutour for the pannell taks instrumentis that my Lordis of Mar and Stirling compeirs with the persewer and assistis this persuite.

It is answerit be my Lord Advocat that the pannell and his prelocutouris may tak instrumentis of the two noble men thair sitting in the heighest roume as noble men may doe, bot naways that thai ar assisters of the persewers in this persuite.

It is declairit be my Lord of Mar and my Lord Stirling that thai have na entreis in this persuite aganis the pannell bot onlie to sie justice ministrat for ather pairtie and in ane freindlie maner to reconceill pairteis at variance.[3]

It is alledget thaireftir be Mr Thomas Nicolsone as procuratour for the pannell[4] that he cannot goe to the knawledge of ane assyse upone this dittay

[1] See legal note 1.
[2] Son of Sir Thomas Nicolson of Cockburnspath. Admitted 20th July 1632; Lord Advocate 10 June 1649. (*Lyon's List* p. 165.)
[3] See legal note 2.
[4] See legal note 3.

quhairin it is lybellit that the pannell crewallie and unmercifullie gave ane deidlie straik to the said umquhile John Crystie in the head with ane bar of ane kist upone the twentie ane day of Januar last off the quhilk straik he deceissit upone the last day of the samyn monethe of Januar becaus no pairtie inflictour of ane wound, quhairof the ressaver of the wound is alledget to have deceissit, can be accuiset *de occiso ubi animus occidendi presumi non potest* for *propositum et voluntas distinguit maleficia et homicida tantum tenetur capitaliter pro homicidio doloso non culposo neque casuali,* but swa it is in the caus lybellit and in the alledget straik gevin be the pannell to umquhile John Chrystie with the bar *animus occidendi presumi non potest* for albeit of the law *in delictis dolus semper presumitur hoc est animus occidendi*; yit the generall presumptione being in favours of the accuser is enervat [*weakened*] and taking away be perticuler and speciall contrair presumptiones, quhilk ar presumptiones exclusive of any intentioun to have killid, and of the law *est presumptio exclusiva animi occidendi si nulla precedat inimicitia inter occisorem et occisum Secunda presumptio est* (quhilk being conjoyntit to the first is fortifeit thairby) *Si homisidium commissum fuit in foro vel in via publica nonnulla presidente innimicitia inter occisorem et occisum*, For it is not presumet that the gever of ane straik in ane commoun marcate and publict way had *animum occidendi* or intensione to kill thepairtie ressaver thairof, quhair he mycht eiselie have bene impeidit frome the prosecutioun of his intentione, and thairfoir gif he had any sic intentione to have killed him he wald have choysein ane moir fit place; [3] *Tertio animus occidendi presumitur et non presumitur* of the law *ex qualitate seu genere armorum quibus vulnus mortuo illatum fuisse dicitur si enim vulnus aut percutio facta fuit cum armis ex quibus vere similiter et ut plurimum percussus mori solet tunc animus occidendi in percussore presumitur si vero cum armis non ad occidendum regulariter et veresimiliter actus vulnus fuit illatum tunc animus occidendi excluditur et vulnus inferens de occiso non tenetur sed de vulnere illato Leg.* 1 *divus. ff: ad legem Juliam de Sicariis ubi propterea juris consultus facit differentiam inter percutionem factam cum gladio et percutionem factam cum clava vel cucuma et Leg: i. C de emendatione servorum ubi an dominus occiderit servum animo occidendi consideratur qualitas instrumenti cum quo percussus fuit servus et Leg: omne delictum si quis commilitonum ff. de remilitari ubi ponit juris consultus differentiam inter vulnus illatum cum lapide,* And this is the oppinione of all the doctouris citit aggreing amongs thameselffs but contradictione *per Phar: quest:* 126 *Num.* 117, And of *Clarus homicidium Num. Quarto versituto dicitur etiam culposo* and moir speciallie *Phar: quest: dicta Num:* 113 affirmes that *animus occidendi non presumitur ex percussione facta cum baculo quanquam in loco corporis periculoso puta in capite nisi histe concurrentibus nimirum nisi ictus et basconate in capite fuerint iterate, et secundo nisi dicatur precessisse capitalis inimicitia inter percussum et percussentem alios non intrat animus occidendi et propterea non mortis pena maxime quando percutiens cum baculo in capite habet penese alia arma ad occidendum aptiora Si utatur armis ad occidendum minus aptis non presumitur animo occidendi vulnus intulisse;* for gif he had had ane intentione to have killid, being maister of airmes moir apt and usefull for the purpois, he wald have maid use of the moir apt airmes, to wit ane sword or ane quhinger and not of ane batone *Ita Phar: dicta quest:* 126 *Num:* 124 *Clarus dicto loco Gomesius de homicidio Num:* 17, and this presumptioun resulting *ex genere armorum* the pannell conjoynes with the preceiding presumptionis exclusive of the intentioun of killing *Excluditur etiam animus occidendi et nono presumitur in eo qui calce vel pede percussit argumento supra allegato quia non sunt arma ad occidendum apta sed ad injuriandum Phari: dicta quest: Num:* 43. *Quarto qualitas percutientis est presumptio excludens animum occidendi ubi animus est in dubio puta si sit bonae famae et ad talia non solitus concurrente qualitate facti et aliis presumptionibus coadjuvatitibus animumque occidendi excludentibus Pha: dicta quest: Num: ibi et* 162 *Bernardus ad Clarum in Homicidium Num:* 13, Bot swait is that all thes exclusive presumptionis of *animus occidendi* ar heir in this caice and in the straik lybellit alledget given be the pannell to umquhill John Chrystie, for quhilk straik the pannell is convenit as ane manslayer, [1] And first *nulla precedebat inimicitia* betwix the pannell and umquhill Johnne Chrystie nather is any lybellit bot on the contrair thair was severall deidis of gratitude and freindschip betwix thaim of befoir and of humane supplieing upoun the pairt of the pannell towardis Johnne Chrystie for eftir that Johnne Chrystie was lifted up from his fall quhich ather he catched casuallie throw the slidrines [*slipperiness*] of the way or possibillie throw his reluctatioun [*struggle*] with the pannell quha was drawing him to confes debtis befoir denyed be the said John Chrystie, the said John Chrystie eftir his fall declairit befoir famous witnessis that he was auchtand to the pannell that same lyttill money the pannell was craiveing him, quhairby it is cleir that the pannell was his merchand howbeit to ane bankerup dettour; lykeas imediatlie thaireftir they went both togidder to ane aill hous and drank togidder and came out togidder to the streitis; [2] secundlie the alledgit straik being given in the hie mercat way (quhair thair was ane concurs of the haill leidges) as the lybell beiris it cannot be presumit that the pannell had any intentioun of killing of the defunct seing he might easillie haif chosen ane moir fitt place; and [3] considdering thair was no proceiding haitrent [*hatred*] betwix the pannell and the defunct, and as the wappones lybellit quhairwith the straik is alledgit to be given (nawayis granting that the pannell had ony suche wappone in his hand bot refuiseing the samyn) is nocht of that soirt of airmes that the pannell wald haif maid use of gif he had had ane intentioun to haif killed the defunct seing he was maister of uther airmes, quhairwith he might haif moir convenientlie effectuat his purpois; and [4] fourtlie,[1] conjoyneing with all the thre preceiding, the pannell his guid fame and honest cayriage in the citie quhair he leveth and cheiflie that he was nocht uset in ony sic ryottis and trubillis, and that perticulerlie to all appeirance he is innocent of the cryme quhilk is now imput to him, the pannell produces ane testimony frome the proveist and bailleis of Sterling, quhairby thay testifie to my Lord Justices the pannell his respectfull cariadge amongst thame, that he was nevir tryit nor fund guiltie of ony publict scandell or offence, and as to this persute moved aganis the pannell thay think it proceidis of malice or greid to get ane compositioun of geir af the puir timerous man, and that thair was no nychtbour about quhair the alledget wrong was done that thay could try to have sene him put violent handis in the man, this testimoniall and recommendatioun is subscryvit be the proveist and foure bailleis upone the tent of Merche 1637; And swa it is cleir out of the pre-

[1] This is a new and novel argument—good character pleaded at the stage of relevancy.

sumptiones abone writtin all being conjoynet togidder, everie on (e) to fortifie ane uther, that the pannell at the alledgit geving of the straik with the alledget bar lybellit (quhilk still the pannell refuissis) was nocht gevin *animo occidendi* and that *animus occidendi in illo actu* can nocht be presumet being excludet be the presumptiones abone mentionat, and thairfore can not be accuset as ane man slayer nor can be put to the knawledge of ane assyse thairupoun; (II) *Secundo* it is alledget that the pannell can not goe to the knawledge of ane assyse as *reus homicidii* upone this dittay beiring that the pannell gave umquhile Johnne Chrystie ane straik upone the heid with ane bar upone the xxi day of Januar last within the burgh of Sterling, and that he deid upone the last day of the said moneth of Januar in Clakmannane, becaus quhair a deidlie wound is nocht gevin albeit the pairtie ressaver thairof die of the wound yit *vulnus inferens non tenetur de occuso* [*sic*] *sed de vulnerato* for of the law only *vulnus mortale inferens tenetur de occiso quod lethale sunt tempore ictus*, And nocht gif it became lethall *ex post facto ex aliqui accedenti extrinseco Puta propter non adhibitum medicum vel propter adhibitum medicum imperitum vel propter negligentiam medici vel propter malum regimen invulnerati,* Bot swa it is that ony wound that was gevin to the said umquhile John Chrystie (the pannell still refuiseing that he gave him ony wound bot gif one he gat) can not be affirmet to haif bene *ab initio vulnus mortale, Primo* becaus *vulnus dicitur mortale vel non mortale ex qualitate armorum cum quibus fuit illatum Puta si armis inferatur ado ccidendum regulariter et veresimiliter aptis vel non aptis*[1] *phar: quest:* 127, *Num:* 57, And that ane battone or the hand or fitt *in nostro casu* ar not *arma ad occidendum apta conjoynet* with the presumptiones contenit in the former alledgeance the pannell referris himselff to the former alledgeance and repeittis the samyn *hoc loco*; [2] *Secundo vulnus dicitur fuisse lethale vel non lethale ex quantitate viz. longitutine latitudine et profunditate vulneris Phar: dicta quest:* 127, *num:* 56 so that gif the wound be not deip bot be ane over struise[2] it is not ane deidlie wound, bot it is trew and of verritie in the caice lybellit that quhan umquhile John Chrystie was raised from his fall quhilk was occasioned throw his strugilling with the pannell that Henrie Bennet, burges of Sterling being present for the tyme, and feiring the fenzednes [*pretence*] of umquhile John Chrystie, come to him to try gif John had catched ony hurt in his heid throw the fall, and haveing luiket his heid all over and rubbet the samyn he fand that thair was no skart [*scratch*] thair nor ony wrong done, and increpat [*rebuked*] and chydit with John Chrystie for his fenzednes [*pretence*] and maid him confes the dett quhilk was in hand and delt with the pannell to geve him some dayis to pay it, and desyret the pannell becaus Johne Chrystie affirmed he was hungrie to goe and geve to him ane chopping [*half pint*] of aill and ane laife [*loaf*]; [3] *Tertio vulnus illatum dici non potest mortale si post illatum vulnus vulneratus post triduum*[3] *ambulaverit de enim casu etiamsi postea breve morcatur non presumitur ex vulnere decessisse sed ex alio aliquo extrinseco accidente Ita glossa in legem primam Cod. de emendatione servorum Clarus homiciduum Num:* 44 *versiculo sed quantum Phar: quest:* 127 *Num:* 73 *Non enim presumitur fuisse vulnus mortale si vulner-*

[1] This is I[3] over again.
[2] This may mean excessive struggling.
[3] See legal note 4.

atus post triduum ambulaverit quanquam non eque sanus fuerit ut antea tunc enim presumitur mortuus ex malo regimine, Bot sa it is that it is offerit to be provin that umquhile John Chrystie nocht only *ambulavit triduo post illatum vulnus* (alwayis refuseing the geving of ony straik or wound), bot also that he was going abrod in the town of Sterling the verrie day of the alledget geving thairof and that he remanit in the town all Sonday thaireftir and all Mononday walking upone the streittis, and that thre dayis or foure eftir the 21 of Januar quhilk was the day of the allegit hurt he went frome the town of Sterling to Cambus and that day and thre dayis thaireftir remanit in Cambus went to uther pairtis about till the saxt day eftir the alledgit giveing of the straik he went to Clekmannane, quhair he died upoun the last day of Jannuar thaireftir, sua that ather his death must be ascryved to some exterior accident yit not knawin seing that thir was nane presentt with him quhair he died, but he deceissit in ane outhous within the town of Clekmannane quhair na uther peopill resoirtit; And gif any is to be suspectit guiltie of his death gif hes died *violenta manu* Johnne Reid is maist suspect in quhais hous he died, and quha is now fugitive haiveing left his labouradge, his haill hous and houshald within four dayis eftir the death of John Chrystie and never as yit returnit; Lykeas it is cleir (albeit that suspitioun on Johnne Reides pairt war not evident be his flight) that the defunct Johnne Chrystie died gif he ressavit any wound *non ex vulnere sed ex malo regimine,* and thaireftir the pannell cannot be accusit for his death his *malum regimen* is proven [4] *Primo ex eo quod in vulnere curando medicum nullum adhibuit*, for of the law *non adhibere medicum vel adhibere imperitum medicum est species mali regiminis Phar: quest:* 127 *Num:* 88, 89, 90; *Secundo* his *malum regimen* is cleir *ex eo* that of the law *dicitur malum regimen quando vulneratus parvi pendendo vulnus die ad solem ad serenum vel ventrum ambulaverit et si moriatur non presumitur ex vulnere sed sua culpa mortuus Pha: dicta quest: num:* 98 quhair he ceitis of *Gaudinus exemplum in rustico qui in capite vulneratus ivit ad laborandum cum bobus ad solem et calefactus mortuus est*[1] *et num:* 37 *dicte questionis* he citis out of *Gramaticus exemplum vulnerati in capite ambulantis per civitatem qui dicitur ipsemet dare causam morti cum deberet stare domi recluisus et clausis fenestris non intuere aevem;* And affirmis the same in a caice lyk unto this presentt caice *de vulnerato qui post tres dies a die illati vulneris profectus est de una villa ad aliam,* but swa it is that the defunct Johnne Chrystie eftir his fall, at quhat tyme the wound is alledgit to haive bene given, walkit up and down the streitis of the town of Stirling thrie dayis thaireftir, walkit abroad in the cuntrie, to the quhilk exces of travell and negligence of cair in the defunct Johnne Chrystie, gif any skaith or harme aryve to him throw his fall the samyn must be imputit thairto and not to the pannell quha possibillie in the strugling betwix him and the defunct might haive occasioned his fall to the grund quhilk fall being in itselff no mortall wound thairthrow the pannell cannot be accusit as ane manslayer, bot aucht to be assoylyeit from the dittay in swa far as slauchter thairby is imputit to him.

It is answerit be my Lord Advocat that all the alledgances aucht to be repellit in respect of the criminall lybell and dittay thairin contenit and takis instrumentis *in quantum* of that pairt of the alledgances quhilk war adducit to liberat

[1] Also founded on by defence in *Crombie*, 22 June 1625, above I.20.

de occiso and only mak him lyabill *de vunerato*, and also that pairt quhair he grantis that the defunct was dettour to the pannell and that the pannell, without warrand of any baillie, pat violent handis into him and caried him be force to his awin hous as to ane privat prissone, quhilk is ane accessioun of ane new cryme to the cryme lybellit, and the pannell being *in actu maxime illicito et violento* is maid inexcusabill ather be casualtarie accident or be the kynd of the wappone quhairwith he straik the defunct of the quhilk he died; And the testimoniall adducit aggravattis the suspitioun of his guiltines be the generall reule *non amo nimium diligentes;*[1] And my Lord Advocat declaires that he will use the confessionis contenit in the exceptionis togidder with the nottour defamatioun of the pannell as ane turbulent man, for the quhilk he hes bene fynit above twentie tymes, and being accusit for ane silver cupp was unlawit in the soume of ane hundreth pundis; and als ane commoun and notorious theife callit Beveradge quha was convict and execut the tyme of his executioun dilaittit the pannell as ressetter of the stowin geir; Lykeas the pannell being indyttit befoir the last Justice air in Stirling and convenit for the caussis foirsaidis fand James Howstane, cordiner in Stirling, cautioun for his compeirance; Quhilk defamationis togidder with the depositionis of witnessis quha ar presentt to be examinat befoir the Judge and assyse and quha war presentt at the giveing of the straikis and saw the defunct founder to the grund and not abill to stand, and of thaim quha saw him at the tyme of his death and his heid swollen to an hudge and monstruous measour greater than twa heides, togidder with the bluidie and blae [*livid*] straikis upoun the rest of the pairtis of his bodie with uther probationis necessar to be usit befoir the assyse.

It is duplyit for the pannell that nochtwithstanding of the reply, the alledgances proponit standis relevant quhairin the pannell declaires that he hes adducit nothing to grant any wound given to the defunct, but his alledgance beiris gif any wound had bene given, still denying the giveing thairof, that the samyn was not mortall; And quhairas the reply insinuatis the alledgances to grant a secund cryme in swa far as they beir the pannell to haive put violent handis in the defunct the samyn is not relevant to infer *crimen privati carceris* for not to that end was the pannell desyring the defunct to goe to his hous bot the ressone was that he wold goe and sie his compt buik quhair he was standing his dettour, quhilk was no *actus illicitus* he being standing hard at the duir; and albeit it had bene *actus illicitus,* quhilk is not grantit, yit *operam dans rei illicite et actui illicito non tenetur de affectu subsequento nisi talis actus de sui natura sit probabiliter destinatus ad subsequntum affectum;* Bot swa it is it caries no ressone to affirme that the act of drawing of the defunct, albeit against his will, was such ane act as of its awin nature it could haive producit the effect that fell out, viz. the death of the defunct; and quhairas the reply beires the testimoniall producit to aggravit the cryme lybellit againes the pannell, it is duplyit that the samyn proves the moir sufficientlie the pannellis guid fame and honest cariadge of the plaice quhair he leived then the persewar John Chrystie his calumnious informatioun imputing crymis and defamatioun to the pannell can doe him any hurt, for the proveist and bailleis of Stirling knawing of the

[1] This was also quoted to the Privy Council in *Oswald* v *Rutherford* (above p. 328), *RPC*[2] VI.636-7. The two cases have much in common.

malicious intent of the persewar and knawing the pannellis guid cariadge and lyfe, might verrie weill be thair testimony informe the Justice; And as to the sinistruous informatioun anent the pannellis diffamatioun maid be John Chrystie, persewar, and cheiflie that he informis my Lord Justice and affirmes that the pannell being arayned for the steilling of ane silver cupp that he was fyllit for the samyn and fynit thairfoir, the pannell takis instrumentis thairupoun, and craives that the samyn may be insert in his instrument; And as to Beveradges confessioun it is the confessioun of a criminall condemned and swa not worthie of my lord Justice eares for *allegatio diffamationis originem suam non trahentis ex ore fidelium est diffamatio;* And as to the cautioun fund befoir the Justice air alledgit to aggravat the pannellis diffamatioun the samyn hes no weight becaus *innocentissimus cuilibet* might have bene citit befoir the Justice air upoun misinformatioun; And that he fand cautioun to compeir at the nixt dyet it was a legall act upoun his pairt bot upoun the pairt of his accuseris and dilaittouris a pregnant presumptioun that they war calumnious dilaittouris, becaus they could not prove quhat was thair laid to his charge; And quhairas the reply beiras that the witnessis salbe producit quha war presentt at the giveing of the straik and uther witnessis quha saw the deid corps of the defunct and that his heid was swollen, that no way waikines the alledgances proponit in thair relevancie; And being fund relevant the samyn sall be proven sufficiently for the pannell might haive given ane straik with ane battone to the defunct (quhilk yit is refuisit) upoun the 21 of Jannuar and his death might haive followit upoun the last of Jannuar and yit his death not to be imputit to the straik and thairfoir not to the pannell albeit he had given straik; And for the force and strenth of the alledgances alreddie producit to evince that the pannell nather had *animum occidendi tempore illati vulneris* nor that *vulnus illatum* was *vulnus lethale* in respect quhairof the alledgances standis relevant.

The Justice continewis this dyet to the morne *decimo septimo Martii* cautioner *ut antea.*

The assyse wairnit *apud acta* ilk persone under the paine of twa hundreth merkis.

(382) [17 March 1637: Colvile J.D.]

Intran.—James Heart, burges of Sterling.

The pannel takis instrumentis of his entrie and protestis for his cautioneris releif.[1]

The Justice, haifing red and considderit the exceptiones and duplyis maid for the pannell and the persewaris answeris maid thairto, be interloquitour findis the summondis and dittay relevant nochtwithstanding of the saidis exceptiones, and remittis the samyn summondis and dittay to the tryell of ane assyse, quhairuponethe persewaris askit instrumentis.

Assisa.—Walter Keir, baxter in Sterling, chanceller; James Gairdin, litster thair; John Moriesone, couper thair; Andro Hagie, elder, fischmonger thair;

[1] See legal note 5.

James Myller, baxter thair; Thomas Meldrum, baxter thair; Johne Blaikburne wobster thair; Johnne Clerk, wobster thair; Johnne Ewing, wobster thair; Andro Ker, dagmaker thair; James Jaffray, merchant thair; Alexander Kirkwoid, wobster thair; Johnne Littilejohn, flescheour thair; Johnne Myller in West Grange; Johnne Dewar, baxter in Sterling.

The persewaris, for cleiring to the assyse of the pannellis guiltines of the cryme contenit in the dittay, produces the witnessis following,[1] desyreing thame to be ressavit sworne and thair depositiones to be judiciallie maid in presens of the Justice assysouris and pairteis bayth persewaris and defender viz. Henrie Bennett, tailyeour in Sterling; Duncane Allane, wobster thair; Johnne Henrie, belmaker thair; William Ewing, tailyeour at Craigmylne,[2] Johnne Melvile, wricht in Alloway [*Alloa*]; Alexander Myller in Cambus; Thomas Moreis in Tulliebody [*by Cambus*]; Johne Stevinsone, tailyeour in Sterling; quhilkis war all sworne and admittit be the Justice and purget of partiall counsall in presens of the pannell and his procuratour.

Henrie Bennet, being sworne anent the hurt or fall gevin be the pannell to Johnne Chrystie and demandit quhat he knawis thairin, depones: he saw nocht the defunct fall bot cuming by and seing him lying the deponer tuik him up, and saw James Heart going fra the defunct and callit upone him to cum bak to help him up, quhilk James Heart did, and ather of thame to wit the deponer and James Heart liftit him up betwixt [them]; depones that he, being siting in his buith neir to the place quhair John Crystie fell, he hard ane man cry 'Allace [*Alas*], I am feld,' quhairupone the deponer come rynning furth and saw the said John Crystie lying in his bak with feit evin up and his heid besyde ane chymnay; knawis nocht quha gave him the fall only saw James Heart going frome him; sayis he askit of James Heart quha gave the fall to John Chrystie, to the quhilk James Heart maid no answer bot come with the deponer and helpit him up; depones he was nocht that waik bot to the deponeris judgement he mycht haif rissin and walkit himselff; and sayis that he hard James Heart say to him 'Flie nocht my gait agane'; depones he saw no bluid upone his heid eftir his uptaking bot thair was ane littill lump behind his lug [*ear*]; deponis that he hard James Heart crave payment of 36 schillingis that John Crystie was auchtand to him, and depones that the deponer did agrie James Heart and John Crystie anent the termes of payment thairof, quhilk was that the samyn sould be payit at two terms, the first terme at Lambes and the uther terme at Witsonday thaireftir, and counsallit thame to tak ane pynt on the blok [*agreement*]; Lykas the said James Heart and John Crystie past and gat ane choppene of aill and ane laif, as the deponer hard, and that they baith choppit [*shook*] handis togidder upone the aggrement foirsaid; demandit gif he saw John Crystie walking on the calsay of Sterling thaireftir, depones he saw him nocht bot hard be repoirt that he was walking thairupoun.

The said Duncane Allane, wobster, sworne and demand[ed] quhat he knawis anent the alledgit slauchter of umquhile John Crystie depones: that he saw James Heart gripping the said John Crystie be the lappis [*folds*] of the cloik

[1] See legal note 6.
[2] Just NE of Stirling.

and drawing him aganis his will down the gait, and that a littill thaireftir he hard on cry 'I am fellit' bot saw na straik gevin nor yit saw him fall; and that Henrie Bennet led up the gait agane and that James Heart was going besyde him quha had no wappone in his hand at all; Farder depones that upone the morne thaireftir being Sonday he saw John Crystie cuming frome the kirk upone his feit himself allane about nyne houris befoir none, and knawis no farder.

The said John Henrie being sworne depones: he saw James Heart and Johne Crystie cumand down the gait togidder, James Heart being upone his richt hand upone the Setterday the day of the allegit hurting of the said Johne Crystie at quhilk tyme he hard James Heart say to him 'I wald haif bene loathe to haif strukin your fatheris sone John' and knawis no farder.

Williame Irving ane of the saidis witnessis, being sworne and demandit quhat he knawis in the premissis, depones he saw the pannell grip John Crystie be the cloik desyreing fra him payment of his dett, and thaireftir desyret him to go to ane bailyie and tuik him down the gait with him to the bailyie quhilk John Crystie refuiset and wald nocht go with him to ony bailyie; depones in his going down the gait with James Heart he saw the James Heart schute [*push*] John Chrystie over in ane close heid, at quhilk tyme he hard Crystie cry eftir he had rissin up 'Allace I am fellit'; depones he saw him nocht fall be resone thair war some houssis betwix him and the deponer; sayis he saw no wappone in the pannellis hand at that tyme; and that a few dayis thaireftir he saw John Crystie walking by the deponeris house towardis Clakmanane and that he went over ane dyke waiklie, in the overgoing of the quhilk dyke he stumblet and fell; and farder knawis nocht.

The said John Melvile in Alloway sworne depones: he knawis nothing anent the hurting of John Crystie be James Heart within Sterling, becaus he was nocht in the town that day, bot declaires eftir John Crystie his death, the deponer being in John Reidis hous in Clakmanane quhair Crystie deid, he saw the defunctis heid gritlie swalled and ane blae straik under his left vayne organe and ane uther blae straik under his left syde and his left airme and schoulder was in the hyde [*skin*] thairof riflet [*injured*] with sum ticheris [*spots*] of bluid wistnet [*dry*] and dry upone his airme, and that befoir the bed quhair he deceissit thair was some mixt spittell with bluid throw thair; and forder knawis nocht.

The said Alexander Myller, sworne and demandit quhat he knawis anent John Crystie his hurting or daith, depones conforme to John Melvill *in omnibus*.

The said Thomas Moriesone, sworne and demandit quhat he knawis concerning the allegit hurt or deid of John Crystie, depones: he being that day in Sterling, he saw James Heart and the defunct going togidder down the hie way in utheris handis, James Heart handing him be the cloik desyreing him ather to pay to him his moneyis or to goe to ane bailyie and that John Crystie refuiset to goe to the bailyie, and that in the meane tyme he struggilt and preisit to be frie of James Heart, at the quhilk tyme he fell bot raise up immediatlie; sayis he hard the said James Heart thaireftir desyre John Crystie to goe with him to sie his compt buik, at quhilk tyme he also fell and raise agane; Sayis James Heart had no wappone at all, and farder saw nocht.

The said John Stevisone sworne depones the day of the said John Crystie his falling and hurting in Sterling the deponer, being in his house or chope, he hard that ane man was fellit in the streit, quhairupone the deponer come furth to the schote [*projecting window*] of his house to understand quhat the tumult was, quhair he only saw James Heart with ane number of folkis going down the gait; and forder knawis not.

[Assize sworn etc.[1] removed to the 'assyse house' etc.]

Re-enterit agane in court, quhair thay all in ane voce, be the judiciall repoirt and declaratioun of the said Walter Keir, chanceller, fand, pronuncet and declairet the said James Heart to be cleane, innocent and acquit of the slauchter of the said John Chrystie; bot the assyse understanding perfytlie that thair was ane strugilling betwix the said James Heart and the said umquhile John Crystie for ane small soume of money auchtand be him to the said James Heart, in the quhilk struggilling the said John Crystie fell to the grund, thairfoir thay intreit my Lord Justice to deill with the said James Heart to geve satisfactioun to the said John Chrystie his puir bairnes and freindis for that ryote, as his Lordschip sall pleis move him thairto, nawayis thairby to infer ony guiltines aganis him for the said allegit slauchter, quhairof the said assyse declairis him innocent as said is; Quhairupoun the pannell as his prelocutour askit instrumentis, disassenting alwayis to the geveing of ony satisfactioun for the allegit ryote.[2]

Thaireftir his Majesteis Advocat protestit, in respect the said James Heart refuiset to geve ony satisfactioun for the ryote be the sight of the Justice, that he mycht haif place to persew him thairfoir befoir the Counsall.[3]

LEGAL NOTES.

1. The most obvious point of attack in the relevancy of these criminal letters, which however was not taken, was that they were self inconsistent. They begin by narrating that on 20th January the victim was given 'ane deadlie straik . . . quhairwith he fell deid to the ground', and end by narrating that he did not die until 31st January. It may be however that the word 'deid' was used here in the sense of unconscious.

2. The oral objection to the presence of the Earls of Mar and Stirling was obviously frivolous. They were entitled to be there as members of the public.

3. The written objections to the relevancy (they were 'read' by the Justice Depute p. 339) are long and involved, with much Latin quotation, and perhaps not very accurately recorded by the clerk (see p. 336). The first was that there were certain presumptions of law which elided the libel: (1) Intention to kill could not be presumed without libelling previous animosity; (2) It is to be presumed from the locus being a public place that there was no previous animosity and no intention to kill; (3) Intention to kill was negatived by the alleged weapon not being lethal and by the alleged blow not being repeated; and (5) by the fact that the parties were on good terms, and by the good character of the accused, as supported by a testimonial from the magistrates. The second was that the death must in the circumstances be ascribed to some further incident or to *mal regimen*, as (*a*) the weapon was not lethal, (*b*) the wound was not deep, (*c*) the deceased walked about after three days; and (*d*) the man in whose house he died in Clackmannan had absconded. There was no hope of these objections being sustained. They involved questions of fact which it would be for the jury to consider. Presumably Mr Nicholson's object was to give the assize, not yet empanelled but no doubt present, the defence version of the incident. No evidence was led in support of them, or attempted to be led.

In the circumstances the Lord Advocate was justified in being brief in his answers, though he was careful to found on those factors in the defence submissions which were prejudicial to the accused. He asserted that it was admitted the panel struck the deceased, and forced him to the panel's house where he was detained. There is no such admission in the record. When the evidence was eventually led there was no witness who even saw a baton. One said the panel had no weapon, and another that he did not see one. Having tried to set up his own good

[1] See legal note 7.
[2] See legal note 8.
[3] No record in extant *RPC* of application for assythement.

character the panel could hardly complain if the Crown alleged some twenty previous convictions for turbulence, one for theft, and an outstanding indictment for reset. No evidence was led as to this record but the assize who were all local would know the position.

4. This is the familiar averment (see *Edward* v *Scrymgeour* 1619, Pitcairn III.467) that if the deceased, after forty days, went about for three days, his wound could not be held the cause of his death. Eight days is substituted for three in *Crawford* v *Crombie* 1625, above I.22. Mackenzie approved of the forty days rule, but here the deceased only survived eleven days. See also *Janet Corsar* 1641, below p. 414.

5. The panel was apparently not confined overnight, but then neither was he prior to trial.

6. This is one of the few cases in which the evidence led before the jury is recorded at length, presumably because in other cases it was generally lodged in the form of depositions. One witness could corroborate another in general terms which suggests that he was present when the earlier witness testified. There is no record of any cross-examination.

7. According to the record the assize were sworn after the evidence had been led, though this is probably an error.

8. The verdict is a special one. The assize must have taken the view that in the scuffle the deceased injured his head on the ground and failed to take care of himself thereafter. But while they acquitted the panel of slaughter they impliedly thought him guilty of 'riot' by which 'assault' was meant, and that he should pay assythment to the relatives. He refused, however, to do so, and the court here had no power to compel him. The Advocate reserved the right to pursue him before the Privy Council. There is no record of the panel claiming the penalty to which he was entitled on acquittal by 1579 cap. 78. He was not entitled to his expenses unless the Justice held the prosecution malicious (1587 cap. 88).

Prefatory Note to L.A. v *Grants in Tulloch.*

This prosecution was part of the general campaign against the lawless McGregors, one of whom had already been dealt with (see vol. I p. 268 above).

The panels were described as 'under the laird of Grant' in the Privy Council order for their arrest and trial on 4th May 1636 (*RPC*2 VI.231-4). On 13th January 1637 the laird was ordered to bring them forth for trial (*ibid* 363; see also 366-7), and on 7th February he produced the first two and lodged a certificate from the local minister that the third was ill, but this did not satisfy their Lordships and he was warded (*ibid* 376-7). This shows that the statutes by which lairds were made responsible for their tenants could be enforced when the Privy Council was involved. On 2nd March 1637 the Privy Council appointed a committee, including the Lord Advocate and Justice Depute, to examine the accused, if necessary by the torture of the boot, all three being by this time in the tolbooth of Edinburgh (*ibid* 397; see also 410, 413[2], 416, 419), and also if necessary to confront them with certain witnesses (*ibid* 418).

The main charge was that of the treasonable slaughter of the Privy Council's commissioner, John Stewart of Drumquhen (of whom nothing seems to be known apart from this incident), in the execution of his duty of apprehending certain McGregors. The latter apparently behaved with great brutality: 'they sett upon him with shotts of hacquebutts and musketts, shott him through the thighes, brake his thigh bones, cutting aff his fingers, cutted aff his head, and danced and made merrie about him a long time' (*RPC*2 VI.366), though this was not attributed to the accused. They were acquitted on this main charge, but nevertheless executed.

Incidentally a dun coloured Spanish bonnet seems to have been the badge of broken men (see below p. 346).

(389) [9 June 1637: Colvile J.D.][1]

Reset of Rebels, Treasonable Slaughter etc. Advocate v *John Grant and others. Convict and hangit.*

Intran.—John Grant *alias* McJokie in Tulliche[2] elder;[3] Patrik Grant McJokie, his eldest sone; John Grant McJokie, younger, also his sone.

[1] Robertson J.D. also sat. See below p. 348.

[2] This Tulloch was in Strathspey, Inverness-shire, in the Grant country, about 4 miles SE of Boat of Garten.

[3] His full name was John Dow Roy McHedrick Grant, *alias* McJokie (see p. 345 below and *RPC*2 VI.410, 413, 416).

Dilaittit for the ressetting of John Dow Gar and utheris his complices[1] notorious rebellis and fugitives within the said John McJokie elder his dwelling hous in Tulliche, and intercomeinoning with the said John Dow Gar, rebell and fugitive, in dyvers pairtis of the cuntray, and remanent crymes contenit in thair dittays eftirspecifeit.

Persewers.—Sir Thomas Hope of Craighall, knycht barronet, his Majesteis Advocat for his Hienes intres; Elspethe Stewart, relict of umquhile John Stewart.[2]

My Lord Advocat producet the dittay quhairof the tennour followis:[3]

Ye ar indyttit and accuiset forsameikle as be dyvers Actis of Parliament maid in the days of our Soverane Lordis umquhile darrest father, King James the Saxt of happie and blissed memorie, and his predicessouris, and speciallie be ane Act maid be King James the Fyft [1540] Par. 7, cap. 97 it is statute and ordanit that na maner of man within this realme wilfullie or wittinglie recept, supplie, menteane, defend, or doe favour to any of our Soverane Lordis rebellis and being at his horne, within thair houssis, landis or boundis, under the pane of deathe and confiscatioun of all thair moveable guidis: And siclyk be the twentie ane Act of his [*James VI's*] first Parliament haldin at Edinburgh in the monethe of December 1567 yeirs it is statute and ordanit that quhatsumevir persone or persones receptis, fortefeis, menteanis, or gives meat, harbourie or assistance to any thevis in thair steilling and thiftious deadis, ather in thair cuming thairto or passing thairfra at any tyme eftir the dait of the said act or intercommones or trystis with thame to that effect be any maner of way without licence of the keiper of the cuntrey had thairto, that the said recepter, fortefier, menteaner, assister, meat gever and intercommoner with sic persones sall be accuiset and persewit criminallie thairfoir as airt and pairt of thair thiftious deadis; as also be the said Act it is expreslie prohibeit that nane tak assuirance or sit under assuirance of thevis, or pay thame blak maill or give thaim meit, drink, ressett, mentinance or supplie under the paine of death, with confiscatioun of all thair guidis; and quhen as any thevis repaires for steilling or reiving in the cuntrie that all his Majesties leidges dwelland within the boundis quhairin they resoirt rys cry, rais the frey, and follow thame alsweill in thair [cuming] as going on hors and foott for redding of the guidis and apprehending of the steilleris to be brocht and presenttit to Justice, and to concur with the awineris of the guidis and thair followeris for that effect under the paine to be haldin pertakeris of the said thift; As also be the 144 Act of his Majesties 12 Par: haldin in Junii 1592[4] it is lykwayis statut and ordanit that nane of his Majesties leidges presume nor tak upoun hand at any tyme thaireftir to recept, supplie, or intercommoun with any tratouris or rebellis, nor to give meit, drink, hous, harbourie or ony uther releiffe or comfort unto thaim, under the same paine for the quhilk they are foirfaltit and declairit fugitives, and that all his Majesties subjectis doe thair exact diligence at the

[1] These were McGregors as later appears (p. 345).
[2] Of Drumquhan, the Privy Council's Commissioner (see p. 346 below, and *RPC*[2] VI.321).
[3] See legal note 1.
[4] Cap. 146 in Glendook, cap. 144 in Skene.

utermost of thair power in searching, seiking, taking and apprehending of the saidis rebellis and in following of thame till they be takin and put furth of the schyre, and then to mak intimatioun to the magistratis of the nixt schyre that the lyk diligence may be done till they be apprehendit; As in the saidis lawis and Actis of Parliament at lenth is contenit; Nochtwithstanding quhairof it is of verritie that umquhill Patrik Gilroy McGregour, Johnne Dow Roy McGregour, his brother,[1] Johnne Dow Gar, John McEan Stalker, and utheris thair complices, haveing risen in oppin and manifest rebellioun againes our Soverane Lordis royall auctoritie be committing of divers thiftis, hearschipes, reiffes, depredatiounes, fyre raiseingis, slauchteris, and utheris odious and treassonabill crymis to their hie contempt of our Soverane Lordis [lawis or auctoritie], oppressioun of his Hienes subjectis, and avowed brek of the peice of the cuntrie, for the quhilkis the foirnamit personis and haill unhappie race of the name of McGregour war denuncit rebellis and put to the horne; Lykeas also letters of publicatioun upoun thair former rebellioun for the crymis abonespecifeit war direct and publeist at the mercat croces of divers heid burrowes of this kingdome, and all our Soverane Lordis leidges thairby inhibeit and dischargit be oppin proclamatioun thairat nawayes to recept supplie intercommoun or keip cumpany with the saidis rebellis under the paines specifeit in the saidis Actis of Parliament; Yit [I] Nevertheles ye the saidis John Grant *alias* McJokie elder, Patrik Grant and John Grant, younger, his twa sones, expres againes the saidis Actis of Parliament and proclamationis following thairupoun [1] in the monethis of Maii, Junii, Julii, August, September, October, November and December 1636 yeiris, at the leist in ane or uther of the saidis monethis, and yeir of God foirsaid, nocht only maist contemptuouslie keipit divers trystis and meitingis with the saidis John Dow Gar, and John McEan Stalker McGregouris rebellis and fugitives abonewritten, recept thaim within the dwelling hous of you the said John McPhadrik Grant *alias* McJokie, elder, your barnes and byres thairof, within the town of Tulliche, furnischt and interteanet thame with meit drink all uther comfortabill supplie and help, at the leist intercomoned with thame in divers pairtis of the cuntrie and within the schirefdomes of Elgyne and Forres; and [2] speciallie ye the said John Grant McJokie, elder, conferrit and intercommoned with the said John Dow Gar in the moneth of Maii last 1636 yeiris within ane aill hous in Rimoir[2] and in the barne thairof, quhair ye and the said John Dow Gar with ane servand of his John McEan Stalker rebellis drank and conferrit togidder ane long space; As also [3] in the moneth of Julii thaireftir, a lyttiill befoir Lambes last, ye the said John Grant *alias* McJokie, elder, of new againe had ane meiting with the said John Dow Gar within the woid of Tulliche, Mr Colene McKenzie, minister, forgaddering with yow and the said John Dow Gar in the said woid in the said ministeris cuming from the kirk of Kincairne [*Kincardine-on-Spey*] quhair ye stayit and conferrit with the said John Dow Gar thair the spaice of ane hour and tuik sneising tobacco togidder; Lykeas [4] in harvest last 1636 ye the said John McPhadrick Grant *alias* McJokie elder had ane meiting and conference within your awin scheillane [*sheiling*]

[1] Ordered to be executed on 26 July 1636 and 1 April 1637 respectively (*RPC*2 VI.301, 427). For the trial of the former see above vol. I p. 268.

[2] Rymore, 1 mile SE of Loch Garden and 2 miles N of Tulloch.

thrie mylles from your awin hous in Tulloche with the said John McEan Stalker McGregour, John Dow Garis brother sone, and ane dum fellow namit Donald, all rebellis fugitives and outlaweris, within the quhilk scheill ye furnischt and interteanet the saidis rebellis with butter cheis milk and uther necessaris ane long spaice conferrit and intercomoned with thame thairintill, contravening thairby the tennour of the saidis Actis of Parliament; Bot also [5] ye, understanding that ane commissioun was given be the Lordis of his Majesties Secreit Counsell to Johnne Stewart[1] for apprehending of the said John Dow Gar and presenting to justice for divers slauchteris and utheris haynous crymis comittit be him as fugitive fra his Majesties lawis thairfoir, and that for putting of the said commissioun to executioun the said John Stewart comissioner had searchit and socht the said John Dow Gar in divers pairtis of the north, and in end in the moneth of December last, haiveing doggit and followit him to the town of Tulliche, ye than, in the said John Stewart comissioner his persut of the said rebell, nocht only refusit and denyit your aid and assistance to his Majesties commissioner in the executioun of the said comissioun, bot also ye, the said John McJokie, elder, Patrik and John McJokies your twa sones, being boddin with swordis, tairdges and gunes, at the leist ye the said John McJokie, elder, and John McJokie, younger, being furnischt with gunes and tairges, assistit and tuik plaine pairt with the said John Dow Gar and his complices, rebellis and fugitives, againes the said John Stewart, comissioner, be schuiting of your gunes at him and his cumpany upoun the xxv day of December within the said town of Tulliche, at quhilk tyme the said John Stewart, commissioner, with Donald McInleithe, ane of his cumpany and assisteris, war tressonablie slaine[2] in the executioun of the said commissioun quhairof ye and ilk ane of you ar airt and pairt,[3]

[II] And siclyk ye the said John Grant McJokie, younger, ar indyittit and accusit for being in cumpany with John Dow Gar and John McEan Stalker with thair complices at Pasche 1635 yeiris or thairby upoun the landis of Glenesk,[4] pertening to the laird of Edzell, and thair thiftiouslie reft, staw and awaytuik fra the said laird of Edzellis tennentis of his landis of Glenesk thair haill guidis geir insicht and plenissing pertening to thame, off the steilling of the quhilkis guidis, geir and plenissing pertening to the saidis tennentis at the tyme foirsaid, ye the said John Grant McJokie, younger, is airt and pairt to the toakin ye had at that tyme ane Spanisch bonnett dune cullourit upoun your heid;[5] And the said McEan Stalker and his complices with quhom ye was accumpaniet at the awaytaking of the said hearschip furth of Glenesk being followit be the awneris of the saidis guidis, as also be John Brabiner and uther cuntrie peopill that assistit thaim for redding and againe bringing of the saidis guidis, ye in defence of the saidis stowin guidis and of your complices, steilleris thairof, presentit ane chargit hagbutt to the said John Brabiner at the coble of Tulliche[6] neir to Colblaine at

[1] Of Drumquhan (*RPC*[2] 10 Sep. 1636, VI.321).

[2] See legal note 2.

[3] There is no reference here to any depositions by the panels on this particular charge, cf. charges II and III.

[4] N of Brechin; Alexander Lindsay was the laird (Forfar Retours no. 242).

[5] This must have been some sort of badge.

[6] This is a different Tullich of which there are two just E of Ballater.

Strathdie betwix Cromar and Braemar, quhilk ye haif confessit be your depositioun to be of verritie.

[III] *Item* ye the said Patrik Grant McJokie ar indyttit and accusit for the crewall slauchter of your guidschires [*grandfather's*] brother sone, namit John Grant, be schuitting him with ane hagbutt throw the body in steid of Johnne McEan Stalker[1] for [? the quhilk slaucht]er ye was laid for the tyme, quhilk ye haive conf[essit be your] depositiounes.

Eftir reiding of the quhilk dittay and accusatioun of the [said John] McJokkie elder, Patrik and John McJokeis his twa sones, t[he Justi]ce finding the samyn to be relevant referrit the said dit[tay] to the said knawledge of ane assyse of the persones following.

Assisa.—William Farquharsone of Auchreachin; Patrik Grant McRobie in Glenbroun; Donald McEane *alias* Grant in Inerlochie; Duncane Andersone of Kynriacrig; Allaster Forbes in Edinglassie; Robert Forbes in Invererntine; Airthour Forbes of Invernochtie; William Reid in Migvie; John Gillandreis in Cobilheuch; Airthour Forbes in Glentarvie; John Couper in Blakhillok; Thomas Gordoun at the mylne of Rappachie, chanceller; James Forbes in Bothane; George Andersone in Tulloche; Alexander Forbes of New.[2]

Quhilkis persones of assyse being ressavit sworne and admittit [etc., narrating that the Advocate repeated to the assyse the Acts of Parliament specified in the dittay, the letters of horning, letters of intercommuning and the pannell's depositions taken in presence of the Justice General, Justice Depute and others, after removing to the assize house][3] fand pronuncet and declairet the said Johnne McJokkie, elder, to be fylet, culpable and convict of the recepting of John Dow Gar rebell and fugitive within his dwelling house in Tullich and intercommoning with him thairintill and in dyvers utheris pairties of the countrie, conforme to his depositiones; As also to be culpable and convict in nocht geving concurrance, aid and assistance to umquhile John Stewart his Majesteis commissioner for taking and apprehending of the said John Dow Gar rebell and his complices in the moneth of December last, accoirding to the commissioun grantit to the said umquhile John Stewart, quha [was] tressonablie slane be the said John Dow Gar, rebell, and his complices in executeing of the said commissioun; bot clanges and acquittis the said John Grant McJokkie elder, Patrik and John his twa sones, of the said John Stewart his slauchter; *Item* lykwayis fand and declairit the said Johnne Grant McJokie younger to be fylet culpable and convict of airt and pairt and being in companie with the committeris of the thift and hearschip upone the laird of Edzellis tennentis of Glennesk conforme to his awin depositioun; And last fand and declairet the said Patrik Grant McJokkie sone to the said John McJokie elder to [be] fylet

[1] See legal note 3.

[2] Auchneachin, possibly Auchanachig NW of Huntly; Glenbroun and Glentarvie have not been traced, but nos. 6-9 and the last four jurymen were definitely from Aberdeenshire (see Aberdeen Sheriff Court Records II.435, III.27, II.454, 270, III.17, II.40, 272, 357, 366, II.27). Edinglassie and Blackhillock are in Strathdon and Kinacraig, now Candacraig, is just NW of Ballater all in the same county. The remaining four may have been from Inverness-shire.

[3] See legal note 4.

and convict of the slauchter of his guidschiris brother sone, conforme to his awin depositioun confessing the samyn.[1] The Justice thaireftir continewis the pronunceing of dome upone thair former convictioun to Wedinsday nixt and ordanit thame in the meanetyme to be tane bak to waird quhill the said day that he may advyset with the Counsall anent the said dome.[2]

(393) [14 June 1637: Sir William Elphingstoun kt., J.G., Colvile and Robertoun JJ.D.]

Doom. John Macjokie and his two sons.

The samyn day John Grant McJokie elder in Tulliche, Patrik Grant and John Grant McJokeis his twa sones, being brocht furthe of waird and presentit upone pannell be the baiilleis of Edinburgh to heir dome pronuncet aganis thame as thay that war convict be ane assyse in ane Justice court haldin within the tolbuithe of Edinburgh be Mr. Alexander Colvile and Mr. James Robertoun, Justice deputtis, upone the nynt day of Junii instant for the crymes contenit in thair convictioun, the Justice at command of the Lordis of Secreit Counsall,[3] be the mouthe of James Grant, dempster of court, decernit and adjudget the saidis John Grant McJokie elder, Patrik and John Grantis *alias* McJokeis his twa sones, to be tane to the burrowmure of Edinburgh and executione place thairof, and thair to be hangit quhill thay be dead and thaireftir to be hung up in yrone cheinyeis within the said place of executioun quhill thay rote and consume; and thair haill moveable guidiis to be escheit and imbrocht to his Majesteis use as guiltie and culpable of the crymes specifeit in thair convictioun, quhilk was gevin out for dome.

LEGAL NOTES.

1. This is one of the few cases where the indictment appears to be narrated in full.

2. It is doubtful if killing the Privy Council's Commissioner was treason. It is not in McKenzie's list of the crimes amounting to treason (see *Criminals* I.vi.xvi).

3. This charge—if accurately recorded—is hopelessly irrelevant for want of specification of time and place.

4. There was no defence counsel, and no interpreter as there had been in an earlier case where—as undoubtedly here—the panels were Gaelic speakers (see above vol. i. p.3). No witnesses were adduced and the Crown relied principally on the panels' depositions taken before 'the Justice General, Justice Depute and others'.

5. This was a discriminating verdict, but by modern standards hopelessly incomplete. The first accused was found guilty of the first charge—receiving and intercommuning with the McGregors—but there is no mention of the second and third accused on this charge, who are by implication acquitted.

In charges II and III the accused are convicted conform to their own admissions on deposition, and the fact that the Crown intended to found on these depositions is libelled in the Indictment. No similar confession by the first panel is referred to in the indictment, but he is convicted by the jury conform to his depositions.

If the present report is correct therefore no evidence was led against any of the panels, other than their depositions.

[1] See legal note 5.
[2] See legal note 6.
[3] No reference in extant *RPC*.

The absence of legal representation was particularly prejudicial to the accused Patrick. He had admitted in a judicial deposition his killing his relative John Grant. The charge against him however—and his admission—was of shooting Grant in mistake for one of the rebels, and it was debateable at this date whether killing 'A' in mistake for 'B' was murder, and whether killing 'A' in mistake for 'B' who was a rebel, was any crime at all.

On the first question McKenzie seems to have had doubts though he thought that the killer should die 'seeing the design of killing a man and not any particular man is murder' (*Criminals* I.xi.xi).

The whole matter was exhaustively argued in *Carnegie of Finhaven* 1728 as a result of which it was finally decided that 'where homicide is intended, it matters not whether the intent take effect in the person meant or in another, the act done being held to partake of the nature of the act intended to be done; (Hume I.22, Burnet, *Criminal Law*, 5, 13, 37 and Appendix I).

In the present case however not only had the panel not intended to kill the deceased. He had admittedly intended to kill a rebel which was no crime at all (McKenzie, *Criminals* I.xi.xix Hume I.187). At this period accidental killing was still considered an offence for which a remission was necessary. The circumstances libelled here, however, hardly warranted the death sentence.

6. This consideration, coupled with the acquittal on the main charge of treasonable slaughter of the Privy Council's Commissioner in the exercise of his duty, may have been the reason why the Justice Depute sought the advice of the Privy Council as to sentence.

(1) [7 November 1637: Colville J.D.]

Thift. Mr Nathaniell Udward contra *Alexander Moubray. Continewit to the* 24 *Novembris.*

Intran.—Alexander Moubray, indweller in Eister Grantoun,[1] at the salt market thairof.

Dilaittit of airt and pairt of the steilling, at the leist resetting, of twentie bollis of salt stowin furth of the salt girnellis [*chests*] pertening to Mr Nathaniell Udwart[2] indweller in Leyth, committit in the moneth of Januar, Februar, Mairche, Apryll, Maii, Junii, Julii, August, at the leist in ane or uther of the saidis monethis.

Persewar.—Maister Alexander Johnstoun, advocat[3] and sister sone to the said Mr Nathaniell Udwart, compliner and as procuratour speciallie constitute be him be vertew and conforme to his letters of procuratorie grantit to that effect subscryvit be the said Maister Nathaniell.[4]

Prelocutour for the pannell.—Mr David Prymrois, advocat.[3]

The pannell takis instrumentis of his entrie and protestit for his cautioneris releiffe.

The persewar producit the letters deulie execut and indorsat, togidder with the said Mr Nathaniell Udwart his letter of procuratorie subscryvit with his hand daittit at Leyth the sevintene day of November instant.

[1] Now a suburb of Edinburgh.

[2] See *RPC*2 VI.294.

[3] Johnstone was admitted Advocate 30 Jan. 1634 (*Lyon's List* p. 112). Primrose was eldest son of Henry Primrose, burgess of Culross; admitted Advocate 25 July 1626 (*Lyon's List* p. 11).

[4] See legal note 1.

The Justice of consent of aither pairtie continewis this dyet to the twentie four day of November instant, and ordanit the pannell to find cautioun for his re-entrie that day under the paines contenit in the Actis of Parliament, quha for obedience thairof fand the laird of Grantoun cautioner for him to the effect and under the paine foirsaid.

The personis of assyse wairnit *apud acta* ilk persone under the paine of twa hundredth merkis.

(6) [24 November 1637: Robertoun J.D.]

Persewer Mr Alexander Johnestoun, advocat, as procuratour and nephew to the said Mr Nathaniell Udwart, persewer of the saidis criminall letters, producet agains the said Alexander Moubray and conforme to the power and procuratioun subscryvet be the said Mr Nathaniell, his uncle, producet in proces, declairit in name of his uncle as persewer foirsaid that at the reaseing of the saidis criminal letters the said Mr Nathaniell was wrangouslie informet of the pannells guiltines of the cryme foirsaid, bot sensyne haveing ressavit certane information of his innocence thairof he, as procuratour foirsaid, in name and be warrand of his said uncle past *simpliciter* fra the said Alexander Moubray his persuite of the cryme foirsaid as altogidder innocent thairof,[1] Quhairupone, the said Alexander Moubray, with Mr David Prymrois, advocat, his procuratour, askit actis and instrumentis; Lykas the said Alexander Moubray on the uther pairt renuncet and past *simpliciter* fra all actioun of sclander or calumnie that may be uset or followit furthe be him agains the said Mr Nathaniell for the allegit cryme abonespecifeit in any tyme cuming, quhairupone the said Mr Alexander Johnstoun askit actis and instrumentis.[2]

LEGAL NOTES.

1. Hume said (II.125) that the Lord Advocate's concurrence was essential to a private prosecution. This is one of the few cases in which such concurrence is not recorded (I.34, 80).

2. Where a private prosecutor failed to proceed he was liable in terms of statutes 1535 c.35, 1579 c.78 to pecuniary penalties, and could also be found liable for the accused's expenses (1587 c.88). No motions for penalty or expenses were made in the present case.

3. In respect of the abandonment of the prosecution, the panel gave up any rights he might have to raise an action of damages for defamation for the accusation of theft.

Prefatory Note in Frendraught v *Glenkindie and others.*

This case has an extensive background and is one of the many incidents in the conflict between the houses of Gordon and Crichton which culminated in the mysterious and tragic burning of Frendraught tower. In 1629 there was a dispute between the complainer, James Crichton of Frendraught, and William Gordon of Rothiemay over fishings on the River Deveron. In June 1629 the latter invaded Frendraught house at Kinnardy (1½ miles S of Aberchirder) and also broke into Frendraught Tower. On 9th January 1630 both were ordered by the Privy Council to keep the peace. In an endeavour to enforce 'letters of treason' apparently for debt, served by a herald 'with displayed coat of arms' Crichton supporters mortally wounded Gordon, who survived only a few days. Crichton himself was exonerated by the Privy Council

[1] See legal note 2.
[2] See legal note 3.

on 11th March 1630 (see *RPC*2 III.401n, 403, 436-437, 485-6). The relations of the dead man made preparations for revenge, but Huntly and Sir Robert Gordon succeeded in producing an apparent reconciliation 'and so all parties having shaken hands in the orchard of Strathbogie, they were heartily reconciled'. The Crichtons agreed to pay a sum of 50,000 merks to Rothiemay's widow 'in composition of the slaughter'. On 8th October 1630 Huntly sent his son, Lord Aboyne, and the young Laird of Rothiemay to escort Crichton in safety from Strathbogie Castle to Frendraught. There they were invited to remain for the night and were housed in Frendraught Tower. During the night fire broke out which destroyed the tower, and six of the Gordon party, including Aboyne and young Rothiemay were burned to death. Lady Rothiemay attributed her son's death—not without justification—to some act of Crichton's and, it was alleged, set upon his tenants a body of moss troopers called the 'licht horsemen' whom she entertained at her house until extruded from it in January 1635 (above i.283, 285). Her trial for this dragged on from 29th July 1636 to 3rd March 1637, when Crichton and the Lord Advocate on the instructions of the Privy Council, deserted the proceedings, she being ordained to reside south of the water of Forth (above i.277-287). She was again tried for herschip in 1638, but abortively (see vol. I 277-287 and below; *APS* V.466; Hill Burton, *Criminal Trials in Scotland* I.202).

The ramifications resulting from 'the fire of Frendraught' figure largely in volumes IV, V and VI of the *RPC* as well as in Scottish ballad literature. The proceedings here printed indicate that many influential people in Aberdeenshire were hostile to Crichton. As late as 26th November 1641 he was still pursuing the Gordons—albeit faintly (see p. 508 below).

(16) [15 December 1637: Robertoun J.D.]

For sindry depredations. The laird of Frendraucht contra *Glenkindie and his tennentis and utheris.* [*Continewit*].

Intran.—Alexander Strauchane of Glenkindie and others.

Compeirit the said day James Creichtoun of Frendraucht,[1] for himselff and as maister to his wrakit [*persecuted*] and oppressit tennentis, and as assignay constitut be thame to the reiffis, hearschipis, thiftis and depredatiounis lybellit, togidder with Sir Thomas Hoip of Craighall, knycht barronet, his Majesties Advocat, for his Hienes intreis, and producit the criminall letters raisit at thair instance againes George, now Marqueis of Huntlie; Dame Hendrita Stewart, Lady Huntlie, his lordschipis mother; John, Erle of Mar; Airthour, Lord Forbes; Sir Alexander Gordoun of Cluny,[2] knycht; John Gordoun of Innermarkie;[2] Sir Robert Inneis of Balveny,[3] knycht; Sir William Forbes of Craigievar,[3] knycht; Michaell Elphinstoun of Quarrell;[4] Sir William Inneis, younger of Balveny; Alexander Strauchane, elder of Glenkindie;[5] and remanent defenderis, as landislordis and maisteris to the rebellis specifeit in the saidis criminall letters, quhairby they ar chargit to haive compeirit this day and plaice, enterit and presenttit thair tennentis and serjandis lybellit, this day and plaice to haive underlyne the law befoir his Majesties Justice and his deputtis for the hearschipes, depredationis, thiftis and oppressionis lybellit, committit be thair saidis tennentis quha ar rebellis and declairit fugitives for the samyne, or els the saidis maisteris to heir thame decernit to mak payment and delyverance to the said laird of Frendraucht and his tennentis of the haill hearschipes lybellit

1 6 miles E of Huntly in Forgue parish, Aberdeen.
2 Cluny Castle 1 mile S of Monymusk, W of Aberdeen; and Invermarkie 6 miles W of Huntly.
3 Balvenie near Dufftown and Craigievar Castle 7 miles NNE of Aboyne.
4 This Quarrell was 3 miles N of Falkirk in Stirlingshire (*APS* VI(2).192b).
5 Glenkindie in Strathdon, 3 miles SW of Kildrummy.

againes thame or of the availles or pryces thairof lybellit incaice of not entrie of thair tennentis committeris thairof, conforme to the Act of Parliament[1] and Generall Band,[2] and upoun the productioun of the saidis letters with the executionis askit instrumentis.

Compeirit Alexander Strauchane, elder of Glenkindie, togidder with Patrik *alias* Peter Moir Forbes in Glenkindie, Alexander Angus thair, John Forbes in Dalrossak, tennentis and servandis to the said laird of Glenkindie, elder, and offerit his saidis thrie tennentis reddie to underly the law for the alledgit hearschipes lybellit as altogidder innocent thairof, and askit instrumentis of his awin and the saidis tennentis entrie for that effect; and in respect of thair compeirance protestit for thair cautioneris releiffe; And as to Robert Kroy alledgit to be his tennent[3] denyis the samyn and swa he cannot be answerable for him.

Compeirit lykwayis Johnne Gordoun of Innermarkie, and offerrit himselff reddie to defend for ony of his tennentis alledgit committeris of the hearschipes lybellit as innocent thairof.

The persewaris viz. James Creichtoun of Frendraucht and his Majesties Advocat, for his Hienes intreis, passis fra the persute of Johnne, Erle of Mar; Michaell Elphingstoun of Quarrell; Sir William Forbes of Craigievar, knycht; and fra the lairdis of Balveny, elder and younger, as maisteris and landislordis specifeit in the sumondis producit for entrie of thair tennentis specifeit thairintill, and desyrit that the haill remanent personis defenderis not compeirand this day as being rebellis and at the horne for not finding of cautioun for that effect may be declairit fugitives fra his Majesties lawis conforme to the executionis producit againes thame, except allanerlie George, Marqueis of Huntlie and his tennentis for quhome he hes purchest suspensioun befoir the Lordis of Secreit Counsall,[4] quhilk suspensioun lyis ever yit undiscussit; And in respect be the Act of Parliament[5] the said laird of Frendraucht as persewar hes in his optioun ather to persew the maisteris for the damnadge and skaith sustenit to him and his tennentis befoir the Justice Generall or befoir the Lordis of Sessioun, and that the cours begune be him befoir the Justice is now interruptit be the said suspensioun, Thairfoir he declaires he will mak his choys of persute befoir the Lordis of Sessioun and suffer this persute intentit befoir the Justice to stay and desert in swa far as concernis my Lord Marqueis his vassellis and tennentis for quhome he is answerabill in respect of the interruptioun abonwrittin.

The Justice continewis this dyet to the morne *decimo sexto* instantis and ordanit cautioun to be fund be the lairdis of Glenkindie and Innermarkie for thair re-entrie and compeirance, as also for the entrie of Glenkindies thrie men, for obedience quhairof compeirit John Sibbett of Glenko and become cautioner

[1] Presumably 1594 cap. 227; but see also 1528 cap. 6.

[2] This was an undertaking signed originally in October 1602 by Border lairds and a few Highland lairds including Huntly (*RPC*[1] VI.825) to which other lairds and chiefs later added their signatures. [See Index to *RPC*[1] VI, under General Bond.]

[3] Evidently the tenants were named in the Indictment.

[4] See *RPC*[2] VI.298.

[5] See 1594 cap. 231 (Glendook); also in *APS* IV.71b, where it figures as cap. 37; in Skene it is cap. 227.

for the said laird of Innermerkies re-entrie the said saxtene day of December instant under the paines contenit in the Actis of Parliament; Lykeas the said Alexander Strauchane of Glenkindie become actit and obleist for himselff and for his awin re-entrie the said day and as cautioner for his saidis thrie men *viz.* the saidis Peter and John Forbessis and Alexander Angus thair re-entrie to the effect and under the paines abonwrittin; Quhairupoun the persewaris askit instrumentis.

(16) [16 December 1637: Robertoun J.D.]

Continewit to the viii of Junii.

Intran.—Alexander Strauchane of Glenkindie, Johnne Forbes in Dalross, Peter Forbes in Glinkindie, and Alexander Angus thair, his thrie servandis.[1]

As they thrie that ar dilaittit of airt and pairt of divers thiftis hearschipes and depredationis committit againes James Creichtoun of Frendraucht and his tennentis, and ar denuncit rebellis and at the horne for the samyn, for the quhilkis thrie tennentis entrie the said laird of Glenkindie as maister is chargit and become cautioun for thair compeirance this day to underly the law for the crymis foirsaidis; And as to Mathow Forbes at the mylne of Glenkindie, for quhais entrie he is chargit, he is deid since the giveing of the charge to that effect, quhilk he referris to the laird of Frendrauchtis awin knawledge and declaratioun.

Persewaris.—James Creichtoun of Frendraucht, and Mr John Oliphant, substitut to his Majesteis Advocat.

Prelocutour for the pannell.—Mr. Thomas Nicolsone, younger.

The laird of Glenkindie, with the said Mr Thomas Nicolsone, advocat, his prelocutour, takis instrumentis of the entrie of the saidis John Forbes, Peter Forbes and Alexander Angus, his thrie men, and offerrit thame reddie to abyd the tryell of the law for any maisterfull thift, reiffe or ressett thairof committit be thame againes the laird of Frendraucht or his tennentis contenit in the lybellit dittay, quhilk is the grund of this chairge direct againes the landislordis, and protestit as procuratour for the laird of Glenkindie that seing he hes satisfiet the charge and enterit his leiving tennentis contenit thairintill that he sall not be troublit, callit, nor persewit for entrie of thir thrie present tennentis now upoun pannell in any tyme cuming.

The Justice continewis this dyet anent the tryell of the laird of Glenkindie his thrie men now upoun pannell for the crymis foirsaidis to the aucht day of Junii nixtocum, and ordanit the laird of Frendraucht to produce ane roll of ane assyse, againes thaim that day, with this instructioun, that gif he failyie in not produceing of ane assyse upoun thame that day he sall not be hard to persew thame thaireftir;[2] And in the meane tyme ordanit the saidis Johnne and Peter

[1] See legal note 1.
[2] See legal note 2.

Forbessis and Alexander Angus to find cautioun ilk ane of thame for utheris compeirance the said aucht day of Junii nixtocum, to be tryit for the saidis crymis under the paines contenit in the Actis of Parliament. For obedience of the quhilk ordinance the saidis John and Peter Forbessis, and Alexander Angus, tennentis foirsaidis, become actit and obleist ilk ane of thaim as cautioneris for utheris re-entrie and compeirance the said aucht day of Junii nixt to the effect and under the paines foirsaidis;[1] Quhairupoun the said Alexander Strauchane of Glenkindie askit instrumentis.

Compeirit the said day John Gordoun of Innermarkie, and declairit that he was chargit at the instance of the laird of Frendraucht, as maister and landisloird to certaine of his tennentis, for entrie of thame this day and plaice to underly the law for the crymis lybellit alledgit done be thaime to the said laird of Frendraucht and his tennentis, and desyrit ane competent day to be assignit to him for entrie of thaim to that effect, in respect of the stormie seasoun of the yeir that they could not haife enterit this day, nather can he furnisch ane cautioner at this tyme within Edinburgh nather for his nor thair entrie, And thairfoir in respect thairof was content of his awin consent to becum actit for his awin compeirance and for the entrie of his saidis tennentis contenit in the lybellit dittay.

The laird of Frendraucht declaires that he insistis againes Innermarkie as maister and landislord to his tennentis, quha ar rebellis for the crymis lybellit, and for quhais entrie he is chargit to presentt thame befoir his Majesties Justice to be tryit thairfoir.

Innermarkie and his tennentis. Continewit to the viii of Junii.

The Justice continewis this dyet for Innermarkie and his tennentis tryell for the crymis foirsaidis to the said aucht day of Junii nixtocum, and ordanit him to becum actit alsweill for his awin compeirance as for the entrie of his tennentis that day under the paines contenit in the Actis of Parliament; For obedience quhairof the said John Gordoun of Innermarkie, of his awin consent, become actit and obleist alsweill for his awin re-entrie as entrie of swa many of his tennentis contenit in the criminall dittay as ar rebellis and fugitives for the crymis lybellit the said aucht day of Junii nixtocum under the paines foirsaid.

The said James Creichtoun of Frendraucht passis *simpliciter* fra Andro Norie in   for the crymis contenit in the letters, quhairupoun Mr Mathow Barclay, advocat,[2] in name of the said Andro Norie askit instrumentis.

Compeirit the said day Mr Mathow Barclay, advocat, as procuratour for Johnne Gordoun of Park,[2] ane of the alledgit maisteris and landislordis contenit in the criminall letters producit be the laird of Frendraucht againes thame, and protestit that na certificatioun sould be given out againes the said John Gordoun as ane of the saidis landislordis upoun the criminall sumondis direct againes thame ather for the said John Gordoun his awin nocht compeirance

[1] It seems remarkable that the accused were accepted as cautioners for each other's appearance.

[2] This is his first appearance; he is not in *Lyon's List*, though a Michael Barclay was admitted Advocate 25 July 1623 (Lyon's *List* p. 11).

[3] Not mentioned above. Probably a son of the Adam Gordon of Park who figures in Watson's case, above p. 319.

this day, or nocht entrie of his tennentis alledgit rebellis for the crymis lybellit to be tryit for the samyne, in respect he is willing to give band, alsweill for his awin entrie and compeirance befoir his Majesties Justice to underly the law for the alledgit crymis lybellit, as to enter and presentt sic of his mentennentis[1] and servandis, alledgit committeris of the saidis crymis, as sall be fund to be dwelland remaneand upoun his landis, rebellis or fugitives for the thiftis, reiffes and oppressionis lybellit, to be tryit and punischt for the samyne, and that at quhat day my lord Justice sall pleis to appoynt for that effect.

Frendraucht contra *Gordoun of Park*. *Continewit to the viii of Junii.*

The Justice continewis the laird of Park and his tennentis tryell to the aucht day of Junii nixtocum for the cryme lybellit, and ordanis cautioun to be fund for him and his tennentis entrie that day to underly the law for the saidis crymis under the paines contenit in the Actis of Parliament, quhairupoun the said Mr Mathow Barclay askit instrumentis.

Compeirit the samyn day[2] Robert Sibbett, sone lauchfull to Sir James Sibbet of Rankelour, knycht barronet, be the compeirance of Mr Mathow Barclay, advocat, as procuratour for him, quha producit ane obligatioun subscryvit be the said Robert Sibbettis hand off the dait the saxtene day of December instant [whereby he] become pledge and souertie for the said John Gordoun of Park that he sall compeir befoir his Majesties Justice and his deputtis in the tolbuith of Edinburgh, or quhair it sall happin the said Justice Generall and his deputtis to sit for the tyme, the said aucht day of Junii nixtocum in the hour of caus, and thair exhibeit and presentt befoir his Majesties Justice the saidis day and plaice, sic of his mentennentis and servandis dwelland upoun his landis as ar rebellis and fugitives for the thiftis, hearschipes, reiffes and depredationis comittit againes the laird of Frendraucht and his tennentis, to underly the law for the samyne, eftir the forme and tennour of the letters direct againes thaim thairanent and under the paines contenit in the Actis of Parliament.

LEGAL NOTES.

1. This case emphasises that the responsibilities of highland landlords for the depredations of their tenants, under the Act 1528 cap. 6, and 1594 cap. 227 (in Glendook) were still being enforced, as they had been recently against the laird of Grant (above p. 343). Glenkindie here produced three of his men at the bar. The laird of Innermarkie appeared personally and intimated that he was ready to defend the charge for any of his tenants, and undertook to produce them on the date fixed for trial—which in the result, however, he failed to do.

2. There is no explanation of Frendraught's failure to cite an assize for the present diet. Warrant for him to do so was contained in the Criminal Letters (Hume II.154; Mackenzie, *Criminals* II.xxi, iv) and it is not clear why the Justice Depute condoned this omission.

3. The case against Sir Alexander Gordon of Cluny was not dealt with.

(42) [8 June 1638: Colvile and Robertoun JJ.D.]

Heirschip. *The laird of Frendraucht* contra *Glenkyndie his tennentis.*

Compeirit the samyn day Johne Forbes, Peter Forbes, and Alexander Angus, tennentis to Alexander Strauchane of Glenkyndie, as thay that become

[1] I.e. persons maintained or supported.
[2] See legal note 3.

actit and obleist, in the buikis of adjournall upone the xvi day of December 1637 last, for thair re-entrie and compeirance befoir his Majesteis Justice and his deputis this day and place in the hour of caus to underly the law for the allegit Heirschipis, reiffis, thiftis and depredationes allegit committit agains James Creichtoun of Frendraucht and his tennentis specifeit in the criminall letters direct aganiis thame thairanent quhairof thay affirmet thame selffis to be altogidder innocent, And thairfoir for tryell of thair innocencie of the premissis offerit thameselffis reddie to abyde the tryell of the law for the allegit crymes abonewrittin, disassenting *simpliciter* to all maner of continuatioun, and in respect that the said James Creichtoun of Frendraucht compeiris nocht this day and place to insist in thair persute for the said allegit crymes, nor yit to produce ane assyse or roll thairof aganis thame for thair tryell accoirding to the tennour of the last act of proces of the dait foirsaid, to the quhilk he standis astrictit bund and obleist thairintill, protestit that nane of thame thre sould be trubillit or persewit for the allegit crymes abonewrittin in ony tyme cuming, and thairupoun thay, with Mr Thomas Nicolsone, younger, advocat, thair prelocutour, askit instrumentis.

Compeirit the same day Sir Thomas Hope of Craighall, knycht barronet, his Majesteis Advocat for his Hienes intreis, and declairet that the certificatioun contenit in the last act of proces anent the saidis John and Peter Forbessis and Alexander Angus, tennentis to Glenkyndie, thair liberatioun and nocht persute for the heirschipis, thiftis, and depredationes committit upone the said James Creichtoun of Frendraucht and his tennentis, can nocht be admittit, in respect the said laird of Frendraucht haifing persewit thame be vertew of criminall letters and thay being charget be vertew thairof at his instance to find cautioun for thair personall compeirance befoir his Majesteis Justice to underly the law for the saidis crymes as being airt and pairt thairof, thay for dissobedience of the said charge war denuncet rebellis and put to the horne and declairet fugitives fra his Hienes lawis as culpable of the saidis crymes, at the quhilk proces of horne the saidis thre persones tennentis to Glenkyndie as yit remanes contemptiouslie nocht relaxt thairfra; and thairfoir desyret my Lord Justice to commit thame to waird to remane thairin unto the tyme thay war examinat upone the factis and deidis contenit in the saidis criminall letters, end thaireftir that ane assyes be summond and thay tryit and puneischet for the saidis crymes.

The laird of Frendraucht contra *Glenkindie his thre tennentis. Continewit to ane xv dayis wairning*

The Justice continewis thir thre persones tennentis to Glenkindie thair tryell for the crymes foirsaidis to ane fyfteine dayis wairning, and ordanet thame to relax thameselffis fra the said proces of horne conforme to the ordour; as also that thay and ilk ane of thame conforme to the last act of proces daitit the 16 of December 1637 last, become actit for entrie and compeirance upone xv dayis wairning befoir the Justice and his deputis to underly the law for the crymes abonewrittin under the panes contenit in the Actis of Parliament, and ordanit that ane assyse be summond upone thame be the said laird of Frendraucht for thair tryell with certificatioun specifeit in the said last act; for obedience quhairof the saidis John and Peter Forbessis, and Alexander Angus, tennentis to the said Alexander Strauchane of Glenkindie, off thair awin frie motive will and consentis become actit and obleist, ilk ane of thame for utheris, as cautioneris and souerteis for uther, that thay and ilk ane of thame sall compeir personallie befoir his Majesteis Justice generall and Justice deputis the thrid day of the nixt Justice air of the schirefdome quhairin thay dwell, or soner quhan or quhair it sall pleis our soverane Lord or pairtie grevit upone fyftene dayis wairning, and thair to underly the law for the allegit crymes of thift, heirschipis, and depredationes committit aganis James Creichtoun of Frendraucht and his tennentis specifeit in the criminall letters direct aganis thame thairanent eftir the forme and tennour thairof and under the panes contenit in the Actis of Parliament; quhairupone his Majesteis Advocat askit instrumentis.

The laird of Frendraucht contra *John Gordoun of Innermarkie his tennentis. Continewit.*

The samyn aucht day of Junii 1638 Johnne Gordoun of Innermarkie being oft tymes callit as maister and landislord to certane his tennentis speciallie expressit and set down in the criminall letters direct and execute aganis him at the instance of James Creichtoun of Frendraucht, quhairby he was lauchfullie charget to haif enterit and presentit thame befoir his Majesteis Justice and his deputis in the tolbuth of Edinburgh the saxtene day of December last, to be tryit and puneisched for the thiftis, heirschipis, reiffis and depredationes committit aganis James Creichtoun of Frendraucht and his tennentis at lenth specifeit in the saidis letters, and in caice of thair nocht entrie and compeirance to heir and sie the said John Gordoun of Innermarkie, as maister and landislord, decernit be decreit of his Majesteis Justice to mak redres and satisfactioun to the persewaris of heirschipis and pryces thairof lybellit accoirding to the probatioun to be led and uset thairintill and Act of Parliament maid thairanent,[1] as he that become actit and obleist in the buikis of adjornall the said xvi day of December last, alsweill for his awin compeirance as for his saidis tennentis and servandis entrie and compeirance this day and place to the effect foirsaid under the panes contenit in the Actis of Parliament, lauchfull tyme of day biddin, and the said John Gordoun of Innermarkie nocht compeirand himselff nor yit enterand ony of his tennentis contenit in the saidis letters to the effect abone expremit, the Justice thairfoir findis the summondis raiset aganis the said Johnne Gordoun of Innermarkie and his tennentis and servandis insert thairintill relevant anent the crymes thairin expremit committit be thame at lenth set down thairintill, and admittis the said summondis and actioun thairin contenit to the persewaris thairof thair probatioun:[2] viz. the factis and deidis lybellit to be provin conforme to the Act of Parliament be twa witnessis and aith of pairtie in maner specifeit thairintill, alsweill anent the quantitie as pryces lybellit in the saidis summondis and assignes the day of nixtocum in the hour of caus for productioun of the saidis witnessis and thair citatioun and giveing of the persewaris oath and thair tryell and examinatioun in the premissis; Quhairupoun his Majesties Advocat askit actis and instrumentis.

[1] 1594 cap. **231.**
[2] See legal note

Laird of Frendraucht contra *John Gordoun of Park and his tennentis of Glenbucket Desertit*

The samyn day robert Sibbald, sone to Sir James Sibbald of Rankelo, knycht, being oft tymis callit as cautioner and souertie for Johnne Gordoun of Park to haife enterit and presentit him, as maister and landislord to his tennentis underwrittin dwelland upoun his landis of Glenbuchet,[1] befoir his Majesties Justice and his deputtis this day and plaice, they ar to say Thomas Torrie in Glenbuchett, William Callum thair, Alexander McRobie thair, William Robertsone thair, Alexander Ego thair, Johnne Rowie thair, William Hay thair, James Watt thair, Johnne Kellies thair, Johnne Braidie thair, and George McRobe thair, and to haife exhibeit the saidis tennentis this day and plaice to haife underlyne the law for the hearschippis, thiftis, reiffis, and depredationis, committit be the said laird of Parkis tennentis dwelland upoun his landis of Glenbuchett, againes James Creichtoun of Frendraucht and his tennentis, in maner specifeit and contenit in the criminall summondis direct at the said laird of Frendrauchts instance againes thame thairanent, as he viz. the said Robert Sibbald quha become cautioner for the said John Gordoun of Park his entrie and compeirance and exhibitioun of the foirnamit personis, his tennentis of Glenbuchett befoir his Majesties Justice and his deputtis this day and plaice to the effect foirsaid; Compeirit Mr Michell Barclay as procuratour for the said Johnne Gordoun of Park and the foirnamit personis, his tennentis of his saidis landis of Glenbuchett, and producit ane discharge maid and subscryvit be the said James Creichtoun of Frendraucht writtin be Johnne Rynd, notter publict, and daittit at Kinnerdie[2] the fourt day of Junii instant 1638 yeiris dischargeing the foirnamit personis, tennentis to the said Johnne Gordoun of Park, of the particuler hearschipis, guidis and geir, availles and pryces thairof, stowin, reft and awaytane fra the said laird of Frendraucht and his tennentis and ressetting thairof, specifeit and contenit in the criminall summondis raisit at the instance of the said laird of Frendraucht and his Majesties Advocat for his Hienes intreis againes the said John Gordoun of Park as maister and landislord to his tennentis abonwrittin thairanent, as also dischargeing all criminall actioun and persuite movet againes thaim thairupoun; And upoun the productioun thairof askit actis and instrumentis; The Justice, in respect of the said discharge producit and red in judgment, with consent of his Majesties Advocat also personallie present, ordanit the said dyet swa far as concernis the said John Gordoun of Park and his saidis tennentis of Glenbuchett and criminall letters direct thairanent to desert; Quhairupoun the said Mr Michell Barclay as procuratour foirsaid for the said John Gordoun of Park askit actis and instrumentis, and protestit for releiff of the said Robert Sibbald, cautioner foirsaid, and of his cautionrie abonespecifeit, quhilk protestatioun the Justice admittit.

Quhilk discharge abonwrittin the said Mr Michell Barclay tuik up againe.

Legal Note

The Act 1594 cap. 231 provided that in the event of the persons complained of not compearing, or compearing but failing to find surety, they are to be denounced rebels, and the

[1] In Strathdon, Aberdeenshire. The Water of Buchat joins the Don above Glenkindie.
[2] 1½ miles SW of Aberchirder.

complainer is to have a choice of civil or criminal action against their landlord, master or baillie or their sureties. The value and quantity of the goods stolen or other damage done is to be referred to the oath of the complainer, and to be proved by two witnesses.

(23) [26 January 1638: Sir William Elphinstoun Lt. J.G., Colville and Robertoun JJ.D.]

Thift. Laird of Frendraucht contra *Lady Rothiemay. Desertit.*

Intran.—Katherine Forbes, Lady Rothemay.[1]

Dilaittit of airt and pairt of the steilling and awaytaking be way of maisterfull thift and stouthreiffe furth of the landis and barronie of Frendraucht, in the moneth of November 1634 yeiris, of the haill guidis, geir insycht and plenissing being within the plaice of Frendraucht, togidder with nyne scoir heid of ky and oxen pryce of the peice overheid twentie pundis, fyve hundreth scheip pryce of the peice overheid thrie pundis, all pertening to the said laird of Frendraucht for the tyme, and remanent crymis contenit in the criminall letters direct at the instance of James Creichtoun of Frendraucht for himselff and as assignay constitut be his wrakit and opprest tennentis dwelland for the tyme upoun the landis and barronie of Frendraucht and utheris landis pertening to him insert in the saidis letters, and als at the instance of Sir Thomas Hoip of Craighall, knycht barronet, his Majesteis Advocat, for his Hienes intreis thairanent.

Persewar.—James Creichtoun of Frendraucht, Sir Thomas Hoip of Craighall, knycht barronet, his Majesteis Advocat, for his Hienes intreis.

Prelocutour in defence.—Mr. Thomas Nicolsone, youngar.

The pannell takis instrumentis of hir entrie and protestis for releife of Thomas Smert of Reidhill hir cautioner and offerrit hirselff reddie to abyd the tryell of the law for the alledgit crymis contenit in the letters as innocent thairof, disassenting to all continuatioun.

The persewar producit the criminall letters with the executionis thairof-quhairby the said Lady Rothemay and remanent defenderis insert thairintill, eftir giveing of the charges to thaim for finding of cautioun to compeir this day and plaice to underly the law for the crymis thairincontenit, ar, for not finding of the said cautioun, denuncit rebellis and put to his Majesteis horne and registrat thairat; and upoun the productioun thairof deulie execut and registrat thairat askit instrumentis; and in respect of the productioun of the saidis letters of horning againes the rebellis insert thairintill desyrit that they sould be declairit fugitives fra his Majesteis lawis as guiltie as culpabill of the saidis crymis.

It is alledgit be Mr Thomas Nicolsone as procuratour for the said Katherine Forbes, Lady Rothemay, that the denunciatioun of horning producet againes hir is altogidder null in respect that schoe, lang befoir the alledgit denunciatioun of hir to the horne, quhilk was upoun the xxvi and penult dayis of December

[1] Earlier proceedings against Mrs Gordon of Rothiemay, were, after many continuations, deserted by order of the Privy Council in 1637 (see above I.277-289). She figures in the *RPC*[2] vol. VI during 1635-37 but apparently not thereafter. See Hume II.405, and introductory note to previous case.

lastbypast and fourt day of Januar instant, at the leist in ane or uther of the saidis thrie dayis, schoe upoun the saxtene day of October lang of befoir fand Thomas Smert of Reidhill cautioner for his compeirance this day and plaice to underly the law for the alledgit crymis abonwrittin, as the act of adjornall maid thairupoun in the selff proportis, and swa schoe haifeing fund the foirsaid cautioun lang befoir the denunciatioun abonewrittin the horning producit againes hir is null *ipso jure*.

To the quhilk it was answerit be his Majesties Advocat that the horning producit is sufficient, nochtwithstanding of the said alledgance, in respect na intimatioun was maid be the pannell to the officer executer of the saidis criminall letters according to the directioun thairof, that cautioun was fund be hir, and that thairupoun ane assyse mycht be sumond be the said officer to this day for hir tryell for the crymis foirsaidis.

Actit to enter upone 20 *dayis wairning.*

The Justice, in respect na assyse is sumond to this day, desertis the dyet abonewrittin againes the said Lady Rothemay, and becaus schoe hes na cautioner in Edinburgh to becum obleist for his re-entrie [*sic* read her], ordaines hir to becum actit and obleist hirselff in the buikis of adjournall for hir personall compeirance befoir his Majesties Justice and Justice deputtis within the tolbuith of Edinburgh, or quhair it sall happin thame to sit for the tyme, at quhat tyme or how soone it sall happin hir to be lauchfullie chargit upoun xx dayis wairning of befoir to underly the law for the crymis abonwrittin and utheris specifeit in the saidis criminall letters, under the paine of fyve thousand merkis money, with this speciall restrictioun and conditioun that the day of hir citatioun and compeirance to be affixt for hir tryell sall be only in ane or uther of the monethis of Junii or Julii in the symmer sessioun; Lykeas his Majesties Justice Generall dischargit the outgiving of ony letters againes hir in the premissis unto the tyme his Lordschip be acquentit thairwith and give warrand and directioun thairanent; Quhairupoun the said Lady Rothemay askit instrumentis and for obedience of the ordinance abonwrittin schoe, of hir awin frie motive, will, and consent, become actit and obleist for hir personall compeirance befoir his Majesties Justice Generall and Justice deputtis in quhat day of Junii or Julii allanerlie it sall pleis his Majesties Justice affix for hir tryell to underly the law for the crymis foirsaidis, schoe being chargit thairto upoun xx dayis wairning under the said paine of fyve thousand merkis; quhairupoun the said laird of Frendraucht askit instrumentis.

Amerciat.

The samyn day Robert Kemp of Vallicraig as cautioner and souertie for James Gordoun in Dauche; *item* John Hamiltoun in Auchbegie as cautioner and souertie for James Gordoun of Letterfurie; and last John Irving of Beltie as cautioner and souertie for Duncane Caddell in Coull and William Nairne in Auchtercowle, being oft tymis callit to haife enterit and presenttit thame befoir his Majesties Justice and Justice deputtis this day and plaice to haive underlyne the law for airt and pairt of the thiftious steilling and awaytaking be way of scheip and thrie hors pertening to Johnne Heislop in Corniehauche, Johne

Horne thair, Robert Duncane thair, and William Stevinsone, tennentis to James Creichtoun of Frendraucht of his landis thairof; and siclyk for airt and pairt of the thiftious steilling and awaytaking af the grund and maynes of Frendraucht of nyne scoir heid of ky and oxen, togidder with fyve hundreth scheip, all pertening to the said James Creichtoun of Frendraucht; and for airt and pairt of the haill remanent hearschipes, thiftis, reiffis and depredationis specifeit and contenit in the criminall letters direct and execut againes thaim and the remanent personis thair complices insert thairintill, at the instance of the said James Creichtoun of Frendraucht and his Majesties Advocat for his Hienes intreis, direct thairanent, lauchfull tyme of day biddin and the foirnamit cautioneris not enterand the personis foirsaidis, for quhome they become cautioun lauchfull tyme of day biddin to the effect abonespecifeit, thairfoir the Justice, be the mouth of James Douglas dempster of court, decernit and ordanit the foirnamit cautioneris and ilk ane of thaim to be unlawit and amerciat in the paines contenit in the Actis of Parliament, *viz.* the said John Gordoun of Letterfurie in the paine of fyve hundreth merkis; the said Robert Kemp of Ballicraig for not entrie of the said James Gordoun in Dauche in the paine of ane hundreth merkis; and the said John Irvine of Beltie for not entrie of the said Duncane Caddell in Cowle, and William Nairne in Auchtercowle for ather of thaim twa, in the paine and unlaw of ane hundreth merkis; and siclyk that the said James Gordoun of Letterfurie, James Gordoun in Dauche, Duncane Caddell in Cowle, and William Nairne in Auchtercowle for thair not compeirance and entrie this day and plaice to the effect foirsaid, sall be denuncit his Majesties rebellis and put to his Hienes horne, and all thair moveabill guidis to be escheit and inbrocht to his Hienes use as fugitives fra his Majesties lawis for the saidis crymis.

Thaireftir compeirit Mr James Ferquharsoune, wryter, as procuratour for James Gordoun of Letterfurie, and alledgit that nather the said Johnne Hamiltoun of Auchbags as cautioner for him, could be unlawit, nor yit the said James Gordoun himselff adjudgit rebell or put to the horne for his not compeirance to underly the law for the cryme foirsaid, becaus be Act of Secreit Counsall all actionis criminall than depending at the instance of the said laird Frendraucht againes the said James Gordoun of Letterfurie, or to be intentit aganes him at ony tyme thaireftir, was dischargit be vertew of the said act; and the Justice and his deputtis also dischargit to proceid againes the said James Gordoun thairanent.[1]

To the quhilk it was answerit be his Majesties Advocat, for the pairt of the said laird of Frendraucht, persewar, that the alledgance foirsaid aucht to be repellit, in respect thair is nothing producit be the proponer for verefieing thairof; and thairfoir the said John Hamiltoun in Auchbegis as cautioner for the said James Gordoun of Letterfurie most remaine unlawit, and the said James Gordoun of Letterfurie himselff, for his not compeirance, to be denuncit rebell and put to his Hienes horne, conforme to the act of adjudicatioun abonwrittin.

[1] James Gordon was baillie to the Marquess of Huntly but among the numerous references to him in vol. VI of *RPC*2 VI this does not appear (cf. p. 472). Letterfourie is 3 miles S of Buckie in Banffshire.

The Justice ordaines the former unlaw to stand anent Letterfuries cautioner, and he himselff to be put to the horne for his not compeirance, but superceidis and continewis the executioun thairof to the secund day of Februar nixtocum, the proponer of the alledgance abonwrittin compeirand and proponeand ane relevant defence quhy the said cautioner aucht not to be unlawit and verefieing the samyn sufficientlie, quhairupoun he sall be hard, utherwayis not to be hard thaireftir; quhairupoun the said laird of Frendraucht and Mr James Ferquharsoune askit instrumentis.

John McEane and others put to the horn.

Item the personis *respective* and particularlie underwrittin *viz.* John McEane at the kirk of Glasch, Patrik Oge in Curgathe, John McKardie thair, Allaster McRobie in Glenkart, Johnne Forbes in Dalrossak, William Roy in Tollaquhill, John Glaschen in Prescheill, Allaster Roy in Tollaquhill, John Forbes in Innerernane, Patrik Roy in Skellater, John Forbes in Tomathone, William Roy thair, and John Forbes of Buchaine, John Gordoun of Auchinnache, James Gordun in Deache, and Jeane Rutherfurd, his spous, Alexander Gordoun of Killihuntlie, James Simme in Hauche, Allaster Ellinslie in Tulliche, Johne Sandisone thair, Donald Ferquharsoune of Monaltrie, Johnne Gordoun of Stragirmak, James Ker in Brayrodak, Johnne Ferreis in Bromehill, James Gillenders, elder and younger, in Tulliche, William Richie thair, Thomas Dow Blair in Aberyeldie, Johnne Jaffray thair, Duncane McGregour and   McGregour, his sone, thair bowmanes,[1] Richard Comert at the mylne of Aberyeldie, Thomas Gordoun at the kirk of Glenmuk, Williame Roy in Balmorall, Patrik Tester thair, William Edwart thair, Allaster Glas *alias* Coutis thair, Findlay McIlkindachie thair, James and John Barreis of Etneiche, Johnne Gordoun in Rawis of Strabogie, George McRobie in Kirkfoule, John Gordoun, kirk officer of Mortlie, Allaster Scott in Tomagillen, Alexander Bissie in Stering, John Gouriache in mylnetoun of Crathie, James Glas in Dalfokar, Thomas Donald in Balmorall, James Cowie at the mylne of Towie, William Lindsay in Cairnecark, Alexander McKay in Newtoun, Johnne Ego thair, Robert Brown in Invercheroche, William Ferrer, James Gordoun of Letterfurie, Jeane Gordoun, relict of umquhill Johnne Gordoun of Auchinhandache, James Alleis of Newtoun,   Done, sone to William Done in Tomallen, [?] Hutcheon, burges in Dalnilthe, Johnne Peirie in Schenwall, George Moir thair, Alexander Malcolme thair, James Burges thair, Margaret Forbes, sumtyme guidwyfe of Skellater and now of Dolasbrachtie, Johnne Fraser, hir spous, for his intries, James Findlay in Brachlie, Robert Caldell in mylnetoun of Inschmarnoche, Robert Gairden in Watternaidie, John Coutis in Grodie, Johnne Thomsone in Staik of Cromar, Patrik Keir in Grodie, Patrik Ker in Belgrennie, Duncane Yairne in Dalbedie, Henry Sector in Inschmarnok, James Coutis younger in Ballachlagane, Johnne Gordoun in Auchindren, Alexander Gordoun in Balnastrone, David Ferquharsoune in Auchinerrer, Duncane Ferrour in Newbiging of Ruthven, George Gillendreis

[1] A bowman was not an ordinary servant. He received the farm stock from his principal and though it remained the principal's property, the bowman received as his payment the increase so far as it exceeded an agreed proportion. (Hunter, *Landlord and Tennant,* vol. I p. 358-9.)

in Wrettoun of Aboyne, William Nicolsone in Culquholtstaine, and his spous, William McRobie in Bellennane, George Michie in Newgrogie, William Snawie in mylne of Melgune, Patrik Ker in Knokfoule, William Ker thair, Patrik Cuik in Bethnie, John Tailyeour in Bogeistoun, Robert Ewin in Quhyt-houssis, William Gresiche in Mostoune, James Garrow in Petintigert, George Smyth in Tulliche, James Ga in Balnacros, Johne Gordoun Brachlie, Andro Mylne at the mylne of Kincraigie, John Symsone in Aucherane, Andro Caddell in Newgrogie, Patrik Ker in Grodie, Johnne Gresiche in Poltilnie, Duncane Nairne in Knokfoule, Thomas Blair in Glenmilk, Thomas Ros in Culs, and Robert Touche in Inschmarnok;[1] being oft tymis callit to haife compeirit befoir his Majesties Justice and his deputtis this day and plaice to haive underlyne the law for the thiftis, hearschipes, reiffis, depredationis and remanent crymis abonwrittin specifeit in the saidis criminall letters, as they and ilk ane of thaim war lauchfullie [chairget] to haife fund cautioun actit in the buikis of adjornall, and for not finding thairof war deulie and ordourlie denuncit rebellis and put to his Majesties horne lauchfull tyme of day biddin; and the foirnamit personis rebellis nawayis compeirand this day and plaice to underly the law for the crymis foirsaidis, thairfoir the Justice be the mouth of James Douglas, dempster of court, decernit ordanit and declairit the foirnamit personis rebellis and ilk ane of thaim to be fugitives fra his Majesties lawis for the crymis *respective* and particularlie mentionat and contenit in the saidis criminall letters, and all thair moveabill guidis to be confiscat and escheit to his Hienes use as fugitives for the crymis foirsaidis, quhilk was pronuncit for dome; Quhair-upoun the said James Creichtoun of Frendraucht askit instrumentis.

(43) [8 June 1638: Colville and Robertoun JJ.D.]

[*Gordon of Invermarkie did not compear and the diet against him was continued to a blank date.*]

(44) [There was produced a discharge by Frendraught dated 4 June 1638 to Gordon of Park and his tenants, in respect of which the JJ.D. ordered the diet to be discharged as against them.]

(27) [7 February 1638]

Mutilatioun. William Rois contra *Malcolme Durward and his sones. Continewit to the xviii day of Julii nixt.*

Intran.—Malcolm Durward and others.

The quhilk day, anent the criminall letters raisit at the instance of William Rois of Cuthilburne[2] againes Malcolme Durward at the mylne of Bonitie,[3] George and Robert Durwardis his sones, and William Forbes in Lairny,[3]

[1] These persons were probably all from Aberdeenshire and Banffshire.
[2] There was formerly a Cuthelburn in Coull parish, and so near the *locus delicti*.
[3] The mill of Bonnyton is in Rayne parish, Aberdeenshire, and Learney is NE of Aboyne.

chairgeing thame to find cautioun for thair personall compeirance befoir his Majesteis Justice and his deputtis this day and plaice in the hour of caus to haife underlyne the law for invaiding, persewing, wounding, mutilatioun and amputatioun of the said William Rois of his richt hand, and straiking away of the mid finger thairof, committit upoun the grund and landis of Coule in Cromar[1] upoun the fyftene day of November lastbypast, compeirit personallie in presens of me, notter publict underwrittin, and clerk deputt to our Soverane Lordis Justice clerk in the clerkschip of justiciarie, and in presens of the witnessis following, Robert Cruikschank, burges of Aberdeine, quha producit the saidis criminall letters deulie execut and indorsat upoun the saidis defenderis, and thairwith in name and behalf of ather pairtie, alsweill persewar as defenderis foirsaidis, lykwayis producit ane letter or testificatioun subscryvit with all thair handis of the dait at Bancherie Ternan[2] the twentie twa day of Jannuar lastbypast, beirand that in respect of the violent storme and tempest of snaw in the north pairtis of this kingdome quahirthrow nather pairtie, ather persewar or defenderis, assysouris or witnessis, summond to this day, war abill to travell without the haizard and perrell of all thair lyves, and that thairfoir be vertew of the said letter of testificatioun baith the saidis pairteis with ane mutuall consent and assent war content that the saidis criminall letters and actioun thairin contenit sould be prorogat and continewit be his Majesteis Justice and his deputtis to the xviii day of Julii nixtocum; Lykas for the saidis defenderis entrie and compeirance that day befoir his Majesteis Justice aither within the burgh of Edinburgh or quhair it sall happin his Majesteis Justice Generall and his deputtis to sitt and hald court for the tyme, producet ane band and obligatioun subscryvit be John Chalmer of Balnacraig, as also subscryvit be the saidis Malcolme Durward, Patrik and George Durwardis his sones, and be the said William Forbes the four defenderis foirsaidis, of the dait the twentie twa day of Januar lastbypast quhairby the said Johnne Chalmer as cautioner and souertie for the saidis foure defenderis obleissis him to enter and present thame and ilk ane of thame befoir his Majesteis Justice and his deputtis in the said tolbuith of Edinburgh, or quhair it sall happin thame to sit and hald court for the tyme, the said auchtene day of Julii nixtocum[3] in the hour of cause, and thair to underly the law for the cryme foirsaid, under the panes contenit in the Actis of Parliament, as the said band of cautionerie beiring the said cautioneris releif subscryvit be the saidis foure defenderis, as also beirand to be registrat in the buikis of adjornall *ad futuram rei memoriam* in the selff proportis; upone the productioun of the quhilkis criminall letters with the remanent writtis abonewrittin the said Robert Cruikschank in name and behalf of aither of the pairteis abonewrittin, alsweill persewar as defenderis, askit actis and instrumentis in the handis of me, notter publict and clerk depute in the said office of Justiciarie. And thairfoir in respect nather the Justice Generall nor Justice deputis war this day within the burght of Edinburgh to the keiping of this dyet protestit that the cautioneris fund alsweill be the persewaris as defenderis sould be fred and relevit of thair cautionerie fund be thame of befoir, and of all

[1] Coull is a parish 3 miles N of Aboyne.
[2] In NW Kincardineshire.
[3] There is no record of a sitting of the Court on the date of this continued diet.

penaltie to be incurrit be ony of thame thairthrow. Quhilkis haill premissis was done within the burgh of Edinburgh and laich tolbuth thairof the said sevint day of Februar in the yeir of God foirsaid, betwix ellevin and twelf houris befoir noone in presence of Mr Andro Williamsone, my sone in law, John Bannatyne, younger, my sone, James Douglas and James [*sic*] Hammiltoun, Justice officeris,[1] witnessis speciallie requyret to the premissis etc. *Ita est Joannes Bannatyne, notarius publicus ac clericus deputatus clerici Justiciarie principalis S.D.N. regis etc.*

LEGAL NOTE

This illustrates the procedure competent where adverse weather conditions made it impossible for the parties to travel to Edinburgh. Non contentious matters were dealt with by the Deputy Clerk of Justiciary in the absence of the Justice or any of his deputes. No doubt the Court had been informed in advance of the position, and this explains why no Justice appeared. The charge should properly have been libelled as Mutilation and Demembration. It was clearly established by this date that a finger constituted a member of the body (Pitmedden I 57).

(38) [17 April 1638: Elphingstoun J.G. and Robertoun J.D.]

Thift. George Weir and another. Convict and hangit.

Intran.—George Weir, sone to John Weir in Colluthie within the boundis of Strabogie,[2] Robert Patersone, sone to umquhile James Patersone, couper in Falkland.

Dilaittit of airt and pairt of the thiftious breking under silence and cluid of nycht in the monethe of November last of ane merchand buithe, perteneing to James Sword, merchand in Sanct Androis, steilling and awaytaking furthe thairof to the number of fourscoir rex dollouris, ten quarteris of Lundoun claithe, and ane pair of trabusschettis [*scales*], quhilkis dollouris war equallie devydit betwix thame, quhairof the said Robert Patersone gat fourtie of the saidis dollouris and the said peace Lundoun claithe for his skair [*share*], and the said George Weir uther fourtie of the saidis dollouris with ane pair of trabuschets, confessit be the said George Weir to be of verritie, and that the said Robert Patersone was in cumpanie with him at the breking of the said buithe, steilling and awaytaking of the money and uthers foirsaidis being thairintill.

Item, the said Robert Patersone for airt and pairt and being in cumpanie with Andro Stewart, sone to umquhile William Stewart, indweller in Berwick, at the steilling of ane napkin with certane moneys being thairintill in the meal merkat of Edinburgh furthe of ane honest manes pouthe [*pouch*] than being within the said mercate, committit within this yeir bygane; *Item,* for steilling and awaytaking of ane uther napkin with ane dollour and ane halff being thairintill furthe of ane honest manes pouthe than being in the mercate of Dumfermeling, committit ten monethe sen or thairby; *Item,* for the thiftious steilling schortlie thaireftir within the town of Dundie and mercate thairof, callit the

[1] James Douglas here makes his first appearance in these volumes. James Hamilton is presumably a mistake for the John Hamilton appointed on 20 July 1636 (above i, 276).
[2] Collithie on the river Bogie, 3 miles S of Huntly in Banffshire.

horse mercate, of ane napkin with aucht pund of turnouris[1] being thairintill, furthe of ane honest manes poutche than being within the said mercate; *Item,* for cutting of ane gentilewomanes purse, the relict of umquhile Robert Alexander, indweller in Leithe, upone the schoir thairof in hir convoying of a friend of hirs to the boitsyde, in the quhilk purse thair was ane gold ring set with ane rubie togidder with thrie dollours and some small money besyde, quhilk purse and moneys with the said gold ring was gottin upone him the tyme of his taking; *Item* for counterfutting, forgeing and devyseing of and useing of ane false and counterfute testimoniall allegit subscryvit be Mr Colene Campbell, minister of Dundie, and twa of the bailleis thairof insert thairintill, beirand him to have bene mareit with Elspethe Patersone, his lemmen [*mistress*], quha is with chyld to him and with quhom he hes keipit cumpanie at bed and buird this half yeir bygane as with his mareit wyfe, quhilk testimoniall is false and feinyeit, counterfute and uset be him as ane trew testimoniall albeit falslie counterfute as said is, and he nevir conjoynet in mariage with the said Elspethe Patersone, his lemmen, committing thairthrow notorious and manifest falset; And last, being dilaittit of commoun thift and pykrie in steilling and cutting of purssis in dyverse mercats and fairs within this kingdome thir dyverse yeirs bygane.[2]

The persewer producet the dittay abonewrittin; and for verificatione thairof producet also the said George Weir his depositione, beiring his confessione of the breking of the said merchant buithe and that the said Robert Patersone was in cumpanie with him at the breking thairof, and was airt and pairt with him at the steilling and awaytaking of his saidis foirscoir dollouris, the peace Lundoun claithe, and trabuschettis abonewrittin perteneing to James Sword, merchand in Sanct Androis, quhilkis war pairtit betwix him and the said Robert Patersone in maner specifeit in thair dittay; As also producet the said false testimoniall forget and uset be the said Robert Patersone, and thairwith lykwayis producet the depositioun of Andro Stewart[3] verefeing and affirmeing the haill remanent thiftis and pykreis [*petty thefts*] abonewrittin to be verritie,[4] and upone the productione thairof askit instrumentis.

Assisa.—Walter Ker, tailyeour, burges of Edinburgh, chancellor; James Wylie, merchand thair; Adam Scot, merchand thair; George Almess, merchand thair; Robert Read, butterman [buttieman?] thair; James Forester, wobster thair; John Corss, tailyeour thair; Robert Cowane, tailyeour thair; John Rob, tailyeour thair; Alexander Read, merchand thair; David King, poultrieman thair; Alexander Gray, cook thair; John Cok, baxter thair; Patrick Menteith, tailyeour thair; James Stewart, tailyeour thair.

The persewer repeittis the depositiones of the said George Weir and Andro Stewart, with the false testimoniall abonewrittin producet be him, for verificatioun of the dittay, and protestit for wilful errour aganis the assyseouris in caice thay acquit the pannell of the crymes foirsaidis.

[1] These were copper coins worth 2d Scots each.
[2] See legal note 1.
[3] Stewart is only mentioned in the record as an accomplice in the second charge in Edinburgh; his connection with the other charges in the other towns is far from clear.
[4] See legal note 2.

[Verdict: guilty.] For the quhilk caus the Justice, be the mouthe of James Grant, dempster of court,[1] adjudget and ordanit the said George Weir and Robert Patersone to be tane to the burrowmure of Edinburgh and to the ordiner place of executione thair, and thair to be hanget quhill thai be dead and thair haill moveable guidis to be escheit to his Majesties use as convict of the saidis crymes, and this dome to be put in executione Thursday nixt betwix twa and thrie houris eftirnone.

LEGAL NOTES.

1. The last charge, if accurately reported here, is wholly irrelevant for lack of specification. Had the panel been been legally represented it would no doubt have been challenged. The pursuer was presumably the Lord Advocate though the record is silent on this matter.

2. The first charge relates to both panels, Weir and Paterson. Weir is not involved in the remaining six charges. Weir admitted the first charge in a pretrial deposition but it is not clear whether he adhered to this at the trial. The fact that the deposition was produced by the prosecutor as proof of the charge suggests that he did not. His deposition was the only evidence against him and in the absence of a plea of guilty, at least by modern standards, such evidence is totally inadequate. The only evidence against Paterson on charge one was the deposition of his *socius criminis*, Weir. There is no suggestion that it was taken in his presence or that he assented to it at any stage. On the remaining charges the only evidence against Paterson is the production of the alleged false testimonial and the deposition of another alleged *socius* called Stewart, apparently taken before trial, and again not said to have been taken in Paterson's presence or that he assented to it. This *socius* was not even adduced as a witness; only his deposition was produced, contrary to the Act 1587 cap. 91 which required all 'reasoning, writtes, witnesses and uther probation and instruction quhatsumever . . . sall be alleged reasoned and deduced to the assize in presence of the party accused . . . and na utherwayes'. There was no evidence whatever that the testimonial was in fact forged. None of the parties whose signatures were alleged to have been counterfeited were adduced as witnesses.

(40) [7 June 1638: Colvile and Robertoun JJ.D.]

Breking kist. Kennydie of Blairquhan contra *James* [sic] *Donan. Desertit.*

[*Intran.*—Thomas Donan.]

Compeirit Frances Mure, brother to John Mure of Achindrane,[2] as procuratour speciallie constitute for James Kennedie of Blairquhan,[2] and producet the criminall letters deulie execute and indorsate, raiset be the said James Kennedie of Blairquhan agains Thomas Donan in Donanstoun,[3] quhairby the said Thomas Donan is charget to find cautioun for his compeirance befoir his Majesteis Justice and his deputis this day and place in the hour of caus to haif underlyne the law for airt and pairt of the thiftious opining and breking up of the chairter kist perteneing to umquhile James Kennydie of Blairquhan, father to the said James Kennydie, his haill evidentis, bandis, writtis and securiteis being thairin, committit in the moneth of Januar 1637 yeiris; and upone the productioun thairof askit instrumentis and protestit for the said James Kennydie now of Blairquhan and his cautioneris releif.

[1] James Grant, the first dempster to appear in this second printed volume, does not seem to have functioned after this year. His last noted appearance was on 20 July 1638 (see below i.297).

[2] Auchendrane House is 4 miles S of Ayr, and Blairquhan Castle 5 miles SE of Maybole.

[3] Dounieston is shown in Thomson's Atlas of 1832 nearly midway between Patna and Dalmellington in the latter parish. The Christian name is wrongly recorded in the marginal note; the report refers to a Thomas Donan.

Compeirit also the said Thomas Donan in Donanstoun, defender, and declairet that he was charget be John Cocherane, messinger, be vertew of the saidis criminall letters to find cautioun for his compeirance befoir his Majesteis Justice and his deputis this day and place in the hour of caus, to underly the law for the allegit crymes abonewrittin specifeit thairintill, quhairof he is altogidder innocent, for his tryell quhairof, and his cautioneris releif, he compeirit and offerit himself reddie to underly his lawfull tryell as altogidder innocent of the samyn, disassenting *simpliciter* to all maner of continuatioun; and in respect na pairtie compeirit (speciallie the said James Kennydie of Blairquhan at quhais instance the saidis letters war direct) to insist in his persute for the allegit cryme thairin contenit, askit instrumentis of his awin compeirance and entrie abonewrittin, and protestit for his cautioneris releif and that na letters or charges sould be direct agains him for the said alledgit cryme in ony tyme cuming, and thairupoun askit actis and instrumentis.

The Justice upone productioun of the saidis criminall letters and executiones thairof, upone consideratioun that the actioun thairin contenit is for abstracting of evidentis and nawayis capitall or criminall, bot that the samyn is altogidder civile and sa competent to the civile Judge to be cognoscet civilie,[1] desertis the saidis criminall letters, and ordanis the cautioneris alsweill fund be the persewar as defenderis to be relevit of thair cautionerie; Quhairupone ather pairtie *hinc inde viz.* the said Frances Mure as procuratour for the persewar and the said Thomas Donan defender askit instrumentis.[2]

LEGAL NOTES

1. The charge was being art and part of the theftuous opening and breaking up of a charter chest belonging to the pursuer's late father, 'his haill evidentis bandis writtis and securities being thairin'. The taking of these contents is not recorded as part of the charge, but the report of the case indicates that the Criminal Letters in fact alleged the 'abstracting of evidentis'. In these circumstances the Justice's finding that the alleged acts were not criminal but a matter for the civil court is unintelligible (see Hume I.57 and 73; McDonald p. 51), particularly since the point was not taken by the defence, and the Justices appear to have acted *ex proprio motu.*

2. It is further difficult to understand why the pursuer's cautioner should have been discharged—since caution was found by him to proceed with the prosecution (1535 c. 35, 1579 c. 78; Gillon I.12; Hume II.127).

[31 January 1639:

Thift. Nisbet v *Craig. Baneist.*

Intran.—Alexander Craig in Nether Craig.[3]

Dilaitit of airt and pairt with John Craig his brother of the thiftious steilling furthe of the ground and landis of Hairschaw of sax scheip, fyve quhairrof pertenit to Jonet Nisbet, wedow in Hairschaw, and the saxt pertenit to William Broun thair, comittit upone the ellevint day of October lastbypast 1638, in the

[1] See legal note 1.
[2] See legal note 2.
[3] Probably Nether Criggie, Eaglesham since he was imprisoned at Polnoon.

dryveing away of the quhilk scheip the space of ane myle and ane halff or thairby aff the ground of the saidis landis of Hairschaw, the said Alexander and his brother, steilleris thereof, being followit and persewit to the outmost border of the landis of Brouncastell, thay left the said sax scheip thereat, and fled and escapit thame selffis, bot being still followit to thair dwelling hous in Nether hous in Nether Craig they war apprehendit and tane to the castell of Polnune, in the whilk thai war wairdit, furthe of the whilk castell the said Johne Craig escapit, and the said Alexander Craig, his brother and theiff marrow, brocht furthe thereof to Glasgow and therefra to Edinburgh to ressave his deservid punaischement.

Persewaris.—Jonet Nisbet, wedow in Hairschaw; Sir Thomas Hope of Craighall, knycht, his Majestys Advocat.

The perseweris producet the letteris and dittay insert thereintill, dewlie execute and indorsat, togidder with ane roll of assyse lawfullie sumond to this day and desyred pro[cess]. Efter reiding of the whilk dittay, the samyn being fund relevant be the Justice, bot the cryme forsaid being altogidder denyit be the said Alexander Craig, defender, the Justice therefoir ordanit the samen to be put to the tryell of ane assyse, whereupone the perseweris askit instrumentis.

Assise.—Williame Patersone in Tempillis; Andro Watson in the Craige; Alexander Davidsone in Braidlet; Robert Strang in Murehous; Thomas Mortoun in Overhous; Mathow Mure in Plewland, chancellor; Archibald Mure thaire; Williame Browning there; John Mortoun in Hairschaw; Williame Young in Scureis; John Faullis thair; Johnne Crawfurd in Woidhous; Johnne Crawfurd, younger thair; James Watsone in Kirkton; Alexander Mukle in Medowfute.

The Advocat takis instrumentis of the sweiring of the assyse and for veriefficatioun of the dittay producet the depositiones of the witnesses following viz. Eliazar Allane in Brouncastell, Johnne Strutheris, dwelland under Bartle Robertoun of Earnok, Mungo Cochrane in Overbrouncastell, Williame Broun in Brouncastell, and Johnne Brouning thair, quha and ilk ane of thame being judiciallie sworne and examinat in presence and audience of the Justice, assysors, and of the said Alexander Craig upone pannell, be thair grit aithe deponit, that in October last the said Alexander Craig and John Craig, his brother, war sene be thame and ilk ane of thame, dryvand befoir thame the sax stowin scheip, stowin and away brocht be thame furthe of the landis of Hairschaw, pertening to William Broun and Jonet Nisbet, and that thai war followit be the saidis witnessis be the space of twa mylls or therby to a burne callit the Smeithburne, whair the said Alexander Craig and his brother left the said scheip; fra the whilk burne thai war lykewayis followit be the saidis witnessis to thair mothers dwelling hous in Nether Craig, and thereftir tane out of the said hous be William Home with certane utheris of the Erle of Eglingtounes schervandis and committit be thame in waird in the castell at Polnune, and festnit in irnes as culpable of the cryme foirsaid, out of the whilk waird or castell the said John Craig, brother to the said Alexander Craig, escapit and fled, and in respect thereof his Majestys Advocat protestit for wilfull errour aganes the saidis persones of assyse gif thai acquit the pannell of the crymes foirsaidis.

[Verdict: Guilty.]

The Justice Generall and Justice Deputtis foirsaidis superseidis and contenowis all pronunciatioune of dome upone the said convictioun untill the tyme thai be advyset withe the Lordis of Secreit Counsall thereanent, and in the meane tyme ordanit the said Alexander Craig to be tane bak to the tolbuithe of Edinburgh and wairdhous thereof, therein to remain in sure firmance in irneis while the pronuncing of the said dome.

(63) [6 February 1639: Elphingstoun J.G., Colvile and Robertoun JJ.D.]

Hugh, Alexander Craig, Baneist;

Intran.—Alexander Craig.

The quhilk day Alexander Craig in Nether Craig, being brocht furthe of waird and presenttit upoun pannell, to heire and sie dome and sentence pronuncet aganis him as he that was dewlie and ordourlie convict be ane assyse in ane court of Justiciarie haldin within the tolbuithe of Edinburgh be his Majesties Justice Generall and Justice deputtis foirsaidis upone the penult day of Januare lastbypast, of airt and pairt of the thiftious steilling of sax scheip perteneing to Jonet Nisbet, wedow in Hairschaw, and William Brown thair, in maner and at the tyme specifeit in the said convictioun, the Justice, be the mouthe of William Andersone, dempster of court, decernit and adjudget the said Alexander Craig to be banischet furthe of this realme and kingdome of Scotland, and to be delyverit for that effect to Captane Walter Murray to serve in the weiris in forane pairtis, and nawayis to returne bak agane within this kingdome or to be fund within the samyn at ony tyme eftir his transportatioun and awaypassing without his Majesties speciall license or warrand, under the pane of deathe to be execute upone him with all rigour. Lykas the saidis Justice Generall and Justice deputtis ordanit him to becume actit in the buikis of adjornall to the effect abonespecifeit. For obedience of the quhilk ordinance the said Alexander Craig of his awin consent become actit and obleist to pas aff this kingdome in service with the said Captane Walter Murray and to remane with him as ane souldier in the weiris and nocht to returne bak to this kingdome nor to be fund thairintill in any tyme cumming eftir his awaypassing without our Soverane Lordis speciall license, under the pane of hanging to be execute upone him with all rigoure but farder dome or proces of law.[1]

LEGAL NOTE

This is the earliest case noticed by Hume (I.91, 361) on which the capital penalty was not exacted for simple theft, but there was an earlier one (above I.224-5, 28 September 1633) where the panel was banished in respect that the theft was 'not grit' (theft of an ox and a mare) and the jury only convicted by a narrow majority.)

[1] See legal note.

(62) [1 February 1639: Colville J.D.]

Uttering Agnes Layng put to libertie and actit to re-enter upone xv dayis warning

[*Intran.*—Agnes Layng.]

The quhilk day in presens of Mr Alexander Colvile of Blair, Justice depute to his Majestie, Agnes Layng, dochter to John Layng within the parochin of Aberdour,[1] nixt to the paroche of Tyrie, committit to waird for airt and pairt with John Gray of the outing of certane fals dollouris at Dustane fair at the kirk of Deir about Yule last, become actit and obleist to compear befoir his Majesteis Justice and his deputtis at quhat tyme or how sone scho be charget upone fyftene dayis wairning, to underly the law for the said allegit cryme under the pane of deid, and thairupone was put to libertie, and this in respect of hir denyell of the said cryme and nae pairtie compeirit to persew hir thairfoir.

LEGAL NOTE

On 26th December 1638 the Privy Council ordered the transmission from Aberdeen to Edinburgh of 'John Gray, tinckler, sometime at the kirk of Tyrie, James Gray in Ellon and Annas Laing, concubine to the said John Gray, who have confest the coyning and outing of false dollers' (2*RPC* VII.103). When the last named appears before the Justice Depute in February she denies the charge, and her alleged confession is not libelled against her. She appears to have been very leniently treated in being released without caution on a capital charge especially in view of the absence of any fixed abode. Nothing more is heard of the case.

(63) [6 February 1639.]

Thift. Richard Lauder. Baneist.

[*Intran.*—Richard Lauder.]

The samyn day Richard Lauder, *alias* Douglas, sone, as he affirmet, to James Lauder, brother to the laird of Lauder, being brocht furthe of waird furthe of the tolbuithe of Edinburgh as he that was tane and apprehendit upone the first day of October lastbypast upone the Hie Streit of the brughe of Hadingtoun and challingit thairupone for the thiftious steilling of ane purse in tyme of mercate, pertening to William Mylne in Balgone[2], furthe of his poutche with certane soumes of money being thairintill, and thaireftir committit to waird be the magistrattis of Hadingtoun, and dureing the tyme of his wairding dyverse cuntrey peaple resorting to the said waird did challenge and accuise him of dyverse poyntis of thift, speciallie William Cairnes and George Rentoun in Pencaitland,[3] fra quhom he had stowin under nycht, furthe of thair dwelling houssis in Pencaitland sevin or aucht yeiris of befoir, ane wob of sey bombasie[4] and ane uther web of lyning with certane lyning yearne perteneing to thame: As also the said Richard being indyttit and accuiset in the monethe of Maii

[1] Near Fraserburgh, Aberdeenshire.
[2] 2 miles S of N. Berwick.
[3] Pencaitland, village 5 miles SW. of Haddington.
[4] Bombasine, a Flemish material.

1636 befoire the proveist and bailleis of the said brught of Hadingtoun and convict be ane assyse of the thiftious steilling of ane purse with certane moneyis thairintill furthe of Alexander Wilsone in Fortoun[1] his poutche, with the quhilk he was tane reid hand; and for dyverse utheris poyntis of thift and pykrie; For the quhilkis he was ordanit to be scurget throw the haill streittis of the said brughe and brunt one the schoulder with the townes burneing irone, bot befoir the executione of the said sentence willinglie and of his awin accord became actit and obleist to depairt furthe of the boundis of the said brughe and haill Sherefdome of Eist Lowtheane, and to be banischet furthe of the samyn and nawayis to returne bak agane or be fund within the boundis foirsaidis at any tyme thaireftire under the pane of daithe: And last the said Richard, being in the monethe of Maii lastbypast tane and apprehendit as ane notorious pyker and commoun theiff and presentit befoire the bailleis of Edinburgh as guiltie of dyverse poyntis of pykrie and thift, was, of his awin consent, actit and obleist in the burrow court buikis of the said brughe to pas aff this kingdome in companie of Leutennent Colonell Stewart to the pairtis of Germanie, thair to serve him in the warris, and nocht to devert himselff frome that service nor to returne within this kingdome at any tyme thaireftire under the pane of hanging but favour, as the severall actis maid thairupone schawin and producet befoire his Majesties Justice under the subscriptiones of Mr Alexander Guthrie, commone clerk of Edinburgh, and of Mr John Hutchesone, commone clerk of Glesgow, and of Mr George Gray, commone clerk of Hadingtoun, beirand him to be banischet furthe of the saidis townes and brughes for thift and pykrie in thameselffis proportis. The Justice in consideratione of the notorietie of the said Richard Lauder his vicious lyfe, and yit mitigatting justice with mercie upone hope of the said Richard his amendiment, ordanit him to be banischet this realme and nawayis to be fund within the samyn at any tyme heireftir under the pane of hanging to the daithe but favour, quhilk sentence the said Richard maist willinglie acceptit and of his awin consent become actit and obleist to depairt and pas aff this kingdome in cumpanie of Captane Walter Murray[2] to serve him in the warris in forane pairtis, and nawayis to returne bak agane within this kingdome or to be fund thairintill at ony tyme heireftire under the said pane of hanging to the daithe; In respect quhairof the Justice ordanit the said Richard Lauder withe the said Alexander Craig to be returned bak to thair waird within the said tolbuithe of Edinburgh thairin to remane quhill thair delyverie to the said Captane Walter Murray to be transpoirtit be him as said is.

Legal Note

This accused was dealt with very leniently. George Weir and Robert Paterson were hanged in the previous year for repeated acts of theft (above p. 365).

One presumes this was a different Richard Lauder from the one sent to the French wars in 1642 (*RPC*[2] VII.573).

Another punishment for theft was perpetual servitude, which involved wearing a brass collar suitably inscribed (see Hume II.544. He deals with this case at I.361). It will be observed that in the burgh court of Haddington the panel was tried by a jury, and that the town possessed its own branding iron.

[1] Fortune is 4 miles NE of Haddington.

[2] Now substituted for Colonel Stewart.

(67) [5 March 1639: Elphingstoun, J.G.]

William Bar. Baneist.

Intran.—William Bar.

The quhilk day in presence of the rycht honorabill Sir William Elphingstoun, knycht, his Majesties Justice Generall, William Bar, lait servand to Sir James Hamiltoun of Reidhall[1] knycht, being brocht out of waird furthe of the tolbuithe of Edinburgh to the laiche counsall hous of the said brughe[2] as being tane and apprehendit and committit to the said waird for the abstracting, steilling and deteneing of fyve silver spones perteneing to the said Sir James his maister dureing the tyme of his service, with the quhilk fang he was challingit and [quhilk] war [in] his possessione the tyme of his taking; Quhilk cryme and offence the said William Bar confessit to be of verritie and cravet Godis mercie and the Justice pardone for the same, and was content to underly the puneischement of scurgeing or burneing one the cheik or ony uther puneisment it sould pleas my lord Justice Generall to injoyne or pronunce aganis him, his lyfe being spairit.

In respect quairof his Majesties Justice Generall, mitigating mercie with justice, ordanit the said William Bar to be banisched this his Majesties kingdome of Scotland and nocht to returne agane within the samyn without his Majesties licence, under the pane of dead; and for this effect ordanit the said William Bar to be delyverit to Colonell Alexander Erskene to pas with him furthe of this kingdome and to serve him in the warris as a souldier; Quhilk sentence abonewrittin the said William Bar of his awin consent willinglie acceptit and imbraicet.

LEGAL NOTE

Hume refers to the case at I.362.

(71) [29 March 1639: Colvile and Robertoun JJ.D.]

Slauchter. Johnne Kennydie. Desertit.

Intran.—Johnne Kennydie in Hallaithes.[3]

Dilaittit of airt and pairt of the slauchter of umquhile Cristell Johnstoun in Lamenbiehill,[4] committit within the town of Lochmaben, upone the nynt day of Februar lastbypast, be geving him ane deidlie straik in the heid quhairof he deceissit upone the fyftene day of the said moneth thaireftir.

Persewaris.—Frances Johnstoun, Andro Johnstoun, David and Archibald Johnstones, as brether to the defunct, Mr Alexander Johnstoun, advocat.

1 By Slateford on the SW. side of Edinburgh.

2 I.e. at the W. end of St Giles Kirk.

3 Halleaths is just E of Lochmaben. For John Kennedy of Haleiths in the Stewartry of Annandale in 1642 see *RPC*2 VII.523.

4 Lammenbie is at NY 1486. See note in 'Place Names and Population, Scotland, 1967'. [H.M.S.O.]

Prelocutouris for the pannell.—Mr Roger Mowat,[1] George Deanes,[2] advocattis.

The persewaris producet the letters deulie execute and indorsate, askit instrumentis thairupoun and protestit for releif of George Johnstoun thair cautioner.

The pannel takis instrumentis of his entrie and offerit himself reddie to underly the law for the cryme contenit in the letters as innocent thairof disassenting to all maner of continuatioun, and protestis for his cautioneris releiff.

The Justice desertis the dyet upone John Kennydie in Hallaithes in respect of the want of assysouris of sic persones as best knawis the verritie in the said matter.

Compeirit Gavin Henrysone in Thorniequhat, John Fareis in Howthat, William Johnstoun in Toddelmure, Nicoll Brown in Apilgirth, Gilbert Skailis in Kameheid, David Hendersone in Cleuchheidis, William Moffet in Blindelbus, Andro Chalmer in Bengaw, George Halyday thair, John Creichtoun thair, John Bell in Drysdaillgait, James Grahame in Corrielaw, David Achiesone in Croftheid, Thomas Moffet in Underwoid and Cristopher Johnstoun in Mylnebank, and declairet that thay war charget be John Mundell messinger to compeir befoir his Majesteis Justice and his deputis this day and place in the hour of caus to pas upone the said John Kennydie his assyse for the slauchter of the said Cristell Johnstoun in Lamembiehill, and in respect of thair compeirance and obedience of the said charge, and that the dyet is desertit be the Justice, askit instrumentis of thair compeirance and protestit that thai nor nane of thame be charget upone this assyse heireftir.

LEGAL NOTES

Although a panel of jurors was present the Justices took it upon themselves to desert the diet on the ground that none of the potential assizers knew anything of the facts of the case. How their lordships satisfied themselves on this matter is not stated, but there must have been some investigation of each individual's knowledge before they could conclude as they did. The case emphasizes—as do many others in these volumes—that the ancient idea still prevailed that the jury should have at least some members who knew something of the incident being investigated. The concept of all the jurors as impartial strangers did not apply (see above i. 37, 48, 50-51, 116; below p. 551). This aspect is not dealt with by Hume who only remarks (II.306-7) that till the new regulations of 1672 the prosecutor made up the List of Assize, who 'were generally from the vicinage of the panel's residence or the *locus delicti*, how distant soever from the place of trial'. In these volumes they are commonly found to be taken from the locus of the crime, and supplemented by Edinburgh burgesses.

(75) [23 August 1639: Colvile and Robertoun JJ.D.]

Sla[uchter]. Erskyne contra William Andersone and utheris, burgessis of Aberdene. Continewit.

Intran.—Williame Andersone, goldsmyth, burges of Aberdene; Alexander Reidfurd, his prenteis and servand; Williame Nicolsone, skynner, burges of Aberdene; James Chrystie, tailyeour, burges thair.

Dilaitit of airt and pairt of the slauchter of umquhile Williame Erskine,

[1] Of Dumbreck, Professor of Civil Law in Aberdeen 1628-40 (*Lyon's List* 157).

[2] Referred to in *Lyon's List* (p. 52) as 'servitor to Robert Burnet of Cringletie, Advocate'. Admitted 19 November 1633.

brother to Thomas Erskine of Balhagardie,[1] committit the xx day of Junii last.[2]

Persewaris.—Thomas Erskyne of Balhagardie as brother, Sir Thomas Hope of Craighall, knycht barronet, his Majesteis Advocat, for his Hienes intereis.

Prelocutouris in defence.—Mr John Nisbet;[3] Mr William Forbes,[3] advocattis.

The persones on pannell takis instrumentis of thair entrie and protestis for thair cautioneris releiff.

The persewaris producet the letters deulie execute and indorsate upone the persones foirsaidis now upone pannell, as also upone David Nicoll ane of the defenderis thairin contenit, quha nawayis compeiris being oft tymes callit, and thairfoir be the mouth of James Douglas, dempster of court, was declairet fugitive fra his Majesteis lawis for the slauchter abonewrittin.

And on the uther pairt the pannell offerit thame selffis reddie to underly the law for the allegit slauchter lybellit as altogidder innocent, and in respect thair is na assysouris present, nor na executioun producet upone thair citatioun be the persewaris, protestit that thair expensis sould be refoundit, and the persewaris cautioner mycht be unlawit for nocht persute, at the leist for nocht productioun of thair dilligence in summonding ane assyse, and that that thai sould nocht be put under new cautioun for thair compeirance to ane new dyet, and producet ane warrand of the Lordis of Secreit Counsall, subscryvit be my lord Erle of Traquair, his Majesteis commissioner *I.P.D.*, for that effect,[4] and askit instrumentis upone the productioun thairof.

To the quhilk the persewaris maid answer: As to the nocht compeirance of the assyse, declairis that the officer executour of the letters *viz.* William Wat, messinger, quha ressavit ane subscryvit roll of the persones to be summond upone the pannellis assyse, hes been seducet and intyset ather to hald up the said assyse roll with the executiones thairof be the moyane [*influence*] of the defenderis or utherwayis hes playid the knave in abstracting the samyn fra the persewaris;[5] and as to the pannellis tryell, desyres that they compair at eftir none in presens of the Justice to be examinat upone the verritie of the fact lybellit and of the forme and maner and uther circumstances anent thair committing thairof; and as to that pairt of the allegeance anent the Counsallis warrand producet be the pannell, answeris that the samyn is clandestenlie purchest *parte non citata*, and thairfoir can nocht be sustenit quhill [*until*] the persewaris be hard.

The Justice continewis the dyet to the morne and ordanit the pannell to re-enter, as also to compeir at eftirnone to be examinat, quhairto the pannellis procuratouris disassentit and adheiris to the warrand producet.

1 Balhagerty is between Laurencekirk and Johnshaven in Kincardineshire. It is odd that the locus is not specified. Its specification in the letters was, of course, essential (Hume II.209).

2 See legal note 1.

3 Nisbet, later Sir John Nisbet of Dirleton, was admitted advocate 20 Nov. 1633, and became Lord Advocate and Ordinary Lord on 14 Oct. 1664 (*Lyon's List* 165); Brunton and Haig, *Senators* p. 389. Forbes was admitted advocate 12 June 1634 (*Lyon's List* p. 741).

4 Not in surviving records of the Privy Council.

5 I.e. he had either been enticed by the accused to conceal the citations or had accepted the assize roll without the intention of executing the citations.

[24 August 1639.]

[The Lord Advocate produced a warrant of Council ordaining parties to appear before them.[1] The Justices accordingly deserted the diet.]

(84) [13 December 1639: Colvile and Robertoun JJ.D.]

Sla[uchter]. *Desertit.*

Intran.—William Andersone, goldsmyth, burges of Aberdene; Alexander Readfurd, his prenteize and servand; William Nicolsone, skynner, burges of Aberdene; and James Chrystie, tailyeour, burges of the said brughe.

Dilaittit of the crewall and unmerciefull slauchter of umquhile Williame Erskene, brothair to Thomas Erskene of Balhagartie, and Alexander Erskene of Barnes, at the least of airt and pairt thairof, committit the twentie day of Junii 1639 in maner specifeit in the letters direct thairanent.[2]

Perseweris.—Sir Thomas Hope of Craighall, knycht barronet, his Majesteis Advocat, for his Hienes intreis; Alexander Keycht, wryter, as procuratour for Thomas Erskene of Balhagartie, ane of the complineris insert in the saidis criminall letters, conforme to ane procuratorie producet be him daitit the 28 of November 1639.[3]

Prelocutouris in defence.—Mr. John Nisbet, Mr. William Forbes, advocattis.

The perseweris foirsaidis compeirand, as said is, producet the criminall letters direct at the instance of Anna Strachane, the relict, Margaret Erskene as dochter, Thomas Erskene of Balhagartie and Alexander Erskene of Barnis, as brether, with the remanent kyn and freindis of the said umquhile William Erskene, and the said Sir Thomas Hope of Craighall, knycht barronet, his Majesteis Advocat, for his Hienes intreis, dewlie execute and indorsate upone the saidis William Andersone, Alexander Readfurd, his servand, William Nicolsone, and James Chrystie, foure of the defenderis foirsaidis thairin contenit and now enterit upone pannell, as also upone David Nicoll in Blaidryne,[4] and Patrik Fergussone sone to Patrik Fergussone, burges of Aberdene, twa of defenderis contenit in the samyn criminall letters, and askit instrumentis upone the productione thairof, and protestit for the perseweris cautioneris releiff.

The persones one pannell with thair prelocutouris foirsaidis askit instrumentis of thair entrie and protestit for thair cautioneris releiff.

My Lord Advocat declairit that he compeirit for his Majesties intreis anent the slauchter abonewrittin; as also the said Alexander Keycht declairis he compeiris as procuratour for the said Thomas Erskene of Balhagarty, compliner, insert in the saidis criminall letters, conforme to the said Thomas his missive letter conteneing his power thairintill to produce the saidis letters of the dait the xxviii of November last.

The pannell takis instrumentis that my Lord Advocat only compeiris as

[1] See legal note 2.
[2] See legal note 3.
[3] See legal note 4.
[4] Not found.

persewer, and that nathair the laird of Pittodrie[1] nor nane of the complineris insert in the saidis letters compeiris to persew the samyn nor to sweir the dittay,[2] and quhairas Alexander Keycht, wryter, as procuratour for Pittodrie, he cannot be admittit, becaus *in criminalibus neque accusator neque reus* can compeir *per procuratorem* seing the pannell is prejudgit [*prejudiced*] thairby of the benefeit competent to him of the law, alsweill in geveing of the perseweris aithe *de calumnia* upone the dittay as in sweiring of the verritie thairof to the assyse; and thairfoir the pannell protestis for thair expensis being verie unjustlie calumniat, vext and persewit for ane cryme quhairof thai ar innocent, alsweill in a dyet preceiding in this mater quhilk than desertit, as now of new convenit be thair perseweris in the secund dyet; And thairfor protestis that thair accuseris absence this day may furneische ane evidence and verificatione to the assyse of thair innocencie, as gif thair accuiseris being present had bene requyret to sweir the dittay producet and had refuiset the samyn.

To the quhilk it was answerit be my Lord Advocat that the maxime is trew for the pannell, but not for the persewers, becaus thai may informe his Majesteis Advocat ather be thame selffis or ane procuratour, and that Alexander Keycht, as procuratour foirsaid, hes producet his warrand and procuratorie; In respect quhairof desyret the summondis to be red and the assyse to be callit.

To the quhilk it was answerit be the pannell that, albeit ane procuratour may informe be ane procuratorie his Majesteis Advocat, yit he cannot sweir the dittay[3].

(85) Thaireftir it is alledget be the pannell and thair prelocutouris that twa thingis ar contenit in the criminall summondis producet aganis thame, the ane for the slauchter lybellit, and the uther for airt and pairt thairof, of the quhilk summondis the defenderis aucht to have had ane just and autentik coppie; bot swa it is that thai ressavet na autentik coppie of the criminall summondis, bot only ane tikit [*abridgement*] nawayis conteneing the circumstances of the tyme, place and maner of the said slauchter lybellit, and swa cannot answer nor defend this day bot most have ane just double of the letters producet aganis thame, and for verificatione of the said alledgeance producet the tykit gevin to thame.

It is answerit be the perseweris that the coppie producet be the pannell is sufficient, and that the executiones of the letters beiris ane coppie to be delyverit to the defenderis, and thairfoir the alledgeance aucht to be repellit in respect of the executione.

It is farder alledget be the pannel that thai accept the summondis producet, and sayis the samyn is altogidder irrelevant and innept, in swa far as the samyn beiris that the pannell darnit [*hid*] neir by the buriall yeard of Aberdene,[4] and dischairget and schote ane muskate at William Erskene quhairof he deceissit, as also it is lybellit alternativelie that David Nicoll schot the schot be the pannellis causeing and hounding out [*setting on*] *etc.*, quhilkis ar incompatable in ane lybell, and swa the persewer, be lybelling alternativlie anent the

[1] Thomas Erskine of Balhagerty was also laird of Pittodrie, e.g. *RMS* IX.1501.
[2] i.e. take the oath of calumny.
[3] See legal note 5.
[4] Probably that of St Nicholas, the parish church; Greyfriars at this date was probably not in use. It is surprising that there was no criticism by the defence of lack of specification.

slauchter abonewrittin, affirmes that the summondis nawayis can be sustenit, *quia qui famosam actionem intendit non debet vagari cum discrimine ne aliene existmationis sed designare certum ff: Lege pretor: dixit de injuriis primo et ibidem quod pretor ait certum est dicere non sub alternatione illud aut illud sed illam injuriame sepassim,* And *Joannes Petrus in forma respontionis rei, libellus est incertus quia alternativus;* And quhairas it is lybellit that the pannell was accessour to the slauchter be hounding out of David Nicoll, the pannell cannot be convenit as hounder out *priusquam constat de mandataria Bartil: Lege et qui reum: si tutituum ff: de furtis qui respondens quod debet constare plene et per testes etc.*

Thaireftir the pannell, notwithstanding of thair former alledgeances and passing thairfra willinglie, offerit thame selffis to the tryell of ane assyse as innocent of the crymes lybellit and thairupone askit instrumentis, and that befoir any answer maid be his Majesteis Advocat to thair alledgeances abonewrittin.

The Justice and Judges foirsaidis,[1] for caisis moveing thame, ordanit the saidis criminall letters, swa far as concernis the saidis four defenderis foirsaidis enterit upone pannell, to desert; to the quhilk desertione the saidis defenderis and thair prelocutouris disassentit and as of befoir willinglie offerit thameselffis to the tryell of ane assyse for the said alledget slauchter as innocent thairof.

The Justice as of befoir, with consent of his Majesteis Advocat, desertis the saidis letters swa far as concernis the saidis four defenderis now upone pannell, and dischairget altogidder the directing and outgeving of ony new letters agains thame for the cryme foirsaid without ane speciall warrand and directione of his Majesteis Justice Generall, Justice Clerk, Justice Deputtis and his Majesteis Advocat for that effect; Quhairupone ather pairteis askit instrumentis.[2]

The pannell and thair prelocutouris in respect of the premisis protestit that thair expensis may be modiefeit be the Justice and refoundit to thame be the saidis perseweris befoir the outgeveing of any new letters agains thame in the said mater, speciallie in respect this is the secund dyet keipit be thame for cleiring of thair innocencie in the premisis, and thairupoun askit instrumentis.[3]

Thaireftir the saidis David Nicoll and Patrik Fergussone, twa of the saidis defenderis contenit in the saidis criminall letters, being oft tymes callit to have compeirit befoir his Majesteis Justice and his deputtis this day and place to have underlyne the law for the slauchter of the said William Erskene, as thai that war laufullie chairget to that effect, and not compeirand, thairfoir the Justice be the mouthe of James Douglas, dempster of court, decernit adjudget and declairit the saidis David Nicoll and Patrik Fergussone, and ather of thame, to be outlawis and fugitives fra his Majesteis lawis, and in that respect ordanit letters to be direct to denunce thame rebellis and put thame to his Hienes horne and all thair moveable guidis to be escheit and inbrocht to his Hienes use as fugitives for the said slauchter; quhairupone his Majesteis Advocat askit instrumentis.

[1] Two Justice Deputes are narrated at the start as sitting together; the reference to the Justice is not understood.

[2] See legal note 6.

[3] See legal note 7.

LEGAL NOTES

1. At neither diet were the *locus* or *modus* specified in the narrative of the charge, but they appear later in the body of the report.

2. The Privy Council warrant does not appear in the extant records, and its effect is unknown. It did not prevent later proceedings. The only reference there to Anderson is as appearing on a delinquents' roll in 1641 (*RPC*² VII.570). He was still alive in 1645 (Aberdeen Sheriff Court Records II.513).

3. At the second diet the panels are charged as principals and not merely art and part as they had been originally—an odd discrepancy at which the panels protested. They had ample justification too for their complaint that they never received 'ane just and autentik coppie' of the criminal letters but only 'a tikit'. By the Act 1555 cap. 33 a 'copy' should have been served which presumably means a full copy or 'just double', although one containing only the essential portions of the charge seems to have been accepted in the first case against Lady Rothiemay in 1636 (I.278 above). The pursuers argued that an execution bearing that 'ane coppie' had been delivered was enough, and it was so held in *Armstrong* 11th Jan. 1605 (Pitcairn II.451). Hume thought any decision that an execution referring to a full copy as having been served was *probatio probata* constituted an 'unwarrantable freedom' (II.244; Armstrong and others 1605, Pitcairn II.451; and Gordon, Pitcairn III.419). In the present case it was perhaps too much to expect Colville J.D. to reverse his own earlier decision. By 1662 'constant practicque of the court' required that a 'full double' be served (Livingstone v Leith 1662; Scott Moncrieff I.53).

4. At the second diet the Lord Advocate appears as first pursuer, whereas at the first the order was reversed. It was unusual but not unknown (see above I.54, 76) for the Lord Advocate to be first pursuer in criminal letters.

5. It seems a good objection for the panels that the individual pursuers were not personally present to take the oaths of calumny. This was not only the oath which was taken before there was any discussion on the relevancy. There was also the oath before the assize after it had been empanelled. Hume deals at length with the former (II.128-9) but not at all with the latter. (See Henryson v Angus 1640 below p. 396.)

6. The report here is unsatisfactory, not only in that the defence withdrew all their legal objections, but also that the Court did not give its reasons for deserting the diet *simpliciter* (p. 378). This was presumably done because the pursuers had produced no assize at the first diet, did not compear personally at the second, and that the Lord Advocate did not wish to proceed alone.

7. The Court did not deal with the motion for expenses. It was presumably made in virtue of the Act 1587 cap. 88, but this only applied where the panels had been 'found innocent and clenged,' i.e., had been acquitted after trial. Here modified expenses are asked as a condition precedent of further criminal letters.

(76) [28 October 1639: Colvile J.D.]

Adulterie. John McCarrell, Irischman. Baneist.

Intran.—John McCarrell.

The quhilk day Johnne McCarrall, Irischman, being at command of Mr Alexander Colvile of Blair, his Majesteis Justice deput, broght out of waird as he that hes bene wairdit thairin this half yeir bygane for adulterie committit be him, as also for ane counterfute coosenar [*cheat*] in fenyeing himselff to be dum and speichles, quhilk eftir his examinatioun he confessit to be of verritie; In presens of the said Justice, off his awin frie and volunter consent, become actit and obleist to depairt and pass af this kingdome as ane baneist man, and to pas away furth thairof in company of Colonell Alexander Erskine to serve him as ane souldiour in the weiris in forayne pairtis, and nocht to returne bak to this realme at ony tyme heireftir under the payne of deid to be execute upone him withall rigour; And thairupone the said John McCarrell was be the Justice ordinance tane bak to the said waird to remane thairin to the tyme he war delyverit to the said Colonell Erskine to the effect abone writtin.

LEGAL NOTE

The panel admitted adultery and feigning dumbness. The adultery was presumably simple and not notour. For the latter the death penalty was competent (1563 c.74). There was no statutory warrant for the penalties of scourging and banishment which were sometimes imposed for simple adultery. Here the conjunction of the adultery charge with one of cheating makes the sentence of banishment by no means exceptional, even where the panel had been in custody for six months (Hume I.454-5).

It is not clear if the feigned speechlessness was an excuse to avoid pleading or as Hume thought (I.362) an additional charge of fraudulent begging. Nor are the circumstances clear in which the panel came to be warded originally. It is stated that he confessed to the adultery and the cheating 'eftir his examination' but the time of this examination and confession is not clear i.e. whether it was before he was originally warded or at the time of the present report. No prosecutor is named and no jury was empanelled, and the panel's six months in ward was apparently terminated by the order of the Justice Depute.

(77) *Apud Edinburgh in pretorio inferiore eiusdem octavo Novembris* 1639 *in presentia mei notarii publici ac clerici deputati in officio Justiciarie,*[1] *ac etiam Jacobi Douglas et Jacobi Kynneir seriandis Justiciario.*[2]

Stouthrief. John Irving of Bruklaw and uthers.

Intran.—John Irving and others.

Compeirit Mr David Heriote advocat,[3] as procuratour for John Ogilvie of Birnes,[4] and producet the criminall letters deulie execute and indorsate, purchest at the instance of the said John Ogilvie of Birnes aganis Johne Irving of Bruklaw,[5] Alexander Irving his brother, Thomas Smyth and Williame Murray servitouris to the said Johnne Irving, James Murray in Bruklaw, George Smyth thair, and Johnne Lesshill messinger, quhairby thay and ilk ane of thame war chairget be vertew of the saidis letters to find cautioun for thair personall compeirance befoir his Majesteis Justice and his deputis this day and place in the hour of caus to underly the law for cuming under silence and clud of nycht to the tour of Brucklaw, houssis and biggingis thairof, occupyit and possessit be the said John Ogilvie and be his servandis in his name, brak up the durris thairof, staw, rest and away tuik furth thairof, be way of maisterfull thift and stouthreif, the haill guidis, geir, insicht plenissing, silver wark, abuilyementis and uther furnitour being thairin pertening to the said John Ogilvie of Birnes and his spous, to the availl of ten thouseand merkis, committit in the moneth of Junii lastbypast, and remanent crymes contenit in the saidis criminall letters, and upone the productioun thairof, askit instrumentis, and protestit for releif of Mr Alexander Lummisdene his cautioner.

Compeirit in lyk maner the saidis John Irving of Bruklaw, Alexander Irving his brother, Thomas Smyth in Bruklaw, George Smyth thair, James Murray thair, and Williame Murray thair, with Johne Dunlope, advocat,[6] as prelocutour

1 John Bannatyne W.S. (see *RMS* IX.437, and above I.59).

2 James Douglas appears several times as dempster, but the only other appearance of James Kinnear in these records is on 6th October 1641 (below p. 463). There were four officers or sergeants (see Gillon I.276).

3 Admitted 1624. Eldest son of David Heriot, goldsmith, Edinburgh (*Lyon's List* p. 101).

4 In the parish of Logybuchan, Aberdeenshire, 3 miles N of Ellon.

5 In the parish of Deer, Aberdeenshire, 3 miles SW of Strichan.

6 Admitted Advocate 1629 (*Lyon's List* p. 64).

for thame, and declairet that thay war charget to find cautioun for thair compeirance befoir his Majesteis Justice and his deputis this day and place to underly the law for dyverse allegit crymes of oppressioun, thift, and stouthreiff at lenth specifeit and contenit in the criminall letters direct aganis thame at the instance of Johnne Ogilvie of Birnes, quhairof thay affirmet thameselffis to be innocent, and that for obedience of the said charge and tryell of thair innocencie thay nocht only fand Alexander Irving of Fortrie cautioner for thame, bot also for the said cautioneris releif and cleiring of thair innocencie of the allegit crymes abonewrittin thay compeirit and willinglie offerit thameselffis reddie to underly the law befoir the Justice for the crymes foirsaidis and utheris quhatsumevir specifeit in the saidis letters; And in respect nather the Justice Generall nor na Justice Depute was present this day and place to put thame to thair tryell for the saidis allegit crymes askit instrumentis of thair compeirance and protestit for thair said cautioneri realeiff, and that na letters sould be direct aganis thame at the instance of the said John Ogilvie for the allegit crymes abonewrittin unto the tyme thair expenssis be refoundit accoirding to the Justice modificatioun.

LEGAL NOTE

This illustrates the procedure where no Justice was available. The Court was held by the Clerk-depute and sergeants. For other instances see Vol. I p. 4 note 4. The claim for expenses was incompetent. The Act 1587 cap. 88 empowering 'the Justice, Justice Clerk and their deputes' to modify expenses of the party accused applied only where he was found innocent after trial.

(79) [27 November 1639: Colvile and Robertoun JJ.D.]

Thift. Replegiat to the regalitie of Lennox.

Intran.—Williame McFarlane in Killiechorrie,[1]

Dilaittit of airt and pairt of the thiftious steilling, conceilling, recepting, and away taking under silence and clud of nycht, in the moneth of Julii lastbypast, of sevin horse and meiris furth of the landis of Waster Findach,[2] and of ten horse and meiris furth of the landis of Glenschervie,[3] extending togidder to sevintene horse and meiris, all pertening to Johnne Gordoun in Midle Findache, John Moreis in Park of Tulliebairne,[4] John Scotland, his sone in law, Gillespik McCleische in Waster Findache, Andro McComeis in Midle Findach, David Moreis, sone to the said John Moreis in Park of Tulliebairne, Patrik Moreis thair, Donald Moreis, his sone thair, and Johnne Dow thair.

Persewaris.—John Dow in Park of Tulliebairne, Archibald McCleische in Waster Findache, for thameselffis and as procuratouris speciallie constitute for the remanent persones foirsaidis, persewaris of the criminall letters, be vertew of thair letters of procuratorie subscryvit with thair handis daitit at Tulliebairne

[1] As appears below, this was in the parish of Luss, W. of Loch Lomond.
[2] In the parish of Crieff.
[3] In Strathearn (see *RMS* IX.867).
[4] Tulliebardine is just W of Auchterarder in Blackford parish.

the xxiiii day of November instant; Sir Thomas Hope of Craighall, knycht barronet, Advocat to our soverane Lord, for his Hienes intreis.

The pannell takis instrumentis of his entrie and in respect thairof protestit for relief [of] John McFarlane of Arochair and Alexander Leach of Coule Kippen his cautioneris of thair cautionerie, and offerit himselff reddie to defend in the said caus as innocent of the saidis crymes.

The perseweris producit the criminall letters deulie execute and indorsate upone the said William McFarlane in Killiechorrie now enterit upone pannell, as also upone the remanent defenderis following insert thairintill, viz. upone Patrik McCondochie Bayne Campbell, sone to Duncane Bayne Campbell in Auchinturen, Donald McInteir, dwelland at the kirk of Strathfillane[5], John McInteir, sone to Donald Dow Moir in Glenkaitland, Patrik McInteir, his servand, Findla McEane Vayne now dwelland in Strathfillane, [name deleted] under the laird of Laweris, John McConeill Voiche in Innerfraschatane under Laweris, Duncane Bayne Campbell in Auchinturen be Wast Strathphillane, and Allaster Over[6] Campbell in Leikchorriche, be vertew quhairof thay ar denuncet rebellis and put to the horne for nocht finding of cautioun actit in the buikis of adjornall to haif compeirit this day and place in the hour of caus to haif underlyne the law for airt and pairt with the aid William McFarlane of the thiftious steilling and away taking under nycht in the moneth of Julii last of sevintene horse and meiris furth of the landis of Glenschervie and Waster Findache, pertening to the persewaris foirsaidis insert in the saidis criminall letters; Lykas eftir the productioun thairof deulie execute and indorsate as said is the saidis Patrik McCondochie Bayne Campbell, sone to Duncane Bayne Campbell in Auchanturen, Donald McInteir, dwelland at the kirk of Strathfillane, under the laird of Laweris, [John] McInteir sone to Donald Dow Moir in Glenkatland, dwelland with Callum McConeill his brother thair and forrester on the northe syde of Corrocheba under the laird of Glennorchie, Patrik McInteir, his servand, Findla McEane Vayne, sumtyme dwelland under the erle of Athole in Glennerkie [*Glenorchy*] and now under the laird of Laweris, Allaster Oure Campbell in Leikchorchie under the constable of Dundie, Duncane Bayne Campbell in Auchinturane, and John McIlvoithe in Innerfressaquhan under the said laird of Laweris, rebellis abone writtin, being oft tymes callit in the said Justice court to haif compeirit personallie befoir his Majesteis Justice and his deputis this day and place in the hour of caus to underly the law for the thiftious crymes abone writtin as thay that war laufullie charget be vertew of the saidis letters be Andro Malloche, messinger, executour thairof to haif fund cautioun for thair compeirance this day and place to the effect foirsaid, lauchfull tyme of day biddin and nocht compeirand, thay and ilk ane of thame for thair absence and nocht compeirance war be the mouth of James Douglas, dempster of the said court, decernit and declairet to be outlawis and fugitives fra his Majesteis lawis and all thair moveable guidis adjudget and ordanit to be broght in to his Majesteis use as fugitives for the saidis crymes, quhairupone the saidis persewaris askit actis and instrumentis.

[5] In the parish of that name between Tyndrum and Crianlarich in W Perthshire.
[6] Presumably 'odhar' or dun coloured.

John McConeill Voich and Duncane Campbell. Continewit to the xxix Januarii 1640.

In the quhilk criminall actioun and eftir the pronunceing and declaratioun of the persones foirsaidis fugitives for the cryme foirsaid, it was speciallie exceptit and providit be his Majesteis Justice, nochtwithstanding of the adjudicatioun and declaratioun abovespecifeit, and that be speciall advyse and consent of the persewaris foirsaidis compeirand as said is, that gif the saidis Johnne McConeill Voiche and Duncane Bayne Campbell compeir personallie befoir his Majesteis Justice and his deputis in ane court of Justiciarie to be haldin be thame within the tolbuthe of Edinburgh the xxix day of Januar nixtocum in the hour of caus, thay to be tryit ather guiltie or innocent of the crymes above writtin conforme to the lawis of this realme, that than and in that caice the foirsaid adjudicatioun and declaratioun of the saidis John McConeill Voiche and Duncane Bayne Campbell, to be fugitives for the crymes abone writtin in swa far as the samyn may be extendit against thame twa allanerlie, sall ceise and be voyde in the selff, utherwayis in caice of failyie and thair nocht compeirance the saidis day and place to the effect foirsaid, the foirsaid adjudicatioun and declaratioun to stand and continew in full force against thame as gif the said provisioun and exceptioun above writtin had nevir bene maid or mentionat; quhairupone the persewaris askit instrumentis.

Compeirit lykwayis thaireftir in the foirsaid actioun and caus criminall judiciallie, Archibald Campbell, brother to Sir James Campbell of Laweris, knycht, quha in name and behalf of ane noble potent Erle, Archibald, Erle of Argyle, Lord Campbell and Lorne etc., heritable Justice of the office of Justiciarie within the boundis of Argyle, Lorne and Kyntyre and north iles of this kingdome, and allegit that the boundis and landis foirsaidis, quhairin the saidis John McInteir, sone to the said Donald Dow Moir, Patrik McInteir, his servand, and Allaster Ower Campbell, ar allegit to have thair dwelling and remaneing, is within the boundis of the said noble Lord his Justiciarie abonewrittin, and thairfoir that thai aucht to have bene convenit and persewit befoir the said noble Erle and his deputtis as Justice foirsaid and onlie Judge competent to thame in the said mater, and protestit as procuratour for the said noble Erle that quhatsumevir proces or declaratour was pronuncet or gevin out this day aganis thame in the said Justice court sould nawayis intreis or prejudge the said noble Erle as Justice Generall within the boundis abonewrittin, quhairin the said delinquentis ar allegit to dwell, nor of replegeing of thame or any uther inhabitant within the boundis of his Lordships justiciarie fra his Majesteis Justice or any uther Judge in criminall materis, bot that thai aucht onlie to be tryet and judget be the said noble Erle himselff as heretable Justice within the boundis abonewrittin, quhairin thai ar allegit to have thair dwelling, as said is, conforme to his Lordships infeftment thairof; and thairupone askit instrumentis.

The persewaris protestit in the contrair, speciallie in respect that thay had uset thair lawfull dilligence in raiseing of letters and executeing the samyn aganis the malefactouris foirsaidis and ilk ane of thame, speciallie aganis the saidis John McInteir, Patrik McInteir, his servand, and Allaster Over Campbell, quha for thair dissobedience of the chargis gevin to thame or denuncet rebellis and put to the horne, and for thair nocht compeirance this day and place to be tryit for the crymes foirsaidis ar lauchfullie decernit and declairit fugitives and outlawis fra his Majesteis lawis for the samyn; And thairupoun in lyk maner askit instrumentis.

Repledgiatione of William McFarlane to the regalitie of the Lennox.

The quhilk day Williame McFarlane in Killiechorrie, being enterit upone pannell, dilaittit, accuset and persewit at the instance of Sir Thomas Hoip of Craighall, knycht barronet, Advocat to our Soverane Lord, for his Hienes intreis in the matter underwrittin, and als at the instance of John Dow in Park of Tulliebairne, [and others as above] off the said William McFarlane his being airt and pairt with his complices in [the horse stealing narrated above]. In the quhilk actione compeirit lykwayis Mr Robert Bruce, advocat,[1] as procuratour for ane noble Prince, James, Duik of Lennox etc. and Lord of the regalitie thairof, quha desyret and requyret the said William McFarlane now enterit upone pannell as dwelland in the town of Killiechorrie within the parochin of Luse, quhilk is ane pairt of the said noble Prince his said regalitie of the Lennox to be repledget fra the said Justice Generall and Justice deputtis thair judgement and jurisdictione to the judgement and jurisdictione of the said noble Prince and his bailleis and baillie deputtis of the said regalitie, conforme to his Graces infeftment grantit to him thairupoun, and [for] verificatione thairof producet the said infeftment grantit to him of the saidis landis and Lordship of the Lennox and regalitie of the samyn, with the instrument of seassing following thairupone, beirand him to be infeft thairintill with priveilledge of repledgatione of all the inhabitantis thairof indyttit for any cryme fra quhatsumevir judges, ather civile or criminall, to his Graces regalitie abonewrittin, his bailleis and deputtis thairof as onlie judges competent for thair tryell, and conforme thairto offerit cautioun of culrache for dew and lawfull administratione of justice upone the said William McFarlane for the crymes foirsaidis, conforme to the lawis of this realme; quhilk desyre of repledgatione abonewrittin in respect of the said noble Prince his infeftment abovespecifeit and privielledge of regalitie thair contenit, producet, red and considderit, the Justice admittit and ordanit cautione of culerache to be fund for the said Lord of regalitie abonewrittin, his bailleis and deputtis thairof, thair dew and lawfull administratione of Justice upone the said William McFarlane, for the crymes foirsaidis specifeit in his dittay, and assignet to the said Mr Robert Bruce, as procuratour foirsaid for the said noble Prince and to his Grace's bailleis and deputtis of the said regalitie of the Lennox, the thrid day of Merche nixtocum for haulding of court and ministratione of Justice upone the said William McFarlane, defender at the instance of the saidis perseweris or any of thame, and that within the tolbuithe of Dumbartane as place appoyntit for halding of the said court of regalitie, and siclyke ordanit cautione to be fund be the said William McFarlane for his entrie and compeirance befoir the said lord of regalitie his bailleis and deputtis thairof the saidis day and place to underly the law for the crymes foirsaidis under the pane of thrie hundrethe merkis, and last asignit to the said Mr Robert Bruce, as procuratour foirsaid the xxvii day of the said monethe of Merche to repoirt to the Justice

[1] Of Broomhall, afterwards a judge (*Lyon's List*, 23).

Generall and his deputtis the said Lord of regalitie his bailleis and deputtis dilligence anent the said William McFarlane his tryell in the premisses under the lyk pane of thrie hundrethe merkis. For obedience of the quhilkis ordinances *respective* abovewrittin compeirit personallie Patrik Gell McFarlane, burges of Edinburgh, quha of his awin consent become actit and obleist as cautioner for the said lord of regalitie, his bailleis and deputtis thairof, that justice sall be ministrat be thame upone the said William McFarlane his entrie and compeirance befoir thame the saidis day and place in the hour of caus to underly the law for the crymes foirsaidis, and to repoirt to his Majesteis Justice and Justice deputtis thair dilligence thairanent betwix and the said xxvii day of Merche thaireftir under the panes *respective* abovewrittin; Quhairupon ather of the saidis pairteis alsweill perseweris as defenderis *hinc inde* with the said Mr Robert Bruce askit actis and instrumentis.

LEGAL NOTES

This is the first case in this (printed) volume of repledging to a regality on finding of caution of culrach (p. 384). For earlier instances see vol. i.70, 129.

It is odd that the Justices Depute gave no decision on the claim of Argyll to exclusive jurisdiction (p. 383) over two of the McIntyres and one of the Campbells, but as they did not compear the point is academic. It is far from clear that the residences of these three fell within the areas described in the Commission to the Earl when he was Lord Lorne in 1628 (see above vol. i.275).

(82) [29 November 1639: Colvile J.D.]

Beiring Hagbutes and Wounding. Mr Robert Watsone contra *Adamesone of Braco and utheris. Declairet fugitives etc.*

Compeiret the said day Robert Neill, wryter,[1] and producet, in name and behalf of Mr Robert Watsone, minister at Grange,[2] the criminall letters deulie execute and indorsate purchest at the instance of the said Mr Robert Watsone and Johnne Gallant, his servand, aganis George Adamesone of Braco,[3] Angus Bayne, his servand, John Stewart in Grange, Symon and Hew Stewartis, his twa sones, quhairby the saidis persones defenderis ar dewlie and ordourlie denuncet rebellis and put to the horne and registrat thairat for nocht finding of cautioun actit in the buikis of adjornall for personall compeirance befoir the Justice and his deputis this day and place in the hour of caus to haif underlyne the law for contravening of the Actis of Parliament[4] in beiring and weiring of hagbutis and pistolettis, invaiding and persewing of the said Mr Robert Watsone and his said servand thairwith, hurting and wounding of ather of thame to the effusioun of thair bluid, and leving thame for deid, and remanent crymes contenit in the saidis criminall letters;[5] Lykas eftir productioun thairof the saidis George Adamesone of Braco, Angus Bayne his servand, Johnne Stewart in

[1] Another instance of a writer appearing for a private prosecutor.

[2] A few miles E of Keith in Banffshire.

[3] 4 miles E of Keith.

[4] See legal note 2.

[5] See legal note 3.

Grange, Symone and Hew Stewartis his twa sones, being oft tymes callit to haif compeirit personallie befoir his Majesteis Justice and his deputis this day and place in the hour of caus to haif underlyne the law for the crymes foirsaidis specifeit in the saidis criminall letters, as thay that war lauchfullie chairget to that effect be Alexander Andersone, messinger, lauchfull tyme of day biddin and nocht compeirand, thairfoir the Justice be the mouth of James Douglas, dempster of court, decernit and declairet the saidis George Adamesone of Braiko [and the others foresaid], and ilk ane of thame, to be outlawis and fugitives fra his Majesteis lawis for the saidis crymes and all thair moveable guidis to be escheit and inbrocht to his Hienes use as fugitives thairfra; Quhairupone the said Robert Neill, wryter, in name of the said Mr Robert Watsone, minister, askit instrumentis and protestit for releif of the said Mr Robert his cautioneris.

Legal Notes

1. The penalties attaching to the carrying and use of firearms are somewhat obscure, and the matter is not dealt with by our institutional authorities with their usual lucidity (see Mackenzie, *Criminals* I.xxxii; Hume I.444).

Parliament first dealt with the matter following a fight in the streets of Edinburgh on 24th November 1567. Birrell (Diarcy) describes the incident as follows: 'At 2 afternoon, the Laird of Airth and the Laird of Wemyss met upon the Hie Gate of Edinburgh and they and their followers fought a very bludy skirmish where there was many hurt on both sides with shot of pistol'. The Privy Council reacted promptly with a proclamation forbidding the wearing of culverins, dags and pistolets or 'sic other firewerks', and ordering that anyone contravening the proclamation should be arrested and tried summarily 'as gif they had committed recent slaughter (*RPC*[1] I.593). Next month Parliament, under reference to the recent incident, followed up with the first Prevention of Crime Act, viz. 1567 cap. 18, which made it an offence for anyone 'of quatsomever estate, degree or condition' to use or carry firearms. The penalty prescribed for shooting with firearms—with certain exceptions—was the cutting off of the right hand. For the bearing, wearing, or use 'outwith housis' of 'onie culverings, dagges, pistolettes or anie uther sik ingine of fire wark upon their persones *or in their companie with them* privatelie or openly' unless with Royal License, the same penalty was prescribed. The offence, then, consisted not only in using or wearing firearms but also being in the company of anyone who did. The penalty prescribed was so savage that unless there were aggravating circumstances, as by being coupled with a conviction for slaughter or other capital crime, there is only one instance traced of it being enforced, viz. Turnbull v Turnbull 1603, Pitcairn II.419. (Hume's attempt (I.444) to explain the sentence in this case as arising from aggravated circumstances is inconsistent with the record. The panel was acquitted of all the charges except bearing and using firearms.) The Statute however was little regarded and in July 1593 the Privy Council alarmed at the prevailing violence in Edinburgh, and on a narrative that 'vile murders have not only been committed within kirks or other places, but even within the burgh of Edinburgh and suburbs thereof ewest [i.e. nearest] to His Hienes palace, to the great hazard of his awin person', commanded the city authorities and the King's guard to search for all hagbuts pistolets worn by any person in the city and palace, and to convey the wearers to prison, the weapons being escheat (*RPC*[1] V.90). Again however the mischief continued and Parliament again intervened. By the Act 1597 cap. 252 the 1567 Act was ratified, various officials were empowered to arrest and prosecute and the penalty of escheat of moveable goods was added. Half this escheat was to go to the prosecutor, but even this failed to improve the situation, and procedural difficulties arose.

Finally by the Act 1600 cap. 6 on a narrative that there was difficulty in trying bearers and users of firearms, and in particular because 'sik as ar guilty eschews their due punishment by declining of the assisouris that best knawes the verity of the fact'—a passage re-emphasising the function of assizers as witnesses—'and other sik subterfuges and delays of lawfull tryell', it was provided that those who had merely borne arms or been in company with such, but without violent use of them, might be tried at the discretion of the Treasurer or King's Advocate, before the Justice or before the King and Privy Council either upon full proof of witnesses or 'oath of party' (i.e. the panel's own admission) (but cf. Mackenzie *Criminals* XXXII.i) with the proviso that if proof was led before the Privy Council amputation should not be incurred but only warding and escheat. Although this Act states there was a practice of trial before the Justice no case has been noted in the sixteenth century. Even before the

Act 1600 c.6 however the Privy Council had dealt with the offence (*RPC*[1] V.127, 382, 395, 465).

After 1600 prosecutions before the Privy Council appear to have been favoured rather than before the Justice. Hume cites a number of cases between 1602 and 1620 (I.444) but the present case is the first for the period 1624-50, others being *Earl Marshall* v *Gordon of Gight* 24th February 1643, and *Peter* v *Cranston* 16th May 1645, neither of which resulted in any decision. The action of the King's Advocate in *Kirkpatrick* v *Douglas* 1611 (Pitcairn III.212) where, when he saw that the major charges were likely to be held irrelevant, he abandoned the subsidiary one of 'beiring and wearing of pistollets', might suggest that the mere carrying of firearms was not then considered serious. Such charges however in the seventeenth century were regularly prosecuted in the Privy Council by the King's Advocate and by private prosecutors, where fines and warding were imposed. In the 1610s and 1620s the King's Advocate not only prosecuted individual offenders or concurred with private prosecutors, but also initiated prosecutions against large batches of offenders, in the same way as he initiated multiple prosecutions of batches of rebels who had remained unrelaxed at the horn (*RPC*[1] XI.503, 542; XII.132, 136; *RPC*[2] I.129, 136, 381). Once an accused had been convened before the Privy Council the Justice was discharged from proceeding criminally (*RPC*[1] XIV.613).

Mackenzie says (*Criminals* I.xxxii.3) that by his time bearing weapons was 'ordinarily libelled as an aggravation rather than a crime'. While his treatise was published in 1678 it would appear to have been compiled prior to 1673, as he does not refer to *L.A.* v *Nicholson* 1673 (Scot) Moncrieff II.165) in which he as counsel for the defence successfully contended that the old statutes were in desuetude in so far as the bearing of arms by a fowler was concerned (see p. 167).

2. Mr Watson had complained on 5th August 1639 to the Presbytery of Strathbogie that 'George Jameson and Angus Bain Mackentosh' attacked him with arms (*Fasti* VI.314). 'Jameson' here is probably a mistake for Adamson. The minister married a daughter of Hew Adamson, burgess of Edinburgh, who may have been a relative of his assailant.

(87) [1 January 1640: Robertoun J.D.]

Treasonable Wounding. Allane Walwoid contra *James Gray and James Reid.*

Intran.—James Reid,[1] paynter, sone to William Reid, customer[2] in the meill mercat of Edinburgh.[3]

Dilaittit for being in companie and airt and pairt with James Gray, skynner, of the tressonable hurting and wounding of Allane Walwoid, servitour to Sir James McGill of Cranstoun Riddell, knycht barronet, ane of the senatouris of the Colledge of Justice,[4] be geving to the said Allane of twa crewall and deidlie straikis behind his bak in the craig [neck] with ane drawin quhinger to the effusioun of his bluid in great quantitie and to the danger and perrell of his lyfe,[5] committit in the moneth of November last under silence of clud of nycht, about sax houris at evin within the burgh of Edinburgh, in the kirk heuch thairof, neir to the Parliament House,[6] the thre Estaittis of this kingdome being sitting in Parliament for the tyme and nocht rissin nor dissolvet, nor yit the effairis of the Kingdome concludit in the said Parliament;[7] And that expres aganis the

[1] The panel had been before the Privy Council for deforcement in 1638 (*RPC*[2] VII.62, 465).

[2] 'One who receives custom or a certain duty on goods' (Jamieson, *Dictionary*).

[3] See legal note 1.

[4] Admitted Lord Ordinary 3 Nov. 1627, created Viscount Oxfurd 1651; reappointed Senator at Restoration (Brunton and Haig p. 283).

[5] See legal note 2.

[6] The late Dr. C. A. Malcolm located this as at the E end of Parliament Square a little W of Exchequer Chambers.

[7] Parliament was only sitting in the most technical sense. In November 1639 as on 31 August it was continued or adjourned to 2 June 1640 (*APS* V.251-5).

lawis and Actis of Parliament[1] of this realme, concluiding the pane and puneischment of treasone to be execute and inflicted aganis and upone all sic as invaidis, strekis, or hurtis ony of his Majesteis peceable and obedient subjectis during the tyme of Parliament and sitting thairof, or neir to the house or place quhair the estaittis of Parliament ar assemlet or convenit, at lenth specifeit in the criminall letters direct thairupoun.

Persewaris.—Sir James McGill of Cranstone Riddell, knycht, ane of the Senatouris of the Colledge of Justice, as maister to the said Allane,[2] quha is seik and nocht as yit convalessit of his deidlie hurtis; Sir Thomas Hope of Craighall knycht barronet, his Majesteis Advocat for his Hienes intreis; quha producet the criminall letters with the executiones thairof.

James Reid continewit to ane xv dayis warning.

The Justice, in respect of the absence and nocht compeirance of the said James Gray, skynner, the principall invaider and streker of the said Allane Walwoid, and for causes moveing him, with advyse of the persewaris, continewis the tryell of James Reid now upone pannell to ane fyftene dayis wairneing; and ordanit the said James Reid to find cautioun for his re-entrie to underly the law for the cryme foirsaid under the pane of thre hundreth merkis money; quha for obedience of the said ordinance fand the said Williame Reid his father, being personallie present, cautioun to the effect and under the pane foirsaid.

Thaireftir the said James Gray, skynner, hantand [practising] in Edinburgh, being oft tymes callit to haif compeirit befoir his Majesteis Justice and his deputis this day and place in the hour of caus to haif underlyne the law for the crewall unmerciefull and treasoneable invaiding, hurting and wounding of the said Allane Walwoid, servitor to Sir James McGill of Cranstone Riddell, knycht barronet, ane of the senatouris of the Colledge of Justice, be geving to the said Allane of twa deidlie straikis in the craig behind his bak with ane drawin quhinger to the effusioun of his bluid in great quantitie, to the perrell and danger of his lyfe, committit be the said James Gray and his complices[3] in the moneth of November lastbypast under silence and clud of nycht, about sax houris at evin, within the burgh of Edinburgh, in the kirk heuch thairof, neir to the Parliament House quhairin the thrie estaittis of this kingdome war sitting in Parliament for the tyme, and nocht being rissin nor dissolvet, nor the effairres of the kingdome nawayis concluidet in the said Parliament, and that expres aganis the lawis and Actis of Parliament of this realme appoynting and concluiding the pane and puneischment of treassone to be inflicted upone all sic as invaidis strekis or hurtis ony of his Majesteis peceable and guid subjectis during the tyme of Parliament and sitting thairof, or neir to the Parliament house and sitting place thairof as at lenth is contenit in the saidis criminall letters, as he that was lauchfullie charget be vertew thairof to haif compeirit befoir his Majesteis Justice and his deputis this day and place to haif underlyne the law for the cryme foirsaid, and to haif fund cautioun to that effect, lawfull tyme of day biddin and

[1] 1593 cap. 177. See Hume I.326.
[2] See legal note 3.
[3] This is the first mention of other accomplices.

nocht compeirand; Thairfoir the Justice, be the mouth of James Douglas, dempster of court, decernit adjudget and declairet the said James Gray to be outlaw and fugitive fra his Majesteis lawis for the cryme abone writtin, And thairfoir ordanit letters to be direct aganis him to denunce him our Soverane Lordis rebell, and to put him to his Hienes horne for his contumacitie and nocht compeirance this day and place to the effect foirsaid, and all his moveable guidis to be escheit and inbrocht to his Hienes use as fugitive fra his Majesteis lawis for the said cryme; Quhairupone the saidis persewaris askit instrumentis.[1]

LEGAL NOTES

1. The record here refers initially to two accused. Later on in the report however there is reference to the crime as committed by James Gray and his 'complices' but without further specification of who these were.

2. Two accused are referred to (Reid and Gray) but only one (Reid) appears. The charge is one of treasonable wounding and the specification is that the complainer was struck twice from behind 'with ane drawn whinger' by Gray the non-compearing accused. With such specification against the principal actor it is difficult to understand what constituted the accession by Reid. No other specification however than that he was 'art and part' was necessary under the Act 1592 c. 153 (see *Hume* II.230; *Mackenzie* I.xxv,2.) In the present report some further specification is given in that Reid is charged as 'being in company' with Gray. One inference from this is that mere presence with the principal actor was sufficient *prima facie* evidence to infer accession. A number of other cases in this volume support this view (see *George Weir and another* 17 April 1638) and it may be that this is still the law (see *H.M.A.* v. *George Kerr and others* (1871) II. *Couper* p. 334 per *Lord Ardmillan* p. 337-8).

3. A master was evidently regarded as having such particular interest in injury to his servant as entitled him to prosecute (see also *Stalker and another* v *Gordon of Haddo* below) but the practice was not invariable (see *Kerr* v *Halyburton*, next case). The side note at the beginning of this case indicates that the servant was the pursuer but this is not borne out by the text. By *Wingate* v *Brain* 17 Feb. 1809 F.C. however, it had become settled that the master had no title to pursue in such cases. In 1882 Lord Fraser thought a master could still sue for civil damages for injury to his servant (*Master and Servant*, 3rd edn., 311) but this view was rejected in *Reavis* v *Clan Line Steamers* 1925 S.C. 725).

4. Reid appeared but was apparently unrepresented. The trial did not proceed against him presumably because the absent Gray was 'the principal invaider and stricker' of the victim. Security was found for Reid's subsequent appearance on fifteen days' warning at any subsequent diet.

(89) [10 January 1640: Robertoun J.D.]

Mutilatioun. James Halyburtoun. Continewit to the xxv Novembris 1640.

Intran.—James Halyburtoun, sone to Thomas Halyburtoun portioner of Mertoun, Thomas Crawmond, indweller in Mertoun.

Dilaitit of airt and pairt of the mutilatioun of Thomas Ker, servand to Andro Ker, younger of Littildane,[2] of his ryght hand, at the leist of twa fingeris thairof, committit in ane or uther of the dayis of October last 1639.[3]

[1] See legal note 4.
[2] Littledean Tower is just across the Tweed from Merton, which is itself 1½ miles NE of St. Boswells in Berwickshire.
[3] See legal note 1.

Persewar.—[the said] Thomas Ker,[1] servand to the said Andro Ker younger of Littildane.

Prelocutour in defence.—Mr David Heriote, advocat.[2]

The pannell takis instrumentis of thair entrie and protestis for thair cautioneris releiff.

The persewar producet the letters and askit instrumentis thairupoun and protestit for his cautioneris releiff.

It is allegit be the pannell that thair is no speciall day or tyme set down in the letters quhan the allegit cryme was committit, and gif the samyn war condiscendit, nocht granting the committing thairof, na proces for mutilatioun quhill the expyreing of yeir and day eftir the committing thairof.

It is anserit be the persewaris[3] that the fact lybellit was committit in October last in ane or uther of the dayis thairof and thairfoir desyret proces.

The Justice, in respect the cryme lybellit was done in October last, quhilk is nocht as yit abone thre monethis, continewis this dyet to the last Wednisdy of November nixt 1640,[4] and ordanit the pannell to find cautioun for thair re-entrie that day in the hour of caus to underly the law for the cryme foirsaid under the panes following, *viz.* the said James Halyburtoun under the pane of thre hundreth merkis, and the said Thomas Crawmond under the pane of ane hundreth merkis; quha for obedience thairof fand Andro Halyburtoun, smyth, burges of Edinburgh, cautioun for thame being personallie present to the effect and under the panes foirsaidis.

The said Mr David Heriote, as prelocutour for the pannell, protestit in his name that quhatsumevir depositioun is maid be him this day extra judiciall nawayis be prejudiciall to the pannell,[5] *viz.* James Halyburtoun, deponent, at the day of his tryell, bot that the samyn depositioun with the qualitie sett down thairintill of his awin defence, haifing gottin thre severall straikis strukin out at him be the persewar befoir the allegit straik gevin to the persewar, may be considderit be the assyse and thairupoun askit instrumentis.

The said James Halyburtoun gaif his aith that he dreidis bodielie harme of the said Thomas Ker and his freindis, and thairfoir desyret cautioun and lawborrows of the said Thomas for his indempnitie.

Secta Pacis.[6]

The Justice ordanit the said Thomas Ker to find the said lawborrows for the said James Halyburtoun his indempnitie under the pane of thre hundreth merkis.

For obedience quhairof compeirit judiciallie James Aytoun, indweller in Kirkcaldie, brother germane to Mr Andro Aytoun, and become cautioun and lawborrus for the said Thomas Ker that the said James Halyburtoun, his men, tennentis, and servandis, sall be hairmeles and skaithles of the said Thomas, and all that he may stope or lat[7] *etc.* under the said pane of thre hundreth merkis money, quhairupone the said James Halyburtoun askit instrumentis.

[1] See legal note 2.
[2] Subsequently himself a Justice Depute, 3 April, 1694.
[3] The plural must be a mistake for the singular as there was no appearance for the Crown.
[4] See legal note 3.
[5] See legal note 4.
[6] *Secta pacis*—lawburrows.
[7] Hinder or allow.

(108) [25 November 1640]

Protest

The quhilk day, in presens of me notter publict and clerk depute in the office of Justiciarie,[1] compeirit personallie James Halyburtoun . . [there follows a narrative of the above proceedings of 10th January 1640].

For the quhilk cautioneris releif and tryell of the said James Halyburtoun his innocencie of the said allegit cryme, he compeirand this day and place as said is, declairet that he willinglie offerit himselff reddie to abyde the tryell of the law for the said allegit mutilatioun as altogidder innocent thairof; and in respect that nather the Justice Generall, nor nane of his Majesteis deputtis, could be had nor war present to the keiping of the said dyet this day and place, nor yit compeirit the said Thomas Ker, persewar, nor na uther in his name, to insist in the said James Halyburtoun, defender, his persute for the said allegit cryme, being oft tymes callit upone to that effect, the said James Halyburtoun askit instrumentis of his entrie and compeirance to the effect abonewrittin and protestit for releif of Andro Halyburtoun, burges of Edinburgh, his cautioner, as also that na letters nor charges sould be direct aganis him for the said allegit cryme at the instance of the said Thomas Ker in ony tyme cuming; Quhilkis premissis war done within the laich tolbuith of the burgh of Edinburgh in the south end thairof, quhair his Majesteis Justice courtis ar commounlie keipit;[2] fencet and haldin, upone the said twentie fyve day of November in this instant yeir of God jmvic fourtie yeiris, in presens of me, notter publict and clerk depute foirsaid in the said office of Justiciarie, as also in presens of James Lawtie, wryter in Edinburgh, Thomas Halyburtoun, cordiner, burges of Edinburgh, James Douglas, Johne Hammiltoun and James Kynneir, all thre officeris of the said office of Justiciarie, witnessis speciallie requyret and present and desyret to the premissis.[3]

Legal Notes

1. This is one of the many cases in which the locus is not specified in the record. Hume regards such specification as 'indispensable' (II.209) but recognises that earlier practice hereon was lax. In the present case the panel was legally represented—indeed his counsel subsequently became a Justice Depute—but curiously no objection was taken to this absence of specification although objection was taken to the want of specification of the exact day of the month. The full indictment or criminal letters, however, rarely enter this record, and it may be that adequate specification was in fact given in the letters here.

2. This is an example—rare in these volumes—of a prosecution by criminal letters without the concurrence of the Lord Advocate. For other examples see I.36 and 86.

3. This is an actual decision that prosecution for mutilation is premature before a year and a day have elapsed. Hume deals summarily with the topic (I.331) but Pitmedden (I.71-2) explains that time is allowed because of the prospect of recovery which does not apply in the case of demembration.

4. The first panel apparently on the first calling of the case made a deposition which is described as 'extra judicial'. In this he apparently admitted having struck the pursuer on one occasion but claimed he was acting in self defence. His counsel's protest is concerned lest the admission be considered at a future trial without the qualification of his having acted in self

[1] John Bannatyne, W.S., see *RMS* IX.437 and above i.59.
[2] This is the most precise specification of where the court sat.
[3] See legal note 5.

defence. He protests that the whole matter of the alleged mutilation and self defence should be considered by the trial jury. It looks as if the extra judicial deposition was used as an intimation of a special defence.

5. On one view it could be assumed that the complainer must have so completely recovered that he did not think it worth while to proceed and had so advised the Court beforehand. The minute however states that neither the Justice General nor Justice Depute 'could be had nor were present' and that the Court was 'fenced' (p. 391). What is significant is that business was transacted in the absence of the judge. For other examples see I. p. 71, 8 Nov. 1639.

(91) [15 January 1640: Colvile and Robertoun JJ.D.]

Thift. My Lord Stormond and his tennentis contra *McChroyter. Desertit.*

Intran.—Moreis McChroyter in Keanlochgar.[1]

Dilaitit of airt and pairt of the steilling of twentie four ky and oxin and foure meiris [*mares*] furthe of the landis of Drumlith,[2] in the monethe of Februar last under nycht, perteneing to John Stewart, Laurance McEwin and John Ower McGilliechallum, tennentis and servandis to Mungo, Vicount of Stormonthe.

Persewar.—Robert Hepburne, advocat, as procuratour for my lord Vicount of Stormond and his tennentis abone writtin, conforme to the procuratorie producet.

Prelocutour in defence.—Mr Johnne Gilmour advocat.[3]

The pannel takis instrumentis of his entrie and protestis for releif of the laird of Auchinbrek, his cautioner.

The said Robert Hepburne, persewar, as procuratour foirsaid declairis that he passes fra the persute of the said Moreis McChroyter for the cryme foirsaid at this tyme, and will nocht insist tharintill, quhairupone the pannell askit instrumentis.

The Justice desertis the letters upone the defenderis foirsaidis thairin contenit and discharges the outgeving of ony new letters aganis thame in the matter abone writtin in ony tyme cuming without thair speciall warrand and directioun to that effect, quhairupoun the pannell askit instrumentis.

Legal Note

This prosecution, in which the Lord Advocate did not concur, had evidently been bought off. Cattle stealing was, of course, a capital offence (see above i.288).

(95) [22 January 1640: Colvile J.D.]

Ryot. Brownes contra *Marioun Symsone, Marioun Cleuch and thair husbandis. Declairet fugitives etc.*

The quhilk day anent the criminall letters direct at the instance of Williame Brown in Skatintie, as father, James and William Brownes, as brither, Agnes Alisone, Jonet and Helene Brownes, as sisteris, Archibald Meane, spous to the

[1] Garelochhead.

[2] Drumleoch, Balquhidder, west of Loch Doine.

[3] The future Lord President of 1661. Admitted advocate, 11 Dec. 1628. (*Lyon's List,* 81).

said Agnes for his entreis, with the remanent kyn and freindis of umquhile Thomas Brown, servand for the tyme to John Vernour in Castellaw,[1] aganis Marione Symsone, the spous of John Melros in Hagis of Foulfuird, and Marione Cleughe, the spous of John Mak thair, chairgeing thame to have fund cautione for thair personall compeirance befoir his Majesteis Justice and his deputtis this day and place to have underlyne the law for the crewall, schamefull, and detestable abuiseing[2] of the said umquhile Thomas Brown upone the xvi day of December lastbypast within the dwelling hous of the said John Melros in Hagis of Foulfuird, be griping the said umquhile Thomas Brown be his legis and airmes violentlie thrawing him bakwardis upone his bak within ane bed, and with thair kneyis and feit leiping upoun his bellie and breist, and thairby bruiseing and breking his haill intrallis and noble pairtis, and thaireftir schamefullie barbarouslie and crewallie rave down his breitches gripit him be his secreit memberis, rudgit and drew the samyn in maist schamefull and detestable maner, brak and bruiset the coddis and stanes of his secreit pairtis and maid him thairby altogidder breathles to resist thair violence and invasione, off the quhilkis hurtis and straikis and schamefull abuises abonewrittin he being careit hame to his maisteris hous quhair he lay bedfast be the space of foure dayis vometting and avoyding bluid baith at his mouthe and secreit pairtis in grit aboundance, and in end upone xxi day of the said monethe of December he deceisset of the saidis hurtis and deidly woundis, as at lenthe is contenit in the saidis criminall letters: The said Williame Brown as father to the said umquhile Thomas compeirand judiciallie and produceand the saidis criminall letters deulie execute and indorsate upone the saidis Marione Symsone and Marione Cleughe and thair saidis husbandis for thair entreisses, quhairby thay for not finding of the said cautione for thair personall compeirance this day and place to underly the law for the cryme foirsaid, being lawfullie chairget be William Wallace, messer [*macer*] to that effect, the saidis Marione Symsone and John Melros hir spous for his entries, and the said Marione Cleughe and John Mak, hir spous, for his entreis, ar denuncet rebellis and put to the horne and registrat thairat; And upone the productione thairof askit actis and instrumentis and protestit for releiff of Thomas Robesone, indweller in the Cannongait thair cautioner, one the ane pairt, and the saidis Marione Symsone and Marione Cleughe, committeris of the cryme foirsaid, and thair saidis husbandis for thair entreisses on the uther pairt, being ofttymes callit to have compeirit befoir his Majesteis Justice and his deputtis this day and place to have underlyne the law for the saidis crymes, as thai that war lawfullie chairget to that effect lawfull tyme of day biddin and not compeirand, war be the mouthe of John Hamiltoun[3] dempster of court, adjudget and declairit outlawis and fugitivs fra his Majesteis lawis for the cryme abonewrittin and all thair moveable goodis ordanit to be escheit to his Majesteis use as fugitives for the samyn.

Legal Note

The charge here libels a series of assaults causing internal injuries from which the victim eventually died. The side note describes the case as one of Ryot. Aggravated and prolonged

[1] 2 m. N of Penicuik.
[2] See legal note.
[3] John Hamilton was appointed one of the four officers and sergeants of the Justiciary Court on 20 July 1636, above i.276.

assault were then described as such. Later 'a great host or multitude of people were predicated' (Hume I.416). It is odd that these two viragos were not charged with slaughter, and that they were charged before the Justice Depute rather than before the Privy Council which usually dealt with Riots.

The locus is the Woodhouselee estate in Glencorse parish, Midlothian, see *Edinburgh Retours* no. 1301.

(102) [15 July 1640: Colvile J.D.]

Sla[*uchter*]. *Pigget* contra *Cuming*. *Desertit*.

Compeirit judiciallie Mr George Cummyng, Minister at Dolles,[1] and haifing enterit himselff upone pannell, with Mr Robert Trotter, advocat, his prelocutour, exponit and declairet that he being callit and convenit befoir his Majesteis Justice and his deputis in ane Justice court, haldin within the tolbuth of Edinburgh be Mr James Robertoun, his Majesteis Justice depute, upone the sevintene day of Januar lastbypast[2] at the instance of Katharene Watsone, the relict of umquhile Johne Piget in Manachtie, Elspeth Pigget in Mynonie,[3] as sister to the said umquhile John Pigget, John Donaldsone, hir spous for his entreis, with the bairnes, remanent kyn and freindis of umquhile John Pigget, and Sir Thomas Hoip of Craighall, knycht barronet, his Majesteis Advocat for his Hienes intreis, to have underlyne the law for allegit airt and pairt of the slauchter of the said umquhile Johne Pigget, committit upone the secund day of September 1639 yeiris in forme and maner specifeit and contenit in the criminall letters direct aganis the said Mr George thairanent, upone the whilk xvii day of Januar last the said Mr George Cuming, compeirand personallie and enterand himselff upone pannell, quha than willinglie offerit himselff to the tryell of the law for the alledget slauchter abone writtin as altogidder innocent thairof, disassenting *simpliciter* to all maner of continuatioun, bot be reasone the persewaris of the saidis letters nawayis producet ane assyse for the said Mr George his tryell in the said mater, the said dyet in that respect was continewit be the Justice to this day, and cautioun for obedience of the Justice ordinance was fund be the said Mr George for his personall compeirance this day and place befoir his Majesteis Justice and his deputis to underly the law for the alledget slauchter abone writtin but farder delay or continuation, with certificatioun to the persewaris of the saidis criminall letters that gif thai compear nocht this fyftene day of Julii instant in the hour of caus to insist in the said Mr George his persute for the said allegit cryme, and produce ane assyse aganis him quhairby he may be fund and tryit aither guiltie or innocent thairof, that the persewaris abone writtin sould nocht be hard to call trouble or persew the said Mr George for the said allegit cryme at ony tyme thaireftir as the act of adjornall maid thairupone contening thairin the certificatioun abone mentionat producet be the said Mr George and red judiciallie in presens and audience of his Majesteis

[1] Dallas, Morayshire, 7 miles S.E. of Forres.

[2] The reference to the ms. is VIII.93.

[3] Minnonie is 3 miles S.S.W. of Gardenstoun in E. Banffshire; Manachtie may be Monauchtie, 6 miles E. of Forres.

Justice of the dait abone specifeit at lenth proportis. Eftir productioun and reiding of the quhilk act of adjornall [of 17 January 1640] the saidis Katharene Watsone as relict, Elspeth Pigget in Mynonie as sister, Johnne Donaldsone, hir spouse, for his entreis, with the haill remanent persewaris insert in the saidis criminall letters being oft tymes callit upone to haif compeirit befoir his Majesteis Justice and his deputis this day and place in the hour of caus to haif insistit in persute of the said Mr George Cuming, now enterit upone pannell reddie to abyde his lauchfull tryell for the said allegit cryme, and to haif producet ane assyse summond upone him for that effect, and nane of the saidis persewaris compeirand to the effect foirsaid lauchfull tyme of day being biddin, the Justice thairfoir accoirding to certificatioun contenit in the former act of adjornall discharget the outgeveing of ony new letters criminall aganis the said Mr George Cuming for the allegit slauchter abone writtin in ony tyme cuming, and he to be frie of all persute to be movet aganis him at the instance of the saidis persewaris as airt or pairt thairof heireftir; quhairupone the said Mr George Cuming and his prelocutour askit actis and instrumentis and protestit for releiff of Leonard Leslie in Balvanie his cautioner, as also that na letters or charges sould be direct or gevin out aganis himselff or that he could be callit trubllit or persewit at the instance of ony pairtie quhatsumevir for the allegit slauchter abone writtin or for being ather airt or pairt thairof in ony tyme cuming, quhilk protestatioun the Justice admittit, quhairupone the said Mr George also askit instrumentis.

LEGAL NOTE

It seems remarkable that the Lord Advocate should have given his concurrence to the prosecution of a minister of the church for slaughter, and then apparently made no appearance at either diet.

(103) [9 October 1640:]

Accidental slauchter. James Mathiesone. Baneist of his awin consent.

Compeirit personallie within the laich tolbuth of Edinburgh, James Mathiesone, cobbler, dwelland at the wast poirt of Edinburgh, as he that was wairdit in the tolbuth of the said burgh for the rasche and accidentall slauchter of umquhile Robert Andersone, sone to John Anderson, tailyeour at the wast poirt, be causing sum stanes roll af the bank or bra [*brae*] of the castell of Edinburgh, in his seiking of certane Jone bullettis,[1] upone the secund day of October instant, be the falling and rowing [*rolling*] down of the quhilkis louse stanes the said Robert, ane boy of nyne yeiris of age, being playing at the fute of the said brae was killed in the heid quhairof he presentlie deceissit.

And being be authoritie of the Lordis of Committie of Parliament committit and keipit in the said waird, the saidis Lordis, upone the supplicatioun gevin to thame be the said John Andersone, father of the bairne, hes ordanit the said James Mathiesone of his awin consent to be baneist this kingdome, and nocht to returne thairin bak agane without his Majesteis warrand under the pane of

[1] Round stones used in the game of 'lang bullet'.

deid; accoirding to the quhilk warrand subscryvit be my Lord of Coupar *I.P.D.* and Robert Hepburne, clerk, daitit the viii of October instant, the said James Mathiesone become actit and obleist of his awin consent to be baneist this kingdome, and nocht to returne thairin heireftir under the pane foirsaid; Quhairupoun the said John Andersone, father to the defunct, askit instrumentis; Quhilk warrand is delyverit to the keiper of the tolbuthe of Edinburgh for the said James Mathiesone his liberatioun furth of the said waird.

Legal Notes

It seems at first sight harsh that the panel—who had no legal representation—should have consented to banishment on this charge—a penalty which was appropriate for slaughter on a suddenty, something much more than accident. Hume, in dealing with Casual Homicide does not mention the case and states that homicide 'by pure misadventure, and by the hand of one who intended no harm' is innocent. Earlier law however took a much less sympathetic view and held all killing to be criminal even if it did not proceed from fault on the part of the accused. Mackenzie (I.xi,9) defines culpable homicide as occurring where 'the murder was not designed, and yet it was committed merely by *accident*'. In such cases the penalty depended on 'the quality of these circumstances which attend the fact'. The Act 1661 cap. 22 provided in terms that homicides by accident or in self defence are no longer to be capital but are to continue to be punishable by assythment or imprisonment. See also Act 1649 cap. 96. These statutes ratified and clarified existing practice. Thus it was necessary for Stair's grandson, afterwards Field-marshall Stair, to obtain a pardon in 1687, though only eight years old, for accidentally shooting his elder brother (*Dict. Nat. Biog.* V.420, A. J. G. Mackay, *Memoir of First Viscount Stair*, pp. 87 and 211, Fountainhall, *Decisions* i.447).

Possibly, however, the brief summary of the charge here invoves a case of *negligent* killing —'some want of due caution and circumspection'—which would bring the case within the category defined by Hume (I.192) where some punishment is due. The record refers to 'rasche and accidental slaughter' and there may have been an element of deliberate disturbance in the reference to 'rolling down' loose stones. Mackenzie (I.XI.16) quotes the example of the mason throwing down stones. If he gives a warning and someone is killed there is no fault, but if he fails to do so then the killing is culpable.

For other examples of killings which might be either accidental or reckless see *RSS* VI. 4 Feb. 1571, and *SHR* 1956 XXXV.182, and *RPC*² VIII.50.

It is perhaps well to add that in the seventeenth century murder was confined to premeditated killing, while slaughter—the libel here—was killing without forethought (Mackenzie I.XI.ii).

The prisoner was warded on the order of the Lords of Committee of Parliament apparently without trial or admission of guilt. His responsibility for the slaughter appears to be assumed.

(104) [4 November 1640: Robertoun J.D.]

Deforcement and mutilatioun. Robert Angus and utheris. Continewit to the morne.

Intran.—Robert Angus, skipper in Bruntieland[1]; Bessie Maw (?Man), his mother, indweller thair; William Gairne, mercheand, burges of Edinburgh.

Dilaittit of airt and pairt of the invaiding, hurting, wounding and mutilatioun of William Henrysone, messinger, in putting of letters of captioun to executioun aganis the said William Gairne, be hurting and wounding him in his richt hand and mutilatioun of his thombe and twa fingeris thairof *etc.* committit within the burgh of Bruntieland the xxiiii day of Maii 1638 yeiris.

[1] Burntisland.

Persewar.—Williame Hendersone, messinger and officer of airmes.[1]

Prelocutour in defence.—Mr Roger Mowat, advocat.[2]

The persewar producet the letters deulie execute upone the thre persones upone pannell, as also upone George Gairne, bailyie of Bruntieland for the tyme and burges thairof.

The persones on pannell takis instrumentis of thair entrie, offerit thameselffis to the tryell of the law for the crymes lybellit as innocent thairof, and protestit for thair cautioneris releif.

Compeirit James Barnes mercheand, and producet ane testimoniall subscryvit be ane of the bailleis of Bruntieland testifeing that George Gairne, burges of Bruntieland, ane of the defenderis contenit in the letters producet, quha is callit and convenit for the cryme foirsaid as airt and pairt thairof, was nocht hable [*able*] to be present this day to justifie his innocencie of the cryme lybellit, and thairfoir desyret the Justice to continew the dyet aganis him to the morne at quhilk tyme he sould be present and offerit cautioun for his compeirance to that effect.[3]

The Justice with the consent of the persewar continewis this dyet aganis the haill persones defenderis, alsweill compeirand as absent, to the morne the fyft of this instant, cautioun being fund for entrie under the panes contenit in the Actis of Parliament.

Compeirit Thomas Wrycht, indweller in Leyth, and become cautioun for the entrie of the thre persones on pannell, and of the said George Gairne, the morne to the effect and under the panes foirsaidis *etc.*

The persones summond to this day to pas upone the assyse wairnet *apud acta* to the morne, ilk persone under the pane of c merkis.

(105) [5 November 1640: Robertoun J.D.]

Past fra.

Intran.—Robert Angus, skipper in Bruntieland, Bessie Man (*sic*), his mother thair, George Gairne, burges thairof, sumtyme bailyie, Williame Gairne, merchand, burges of Edinburgh.

Dilaittit of airt and pairt of the mutilatioun of Williame Hendersone, officer of airmes, in the executioun of his office in taking and apprehending of the said William Gairne his Majesteis rebell for the tyme, be vertew of letters of captioun raisit aganis the said William Gairne at the instance of Thomas Garscher, be invaiding of the said William Hendersone and mutilating him in his richt hand, at the leist of his thombe and twa formest fingeris thairof, committit within the burgh of Bruntieland upone the xxiiii day of Maii 1638 yeiris *etc.*

Persewar.—Williame Hendersone, officer of airmes.

Prelocutour for the pannell.—Mr Roger Mowat advocat.

[1] See legal note 1.
[2] Admitted advocate 17 Jan. 1611. Professor of Civil Law at Aberdeen, 1628-40.
[3] See legal note 2.

The pannell takis instrumentis of thair entrie, offerit thameselffis to the tryell of the law as innocent of the crymes contenit in the dittay, disassenting *simpliciter* to all farder continuatioun, and protestis for thair cautioneris releif.

The pannell thaireftir with thair said prelocutour protestis, eftir reiding of the dittay and thair accusatioun of the cryme foirsaid thairin contenit, that incaice thay be absolvet be the assyse of the crymes lybellit that conforme to the Act of Parliament [1587 cap. 88] thair expenssis be modifeit be the Judge and the persewar compellit to mak payment thairof at the leist to [be] keipit in waird quhill thay be satisfeit of the samyn.[1]

The persewar refuiset to geve his aith upone the verritie of the dittay that the pannell war airt and pairt of the cryme thairin contenit; quhairupone the pannell askit instrumentis.[2] And siclyk the pannell be thair grit aith swore and declairet that thay war altogidder innocent of the saidis crymes, and gif ony hurt be ressavit the tyme lybellit that thay nor nane of thame war present upone the ground quhair the samyn was committit.

The persewar thaireftir passis *simpliciter* fra the persute of William and George Gairnes for the crymes foirsaidis, as also passis *simpliciter* fra the persute of the saidis Robert Angus and Bessie Maw (?Man), his mother, *jure lite et cause* for the haill crymes lybellit. Quhairupone the haill persones on pannell with thair said prelocutour askit instrumentis, and nochtwithstanding of the said persewar his passing fra thair persute, offerit thameselffis as of befoir to be tryit be the assyse present at the bar as innocent of the saidis crymes, and thairupone askit actis and instrumentis, and protestit in respect of the premisses that na letters nor chairges sould be direct aganis thame at the instance of the said William Hendersone, or at the instance of ony uther pairtie persewar quhatsumevir, for the allegit crymes abonewrittin in ony tyme cuming, quhilk protestatioun the Justice admittis *etc.*

Legal Notes

1. The Lord Advocate's failure to concur in a prosecution for deforcement, in which the public interest was clearly involved, suggests there was no real case against the panels (see Hume I.399). It seems likely that matters were settled out of court.

2. It is remarkable where the panels were represented by counsel, that a merchant was allowed to appear at the bar for one of the accused; that the certificate he produced of that accused's inability to appear—on a ground not stated—was from a baillie, and not from a doctor or minister; and that it was accepted as sufficient cause for a day's continuation. That he appeared the next morning suggests there was little wrong with him, but so far as the record is concerned the Court does not appear to have investigated his non-appearance further.

3. The panel's motion was that in the event of their being absolved by an assize they should be entitled to their expenses. After further procedure however (see note 4 below) the pursuer deserted the pursuit and the claim for expenses was not renewed. This was conform to the letter of the Act 1587 c. 88 which only empowered the Court to modify the panels' expenses where they were 'found innocent and clenged' of the accusation. Here no jury was empanelled, though assizers were present in court, and the case concluded with the Justice Depute accepting the panel's protestation that no further proceedings at the instance of the pursuer should be competent.

4. Whenever the pursuer declined the oath of calumny then the Court deserted the libel Hume II.129). See also above *L.A.* v *Anderson* 1639 p. 376. Here in addition to the pursuer refusing the oath of calumny the panels declared on oath that they were innocent. Following on these two stages of the process the pursuer deserted *simpliciter*.

[1] See legal note 3.
[2] See legal note 4.

(106) [11 November 1640: Robertoun J.D.]

Sla[uchter]. James Graham. Deserted.

Intran.—James Grahame in Drumfad.[1]

Dilaittit of airt and pairt of the murthour and slauchter of umquhile Johne Hadden, servand to the said James Grahame, committit within his awin dwelling hous of Drumfad, barnes or byres thairof, committit in the moneth of Februar last.

Compeirit judiciallie Mr William Sterling, wryter, with George Hadden burges of Edinburgh, and producet the criminall letters deulie execute and indorsate purchest at the instance of Grissell Scobie, relict of umquhile Williame Hadden in Balhaddie,[2] as mother to umquhile Johne Hadden, servand to the said James Grahame for the tyme, aganis the said James Grahame, chairgeing the said James Grahame to find cautioun for his personall compeirance befoir the Justice and his deputis this day and place in the hour of caus to haif underlyne the law for the slauchter and murthour of the said John Hadden, his servand for the tyme, committit in the moneth of Februar lastbypast, in forme and maner specifeit in the saidis letters, and upone the productioun thairof askit instrumentis and protestit for releif of the said George Hadden as cautioner for repoirting of the saidis letters deulie execute and indorsate at the raiseing of the samyn.

The pannell takis instrumentis of his entrie and protestis for releif of Mr James Grahame, minister at Comerie, his cautioner, and willinglie offerit himself to the tryell of the law for the allegit cryme abonewrittin as innocent thairof, disassenting *simpliciter* to all maner of continuatioun.

Thaireftir it was declairet be the said Mr Williame Sterling, producer of the saidis criminall letters, that the said Grissell Scobie, mother to the defunct, sen the raiseing and executeing of the saidis criminall letters is depairtit this lyfe and sa na uther persewar being insert in the saidis letters the dyet behovet to desert, and new letters grantit in favouris of the nerrest of kyn to the said umquhile Johne Hadden to persew for his slauchter and ane competent day affixt to thame for that effect, and thairupone askit instrumentis.

To the quhilk it was answeirit be the said James Grahame, defender, that he altogidder dissassentit to the deserting of the said dyet, and thairfoir as of befoir he offerit himselff than instantlie to the tryell of the law for the said alledget slauchter and murthour lybellit as altogidder frie and innocent thairof and of the haill circumstances of the samyn *ut libellatur*, speciallie in respect that he himselff is ane aget man past thre scoir fourtene yeiris, and hes travellit in his cuming to this burgh frome his awin hous ane tedious and long jornay to the keiping of this dyet in this winter seasone and tyme of yeir and that only to be tryet of the allegit cryme abonewrittin and cleiring of his innocencie thairof, and thairfoir protestit in respect of his obedience at this tyme and na dilligence is used be his persewaris in following out of his persute for the said allegit cryme, quhairof he is maist innocent, that he mycht be *simpliciter* assoilyeit

[1] Between Gleneagles and Blackford, Perthshire.
[2] Balhaldie is 3 miles NE of Dunblane.

frome the said criminall persute and that na letters nor charges sould be direct aganis him for the said allegit cryme at the instance of quhatsumevir pairtie persewar in ony tyme cuming and thairupone askit actis and instrumentis.

The Justice in respect of the daith of the said Grissell Scobie, persewar of the saidis criminall letters, and of the notorietie thairof, desertis the saidis criminall letters and dyet abonespecifeit sett down thairintill, and discharget the outgeveing of ony new letters aganis the said James Grahame for the allegit cryme abonespecifeit unto the tyme his Lordship be first acquentit thairwith and geve his expres warrand for that effect; Quhairupone ather pairtie askit actis and instrumentis.

LEGAL NOTE

The appearance of a writer at the bar though unusual was not unprecedented (see Adamson of Braco and others above). There are a number of later instances.

Where the Lord Advocate did not concur, apparently criminal letters were spent on the death of the private prosecutor. But the diet was deserted only *pro loco et tempore* and not *simpliciter*.

(116) [7 April 1641: Robertoun J.D.]

Theft or Reset. James Bailyie. Past fra.

Intran.—James Bailyie in Braidleyis.

Dilaittit of airt and pairt of the allegit thiftious steilling, at the leist thiftious ressetting, of ane blak gray horss fra Patrik Tait in Thoirnylie, quhilk was stowin be Alexander Prenteis in Inglistoun Brig, of the ground and landis of Thoirnylie, upone the xiii day of November last be way of maisterfull thift and stouth reid, and thaireftir recept be the said James Bailyie af the said Alexander Prenteis principall steiller thairof his handis *etc.* as the dittay beiris.[1]

Persewaris.—Patrik Tait in Thoirnylie, Sir Thomas Hoipe of Craighall, knycht barronet, his Majesteis Advocat for his Hienes intreis.

The persewar producet the letters deulie execute and indorsate upone the said Alexander Prenteis in Inglistoun Brig and the said James Bailyie in Braidleyis, quhairby thay ar chargit to find cautioun for thair compeirance this day and place to underly the law for the cryme foirsaid, and that the said Alexander Prenteis, for his dissobedience in nocht finding of the said cautioun, hes past to the horne and sa becum fugitive for the said cryme, at the quhilk hoirning he is registrat, and upone the productioun of the saidis letters with ane roll of assyse summond upone the said James Bailyie now upone pannell he askit instrumentis and protestit for his cautioner his releif.

The pannell takis instrumentis of his entrie and protestis for relief of David Newlandis, merchand, burges of Edinburgh, his cautioner; And as to the allegit cryme specifeit in the criminall letters producet aganis him ather for steilling or thiftious recepting of the horse lybellit denyis the samyn bot affirmes that he bocht the samyn lawfullie in presens of famous witnesses at the bar, and sa can

[1] The locus of the case is SE of Paisley.

nather be estimat the steiller nor receptor of the said horse, quhilk horse he hes brocht with him to this burgh of Edinburgh, and is willing to restoir and delyver him to the said Patrik Tait persewar, he alwayis geving his aith and faithfull declaratioun that the samyn is the horse that he alledges to be tane af the ground of his landis of Thoirnylie, and that the said horse pertenit to him at that tyme, but prejudice nevertheles of his actioun of warrandice aganis the persone that sauld the said horse to him.

Thaireftir the said Patrik Tait, persewar, being deiplie sworne and demandit gif he hes sene the hors lybellit since the bringing thairof to Edinburgh be the pannell, and gif it be his awin propper hors quhilk was tane af his landis of Thoirnylie the tyme lybellit, declairet be his grit aith that the said horse is his awin horse quhilk he wantit, and that he hes sene the samyn in the pannellis stable in Edinburgh quhair he presentlie standis, and that he is content to tak him bak agane, and thairfoir past *simpliciter* fra the pannellis persute for the cryme lybellit the said hors being delyverit to him presentlie, but prejudice alwayis of his civile actioun and persute competent to him aganis the pannell for damnage, intreis and proffeittis of his said horse daylie sen the awaytaking thairof, befoir the Judge ordiner as accoirdis of the law; quhairupone the said James Bailyie askit instrumentis and desyret the said Patrik to go with him and ressave his said horse af his handis.

LEGAL NOTE

The case presents a number of remarkable features. The panel is charged with being 'art and part' of the theft of a horse, or alternatively with reset thereof. That the charge properly is simply one of reset is clear from the latter part of the narrative. The horse is said to have been stolen by one Alexander Prentice and thereafter 'recept' by the panel from Prentice. At the outset the panel states a defence of having bought the horse openly before witnesses who are available to give evidence. He further offers there and then to restore the horse to the pursuer if he identify it on his oath. No jury was empanelled but the pursuer having sworn that the horse was his property, abandoned the charge on the basis that the horse be delivered to him. It is remarkable that the Lord Advocate should have concurred in a prosecution where no criminative circumstance attached to the panel, and where the pursuer was content to accept the return of the horse. It is even more remarkable that, having given his concurrence, he did not proceed with the charge notwithstanding the private prosecutor's attitude.

Each party was careful to reserve his civil right: the panel for breach of warrandice against the thief who sold him the horse; and the pursuer against the panel for damages for loss of use of his animal.

(117) [9 April 1641: Robertoun J.D.]

Treasonable Usurpation. Irwings etc. contra *Maxwall of Bromeholme. Continewit to the xxiii Junii nixt.*

Intran.—Johne Maxwall of Bromeholme.[1]

Dilaitit of airt and pairt of the tressonable usurpatioun of our soverane Lordis authoritie in putting violent handis on the persones of umquhile Rosie Baittie, the relict of umquhile Hectour alias Ekkie Irving in Auchinraven,[2]

[1] Broomholme or Brownholme $2\frac{1}{2}$ miles SE of Langholm.
[2] Auchenrevin is north of Langholm.

and umquhile William Irving, hir sone, streking up of the durris of his dwelling in Auchinraven, taking hir and hir said sone violentlie furth thairof under nycht, binding thame with coirdis, and carieing thame as captives and prissoneris to the Watter of Ew [*now Ewes Water*] neir to the place of Langholme, in the quhilk watter thay war crewallie drownet and murdreist to deid be the said John Maxwall and his complices, thay being his Majesteis peceable subjectis, and the said John Maxwall haifing na power or commissioun to that effect nor na dome nor sentence or preceiding tryell uset or gevin out aganis thame for ony cryme befoir ony Judge ordiner ather criminall or civile[1] committit in the moneth of November imvic twentie ane yeiris.[2]

Persewaris.—Margaret Irving, dochter to Rosie Baittie and sister to William Irving, hir sone; Daniell Irving, brother in law to the said Rosie and uncle to the said William Irving, hir sone; Sir Thomas Hope of Craighall, knycht barronet, his Majesteis Advocat for his Hienes intreis.

Prelocutouris in defence.—Mr James Baird, Mr Thomas Nicol[son], advocattis.[3]

(118) The persewaris producet the criminall letters deuly execute and indorsat raiset at the instance of Walter Scott of Thirlestane, Robert Scott his brother germane, John Murray in Bankhous, as sister sones, Williame Airmestrang of Kynmonth, Williame Baittie in Watcarrick, Richerd Airmestrang in Woidheid, Johnne Airmestrang of Sark and William Airmestrang his brother, all neir freindis and kinsmen with the remanent kyn and freindis of umquhile Rosie Baittie, relict of umquhile Hectour alias Ekkie Irving in Auchinreven, and umquhile William Irving hir sone, ane young boy betwix threttene and fourtene yeiris of age[4] allanerlie, and Sir Thomas Hope of Craighall, knycht barronet, advocat to our Soverane Lord for his Hienes intreis, aganis the said Johne Maxwall of Bromeholme, quhairby he is charget be Johne Richardsone, messinger, to find cautioun for his compeirance befoir his Majesteis Justice and Justice deputtis this day and place in the hour of caus to underly the law for the crymes foirsaidis; And upone the productioun thairof askit instrumentis and protestit for releif of James Johnstoun of Lanerk, cautioner for repoirting and persute of the samyn.

The pannell askit instrumentis of his entrie and compeirance and protestit for releif of Wa (Walter?) Airmestrang of Bigholme his cautioner, as also takis instrumentis that nane of the persewaris abonewrittin compeiris this day to persew him for the allegit cryme abone specifeit (except his Majesteis Advocat) thay being oft tymes callit upone to that effect.

[1] See legal note 1.
[2] November 1621 must be a clerk's error for November 1623 which is the date of the extract conviction produced (p. 403 below). The accused was not a baillie-depute till 7th February 1622 (p. 403 below). But 1621 is repeated at p. 406 below. Confusion becomes more confounded when the Lord Advocate is reported as saying in argument (p. 406 below) that the thieves were taken violently from their homes in January 1621. It seems improbable that they would be imprisoned without trial from January to November whatever the year. The 19 years mentioned at p. 406 fits in with 1623. See *RPC*[2] VII.451.
[3] Probably Nicolson. No Thomas Nicol is listed in *Lyon* for this period.
[4] See legal note 2.

My Lord Advocat takis lykewayis instrumentis that the said Margaret Irving, as dochter to the said umquhile Rosie Baittie and sister to the said umquhile William Irving, the young boy, compeiris as persewaris and informeris to his Lordship in this persute, togidder with the said Daniell Irving, uncle to the boy and brother in law to the mother, quha ar the speciallis of thair kyn and informeris to his Lordship in this persute.

Eftir reading the former letters and dittay specifeit thairintill it is allegit be the pannell and his prelocutouris that he can nocht pas to the knawledge of ane assyse for the allegit cryme lybellit becaus quhatsoevir thing was done be him in that matter *est jure factum*, in respect that the said Rosie Baittie and hir sone William Irving, being baith apprehendit and tane for certane poyntis of thift contenit in thair dittayis, dilaittit, accuset and persewit thairfoir befoir the said Johnne Maxwall of Brumeholme, now upone pannell, as judge and bailyie of the lordship of Eskdaill *etc.* in ane fencet court haldin be him at the Langholme the xxii day of November 1623 yeiris, and being put to ane assyse for the saidis thiftious crymes war be the said assyse deulie and ordourlie convict of the saidis crymes and fund guiltie thairof, quhairupone the dome and sentence of daith was pronuncet and gevin out aganis the said Rosie Baittie and William Irving hir sone, and the samyn dome accoirdinglie was put to executioun; And for verificatioun thairof producet nocht only ane act of court of the lordship of Eskdaill haldin at the Langholme be ane noble lord Robert, Erle of Nithisdaill, Lord Maxwall, Eskdaill *etc.*, and be James Maxwall of Kirkconnell his lordship's brother and bailyie, upone the sevint day of Februar imvicxxii yeiris quhairby the said John Maxwall of Bromeholme is sworne and admittit bailyie depute of the said lordschip of Eskdaill, Ewisdaill, and Wauchope daill etc., bot lykwayis producet thairwith the said criminall proces or rolment of court led and deducet aganis the saidis Rosie Baittie and William Irving hir sone, off the quhilkis act of bailyerie and rolment of court the tennour respective followis: In the first, the foirsaid act of bailyierie: The court of the lordship of Eskdaill haldin at the Langholme be ane noble and potent Erle, Robert Erle of Nithisdaill, Lord Maxwall Eskdaill etc., and James Maxwall of Kirkconnell, his brother and bailyie, upone the sevint day of Februar the yeir of God imvic twentie twa yeiris, suitis callit, court affirmet James Airmestrang officer etc.: The whilk day Johne Maxwall[1] brother to Archibald Maxwall of Cowhill, is admittet bailyie depute of the lordship of Eskdaill, Ewisdaill and Wauchopedaill, and of the barroneis of Carutheris, Middilbie, Bengall, Trailtrow, Kyrkconnell, Logane, Neatoun, and Springkal, quho being tane sworne *de fideli administratione* in the saidis deputrieis during the said noble Erle and his brotheris Will and pleasour, is admitit in bailyie depute as said is, quhairupone the said Johne Maxwell askit instrumentis and act of court. *Sic subscribitur* Nithisdaill, James Maxwall, John Young *ac clericus dicte curie.*

Followis the tennour of the said rolment of court: The barrone and bailyie court of the lordship of Eskdaill, Ewisdaill, Wauchopedaill, haldin at the Langholme the twentie twa day of November 1623 yeiris, be Johne Maxwall of Bromeholme, bailyie of the saidis lordships and barroneis, suitis callit, court affirmet be James Airmestrang in Poquharling, officer, George Airmestrang

[1] This was the panel, John Maxwell of Broomholme.

dempster: The whilk day Rosie Baittie in Irving, relict of umquhile Hectour Irving thair, and Williame Irving, hir sone, being enterit on pannell war indytit and accuset be the persones persewaris particularlie inder namet **(119)** and Williame Airmstrang, callit of Bigholme, procurator fiscall of the said court, for the crymes of thift and utheris perticularie eftir specifeit the said Rosie Baittie and her said sone war content to pas and abyde the tryell of the persones of assyse under namet quha war lauchfullie summond for that effect, thay ar to say Thomas Littill of Mekildaill, Walter Scott in Burnfute, George Bell, smyth in Arkinholme, William Airmestrang in Walles, Adame Pott in Stable Gordoun, Andro Irving in Holmeheid, Johnne Murray in Turnerholme, Hab Ellote in Enzieholme, Gib Ellot, his sone thair, Williame Fruide in Langholme, Michaell Scott in Turnerholme, Thomas Gray, mason in Langholme, John Patie thair, Thomas Murray in Irving, and Patrick Grahame thair, quhilkis persones of assyse abone writtin war all solempnelie sworne upone thair grit aithes judiciallie be the said bailyie to pas upone the foirsaid assyse; Thaireftir compeirit Robert Littill in Caltoun, personallie present in judgement with the said procuratour fischall, quha inditit and accused the said Rosie Baittie and William Irving hir sone of the thiftious steilling and awaytaking fra him of ane quhyte homell yow [*dishorned ewe*] furth of the landis of Caldtoun in the moneth of September than begane ane yeir. Thairefter compeirit Meg Irving in Car with the said procuratour fischall, quha lykwayis accuset the said Rosie Baittie and the said William Irving hir sone for the thiftious steilling and away taking fra hir of sevin scheip furth of the landis of Car in the moneth of September then lastbypast; And siclyk compeirit Cristopher Airmestrang in Stubholme judiciallie with the said procuratour fischall, quha lykwayis accuset the said Rosie Baittie and the said Williame Irving hir sone for the thiftious steilling and away taking fra him of foure scheip furth of the landis of Stubholme in the said moneth of September than lastbypast; And last compeirit Johnne Cawert in Woodhousleis personallie with the procuratour fischall in judgement, quha accuset and indyttit the said Rosie Baittie and Williame Irving hir sone for the thiftious steilling and away taking of four scheip furth of the landis of Woidhousleyis upone the nyntene day of November instant;[1] And last of all the said Rosie Baittie and Williame Irving, hir sone, being accuset be the procuratour fischall for commoun thift, resset of thift, infang, outfang and pykrie etc.

The foirsaid persones of assyse haveing removet thameselffis out of judgement, and being incloset secreitlie with thair clerk[2] undernamet, thay electit and choiset the said Walter Scott in Burnefitt in chancellour of the said assyse, quha causet the clerk undersubscryveand of new reid the saidis perticuler dittayes to the said chanceler and remanent persones of assyse abone namet; quha, being weill and ryplie advyset thairanent, being demandit be the said chanceller upone the perticuler declarationes as thair consciences sould dyte thame thairintill be thair severall voittis, and all in ane voce fand and declairet the saidis Rosie Baittie and William Irving hir sone and aither of thame guiltie and foull of the thiftious steilling and away taking fra the said Robert Littill

[1] I.e. only three days before the baron court trial. It is unusual for the evidence to be recited.

[2] See legal note 3.

of ane quhyte homell yow furth of the landis abone specifeit the tyme foirsaid; and siclyk fand and declairet the said Rosie Baittie and William Irving hir sone, and ather of thame, guiltie and foule of the thiftious steilling and away taking of the said sevin scheip fra the said Meg Irving furth of the saidis landis of Car the tyme foirsaid; and lykwayis fand and declairet the said Rosie Baittie to be foule and guiltie of the thiftious steilling and away taking of the saidis foure scheip fra the said Christopher Airmestrang furth of the saidis landis of Stubholme the tyme foirsaid, and fand and declairet the said William innocent thairof; and als thay fand and declairet the said Rosie Beattie and the said Williame Irving hir sone and aither of thame guiltie and foule of the thiftious steilling and away taking of the saidis four scheip fra the said Johnne Cowert furth of the saidis landis of Woidhous the tyme foirsaid, in respect of the said Rosie and hir said sone thair judiciall confessioun befoir the said judge and remanent persones of assyse abone writtin befoir thair incloseing of the last poynt and dittay abone writtin; And als in respect of the foirsaidis persones accusearis abone namet **(120)** thair solempne aithes gevin to the said judge, ilk ane of thame for thair awin pairtis of the dittayis and accusationes abone writin, that the samyn war trew and lauchfull as thay sould answeir to God; And last the said Rosie Beattie and Williame Irving hir sone war lykwayis convict of commoun thift resset of thift infang outfang and pykrie; And thaireftir the said chancellour of assyse, re-entering in judgement, agane declairet to the said judge in presence of the saidis persones accuset the perticuler determinatioun of the saidis persones of assyse; And thairfoir the said Johnne Maxwall, bailyie and judge abone namet, ordanit the said Rosie Beattie and William Irving, hir sone, to be takin to the Watter of Ewis at that pairt thairof callit the Greine, and thair thay and aither of thame to be drownet in the said watter to the daithe; Quhairupone the said Dempster gave dome. Extract furth of the courte buikis of the said lordship and barroneis be the clerk of court thairof undersubscryveand under his subscriptioun manuall *Sic subscribitur* Walter Scott chanceller, Johne Maxwall, S. Young clerk.[1]

My Lord Advocat, eftir productioun and reiding of the said rolment of court, askit instrumentis thairupoun, and alleget the samyn to be null *ipso jure* being the rolment of ane barroun court, in respect na barronie within this kingdome hes power to sit or judge ony theif without he had bene takin with the fang and reid hand, nather is my Lord of Nithisdaill his infeftment producet, and gif it war producet it beiris only for infang and outfang thift,[2] and gif it war infang quhilk [it] is not, it was only competent to the shereff quha could nocht proceid without a fang and that upone fyftene dayis citatioun and could nocht tak thame out of the houses without citatioun,[3] and be this rolment of court, producet be the pannell, it beiris no citatioun at all, lykas *de facto* it sall be provin[4] out of thair houses and sistit and brocht to this pannell within twelff

[1] See legal note 3.

[2] Terms used in feudal charters granting jurisdiction infangthef—the rights of trying and punishing a thief caught with the goods on him within the jurisdiction of the holder of the charter; outfangthef—the right of trying a dependent accused of theft, caught with the goods on him, outside the jurisdiction of his lord. Innes, *Scotch Legal Antiquities*, p. 58.

[3] See legal note 4.

[4] The sense demands that there must be added here such words as 'they were taken'.

dayis thaireftir. *Secundo* the act of court meittis nocht the dittay, quhilk is foundit upone the violent taking of the persones murthouret furth of thair awin hous and that in the moneth of Januar 1621. Item his Majesteis Advocat takis instrumentis of the tennour of the Rolment of Court producet and protestis it be nocht gevin up nor that the tennour thairof be changed.

It is duplyit for the pannell that the defence abone writtin proponit be him standis relevant nochtwithstanding of the reply proponit be my Lord Advocat as being foundit upone the rolment of court of the barrony of Eskdaill, quhilk beiris that the pannell thairin indyttit war accuset and convict of commoun thift, infang, outfang, and pykrie, lykas in supplement of the said rolment of court it is offerit to be provin be witnesses instantlie at the bar that the persones pannellit contenit in the said rolment of court war treulie tane with reid hand with all the fangis lybellit in the said rolment of court, at the leist of ane or uther of thame. *Secundo* the rolment of court is the verdict of ane ordiner judge standing unreducet, and the nullitie proponit aganis the same is nocht ane intrinsicall nullitie of the rolment quhilk can tak it away *hoc loco* be way of reply eftir so mony yeiris taciturnitie be the space of nyntene yeiris. *Tertio* that nullitie of the rolment beiring the samyn nocht to carie a citatioun of the pannell thairin contenit is in nullitie, becaus the rolment of court aucht nocht to beir that the pairtie was cited bot that the pannell enterit upone pannell sic ane day, and quhan the rolment sall be reducet *ex hoc capite* that the pannell was nocht cited, than in the caice of necessitie of citatioun it sall be provin that thay war cited at the leist takin reid hand. *Quarto* that pairt of the reply beiring the pannell to have takin Rosie and hir sone out of hir hous and presentit thame within twelf houres to the judgement quhairupone instrumentis is taken be the pannell and his prelocutiouris, and now it is allegit that thair was no wrong done be the pannell in apprehending thame and presenting thame to judgement within twelff houres, becaus thay war apprehendit reid hand and thaireftir tryit, [found] guiltie, condempnet, and put to daith, swa that the rolment producet cleirlie meittis the dittay. *Quinto* the rolment producet, being ane standing sentence, standis relevant nochtwithstanding of the reply foundit upone reid hand, in respect of the inveterat custome of barrone courtis of citatioun, convicting, and condempning of malefactouris nocht takin reid hand.

It is answerit that the probatioun of fang to be now takin eftir the daith of the pairtie is contrair to the rolment of court producet, and na probatioun can be ressavit bot that quhilk is verifeit be the rolment of court itselff. To the **(121)** secund, the nullitie is *nullitas juris* becaus the propositioun is foundit upone the commoun law of the kingdome nevir yit questionat and weill knawin to the Justice, and the assumptioun that it is ane barrone court it is verifeit be the selff and is intrinsicall; And to the remanent repeittis the answer maid to the first.

It is quaudrplyit be the pannell that howbeit it war *nullitas juris* yit thair is no intrinsick fault in the rolment of court. *Secundo* it may be suppleit be the depositiones of witnesses for manteneance of the rolment of courte producet. *Tertio* the rolment of courte being ane rolment of ane inferiour judge the want of expressioun of reid hand may verrie weill be supleit *ut supra*.

The Justice continewis this matter and his interloquitour in the premisses to the xxiii day of Junii nixtocum, and ordanis the pannell to find cautioun for his re-entrie and compeirance that day to underly the law for the cryme abone writtin under the pane of ane thousand merkis: For obedience quhairof compeirit judiciallie John Maxwall younger of Kowhill, quha become cautioun for the entrie of the said John Maxwall of Bromeholme his uncle the said xxiii day of Junii nixtocum to the effect and under the pane foirsaid, lykas the said John Maxwall of Bromeholme band and obleist him his aires and executouris to releiff his said cautioner of the premisses.

(131) [23 June 1641: Robertoun J.D.]

[The record here repeats the earlier minute.]

(132) The said Johnne Maxwall compeirit with his saidis prelocutouris and offerit himselff reddie to defend in the said matter this day and place and askit instrumentis thairupoune on the ane pairt. Lykas the persewaris speciallie nominat in the saidis criminall letters with the saidis Margaret Irving, dochter to the said umquhile Rosie Beattie and as sister to the said umquhile William Irving, sone to the said Rosie, with the said Daniell Irving as brother in law to hir and as uncle to hir said sone, being oft tymes callit to haif compeirit this day and place to haif insistit in the said John Maxwall his persute for the saids alledget crymes on the uther pairt, and nane of the persewaris foirsaidis compeirand to that effect except the said Sir Thomas Hope, his Majesteis Advocat for his Hienes intreis, quha producet his Majesteis perticuler letter signed with his Majesteis hand, quhairof the tennour followis: 'Charles R. To our trustie and weilbelovit concellour Sir Thomas Hope, knycht barronet, our Advocat of our kingdome of Scotland; trustie and weilbeloved counsellour we greete you weill: We ar informed that, in the actioun persewit be you for our interrest aganis Johnne Maxwall, bailyie depute to the Erle of Nithisdaill, it dois appeir by the rolment of the court that the executioun was done by ane fair and legall procedour of judgement and convictioun by ane assyse; bot nevertheless that by the negligence or corruptioun of the clerk, it is nocht thairin exprest, that thay war takin with the fang, and thairfore that in the rigour of the law the defender may possiblie run in the danger of wilfull murthour. We thairfore taking into our Princlie consideratioun, both the prescriptioun of many yeiris, and the defenderis offer to prove that the defunctis war taken reid hand, as lykwayis that in equitie so small ane oversight or informalitie aught nocht to be ballancet with the lyfe of ane subject, equallie executeing the lawis and cled with sufficient authoritie thairanent, have thoght fitt to will and requyre you to desist frome ony furder prosecutioun thairof till our forder pleasure be knowin, and with all to intimat this our sense thairof to our Justice Generall or deputtis that no forder proces, till our said pleasure be forder knowen, be granted thairin, in which nocht doubting of your care and dilligence wee bid you fairweill. Gevin at our court at Whytehall this 10 of Junii 1641.'

And accoirding thairto and for obedience thairof [the King's Advocate] desyret this dyet to be desertit.[1]

[1] See legal note 5.

The Justice, accoirding to his Majesteis letter abone writtin and his Hienes royall will and plesure thairin expressit, desertis the saidis criminall letters and persute mentionet thairintill; Quhairupone the said Sir Thomas Hope his Majesteis Advocat, and the said Johnne Maxwall of Bromeholme, *hinc inde* askit actis and instrumentis; And nochtwithstanding thairof the said Johne Maxwall in all humilitie desyret that the witnesses to be uset be him for proving that the said Rosie Baittie and William Irving hir sone, convict and legallie execute for thift, war tane reid hand with the fangis lybellit in the rolment of court, at the leist with ane or uther of thame, the saidis witnesses being present at the bar, that thai mycht be examinat and thair depositiones to remane in proces; To the quhilk his Majesteis Advocat disassentit. The said John Maxwall of Bromeholme askit instrumentis of his compeirance this day and place, and in respect thairof protestit for releiff of Johne Maxwall of Kowhill, his cautioner, of his cautionerie, and that he himselff sould not be callit or persewit for the allegit crymes abone writtin in ony tyme cuming etc. etc. Quhilk warrand or discharge of his Majesteis gevin to my Lord Advocat for desisting in this persute is delyverit up to Mr David Crawfurd, his Lordships servand, quha seud for the samyn to be keipit be his Lordships selff for his warrand.[1] D. Crawfurd.

Legal Notes

1. The charge was laid as for 'treasonable usurpation of our Sovereign Lords authority' by seizing persons and putting them to death by drowning, the accused 'having na power or commission to that effect, nor na dome nor sentence given. The critical factor was the allegation, borne out by the record of the Baron Court that the deceased were not taken 'with the fang'. The King's letter implies that if in fact the Irvines were sentenced to death for theft when they had not been apprehended with the stolen property on them, the Baron baillie's sentence would have constituted wilful murder.

2. The Lord Advocate attacked the execution of the Irvings on the technical grounds that the Baron Court had no jurisdiction unless the thief was taken redhanded and the Baron Court record produced here contained no such statement. The deceased William Irvine, however, was a boy of 13-14 according to the Criminal Letters, and it is surprising that no attack was made upon the execution of a person so young. Mackenzie (*Criminals* I.i.v.) accepted that a minor was liable to prosecution for crimes 'if dole can be proved'. He had however reservations on the criminal liability of a minor charged Art and Part. There is no specification in the Baron Court record of the part played in the thefts by the boy. In any event it was the invariable practice to mitigate the penalty where a pupil or minor was involved. Hume (I.33-34) found no case of a death sentence ever imposed on a pupil. Non-age was accepted by the Privy Council as a ground for reducing a death sentence for theft to one of banishment (*RPC*[1] 1612 ix.372; see also *Clark* v *Inglis* 1532 Pitcairn I.160). Hume dismisses this case in a footnote (I.195) but Burnett (*Criminal Law* p. 59), discussing homicide in discharge of public duty, realised its importance and printed it nearly in full in appendix p. xvi. He considers it unique—apart from another in 1714 which did not proceed further than a debate on relevancy.

3. The record of the proceedings in the Baron Court is unusually elaborate. It describes the calling of cases, and the fencing of the court ('court affirmet'). The accused was charged at the instance of the Procurator Fiscal and the individual complainers. A jury of 15 was sworn and each complainer appeared personally and testified on oath (p. 404) against the accused. The jury retired, along with the clerk of court, and elected a chancellor who had the clerk read over the charges again. After being 'ryplie adviset' the chancellor asked each juror how he voted. A verdict was returned on each charge 'in respect' of the panel's judicial confession 'before the jury was enclosed' and in respect of the evidence given on oath by the complainers. It is not clear if the judicial confession was restricted to the second last charge or covered all the charges. If the former it appears that one witness to each charge was considered sufficient, particularly when the jurors were entitled to use their own knowledge.

[1] See legal note 6.

4. The Lord Advocate was well founded in his argument that the Baron Court like the Sheriff Court had no jurisdiction to try theft other than when the panel was taken 'red hand' or with the fang i.e. with the stolen goods in his personal possession or at his dwelling place; otherwise only the Justice Court had jurisdiction. (Mackenzie, II, XIII.iii). But officers of court had right of search—a process known as 'dakering' or 'rancelling for theft' (see *Spalding Club Misc.* II.129-30, 133, 137; Carnwath C.B. p. cvii; *Fife* xxxviii).

5. This is one of the very few examples of interference by the Sovereign with the course of justice, but it was probably justified by the fact that the prosecution was founded on a technicality. The correct procedure however would have been for the Privy Council to take precognition of whether in fact the Irvings were caught red handed. No reference has been traced in the Privy Council record.

6. It is difficult to discover what really lay behind this prosecution. The alleged crime was stale by almost twenty years. The Criminal Letters were taken out in the name of next of kin of the deceased none of whom appeared as pursuers at the bar. The panel's protest at their absence is met by the Lord Advocate's assertion that they in fact compear as pursuers and his informers, but this does not explain their absence from the record. The pretext for the prosecution may indeed have been political. Later in 1643 Broomholme was generally considered to have been implicated in Lord Nithsdale's conspiracy to invade Scotland (see *RPC*[2] VII.451) and it may be that the present proceedings were designed to harrass a political opponent.

[21 April 1641: Robertoun J.D.]

Murthour. John Andersone and uthers. Assysoris amerciat.

Intran.—William Andersone in Ardoyne,[1] John Andersone, his father thair, James Andersone, his son, brother to the said William Andersone, Patrick Watsone in Newtoun.[2]

Dilaittit of airt and pairt of the crewall slaughter and murther of umquhill William Davidsone, sumtyme of Pitbeishaugh,[3] comittit in the moneth of December lastbypast 1640.

Persewaris.—James Davidsone, brother to the defunct; Sir Thomas Hope of Craighall, knyt barronet, his Majesties Advocat.

Prelocutor in defence.—Mr Thomas Nicolsone, younger.

The pannell takis instrumentis of thair entrie and protestis in respect of thair compeirance for thair cautioners releiff.

The persewer, James Davidsone, producet the letters and dittay insert therein with the executiones thereof execute aganis the persones on pannell, as also deulie execute and indorsate upone George Andersone, sone to John Andersone in Ardoyne, quhairby the said George Andersone is lauchfullie chairget to have found cautioun for his personall compeirance befoir the Justiciar and his Deputis this day and place in the hour of caus to have underlyne the law for the murthour and slaughter abone wrettin of the said umquhile Williame Davidsone and for his dissobedience in nocht finding of the said caution is denuncet rebell and put to the horne and r[emaines] thairat: Lykas the said George Andersone

[1] $1\frac{1}{2}$ miles NW of Oyne, Aberdeenshire.
[2] In parish of Garioch, Aberdeenshire.
[3] Pitbee is near Pitcaple, 3 miles E of Oyne.

eftir productioun of the saidis letters of horning aganis him being ofttimes callit to have compeirit this day and place to have underlyne the law for the cryme foirsaid as he that was lawfullie charget be Lancelote Leslie, messinger, to that effect lawfull tyme of day biddin and nocht compeirand, and quha for his nocht compeirance was be the mouth of James Douglas Justice, officer and dempster of court, declairet fugitive for the said slaughter etc. and all his moveable guids ordanit and adjudget to be escheit and inbrocght to our Soverane Lordis use as fugitive for the said cryme, the persewaris foirsaidis askit instrumentis thereupon and protestit for their cautioneris releiff.

My Lord Advocat eftir productione of the letters and qualificatioun of that part of the lybell quhair it is said that the persones pannellit and thair complices lay in wait, condiscendis as followis, viz. that the defunct and the committeris of the slaughter lybellit of within the oisler hous or innes of Robert Cattoche in Staneboig haveing cum frae the mercat keipit that day at the Kirk of Insche and soupet in the said Robert Cattache his hous in Staneboig, eftir sopper thay all meiting togidder in the said hous pertaining to the said Robert Cattoche thay fell out in evill woirdis, speciallie betwixt the defunct and Williame Andersone now upone pannell, and eftir woirdis the defunct haveing nather sword nor quhinger the said William Andersone with his complices drew swordis to persew the defunct of his lyf and who than, be the [indecipherable] and that the said William Andersone with the rest of his complices past out of the house leaving the defunct in the house himselff allane quha supposet that upone this thair away passing out of the said house that thay had past to thair severall hames or housses, bot that they remanet closelie and darnetlie about the dur of the said oisler house to ten hours at nyt and eftir, And quhan as the defunct therefore come furth himselff allane the said William Andersone with his complices foirsaids being about the durris of the said hous thay mett him with straikis gevin be thame to him on his heid ane or mae quhairwith thay fellit him cauld deid; Quhilkis war done be the said William Andersone or be George Andersone, his brother, and thaireftir fled to thair houss, and the said William Davidsone deceissit thereof upone the morne thereftir about twelff houres and quhan he was bureit the bluidie fork with the quhilk he was persewit was fund in the hous of the said William Andersone standing behind the his pantrie dur (*sic*); whereupon the said William Andersone fled his hous and absentit himselff the space of fourtie aucht hours as being conscious to his own guiltines.

Thaireftir it is allegit be the persones on pannell and be Mr Thomas Nicolsone, advocat, thair prelocutor, that the dittay is nawayes relevant nather can thay pas to the knawledge of ane assyse thereupone in sua far as it conteins nocht the day of the allegat committing of the cryme, for albeit be the cours of law the accuser or persewar be nocht obleist to condiscend upone the speciall day quhen the cryme alledget is comittit bot allanerlie on the moneth and yeir, yet gif the pannel be prejudget be the omissioun of the day, that day most be necessarlie condiscendit upone. This is verrae weill knawin to my Lord Justice be the comone opinionis of all laweris, and gif the persewar will condiscend upone the day, the panell John and James Andersones will offer thame to prove that upone that day of the allegit comitting of the cryme, speciallie at that tyme of the day, viz at the glomeing of the nyt, that thay war nocht with George Andersone, the special malefactor, in the place quhair the malefice is comittit, bot that William Andersone finding his brother George wavering [?] in wordis with the defunct in Staneboig in the house of Robert Cattoch that he delt with his brother to cum away fra the defunct, and that he brocht his brother away and convoyit him halfway towards Ardoyne whilk is ane half myle distant from Stanebog [?boig] being accompaneit with Andro Baittie, Robert Watsone and William Sandersone, and that in the midis of the way his brother falling cumersoune he left his brother, the malefactor, thas and past hame to Ardoyne in company with the thre foirnamet persones and went and drank in ane pynt of aillis house [sic] with Robert Watsone, and therefter past hame to his awin house in Ardoyne, and that befoir he went to drink with Robert Watsone he went to his father, Johne Andersone, and desyrit him to goe to his son George, the malefactor, and to attend upone him becaus he was in drink and had swaggerit with the defunct and that the said John, the father, was nocht in Ardoyne the tyme of the comitting of the slaughter; Quhilk defence as it is relevant of itself not being ane naiket negative as it may be supposet bot ane coactat negative with positive circumstances so it sall be provin be famous witnessis.

My Lord Justice indulges that favor to the panell that thay may have his Lordships warrand to sumond the witnesses.

It is ansyrit tharto be his Majesties Advocat that the lybell with the declaratioun is most relevant without condiscending upone the day of the slaughter and the exceptioun proponet is contrar to the lybell *et . . . . negativa Li . . . . cum scripta loco et tempore* nor yet implicite *firmativo quod fuerunt alibi* is relevant nawayis *in criminalibus* in respect whereof the dittay standis relevant, and becaus thair is nocht ane sufficient number of assyse present wha best knawis the verritie of the panellis thair guiltiness of the said slaughter, desyret that the witnessis following myt be callit upone, sworne and admittit, wha ar present at the bar to give thair testimonie and declaratioun what thay knaw of the slaughter above writtin and gif the persones on panell be guiltie or innocent of the samyn.

The Justice continewis this dyet to the last day of June nixtocum, and, with consent of the defenderis, ordanit the witnesses following viz. John Cruikshank in Kirktoun of Oyne, Robert Cattoche in Stonebrig and James Neische, tailyeor in Torreis, to be sworne and ressavit and thair depositiones to be tane to remane in proces to the said day; quha being callit upone and compeirand and solemnlie sworne to declair the verritie, war ordanit to attend upone the morne to be examinat be my Lord Justice and thair examinatioun and depositiones to be alss lawfull and sufficient as gif thai war examinat in presence of the judge and assyse in judgement, to the whilk examinatioun of the saidis witnesses and taking of their depositions in the premisses the panell with thair prelocutors consentit.[1]

The Justice ordanit the panell to find caution for their re-entrie and compeirance the said last day of June nixt in the tolbuth of Edinburgh to underly the law for the said slaughter, ilk ane of thame under the pane of fyve hundrethe merkis. For obedience whereof compeirit judiciallie William Leslie younger of Hilbray and Thomas Gordoun, callit of Bruchlie, servitors to my Lord Gordoun, wha and ather of thame become cautioneris and soureties, conjunctlie and

[1] See legal note 1.

severallie, for the said John Andersone and Williame Andersone his sone thair entrie and compeiring befoir his Majesties Justice and his deputis the saids day and place to the effect foirsaid, under the said paine of vc merks for ather of the saids John and Williame Andersones; lykeas the saids John and Williame Andersones obleist thame conjunctlie and severallie to releif thair said cautioneris of their cautionerie and of the penaltie above writtin.

Compeirit lykewayis George Leith of Overhall and become caution for the said Patrick Watsone in Newtoun his re-entrie and compeirance the said day and place to the effect and under the paine foirsaid, and last compeirit Robert Cattoch in Stanebrig and become cautioun for the said James Andersone to the said John Andersone his entrie and compeirance the saids day and place to the effect and under the said payne of fyve hundreth merkis money; lykeas the said James Andersone and Patrick Watsone obleist thame severallie for thair owin partis to releiff thair saidis cautioneris of the premissis.

(133) [30 June 1641: Robertoun J.D.]

Murthour. John Andersone and utheris. Assysoris amerciat.

Intran.—Johnne Andersone in Ardoyne; Williame Andersone, James Andersone, his twa sones thair; Patrick Watsone in Newtoun.

Dilaitit of airt and pairt of the crewall murthour and slauchter of umquhile William Davidsone, sumtyme of Pitbeishauch, committit in the moneth of December lastbypast at the oisler [*ostler*] hous or innes of Robert Cattoche in Stanebrig.

Persewaris.—James Davidsone, as brother to the defunct; Elspeth Smyth, the relict; Williame Davidsone, eldest sone of 13 yeiris of aige allanerlie; George Davidsone, also sone ane young chyld in his motheris airmes;[1] Sir Thomas Hope of Craighall, knycht barronet, his Majesteis Advocat for his Hienes intreis.

The persewaris takis instrumentis of the productioun of the letters of assyse with the roll and executiones thairupoun, the principall letters being producet be thame upone the xxix day of Apryle last,[2] and the tryell of the persones upone pannell being that day continewit be the Justice to this day, And thairfoir desyret Justice to be ministrat.

The persones on pannell askit instrumentis of thair compeirance and offerit thame selffis reddie to underly the law for the allegit cryme abone writtin, being innocent thairof; And in respect the assyse being callit upone and nane compeirit bot sax persones allanerlie, and that the remanent persones summond ar unlawit for thair nocht compeirance, as also seing this is the secund dyet keipit be the pannell for cleiring of thair innocencie of the said allegit cryme, protestit that na letters or charges sould be direct agains thame at the instance of ony pairtie persewar for the cryme foirsaid in ony tyme cumming, speciallie in

[1] See legal note 2.
[2] A mistake for 21st April.

respect that the pannell hes summond witnesses be warrand of his Majesteis letters grantit be delyverance of the Lordis of Sessioun to verriefie to the Justice and assyse[1] that thai war nawayis present upone the grund quhair the slauchter lybellit was committit, and war nather airt nor pairt thairof.[2]

The persewaris protestis for ane new dyet to be affixt be the Justice for tryell of the pannell anent the slauchter abone writtin, in respect that the dyet affixt to this day is desertit for want of assysouris, quhilkis are detenit and stayit at hame be the procurement and instigatioun of the persones on pannell or thair freindis; and quhairas that the saidis witnesses ar present the persewaris consentis to thair examinatioun leist be thair deceis the persewaris probatioun sould ceise quhan evir this persute sall be of new agane walknet [*wakened*], under protestatioun alwayis that the saidis persewaris nawayis aggreis that the poyntis quhairupone thay ar to be examinat ar relevant in law.[3]

The pannell protestit in the contrair and that na new letters be grantit, nor na new dyet be affixt for persute of thame for the cryme foirsaid, in respect the pannell offeris thame to prove be assysouris at the bar that James Davidsone, ane of thair persewaris, transactit with the assysouris nocht compeirand, and componet with thame the tyme of thair citatioun to this dyet be taking money frome thame to stay and abyde at home.

The Kingis Majesteis Advocat declairet that he is content that the said James Davidsone and the officer executour of the letters be tryit legallie swa that the pure woman and hir bairnes ressave na prejudice thairby.[4]

The quhilk day Johnne Thomesone in Rothena, Johne Reid in Myretoun, Thomas Kempt in Smalburne, William Allerdyce in Logyaltoun, George Allerdyce thair, Robert Nevene thair, James Durna in the Buss, Williame Durna thair and James Knycht in Ardoyne being oft tymes callit to haif compeirit befoir his Majesteis Justice and his deputis this day and place to haif past upone the assyse of Johne Andersone in Ardoyne, William and James Andersones his twa sones thair, and Patrik Watsone in Newtoun, for airt and pairt of the crewall slauchter of the said umquhile Williame Davidsone sumtyme of Pitbeishauch, committit in December lastbypast, as thay and ilk ane of thame that war lauchfullie summoned be Johnne Gairdin messinger, be vertew of his Majesteis letters of assyse direct at the instance of James Davidsone in Auldrane, as brother, with the remanent kyn and freindis of the said umquhile Williame Davidsone sumtyme of Petbeishauch, and Sir Thomas Hope of Craighall, knycht baronet, his Majesteis Advocat for his Hienes intreis, all personallie apprehendit [*cited*] to haif compeirit to pas upone the saidis defenderis assyse this day and place for the cryme foirsaid, lawfull tyme of day biddin and nocht compeirand; The Justice thairfoir be the mouth of James Douglas, dempster of court, decernit and adjudget the foirnamet persones of assyse for thair nocht compeirance to be unlawit and amerciat in the pane of ane hundreth merkis money ilk ane of thame.

[1] See legal note 3.
[2] See legal note 4.
[3] See legal note 5.
[4] See legal note 6.

Legal Notes

1. The Act 1587 c. 69 required that the 'hail probation' be led in the presence of the assize and accused. The procedure adopted here and elsewhere in this collection however (e.g. p. 463) illustrates that contemporary construction did not require the witness to give detailed testimony before the trial court. He might simply assent to the terms of his deposition produced to him and it would appear from the Justice Depute's interlocutor in the present case (p. 411) holding 'thair examinatioun and depositiones to be alss lawfull and sufficient as gif thai war examinet in presence of the Judge and assyze in judgement,' that he, with the consent of the defence was prepared to hold production of these depositions to the assize, of themselves to amount to probation led in the presence of the assize. See note 5 below. When the dead Earl and Master of Gowrie were tried by Parliament for treason arising out of the incident at Gowrie House (1600) the Lord Advocate produced all the depositions of witnesses examined before the Lords of the Articles with those of other witnesses. These being 'red, seen and considered by all the Estates of Parliament in presence of the King's Majesty and they therewith being ripely advised . . . found decerned and declared' both accused guilty (Barbe, *Tragedy of Gowrie House*, p. 103).

2. The widow and children do not appear as pursuers at the original diet. The deceased's eldest son of 13 years and a younger son still 'in his mother's airmes' are now listed as individual pursuers. It is remarkable that their title is not challenged. Concourse of tutor or curator had been required from at least 1597, and it was open to a minor to invite the Court to appoint a Curator *ad litem* in such a process (Mackenzie II.xix.iii). The mother was not regarded as curator to her children in such a pursuit (Mackenzie II.xix.4; Stair I.vi.2).

3. Mackenzie (II.xxii.11) and Hume (II.398) erred in thinking that warrants to cite witnesses for the defence were not issued before the Restoration. At least by this date the matter appears to have been one for the discretion of the Justice Depute which he might decline to exercise. In the present case, where a detailed defence of alibi was advanced, he did exercise it in favour of the accused. There is no apparent reason why this warrant was inoperative but the panels obtained a further warrant from the Court of Session, and the case is authority for the view that a warrant to cite defence witnesses in a criminal case, could also be obtained from the Court of Session, at least in the case of a special defence. The point was argued in Corsair's case, see below p. 419.

4. The specification of the special defence of alibi had been intimated at the first diet. See p. 410 above.

The fact that the panels plead not only absence from the locus but also that they were neither art nor part of the slaughter suggests that accession by prior concert, though there was no immediate assistance at the time of the crime, was recognised.

5. Without conceding that alibi was a relevant defence, the pursuers agree here to the unusual procedure of examining the defence witnesses, cited by warrant from the Court of Session, in the absence of a jury. They could hardly do otherwise in view of the defence having consented to the pursuers' witnesses being similarly examined at the earlier diet. See note 1 above. The absence of any challenge by the Advocate of the relevancy of the defence stated suggests he thought the defence a good one. Hume refers to this case (II.405).

6. No third diet was fixed, presumably because of the mutual contentions that the absence of jurors was due to the instigation of the panels or pursuers. The Lord Advocate's attitude was that this must be investigated and nothing done which might prejudice the widow and her children.

(124) [23 April 1641: Robertoun J.D.]

Sla[ughter]. Janet Corsair. Acquit of the slauchter of umquhile James Johnstoun.

Intran.—Jonet Corser, sister in law to Robert Watsone, indweller in Leith.

Dilaitit of crewall slauchter of umquhile James Johnstoun, sone to Thomas Johnestoun, indweller in Leyth, ane young boy of aucht yeiris of aige or thairby, committit within the town of Leyth in the moneth of August 1640 yeiris be gripping him with hir handis be his twa lugis or eares, and lykwayis be the chyn and choukis [*cheeks*] and casting him with grit force and violence to the ground upone his bak, and thaireftir geving him dyvers and deidlie straikis with hir handis, faldit neves [*fists*], kneyis and feit, in dyvers pairtis of his body, and possing [*pushing*] him in the breist, bellie, bak and sydis, and breking thairby of his haill intrallis and noble pairtis within him, to the effusioun of his bluid, quhairof he nevir convalessit, bot being tane up be his father and mother and borne hame to thair hous and sichtit [*examined*] thair, was fund ane crewall straik and hurt gevin to him in his secreit pairtis betwix his wame and his fundament, and ane uther straik under his chyn grittumlie swellit, and was thaireftir put in his bed with mony uther bauch and blae [*sorry and blue*] straikis in dyvers uther pairtis of his body gevin be the said Jonet Corser to him, swa that he remanet in grit dollour and payne of the saidis deidlie straikis under the cure of doctouris and chirurganes, droyneing [*pining*] away the space of nyntene oulkis [*weeks*] togidder, nevir haifing habilitie to cum out at the dur, and in end upone the xxiii day of January 1641 lastbypast deceissit thairof.[1]

Persewars.—Thomas Johnestoun, indweller in Leyth as father; Helene Johnestoun, his spous as mother; Sir Thomas Hope of Craighall, knycht barronet, Advocat to our Soverane Lord for his Hienes intreis.

Prelocutour in defence.—Mr Thomas Nicolsone, younger, advocat.[2]

The pannell takis instrumentis of hir entrie and compeirance and protestis for releif of Robert Watsone, indweller in Leith, hir cautioner of his cautionerie.

The persewaris producet the letters deulie execute and indorsate, askit instrumentis thairupone and protestit for thair cautioneris releif.

My Lord Advocat declaires that he insistis upone this lybell *pro defuncto occiso saltem lethaliter vulnerato vel contuso; ad penam mortis si inveniatur occisus; et ad penam vel multam extraordinariam si tantum inveniatur contusus et non ex vulneribus vel contusionibus decessisse.*[3]

It is alledgit for the pannell that schoe can nocht pas to the knawledge of ane assyse for the alledgit slauchter of the defunct chyld by the alledgit straikis lybellit and inflicting thairof, becaus, howbeit that illative [*inferentially*] thay be termed deidlie hurtis in the lybell, yit it be the straine of the lybell it is cleirlie constant [*established*] that nane of the straikis or hurtis lybellit (giveand and nocht grantand that ony was gevin) war not[4] *vulnera lethalia*, in swa far as the lybell beiris that the alledgit straikis and hurtis war gevin in August last, and that the chyld deceissit upoun the twentie thrie of Januar thaireftir be the spaice of half ane yeir eftir the alledgit geveing thairof, for of the law *vulnus non presumitur lethale neque presumitur defunctus decessisse ex vulnere si post quadraginta dies ambulaverit sed presumitur decessisse vel ex malo regimine vel ex incuria vel ex infirmitate super veniente*, and swa heir the defunct chyld haveing survivit fra the tyme lybellit of the geveing of the alledgit straikis be the spaice **(125)** of ane half yeir he can not be said to haif diet of the woundis lybellit; cheiflie considdering that it is offerit to be provin be witnesses present at the bar

[1] A fuller recital of the charge is given below p. 421.

[2] He became Lord Advocate on 10 June 1649; his father Sir Thomas was also a member of the Bar. (*Lyon's List* p. 165).

[3] I.e. the L.A. wished to plead alternatively for either slaughter or wounding.

[4] There seems to be an unintentional double negative in the text here.

that some twa or thrie monethis or thairby eftir the said moneth of August the chyld walkit abrod in als guid helth, gif nocht better, as he was befoir the moneth of August, at the leist in suche ane qualitie of his health as was not compatibill with ane mortall wound, viz. that he cam to the hous of Johnne Mathesone, schole maister in Leith, with twa of the defunctis brether quho was in the schole, and that he played himselff with the childrene of the schole albeit not at the schole, and this sal be provin be the said Johnne Mathesone, present at the bar, that it was ane moneth, twa monethis or thrie monethis or thairby eftir the said moneth of August; Lykas also it is offerit to be provin be Johnne Wilsone, tailyeour in Leith, William Merschell and James Turnbull, officeris in Leith, that ane moneth, twa moneth, thrie moneth or thairby eftir the said moneth of August thay saw the defunct chyld playing him upoun the streat, in respect quhairof the straikis lybellit can nevir be said to be deidlie woundis as quhairupoun to infer *penam homicidii* against the pannell.

Secundo, it is alledgit for the pannell that, quhairas my Lord Advocat hes bene pleaset to declair the dittay that his Lordship insistis in sic termes as is contenit in the declaratione, that the pannell in law is not obleist to anser thairto in swa far as the declaratioune craves the pannell to be puneischit *pena extraordinaria* in caice the straikis be nocht found lethall, becaus thair is no suche conclusioun in the dittay, and it is to mak up ane new dittay quhairunto the pannell is not haldin to answer, cheiflie sieing the dittay is not raisit at the instance of his Majesties Advocat bot at the pairties.[1]

Tertio, it is alledgit for the pannell that the persewar cannot be hard to eik [*add*] at the bar ony aggravatting qualitie to his dittay, viz. the effusioun of bluid, and craves that the pannell may not be haldin to answer to the dittay with the said additioun.

It is answerit be the persewaris that the exceptioun is nowayis relevant, and hes nather the ground of law nor practique, civile nor municipall, for of the law *illud est lethale vulnus ex quo sequitur mors,* and thair is no consideratione had of the intervall of tyme *ubi vulneratus processit a malo in peius* without recoverie, and this is cleir *per legem ait lex ff. ad legem aquiliam* and *Julius Clarus* 5, *homicidium numeris* 43 *and* 44, *and Baptista numero* 154, quhair thay say *quod haec est communis opinio non habito respectu ad spatium temporis etiam si moreretur post octo menses.*

Item, answerand to the secund exceptioun subjoynet to the said first aledgeance, the samyn is nowayis relevant and is contrair to the lybell, beiring that the defunct deceissit of the woundis and contusiones lybellit, lykas in fortificatioun of the lybell it sall be provin to the assyse that the bairne keipit hous and nevir convalessit bot still remainet under cure of Doctor Polutius and Patrik Johnestoun, chirurgane, till the tyme of his death, and the qualificatioun of the boyis comeing furth to the schoole and playing himselff abroad is nawayis relevant nocht condiscending *quanto tempore*, for ane bairne haiveing ane deidlie wound upoun him, quhilk be tyme micht procure death, micht goe to the schoole and remaine for ane schoirt tyme als lang as the paine was at him and returne home to his bed and to his cure, and na sic probatioun can be ressavet

[1] This implies that in an indictment more latitude was allowed to the L.A. than when he concurred in criminal letters, but see Hume II.281.

at the bar be witnesses quhill [*until*] first the judge discuss the exceptioun quhilk was nevir found relevant in ony judgement bot the lybell fund relevant and referrit to ane assyse, speciallie sieing it is offerit to be provin to the assyse *quod vulnus et ulcus* [*ulcers*] *ex vulnere* being upoun the bak of his balcod [*scrotum*] ran and matteret, haifing ane tent [*extent*] of a finger lenth, continewallie till his death.

Secundlie, as to the objectioun maid aganis the declaratioun, the samyn is **(126)** nawayis relevant becaus the declaratioun tuitches no pairt of the cryme lybellit, bot only explanes the conclusioun, and nocht be way of extentioun bot be way of restrictioun, lykas the declaratioun is impliceitlie comprehendit under the conclusioun of the summondis quhilk beiris the pannell to be puneischet conforme to the lawis of the kingdome.

To the thrid repeittis the same answer, the effusioun of bluid nocht being ane aggravatting circumstance bot rather diminiteve in respect of the uther circumstances, the quhilk ar more violent and pregnant.

It is duplyit for the pannell that that pairt of the defence foundit upone the law *de vulnere lethali* standis relevant nochtwithstanding of the reply, and that it is the opinioun of Clarus in the citet place that *etiam si vulneratus processit de malo in peius: secundum sententiam* Angeli, *nullus lethaliter vulneratus potest quadrgainta dies*, and than of his opinioun he sayis *si tamen vulneratus post illatum vulnus per triduum ambulaverit, de casu etaim si postea moriatur non presumitur ex vulnere decessisse*; And it is offerit to be provin that ane moneth, twa, thre monethes or thairby, eftir the moneth of August lybellit the chylde went to schoole and played abrode thre, foure, fyve, or sax dayis, gif it be neidfull. Lykas it is offerit to be provin be witnessis present at the bar that ane moneth or thairby eftir August lybellit that the tyme of the great seiknes of the pox quhilk raget amongst the childrene in Leith and Edinburgh, that the chyld had the pox and recoverit thairof, so that gif the wound had been deidlie the chyld could nocht have eschewit daith with the accessioun of sa mortall ane disease as the pox was, and that he recoverit of the pox, and was in guid health, so that he went abrode without durris [*out of doors*].

Secundo, it is duplyit for the pannell that the defence, howbeit it be in some soirt contrair to the lybell, gif contrair be understuid to elyde the lybell, yit it is more pregnant nor the lybell and moir favorable; moir pregnant because positive, and the lybell is negative, and at the best the lybell is bot putative viz. that he nevir recoverit; bot the defence is positive that he was in guid health because he went abroode; and the defence is moir favorable nor the lybell and reply, becaus it is *in favorem rei ad extendendum delictum*: And to that pairt of the reply quhairby it is alledget that the wound and the byle [*boil*] remanet and ran to the death of the chyld, it eleidis nocht the relevancie of the defence, for the defence is *si vulneratus post quadraginta dies ambulaverit per triduum. non presumitur decessisse ex vulnere;* Lykas, in fortificatioun of the defence, it is offerit to be provin that the bairne deit of ane uther diseas, viz. of the fluxes, and that *nullo modo laborabat sed sanus erat in inguine*, and this sall [be proven] be Patrik Johnstoun, chirurgane, quho visseit the chyld bothe befoir and eftir his death.

To the reply aganis the secound defence that thairfoir the defence is relevant becaus the declaratioun does nocht tuitch the lybell, nather can the lybell be said implicite to contene the declaratioun, becaus gif the cryme of slauchter had nocht bene lybellit the course of justice in the strick [*strict*] way of the lybell could nocht have proceidit against the pannell; and as to that pairt of the reply anent the meaning of the lybell it is duplyit that howbeit the additioun does nocht aggravat the cryme; yit it aggravattis the nature of the wound *in genere vulneris*, quhilk is ane cleir changeing of the lybell.

The Justice continewis this matter to Tysday nixt the 27 instantis, and ordanit the pannell to find cautioun for hir re-entrie that day; the assyse wairnet *apud acta* to the said day; lykas Robert Watsone, indweller in Leyth, being present, become cautioun for the pannell hir re-entrie under the panes contenit in the Actis of Parliament.

(126) [27 April 1641: Robertoun J.D.]

The Justice be interlocutour declaires he will nocht admit my Lord Advocat his declaratioun *hoc loco* and in this dittay; reservand to the pairtie persewar to persew *pro vulnerato aut contuso* upone a new lybell or dittay, and remittis this matter *pro occiso* to the knawledge of ane assyse to be tryit and cognoscet be thame accoirding to thair knawledge and conscience.[1]

Assisa.—Patrick Johnestoun, chirurgeon in Leyth, chanceller; Johnne Wilsone, tymmer (*timber*] man thair; Dr John Polutius, doctour in physick:[2] Thomas Harlaw, elder, mealmaker in Leyth; Thomas Harlaw, younger, thair; James Hammiltoun, mealmaker in Leyth; John Meggat, workman thair; Andro Harlaw, tailyeour thair; Robert Makconnell, brouster [*brewer*] thair; James Aliesone, customer [*exciseman*] thair; William Thomesone, airmorar in Edinburgh; Mungo Symsone, buikseller thair; James Leirmonth, skynner thair; Johnne Reid, indweller in Leith; James Johnstoun, couper in Calton.

My Lord Advocat takis instrumentis for the sweiring of the assyse.

Thaireftir my Lord Advocat desyret that the father and mother of the chyld, quha ar persewaris of this dittay, thair aithes mycht be tane upone the treuth thairof, quha, being ather of thame solemnelie sworne, declairet that the dittay is trew in the selff as the samyn is lybellit, and that thair bairne deceissit of the straikis mentionet thairintill.[3] Quhairupone my Lord Advocat also askit instrumentis, and protestit for wilfull errour aganis the assyse gif thay acquit the pannell of the cryme of slauchter abonewrittin.

The persones of assyse, for cleiring to thame of the veritie of the factis and deidis lybellit and thair better informatioun thairintill, maist humblie desyres my Lord Justice that the foure witnesses nominat be the pannell presentlie at the bar[4] may be receavet, sworne, and admittit be his Lordship to mak thair judiciall declaratioun, in his Lordships, the pairties als weill persewaris as defender presens, and in thair presens as assysouris, befoir thair passing furth of judgement.

[1] See legal note 1.
[2] See legal note 2.
[3] This is the second oath of calumny before the assize as opposed to the first oath taken before the Justice Depute at the start of the proceedings.
[4] Named at p. 416 above.

To the ressaveing of the quhilkis witnesses my Lord Advocat disassentis, and allegit that thai can nocht be ressavit, because [1] it was nevir done befoir in this judgement, and [2] it is done only *ad instantiam partis;* [3] thair is no witnesses summond to this day, and gif thay be, it is at the desyre of the pairtie defender, quhilk is ane lawfull objectioun to repell ane witnes in ane civile caus of ane hundreth pund, *multo magis* in ane caus criminall.

It is answerit for the pannell to the first objectioun, that the samyn is naways relevant, becaus it is confessit be my Lord Advocat that gif the persewar use witnesses the defender may also use, quhilk hes been done, and swa, albeit na witnesses be uset be this persewar, nevertheles the pannell aucht to haif witnesses ressavit for cleiring to the assyse of hir innocence quhilk is most equitable, speciallie seing thair is no contrair practique allegit bot only that it was nevir done, quhilk possiblie hes bene becaus that witnesses hes bene producet to the assyse. To the second, it is verrie ressonable that the pannell may desyre the assysoures to crave all maner of informatioun thay can and speciallie the examinatioun of witnesses.

(128) To the 3 it may nocht be respectit becaus it hes evir bene refuiset in this judgement to geve warrand to persones pannellit to summond witnesses, and so the pannell most ather deale with thame to compeir voluntarlie and declair the verritie, or than [*then*] the pannell most be content to suffer death for nocht probatioun of thair innocencie: in respect quhairof the witnesses aucht [to] be ressavit.

It is answerit be my Lord Advocat that the Act of Parliament in anno 1587 cap. 90[1] prescryves the ordour for ressaveing of witnesses and probatioun at the instance of the persewar only, and thair is no warrand to ressave witnes at the instance of the defender, and the Justice, at the leist the Lordis of Sessioun quha directis criminall letters, hes bene in use to grant letters to the persewar for summonding of witnesses, by and besyde the assyse, wald nevir have refuiset to haif gevin warrand to this pannell to summond witnesses gif scho had supplicat thairfoir, and the preparative to ressave witnesses nocht being citit bot *ad rogatum partis* cayreis with it gritter prejudice and novatioun in this judgement nor aucht to be uset considdering that the interloquitur for thair ressait will be ane dangerous preparative [*precedent*] in tyme cuming.

To the quhilk it is duplyit for the pannell, that the Act of Parliament 1587 is nocht exclusive of witnesses to be adducet be the pannell bot is meirlie in favoures of the pannell introducet for taking away the great abuse of leiding the persewaris probatioun outwith the presens of the persones pannellit; thairfoir the persewaris probatioun was ordanit to be led in presens of the assyse and the pannell, bot the Act excludis nocht the pannell to use witnesses, bot on the contrair in the end of the Act ordanis the pannell to have procuratouris to propone thair lawfull defences, and gif the proponeing of ane defence be indulget to the pannell the proveing thairof most follow be consequence lykas the 91 Act of that same Parliament[2] ordanes the assysouris gif thay have ony doubtis thay ar ordanet to propone the samyn in judgement; and now adheirand thairto the assysouris craves for thair resolutioun to have the witnesses ressavet. And

[1] Glendook cap. 91.
[2] Glendook cap. 92.

to the rest of the reply the pannell oppones the custome of the court for ressaveing of witnesses to the assyse. And it is eikit be the pannel that John Mathesone, scoolemaister, quha is nominat to be ane of the witnes is nocht cum heir so meikill *ad instantiam partis* as he is cum *ad instantiam accusatoris* being summond to pas upone the assyse, and swa the persewar can mak na objectioun aganis him.

It is answerit be the persewar that, albeit he be summond upone the assyse, yit the persewar hes nocht uset him, and nocht being uset be the pannell he mycht have past away.

Thaireftir the haill assyse cravet earnestlie at my Lord Advocat that the witnesses mycht be ressavet, but prejudice of his Lordships objectiones to be proponit aganis thame, to the quhilk my Lord Advocat assentit provyding it be nocht ane preparative [*precedent*] heireftir and thairupoun askit instrumentis.[1]

Williame Merschell, officer in Leyth, producet as witnes be the pannell, being deiplie sworne and demandit quhat he knawis anent the hurtis gevin to umquhile James Johnstoun, depones be his grit aith that he knawis nothing thairof, bot declairis that about Mertinmes last, a twa monethes eftir August or thairby, he saw the boy walking up and down the town of Leyth in guid helth to his appeirance. Lykas betwix Mertinmes and Yule last the boy come with his mother to the deponeris hous, his father being than in waird, at quhilk tyme the boy, to the deponeris judgement, was haill and feir and frie of ony hurt.[2] And being interrogat quhat he knawis anent the boyis daith, and gif he deceissit of ony flux, depones he knawis nothing thairof, bot be repoirt that he sould have deit of ane flux; and farder knawis nocht.[3]

James Trumble, producet as witnes be the pannell, and deiplie sworne to declair the veritie, depones that he is ordiner officer in Leyth, and that Thomas Johnesoun, the defunctis father, being wairdit in the tolbuth of Leyth, the defunct with his mother come dyvers tymes in his motheris hand in guid helth to the deponeris hous, and namelie that he come dyvers tymes eftir August, in September and October, in dyvers dayis of the saidis monethis speciallie betwix Mertinmes and Yule last; as also depones that he come to the said Thomas Johnstoun his hous father to the boy, quhair he saw the defunct with the rest of the bairnes of the hous airlie in the moirning, befoir aucht houris, lying togidder in ane bed, all in guid helth, without ony hurt or seiknes eftir August last.

Johne Mathiesone, scole maister in Leyth, witnes ressavit for the pannell, being sworne, depones upone his conscience that he saw the boy James Johnstoun four or five severall tymes within his scoole, in his brethers company, betwix the letter end of August and November last, in perfyte helth without ony hurt or menyie [*cause of complaint*], to the deponeris judgement, in ony pairt of his body.

(129) Upone the examinatioun of the quhilkis witnesses and thair judiciall declaratioun, the pannell askit instrumentis, and protestis, in caice scho be acquit be the assyse of the cryme lybellit, that schoe may have the benefit of the

1 See legal note 3.
2 Whole and sound, or hearty, see Pitcairn III.467.
3 See legal note 4.

Act of Parliament [1587 cap. 88] for refounding of hir expenses being fund innocent be the said assyse.

The persewaris protestit in the contrair in respect of the Justice interlocutour.

Jonet Corser acquit of the slauchter of umquhile James Johnstoun ane young boy etc.

The quhilk day Jonet Corser, sister in law to Robert Watsone, indweller in Leyth, being enterit upone pannell dilaittit, accuset, and persewit at the instance of Thomas Johnestoun, indweller in Leyth, as father, Helene Johnestoun his spous as mother to umquhile James Johnestoun, thair sone and Sir Thomas Hope of Craighall, knycht barronet, advocat to our soverane Lord for his Hienes intreis, off the cryme underwrittin specifeit in hir dittay *viz.* forsamekill as in the moneth of August lastbypast imvic and fourtie yeiris thair being twa young bairnes, the ane a sone, the uther a dochter of the said Robert Watsones, playing thameselffis foiranent the dur of thair fatheris house lyand *contigue* with the said Thomas Johnestoun his dwelling house, and the saidis twa young childrene in thair pastyme being rynand round about quhilk disseit thair branes, ane of thame falling to the ground and hurting uther to the effusioun of thair bluid, quhairby the bairne that fell to the ground geving ane grit cry, the said Jonet Corser hearing the cry, come out of the said Robert Watsones hous, quhairin scho was for the tyme, and seing the bairne bleiding, come in ane grit radge and furie to the said umquhile James Johnstoun, sone to the said Thomas, being ane young boy about aucht yeir auld or thairby, quha at that tyme was playing himselff allane at the dur of his said fatheris dwelling hous, nawayis being in the company with the said Robert Watsones bairnes, bot being in sober and quyet maner for the tyme, and thair the said Jonet Corser ran upone the said James Johnestoun, being only aucht yeiris of aige as said is, and first with hir handis violentlie grippit and tuik him up be his twa luggis and eares, and thaireftir be the chyn or choukis and slang him to the ground with great violence upone his bak, and nocht satisfeit thairwith maist barbaruslie and crewallie with hir faldit nevis, kneyis and feit, possit and strak him in the breist, bellie, bak and sydis to the effusioun of his bluid, quhairby the said young chyld was altogidder confoundit and maid senseles with the saidis straikis; Quhairupone the said young boy his father and mother cuming out of thair hous, and heiring of the grit abuse done to thair bairne, and seing him crawling on the ground in that pitiefull estait, thay tuik him up and cayreit him hame to thair house, and being sichted throw his haill body thay fand ane crewall straik gevin to hym be the said Jonet Corser in his secreit pairtis betwix his wame and his fundament, and ane uther under his chyn quhilk grittumlie swallit, with mony bauch and blae straikis in dyvers pairtis of his body, and his haill intrallis and noble pairtis to be brokin and bruset within him swa that he nevir convalessit, bot remaneing in grit dollour and payne of the saidis deidlie straikis under the cure of doctouris and chirurganes, nevir being of habilitie to cum out at the dur, daylie dwyneing and pyneing away be occasioun of the saidis crewall straikis and deidlie woundis; In end uppone the xxiii day of the said moneth of Januar last he deceissit thairof, and swa was crewallie and unmerciefullie murdreist and slane be the said Jonet

Corser; and scho was and is the only committer, airt and pairt thairof; For the quhilk scho aucht and sould be puneisched conforme to the lawis of this realme, as at lenth is contenit in the said dittay.

Quhilk being altogidder denyit be the said Jonet Corser to be of verritie, the Justice, nochtwithstanding of divers alledgeances maid be the said defender and hir prelocutour aganis the said dittay and relevancie thairof, quhilkis war repellit in respect of the dittay and the answeris maid in fortificatioun of the samyn, referrit and remittit the tryell of the said slauchter to the knawledge of the persones of assyse eftir following to be tryit and cognoscet be thame accoriding to thair knawledge and conscience, they ar to say Patrik Johnestoun, chirurgane in Leyth [etc. as above], quhilkis persones of assyse being ressavit, sworne, and admittit eftir accusatioun of new agane be dittay of the said Jonet Corser in thair presence and audience of the cruell slauchter and murthour of the said umquhile James Johnestoun, ane young chyld of aucht yeiris of age, committet in maner and at the tyme abone writtin, and of the haill circumstances thairof specifeit in the said dittay, quhilk was altogidder denyit be hir to be of verritie, bot be the contrair it was constantlie affirmet and allegit be hir and hir prelocutour, lykas scho offerit hirselff to prove be famous witnesses present at the bar, that eftir the moneth of August lybellit, quhilk is the tyme of the alledget geving of the straikis quhairof the chyld is alledgit to haif deceissit, quha deceissit nocht quhill the xxiii day of Januar thaireftir as is confessit in the dittay, that the said James Johnestoun, the young boy, ane moneth, twa moneth, or thre monethis eftir the said moneth of August lybellit, he went to the scoole and played abrode at dyvers tymes in guid helth without ony hurt or menyie and eftir the examinatioun of Johnne Mathiesoun scolemaister in Leith, William Merschell and James Trumbill, officeris in Leith, as witnesses sworne and admittit be the Justice judiciallie in presens of the said assyse to declair the verritie in the premisses, the saidis persones of assyse removet altogidder furth of court to the assyse house quhair first thay electit and chooset be pluralitie of voittis the said Patrik Johnestoun in chanceller, thaireftir thay ressonet and voittit upone the poyntis of the said dittay and being ryplie and at lenth advyset thairwith and with the alledgeances maid be the said Jonet Corser and hir prelocutouris and answeris maid thairto be his Majesteis Advocat, as also with the depositiones of the saidis witnesses all sworne and examinat judiciallie in face of judgement in thair presens and audience, thay re-enterit agane in court quhair thay, be the oppin declaratioun of the said Patrik Johnestoun, chanceller all in ane voce, fand, pronuncet, and declairet the said Jonet Corser to be cleane, innocent, and acquit of the slauchter of the said umquhile James Johnstoune, the young chyld sone to the said Thomas Johnstoun, and of airt and pairt thairof; Quhairupone the said Jonet Corser and hir prelocutouris askit instrumentis, and protestit, in respect that scho is fund cleane and innocent of the allegit cryme abone writtin be the haill foirnamet persones of assyse, that scho may have the benefeit of the Act of Parliament [1587 cap. 88] for refounding to hir of hir expenses maid be hir in this hir wrangus and malicious persute.

Legal Notes

1. As Hume points out (II.281) the J.D. took a strict view in favour of the panel in ruling (above p. 418) that the L.A. could not extend the criminal letters in which he concurred so as

to charge alternatively murder or wounding. He was forced to proceed on the original charge of murder, reserving the relatives' (but not his own) right to bring a new dittay for the lesser charge.

2. The inclusion in the assize of the two doctors who had treated the child shows how little the functions of witness and assizer were distinguished in the seventeenth century. The schoolmaster referred to in the pleadings was among those cited for jury service. When he was omitted from the jury, he was adduced as a defence witness. See above, pp. 418-420. The terms here of the remit to the jury to try the case 'according to their knowledge and conscience' clearly expect them to use their own knowledge.

3. In this extraordinary and illuminating case the Crown apparently led no evidence at all, apart from taking the oath of calumny from the deceased child's parents, and lodged no documents. Under modern procedure a direction to the jury to return a verdict of 'not guilty' would have been inevitable. But counsel for the defence made no such motion. Instead the assize *ex proprio motu* asked that the four witnesses mentioned by him in his legal submissions should be examined, and the L.A. objected. To modern practitioners this attitude appears inexplicable. But his Lordship can hardly be blamed for his attitude, since when he appeared for the defence in *Edward* v *Scrymgeour* 1619 (Pitcairn III.467) he was refused a proof in exculpation in a case of slaughter (p. 471), though he cited an unreported precedent of 1614, *Strauchan* v *Johnston* (see Hope's *Major Practicks* VIII.xv.12; not in vol. V of Books of Adjournal). The L.A. then pled general practice to which treason, he said, was a statutory exception under 1587 cap. 91, a very doubtful interpretation of the Act. The Crown advanced three reasons: (1) 'It was nevir done befoir in this judgment,' which presumably means no precedent in this Court, to which Mr. Nicolson naturally replied that never before had the Crown led no evidence. (2) In any event, said the L.A., witnesses should only be called at the instance of the panel, to which the obvious answer was that if the assize wanted information, justice required that they should have it. (3) While 1587 cap. 90 (in Glendook cap. 91) makes no express provision for citing witnesses for the defence, as matter of practice, so said his Lordship, a warrant would have been issued either by the J.D. or the Court of Session. This view of practice was sharply challenged for the panel, it being alleged that defence witnesses could only be brought by means of persuasion to the Justice Court, a view supported by Mackenzie's statement of early practice (II.xxii.1; Hume II.398). But in the cases of *William Aird* 1639 (Hume II.258), and *John Anderson* 1641 (above p. 409), such warrants were granted. Mr. Nicolson further added that one of the four had been cited by the Crown 'to pas upone the assyze', to which it was answered that he had not been 'used' by either party and so was free to leave the Court. This may suggest that both parties had the right to select a certain number of jurors, an idea which is not reflected in Hume (II.306) and for which no other evidence has been traced, or it may mean that a witness, having been cited for jury service and not empanelled, could then be used as a witness for either side.

The L.A. wisely withdrew his objections, as there could be no doubt that the J.D. would have repelled them. Hume refers to the case only casually (II.398n), but despite the L.A.'s protest that it be not regarded as a precedent, in fact it was so. It sounded the death knell of the old view that the defence should be denied the opportunity of leading any evidence at all in exculpation. The view formerly taken was, that if the prosecution witnesses failed to establish the charge, the panel as entitled to an acquittal, and required no proof in replication. If the prosecution witnesses proved the charge, it would encourage perjury to allow the panel to lead evidence supporting a defence. 'To admit contrary probation were to open the door to perjury' (McKenzie II.xxii.2). Special defences were originally the only exception (see McKechnie 'Judicial Process upon Brieves' p. 12) and the following case (Hume II.297).

4. It would be difficult to find a worse example of hearsay evidence than that of common report on p. 420 above, but it was, as the present record proves, regularly used, especially in witchcraft cases.

Prefatory Note to Argyll v *Mr. John Stewart*

This was another prosecution for Leasing-making—'the old mystery of iniquity in Scots Law' (Hallam, *Constitutional History* III. p. 287)—by slandering a nobleman in suggesting that his political activities amounted to near treason, like that of Lord Ochiltree in 1631 (above I.170), but this time pressed to a fatal conclusion. The law here was such that no man engaged in political affairs or expressing views thereon could be considered safe.

Mr. John Stewart, like his father, Commissary of Dunkeld, was well known in Athol. As a pawn in the contest between Montrose and Argyll, who respectively followed him to the scaffold in 1650 and 1661, he was described by Mark Napier (*Memorials* II.903) as 'the first sacrifice in the shambles of the Covenant'. There can be no doubt that in the disturbed state of the country, these proceedings were designed to intimidate any, and in particular the party of Montrose, opposed to, or tempted to oppose, the Presbyterian party. The Committee of Estates made this clear. In their remit of the case to the Justice Court they claimed that the statutory penalties 'aucht and suld be execute . . . in maist examplar manner to the terror and example of others to abstain from making of the lyk fals lyes and calumnies'.

The indictment charged the malicious spreading of falsehoods about Argyll calculated to cause discord between the King and Parliament (p. 428). The panel was charged with acting 'furth of . . . maliscious wicked and devillische disposition and perverse desyre of revenge' against the Earl of Argyll 'and consequently against the hail body of the Estait of this Kingdom' in that he 'forged, invented, malisciously devyset' and published by word and writ certain falsehoods.

Head I averred that the panel had told 'to diverse persons' that Argyll's agent, in March 1639, tried to persuade men from Atholl to subscribe a band to follow the Earls of Argyll and Athole; that his agent had tried to persuade the Laird of Weyme, his sons and people to sign a band to follow the Earl . . . without any relation to the publict; and finally that Argyle took a band from 'some cuntrie men in Mar and Garioch' whereby they undertook to do and perform to him whatsoever he required. In each case the gravamen of the allegation is that the alleged bands did not except the allegiance of the signatories to the Crown, and thereby brought Argyll within the statutes proscribing Leagues and Bands under which he could be held guilty of sedition and subjected to severe penalties (1424 c. 30, 1457 c. 77, 1491 c. 34, 1503 c. 87, 1555 c. 43, 1585 c. 12).

Head II averred that the panel alleged in June 1640 in Glenlyon, that Argyll had stated that Parliament would depose the King, and by repeating this to diverse persons sought to engender discord.

Heads III and IV charged the panel with repeating the allegation to Lt. Col. Stewart who in turn reported it at court to the Earl of Traquair, and charged him later with writing to Traquair in similar terms, and also relating them to Montrose.

All this the panel is said to have freely confessed before the Committee of the Estates of Parliament. This committee had investigated the matter both by writ and witnesses, had examined the panel on oath before them, and had concluded by finding that the libel relevatly charged the crime of leasing making and that the accused was guilty thereof. It may be that it was only because the matter was dealt with by a Committee of the Estates that they did not proceed to sentence but remitted the panel to the Justiciary Court 'to be punished for the said crymes' in a 'maist exemplarie manner'. It would however have been competent for them to pass sentence (Mackenzie II.iii.3; Rait, *Parliament*, 66, 376-7). Napier suggests that the move to have the matter remitted to the Justiciary Court was at Argyle's instigation.

The attitude of the Lord Advocate was that the charges had been tried before the Committee of the Estates, but he moved the Court that the accused be put to the knowledge of an assize for the crimes in question with the Decreet of the Committee as proof. The panel does not appear in *Lyon's List* as an advocate, but he must have been a trained lawyer, and though not legally represented was prepared with a number of preliminary pleas; first: that the Lord Advocate needed a special warrant from the King to pursue an offence against the Sovereign; secondly: that in any event to calumniate one subject to another was not a contravention of the statutes libelled, and Traquair had ceased to be Commissioner, and so did not represent His Majesty. He accepts that the allegations attributed to him are scandalous, but though such, do not come within the statutes libelled. At most he concedes he is liable to censure as a slanderer and is willing to give Argyll satisfaction therefor. He made a number of other submissions, viz. (1) that the Estates had agreed to meet to consult only, but not to conclude any matters. If there was contention the matter should be continued until the King was present; (2) that his plea of guilty related only to Head II and meant not that his allegation was fabricated but that he had misunderstood what Argyll had said, and that his allegation about the bands was not invented but based on information received, and so was not malicious. Finally he submitted that all the evidence had not been heard, that witnesses for the defence had still to be examined, and until this had been done the process could not be held to be closed.

The Lord Advocate in reply relied on the terms of the statutes libelled, and on the panel's admission before the Committee of Estates, which was unconditional and could not be withdrawn (cf. below John M'Kathie and others, 20th November 1646 where a judicial declaration was 'past fra'). As to his title to prosecute he claimed that where a private party pursues his own injuries the Lord Advocate might not refuse his concurrence and assistance,if asked, unless he was expressly prohibited by the King.

In the light of the temper of the time and the Decreet of the Committee it is not surprising that none of the panel's submissions were sustained—apparently not even that which sought to adduce further witnesses before the assize. When the assize was empanelled 'the dittay and the whole circumstances as contained in the Decreet' were remitted to them. When the panel was interrogated he 'repeated' his 'admission,' though whether to the whole libel or only to Head II is not clear. The report does not reveal precisely what evidence the jury acted on. It refers to the 'hail circumstances and qualifications producet for verification thairof', and it would appear that the Decreet of the Committee and the panel's confession constituted the evidence. They unanimously found the panel guilty as libelled.

There is no hint in this record of the fact that the originator of these charges was Montrose, who suspected Argyll's ambitions and formed a group called 'the plotters'. According to Montrose's contemporary account he met the accused, Stewart of Grandtully, and Atholl at Scone early in Feburary 1641, and heard from them reports of Argyll's speeches. As Walter Stewart was going to Court on his own affairs he was commissioned to persuade, not Traquair, but the Duke of Lennox (who was a Stewart) to have the King come north to deal with Argyll (Napier's *Memorials* I.295, *et seq.*). Montrose spoke of the reports to his friend, Mr. Robert Murray, minister of Methven. He in turn mentioned them to Mr. John Graham, minister of Auchterarder, who repeated the story to the Auchterarder Presbytery, whence it came to the ears of Argyll. When Murray and Graham were asked for their authority they named Montrose who accepted responsibility and named his witnesses including the accused. The witnesses were examined but all proved unsatisfactory except the panel who on 31st May repeated his allegations. 'My Lord,' said he to Argyll, 'I heard you speak these words in Atholl, in presence of a great many people, whereof you are in good memory,' whereupon he was sent to the Castle (Napier, I.301, 308, 304; Bp. Guthry's *Memoirs*, 2nd edn. 1748, pp. 92-93). There he changed his mind. Either he lost his nerve or succumbed to threats or inducements, probably also to torture. He speaks in his recantation of 'the infirmitie and weekness of my bodie and spreet' and of 'not being able in respect of my weakness ather to stand or gang' (Napier I.298). The Committee instructed Lord Balmerino who had cause to know something of the law on leasing-making, having himself been convicted of the crime (see above I. p. 230): and Gibson of Durie (next year created Lord President) to interview him. Guthry (*Memoirs* p. 93) alleges he was tampered with by them. As a result he withdrew the allegations against Argyll and in a written Recantation admitted he had forged them out of malice (Napier I.297-8). Later he was examined by a Committee of the Estates consisting again of Lord Balmerino, Sir Thomas Hope and a burgess named Edgar. Besides recanting, the panel described discussions between Montrose, Napier and others, and that it was on their instructions that the report of Argyll's speeches had been sent to the King by Walter Stewart. (Guthry, 93-94; Napier, I.328). This recantation is printed in Napier (297-299). His explanation of the second charge was that Argyll had been speaking of kings in general, and that he wrongly attributed the words to Charles I (Napier, I.299-300). The Lord Advocate's second son, Sir Thomas Hope of Kerse, soon to be Lord Justice-General, wrote on 7th June 1641, describing how Walter Stewart the messenger had been intercepted on his way back from London between Cockburnspath and Haddington, and taken to Balmerino's lodging where Kerse joined them. There were found concealed in his saddle *inter alia* a letter from His Majesty that he would attend the next Parliament in Scotland 'to satisfy my people in their religion and just liberties,' papers written in what subsequently appeared to the Committee of Estates to be cypher, and what was called 'a signatour' of the chamberlainry of the Bishopric of Dunkeld to Mr. John Stewart, the panel, with a blank for a pension to Mr. John, but unsigned (Napier I.279). The indictment alleged he had been promised by Traquair the vast sum of £200 sterling a year (p. 433 below). Walter Stewart went to the Castle and so did Montrose.

According to Bishop Guthry, who attended Mr. John during the last hours before his execution, and to Napier, Montrose's biographer, the confession was false and was induced by a promise of Argyll that his life would be saved (and since an unproved charge of treason amounted by itself to treason, his life was in jeopardy if he could not prove his charges), and that he would be given preferment. Guthry narrates that the condemned man bitterly lamented 'the bearing of false witness against himself when he found that the course whereby he thought to have rescued himself from suffering proved the reason of it; this made him querulous against himself as being the causer of his own death'. Spalding reporting the talk of the country said he 'bade be all the speeches he spoke and went to death therewith' (*History* I.333; Guthry, 94; Napier, 297). Both authors stoutly maintain his innocence and certainly the phrase in his deposition bearing 'as not being able in respect of my weakness ather to stand or gang' (Napier 298) makes the inference of torture inescapable. The Parliamentary records for this critical period are defective, but the charge narrates that on 2 July 1641 a Committee of Estates exonerated Argyll, (p. 435) and on the 6th it found Mr. John guilty (below p. 431).

The Estates gave leave for the Justice Court to sit during Parliament and he was hustled into the dock on 21st July (p. 436), while Montrose was powerless to help him. Owing to his pre-trial before the Committee his conviction was a certainty, and he was beheaded at the cross of Edinburgh on the 28th (p. 442). The day before, the Committee refused his appeal for remission or prorogation of sentence as a matter already dealt with by the Criminal Court

—a spurious reason. The fact was they had themselves condemned him in advance. According to Guthry (94), Argyll and the Lord Advocate (Kerse's father) feared that if was pardoned the public would think he had been bribed to recant. They probably did think that, in any event. Baillie thought his execution was 'necessare to make an example: so much the more as his friends, for whose pleasure his lies were invented, were giving out that all was but collusion betwixt him and Argyll who undoubtedly would purchase him a full remission'. From Argyll's point of view and for his vindication he was better out of the way and it is difficult to believe that his (Argyll's) alleged approach to the Lord Advocate to see if a more lenient sentence could be imposed was sincere (Guthry p. 94-5). Walter Stewart was proceeded against before the Estates on 23rd and 24th July, and the other alleged Montrose Plotters were investigated on 4th-5th August (*APS* V.335-6, 664-7).

It is only right to add that Bishop Guthry's account is controverted in Malcolm Laing's *History* (2nd edn., 1804, III.199), where it is asserted that Argyll's well known discretion excludes the possibility of his having acted as the accused said he did, and that certain depositions prove the latter's guilt. Few lawyers however are impressed by the inherent improbability of any charge, and the depositions printed in the *APS* are neutral in character (V.637-9). Those preserved in the Advocates' Library (Woodrow LXV) were carefully examined by Napier, and he rejects Laing's conclusions upon them (*Memorials* I.309). Having regard to the relations between King and Parliament at this date the suggestion that the accused's allegations made matters worse is fantastic. The case produces an uncomfortable feeling, as it did among contemporaries. 'This gentleman,' said Spalding, 'is cruellie execute for words, not before our ordinar Justice or Sheriff Courts according to our Scottish laws but before ane new in-come Committee-Court' (*Trubles* I, 333). Even Baillie, by no means favourable to the accused, had his misgivings. The panel, he said, was 'condemned to die by an old Act of Parliament . . . It is true that none ever died for so transgressing that Act, and Balmerinoch being condemned for an alleged transgression was thought to have gotten great wrong and the preper ative may prove very dangerous. Whereupon some of the Justices were very scrupulous to pronounce sentence.' It is only too likely that if, as he said at his trial (p. 439), he misinterpreted what Argyll said, and was misinformed as to what he did, he did not act maliciously, and had good reason to report matters to authority as a good citizen. The conclusion, that this was a political murder designed to intimidate opponents of the ruling party, is irresistible. Hume's comment (II.16) is that the case 'bears strong marks of the factious and hypocritical temper of the times'. It has the familiar hallmarks of political trials in all ages. The Lord Advocate's anxiety to secure a conviction is shown by his having libelled an Act of Parliament of 1457 which had so far fallen into oblivion that it was omitted from the edition of the statutes then current, which was Skene's of 1597, and was later omitted from Glendook's edition. If Baillie is right that Stewart was the first to die for this crime—in Nicoll a few years earlier the sentence had been banishment (above I. p. 222)—he was not the last. Arnot (125) concludes his account of the matter by noting with satisfaction that 'the son of this very prosecutor fell by an iniquitous sentence on this very charge of leasing making' (see Hume I.350).

(135) [21 July 1641: Colvile and Robertoun JJ.D.]

Forgeing of false leyis and calumnies. Argyle contra *Mr John Stewart. Convict et decollet.*

Assessores to the Justice.[1]—My Lord Elphingstoun; My Lord [Leirmonth] of Balcomy; John Sempill provest of Dumbarten; William Rig of Eddernie.[2]

Intran.—Mr Johne Stewart, son to Mr James Stewart of Ladywall.[3]

Dilaittit of the making forgeing venting and divulgeing of certane fals leyis and calumneis contrair to the Actis of Parliament specifeit in his dittay.

1 These assessors were only appointed the day before, and on the day of the trial Elphinstone as related to Argyll, honourably asked to be excused. He was ordered, however, by, Parliament to do his duty (*APS* V.314, 315). See legal note 1.

2 Athernie (here Eddernie) was in Fife (see *RMS* VIII.413). Rigg had lands in other parts of Scotland (see e.g. Stirling Retours, 180), many of which he held of the Lord Advocate (*RMS* IX.620).

3 Ladywell is at Dunkeld, of which the panel was Commissary.

Persewaris.—Archibald, Erle of Argyle etc.; Sir Thomas Hope of Craighall, knycht barronet, his Majesteis Advocat, for his Hienes intreis.

Compeirit George Campbell, servitour to Archibald, Erle of Argyle etc., and producet ane supplicatioun gevin in to the Estaittis of the Parliament now sittand, with ane delyverance upone the bak thairof subscryved be my Lord Burghlie preses *I.P.D. Parliamenti*, quhairof the tennour followis: My Lordis and utheris of the Estaittis of Parliament, unto your Lordships humblie **(136)** meanis and schawis your Lordships servitouris Archibald, Erle of Argyle, and Sir Thomas Hope of Craighall, his Majesteis Advocat, that quhair befoir, the downsitting of this present Parliament thair was ane criminall persute intented and depending at our instance befoir his Majesteis Justice Generall and Justice Deputtis against Mr Johnne Stewart, sone to Mr James Stewart of Ladywall, for certane wicked and pernicious fals leasingis and calumneis maist maliciouslie forged, vented, and devulged be him, tending nocht only to the great hurt and prejudice of me, the said Erle of Argyle in my persone, credeit, honour, and estait, bot also to the engendring of discord betwixt our dread Soverane, the Kingis Majestie, and the Estaittis of Parliament, the dyet of the whilk criminall persute is set to be within the tolbuth of Edinburgh upone the xxi day of Julii instant, and seing in tyme of Parliament Justice courtis can nocht weill be haldin without warrand frome the Parliament swa that the said Justice Generall nor Deputtis can nocht hald the said Justice Court nor proceid to the doeing of justice in the said matter without your Lordships warrand,[1] heirfoir we maist humblie beseik your Lordships and utheris of the Estaittis of Parliament presentlie convenit to be pleased to grant warrand to the saidis Justice Generall or Justice Deputis, thair clerkis, officeris and haill memberis of court, for holding of the said Justice court to the finall end thairof, and to dispense with thaime [*sic*] and the assyse thairanent, nochtwithstanding of the sitting of the Parliament, and your Lordships answer; *Sic subscribitur*, Sir Thomas Hope. Followis the delyverance on the bak thairof: *Apud* Edinburgh *vigesimo Julii* 1641: The haill Estaittis of Parliament, upone goode considerationes grantis the desyre of the supplicatioun within writtin; and farder the Estaittis nominattis and gevis the Lord Elphingstoun, the Laird of Athernie, Johnne Semple, Commissioner for Dumbarten, and Sir James Leirmonth of Balcomie, knycht, ane of the Senatoures of the Colledge of Justice, to be assessouris to the Justice Generall or his Deputtis in the haill proces within specifeit; And ordanis the procuratouris for the Estaittis to concur with the Kingis Advocat in the persute within writtin *Sic subscribitur* Burghly, *I.P.D. Parliamenti etc.*; *Item* the Estaittis of Parliament adjoynes the four persones abone writtin to the Justice or his deputtis in the proces within writtin or ony thre of thame, quhich number thay appoint to be ane quorum: *Sic subscribitur* Burghly *Praeses, I.P.D. Parliamenti.*[2] Eftir production and reiding of the quhilk suplicatioun with the delyverance abone writtin beiring thairwith the nominatioun of the assessouris abonewrittin, lykas the saidis assessouris, being judiciallie present and being sworne be the Justice, gave thair aithes *de fideli administratione*, quhairupone the said George Campbell askit instrumentis.

[1] See legal note 2.
[2] *APS* V.314.

The pannell thaireftir being demandit gif he had ony procuratouris to defend, or gif he had ony thing to say quhy the dittay producet agains him sould nocht pas to the knawledge of ane assyse, for answeir thairto declairet that he nather hes nor wald use ony prelocutouris in this matter, becaus he haifing socht thair advyce it was schawin be thame to him that thay could nocht defend for him in respect that the crymes specifeit in his dittay war confessit be him in presens of the Committie of Estaittis, and that he had submittit himselff to the Parliament.[1]

My Lord of Argyle as persewar, being present, representit to the Judges the necessitie of his attendance at the Parliament, and thairfoir cravet licence to repair thairto schawing that his Majesteis Advocat wald supplie his absence in persute of the pannell for the crymes contenit in his dittay, bot gif the Judges heir have necessarlie to do with his awin presence he sould returne upone adverteisment, and thairfoir cravet licence to remove for the present.

Thaireftir his Majesteis Advocat producet the dittay agains the pannell desyreing the samyn to be red, quhairof the tennour followis: Mr Johne Stewart, sone to Mr James Stewart of Ladywall, ye ar indyttit and accuset; Forsamekill as albeit be the commoun law of all nationes, municipall lawis and Actis of Parliament of this kingdome, speciallie be the 43 Act of the secound Parliament of our Soverane Lordis most royall Ancestour King James the First[2] of everlesting memorie it is expreslie provydit, statute, and ordanit be the King and haill Estaittis of Parliament that all leasing makeris and telleris of thame quhilk may engender discoird betwix the King and his people, quhair evir thay may be gottin, sall be challanget be thame that power hes, and sall tyne lyfe and guidis to the King, quhilk Act is thaireftir repeitted be ane uther Act of Parliament maid also be his Majesteis darrest ancestour, King James the Secound, in his 14 Parliament cap. 100,[3] and siclyk thaireftir be his Majesteis darrest grandsire King James the Fyft Parliament 6,[4] the samyn Actis of Parliament ar renewit, ratifeit, and approven, and ordanit to be put in executioun in all poyntis, in lyk maner be the 205 Act of the fourtene Parliament haldin be our Soverane Lordis darrest fader King James the Saxt of happie and blissed memorie in the moneth of Junii 1594 yeiris, intitulat against leasing makeris,[5] the saidis thre severall Actis of Parliament maid against leasing makeris ar expreslie ratifeit and ordanit to be put to executioun in all tyme cumming, lykas also in the lait Actis of Parliament maid be the thre Estaittis of this Kingdome in the moneth of Junii 1640,[6] to the quhilk the Kingis most excellent Majestie hes gevin his royall assent in the articles of treattie, the haill former Actis of Parliament maid against leasing makeris ar renewit and revived; Nochtwithstanding quhairof it is of veritie that ye, the said Mr Johnne Stewart, expres contrair to the saidis lawis and Actis of Parliament, schaiking of all feir of the Almychtie God, regaird of religioun and guid conscience, furth of your malicious wicked and devillische dispositioun and perverse desyre of revendge against his Majesteis richt trest

1 See legal note 3.
2 1424 cap. 43.
3 Referred to but not printed in Glendook and Skene (see *APS* II.52).
4 1540 cap. 83.
5 1594 cap. 209 in Glendook, 'Anent leasing-makers and authors of slanders.'
6 *APS* V. (1639) 604, 667; (1640) 289 cap. 41.

cousing and counsallour, Archibald, Erle of Argyle etc. his lyfe, honour, and estait, and consequentlie against the haill body of the estait of this Kingdome,[1] upone whome the fals leyis and wicked calumneis eftir specifeit (hatched and invented be you the said Mr Johne) reflexis and trinches, nocht only maist falslie and intreulie have ye, the said Mr Johne, forget, invented, and maliciouslie devyset, the fals and odious leies and calumneis respective and particularlie eftirfollowing, bot also hes vented, publeisched and as ane impudent and affronted leyar hes divulget the samyn in dyverse places to sindrie persones bothe be word and writt in maner and at the tymes respective and particularlie underwrittin; viz [I (1)] ye the said Mr Johne Stewart maist falslie maliciouslie and as ane impudent liear and calumniatour, have spokin and averred to dyverse persones that [Mungo Campbell] the Laird of Laweris, younger, and the barrone of Comerie, namet Alexander Menzeis, in name and to the behove of the said Archibald, Erle of Argyle, presented ane band to be subscryvet be the said Athole men than being at Logierait with the Erle of Athole, in the moneth of Merch 1639 yeiris, the tennour quhairof was (as ye the said Mr Johne falslie repoirted) to follow the saidis Erles of Argyle and Athole; [2] Lykas ye the said Mr Johne, as ane impudent liear, have maist falslie and untreulie spokin and affirmed to dyverse persones and in dyverse places that quhan some of the Erle of Argyle his people (quhome ye named to be his airmy) war at Balloche,[2] goeing for the brig of Die in *anno* 1639, that thair was ane uther band presented in Weyme[3] be [John Campbell] the laird of Glenlyone and the barrone of Comerie in the said Erle of Argyle his name, quhilk was prest to be subscryvet be [Sir Alexander Menzies] the laird of Weyme his sones and people, the tennour quhairof was as ye the said Mr Johne maist untrewlie did affirme, to follow the said Erle of Argyle without ony relatioun to the publict, quhilk band ye affirmed that ye saw and red; [3] and siclyk ye the said Mr Johne as ane impudent liear have maist falslie and untreulie said and affirmed to dyverse persones that thair was ane band takin be the Erle of Argyle of some countriemen in Mar, Garioche and in thaise boundis, the tennour quhairof was absolutelie to the said Erle of Argyle himselff to doe and performe to him quhatsoevir he sould requyre at the subscryveris handis, the coppie of the quhilk band ye the said Mr John have affirmed most falslie that ye saw in Robert Farquharsone of Innercald his hand in presens of Johne Stewart of Scheirglas, John Stewart of Innercharnochan[4] and utheris; Quhilkis wicked and abhominable leyis swa maid and devysed be you upone and concerning the saidis bandis was to draw the said Archibald, Erle of Argyle, within the comptis of the Actis of Parliament and perrell thairof maid against legues and bandis quhilkis ar puneischeable as seditioun, and of thair awin nature tendis to ingender discord betwix our most gracious soverane the Kings most excellent Majestie and his lordis and barrones.[5]

1 This seems an obvious *non sequitur*.

2 Now Taymouth Castle.

3 Near Aberfeldy.

4 The latter was charged with resetting rebels on 7 February 1637 (*RPC*² VI.375). The former and the latter's son were out with Montrose in 1645 (*APS* VI. Pt. 1. 31). Shierglass is 1 mile SE of Blair Atholl; Auchanachie (?=Innercharnochan) is 4½ miles NE of Huntly.

5 See legal note 4.

[II] And farder ye the said Mr Johne have bene swa impudentlie fals, perverse, and wicked in your devillische and monstrowus plottis and hellische devyces nocht only against the said Archibald, Erle of Argyle, his honour and estait, bot **(138)** also against the staittis of Parliament of this kingdome, in swa far as ye have maist falslie affirmet to dyverse persones of all qualiteis and rankis alsweill be word as be writt, that the said Archibald, Erle of Argyle, in his tent at the fuird of Lyoun[1] in the moneth of Junii 1640 yeiris did affirme in ane discourse had and maid be him to the said Erle of Athole and the rest of the Athole prissoneris being thair for the tyme, (quhairof ye the said Mr Johne was ane), that the Parliament haldin in the moneth of Junii 1640 yeiris wald have begune at the deposeing of the King frome his Majesteis regall power and soverane auctoritie, and how evir thay had continewit the doeing of it at that tyme yit that it wald be first thing that thay wald begyn at in the nixt sessioun of Parliament.[2]

[III] Lykas ye, the said Mr Johne, nocht only have maist maliciouslie and wickedlie forged, invented, plotted and devysed the saidis notorious and montrowus leis and fals calumneis against the said Erle of Argyle, intending thairby no les nor his Lordships utter overthraw and ruinatting of his lyfe, honour and estait, bot also by the same your devillisch purpois and intentioun to mak the said noble Erle of Argyle odious to the Kingis most excellent Majestie his prince and soverane, and seditiouslie to engender discord and dissentioun betwix his Majestie and the Estaittis of Parliament of this his Hienes kingdome, hes vented, dispersed, and devulged the saidis odious lieis and fals calumneis to dyverse and sindrie persones of all rankis and qualiteis, bothe be word and writt, and namelie ye the said Mr Johne did vent and devuldge the saidis devillisch and notorious lieis and fals calumneis to Leutennent Colonell Walter Stewart at that tyme, quhan as ye war confynet within the burght of Edinburgh betwixt the monethis of Julii and November 1640 yeiris, lykas the said Colonell Walter Stewart repairing thaireftir to Court [in London] impairted the saidis wicked leyis and calumneis to the Erle of Traquhair and informed him thairof, and the said Leutennent Colonell Stewart, eftir his returne frome court in the monethe of Merche last, (ye and the said Leutennent Colonell meitting togidder within the burgh of Edinburgh), the said Leutennent Colonell askit of you gif ye rememberit of the discourse betwix him and you the tyme foirsaid of your confynement, quhairby ye the said Mr Johne, had related to the said Leutennent Colonell Stewart the foirsaid damnable and detestable lie and fals calumnie anent the deposeing of the Kings Majestie frome his royall governament be the Estaittis of Parliament, quhairunto ye, the said Mr Johne, maid answeir that ye did remember, at quhilk tyme ye, the said Mr Johne, did repeit and renew the said wicked and abhominable discourse and fals calumneis, quhilk discourse the said Leutennent Colonell Stewart tald to you, the said Mr John, that he had impairted the same to some at court and namelie [particularly] to the said Erle of Traquair, quho earnestlie desyret to know the certantie thairof; Lykas ye the said Mr John at the desyre of the said Leutennent Colonell Stewart, drew up and delyverit at that same tyme to the Leutennent Colonell the foirsaid

[1] The ford was just E of Fortingall.

[2] For an account of the incident see the *Memoirs* of Henry Guthry, Bishop of Dunkeld, 2nd edn., 1748, p. 24-6.

wicked and fals lie in writt under your hand, and thairwith ye than also wrait ane letter direct to the said Erle of Traquair beiring the saidis fals leyis and calumneis anent the deposeing and degraiding of the Kingis Majestie frome his Hienes royall power and governament at the tyme and in maner foirsaid, the quhilkis paper and letter contening the saidis fals and damnable leyis the said Leutennent Colonell Stewart delyverit to the said Erle of Traquair at court with his Majestie, quha in your opinioun had bene than standing his Majesteis Hegh Commissioner undischarged, quhilk is alyk as gif ye the said Mr John had spokin and delaited the saidis fals leyis to the Kingis Majestie himself;[1]

[IV] And ye, the said Mr Johne, nocht being content to vent the saidis wicked speches, fals calumneis and leyis to the said Leutennent Colonell Stewart, and to informe the said Erle of Traquair thairof be your letter, ye have lykwayis ventit, spokin, and divulget the foirsaidis haill wicked and fals leyis and claumneis to the Erle of Montrois and dyverse utheris persones of severall rankis, and, out of ane deip haitfull and precogitat malice agains the said Archibald, Erle of Argyle, his honour, credeit, and estait, and reflecting gritlie upone the haill Estaittis of Parliament, hes gevin and sent ane paper contening in writ the saidis haill wicked and malicious leyis and calumneis to the said Erle of Montrois; quhilkis wicked and pernitious leyis and calumneis ar of suche ane heiche and abhominable strayne that the samyn tendit nocht only to the said Erle of Argyle his utter ruyne bot also to the ingendring of discord betwix the Kingis Most Excellent Majestie and his saidis Estaittis of Parliament, lykas ye the said Mr
(139) John being convenit befoir the Committie of Estaittis of Parliament,[2] and being dyverse tymes examinat upone oath befoir thame anent the saidis dâmnable leyis and fals calumneis, haill circumstances and qualificationes thairof, ye be your judiciall confessioun maid and subscryvit be you in presens of the saidis Lordis, have granted and confessit the haill premisses, and that the samyn war fals leyis and calumneis falslie forged be you and vented be you as said is; And quhat is nocht proven be your confessioun is provin be witnesses as is cleir and evident be the act and decreit eftir specifeit; Lyk(as) the said Committie of Estaittis haveing tane all lawfull tryell bothe be writt and witnesses concerning the saidis leyis and calumneis, and haveing at lenth sene and seriouslie considderit the same with youris the said Mr Johnes awin confessioun and missive letters subscryvit be you, thay be thair decreit of the dait at Edinburgh the saxt day of Julii instant have fund the haill heidis poyntis, and articles of the saidis dittayis, with the haill qualificationes thairof abonewrittin and contenit in the said decreit beiring the samyn crymes to be manifest leasingis, tending nocht only to the said Erle of Argyle his utter ruine, bot also to the engendering of seditioun and discord betwix the Kingis Majestie and his Estaittis of Parliament sufficientlie verifeit and proven; And thairfoir the saidis Lordis and utheris of the Committie of the Estaittis of Parliament have fund and declairet you, the said Mr John Stewart, nocht only to be culpable and guiltie[3] alsweill of the making of the saidis wicked and fals leasingis and calumneis anent the saidis thre bandis alledget presented

1 See p. 433 below.
2 There is no record of this in *APS*.
3 See legal note 5.

and takin be the said Archibald, Erle of Argyle, and utheris persones foirsaidis, as of the wicked forgeing, inventing and devyseing of the saidis most damnable and abhominable leasingis and calumneis anent the deposeing of our Soverane Lord frome his Majesteis royall power and governament be the saidis Estaittis of Parliament, bot also to be culpable and guiltie of the said malicious venting, disperseing, and devulgeing of the samyn haill wicket and abhominable leasingis and calumneis respective and particulerlie abonewrittin both be word and writt, in maner, forme, and to the effect abone specifeit, quhilkis wicked, odious, and pernitious leasingis and calumneis swa forget, invented, devysed and maliciouslie vented, dispersed, and devulget be you, the said Mr John Stewart, as said is, the saidis Lordis and utheris of the Committie of Estaittis hes fund and declaret be thair said decreit to be prohibeit be the saidis Actis of Parliament and to fall within the compas thairof, and that ye the said Mr Johne throwe your wicked and malicious forgeing, inventing, devyseing, venting, disperseing, and divulgeing of the former wicked and damnable fals leasingis and calumneis, as said is, have contravenit the tennour of the saidis Actis of Parliament; And thairfoir be thair said decreit hes remittit you to the Justice Generall and Justice Deputis to be puneischet for the saidis crymes accordinglie, as in the said decreit at lenth is contenit; The quhilkis panes and puneischment mentionat in the saidis lawis and Actis of Parliament aucht and sould be execute upone you in maist exemplarie maner to the terrour and example of utheris to abstene fra making of the lyk fals leyis and calumneis venting and devulgeing thairof in tyme cuming etc. Eftir reiding of the quhilk dittay and accusatioun of the said Mr Johnne of the crymes foirsaidis thairin contenit, my Lord Advocat askit instrumentis of the reiding thairof, quhilkis factis and deidis mentionet thairin his Majesteis Advocat declairet that thai war tryit and verifeit befoir the Lordis and utheris of the Committie of the Estaittis of Parliament, and for verificatioun thairof producet the said decreit of Committie, quhilk his Lordship desyret to be lykwayis publictlie red, off the quhilk decreit the tennour followis: [*Decree of Committee of Estates*].

At Edinburgh the saxt day of July the yeir of God jmvic fourtie ane yeiris: Anent the supplicatioun or bill of complent presented and gevin in to the Lordis and utheris of the Committie of the Estaittis of Parliament[1] be ane noble Erle, Archibald, Erle of Argyle etc. against Mr Johne Stewart, sone to Mr James Stewart of Ladywall, makand mentioun that quhair, albeit be the commoun
(140) lawis and practique of this realme, and namelie be the 43 Acts of the secound Parliament of King James the First, it is ordaned be the King and haill Parliament that all leasing makeris and telleris of thame, quhilk may engender discoird betwix the King and his people, quhair evir thay may be gottin, sall be challanged be thame that power hes, and tyne lyfe and guidis to the King, and be the 205 Act of the 14 Parliament of King James the Saxt intituled anent leasing makeris the former Act is ratifeid and approvin, yit nocht withstanding thairof the said Mr John Stewart haveing schaikin af all feir of God and regaird of religioun and conscience, out of ane malicious wicked, and devillische dispositioun, and unjust desyre of revendge against the said Erle of Argyle, hes nocht only forged invented, and devysed the fals wicked and odious calumneis

[1] No record in *APS*.

and leas respective and particularlie eftir following, bot also hes ventet publeisched and divulged the samyn in dyverse places to sindrie persones bothe be word and wreat in maner and at the tymes particularlie underwrittin, viz. [the above particular occasions are repeated here in the record *ad longam* and are omitted here, except for the incident relating to the Earl of Traquair at p. 430 above which is elaborated as follows] . . . And quhilkis paiper and letter contening the said fals and unhappie discours the said Lieutennent Colonell Stewart delyverit to the said Erle of Traquair and quhilk abhominabill lie and calumnlie swa forgit, emittit, disperst, and divulgit be word and writt be the said Mr Johnne at severall tymis and to severall personis and speciallie to the said Erle of Traquair being than at court moist be presumit to haife beine impairtit be the said Erle to the Kingis Majestie, and the said Mr Johnne in swa doing hes beine ane maker and teller of leasingis to the King upoun and againes his peopill and loyall subjectis to make discoird betwix thame in swa far as he hes maid and impartit the saidis leasingis to the Kingis Majesties principall thesaurer and his Majesties lait Heigh Commissioner for the Parliament, haifeing in the oppinioun of the said Mr Johnne both the saidis offices in his persoune standing undischargit, quhilk is alyke in effect to the said Mr Johnne as gif he had tald the saidis leasingis to the Kingis Majestie himselff, seing the thesaurer is he at quhais instance the crymis and offences contenit in the saidis leaseingis ar propper to be persewit in the King his name for his Majesties intreis, and also that he quha in the said Mr Johnne his oppinioun was his Majesties Commissioner and so supreame Judge representing his Majestie to cognosce of such crymis and offences, and also the said Erle being ane of his Majesties Privie Counsallouris and being for the tyme actuallie and frequentlie conversant about his Majesties persoune at court fuirth of the kingdome, and haifeing thairby faceill [facile] and easie access and opportunitie to acquent his Majestie with these devlisch purpoisses for sawing of discoird betwix his Majestie and his good subjectis, and to hatche and invent ane grund of recriminatioun againes the said Erle of Argyll as ane of his Majesties subjectis (quhome he constructit be reassoune of the said Erle his plaice and commissioun quhairin the saidis Estaittis did imploy him against thair enemeis) to be a furtherer of the persuitt aganes the said Erle befoir the Parliament as ane enimie to the King and kingdome;[1] And quhilk Erle did so earnestlie imbraice the occasioun of the said Mr Johnne his leyis, that he causit offer to him ane pensioun of twa hundreth pund sterling be yeir duiring his lyftyme to abyd be and furnisch probatioun of the saidis leaseingis, quhilk the said Mr Johnne hes confest in his depositioune; Lykeas it is maist probabill that be the said Mr Johnne Stewartis leying to the said Erle of Traquair the same hes come to his **(142)** Majesties eare and knawledge be the said Erle, seing his Majestie, eftir that the said Mr Johnne had acquentit the said Erle thairwith, did earnestlie insist with the Commissioneris of Estait being than at court to pas fra the said Erle of Traquair and the persuitt intentit againes him befoir the Parliament, or els that thair micht be reservit to his Majesties actioun or persuitt befoir the Parliament or uther Judges againes any uther noblemen quha had assistit and

[1] The text here is confused but the meaning is that the accused understood that Traquair was bound *ex officio* to take up the case against Argyll.

countenanced the guid caus, to quhais chairge he micht lay any capitall cryme nochtwithstanding of the Act of Oblivioun or pacificatioun maid or to be maid, quhilk insisting and reservatioun cannot be bot vehementlie presumit to haife risen from the said Mr Johnne Stewartis fals leaseingis to the Erle of Traquair and suggestit be the said Erle to the King againes the Parliament, and the said Erle of Argyll for his forwardnes in the publict guid caus, and in so far as he hes maid and told the saidis leaseingis upoun and againes the said Erle, being imployit be vertew of ane commissioun put and imposit upoun him be the saidis Lordis and utheris of the said Committe of Estaitts for composeing and taking ordour with the enemeis of the King estait, and kingdome within Athole and utheris pairtis, it is alyk in effect as gif he had maid and told the saidis leaseingis againes the Estaitts representing the haill body of his Majesteis loyall subjectis, quhilk making and telling of leaseingis conteaning the forgit, odious, fearfull crymis and offences thairin set down, to the King, his thesaurer, and Heigh Commissioner, undischargit in the oppinioun of the said Mr Johnne as said is, upoun and againes the Estaitts and thair Commissioner, and his cariadge in the discharge of his commissioun as such leaseingis as micht engender discoird betwix the Kingis Majestie and his peopill, and so fallis directlie under the saidis Actis of Parliament and deservis the paines and punischmentis thairincontenit; Lykeas the said Mr Johne, not being content to vent the saidis wicked speiches, calumneis, and leyis to the said Lieutennent Colonell Stewart and to informe the said Erle of Traquair thairof, be his said letter hes lykwayis ventit, spokin, and divulgit the foirsaidis haill leyis and calumneis to the Erle of Montrois and diverse utheris personis of severall rankis, and hes given and sent ane paiper contening in writt the saidis haill wicked and malicious leyis and calumneis to the said Erle of Montroiss out of ane deip haitfull and precogitat malice againes the said Erle of Argyll, his honnour, credit, and estaitt, and reflecting greatlie upoun the saidis estaitts of Parliament, quhilkis wicked and pernicious leyis and calumneis ar of such ane height and abhominabill straine that the samyn tendit not only to his utter runie bot also to the engendering of seditioun and discoird betwix the Kingis Majestie and the Estaitts of Parliament; Lykeas the said Mr Johnne Stewart be his depositionis and missive letteris takin and lying befoir the said Comitte of Estaitts hes cleirlie confest the wicked forgeing, inventing, and devyseing of the said damnabill and abhominabill lie and calumnie anent the deposeing of the King be the Parliament and his malicious venting dispersing and divulgeing thairof in maner abovewrittin; Lykeas also it is cleir and manifest be the saidis depositionis, and the depositionis of utheris, takin **(143)** befoir the said Committee that the first three speiches ventit be the said Mr Johnne anent the presenting and pressing of the saidis three bandis to be subscryvit as said is ar fundin be the tryell, takin befoir the said Committie, to be manifest leyis and calumneis, as the saidis depositionis and missive letteris takin and lying befoir the said Committe will cleirlie instruct, and be the quhilkis depositionis the said Committe of Estaitts will also find that the said Mr Johnne hes perjurit himselff in sindrie poyntis, and seing by forgeing, inventing, and dispersing of the saidis wicked, fals, and treicherous calumneis and leyis, and by venting, disperseing, and divyseing and divulgeing thairof to dyverse persones off all rankis and qualiteis and in diverse places, both be word and writt, as is cleir and manifest by dyverse depositiones emittit be the said Mr

John befoir the said Committie of Estaittis and missive letters under his awin hand, the said Mr Johne Stewart hes contraveind the saidis Actis of Parliament and hes incurret the severall panes and puneishement thairin contenit, desyreing the said committe to be pleased to tak the premisses, togidder with the said Mr John his awin depositiones and missive letters and all uther depositiones concerning the saidis leyis and calumneis, seriouslie to thair consideratioun, and to geve furth thair judgement and determinatioun anent the cleiring of the said Erle of Argyle his innocencie, and vindicating of him his name, honour, and credeit frome the saidis wicked, abhominable, and malicious leyis and calumneis, and anent the puneischment deu to the said Mr Johne for the same be the saidis lawis and Actis of Parliament and all utheris lawis and actis maid thairanent, as the said Committee of Estaittis sould think fitt and expedient, as the said supplicatioun or bill of complent at lenth beiris. Eftir publict reiding of the quhilk supplicatioun or bill of complent in presens of the said Committie, upone the secound day of Julii instant, the same was be thair warrand delyverit to the said Mr Johne Stewart to sie, and he was ordaned to be reddie to answeir thairto quhan the said Committie sould desyre; and than it was also ordanit in presence of the said Mr Johne and in his heiring that ony freindis or laweyris he pleased to call for sould have frie acces to repair to him that he might advyse and consult with thame in the bussines; And the said Mr Johne being this day callit for and brocht befoir the said Committie and haveing reproduced in judgement the said supplicatioun or bill of complent he was desyret to geve answeir to the same, quha declaired he wald mak no answeir to the said supplicatioun or bill of complent bot declairet he pleidit guiltie, and referred himselff in the said Committeis will and the said Erle of Argyle's, quhome he declairet to be frie of all the foirsaidis leasingis and calumneis alledged be him and contenit in the foirsaid supplication, quhilk declaratioun he subscryvit with his hand upone the foirsaid bill of complent whilk was delyverit to him of befoir upone the said secound day of Julii instant and reproduced be him this day in judgement as said is; and thaireftir both the saidis pairteis being removed, and the saidis Lords and utheris of the said Committie of Estaittis of Parliament haveing at lenth hard, sene, and seriouslie considderit the said supplicatioun with the said Mr Johne his awin depositiones, confessiones, missive letters, and haill remanent depositiones and declarationes and uther tryellis lying and takin befoir thame in the said matter, with his awin judicial declaratioun and confessioun this day in presens of the said Committie subscryvit with his hand as said is, togidder with the decreit gevin and pronuncet be the said Committie upone the said secound day of Julii instant quhairby the said Erle of Argyle is cleired, fred, and *simpliciter* assoilyeid, fra all the wicked odious damnable and fals leasingis and calumneis abone mentioned, and being thairwith ryplie and at lenth advyset the saidis Lordis and utheris of the Committie of the Estaittis of Parliament, findis and declaires the said Mr Johnne Stewart not only to be culpabill and guiltie, alsweill of the making of the saidis wicked and fals leaseingis and calumneis anent the saidis three bandis alledgit presentit and takin be the said Erle of Argyll and utheris personis foirsaidis, as of the wicked forgeing, venting, and devyseing of the said moist damnabill and abhominabill leaseing and calumnie anent the deposeing of our said dread Soverane the Kingis Majestie be the Parliament. Bot also to be culpabill and guiltie of the said malicious venting, dispersing, and divulgeing of the samyn haill wicked and abhominabill leaseingis and calumnies respective, and perticularlie abonewrittin, both be word and writt, in mainer, forme, and to the effect abovespecifeit, and quhilkis wicked odious and pernicious leaseingis and calumneis swa forgit, inventit, devysit, and maliciouslie ventit, disperst and divulgit be the said Mr Johnne Stewart as said is, the saidis Lordis and utheris of the Committe findis and declairis to be prohibeited be the saidis Actis of Parliament and to fall within the compas thairof, and that the said Mr Johnne throw his wicked forgeing, inventing, devyseing, venting, dispersing and divulgeing of the saidis wicked and damnabill fals leaseingis and calumneis as said is, hes contravenit the foirsaidis Actis of Parliament, and thairfoir the said Committee of Estaittis remittis the said Mr Johnne Stewart to the Justice Generall or his Deputtis to be puneist for the saidis crymis accordinglie, becaus the said Committe fand the haill heidis poyntis and articles of the said supplicatioun or bill of complaint abonespecifeit with the haill qualificationis thairof abonewrittin beiring the samyn to be leaseingis, tending not only to the said Erle of Argyll his utter ruine, bot also to the engendering of seditioun and discoird betwix the Kingis Majestie and the Estaittis of Parliament, sufficientlie verefiet and provin, as was cleirlie understuid to the said Committe, and thairfoir they haife fund and declairit the said Mr John to be guiltie and remittit him to be punischt in manner abonementionat *Extractum de libris actorum dictorum Commissionariorum per me etc. Sic subscribitur* A. Hepburne.

My Lord Advocat askit instrumentis of the reiding of the said decreit in the presence and audience of the Justice and assessouris, and desyret conforme thairto that the said Mr Johne may be put to the knawlege of ane assyse for the crymes foirsaidis specifeit in his dittay and decreit producet for verificatioun thairof.

The said Mr Johne Stewart, being inquyret quhidder he had anything to say quhy the dittay producet, and the decreit with the verificatioun, sould nocht be put to the knawlege of ane assyse; [1st Defence, Head I] Quha for answer thairto declairet that he objectis agains my Lord Advocat his compeirance, and allegit that nochtwithstanding of the lybell and summondis producet agains him, quhilkis ar foundit upone the Actis of Parliament, it is trew and of verritie that the Actis mentionet thairin ar only conceavet in favour of the Kings Majestie and his royall predicessouris, agains sic as makis leasingis and scandalous speiches against thair royall persones and against his counsallouris, and thairfoir he can nocht be accuset for brek of the saidis Actis, nor incur the panes thairin contenit, seing thair is nothing provin nor declairet agains the pannell quhilk may infer ony leasing or scandalus speach agains his Majesteis royall persone, nather can he be convenit nor persewit for the saidis factis contenit in the lybell and dittay at the Kingis Majesteis his Advocatis instance, for his Majesteis intreis, without his Lordship, as Advocat, have ane speciall warrand under his Majesteis hand for that effect; [Head II] And as for the speich and calumneis quhairupone the pannell is now accuset, being only spokin be him of ane subject to ane subject, nawayis prejudiciall to his Majesteis honour and dignitie, can nevir bring him under the compas of the saidis Actis of Parliament conforme to the desyre of the lybell and dittay, seing the pannell nevir aither by letter or word did dilait ony speiches as the lybell beiris to his Majesteis selff against the Erle of Argyle; And, quhairas it is alledgit that he acquented **(145)** the Erle of Traquair thairwith be his letter, quhilk is alsmuche as gif he had acquented the King himselff, he being (as the pannell thocht) at that tyme Heigh Commissioner, it is answerit thairto that lang befoir that tyme it was trew that befoir the ressait of that letter, (gif he did ressave the samyn), the said Erle had dimittit his place as Commissioner, at the leist the Estattis of this kingdome upone guid respectis and considerationes moveing thame at the prorogatioun of ilk tyme of the Pairliament did tak dyverse protestationes against him that his commissioun was becum ineffectual, and that he sould nevir be Commissioner as the saidis protestationes beiris, so that the sending of the said letter be the pannell to the Erle of Traquair can infer no farder danger against him nor as gif he had sent the samyn to ony uther particular persone, nather is thair ony thing produced for preveing of the said letter or ony thing thairof to have cum to his Majesteis knawlege; [Head III] And howbeit he war guiltie of the factis contenit in the said lybell and dittay in swa far as concerned the said Erle of Argyle, quhilk the pannell confesses is scandalus, yit be the lawis of this realme the samyn can nocht cum under the compas of the saidis Actis of Parliament, bot only that he be censuret thairfoir as ane sclanderar befoir the Judge ordiner, and in place of ony satisffactioun that he sould be injoyned to doe be the ordinar Judge to the said Erle for his calumneis and utheris spokin be the pannell against his Lordship, he is now, as of befoir, content to mak ony satisffactioun and obedience to his Lordship that his Lordship will demand, hoiping that his Lordship out of his generous goode mynd and dispositioun will accept thairof, nochtwithstanding of ony decreit gevin be the Committie in contrair of the pannell and summondis and dittay raiset thairupone, seing that in respect of the pannell his voluntar and ingenowus confessioun, the probatioun led agains him, the decreit of the Committie thairupoun, the imputation of thaise calumneis redoundit to the pannell himselff and nawayis to the said honorabill Erle and hoipes that his Lordship will nevir incroache farder upone him.

(145) To the whilkis it is answerit be his Majesteis Advocat [1] that the Act of Parliament fra the begynning James I cap. 43,[1] is only maid against leasing makeris and telleris of thame of his Majesteis people quhilk may ingender discord betwix the King and thame, quhilk be the said Act is puneischeable be tynsall of lyfe and guidis, quhilk is cleared be the Act of Parliament King James the Fyft Parliament 6 cap. 83,[2] quhilk relaittis and explanes the said Act maid be King James the First, and ratifeis the samyn, referring the said first Act '*per expressum*' to leasing makeris of barrones, great men and leidges and for puneischment to be put to thame thairfoir, and be the said Act of King James the Fift and na soner the statute agains leasing makeris was maid reciprock and mutuall and extendit to lesing makeris against his Majestie to his barrones and leidges, quhilkis Actis of Parliament ar frome tyme to tyme ratifeid and renewit in maner contenit in the dittay and decreit; [2] And gevand that the Act war sic as the pannell alledges, quhilk is nocht grantit bot the contrair cleirit as said is, yit seing be the pannell his awin confessioun thair is ane cryme committit be him agains the Erle of Argyle, being ane noble man of eminent

[1] 1424 cap. 43.
[2] 1540 cap. 83.

qualitie quhais lyfe, honour, and estait was drawin in questioun be the saidis leasingis and calumneis, the said Erle had and hes his awin propper persute and accusatioun against the pannell; [3] And quhair it is alledget that his Majesteis Advocat can nocht persew without his Majesteis warrand, it is answerit that his Majestie hes ane double entreis, ane personall and perticular, and the uther generall, as soverane King '*et pater patrie*', and in the first it is granted that the Advocat may nocht persew without ane warrand frome his Majestie, bot for the uther the lawis, Actis of Parliament and inviolable custome observet in the kingdome, and speciallie in Justice courtis, makis cleir that quhair pairteis persewis thair awin perticuler injureis and crymes, the Kingis Advocat being requyret may nocht refuis his concurrance and assistance except he have ane expres prohibitioun frome his Majestie,[1] nather dois ony advocat persew befoir the Justice assisting a pairtie bot the Kingis Advocat, bot quhair the pairtie is silent and will nocht persew thair is ane Act of Parliament in *anno* 1587 quhilk is permissorie bot nocht mandatorie quhairby it is declared cap. 76[2] that the Kingis Majestie, his Thesaurer and Advocat may persew all crymes without the **(146)** partie, according to the quhilk Act of Parliament the Advocat may persew all crymes, bot nather he nor his predicessouris did ever persew or can be urgit to persew, without expres warrand from his Majestie, bot the caice of this present persuitt is not upoun the poyntis quhairin the Advocat must haife his Majesties warrand bot upoun Actis cleirlie maid in favouris of the subjectis and persewit in the subjectis name with concurrance of his Majesties Advocat; And as to the remanent poyntis of the said alledgance oppones thairto the decreit of the Lordis of Committe, quhairby it is fund againes the pannell compeirand they ar sic and of that qualitie as fallis directlie under the compas of the Actis of Parliament quhairupoun the dittay is foundit; And for the last poynt in cumming in my Lord Argyllis will he himselff craived justice.

It is duplyit be the pannell that the decreit given be the Committe of Estaitts againes him upoun his declaratioun and probatioun takin be thame againes him in all humilitie he reverenced thair judicatoris, bot in respect that it was decreed and agreit upoun be the Estaitts of this present Parliament that matteris mycht only be consultit upoun bot not concludit in caice that no pairtie objectit in the contrair, bot gif any pairtie sould compeir and object that the determinatioun of the sentence and the conclusioun againes thaim sould be continewit till his Majestie war presentt; And seing this persuitt againes the pannell dependis and resultis upoun the said decreit given be the said Committe against him in mainer foirsaid, it cannot be ane effectuall decreit till the samyn be ratified in Parliament, he humblie craives that this proces befoir the Justice may be continewit till the conclusioun of the Parliament

It is answerit be my Lord Advocat that thair [is] nothing producit to verefie, nor can be producit to verefie this alledgance, and gif it war it could not be opponed to this persuitt for twa ressonis: First, becaus the decreit is given befoir the sitting of the Parliament upoun the fyfteine day of Julii instant; And nixt, becaus the decreit is given againes the pannell compeirand and confessand, quhilk both ar verefied by the decreit producit.

[1] See legal note 6.
[2] 1587 cap. 77 in Glendook.

Secundo it is alledgit be the pannell [2nd Defence, Head 1] that his meaning in pleading of himselff guiltie of the crymis contenit in his dittay and the decreit producit, was only concerning that speich spokin be the Erle of Argyll at the fuird of Lyoun, quhairas his Lordship haifeing spokin generallie of kingis he tuik it to haife beine spokin of our King and of the presentt tyme, quhilk he diverse tymis in his former depositionis hes declairit, and quha as he said that out of ane desyre of revynge he did vent the said speiche againe, he dois not meane contryveing or making up of these speiches, bot only reveilled thame as he consavit they war spokin at that tyme; And [Head II] for the rest of the bill he acknawledged no guilt in him, for quhat he spak concerning these bandis was by informatioun of utheris for the maist pairt and hes given dettouris for evrie perticular thairincontenit so quhat hes beine spokin by him thairanent he confesses to his awin knawledge it is *falsum sed non mendacium.*

My Lord Advocat takis instrumentis of the pannellis confessioun *pro tanto* anent the speich at the fuird of Lyoun, quhilk is the maist pernitious and damnabill speiche contenit in the lybell and reflectis maist upoun the persewaris lyfe, hous and estaitt, and upoun the haill bodie of the Estaitts of Parliament, being not only tressonabill (gif it had beine trew) bot the heighest and maist transcendent poynt of tressone and treacherie to intend the deposeing of our gratious **(147)** Soverane fra his throne; And als to the uther poynt of the dittay anent the three bandis, quhilk the pannell in his declaratioun seames to schwue [show] as that quhilk he nather confest nor pleadit guiltie for, this is contrair to the act and decreit of the Estaitts producit, quhairby it is evident that the pannell, upoun the secund day of Julii instant, ressavit the haill bill of complaint fra the Committe to be advysit upoun and gat the dilatioun of four dayis to answer, and being than askit quhat he could say aganes the bill, declairit he wold mak no answer to the supplicatioun bot wold plead guiltie, quhilk being movit upoun the haill bill and generallie answerit includis the haill poyntis and articles of the bill quhairof thir three bandis is ane; And, but prejudice of this answer, quhilk cleirlie elydis the subterfuge of ane partiall pleading guiltie, it is farder answerit that the foirsaid poynt anent the three bandis is not only provin be his confessioun and pleading guiltie foirsaid, bot also be these quhome he namit dettouris or authoris, quha being all examinat befoir the Committe hes unproven his speich and hes deponit the direct contrarie thairof to be of verritie, lykeas be the decreit producit, this poynt is fund to be fullie provin; And, quhairas the pannell wald alledge that his speich will not infer him to be ane contryver bot only ane repeiter of that quhilk he hard of utheris, it is a thing to be lamented quhilk utherwayis was spokin be ane verrie wyse polititiane *quod quando quis mendacium excogitat saepius repetendo inducit seipsum credere*; And for the distinction quhilk the pannell induced betwix *falsum et mendacium* they may haife it in the generall consideratioun of twa thingis distinct *in natura* bot *in actu* they ar never separated.

It is alledgit be the pannell that his pleiding himselff guiltie cannot be tane generallie for the haill lybell in respect that thair was ane secund acknawledgment subjoynit quhilk concernit the bandis, quhairby he declairit the Erle of Argyll to be frie of all these calumneis according to his knawledge, and the pleading of himselff guiltie was for these speiches at the fuird of Lyoun; And quhairas it is affirmit in the decreit that all these bandis ar provin to be contrair be the witnesses producit the pannell alledgis that the haill witnesses producit be him ar not examinat as yit, and untill the haill witnesses be examinat the proces cannot be haldin as cloisit.

My Lord Advocat opponis the decreit for answer thairto.

The Justice continewis this dyett to the morne the twentie twa instantis, and ordanis the pannell to be returnit bak to his waird. The personis of assyse wairnit *apud acta* to the said day ilk persone under the paine of fyve hundreth merkis.

(147) [22 July 1641: Colville and Robertoun JJ.D.]

Assessores ut in precedenti actu.

Intran.—Mr Johnne Stewart, son to Mr James Stewart of Ladywall.

(148) Dilaittit of the fals leyis and calumneis contenit in his dittay befoir expressit.

Persewaris.—Sir Thomas Hoip of Craighall, knycht barronet, his Majesties Advocat for his Hienes intreis; Archbald Campbell, brother to the laird of Laweris, for the Erle of Argyll.

My Lord Advocat befoir interloquitour producit the blak printed Actis of Parliament for instructing that poynt of dittay foundit upoun the 100 Act of King James the Secund Parliament 14,[1] in respect that Act intitulat of leaseing makeris and telleris of thame is omittit in the laitt printed Actis [i.e. Skene's] and nocht contenit thairin; and also for removing all scrupill repeittis as ane pairt of the dittay the haill circumstanceis and qualificationis contenit in the decreit of the Committe alreddie producit and craives the Justice answer.

The Justice continewis this dyet to the morne the twentie thrie instantis, and ordanis the pannell to be returnit bak to his waird.

The personis of assyse wairnit *apud acta* ilk personne under the paine of fyve hundreth merkis.

[23 July 1641: Colvile and Robertoun JJ.D.]

Assessoures.—Alexander, Lord Elphingstoune; Sir James Lermonth of Balcomy; William Rig of Eddernie; Johnne Sempill, proveist of Dumbartane.

Intran.—Mr Johne Stewart sone, to Mr James Stewart of Ladywall.

Dilaittit of the fals leyis and calumneis contenit in his dittay.

Persewaris.—Sir Thomas Hope of Craighall, knycht barronet, Advocat to our Soverane Lord etc.; Archibald Campbell in name of my lord of Argyle.

Mr Johne Stewart, being demandit, befoir the pronunceing of interloquitour, gif he had ony farder to say in his awin defence, for answeir thairto declairet he had no farder to say, quhairupone my Lord Advocat askit instrumentis.

[1] 1457, The Black Acts 1566 fol. xlv. Referred to, but not quoted, in Glendook.

Thaireftir my Lord Advocat declairet that he conjoynit togidder all the poyntis of the dittay, viz. the leyis upone the thre bandis, and the last great lie at the fuird of Lyoun anent the deposeing of the king, with the haill circumstances and qualificationes contenit in the lybell and decreit producet, with this declaratioun alwayis—that albeit that gif the thre bandis be nocht provein (quhilk yit is cleirlie proven be the decreit producet) yit that last lie of the speich spokin at the fuird of Lyoun anent the deposeing of the King is be the selff allanerlie relevant to infer the conclusioun of the summondis and dittay.

The Justice with advyce of the assessouris remittis the dittay as it is conjoynet be the Kingis Majesteis Advocat, and with his declaratioun viz. (that albeit the leyis of the thre bandis sall nocht be fundin proven yit that last great lie anent the speach quhilk was said to be spokin at the fuird of Lyoun concerning the deposeing of the Kings Majestie is be the self allanerlie relevant to infer the conclusion of the summondis), as also the haill circumstances and qualificationes **(149)** contenit in the decreit of the Committie producet repeittit be my Lord Advocat as ane pairt of the dittay, to the knawledge of ane inqueist, quhairupone his Majesteis Advocat askit instrumentis.

Assisa.—Sir Patrick Douglas of Kilspindie; David Dumbar of Enterkyn; Robert Drummond of Medhope; George Leslie of that ilk; Mr George Windrahame of Libbertoun; Mr William Cuninghame of Bromehill, chanceller; Johne Kennydie of Knokdaw; Mr Alexander Kennowie of Northbank; Alexander Ingles of Inglestoun; John Rynd, merchand burges of Edinburgh; James Barnes, merchand burges of Edinburgh; Mr James Scot, merchand burges thair; George Wauchope, merchand burges thair; Johne Edzer, merchand burges thair; Mr Alexander Eleis of Monthulie.

My Lord Advocat takis instrumentis upone the sweiring of the assyse and of the reiding of the dittay in thair presens and audience, and of the reiding of the decreit of the Committie of Estaittis and haill circumstances thairin contenit quhilk the said Committie of Estaittis hes fund provein, as also upone the pannellis judiciall confessioun renewit this day befoir the Justice and assessouris off that odious and detestable poynt spokin at the fuird of Lyoun anent the deposeing of our gratious Soverane, and in respect thairof protestit for wilfull errour agains the assyse gif thay sould acquit the pannell of the leyis and calumneis above writtin.

Thaireftir the said Mr Johne Stewart, being demandit in presens of the haill assyse anent the leyis and calumneis abone writtin contenit in his dittay and his renewit confessioun thairof abone specifeit, he in thair presence and audience repeittit the said confessioun,[1] quhairupone his Majesteis Advocat lykwayis askit instrumentis.

Mr John Stewart convict et decollat.

Quhilkis persones of assyse, being chosen sworne and admittit, eftir accusatioun of the said Mr Johne Stewart be dittay of the haill odious crymes foirsaidis mentionet thairintill, thay removet altogidder furth of court to the counsall

[1] See legal note 7.

hous neir to the said tolbuith, quhair first be pluralitie of voittis thay electit and chuiset the said Mr William Cunninghame of Bromehill in chanceller, thairefter reasonet and voitted upone the haill poyntis and crymes contenit in the said dittay, and upone the haill circumstances and qualificationes producet for verificatioun thairof, and being ryplie and at lenth advyset thairwith and with the said decreit of Committie of Estaittis haill circumstances and qualificationes contenit thairintill, togidder with the said Mr Johne Stewart his awin judiciall confessioun maid be him in judgement, alsweill befoir the Justice and assessouris as in presens and audience of thame selffis as persones admittit upone his assyse, speciallie with his confessioun renewit be him in judgement anent that odious and detestable lie alledgit spokin at the fuird of Lyoun concerning the deposeing of our most gracious Soverane, thay re-enterit agane in court, quhair thay all in ane voce, be the judiciall declaratioun of the said Mr Williame Cuninghame chanceller, fand pronuncet and declairet the foirsaid dittay to be cleirlie and sufficientlie proven, and the said Mr Johne Stewart to be fylet, culpable and convict of the haill crymes contenit thairintill; Quhairupone instrumentis was tane be his Majesteis Advocat, and be Archibald Campbell in name of the said noble erle, Archibald, Erle of Argyle; For the quhilk caus the Justice be the mouth of Patrick Barrie, dempster of court, decernet, adjudget and ordaned the said Mr Johne Stewart to be takin to the mercat croce of Edinburgh upone Wedinsday nixt being the xxviii of Julii instant, and thair his heid to be strukin frome his body, and all his moveable guidis to be escheit and inbrocht to our Soverane Lordis use, as culpable and convict of the making, forgeing, venting and divulgeing of the wicked and monstrowus leyis and fals calumneis contenit in his dittay; Quhilk was pronuncet for dome.

Legal Notes

1. Assessors were not usual, though there are four instances above (i.18, 230, 257, 273), all apparently appointed by the Privy Council. This is the only case noted by Hume (II.15-16) where they were appointed by Parliament. The Privy Council Register casts no light on this sinister case, as there are no surviving records from November 1639 to November 1641 (*RPC*[2] VII.141n). Assessors were not popular in the country, and John Spalding (*Trubles*, I.333, 1829, p.244), says 'this gentleman is cruellie execute for words, not before our ordinar Justice of Sheriff Courts, according to our Scottish laws, but before ane new in-come Committee-Court'. See Napier, Montrose, I.301.

2. The Justice Court did not sit during Parliament, as was reflected in (*Barrie* v *Rogers and Others* and *Stalker and Others* v *Gordon*, 1641, above p. 505, and below p. 485), though there the day was that of the actual riding of Parliament.

3. This alleged confession before the Estates of Parliament is not recorded in the *APS*, and one is left in doubt as to whether the case was really hopeless or whether advocates were afraid for political reasons to take it up.

4. The gist of charge I (p. 429) was that Argyll had taken bonds of manrent without the usual clause reserving allegiance to the Crown. Under 1587 chap. 12 parties to such bonds were to be treated as 'movers of sedition and unquietness'.

5. This is the first case noted where the panel had already been convicted in Parliament before his trial in the Justice Court began (see p. 431), the injustice of which is obvious. There is one case, however, where the Estates intervened to order the Justice to desert a diet in a prosecution for false measures (*L.A.* v *Neilson and Others*, 1625 above i.30-32).

6. It was submitted by the Crown (p. 438) that the L.A. was bound to give his concurrence to a prosecution by a private prosecutor—a very doubtful view. This was not the view of later times, when, if he refused, the Court might authorise the private prosecutor to proceed alone or direct the L.A. to give his concurrence (*J. & P. Coats Ltd.* v *Brown*, 1909 S.C. (J.) 29).

7. The panel finally gave the case completely away by admitting before the assize that his confession was genuine (p. 441). No doubt he hoped for a remission, but none was forthcoming. See prefatory note.

(156) [30 July 1641: Robertoun J.D.]

Sla[*ughter*]. *William Fraser. Convict et decollat.*

Intran.—William Fraser, fute mercheand [*pedlar*] in Fraserburgh.

Dilaittit of the crewall slauchter and murthour of umquhile Edward Skollay, sone in law to David Currour of Fingask,[1] committit within the dwelling hous of umquhile Johne Lyell in Fraserburgh, upone the xxiii day of Apryle 1639 yeiris, be geving him dyvers straikis in his body, speciallie ane crewall and deidlie strak throw his richt palpe [*breast*] with ane quhinger [*small sword*], quhairof he presentlie deceisset, and for the quhilk slauchter he being chairget be vertew of criminall letters to find cautioun actit in the buikis of adjornall for his personall compeirance befoir the Justice and his deputis the xxvi day of July thaireftir, he past to the horne and was declairet fugitive for the slauchter abone writtin, quhairupone he, be vertew of letteris of captioun, is taken and brocht frome Aberdene to Edinburgh and committit to waird within the tolbuth thairof, and is also excommunicat and lyne under the sentence thairof sence the moneth of August 1640.

Persewaris.—Jeane Currour, the relict of umquhile Edward Skollay; Sir Thomas Hope of Craighall, knycht, his Majesteis Advocat for his Hienes intreis.

Prelocutouris for the pannell.—Mr David Heriote, advocat.[2]

The persewaris producet ane deliverance of the Estaittis of Parliament, granting licence to the Justice[3] to sitt and hald court and minister justice upone the said William Fraser for the slauchter abone writtin, daittit the 27 of July 1641, subscryvit be my Lord Burghlie,[4] President of Parliament *I.P.D. Parliamenti.*

The pannell, eftir reiding of the dittay and his accusatioun be vertew thairof of the crewall slauchter abonewrittin, desyret of my Lord Justice continuatione of his tryell to the morne, in respect he nather hes spokin with freind nor procuratour in this matter being keipit in close prissone, and that it is nocht fourtie aucht houris since he was summond to this Justice court and gat the coppy of his dittay.[5]

To the quhilk continuatioun or delay the persewaris deiassentis, alwayis [in any event] gif my Lord Justice will condiscend thairto, desyret that the witnesses to be producet be thame, quhilk ar present at the bar for cleiring of the pannellis guiltines of the cryme lybellit, may be examinat,[6] and that thair depositiones of consent of pairtie may be declairet to be als lawfull and valide as gif thai war examinat befoir the assyse in judgement, reservant and pannellis

1 2 miles W of Old Meldrum, Aberdeenshire.
2 See *Lyon's List*, p. 101.
3 *APS* V.312.
4 Robert Arnot, 2nd Lord Balfour of Burleigh see *Scots Peerage* I.542-3; *I.P.D.*=*in praesentia dominorum.*
5 See legal note 1.
6 The necessity for this is not clear. See legal note 2.

objectiones *contra probationem* as accoirdis of the law; Quhairupone the witnesses following being callit, *videlicet* My Lord Sindlair, Mr William Davidsone, schireff depute of Aberdene, William Sinclair, William Alexander and David Tailyeour, servitouris to the said Lord Sinclair,[1] war sworne and ressavit eftir objectiones wes maid aganis thame be the pannell, quhilkis objectiones being referrit to the saidis witnesses oathes and thay sworne thairupone denyit the samyn be thair great oathe.

The pannell thaireftir desyret reservatioun of his defences etc.

My Lord Advocat with the pairtie persewar disassentit for all reservatioun of defensses, except allanerlie the objectiones to be proponit be the pannell aganis the depositiones of the witnesses.

The pannell adheires to the continuatioun grantit be the Judge,[2] quhairin all his defensses ar reservet, and [protestis] that in equitie he aucht to haif continuatioun grantit to the morne for the reasones foirsaidis; to the quhilk the persewar disassentis. The Justice ordanit the pannell to propone his defences aganis the relevancie of the dittay gif he ony hes.

Compeirit Mr David Heriote, as procuratour for the laird of Fillorthe,[3] and allegit that the said laird of Phillorthe is infeft in the regalitie of Fraserburgh, beirand power to repledge, and conforme thairto cravet the pannell to be repledget, he being ane **(151)** inhabitant within the said regalitie, and for verificatioun thairof producet the extract of ane act of adjornall of the dait the 26 of July 1639[4] yeiris, quhairin the said laird of Phillorth his infeftment was producet with ane ratificatioun thairof, quhilk the Justice tuik to his consideratioun anent the discussing of the samyn.

It is answeirit be his Majesteis Advocat that the pannell can nocht oppone repledgiatioun, becaus he hes consentit that the Justice be judge in swa far as he hes craved a delay to the morne, and for obtening thairof hes consentit[5] to the examinatioun of the witnesses to be producet be the persewar, and that thair depositiones sall work alsmeikill as gif thay war tane befoir the assyse. Lykas fyve witnesses being severallie callit he hes proponet objectioun declinatour aganis all the witnesses, quhilkis objectiones war referrit to the witnesses oathes and quhairupone thay have sworne, and nochtwithstanding thairof the witnesses admittit and thair aithes takin to depone, eftir the quhilk, the Judge and judgement swa acceptit, that the pannell can nocht returne to ane repledgeatioun, quhilk is a declinatour of the awin nature and quhilk na pairtie can be hard to propone *post exceptionem vel dilatoriam vel peremptoriam* proponet and discussit. Nixt, geivand thair war place for repledgeatioun or declinatour, quhilk is nocht grantit, yit this repledgeatioun can nocht be admittit, becaus to the lawfulnes of ane repledgeatioun be the law and custome of this kingdome thir thingis ar necesserlie requyret: (1) that the pairtie desyret to be repledget dwellis actuallie and presentlie and immediatlie befoir the repledgiatioun within the regalitie; (2) that the repledgear schaw ane lauchfull rycht to repledge;

[1] As later appears (p. 449 below) none of these were eye witnesses.
[2] Evidently an interlocutor had been pronounced to that effect, which the clerk has omitted.
[3] Alexander Fraser, 1st Lord Saltoun of the name of Fraser.
[4] Recorded at p. 75 of vol. vi.
[5] No consent has yet appeared in the record.

(3) that he, or his procuratour personallie constitute to repledge that same persone, quha is accuset criminallie befoir the Justice, compeir and produce thair richt; and (4) gif it be fund relevant to find cautioun of cullerauch[1] for administratioun of justice upone the pairtie accuset within fourtie dayis thaireftir, or sic uther tyme or space as the Justice sall prescryve, and to repoirt the samyn to the Justice at the tyme to be appointed be him: Quhilkis all ar deficient and inlaiking [*lacking*] in this alledgeance; for first the pannell dwellis nocht within the regalitie, bot continuallie since the committing of the cryme (quhilk was in Apryle 1639) hes dwelt within the schirefdomes of Aberdene, Banff, Elgin, and Invernes, lykas the Justice Generall hes proceidit to doe justice aganis the pannell be ceitting him to compeir befoir him to underly the law, quhairupone he was declairet fugitive and is takin and apprehendit be captioun be the schireff of the schyre[2] and proveist and bailyeis of Aberdene, and be warrand of the Committie of Estaittis broght fra Aberdene to the prissone of Edinburgh and hes remanet thir auchtene dayis, fra the quhilk he is brocht to his tryell heir. Nixt it is nocht verifiet nor schawin that the laird of Phillorth hes ony richt of regalitie, nor ony procuratorie frome him, and quhairas thay produce ane pretendit Act of Adjornall befoir the Justice, daittit the 26 of Julii 1639, quhairin it is alledget that uther twa persones being persewit befoir the Justice at the instance of Jeane Currour, ane of the persewaris, for the slauchter of hir husband, that the laird of Phillorthe[3] thairto was producet beiring regalitie with ane ratificatioun thairof in Parliament, that can nocht be respectit for thir causes: first, becaus in that persuit na pairtie persewar compeirit and swa no judgement; 2, [sic] No alledgeance proponit, verefeit nor admittit concerning the said repledgeatioun of regalitie, bot allanerlie ane protestatioun maid be the producer of the saidis writtis, quhilk is nawayis admittit be the Justice bot only reservet to the awin [*proper*] tyme and place quhilk is now, and except at this tyme all the perticuleris abone specifeit necesserlie for ane lawfull repledgeatioun be presentlie producet and verifeit no repledgeatioun can be admittit, speceallie in respect the repledgeatioun mentionat in the said Act is for twa persones, quhairof nane of thame is now accuset, and all repledgeationes ar and most be personall and of the same persones quho ar accuset; nixt because the productioun maid at the said dyet was nocht sufficient in law, thair being ane chairtour producet without ane seasing; 3, becaus, albeit, the same persones war now upone pannell, yit the laird of Phillorthes repledgeatioun (albeit he himselff war personallie present and producet ane perfyte richt) could nocht be admittit, in respect he hes nocht done justice be the space of twa yeiris;[4] and as for this pannell he is nocht resident within the regalitie bot within the schirefdomes *ut supra etc.*

(152) It is answeirit be the pannell that thair was no consent grantit be him bot upone ane expres recervatioun of all his defenses quhairof this defence of

[1] I.e. that justice would be done; see Hume II.30 where it is called 'Culreach'; for other examples see pp. 70, 124, 264.

[2] William, 7th Earl Marischal.

[3] Some such word as 'title' has been omitted here, consisting of the 'writs' and 'charter' hereinafter mentioned.

[4] I.e. since April 1639.

repledgeatioun is ane, and it is nocht ane declinatour exceptioun, becaus it is ane peremptour, it being proponet be the pannell under protestatioun that he nawayis acknowledges the fact beiring [*sic*] ane lawfull defence of repledgeatioun *penam hac instantiam*, and swa being proponet peremptorie the haill defenses being reservet as is knawin to the Judge, and thair war no witnesses sworne nor admittit bot efter that the pannellis haill defenses war reservet; And quhair it is alledgit that eftir a dilatour proponet the pannell can nocht propone a declinatour, it is answerit that, althocht a dilatour be proponet to be granted reserveand the pairteis haill objectiones, he may lawfullie propone ane declinatour quhilk is proponet peremptorie and verefeit as this of repledgeatioun, quhilk is verifeit be the Adjornall Act beiring the infeftment to be producet in ane caus persewit at the instance of the same persewar aganis utheris persones challanged and convenit for the same cryme as speciall actouris and committeris of the same slauchter. It is answeirit to the secund that the alledgeance foundit upone the repledgeatioun is relevant, becaus the pannell (craveing to be repledget) the tyme of the allegit fact had his actuall residence within the regalitie, and had, and as yit hes, his actuall residence within the regalitie, and had, and as yit hes, ane merchand buithe or chope [*shop*] thair, and it is sufficient for ane lord of regalitie to repledge any pairtie accuset gif he can qualifie that the tyme of the alledget deid the persone dwelt within the regalitie; And albeit it be alledget that since the fact he hes had his residence in Invernes, Aberdeine *etc.* ay and quhill [*until*] he was takin with letters of captioun and brocht over to Edinburgh and cittit [*cited*] befoir the Justice, that is nawayis relevant to stop the lord of the regalitie to repledge any pairtie accuset befoir the Justice, seing the lord of regalitie hes power to repledge, he qualifieing the pairtie to haife had his actuall residence within the regalitie the tyme of the fact; and altho he had beine quhyllis at Aberdeine and Invernes being ane traveller, becaus he was callit ane fute merchand by his travelling through these boundis, [they] cannot be callit his residence, bot the pairt quhair he was borne, bred and had his continuall residence and hes his merchand buithes thair yit quhilk is within the regalitie. And quhair it is alledgit that the pairtie repledger sould compeir personallie or be his prelocutour and produce ane lauchfull infeftment and offerrit to find cautioun to doe Justice within the tyme forescryvit to him be the Justice, it is answeirit that the repledger compeiris be Mr David Heriot, his prelocutour, and being ane advocatt neidis not ane procuratorie, and gif neid beis sall produce ane procuratorie, and produced the Act of Adjornall beiring the laird of Philorth his infeftment and ratificatioun, and offeris to find cautioun and to repoirt the samyn the tyme to be proscryvit be the Justice. And quhair it is alledgit that the tyme the adjornall act was maid thair was not a persewar, and that thair was no defence admittit or proponit upoun the repledgiatioun bot only ane protestatioun maid and it was not thir pairteis was convenit, and ane defence of repledgiatioun moist [*must*] be personall upoun the pairtie, it is answeirit that we oppone the Adjornall Act, quhilk was one in ane lawfull fencit court; and althocht thair was no defence proponit thair, bot ane protestatioun maid, it is answeirit the Act is not usit as ane grund of the repledgiatioun or to be ane defence to haif beine proponit then, bot Philorth proponing now ane defence upoun the replediatioun, repledging this pairtie pannellit he used the Act for verifieing that the infeftment was producit togidder with the ratificatioun, at quhilk tyme the Judges then tuik it to thair consideratioun; it is answeirit that the defence foundit upoun the repledgiatioun was relevant nochtwithstanding of the not doeing of justice, becaus the laird of Philorth was never requyrit be any pairtie, and lykeas he will qualifie that the **(153)** doer of the deed dwellis not within the regalitie and so he had no power of him.[1]

It is answerit be my Lord Advocat that both a declinatour and a dilatour ar perremptorie instantis, bot that is not the questioun bot quhither gif eftir a dilator proponit be the Judge, and eftir sweiring of witnesses be consent of the pannell to the effect he might haif dilatioun to the morne, and eftir the pannellis proponing of objectionis againest the witnesses and referring the samyn to witnesses oath quhairupoun they war sworne, and eftir the saidis witnesses war admittit and sworne to tell the treuth *in causa* befoir the Justice, the pannell and his procuratour might ather desyre reservatioun of defenses declinator, or gif, albeit desyrit and reservit, the reservatioun can includ a declinator, that is the questioun. And for cleiring heirof, First, opponis the minuttis of the proces quhilk beiris the proponing of the declinator, the consent to the examinatioun of the witnesses and thair depositioun to be als valeid as gif they war takin befoir the assyse, and als eftir sweiring of the witnesses and admissioun thairof, and never befoir, the procuratour for the pannell cravit reservatioun of his defenses. Nixt, albeit it war not so, quhilk is direct contrair to the proces, for quhen he cravit reservatioun the Advocat opponit againes it and becaus the Justice thocht it not ressonabill commandit the pannell to cum to his defenses, yit it is impossibill that under that reservatioun gif it had beine grantit (quhilk is no) a declinator could haife beine comprehendit, becaus *hactenus judicavit in processu*, and it is impossibill that he can [be] both judge and no judge in *eadem instantia processus*. *Item* as to the rest of the answeiris my Lord Advocatt repeittis his former replyis.

To the quhilk it is answeirit for the pannell that, altho he proponit a dilator craving a delay quhill he had spokin with his procuratouris and freindis, and quhilk was grantit conditionallie reservand all the pannellis defenses under the compas cuiuis [*sic*] this declinator,[2] and the pannell nawayis consentit to the ressaveing of any witnes bot upoun expres conditioun of the reservatioun of his haill defenses, off the quhilk this is ane; And gif my Lord Advocatt will oppone that eftir the witnesses sworne that the pairtie cannot cum to ane declinator the pannell will reseill [*resile*] fra that consent and will adher *mordicus* [*firmly*] that except his haill defenses had beine reservit he wold never haife consentit, nayther does he consent bot affirmes that na witnes can be ressavit except in presence of the assyse conforme to the Act of Parliament [1587 cap. 91]; And quhair it is alledgit that the judge, eftir the Advocattis protestatioun anent the not admitting of the[3] urgit the pairtie defender to cum to his defenses, that was only except the pannell wold pas from the repledgiatioun or say [*speak*] to it presentlie quhilk he hes done, and altho the pannell wold not propone it Philorth's pro-

[1] This implies that the court seeking to repledge had formed the conclusion that another person than the present accused was responsible for the crime.

[2] Apparently meaning 'including this declinature of jurisdiction'.

[3] Some words are omitted here referring either to the protest for a postponement or to the witnesses.

curatour compeiris and proponis it, and repeittis the act quhair the infeftment was producit, and the notorietie thairof knawin to my Lord Advocatt.[1]

The Justice continewis this dyet to the morne, the last of this instant, and ordanis the pannell to returne to his waird. The persones of assyse wairnit *apud acta* ilk personne under the paine of twa hundreth merkis.

(154) [31 July 1641]

Maister David Heriott as procuratour for the pannell takis instrumentis that the defence proponit be him yesterday was for the laird of Philorth, and protestis quhatever be the judges interloquitour thairintill that the samyn wrong not the laird of Philorth his right of regalitie.

The Justice repellis the exceptioun of repledgiatioun, in respect thair is nather infeftment nor procuratorie producit, nor any Act of Adjornall beiring any pairtie ever to haife beine repledgit from this court to the laird of Philorth his regalitie be vertew of his infeftment, quhairupoun the persewaris askit instrumentis.[2]

The pannell, befoir the proponing of ony defence be him againes the dittay, producit his relaxation fra the horne, daittit the secund and thrid dayis of Julii 1641, and takis instrumentis upoun the productioun thairof etc.

It is thaireftir alledget be the pannell that the dittay as it is conceavet beiring ane taikin [*token*] that he did the deid lybellit, he was fugitive, and that he went to ane schip to escaip as ane passinger, and changet his name, ar nawayis relevant as positive pairtis of the dittay, nor can be qualifeit or fund relevant to infer the deid to have bene done be the pannell; For albeit he went to the horne that was throu nocht lawfull citatioun, lykas thair is foure or fyve cited quhilk lykwayis went to the horne, and so sone as the pannell gat notice he relaxt himselff. And as to his going to the schip it can nevir be respectit as ane positive pairt of the dittay, becaus he is ane merchand and travellit be sea in the exerceis of his calling.

My Lord Advocat takis instrumentis of the relaxatioun producet and dait thairof, and of the reasone of the relaxatioun, that the charge came nocht to his knawledge he being out of the countrie, quhairas be his awin confessioun it sall be proven he nevir went out of the countrie. And as to the alledgeance proponet my Lord Advocat declaires that he uses nocht that poynt of the dittay as ane relevant pairt *per se*, bot as ane adminicle, and leist ony scruple sould aryse thairupoun, haldis the samyn as nocht insert in the lybell, bot will propone the samyn to the assyse etc.[3]

(155) *Assisa*.—John Ramsay, burges of Fraserburgh; Michaell Brodie in Fraserburgh; Archibald Thomesone, burges of Edinburgh; Johne Miller, servitor to Drumkilbo; Johne Younger in Fraserburgh; Patrik Johnstoun, tailyeour in Edinburgh; Thomas Nicoll, lorymer there; John Malcolme, herauld thair, chancellor; George Norie, indweller in Edinburgh; James Lychtbodie,

[1] See legal note 3.
[2] See legal note 4.
[3] I.e. it was only in the dittay as giving fair notice to the accused of the evidence to be led.

mercheand thair; David Kinloch, skinner burges of Edinburgh; William Salmond, mercheand burges thair; Frances Brown, merchand burges thair; John Brown, mercheand burges thair; George Thrid in Phillorthe.

My Lord Advocat takis instrumentis of the sweiring of the assyse, as also of reiding of the dittay to the assyse, and desyret my Lord Justice, for the assyse farder informatioun to tak the gentilwoman, the defunctis relict, hir oathe upone the verritie of the dittay;[1] quha, being sworne on hir salvatioun and damnatioun at the day of judgement, declairet be hir great oath that Williame Fraser now upone pannell, was the only man and no uther that murdreist Edward Skollay, hir husband, and that the ground and quarrell thairof was for ane stalf betwix hir husband and the pannell in the pannellis awin chope in Fraserburgh; Quhairupone my Lord Advocat askit instrumentis.

Thaireftir his Majesteis Advocat desyret that my Lord Sinclair[2] with the remanent witnesses befoir nominat may be callit upone to geve thair publict declaratioun to the assyse quhat thai knew concerning the pannellis guiltines of the slauchter contenit in the dittay.

Compeirit my Lord Sinclair quha, being solempnelie sworne in presens of the assyse, declairet be his great oath that his Lordschip being at Aberdene the tyme of the pannellis taking and bringing furth of the schip to the magistrattis of Aberdene, his Lordschip was desyreous to sie the pannell, and the cause thairof was that it was repoirted to his Lordschip that the schip quhairin the pannell was imbarkit was past two myles of [*off*] the schoir and under saill with ane fair wynd, but stoppit and wald nocht goe forwardis,[3] quhairupone his Lordschip was curious to sie the man, and the pannell cuming befoir his Lordschip fell down upone his kneuis and craved mercie; at quhilk tyme my Lord askit him how that unhappie murthour fell in his hand, who answeired that the defunct and he fell in ane quarrell for ane stalff [*staff*], and that he thaireftir hard that the defunct had fellit his brother, quhairupone the pannell ran to the house of John Lyell,[4] quhair the defunct was for the tyme, and haveing cum in to the said house fand him and Gilbert Wairdane, gairdner to the pesewaris father, bot at that tyme thair was ane or uther tuik the pannell be the gairdeis [*arms*], and he haveing fred himselff in the verrie freeing he strak the defunct with ane quhinger in throu the richt palpe, thinking only to have strukin him throu the airme; And furder deponet that the pannell said that he was urgett to it, being persewit a day befoir be the defunct, bot it was answeirit to him be Capitane Sudderland, ane of his Lordschips capitanes, that, albeit he had wronget him the day befoir, yit he sould nocht have socht the defunct in the house quhairin he was; and depones that this was spokin in presens of twa bailyeis, *videlicet* bailyie Mortymer and bailyie Leslie, as also in presens of threttie gentilmen and utheris than being in his Lordschips ludgeing.

Mr Williame Davidsone, schireff depute of Aberdene, being lykwayis sworne in presens of the assyse, deponet *in omnibus* conforme to my Lord Sinclair, with this additioun that he as schiref depute, haifing searchet the pannell for wappones, the pannell said quhat neidis any searche, I will nocht put handis in my

[1] A good example of the oath of verity follows.
[2] John, 9th Lord Sinclair.
[3] I.e. it was regarded as a miracle, see p. 453 below.
[4] The widow in her oath of verity gave a different locus namely the accused's shop.

selff, for this fact quhairof I am accuset, thank God I am in ane better caice, and I hope to change for the better, quhilk was spokin be the pannell befoir he come up to my Lord Sinclairs hous; and quhan he come thair he thocht him to be ane verrie penitent man for the fact, and rememberis that the pannell said quhan he strak the defunct that the defunct was abone him.

(156) Williame Sinclair, servitour to my Lord Sinclair, being sworne depones *in omnibus* conforme to my Lord Sinclair.[1]

David Tailyeour, servand to my Lord Sinclair and servand in his Lordschips regiment,[2] being sworne depones that, he haveing interrogat the pannell quhan he come thair to Aberdene, the pannell answeirit yisterday he being tane for the slauchter of Edward Skollay, and the deponer being arguent with the pannel of befoir said to the pannell 'I am sorie for the accident I heir ye have committit,' quho answeirit, 'I am sorie for it myselff, bot I hope it sall bring me to ane gritter licht'.

Williame Alexander, also servand to my Lord Sinclair, being sworne depones that he hard the pannell say in my Lords ludgeing that he did the wrong negligentlie and thocht only to have struckin him in the airme, bot strak him throuch the richt palpe.

The assyse craved that Edward Cairny may be hard,[3] quha being sworne depones that he knawis nothing of the slauchter bot allanerlie that be the commoun bruit of the countrey, the pannell was the man that did it.[4]

Thaireftir my Lord Advocat producet ane testimoniall subscryvit be the Moderatour, the clerk and nyne uther ministeris of the presbiterie of Deir, and desyret the samyn to be red to the assyse, quhairof the tennour followis: The presbiterie of Deir haldin at Strechen octavo Julii 1641: We, the bretherene of the presbiterie of Deir, testifeis be thir presentis to our verrie honorabill Lordis, barrones and utheris on the Committie of Estaittis that we being directed be the Synode of Aberdeen to goe to Fraserburgh and thair to try the qualitie of the murthour of umquhile Edward Skollay, husband to Jeane Currour, committit[5] be William Fraser, fute mercheand, did accoirding to the said ordinance convene at Fraserburgh, and, eftir dew tryell and examinatioun of dyvers witnesses, fand it to be ane most wylde and wilfull murthour: And, upone the said tryell and complent of the said Jeane to the last Generall Assemblie haldin at Aberdene,[6] the said Assemblie did ordaine the said Williame to be excommunicat thairfoir, quhilk accoirdinglie was done be umquhile Mr Williame Forbes, minister thair; Be thir presentis subscryvit with our handis, day, yeir and place foirsaid: *Sic subscribitur* Mr George Clark, minister at Aberdour in Buchane, Moderatour of the said presbiterie; Mr William Jaffray, minister at Auchrydie[7] and clerk to the presbiterie; Mr James Mairtene, minister [at Peterhead]; Mr Williame Davidsone, minister at Rathane; Mr William Hay, minister at Crimond; Mr Thomas Reres, minister at Conney [*sic* for *Lonmay*]; Mr A. Mairtene, minister

1 I.e. another witness of concurring testimony.
2 The Fife Regiment of Foot.
3 See legal note 5.
4 I.e. hearsay evidence.
5 His guilt was assumed.
6 I.e. in 1640 (Peterkin, *Records of the Kirk of Scotland*, p. 278).
7 Auchreddy, now New Deer.

at Deir; Mr William Scott, minister at Strechin; Mr Airthour Forbes, minister at Pitsliego; Mr Alexander Irvine, minister at Langsyde;[1] Mr Williame Fraser, minister at Tyrie. Upone the reiding of the quhilk testimoniall to the assyse my Lord Advocat askit instrumentis.

Thaireftir Mr Alexander Mairtene, minister at Deir, being sworne in presens of the assyse depones that the presbiterie heiring of this filthie murthour was commandit be the provinciall assemblie of Aberdene[2] to tak tryell quhidder the slauchter was accidentall or wilfull, and to this effect examinat four or fyve witnesses in Aprile, May, Junii or thairabout in *anno* 1640, the pannell his father being present with Mr William Stewart, nottar, and thay hard to object against the witnesses; And eftir provatioun it was fund that the samyn was nocht accidentall bot wilfull murthour committit be this pannell; quhilk being repoirted to the General Assemblie, thay ordanet him to be excommunicat, lykas he was excommunicat be umquhile Mr William Forbes minister at Fraserburgh; And farder depones that the pannellis father, eftir the excommunicatioun, presentit dyvers supplicationes beiring the name of the pannell thairintill and desyreing that he micht be admittit to his repentence upone his humble confessioun, becaus he could nocht be at rest for the sentence of excommunicatioun following upon the bluid, and als offeret to geve assythement to the pairtie, and desyret ane number of the ministeris to goe to the relict and deill with hir and hir freindis to accept of assythment for the slauchter.[3]

Mr Williame Jaffray, minister at Auchrydie, sworne befoir the assyse, depones conforme to Mr Alexander Mairtene *in omnibus*.

Andro Fraser, father to the pannell, sworne judiciallie, grantis that he was in Fraserburgh with Mr Williame Stewart, nottar, and was present at the examinatioun of the witnesses, and that he gave in ane supplicatioun to have his sone relaxt be the presbiterie fra his excommunicatioun, bot denyit the offer of assythment and allegit the witnesses quha war ressavit war sic as could nocht be witnesses, *videlicet* the relictis brother and hir fatheris servand. The twa **(157)** ministeris befoir deponing, being confronted with the said Andro Fraser, the father[4] in the premisses declairet that bothe thaise twa witnesses, *videlicet* the relict hir brother and hir fathers servand, war repellit for beiring witnessing, and all utheris aganis quhome the pannell had ony lawfull exceptioun.[5] Thaireftir the said Andro Fraser, being sworne and demandit gif he had ony warrand frome the pannell his sone, denyis that he had ony directioun or allowance frome his sone, bot that some freindis imployet him; being askit what war theis freindis, sayis his brother was one and that he acquented his freindis with the presbitereis answeir to his supplicatioun; and, being askit quhat war the uther freindis, depones the commoun people.

My Lord Advocat producet thaireftir the act of the Generall Assemblie of Aberdene, daittit primo Augusti 1640, beiring that it is notourlie knawin that umquhile Edward Skollay, husband to Jeane Currour, was schamefullie and crewallie murdreist be Williame Fraser, chopman, quhilk murthour and maner

1 Langsyde=Longside.
2 I.e. the Synod.
3 See legal note 6.
4 See legal note 7.
5 See legal note 8.

thairof is verifeit in presens of the presbiterie of Deir, and also producet the sentence of excommunicatioun, daittit the threttie day of August 1640 yeiris, subscryvit be umquhile Mr Williame Forbes, minister at Fraserburgh, of the quhilk act of Generall Assemblie the tennour followis: *Apud* Aberdene primo Augusti 1640 act. sess. 5, anent the supplicatioun gevin in to the Generall Assemblie be Jeane Currour, wedow of umquhile Edward Skollay, infeinzeis[1] that, quhair as is nottourlie knawin my said umquhile husband was chamefullie and crewallie murdreist be William Fraser, chopman in Fraserburgh, and now gentilman to the laird of Streichane upone the 23 of Apryle 1639, under silence and clud of nycht within the town of Fraserburgh, quhilk fact is verifeit and proven anent the said murthour in presens of the presbiterie of Deir, and thairfoir accoirding to the constitutiones of this kirk I humblie desyre that the ecclesiastiall swoird of excommunicatioun may be drawin aganis the said William Fraser and that he be summerlie excommunicat for the said bluidie murthour that thaireftir I may persew him befoir the civile judge[2] that he may be puneist for his demereittis and your wisdomes answeir. Quhilk supplicatioun abonewrittin being oppinlie red in audience of the Assemblie, and the desyre thairof fund be thame to be reasonable, thay ordanit the minister of the place quhair the murthour was committit to pronunce and geve furthe the sentence of summer [*summary*] excommunicatioun against the murtherour, and recommendit the prosecuteing of captioun aganis him to the Erle of Merschell, quha is Schireff in theas boundis, quhome the Assemblie earnestlie intreattis to further by all lawfull meanes; and siclyk the Assemblie, eftir thay had poiset [*questioned*] the laird of Strechin, (being personallie present as ane Commissioner of the Assemblie), upone the keiping of the murtherar in his service, he absolutelie denyit that he was in service with him, or in his company. The Assemblie thairupoun dischairget the laird of Streachin ony wayis to recept him thaireftir, and gif he did to be lyable to the puneischment prescryvet be the lawis of this kingdome. Extractit furth of the buikis of the Generall Assemblie haldin at Aberdene be me James Murray, clerk depute to Mr Archibald Johnestoun, clerk to the Generall Assemblie, witnessing my signe and subscriptioun manuale: *Sic subscribitur* J. Murray, clerk depute, etc. Followis the sentence of excommunicatioun: Upoun the threttie day of August 1640 I, Mr William Forbes, minister of the gospell at Fraserburgh, accoirding to the ordinance of the Generall Assemblie, excommunicated in the kirk of Fraserburgh, Williame Fraser, chopman, for murtherring of Edward Skollay, and this I testifie be thir presentis; writtin be the hand of Johne Ogstoun, sessioun clerk in Fraserburgh, and subscryvit with my hand the xxiii day of November 1640. *Sic subscribitur* Mr William Forbes, minister at Fraserburgh.

As also his Majesteis Advocat repeittit the letters captioun producet quhair the pannell beiring his denunceatioun to the horne for nocht compeirance befoir the Justice the 26 of July 1639, quhilk is within fyve weikis eftir committing of the fact; and als repeittit the letters of relaxatioun producet be the pannell, quhairby he is relaxed upone the secunde and thrid dayis of July 1641 yeiris fra

[1] Probably a mistranscription of 'insenses' i.e. informs; no Scottish examples of its use traced and it is not in Jamieson.

[2] I.e. civil as opposed to ecclesiastical.

the proces of horne execute aganis him; and als producet the pannellis judicial **(158)** depositioun and confessioun maid befoir Mr Alexander Colvile, Justice Depute, upone the xxii day of Julii instant, quhairin he confesses that he changet his name fra Williame Fraser to Williame Rois; and siclyke repeittit the pannellis judiciall depositioun takin befoir Mr James Robertoun this day, quhairin he grantis that the quarrell and grudge betwix him and the defunct to be ane cuff gevin be the defunct to him a thre dayis befoir the fact, and grantis that he come to the house quhair the defunct was to drink ane pynt of aill, and grantis that he gat bak his quhinger that same nycht quhilk was sent to him be his father etc.

In respect of the quhilkis probationes be witnesses and writ as said is, producet be his Majesteis Advocat, and seing the probatioun is so cleir and evident be the pairteis confessioun, be the probatioun led befoir the presbiterie, be the depositiones of the ministeris, and haveing all the indices requyret of the law concurring to the probatioun of ane slauchter committit within the house and chalmer quhair the defunct was for the tyme, *videlicet* Johne Lyellis house, and befoir that accoirding to the pannellis confessioun a thre dayis of befoir the defunct had gevin him ane cuff, and that same nycht of the slauchter, or upone the morrow, the pannell fled out of Fraserburgh and within twa monethis thaireftir was persewit befoir the Justice and put to the horne, at quhilk he remanet above twa yeir till the tyme he was takin; *item* the miraculous staying of the bark quhairin he was goeing away haveing ane fair wind;[1] the changeing of his name fra William Fraser to William Rois, his craveing of mercie for the fact in remoirse of conscience testified be ane noble man *videlicet* my Lord Sinclair, and be ane judge, *videlicet* the Schiref depute of Aberdene; togidder with the ministeris depositiones; quhilkis all concurring ar ane maist cleir and evident probatioun to the assyse to fyle him of this bluid, togidder also the commoun and universall bruit of the countrie, and the pannellis confessioun maid be him selff that he knew nane to have splane [*spleen*] against the defunct bot himself;[2] quhilk is repeittit be my Lord Advocat to the assyse, togidder with the persewaris aithe, with the act anent the pannellis excommunicatioun. The Advocat protestis for wilfull errour gif thay acquit.[3]

The pannell with Mr David Heriote, his prelocutour, takis instrumentis of the productioun of the writtis, and of the depositiones of the witnesses led, and of thair declarationes maid, and that nather of thame doeth prove the positive pairt of the dittay quhilk is only fund relevant, *videlicet* that the defunct sould have bene murdreist be the pannell; And as to the declaratioun maid be my Lord Sinclair and remanent witnessis, it can nevir prove aganis the pannell geveand that the pannell had spokin it, quhilk is denyit, becaus it is extra judiciall confessioun, and of the law *confessio extra judicalis nihil operatur ad plenam probationem*; And althoe the pannell wald confes in judgement it wald nocht be ane ground to condempne him except the fact war cleirit to have bene done be him, and the law sayis *ubi aliter non apparet de crimine quam per confessionem ipsius rei, non debet reus ex sua sola confessione condemnari,* that is to say quhair

[1] This phenomenon was what had caused Lord Sinclair to interview the panel.
[2] Neither of the last two items could have any weight in a modern trial. See legal note 9.
[3] See legal note 10.

the delict and cryme is nocht cleirlie provin, the naikit confessioun of the pannell can nocht condempne him, ye althocht he confessed it in judgement, mekall mair this pretendit and nocht grantit extra judiciall confessioun, quhair the cryme is nocht cleirlie provin to be done be the pannell, can [not] be ane ground to ony assyse to condemne him; this is cleir in the first law of the secund title of the Digestis *de confessis* and bakit [supported] be Julius Clarus *questione* 55a his fyft buik.

Finali; And gifand he had confest, ane single confessioun is nocht ane ground to condemne him, as is cleir in the law, *unica confessio non sufficit*, as is cleir in the first law of the title ff. *de questionibus*; swa that the pretendit declaratioun of the pannell, quhilk is now denyit be the pannell, can nevir be ane grund to the assyse to convict him, the relevant pairt of the dittay anent the cryme allegit committit be the pannell nocht being provin. And as to the depositiones of the witnesses, and namelie [*particularly*] of the ministeris and the allegit tryell tane be thame, can nevir be respectit, becaus the samyn was ane unwarranted probatioun and ane unlawfull, the pairtie nocht being cited, nor na litiscontestatioun maid agains him, and ony witnesses that war ressavet thay war witnes ressavit befoir litiscontestatioun, the pairtie nocht being cited, and *Julius Clarus* in his 45 questioun sayis *Quod testes recepti ante Litiscontestationem nullam fidem faciunt contra reum cum sint examinati reo non citato*, that is to say, witnes resavit befoir litiscontestatioun, the pairtie nocht being cited, can nevir mak fayth aganis him, for gif he had bene cited he wald haif objected aganis the relevancie of his lybell, the verritie of the deid, and the unlawfulnes **(159)** of the witnesses. And quhar thay affirme that the pannellis father compeirit it is cleirlie confest, he being confronted with the witnesses that he had no warrand of the pannell: swa theise unwarrantable proceidingis can nevir be ane ground to the assyse to mak the pannell guiltie of the fact, it nocht being provin. And as to the alledget depositiones of the pannell himselff, maid to Mr Alexander Colvile and Mr James Robertoun, thair is no ground in thame to be ane warrand to the assyse to mak the pannell culpable or to convince him of the fact; the fact itselff, quhilk is only thair pairt to try, nocht being provin; and, albeit thair wald appeir to be vidimuses [?witnesses] and presumptiones, yit thay ar no cleir ground to infer the fact lybellit to have bene done be the pannell; and as to the letters of hoirning and excommunicatioun mentionet, thay can be na ground to the inqueist, becaus his hoirning proceidit he nocht being lawfullie chairget nor cited, nather can it be instructed that he was lawfullie charget; and altho he had bene lauchfullie charget and went to the horne, it can be no ground to infer that, althought he gaid to the horne, thairfoir he committit the deid: that followis nocht. And as to the excommunicatioun it proceidit upone his contumacie, becaus he compeirit nocht to answeir, bot he is nocht excommunicat becaus he murdreist the defunct; and quhairas the warrand wald appeir to beir that it being tryit that he committit it, that tryell as said is was unlawfull, the pairtie not being cittet, and sa can be na ground to the assyse of convictioun; for all that the assyse hes to try is quhidder or no the pannell murdreist the defunct, quhilk is only fund relevant, and nane of the foirsaidis presumptiones can cleir the same.

It is answeirit be my Lord Advocat that, albeit confessioun extrajudiciall be the selff allone in some caices will nocht suffice for condemnatioun, yit be all laweiris it is aggreit that, quhair uther indices, presumptiones, conjectouris, concurris, the samyn joyntlie ar ane sufficient ground for convictioun, speciallie quhair the cryme is nocht probable be witnes, bot committit in secreit and in ane hous quhair the defunct was, and nane thair at the committing of the fact bot the defunct and the pannell, except ane Gilbert Wardon, quhome the pannell alledges to be present, and this man being uset as ane witnes was castin [*spurned*] be the father quho compeirit befoir the presbiterrie of Deir, and this is cleir be Pharinacius, speciallie quhair the confessioun is nocht only doublett bot also maid befoir ane gritt number *videlicet* threttie persones, and also quhair it is maid upone remorse for exoneratioun of conscience as this is; and this all concurris: preceiding quarrell, slauchter within thre dayis; comeing to the house quhair the man was; flight immediat; accusatioun of pairtie befoir the Justice; his going to the horne; remaneing thairat twa yeir; the commoun bruit and fame; the ministeris depositiones; the Assembleis excommunicatioun becaus of the deid provin; his confessioun befoir noblemen, judges and utheris famous witnesses; his awin confessiones; the change of his name; and the miraculous staying of the bark quhair he was takin; And as to the remanent repeittis the haill writtis.

It is answeirit be the pannell that quhair the Advocat manteanes that the extra judiciall confessioun, althoght be itselff in some caices it could not prove, yit haveing so mony presumptiones conjoynet togidder as is heir and that the fact was so secreitlie done, that it could nocht be provin be witnesses, it is answeirit thairto be the pannell that althocht that held in some caices, quhilk is nocht granted, it can nevir prove heir quhair the deid is nocht secreitlie done, becaus be the persewaris awin lybell it was condiscendit that thair war sundrie complices and be thair awin hoirning gif ony be it will be cleir that thair war sevin or aucht persones within the hous the tyme of the alledget fact quhairof thair is some gone to the horne, so it can nocht be callit secreitlie to have bene done it being in ane innes [*inn*], upone fair day licht, betwix thre and foure eftir noone, swa it being such ane publict deid could nocht be secreitlie done; The quilk the pannell craved the assyse to advert unto, protesting gif thay fylet the pannell of this fact, he nocht confessing the samyn bot denying it altogidder, for manifest and wilfull errour.[1]

My Lord Advocat protestit in the contrair gif thay acquit etc.

Quhilkis persones of assyse being ressavit sworne and admittit, eftir accusatioun of the said Williame Fraser be dittay in thair presens and audience, and repetitioun of the probatioun thairof, alsweill be writ as witnesses be the persewaris, and of the pannellis answeiris and objectiones maid thairto, thay removet altogidder furth of court to the assyse hous, quhair thay electit and chooset be pluralitie of voittis the said Johne Malcolme, herauld, in chanceller, thay thaireftir reasonet and voitted upone the poyntis of the said dittay and haill qualificationes thairof, and being ryplie and at lenth advyset thairwith, re-enterit agane in court, quhair thay all in ane voce be the repoirt and judiciall declaratioun of the said Johne Malcolme, chanceller, fand pronuncet and declairet the said Williame Fraser, now upone pannell, conforme to the depositiones maid

[1] See legal note 11.

judiciallie be my Lord Sinclair, Mr Williame Davidsone, Schiref depute of Aberdene, the ministeris depositiones, and remanent witnesses sworne and examinat in thair presens and audience, to be fylet, culpable and convict of the crewall slauchter and murthour of the said umquhile Edward Skollay committit be him in maner and at the tyme specifeit in his dittay, quhairupone the said Jeane Currour, persewar, with his Majesteis Advocat askit actis and instrumentis.

The Justice continewis the pronunceing of dome upone the former convictioun aganis the pannell till Tuysday nixt, to the effect he may be advyset with the Lords of Parliament now sitting anent the forme and maner of the pannellis puneischment, and ressave thair Lordschips resolutioun and answeir thairintill; ordaining the pannell to be returnet to his waird to remane in irones quhill the outgeving of the said dome.

(160) [4 August 1641: Colville and Robertoun JJ.D.]

(161) The samyn day Williame Fraser, merchand in Fraserburgh, being brocht out of waird and presentit upone pannell to heir dome pronuncet against him, as he that was deulie and ordourlie convict be ane assyse in ane court of Justiciarie haldin within the tolbuthe of Edinburgh be Mr James Robertoun, advocat, Justice Depute, upone the last day of July last past, of the crewall murthour and slauchter of umquhile Edward Skollay in Fingask, committit be him in maner and at the tyme specifeid in his dittay, and convictioun following thairupone, quhilk dome and pronunceatioun thairof was continewit be the Justice unto the tyme the Parliament, now sitting, war maid acquent with said convictioun, and thair Lordschips advyse and resolution war gevin anent the forme and maner of the said William Fraser his puneishment, and ane supplicatioun gevin to thair Lordschips for that effect, off the quhilk supplicatioun the tennour followis: My Lordis of Parliament unto your Lordschips humlie meanis and schawis we your Lordschips servitouris, Maisteris Alexander Colvile[1] and James Robertoun Justice Deputtis, that quhair upone Setterday last, being the last day of July lastbypast, Williame Fraser was be ane condigne assyse convict in ane Justice court of the slauchter of umquhile Edward Skollay, upone presumptiones, indices and extrajudiciall confessioun without ony depositioun of witnesses present at the committing of the fact, or of the malefactouris confessioun in judgement, and seing be the lawis of the best governet nationes and custome of justice courtes observet heirtofoir, the advyce of the supreame Judge is necesserlie requyret in sic caices[2] for pronunceing of dome upone malefactouris convict as said is, we thairfoir doe in all humilitie beg your Lordschips ordour and advyce thairanent with your Lordschips answeir. Followis the delyverance thairupoun *tertio Augusti* 1641:[3] This petitioun being red in Parliament, remittis the same agane to the Justice to proceid against the convict persone accoirding to the lawis of this kingdome. *Sic subscribitur* Burghlie *I.P.D. Parliamenti,* Conforme to the quhilk the Justices,

[1] See legal note 12.
[2] See legal note 13.
[3] *APS* V.321b.

be the mouth of Patrick Barrie, dempster of court, adjudget decernit and ordanit the said William Fraser, upone Mononday nixt, the nynt of this instant, to be tane to the mercat croce of Edinburgh, and thair his heid to be strukin frome his body, and all his moveable guidis to be escheit and inbrocht to our Soverane Lordis use, as culpable and convict of the said slauchter, quhilk was pronuncet for dome.

Legal Notes

1. The panel was not granted the usual *induciae* of fifteen days, recognised as the rule from *Quoniam Attachiamenta* (ch. 2.3; Hume II.257). Hume however suggests that the rule only applied to panels who were at liberty and were summoned on criminal letters. In the present case the panel had been at the horn for about two years and was in custody, having been brought from Aberdeen to Edinburgh where he was cited on a 48 hours induciae. He had every justification for his complaint that he did not have time to prepare his defence.

2. The motion is an extraordinary one, and contrary to the Act of 1587 chap. 91. This course however was adopted in *Cheyne* v *Mowat* 1642 below p. 464 and of consent in *Davidson* v *Anderson* above p. 409. In the present case, though 'sworn and received' before the debate on the relevancy, the witnesses do not in fact appear to have deponed until the appropriate stage. It may be that it was merely the competency of the witnesses that was decided at this early stage. The panel challenged certain of them on grounds not specified, but which were referred to their great oaths. Thereafter they were admitted as competent witnesses.

3. The Lord Advocate's argument that by asking for a continuation of the diet and allowing witnesses to be sworn, the panel had precluded himself from excepting to the jurisdiction of the Court by seeking repledgiation to another court, seems highly technical.

4. Repledging was refused because of non production of either (*a*) the regality infeftment, and a procuratory to found on it, or (*b*) evidence of a former repledging from the Justice Court to that regality. This again appears a highly technical decision as the infeftment had been produced in this Court in earlier proceedings for this very murder (ms. VI.75). Time was not even granted for further investigation. Instances of successful repledging will be found above (I.69, 129, 263, 275). For the procedure generally see Dickinson, *Fife Sheriff Court Book* 344.

5. This is another instance of the assize asking for evidence (see above p. 414 Janet Corser 23 April 1641) which suggests that some of them must have had personal knowledge of the incident, and of those who could speak to it, and were entitled to use it.

6. The pre-trial procedures before the Church Court here are remarkable and must have been highly prejudicial to the panel. Before the Synod and Presbytery his responsibility for the killing was assumed, and the Synod directed the latter to 'try the qualitie of the murthour'. This they did, and after 'dew tryell and examination of diverse witnesses' but in the absence of the accused, found the killing 'to be ane most wylde and wilful murthour' on which, following a petition by the widow to the General Assembly, excommunication passed. The Lord Advocate produced to the assize as adminicles of evidence on the present charge *inter alia* a testimonial signed by the members of the Presbytery who conducted this trial, and the relevant Act of Assembly. He also adduced two of the ministers who had been members of the Presbytery to testify to the proceedings before them. The decision of another court, therefore, was accepted as competent evidence against the accused albeit the Privy Council had taken the view that a Presbytery 'were not judges of the fact' and should not put an accused to his oath for adultery (*RPC*[1] XIV.619). For other examples however see above I.47-51, 105-6. For the relevance of a decision before another court in modern practice see Law Reform (Miscellaneous Provisions) (Scotland) Act 1968, Part III.

7. This is an unusual step—the confrontation of contradictory witnesses—which is a feature of the continental inquisitorial system. The witness—the panel's father—having deponed to certain happenings before the Presbytery, the two ministers, who had earlier given evidence, were recalled and according to the report were 'confronted' with the father, and given the opportunity to rebut the evidence he had given. Hume does not mention the matter. For another example see above I.107.

8. The law as to whether near relatives of the prosecutor were competent witnesses was unsettled even in Hume's day (II.345-6) but he cites cases of 1669 and 1709 in which objections to them were repelled (Scott Moncrieff I.307). The Church evidently took a strict view in favour of the panel.

9. This illustrates that hardly any evidence however remotely relevant to the charge was considered incompetent to go before the jury. Many of the factors relied on here by the Crown would be unexceptionable today—circumstantial evidence in the form of the panel changing his name, and trying to flee the country; evidence of admissions against interest to a number of witnesses, and of the panel's demeanour when making them; evidence of judicial declarations made by the panel before two Justice Deputes. In addition to these however the Crown founded on the stopping of the boat taking the accused abroad, notwithstanding 'ane fair wynd' i.e., a miracle; and on 'the common bruit of the countrey' i.e. hearsay. Indeed in his address the Lord Advocate referred to 'the commoun and universal bruit of the countrie' in the same sentence as he referred to the panel's confession. He also relied strongly on the documentary and oral evidence of the proceedings before the Presbytery and General Assembly; and drew a sinister inference from the panel's having been outlawed for non-compearance for this crime for some two years.

10. The jury were empanelled and the Crown evidence led before them. Thereafter the record reports at unusual length the submissions of prosecution and defence counsel. Each spoke twice, and the defence had the last word. The Lord Advocate's first speech reads like an address to the jury. It is not at all clear however whether the first defence speech was directed to bench or jury or both. In it, objection is taken to the competency of some of the evidence led, and counsel is reported as quoting Latin maxims, the Digest, and Clarus to support his argument. The question of the sufficiency of an extra-judicial confession is also debated. It looks very much like submission that certain evidence should not go to the jury and that there is no case for the jury to consider. It is unlikely that the jury would make much of the Latin quotations. It is however too early for the concept of 'withdrawing a charge' or a direction on law to the jury. The whole learned debate proceeded in front of them and in his second speech, defence counsel specially craves the assize to consider certain submissions on the facts.

In the argument the Lord Advocate seems to have conceded that an extra-judicial confession would not *per se* be a sufficient basis for a conviction. The defence went further and submitted that a plea of 'guilty' in court would not be sufficient either, which was contrary to practice. Hume (II.321) and Royston (Notes 257) misrepresent the case by implying that the conviction was solely based on the confession whereas there were many other circumstances on which the prosecution was entitled to found.

11. The defence protest for error against the jury, if they convicted, was pointless. The Act 1475 cap. 63 dealing with wilful error is only concerned with unjust acquittals. Mackenzie (*Criminals* II.xxiii.12) opines that if an assize were to condemn 'without any probation or by palpable iniquity' they might be liable at common law, and Balfour (266) appears to support this. There is however no known instance of proceedings against a jury who convicted as opposed to one which acquitted.

12. It is not clear what right Colville J.D. had to join in the petition to Parliament since he was not the trial judge.

13. In the absence of eyewitness evidence of the crime, or a confession to it by the accused, the Justice Court at this period declined to pronounce sentence, but referred the matter to Parliament as the supreme judge. Hume refers to the case (II.507) as showing that while Parliament's advice might be sought by the Court, there was no appeal to Parliament by the accused.

(160) [4 August 1641: Colvile and Robertoun JJ.D.]

Slaughter. Patoun contra *Wilsone and his spous. Past frae.*

The quhilk day anent the actioun and caus criminall persewit befoir his Majesteis Justice Generall and Justice deputis upone the xxi day of Julii lastbypast at the instance of James Patoun in Eister Adie,[1] as father with the brether and remanent kyn and freindis of umquhile Johne Patoun, sone to the said James, aganis Andro Wilsone, gairdner in Adie, and Iden Cuthbert his spous, for allegit airt and pairt of the slauchter of the said umquhile John Patoun,

[1] Aldid in Fossoway parish, Kinross-shire.

committit upone the first day of Julii last, in maner specifeit in the criminall letters direct aganis thame thairanent, quhilk dyet with the said Andro Wilsone and his said spous tryell of thair guiltines or innocencie of the said slauchter was continewit to this day, as the act of adjornall maid thairupone of the dait foirsaid proportis;[1] The said James Patoun in Eister Adie, father to the said umquhile Johne Patoun, compeirand personallie in judgement as persewar on the ane pairt, and on the uther pairt, Johne Wilsone, eldest sone to the said Andro Wilsone, gairdner, his father and as cautioner for him and for Iden Cuthbert, his mother, spous to the said Andro, compeirand also personallie, with Mr Thomas Nicolsone, younger, advocat, and Johne Myller, wryter to his Majesteis signet,[2] as prelocutouris for the said Johne Wilsone, quha declairet that the said Andro Wilsone and Iden Cuthbert his spous war nocht as yit convaleschet of thair seiknes with the quhilk thay haif bene visseit thir twa monethis bygane, the verritie quhairof is sufficientlie knawin to the said James Patoun, persewar, himselff, to quhais answeir and declaratioun thairanent the said Johne Wilsone referrit himselff, and thairfoir demandit of the said James Patoun gif he wald insist in persute of the said Andro Wilsone and Iden Cuthbert his spous for the slauchter abonewrittin, quhais innocencie thairof is cleirlie knawin to the said James himself, and that the saidis Andro Wilsone and his said spous war nawayis accessorie to the said slauchter, nor war nather airt nor pairt to the samyn, quhilk was testifeit judiciallie to my Lord Justice be the declaratioun of Mr Laurence Merser, minister at Fortoquhy [Fossoway], James Creichtoun, bailyie of Adie,[3] and Alexander Patoun thair, compeirand judiciallie this day and testifeing the samyn, to be of verritie,[4] speciallie in respect the said slauchter was committit be James Wilsone, sone to the said Andro quha hes past to the horne, and hes tane the said cryme upone him, and remanes fugitive thairfoir, nather his father nor mother being on the ground quhair the said slauchter was committit at the tyme of the committing thairof. For answer thairto the said James Patoun as father for himselff and in name of the remanent persewaris insert in the saidis criminall letters, upone provisioun and expres conditioun following, *viz.* that the said Andro Wilsone, his spous and thair haill famelie betwix [*between now*] and Mertimes nixt, remove thameselffis af the boundis of Aldie and landis thairof, and nocht to return thairto thaireftir, quhairby the father, brether and remanent kyn and freindis of the said umquhile Johne Patoun may ony wayis be irritat or provoikit to offence heireftir, and to find cautioun for that effect, he, *viz.* the said James Patoun, past *simpliciter* fra the persute of the saidis Andro Wilsone and Iden Cuthbert, his spous, for the slauchter abonewrittin. Quhairupone the said Johne Wilsone askit actis and instrumentis and of his awin consent become actit and obleist, as cautioner for the said Andro Wilsone, his father, that he and the said Iden, his spous, thair bairnes, servandis and hail famelie sall remove thameselffis af the ground of the saidis landis of Adie betwix [date omitted] and the said terme of Mertimes nixt, and nocht to returne thairto at ony tyme thaireftir, nather yit to irritat or provoik the said James Patoun or

[1] See legal note 1.
[2] See legal note 2.
[3] Presumably baron baillie of the barony of Aldie.
[4] See legal note 3.

his sones nor na uther of the kyn and freindis of the said umquhile Johnne Patoun to ony offence in the meane tyme, under the pane of ane hundreth pundis money to be payit to the said James Patoun in caice of failyie or contravening of the premisses; Quhairupone the said James Patoun also askit instrumentis. The Justice, in respect of the said persewair his passing fra the persute of the saidis Andro Wilsone and of Iden Cuthbert his spous for the allegit cryme abone-writtin, desertis the foirsaid dyet upone the said Andro Wilsone and his spous and discharget the outgeving of ony criminall letters aganis thame as being ather airt or pairt of the slauchter abonespecifeit in ony tyme cuming; Quhairupone ather pairtie *hinc inde* askit actis and instrumentis.

Legal Notes

1. This is a curious case. The charge against the panels, who were husband and wife, was art and part of a slaughter. They were represented by their eldest son who appeared with counsel and a writer to the signet, and intimated that his parents were unable to attend because of sickness. The defence then demanded to be told if the prosecutors meant to proceed, produced three witnesses to testify to the panels' innocence, and named another son who had been outlawed as the person responsible for the crime. The case was settled by the private prosecutors deserting *simpliciter* on condition that the accused and their whole family removed themselves permanently from the district to prevent the kin and friends of the deceased being 'irritat or provoikit to offence heirefter'.

2. This is one of the rare appearances of a W.S. as to which see also *Jordan* v *Edmonston* 1641 below.

3. The purpose of the minister and two others testifying at this stage—in the absence of panels and of assize—can only have been to strengthen the defence demand that the pursuer desert the case. They stated that the accused had not been present where the crime was committed and further that in fact it had been committed by one of their sons. This however hardly amounts to a special defence of alibi since it is not stated where they had been at the relevant time (see *Davidson* v *Anderson* 1641 above p. 409). This is one of the first cases noted of impeachment of a third party.

(161) [6 October 1641]

Thift. Hoirning producet. Campbellis et *Stewart* contra *The Clandonald and utheris.*

The quhilk day, in presence of me nottar publict clerk depute in the office of Justiciarie,[1] and witnessis underwrittin, compeirit personallie George Campbell, clerk to ane nobill and potent Erle Archibald Erle of Argyle, Lord Campbell and Loirne *etc.*, and producet the criminall letters deulie execute and indorsate raiset at the instance of Alexander Campbell, lawfull sone to Archibald Campbell of Innerraw,[2] Patrick Campbell of Aucherehaw,[3] and Margaret Stewart relict of umquhile Johne Stewart of Letterchunay,[4] aganis Johne Moir McDonnald in Innergarrie,[5] Ferquhar Makdonnald VcBeane his servand, Donnald McDonnald VcBeane, his bowman, Donnald Dow McWilliame VcMeghneis tennent to the said Johne Moir McDonald, chairgeing thame to have fund cautioun

[1] John Bannatyne, W.S.

[2] Inverawe by Taynuilt.

[3] Acheraw by Barcaldine?

[4] Lettirschewnay in Appin.

[5] This Invergarry was W of Loch Oich in the Great Glen in Inverness-shire.

for thair personall compeirance befoir our Soverane Lord Justice and his deputtis this day and plaice in the hour of caus to have underlyne the law for the severall and perticular thiftis efter following specifeit and contenit in the saidis criminall letters viz:—for the thiftious steilling of ane twa yeir auld hors ane meir and ane fillie, pryce thairof four hundreth merkis pertening to the said Alexander Campbell furthe of the landis of Innercharnane in Glennaeties[1] in the moneth of September imvic and fourtie yeiris; *Item* for the steilling of thrie hors fra the said Patrick Campbell in the moneth of August imvic threttie nyne yeiris furth of the landis of Barnamuck in Benedealock,[2] pryce of the saidis thrie hors thrie hundreth merkis; And last for steilling of uther thrie hors pryce thairof thrie hundreth merkis, pertening to the said Margaret Stewart furthe of the landis of Sassacloche[3] in Appin in the said yeir of God imvic threttie nyne yeiris; Be vertew of the quhilkis letters and executiones thairof, and for nocht finding of the said cautioun, the saidis persones defenders perticularlie abonenominat and ilk ane of thame ar denuncet rebellis and put to the horne and registrat thairat as fugitivis fra his Hienes lawis for the saidis thiftious crymes.[4] Upoun the productioun of the quhilkis criminall letters, dewlie execute, indorsate and registrat as said is the said George Campbell askit actis and instrumentis and protestit in respect of the productioun and repoirting thairof for releiff of Dougall Campbell fier of Innerraw, cautioner fund be the persewaris of the saidis letters at the raiseing thairof of his cautionarie and of all penaltie or unlaw to be incurrit be him thairthrow. This was done within the laich tolbuithe of Edinburgh in that pairt thairof quhair his Majesteis Justice and Justice deputtis ordinarlie sittis and haldis Justice courtis[5] betwix alevin and twelff houris befoir noone, day, moneth and yeir of God foirsaid in presence of Lauchlane Makintosche, brother germane to Williame Makintosche of Torcastell, Johne and George Bannatynes my sones, James Douglas Johne Hamyltoun and James Kynneir Justice officeris, witnessis speciallie requyrit and desyrit to the premissis.

Hoirning producet. McIntosches and Myller contra *The Clandonald and utheris.*

The samyn day in presence of me, nottare publict and clerke depute in the office of Justiciarie, and of the witnessis underwrittin, compeirit personallie Lauchlane McIntosche, brothair germane to William McIntosche of Torcastle, as maister,[6]   McQueane, the relict of umquhile Lauchlane Makintosche, Angus McIntosche, as brother to the said umquhile Lauchlane, servand for the tyme to the said Williame Makintosche of Torcastle, Angus, John and Allaster Milleris, as brither to umquhile William Miller, also servand for the tyme to the said William McIntosche of Torcastle, with the remanent kyn and freindis of the saidis umquhile Lauchlane McIntosche and William Miller, and Sir Thomas Hope of Craighall, knycht barronet, Advocat to our Soverane Lord, for his

1 Invercharnan in Glen Etive at the head of Loch Etive in Lorn.
2 Barnamuc in Benderloch is towards the head of Glen Creran.
3 Presumably a slip for Fasnacloich in Glen Creran.
4 See legal note 1.
5 Another example of the master pursuing for the murder of his servant, the master being represented by his brother. See also Gray v Reid II.387.
6 Torcastle is 4 miles NE of Fort William.

Hienes intreis, aganis John McDonald in Innergarie, John McDonald, younger, his brother, Allexander McDonald in Culleachie,[1] also his brother, Rorie McGillespik, John McCouill VcEane, Allexander McGillespik, Allaster McCouill VcGorie, Dougall McConnochie VcInnes, Angus McGilliechallum VcConnochie, Rorie Dow McInnes Roy, all servandis and followeris of Angus McDonald of Glengarie, Donald McCouill VcEane Vayne in Strouthroak, John Couill in Achnaddarache,[2] Allane McAllane VikInnes, and [ ] Makallanes, his twa sones, Angus McEane VcInnes Oig in Kyterack, Johnne Bayne McInnes VcAllaster in Killmen, John McEwin VcEane Ovistich in Fothiein,[3] Johnne McInnes VcDonald VcAllane thair, Donald Ovir his brothair thair, Johnne McCouill VcEane Voir in Dain, Neill McCouill Vig Ewin Roy in Keltir, Donald Oig McCouill Bowie VcEwin in Drenachan,[4] John McEwin VcEane Dowie in Lagane,[4] all tennentis and servandis to the said Angus McDonald of Glengarie and dwelland upone his landis, Duncane McMairtene *alias* Camrone of Letterfindlay,[5] John McRorie VcConnochie in Stronnaba,[5] servand to the said Duncane McMertene, Allaster Dow McCouill VcAllaster VcEwin, servand to Thomas Fraser of Ardache, Allaster Beg in Aberchaldour, brother to the said Allaster Dow, [ ] McConnochie, sone to Gillespik McConnochie, officer in Aberchaldour, Angus McRonald VcAllane in Ardibeg, Donald McEane VcEwin Duy Donald McInnes VcAllane VcInnes Voir in Schian[6], with his twa uncles Allane [ ] McInnes Voiris, chairgeing thame to have fund cautione for thair personall compeirance befoir his Majesteis Justice and his deputtis this day and place in the hour of caus to have underlyne the law for airt and pairt of the slauchter and crewell murthour of the saidis umquhile Lauchlane McIntosche and umquhile William Miller, servandis to the said William McIntosche of Torcastle, committit at the poirt [*harbour*] of Innernes upone the fyftene day of August lastbypast[7] in forme and maner specifeit in the saidis criminall letters, be vertew of the quhilkis criminall letters and executiones thairof and for not finding of the said cautione the haill foirnamet persones defenderis perticulerlie abone expremit, and ilk ane of thame, ar denuncet our Soverane Lordis rebellis and put to his Hienes horne as fugitivs fra his Majesteis lawis for the saidis crymes.[8] Upoun the productione of the quhilkis criminall letters dewlie execute and indorsate and registratione thairof as said is, the said Lauchlane McIntosche, brother germane to the said William McIntosche of Torcastle, as cautioner and souertie for repoirting and persuite of the saidis criminall letters at the reaseing thairof, askit actis and instrumentis and protestit in respect of the productione of the samyn for his releiff as cautioner foirsaid and for all payment of any payne or unlaw to be incurrit be him thairthrow. This was done within the laighe tolbuithe of Edinburgh in that pairt thairof quhair his Majesteis Justice and his deputtis ordinarlie sittis

[1] Cullachy is just N of Loch Oich.
[2] Achadh nan darach is 3 miles N of Invergarry Castle.
[3] Faichen is between the Castle and Loch Garry.
[4] Drynachan is on the W bank of Loch Oich and this Laggan just S of that loch.
[5] Letterfinlay and Stronenaba are on the E bank of Loch Lochy.
[6] The remaining places have not been identified.
[7] This was a Sunday, see *RPC*[2] VII.561.
[8] This was done on 20 Sept. 1641, *RPC*[2] VII.173.

and haldis thair Justice courtis betwixt ellevin and twelff houris befoir none, day, monethe and yeir foirsaid in presence of George Campbell, ordiner clerk to ane noble and potent Erle, Archibald, Erle of Argyll, Lord Campbell and Lorne, Johnne and George Bannatynes, my sones, James Douglas, John Hamiltoun and James Kynneir ordiner officeris of the said court of Justiciarie, witnesses speciallie desyret and requyrit to all and sindrie the premissis.[1]

Legal Notes

1. Argyll might have dealt with these charges at Inverary as offences committed within his jurisdiction (see Cameron, *Argyll Justiciary Records*, 1664-1705.I.x). It may however be that the residence of the accused was treated here as determining the court to which he was to be cited, and this Invergarry was in Inverness. Mackenzie (II.II.12) recognised the *forum originis* and the *forum domicilii* of the accused as well as the *forum delicti commissi* as competent courts. Cf. Hume's view that the *forum delicti* is 'the prime and most proper forum in criminal matters' (II.57).

2. These two hornings against the McDonalds of Invergarry, cadets of Glengarry, have no particular legal interest except as showing the practical difficulties of obtaining redress for crimes committed in the highlands by the ordinary processes of the criminal law. The history of the murder charge here shows how recourse was had to other means.

Old Angus McDonald of Glengarry (then styled Donald McAngus) had been before this Court in 1626 for illegally putting two men to death, but was saved by the intervention of the Privy Council (I.557, 558, 565, for a similar case see Douglas of Drumlanrig 1602 *RPC*[1] VI.473, 481). While in Edinburgh in the winter of 1641 he was cited before the Privy Council by Macintosh of Torcastle one of the pursuers in the murder charge (who pursued as master of the victims) on a supplication that as titular chief and master he should be committed to ward until the accused in that charge, who had been outlawed on 6th October, 1641, were produced to answer it. His grandson (also Angus) appeared for him. In respect that the old man was 'near ane hundreth yeeres of age' and the grandson in fact managed the estate and was followed and acknowledged as chief, their Lordships on 3rd December, 1641, ordered the latter to find caution for the compearance of the accused. Young Angus refused and was imprisoned (see *RPC*[2] VII.173-4).

After confinement for 'ane long space,' first in the castle and then in the town, he was allowed to go north to arrange redress, on caution to reappear before the Council on 1st January, 1643. Parties met at Inverness on 29th October, 1642 and Glengarry proposed that the three principal accused (who were his uncles; John, younger, being designed as 'of Slisgarrow') would submit to the decision of named arbiters and he himself (though altogether innocent) would guarantee the assythment awarded. Torcastle and his friends however refused these terms 'alluterlie' (utterly), on the ground that they were not *bona fide* and would never be implemented (see *RPC*[2] VII.559-563). The next move was that Glengarry's friends presented to the Privy Council an instrument by responsible persons that the satisfaction offered was reasonable. Finally on 24th January, 1643, he found caution in the sum of 10,000 merks that he would keep ward in Edinburgh till he and his cautioner lodged a band by them that they would see the arbiters' award obtempered (see *RPC*[2] VII.580-581, 592). The case then disappears from the records.

Prefatory note to Cheynes v *Mowat and Ors., Shetland*

This demembration case figures often in the records of the Justice Court and Privy Council over the period 1641-43, and is several times referred to by Mackenzie, Pitmedden and Hume. There had apparently been 'secret grudges' between the parties (p. 473 below), and these flared up at the time of a head court at Scalloway in November, 1638, there being scuffles on the 9th and 10th.

The Mowats and the Nivens were litigious people, and there was a prolonged process between them before the Privy Council in 1624, when the Mowats were friendly with the Cheynes (*RPC*[1] XIV.717-776). The three Niven brothers were all notaries public, and should have known how to behave, but Ninian Niven was well known for violence and chicanery. (F. J. Grant, *Zetland Family Histories*, 1907, pp. 207-208).

[1] See legal note 2.

The first stage of this prosecution was on 10th November, 1641, when the prosecutors failed to appear. As a consequence their cautioner was fined for having been responsible for the panels being brought 300 miles to Edinburgh, waiting there ten weeks in anticipation of the trial, and then not compearing themselves. Later after being warded in Scalloway Castle, two of the panels escaped; one at least was rearrested, and three of them were taken to Edinburgh in January, 1642.

In June James Mowat and Ninian suffered a 'sudden inconvenience' by being mysteriously burnt with a blast of powder in the High Street, such that they were unable to leave their lodging without 'hazard of their lives,' which led to several continuations.

Ultimately on 15th July, 1642, all three were brought to trial, the evidence having been taken in advance, on interrogatories, before the Justice Depute of consent of parties, before the relevancy of the charge had been determined (p. 471 below). After hearing the depositions read the assize rejected a plea of self-defence, and convicted the panels of being each art and part in the wounding (p. 480). The Justice Depute referred the question of sentence to the Privy Council, who tried unsuccessfully to get the parties to settle their differences. All three were then found liable jointly and severally in assythment to the complainers and in a fine to the Crown. In 1643 discharges were registered (p. 484), and the case disappears from the records.

(163) [10 November 1641: Robertoun J.D.]

Mutilatioun. Act. Cheynis contra *Nevingis* et *Mowat.*

The quhilk day compeirit personallie Mr. James Mowat of Ollaberie[1] and Niniane Neving of Windhous,[1] quha exponit and declairit that thai and ather of thame, togidder with James Neving, brother to the said Niniane and John Neveing also his brother, war chairget be vertew of criminall letters reaset at the instance of Mr Patrik Cheyne of Valley,[2] Laurance and James Cheynes, his brether, Mathow Sinclair, sone to Laurance Sinclair of Ustnes,[2] Robert Irving, servitour to the said Mr Patrik, and Gilbert Hay, servand to Gilbert Bisset of Mewie,[3] to have fund cautione for our [*sic*] personall compeirance befoir the Justice and his deputtis, this day and place, to have underlyne the law for alledget airt and pairt of the hurting, wounding and mutilatione of the saidis Mr Patrik Cheyne, of the saidis Mr Patrik Cheyne of his left hand, Laurence Cheane, his brother, of his rycht hand, and of the alledget hurting and wounding of the saidis James Cheane, Mathow Sinclair, Robert Irving, and Gilbert Hay in thair headis, armes, legis and utheris pairtis of thair bodeis to the effusione of thair blood,[4] alledgit committit upone the nynt day of November 1638 yeiris neir to the castell yett of Skalloway[5] at ane schiref head court of the schirefdome of Zetland, keipit and haldin that day be James Sinclair of Skalloway and Johnne Aitkin, commissar, schireff deputtis of the said schirefdome, in maner specifeit in the saidis criminall letters; off the quhilk alledget crymes thay affirmit thameselffis to be altogidder innocent. Lykas for tryell thairof thay nocht onlie fand Andro Bruce of Munes cautioner to the effect foirsaid, bot also for the said cautioneris releiff and cleiring of thair awin innocencie of the crymes foirsaidis

[1] Ollaberry is on the W side of Yell Sound, Northmaven Parish, Mainland, Shetland, and Windhouse at the SE end of Whale Firth on the island of Yell.

[2] Vaila, an island on W coast of Walls parish, Mainland. Ust Ness is in the parish of Whiteness, near Scalloway. For the Cheyne brothers see *Zetland Family Histories*, 48-49.

[3] Mewie or Neving is in Sandness parish.

[4] See legal note 1.

[5] Scalloway is 5 miles W of Lerwick.

as said is, compeirit this day, and willinglie offerrit thameselffis reddie to abyde the tryell of the law for the samyn as altogidder innocent thairof, disassenting *simpliciter* to all maner of continowatione; And in respect nane of the perseweris foirsaidis insert in the saidis criminall letters compeiris this day and place to produce the samyn dewlie execute and indorsate agains thame, nor to insist in thair persuit for the saidis alledget crymes mentionat thairintill, being oft tymes callit upone to that effect, the saidis Mr James Mowat and Niniane Neveing haveing travellit frome thair awin housis to this brught of Edinburgh, quhilk is mair nor thrie hundrethe myllis in distance and remanit this ten oulkis [*weeks*] bygane within this said brught attending upone the keiping of the said dyet, to thair great and exterordiner chairgcs sustenit be thame thairthrow, thay thairupone askit instrumentis of thair compeirance and protestit for releiff of the said Andro Bruce of Munes, thair cautioner, and that na letters or chairges sould be direct agains thame at the instance of the perseweris abonewrittin for the said alledget crymes in any tyme cuming, and in caice of raiseing thairof protestit that cautione be fund be the perseweris for refounding to thame of thair expenssis conforme to the Justice modificatione.

The samyn day John Dingwall, burges of Creall [*Crail*], being oft tymes callit as cautioner and souertie for reporting and persuite of the criminall letters and persewing thairof reaset [*raised*] at the instance of [the said complainers] aganis Niniane Neving of Windhous, James Neveing of Skethbrught,[1] John Neveing of Luning,[1] Mr James Mowat of Ollaberrie, and Gilbert Mowat of Collafirthe,[2] chairgeing thame to find cautione for thair personall compeirance befoir his Majesteis Justice and his deputtis this day and place in the hour of caus to have underlyne the law for airt and pairt of the hurting, wounding and mutilatione of the said Mr Patrik Cheyne of his left hand, of the said Laurance Cheyne, his brother, of his rycht hand, and hurting and wounding of the saidis James Cheyne, Mathow Sinclair, Robert Irving and Gilbert Hay in thair headis, armes, leggis and utheris pairtis of thair bodie to the effusione of thair bluid committit the nynt day of November 1638 neir to the castell yett of Skalloway in maner specifeit in the saidis criminall letters, lauchtfull tyme of day biddin, and the foirnamet persones perseweris of the saidis letters with the said John Dingwall, thair cautioner, nawayis compeirand to produce the samyn dewlie execut and indorsate and to insist in the persuite of the saidis defenderis for the crymes abonewrittin insert thairintill, the Justice thairfoir, be the mouthe of James Douglas, dempster of court, decernit and ordanit the said John Dingwall as cautioner foirsaid to be unlawit and amerciat in the paynes contenit in the Actis of Parliament, *viz.* for not reportting of the said letters and persuite thairof aganis the said Niniane Neving of Windhous, James Neveing of Skethburghe, John Neveing of Luneing, Mr James Mowat of Alloberrie, and Gilbert Mowat of Collafirthe for ilk ane of thame in the payne of twa hundrethe merkis.

NOTE

The case shows that the King's writ ran in Sheltand.

It is remarkable however that the Lord Advocate did not appear at this or the continued diet to support a prosecution for mutilation at a head court. He does not appear in the process until the diet of 8th June, 1642.

[1] Not traced. There is a Lunning in Lunnasting parish, NE Mainland.

[2] Collafirth is 2 miles NE of Ollaberry. This panel has not been mentioned earlier.

There appears to have been no award of expenses to the panels under the Act 1587 cap. 88 for their being kept ten weeks in Edinburgh after travelling 300 miles from home for the purpose of the trial. The fining of the prosecution was no reparation to the panels.

(181) [7 January 1642: Colville and Robertoun JJ.D.]

Continewit to the viii of Junii nixt

Intran.—Niniane Neveine of Windhous, Johnne Neveine of Lowning [*Lunnine*] his brother, Mr James Mowatt of Ollaberrie.[1]

Dilaittit [as before], eftir the comitting of the quhilkis crymis the saidis Mr James Mowatt and Gilbert Mowatt,[1] being comittit to waird within the castell of Skalloway, be command of James Sinclair, schiref deputt of Zeitland, for the tyme to remane thairin quhill cautioun had beine fund be thaim for keiping of his Majesteis peice, the samyn waird was tressonablie brokin be thame and they fled and escaipit furth thairof in heigh and proud contempt of his Majesteis auctoritie and lawis.[2]

[Continued to 8 June 1642.]

(215) [8 June 1642: Colvill and Robertoun JJ.D.]

Mut[*ilatioun*]. *Mr Patrik Cheane and his brother* contra *Nevenes* et *Mowat. Continewit to the tent instantis.*

Intran. eodem octavo Junii.—Johnne Neveine of Lowning.

Dilaittit [as above].

Persewaris.—Mr Patrik Cheyne of Valley; Laurence Cheyne, his brother; Sir Thomas Hoip of Craighall, knycht barronet, his Majesteis Advocat, for his Hienes intreis.

Prelocutouris in defence.—Mr Rodger Mowatt, Mr Thomas Nicolsone, advocattis.

The pannellis procuratouris producit ane supplicatioun given in to the Lordis of Secreit Counsall[3] anent the suddane inconvenience befalling to the said Mr James Mowat and Niniane Neveine be haifeing thair bodies and faices brunt with powder upoun the saxt of Junii instant, quhairthrow they ar not of abilitie to cum out of thair ludgeingis for keiping of this court without the haizert of thair lyves, togidder with the saidis Lordis delyverance upoun the bak thairof, subscryvit be my Lord Chancellour, recomending to the Justice the tryell of the verritie thairof, and to [?of] the chyrurgiainis attestatioun thairupoun;

[1] The case against James Niven and Gilbert Mowat seems to have been dropped.
[2] On 13th January, 1642, Mr. James Mowat and Ninian and John Niven were liberated by the Privy Council, James evidently having been rearrested (*RPC*[2] VII.517).
[3] Not in extant records of *RPC*.

quhilk eftir tryell being fund of the verritie of the said burning, Ordanis the Justice to continew the dyet to sic tyme as he thinkis expedient; And thairwith lykwayis producit the attestatioun of David Douglas and James Rig, chyrurgaine, under quhais cuir the saidis twa personis ar for the presentt, testifeing be thair subscriptioun and oath that they ar so pitifullie brunt, hurt and deformit of thair faices, feitt and handis that they ar lying bedfast and cannot cum furth of thair ludgeings to any publict plaice; And in that respect and of the Counsallis warrand anent the tryell of the premissis desyrit the Justice conforme to the saidis Lordis ordinance to continew thair tryell quhill they be cuirit and of abilitie to travell.[1]

The Justice continewis this dyet to Fryday nixt and ordanis cautioun to be fund for the haill thrie defenderis entrie that day; conforme to the quhilk ordinance compeirit Thomas Wrycht, burges of Edinburgh and indweller in Leyth, quha become cautioun for the saidis Mr James Mowatt, Niniane Neveine and Johnne Neveine thair entrie the tent day of Junii instant, ilk ane of thaime under the paine of fyve hundreth merkis.

(221) [10 June 1642: Colvill and Robertoun JJ.D.]

Continued to 15 June 1642 for same cause.

(224) [15 June 1642: Robertoun J.D.]

Continued to 22 June 1642 for same cause.

(228) [22 June 1642: Colvill and Robertoun JJ.D.]

Continued to 24 June 1642 for same cause [. . . in respect that Niniane Neveine of Windhous brother to the said Johnne is not fullie cuirit of his hurt ressavit be him of the blast of powder . . .'].

(230) [24 June 1642: Colvill and Robertoun JJ.D.]

Continued 'with consent of pairtie' to 1 July 1642 for same cause.

(232) [1 July 1642: Colvile and Robertoun JJ.D.]

Continued to 6 July 1642.

[1] See legal note 2.

(234) 6 July 1642: Colville and Robertoun JJ.D.]

Continued to 13 July 1642 'And this meanetyme [the Justice] desyres Sir William Dick of Braid, knycht, lait proveist of Edinburgh to travell (travail) with ather pairtie anent the taking away of this persute be aggrement etc.'

(234) [13 July 1642: Colvile J.D.]

Continued by the Justice to 15 July 1642 'in respect of the absence of Mr James Robertoun, Justice depute, his collig'.[1]

LEGAL NOTES

1. They were not charged *eo nomine* with demembration, though in Pitmedden's view (I.57) destruction of a thumb or fingers as here (p. 464) amounted to this. As to the difference between mutilation and demembration see Pitmedden I.4.

2. The Justices seem to have accepted the medical certificates without evidence led though the Privy Council had directed them to 'try the verity' of the matter. This was evidently the practice as in *Taylor v Norrie* 1642, below p. .

3. The reason given by Colville J.D. for the final continuation was probably based on the fact that he and his colleague had sat together to take the evidence of the witnesses the previous December.

(237) [15 July 1642: Colvile and Robertoun JJ.D.]

Intran. eodem die.—Mr James Mowat of Allaberrie, Niniane Neveing of Windhous, John Neveing of Lownane, his brother.
Dilaittit [as above].

Perseweris.—Mr Patrick Cheyne of Valay, Laurance Cheyne his brother, Sir Thomas Hope, his Majesteis Advocat.

Prelocutouris in defence.—Mr Rodger Mowat, Mr Thomas Nicolsone, Mr Patrik Pitcairne,[2] advocatis.

The pannell takis instrumentis of thair entrie and protestis for thair cautioneris releiff.

Convict.

My Lord Advocat as persewer declairis that he insistis upone the criminall summondis aganis the pannell for hurting, wounding and mutilatione allanerlie of the said Mr Patrik and Laurance Cheynes in maner specifeit thairintill, and passis fra the remanent poyntis lybellit *pro loco et tempore*.[3]

It is dyseret be the pannell and thair prelocutouris[3] that conforme to dyverse

[1] See legal note 3.
[2] This presumably means he passed from the charges of wounding the others named above.
[3] At this hearing the panels had a third counsel also appearing for them, Mr. Patrick Pitcairn, admitted advocate 13th November 1634, and described in *Lyon's List* 172 as 'servitor to Sir James Oliphant'.

supplicationes maid and gevin in be thame to the Justice for ressaveing of witnessis to be producet be thame for proveing of thair exceptione, that gif any hurt or wound was gevin to the persewers be thame, it was done be the pannell in thair awin defence, being persewit of thair lyffis be the said Mr Patrik and Lawrance Cheynes the tyme lybellit, quhilkis witnessis ar present at the bar, and thairfor desyres as of befoir thaim to be ressavit and examinat.

It is answerit be my Lord Advocat that the desyre of the panell is unjust and aucht to be repellit in respect of the stait of the proces, quhairin witnessis producet be the persewers, quha war ceitit be the Justice precept and the panell lykways ceittit to heir thame ressavit to ane certane day thaireftir, at quhilk tyme the witnessis war not only ressavit bot examinat, alsweill upone interogatouris gevin in be the pannell and thair procuratouris as thai pleaset to set down as upone the said persewers interogatouris producet be thame, quhilk is verefeit **(238)** be the productione of the saidis interogatouris and the justice examinatione of the witnessis thairupone.

It is alledget for the pannell that the opponeing of the estait of the proces aucht to be repellit, becaus be the minutis of proces it is cleir that the panell hes evir bene requyreing witnessis to be ressavit for proveing of thair said exceptione and thair desyre thairin was evir refuiset howbeit of equitie it aucht till have bene grantit seing as thair is an patent legall way set down for the persewers probatione uset be thame, swa my lord Justice will be pleaset in the way of justice to efford and prescryve a way to the pannell for proveing of thair lawfull defenssis; And farder the examinatione of witnessis is naways contrar to the pannellis present desyre, becaus gif the witnessis be uncleir or contrair in thair answeris to the interrogatouris the panell aucht baithe to have thame re-examinat and uther witnessis examinat for cleiring of the verritie; And farder the pannell takis instrumentis of the proponeing of thair former desyre and protestis that gif any assyse pas upone this dittay protestis that the said assyse may tak consideratione of the panellis thair frequent desyre evir since the begyning of this proces, quhilk desyre tendis only to the cleiring of the pannellis innocencie and for cleiring the doubtfulnes and contrarieteis of the witnessis depositiones alredie ressavit, and that in respect of the refuisall of the pannellis just desyre that the assyse have na respect to the dowbtsomenes and contrair depositiones of the saidis witnessis.

The Justice findis proces notwithstanding of the desyre proponit be the pannell.[1]

My Lord Advocat takis instrumentis of the Justice repelling of the panellis desyre as injust and contrair to all law and practique, that eftir the paynfull examinatione of witnessis be the Justice and thair depositiones and considarit be the pannell and his procuratouris, the pannell thaireftir sould crave witnessis to be ressavit and examinat.

It is answerit for the pannell that thai tak instrumentis that my Lord Advocat alledges no uther reasone quhy ather in law or in practique the desyre of the pannell is unreassonable bot only becaus witnessis have bene examinate alreddie in this proces upone the pannellis interogatouris, and that the depositiones ar sene be the pannell and thair procuratouris; And farder it is alledget for the

[1] See legal note 1.

pannell that that is na relevant caus to refuis thair desyre becaus be the Act of Parliament the depositiones of witnessis in criminall caussis ar ordanit to be tane in presence of the pannell, and thairfoir the publicatione of the depositiones cannot be objectit[1] bot *receptio testium vel re-examinatio testium post publicationem depositionum* hes only place in thais judgement seattis quhair witnessis ar examinat *extra presentiam partis,* bot befoir my Lord Justice quhan the depositiones of any witnessis is taikin, in presence of the pannell, ather judiciallie or extrajudiciallie be way of precognitione *ex officio*, gif the dyet thaireftir continow and gif the pannell urge the summonding of uther witnessis or re-examinatione of the first examinat witnessis for cleiring thair dubious or contrair depositiones, notwithstanding of any precedent examinatione, in equitie it aucht to be grantit to the pannell least [lest] that ather the pannell suffer in thair innocencie or that the assyseouris for fault of just informatione or probatione proceid to any injust or rasch sentence of convictione. Lykas dayis war **(239)** grantit be my lord Justice to the pannell, according to thair desyre, quhilk the pannell referris to the Judges thair memorie, bot in the tumult quhilk was in the hous or tolbuith that day was mistakin be the clerk in the delyverance of [on] the pannellis supplicatione.

The Justice ordanis the pannell to proceid to thair defense, give thai any have, aganis the relevancie of the lybell.

The pannell with thair prelocutouris, adhearing to thair former desyre, alledges that thai cannot be convenit for the alledget mutilatione of the perseweris becaus thair is noe legall or lawfull testificate producet schawing that the perseweris or ony of thame ar mutilat.

To the quhilk it is answerit be my Lord Advocat that the alledgeance aucht to be repellit in respect of the dittay quhilk is relevantlie lybellit, and quhat consistis *in facto* baithe for the wounding and mutilatione lybellit sall be verefeit to the assyse *suo loco*.[2]

Secundo it is alledget for the panell be thair procuratouris that the dittay is not relevantlie lybellit in the poynt of wounding, nawayis condischending quhat woundis war gevin or in quhat pairtis of thair bodie.

It is answerit be my Lord Advocat that the former alledgeance aucht to be repellit in respect of the dittay.

Tertio it is alledget for the pannell that, giveand and not grantand that any mutilatione was committit aganis the persewers the tyme lybellit, yit the pannell cannot be convenit thairfoir criminallie becaus of the law all crymes committit or woundis gevin be a pairtie quha is assalltit and set upone be the persones woundit or ressavers of that wound, ar impuneischable, and the pairtie assalter *ut primis* agressor of the law is puneischable for his onsetting, and the pairtie alledget wounder aucht to be assoilyeit fra the wound becaus *ipse vulneratus dedit causam rixe et sibi imputare debet quod vulnera receperit*; And trew it is that the day of the alledget mutilatione lybellit and severall dayis befoir the perseweris, at the least Mr Patrik Cheyne, accumpaneit with twentie or threttie of the Kingis leidges all boddin in feir of weir, came to the town of Skalloway, braging and bosting to set upone the Neveingis and the Mowatis, lykas the verie

[1] See legal note 2.
[2] This point was unsuccessfully taken in *Fletcher* v *Ramsay* 1635, p. 315.

day of the alledget committit mutilatione, the persewer, Mr Patrik Cheyne, accumpaneit with ten or twelff of his saidis assosiattis, quhairof his brother Lawrance was ane, set upone the panell Niniane Neveing, he being himselff allane, persewit and invaidit him at the yet of the castell of Skalloway, thay being ten for ane, quhan thair was [nane] to help or defend the said Niniane in that his persuite bot himselff. Lykas the rest of the pannellis, *viz.* Mr James Mowat and John Neveing, comeing *ex post facto* and at severall tymes to the tumult upone the hearing thairof, war lykways assaltit and set upone be the persewers and thair assosiattis; And thairfor the panell cannot be convenit for any alledget mutilatione lybellit the samyn haveing bene (still refuiseing the samyn) done in the panellis thair awin defence in maner abone mentionat; And this the pannell offeris thame to prove be witnessis present at the bar, quhilk defence is proponit be the pannell thay always refuiseing and denying that thai or any of thame did mutilat the persewers or any of thame.

My Lord Advocat answerit that the alledgeance aucht to be repellit as contrair to the dittay, and that na probatione can be ressavit be witnessis *in statu cause quo nunc est* bot allanerlie be the assyse.

(240) The Justice remittis this mater and tryell thairof to the knawledge of ane assyse quhairupone my Lord Advocat askit instrumentis.

Assisa.—William Craigie of Gairsay in Orknay; Edward Sinclair of Gyer; John Cromertie of Skea; Harie Elphingstoun of Calderhall, chancellour; Archibald Couper merchand in Edinburgh; John Kennedie, merchand thair; John McKeane merchand thair; William Silsone, elder, in the Cannongait; William Wilsone, younger, thair; William Cokburne of Skirling; John Mortymer of Craigievar; George Ker of Ormeistoun; Henrie Robertsone, merchand in Edinburgh; Captane Alexander Hurrie; Gilbert Somervell in Edinburgh.

My Lord Advocat takis instrumentis of the sweiring of the assyse.

Compeirit Sir William Dick of Braid, knycht, lait proveist of Edinburgh, and protestit that this persuite of mutilatione and proceiding thairintill befoir the Justice be not prejudicial to his rycht he hes of his Majestie of his office of Justiciarie within the boundis of Orknay and Schytland.[1]

My Lord Advocat for verificatione of the dittay to the assyse producet the depositione of the witnessis ressavit and examinat befoir the Justice be consent of pairtie, and quha was examinat bothe upone the perseweris and pannellis interogatouris, and repeittit the interogatouris gevin in be the pannell and markit be the clerk quhairupone the witnessis was examinat, and desyret the saidis depositiones to be red, and speciallie that minute of proces beirand that Mr Thomas Nicolsone compeirit as procuratour for the panell and objectit aganes the ressaveing of the witnessis, quhairupone instrumentis was askit be the persewers, and also consentit that the dyet affixt to [*fixed for*] the sevint of Januare sould be prorogat to the aucht day of Junii upone cautione, off the quhilkis depositiones the tennour followis.[2]

[1] This explains no doubt why he had been asked by the Court on 6th July, 1642, to try and settle the whole business (above p. 468). See legal note 3.
[2] See legal note 4.

Apud Edinburgh quinto Decembris 1641 in presence of Mr Alexander Colvile and Mr James Robertoun, Justice deputtis to our Soverane Lord.

Alexander Forbes, mareid, dwelland in Zeatland, of the aidge of thriescoir yeiris, sworne deiplie; being demandit gif he knawis the perseweris and defenderis sayis he knawis thame bothe; farder depones he was present upone the nynt of November jmvic threttie aucht yeiris at the Castell of Skalloway, and saw bothe the perseweris and defenderis at the said castell at the halding of the schirff court that day; depones he hard of ane swable [*squabble*] that nycht befoir the mutilatione, bot knawis not quha was the first provoker; depones that the nixt morneing upone the tent of November a litle eftir the sune ryseing he went in to the castell of Skalloway to speik with Mr Harie Aitkyn, comissar and schireff; depones the commissar was in his bed, and that he saw within the castell Mr James Mowat, Niniane and John Neveingis, James Neveing and Gilbert Mowat thair; depones at that tyme Mr Patrik Cheyne was walking within halff ane bow schott to the said castell, and Lawrance his brother was about ane pennystane [*quoit*] cast befoir Mr Patrik; And depones that Mr Patrik Cheyne had not ane sword about him at that tyme; depones that Niniane Neveing and Mr James Mowat being within the castell saw out at ane window the said Mr Patrik and his brother Lawrance walking, and that the said Niniane came presentlie down out of the said castell and went to Lawrance Cheane and **(241)** thrust his clock under his left airme uttering thir speatches to the said Laurance 'Will ye byd at the wordis ye spak yisternycht?', and with the speiking of thais wordis the said Niniane drew his words and invaidit the said Lawrance thairwith; depones eftir drawing of swordis thair repairit about halfe ane dussane to ather syde and faucht for the space of ane quarter of ane hour or thairby till sutche tyme as James Sinclair of Skalloway, Mr Johne Edmeistoun, minister,[1] Gilbert and Walter Craigeis, William Myller, Robert Brown, and dyvers utheris with Andro Bruce of Munes, come and separate thame; depones that Mr Patrik and Lawrance his brother war woundit at that tyme be the said Niniane Neveing, Mr James Mowat, and remanent persones foirsaidis thair assisteris, at the least be ane or uther of thame; depones he hard not the pairtie defender brag of the fact thai had done; depones he knawis nothing of the thrid interrogatour, depones he knawis nothing of the fourt interrogatour. Depones that the defenders immediatlie eftir the tuilzie war committit to ward, bot knawis not how thai brak it[2] or gif thai did refuis to find cautione or not.

Gilbert Craigie, of the aidge of xxviii yeiris, unmareid, dwelling in Skalloway, sworne deiplie; depones that upone the nynt day of November 1638 the deponer being in Walter Craigeis hous, his brother, he saw Laurance and James Cheynes and Gilbert Mowat drinking togidder at the buird, and Niniane Neveing with thame; the deponer went furthe to ane uther hous to get ane pynt of beir; depones he hard not the wordis that past betwix thame, and quhan he came agane thai war come out of the hous to the yeard, and that thai had drawin swordis and battones in thair handis, quhilk was about mydnycht; farder

[1] Of Gravaland, minister of Mid Yell or Reafirth parish, see *Fasti* VII.302; he and James Sinclair complained to Parliament on 17th March, 1641, of the wrongs done by Mowat and Ninian Niven (*APS* V.425, 713; see also 633).

[2] See above p. 464.

depones that thai war seperat that nycht without any skeathe done be ather of thame be uther, and that the deponer convoyit Lawrance and James Cheynes to Mr Patrikis chalmer, quhair the said Mr Patrik was lying in his bed for the tyme; and generallie knawis not quhilk of the pairteis injured or provocked uther that nycht; depones that upone the morne thaireftir he saw Niniane Neveing come to Lawrance Cheyne and ask him 'Quhat man am I this day?', to whom he answerit 'The same man ye war yisternycht'. Thaireftir the said Niniane said thir wordis, 'Than have withe the man'. Yit nevertheles the deponer, becaus he was working in his schip, cannot say quhich of thame drew first, bot that be all appeirance Niniane was the first drawer; farder declairis that thair was nane to hurt the said Laurance and Mr Patrik Cheynes bot the Neveingis and Mowattis, and that thai war the doers of it; depones that Mr Patrik Cheane at that instant had not his sword about him till his boy brocht it to him; and last declairis that Mr Patrik was not present the first nycht eftir the swable; and this is all he knawis: *sic subscribitur*, Gilbert Craig.

Walter Craigie, of the aidge of fourtie yeiris, mareid, dwelling in Skalloway, sworne deiplie; being demandit quhat he knawis in this mater, depones he knawis nothing quhat was done the tyme of the feght upone the tent day, bot eftir thair redding he come and saw thame all bleeding; bot upone the nynt day the nycht befoir that Neniane Neveing, Lawrance and James Cheynes, with John Cheyne of Assilmonthe, war drinking at the deponeris buird, and that thairfell out some hot speiches amang thame, *viz*. Lawrance Cheyne alledget that Thomas Mowat had spokin some disgracefull speatches and wischet that he wald byd be thame and mak thame guid, quhairupone Niniane Neveing answerit that gif he wald not doe it himselff that he had some freand wald doe it for him, to quhom Lawrance Cheyne replyet 'Will ye be the man?' quha answerit; 'Gif he have not neirer freandis nor I, it may be I will', to quhom Lawrance answerit with ane great aithe that he durst. In the meane tyme Johnne Cheane of Essilmonthe sayis to Laurence 'Ye ar to rasch in your speiche', quhairunto Laurence answeirit 'May I nocht speik to ane scheip theif',[1] quhairupone thay start all to thair feit **(242)** and to thair airmes; bot war haldin and separat, so that thair was no skaith that nycht; And being speciallie interrogat what war the woirdis that Laurence challanget Thomas Mowat of, he can nocht declair, and that in the meane tyme of the thorstering [*argument*] at the buird Gilbert Mowat and John Nevene war sitting at the fyre syde at ane pynt of aill; And declaires that befoir the woirdis fell out betwix Laurence and Niniane thair had past some woirds betwix Laurence and James Cheanes and Gilbert Mowat, bot that thay war separat be the company and Gilbert came willinglie to the fyre syde and satt down, and that Gilbert Mowat and James Cheane drank togidder; And last of all the deponer declaires that thair was some secreit grudges betwix the pairteis befoir this meitting twa yeir of befoir, bot knawis nocht quhat it was: *Sic subscribitur*, Walter Craige.

Hew Groitt, merchand, of the aidge of fourtie yeiris, mareit, dwelling in Skalloway, sworne deiplie; depones he knawis nothing what past betwix the pairteis the first nycht *nisi ex relatu*, because he was nocht thair; and as to quhat fell out upone the morne thaireftir the tent of November, knawis only this far,

[1] This today would support a plea of provocation, but not self-defence.

that quhan the tuilyie [*struggle*] fell out, James Sinclair, schireff, send for the deponer to cum and accompany him, and thair going alongis fand that Mr Patrik and Laurence Cheanes war bothe hurt and both thair swoirdis brokin and dung out of thair handis; only the deponer affirmes that no uther body could geve the Cheanes the hurtis bot the Nevenes and Mowattis, becaus thair was no uther body opposet to thame at that tyme, and that thay war hurt befoir the redderis come.

William Myller, sailler in Skalloway, of the aidge of fourtie yeiris, mareit, and deiplie sworne; depones he knawis nathing quhat was past the first nycht betwix the pairteis, and as to quhat past the day of the feght, depones he was in Walter Craiges bark [*ship*] whan he hard the fray, and that Mr Patrik was hurt and fallin befoir he come to thame, and that in his cuming he saw Mr Patrik fall; And knawis nocht particularlie quha gave the Cheynes the straikes, bot that it was ane or uther of the defenderis *viz.* the Mowattis or Nevenes, becaus thair was no uther to geve thame the wounds, and that thay war hurt befoir the redderis come.

Magnus Wischart, sailler in Yell, mareitt, of the aidge of fyftie yeiris, sworne deiplie; depones he knawis nothing the first nycht *nisi ex relatu*; depones the nixt moirning the tent of November Niniane, John, and James Nevenes he saw thame croce the dur of Mr Patrik Cheane his ludgeing hous, quhan thay neidit nocht to have come that way; depones that twa houris thaireftir the said Mr Patrik went eistward to the castell, and that the saidis Nevenes followit immediatlie the foote stepis of the said Mr Patrik; depones it was at that tyme thay yockit [*jostled*], bot he saw nocht the maner of the rancounter, and saw nothing till he saw Mr Patrik lying upone his bak and the said Niniane streking at him; depones it was Niniane that hurt Mr Patrik, and some of the defenderis hurt Laurence, bot knawis nocht which of thame.

Robert Brown, unmareit, sailler in Skalloway, of the age of xxiiii yeiris, sworne deiplie; depones he knawis nothing of the first nycht of the outcast, bot was in Walter Craigeis bark; and as to the morne thaireftir saw nothing ather becaus thay war all seperat of befoir he come; and that thair was no uther men to wound thame bot the Nevenes and Mowattis.

Patrik Wirk, indweller in Leyth, bot borne in Skalloway, unmareid, sworne deiplie; depones he knawis nothing quhat was done the first nycht, and as to the morne *nihil novit* becaus he was foure myles out of the towne.

Williame Mortoun, mercheand, mareit, in Skalloway, of the adge of xxiiii yeiris, sworne deiplie; depones he knawis nothing quhat was done the first nycht, bot quhat he hard be utheris, and as to the morne thaireftir can nocht tell quhilk of thame sett upone uther, bot hard be repoirt that Niniane Nevene was the first onsetter or provoiker; and saw Laurence and Niniane ather of thame invaid utheris with swordis; farder depones that he saw Mr Patrik lying upone his bak, and gif Niniane Nevene had nocht bene haldin be ane Johne Petersone he had rune ane sword throw Mr Patrik.

James Johnestoun, wright in Skalloway, mareit, of the aige of fyftie yeiris, deiplie sworne; being interrogat aganis Niniane and John Nevene, depones he knawis nothing quhat was done the first nycht, and as to the morne he knawis nocht quha was the first onsetter or provoiker, bot in the ending of the tuilyie the deponer come with oares in his hand and past betwix the pairteis as ane redder [*settler*] with the guidman of Skalloway, his maister; and can nocth speciallie declair quha it was that woundit Mr Patrik and Laurence Cheanes, bot it behoved to be the Nevenes and Mowattis, becaus thair was na uther to doe it: *Sic subscribitur,* Ja: Johnstoun, A. Colvill, Ja: Robertoun.

The pannell, in swa far as concerns the depositiones adducet for probatione of the dittay, and in swa far as thai ar alledget be my Lord Advocat to have bene ressavit of consent of the pannell, earnestlie desyres the assyse to tak notice of the bill gevin in be the persewers quhairupone the witnessis war ressavit, beiring some pretendit reassones quhy thai sould have been ressavit, and of the minute of proces beiring the pannell thair advocattis compeirance for thame and thair advocattis objectiones aganis the witnessis, and thair advocattis consenting to the continuations of the dyet, and that the assyse wald considder that thair is na menute extant schawing that the pannell and thair procuratouris did consent to the ressaveing of the witnessis, bot be the contrair the witnessis being desyret one the perseweris bill or precept thay most be presumet to have bene ressavit becaus of the reassones thairof and at the persewers desyre as trewlie it was; And as to the consent of the continuatione of the dyet that is ane other thing than to consent to the ressaveing of the witnessis, for the panell mycht have assentit to the ane to wit, the continuatione, and not to have gevin his consent to the uther; And quhair my Lord Advocat wald infer the pannellis consent to the ressaveing of the witnessis upone the pannellis ingeveing of interogatouris to be speirit at the witnessis that inference is most unrelevant, becaus the witnessis being ressavit be ordour of Justice and not be consent, it is lawfull to the pairtie haveing intreis to give in interrogatouris to the witnessis, and thairfoir the ingeveing of interrogatouris the witnessis is not ane guid argument to infer the pannellis consent to the ressaveing of thame, utherwayis all processis quhairin interrogatouris ar gevin to the witnessis be the defender, the defenderis most be haldin as ane consenter to the ressaveing of the witnessis, quhilk is absurd.

My Lord Advocat takis instrumentis of the reading of the depositiones in presence of the assyse, and thaireftir producet the subscryvit declaratione of James Rig, David Douglas, James Scot, Alexander Pennycuik, and Andro Brown, daittit at Edinburgh the twentie aucht day of Maii 1642,[1] testifieing the mutilatione of the said Lawrance Cheyne, as also the uther declaratione subscryvit be the said deacone and four maisteris of the chirurgeans anent the mutilatione of Mr Patrik Cheyne of the samyn dait, and thairupone askit instrumentis, and in respect of the evident and cleir depositiones maid be the witnessis and of the evidence of the mutilatione testifeit be the deacone and maisteris of the chirurgeanes be thair subscriptiones quha ar sworne in thair awin craft and calling, and to quhome only faithe is to be gevin, protestit that the assyse sall find the lybell provein conforme thairto, and siclyk sall find the panell guiltie of the crymes thairin contenit *viz.* of wounding and mutilatione of the saidis perseweris; And protestis gif thai doe utherwayis for the pyne of wilfull erroure.

It is objectit be the pannell and thair procuratouris agains the depositiones of Alexander Forbes that his depositiones cannot be respectit, becaus it is offerit to be provein be honest and famous witnessis at the bar that the said Alexander

[1] No record in Books of Adjournal.

Forbes is ane infamous persone and hes bene convict of mensweiring of himselff within the cuntrey quhair he dwellis, and thairfoir his depositiones aucht to have na faithe, speciallie in respect he was puneist be the Judge and be his lying in prissone thairfoir; and this objectione agains him aucht to have place withe the assyse albeit it was not objectit at the first tyme quhen he was ressavit becaus the pannell war in prissone the tyme of the ressaveing of the saidis witnesses, and the gentilmen be quhome the pannell will prove presentlie this exceptione war not in this cuntrey the tyme of the ressaveing of the saidis witnessis. Farder the said Alexander Forbes his depositione beiris not mutilatione bot only wounding, and in swa far as it beiris wounding aucht not be respectit, becaus it is bothe doubeous and uncertane anent the wound, not specifieing the place and in quhat pairtis of the bodie the woundis war gevin; As also dois not condischend upone the pairteis geveris of the woundis, the depositiones naways condischending quhilkis of the persones one pannell gave the woundis, bot beiring allanerlie that Mr Patrik and Lawrance Cheynes war woundit at that tyme be the saidis Niniane Neveing, Mr James Mowat and the remanent perseweris [*sic*, *lege* defenderis] foirsaidis thair assisteris at the least be ane or uther of thame; And thairfoir *tamquam depositio incerta* it aucht to have na credeit with the assyse, bot rather aucht to be suspectit as being to [*too*] favourable for the perseweris smelling of partialitie, quhilk is probable be the deponers deponeing *super visu alieno*, quhilk is impossible for a witness to doe; the witnes mycht weill have said that he hard the pannell say that thai saw thame out at the castle window, bot *affirmare non potest actum visus alieno, viz.* that the pannell saw the perseweris. Lykwayis the suppressing of the verritie in severall circumstances probablie inferis ane suspitioun of partialitie, for quhair the deponer affirmes that Mr Patrik Cheane was standing within a bow schote to the castle and his brother befoir him he to [*too*] favourably forgettis to tell how far within a bow schoot Mr Patrik Cheyne stuid fra the castle, for the treuthe is he stuid neir to the castle within the cast of ane cannon billot, quhilk he will not deny himselff; *Secundo* the deponer forgettis to tell that Mr Patrik and his brother stood thair and twelff or fourtene with thame; *Tertio* quhair the deponer declairis that Mr Patrik had na sword about him, forgettis to tell that his man had a twahandit sword at his bak as the perseweris will not deny and we will prove; *Quarto* this depositione of Alexander Forbes aucht to have no faithe bot to be rejectid as false and untrew conteneing a manifest untreuthe in the pairt thairof quhilk in effect is his *causa scientiae* in swa far as his depositione beiris that the day of the ryot lybellit the deponent went into the castle of Skalloway to speik with Mr Harie Aitkyn, comissar, quhairas *in rei veritate* Mr Harie Aitkyn was not in Zetland for four yeiris befoir, and this the perseweris will not deny especiallie if it be referrid to thair aithes and may be provein be witnessis.

Gilbert Craigie, his depositione proves nothing: 1°, becaus he deponis nothing aganis the mutilatione; 2° the depositione is contrair to itselff in swa far as the deponent affirmes that he hard quhat discourse past betwix Niniane Neveing and Lawrance Cheyne quhan thai met at the castle the day of the ryot lybellit, and confessit he hard Ninion's questione and Lawrance his answer and Niniane's reply, and yit he affirmes he was working in a schip and soe could not sie quha was the first onsetter, quhairby it cleirlie appeiris that he being in the schip could not hear quhat thai war saying upone the land, the schip being twa pair of buttis [*bowshots*] so that it was impossible to him to hear quhat discourse was betwixt thame the depositione beiris; becaus he was working in the schip he could not hear, quhilk cleirly contradictis that pairt quhairby he affirmes, that he hard thair discourse, seing the sight is moir quick nor the ear; 3° the depositione aucht not to be respectit for the pairt of wounding, bot most be presummet beyound verritie favourable deponit in favour of the persewer, seing the deponent quhan he hes affirmet that he knawis not quho was the first onsetter is not aschamed to affirme in the depositione that be all appeirance Niniane was the first onsetter and drawer haveing noe reassone for the same, and it is cleirlie evincet that quhat he affirmes he hard Niniane say to Lawrance was noe treuthe bot a fictione of the deponer for *per rerum natura* it was impossible he could hear; 4°: the depositione aucht not be respectit as being in the poynt of wounding dowbious, affirmeing that the Neveingis and the Mowattis woundit the perseweris, bot not telling quho woundit thame nor in quhat pairt of the bodie thai war woundit thair haveing bene many moe swordis than the pannellis or the perseweris ather; *Quinto* it is meirlie favourable in behalff the perseweris and schawis partialitie and subornatione in swa far as in his declaratione concerneing the swable the nycht befoir, he sayis he saw thame with thair drawin swordis quhilk is trew in respect of the perseweris, bot this deponent being examinat could declair that none of the defenders had swordis at that tyme; *Sexto* the deponer schawis his partialitie in affirmeing that the nycht of the swable befoir he convoyit Lawrance and James Cheynes to thair ludgeings, bot suppressithe in favouris of the persewer that quhan thai came neir to the ludgeing, the said Lawrance and James Cheanes, being drawin away frome the swable by thame, brak aff and ran frome thame with a schout, and bak agane they ran to meit with Niniane and Gilbert Mowat, and meitting thame upone the way set upone thame of new agane as thai war cuming to thair ludgeingis, and now haveing gottin thair swordis Niniane and Gilbert Mowat, had thai bene set for thair lyffis, as is lybellit thay mycht have killed thame that nycht haveing gottin thair swordis in thair handis for gairding of thair persones, especiallie being in thair awin defence thay war forcet to straik out and the perseweris fell at thair feit *viz.* Lawrance Cheyne; all quhilk is knawin to the haill cuntrey; *Septimo* Gilbert Craigeis depositione and Alexander Forbesis disagrie in swa far as Alexander Forbes maliciouslie affirmeth that Niniane without any more adoe came to Lawrance and said 'Will you byd at the wordis you spak yisternycht' and drew his sword and strak at him, bot Gilbert Craigie makis a questione by Niniane, ane answer by Lawrance, and a reply by Niniane agane, different in all termes frome the former.

Walter Craigis, his depositione, disclames all knawledge of the fact, and makis a declaratione of the straikis the nycht befoir conteneing a mistaking of the speatches that past betwix the perseweris and the defenderis declairing that thai went to airmes bot suppressethe quhich of the pairteis it was that went to airmes, (to wit) that it was only Lawrance and James Cheynes that did soe, and that Niniane and Gilbert Mowat had not a sword; lykas he was witnes that the oneset maid by Lawrance and James Cheynes that same nycht was maid be thame by the waysyde, and this he suppressithe, that Niniane, gif he had bene willing to have set upone thame for ane evill turne (as is alledged he was upone the morrow), mycht have actit that same nycht, as also it includethe a meire untreuthe, (as the perseweris being interrogat will declair), that John Neveing was not thair that nycht, and soe will the deponer himselff being re-examinat, quhich all schawis thair partialitie and manifest wrangous depositione quhilk cannot mak aganis the defenderis.

Hew Groote, his depositione proves nothing, nather quho was the first onsetter or wounder, and gif his depositione war positive in any poynt it aucht not to be respectid, becaus the deponer thairin bewrayis (betrays) his partialitie and favour to the persewers by taking upone him the Judges pairt to prejudicate the persones one panell by infering upone thame that thai behovet to be the wounderis of the Cheynes without any reasone; and as to the twa reassones contenit in the depositione thay ar contrair to the depositione becaus the depositione beiris that thai war woundit befoir he came, and swa he could not knaw quither thair was any uther bodie opposeit or not, and thairfoir the deponeris partialitie is cleir in concluiding ane *illative* guiltienes upone the persones one pannell upone ane reassone quhich the deponent in his depositione hes beleit.

William Myllere, his depositione proves nothing, nor (gif it did) aucht to be respectit for the same reassone that is objectit aganis Hew Grote.

Magnus Wischerte, his depositione aucht not to be respectid for thir reassones: 1° becaus, quhair it affirmes the Neveingis crocet Mr Patrik Cheynes ludgeing quhair thai neidit not to have cum that way, it is offerit to be proven that the Neveingis war ludget in that hous, quhairby the deponer is cleirlie convincet of partiall favour quhich he careis to the perseweris deponeing that quhilk is not of verritie; *Secundo* becaus his depositione is contrair to Alexander Forbessis, for quhair Alexander Forbes affirmes that the Neveingis war in the castle and onlie saw the Cheanes out at the window, the deponent affirmes that the defenderis followit the Cheynes to the castle and set upone thame, and swa Alexander Forbes and Magnus Wischert being contrairie to uther nather of thair depositiones aucht to be respectit; *Tertio* quhair the deponer affirmes that Mr Patrik Cheane was hurt by Niniane, and Lawrance by John Neveing the same aucht not to be respectid because it is contrair to the depositione, for as the depositione beiris the deponent saw nothing till he saw Mr Patrik Cheyne lying upone his bak, and yit he affirmes that Niniane hurt him quich he cannot affirme *ex visu* becaus Mr Patrik was fallin befoir he cam; *Quarto* the depositione concerneing Lawrance is dubious and uncertane *nulla causa scientiae reddita* that he saw and swa cannot be respectit.

Robert Brown, his depositione proves nothing, becaus thay war all seperat befoir he came.

Patrik Wirkis depositione proves nothing becaus he was absent.

Williame Mortoun, his depositione proves nothing, seing he depones onlie *ex auditu* that Niniane Neveing was the first onsetter bot saw it not, and depones not that he saw any straikis gevin.

James Johnstoun, his depositione proves nothing.

And finallie thair is nane of the depositiones of the witnessis that proves ony positive wound in Mr Patrik Cheynes thombe and Lawrance his finger, quhilkis ar the pairtis of the bodie quhair the mutilatione is alledget to be.

My Lord Advocat takis instrumentis of the sweiring of the dittay be the perseweris, and also that the pannell did requyre thair aithes bot thaireftir past fra thair aithes;[1] as also takis instrumentis that Mr Patrik Cheyne, persewer, hes deponit that the pairteis pannellit war and are all airt and pairt of his mutilatione; *Item* takis instrumentis that Lawrance Cheyne being sworne declairit be his great aithe that the lybell was trew, and that the pairteis impannellit ar all airt and pairt of his mutilatione.

The pannell takis instrumentis of the perseweris thair aithes and declaratione maid be thame, and desyres the assyse to tak notice of the uncertanetie thairof and that, albeit thair war na uther probatione or presumptione for the innocencie of the pannell, yit thai aucht to pronunce the pannell innocent of the mutilatione and woundis lybellit, because the perseweris, *viz.* Mr Patrik and Lawrance Cheynes, haveing ressavit bot ane wound, everie ane of thame, quhairwith thai ar alledget to be mutilate, yit thai cannot condischend upone thair aithe quhich of the thrie persones one pannell gave the saidis woundis, and it was impossible that ane wound could have bene gevin be thame all thrie; And chieflie for Mr James Mowat the persewers refuissis to cleir thair depositione, and to affirme that he woundit thame and thairfoir the persewers depositione being dubious and incertane becaus generall, cleirlie proves the innocencie of the haill pairteis impannellit.[2]

The perseweris being desyret to cleir thair oathe quither or not the persones one pannell set upone thame, and if the haill persones one pannell war present upone the ground with drawin swordis and persewing thame, and gave to thame the straikis quhairof thai war mutilat, the saidis persewers deponit be thair great oathes the samyn to be of verritie; quhairupone my Lord Advocat askit instrumentis.

The pannell alledges, aganis the chirurgeanes testimoniallis producet, that the samyn aucht not to be respectit becaus they beir not the chirurganes testifiecationes to be gevin be thame upone thair saull and conscience, quhilk aucht to have bene done, for as in civile caussis the testimoniall of a minister and of ane phisitiane (quhilkis ar men of gritter faith and respect nor chirurgeanes) thair testimoniallis will not be relevant in judgement nor ressavit without thair wordis of asseveratione upone thair saull and conscience; lykas the Lordis of Sessione and Secreit Counsall refuiset to ressave a testificatione uset be the same panell subscryvit by chirurgeanes becaus it wantit saull and conscience.[3]

Finallie, the said Mr. James Mowat and remanent persones upone pannell declairithe that thai war content the assyse incloise thameselffis and goe one upone the depositiones alreddie ressavit, without examinatione of thair witnessis, quhairupone the perseweris askit instrumentis.

Mr James Mowat, Niniane Nevene, John Nevene. Convict of mutilatioun of Mr Patrik Cheane and Laurence his brother.

Quhilkis persones of assyse being ressavit, sworne and admittit, eftir accusatione be dittay of the saidis Mr James Mowat of Ollaberrie, Niniane Neveing

[1] This is self-contradictory unless it means that the pursuers took an oath of calumny before the jury was empannelled, but the panels did not ask an oath of verity at the end of the trial. In any event the oath of verity was ultimately taken.

[2] See legal note 5.

[3] See legal note 6.

of Windhous and John Neveing of Luneing, his brother, of airt and pairt of the hurting, wounding and mutilatione of the said Mr Patrik Cheane of Valey of the thombe of his left hand, of the said Lawrance Cheyne, his brother, of the foirmost finger of his rycht hand, in maner and at the tyme specifeit in thair dittay, than removet altogidder furthe of court to the counsallhous of the said tolbuithe, quhair thay, be pluralitie of vottis, electit and choyset the said Harie Elphingstoun of Calderhall in chancellour of the said assyse, thaireftir reassonet and voitit upone the poyntis of the said dittay, and being ryplie and at lenthe advyset thairwith, and with the depositiones of the witnessis and uther probatione uset and producet be the perseweris for proveing of the pannellis guiltienes of the crymes foirsaidis, togidder with the pannellis objectiones maid against the said probatione, thay re-enterit agane in court quhair thay be the report and declaratione of the said Harie Elphingstoun, chancellour, all in ane voce, fand, pronuncet and declairit the saidis Mr James Mowat, Niniane Neveing and Johnne Neveing to be fyllet culpable and convict of airt and pairt of the wounding and mutilatione of the said Mr Patrik Cheyne of the thombe of his said left hand, and of the said Lawrance Cheyne his brother of the foirmost finger of his said rycht hand in maner specifeit in thair dittay; quhairupone the said Mr Patrik Cheyne for himselff and in name of his said brother askit actis and instrumentis.

The Justice, in respect of the former convictione of the saidis Mr James Mowat, Niniane and John Neveingis, of the saidis crymes of mutilatione, ordanit thame to be committit to waird within the tolbuithe of Edinburgh untill the tyme the Counsall be acquentit with the said convictione and gif ordour anent thair dome and puneischement.

[21 July 1642: Privy Council.]

[Commissioners appointed to deal with Mr Patrik Cheyne, Mr James Mowat, and others from Orkney and Shetland presently in process before the Council or Justices, to settle their cases by agreement and to report. This evidently proved abortive (see *RPC*2 VII.304).]

Legal Notes

1. Before the libel was held relevant or any jury empanelled, the witnesses for the prosecution had been cited before the two Justice Deputes presently presiding, and in December 1641 had been examined on oath or 'interrogatories' for both parties in the presence of the panels. When the trial started on 15th July 1642 the defence attempted to introduce a plea of Self Defence and to call witnesses, who were present at the bar, to support it. According to the defence they had repeatedly attempted 'since the begynning of this process' to have the evidence of these witnesses heard by the Justice Depute, but without success. In support of their contention they refer to 'the minutes of process'. The present minutes however do not refer to any such motion. Later in their argument the defence goes further and alleges that 'dayis war grantit' by the Justice to the panel (i.e. for adducing defence witnesses) and in the absence of any record in the minutes refers this matter to the Justices' own memory. It is an interesting sidelight on the conditions on which these courts could be held, that the reason given for the clerks failure to record the defence submission was 'the tumult quhilk was in the house or Tolbuith that day'. The Lord Advocate did not concede the alleged earlier motions by the defence but opposed their request at the start of this trial 'in respect of the state of the process' *viz.* that the evidence having been taken on interrogatories, it was too late now to examine

defence witnesses to support the special defence. The position seems to have been that Sir Thomas Hope was objecting not to any defence evidence at all as incompetent (as he had done in Johnston v Corsar 1641, above p. 414) but to such evidence at this late stage. The Justice Deputes, in the result, held that it was now too late to adduce defence witnesses and the panels were told to advance their objections to relevency 'gif thai any have', which shows the way the Court's mind was tending. Whether the defence plea was rejected in respect that the motion came too late in the special circumstances of this case, the whole evidence having been taken earlier, as the Lord Advocate argued, or because the defence of self-defence was contrary to the libel as Sir George Mackenzie (II.xxi.II) and Arnot (p. 173) thought, is not stated. The defence however did not give up the point. They protested that their many requests to adduce their witnesses should be brought to the jury's attention. In their arguments on relevancy they submitted a plea of self-defence. In their submissions to the jury they founded on self-defence, and apparently ignoring the Court's ruling, referred to witnesses whom they would subsequently adduce to establish their defence! At the end of the case, it is true, they intimated that they did not wish to call any evidence, but one would have thought it had already been decided that they could not do so. Though denied the right to call witnesses, their plea of self-defence was left to the jury on the evidence already taken. By the interlocutor on relevency the Court remitted the whole matter—charge and defence—to the knowledge of the assize—as had been done in a number of earlier cases (Hume II.286-7).

2. The defence concession here—that no objection could be taken to the use by the prosecution in evidence of depositions of witnesses taken in the presence of the accused but outwith the presence of the jury—is contrary to the now accepted interpretation of the Act 1587 c. 91, but illustrates its contemporary interpretation. The Act required that the 'hail accusation, reasoning, writtes, witnesses and other probation and instruction quhatsumever of the crime sall be alleged, reasoned and deduced to the assize in presence of the party accused in face of judgement and na utherwayes'. The view accepted by both sides without any argument and by the Court in the present case is that statements taken on oath by the Justice Deputes in the presence of the panels and prior to the trial, can be placed before the jury—read to them —as evidence in the case without the actual witness being adduced either to testify or to ratify the precognition. Several examples of similar procedure are quoted in Hume II.405-6; see also Alexander Gylour, below p. 518. Such irregularities only ceased after the establishment of the High Court of Justiciary in 1672 (Hume II.406).

3. Pitmedden (I.66, 78) regarded this as a refusal of repledgiation but the point was not argued. The intervention was to ensure that the failure to repledge in the present case did not prejudice the right to do so in the future.

4. The prosecutors' proof consisted in the depositions taken earlier before the two Justice Deputes being read to the jury and in the production of two 'Declarations' (not on soul and conscience) signed by the Deacon and four Masters of the Chirurgeons Craft describing the injuries on the complainers. The depositions are given in full—as also are the defence criticisms of them. Clearly a jury could expect to be addressed at length and in detail on the evidence where the panels were legally represented. The criticisms here include such matters as the competency of witnesses, their bias, partiality, unreliability and previous bad character. Absence of specification and contradictions in the evidence are stressed, as are discrepancies between various depositions. Submissions are made on the improbability of the witness's testimony and the improbability of his being able to see or hear what he says he did. Further the defence took full advantage of the opportunity presented by the witness's statement being available when the witness was not, by seeking to amplify the statement from the bar by alleging facts to which the witness could have testified but because he 'forgettes to tell' had not done so.

5. Pitmedden deals with this argument at I.88. It ignores that where all are guilty art and part it does not matter who struck the blow. It had been settled in two cases in 1635 (Thomson v Gillespie, Thomson v Hill, 10 July 1635 and Fletcher of Benshaw v Ramsay, Lindsay and Lord Spynie) that 'if more than one be conveen'd for mutilation or demembration as Actors, Airt and Part, all of them may be insisted against, and it will be no good defence for any of the panels, that there is but one wound which could only be given by one as principal percusser who ought to be condescended on and first discussed' (Pitmedden, I.88). The charge against the panels here was of acting art and part, and it was a verdict in these terms that was returned.

6. The argument is that a testimonial from a minister, physician or chirurgeon required to be on soul and conscience conform to practice in the Court of Session and before the Privy Council. Such an objection however had already been disregarded in Crawford v Scott I.166. See also p. 515.

(258) [5 August 1642: Sir Thomas Hope of Carse, kt., J.G.[1]]

Dome pronuncet upone Mr James Mowat, Niniane Nevene, John Neveing for mutilatioun of Mr Patrik Cheane and Laurence Cheane his brother.

The quhilk day Mr James Mowat of Allaberrie, Niniane Neveing of Windhous, and John Neveing of Luneing, his brother, being brocht furthe of waird, furthe of the jeoll or tolbuithe of Edinburgh be the bailleis thairof at command of my lord Justice Generall and presenttit upone pannell to hear dome and sentence pronuncet aganis thame, as thai that war dewlie and ordourlie convict in ane Justice court haldin within the tolbuithe of Edinburgh upone the fyftene day of Julii lastbypast be Mr Alexander Colvile of Blair and Mr James Robertoun, advocat, his Majesteis Justice deputtis, off airt and pairt of the hurting wounding and mutilatione of Mr Patrik Cheane of Valay of the thombe of his left hand and making him impotent thairof as also of hurting, wounding and mutilatione of Lawrance Cheane his brother of the foirmest finger of his rycht hand, in maner and at the tyme specifeit in thair said convictione, compeirit the said Mr Patrik Cheane of Valay and Lawrance, his brother, and producet ane Act of the Lordis of Secreit Counsall of the dait the xxix day of Julii lastbypast anent the pronunceatione of the dome and sentence underwrittin, quhairof the tennour followis [in *RPC*[2] VII.312].

Eftir the productione and reading of the quhilk Act of Counsall the Justice Generall, be the mouthe of James Douglas, dempster of court, decernis and ordanis the saidis Mr James Mowat of Allaberrie, Niniane Neveing of Windhous, and John Neveing his brother, to mak payment and satisfactione of the soume and fyne of ane thousand pundis money of this realme to the said Mr Patrik Cheane and Laurance Cheane, his brother, as pairteis mutilat, and siclyk to mak payment to his Majesteis Thessaurar, and under ressavers in his Majesteis name and to his Hienes use of the soume of thrie hundrethe merkis money foirsaid for the said cryme of mutilatione;[2] as also to find sufficient cautione actit in the buikis of adjornall for thair keiping of his Majesteis peace under the paynes following, *viz.* the said Mr James Mowat under the said payne of twa thousand merkis specifeit in the said Act of Counsall, and ather of the saidis Niniane and John Neveingis under the payne of fyve hundrethe pundis also specifeit in the said Act; and lykwayis ordanis thame and ilk ane of thame to stay and abyde in waird quhill thay pay the saidis fynes and find the said cautione as also for passing of thair remissione for the said mutilatione; Quhairupone the said Mr Patrik Cheyne and Lawrance his brother askit actis and instrumentis. For obedience of the quhilk pairt of my lord Justice ordinance anent the finding of the said cautione for keiping of his Majesteis peace, and passing of the said remissione, compeirit judiciallie Williame Bruce of Symbester, quha become pledge and souertie for the saidis Mr James Mowat of Allaberrie, Neniane Neveing of Windhous, and John Neveing of Luneing, his brother, that thai and ilk ane of thame sall observe our Soverane Lordis peace, keip good reule and quyetnes in the cuntrey, with Mr Patrik Cheane of Valay and Laurance Cheyne

[1] His appointment is in the record on 7 July 1642; see p. 532.
[2] See legal note.

his brother, and that the saidis Mr James Mowat, Niniane and John Neveingis nor nane of thame nor na utheris of thair causeing, sending, hounding out, command, resset, assistance or ratihabitione quhom thai may stope or late, sall onnawayis invaid, molest, harme, truble or persew the saidis Mr Patrik and Lawrance Cheynes, thair men, tennentis, or servandis, directlie or indirectlie, in tyme cuming, in thair persones, landis, goodis or geor, for quhatsumevir caus, dead or occasione bygane, utherways nor be ordour of law and justice, under the paynes following, *viz.* the said Mr James Mowat under the said payne of twa thousand merkis money; and ather of the saidis Niniane and John Neveingis under the said payne of fyve hundrethe pundis money; as also that the said Mr James Mowat, Niniane and John Neveingis, sall pas and expeid thair remissione throw the registeris and seallis for the said mutilatione; Lykas the saidis Mr James Mowat, Niniane and John Neveingis, being personallie present become actit and obleist to warrand freathe and releive the said William Bruce of Symbester thair cautioner, his airis and executouris, ilk ane of thame, respective for thair awin pairtis, of his cautionrie abonewrittin and of all danger to be incurrit be him thairthrow.

The samyn day the saidis Mr James Mowat, Niniane and John Neveingis, desyret of my lord Justice cautione and lawborrows of the said Mr Patrik and Lawrance Cheanes for thair indempnetie in respect be thair great aithes thay declairit that thai dred thaim bodilie harme. The Justice in respect of the geveing of the saidis Mr James Mowat, Niniane and John Neveingis thair soleme aithes in the premissis ordanit the saidis Mr Patrik and Lawrance Cheynes to find sufficient cautione for the saidis persones indempnitie in thair persones landis and guidis in tyme cumming, *viz.* the said Mr Patrik under the payne of ane thousand merkis, and the said Lawrance his brother under the payne of fyve hundrethe merkis money. For obedience quhairof compeirit personallie Mr James Cheane, wryter to his Majesteis signet, and of his awin consent become cautione, souertie and lawborrus for the saidis Mr Patrik Cheane of Valay, and Laurence Cheane his brother, that thay sall nawayis truble nor persew Mr James Mowat of Ollaberrie, Niniane Nevene of Wyndhous and Johnne Nevene of Lownane nor nane of thame in thair bodeis, landis, takis, possessiones, guidis nor geir, and that thai thair wyfes, bairnes and servandis sall be hairmeles and skaithles of thame and nawayis trubillit or molestit be the saidis Mr Patrik and Laurence Cheanis, nor be na utheris of thair causing, sending, hounding out, command, resset, assistance and ratihabitioun quhome thay may stope or lat, in tyme cuming utherwayis nor be ordour of law and justice under the panes foirsaidis; *viz.* for the said Mr Patrik Cheane under the said pane of ane thousand merkis, and for the said Laurence Cheane his brother under the said pane of fyve hundreth merkis. Lykas the saidis Mr Patrik and Laurence Cheanes obleist thame, conjunctlie and severallie, thair airis and executouris, to warrand freith and releive the said Mr James Cheane, thair cautioner, his airis and executouris, of his cautionerie abonespecifeit, and of all danger, penaltie, and utheris charges quahtsumevir to be incurrit be him thairthrow; Quhairupone Mr Patrik Pitcairne, advocat, as procuratour for the saidis Mr James Mowat, Niniane and John Nevenes askit instrumentis in thair names: In witnes quhairof the saidis principallis and cautioneris hes subscryvit this present act with thair handis day, yeir and place foirsaid, Ja: Cheyne, Pat: Cheyne, Laurenc Cheyne.

(323) [25 August 1643: Colvile J.D.]

[Registration of Discharges (i) by Cheynes for £1000 in name of assythment and satisfaction, dated 8 August 1642, and (ii) by H.M. Receiver of Fines for 300 merks, dated 27 August 1642.]

Legal Note

The sentence in this case involving damages and fine—which is noted in Pitmedden (II.192) and Hume (I.330)—is typical of the disposals 'daylie practised' in the Justiciary Court in such cases in the 17th century. The penalty was at the discretion of the Court but Pitmedden (II.192) speaks of the Court 'as in use to decern in a sum of money to be payed by the panel . . . to the party injured, for all he can ask or crave, either for Damages or Punishment, except the Delinquency be very atrocious, and then they also Imprison or banish the Delinquent: likewise they modify a Fine to be pay'd to the King (especially if the Crime be Demembration) and the Delinquent finds Caution to satisfy the Damages and Fynes decerned or to go to Prison till he pay: He is also Burthened to procure a Remission, and for that effect the pursuer is Decerned to give him a letter of Slains.' No recorded instance of capital punishment for Demembration or Mutilation has been traced, except when combined with Hamesucken (*LA* v *Crombie* above I.291). Both Pitmedden and Hume (*op. cit.*) considered the question of whether this was competent under the implication of the old statutes which ranked Mutilation and Demembration with Homicide and other capital crimes, but agreed with McKenzie (*Observations*, p. 147) that it was not. The Crown considered these old statutes to be in desuetude at least by 1608, when it wrote that 'it was not usual in this Nation to inflict the pain of death for the crime of Demembration' (Pitmedden II.193). The most singular disposal occurred in a case that did not go to trial. In *Clerk* v *Inglis* (1532 Pitcairn I.160) where a minor was accused of mutilation, James V personally intervened and 'because of his (i.e., the accused's) lessage and innocence he standis in, being bot ane barne quhom we have sene brocht in our presence,' prohibited further proceedings and ordained the accused to 'pass . . . beyond the sey to the sculis . . . and thare to remain and abyde for the space of sevin zeris'.

Prefatory Note to Stalker v *Gordon of Haddo*

The charge in this case arose from an incident during the so-called 'Trot of Turriff' on 14th May 1639. In the early part of the year Montrose, then in command of the Covenant forces, came north to neutralise Huntly who had been appointed the King's Lieutenant for the North-East, with the present first accused as his second in command. While in the north Montrose was joined by local Covenant sympathisers including Lord Fraser, one of the present pursuers. Aberdeen was occupied and in April, Huntly, after a promise of safe conduct, was taken by the Covenanting army to Edinburgh. On the departure of that army the Covenanters of the north-east appointed a meeting of a committee to be held at Turriff, which included Lord Fraser. The Gordons and Huntly's followers resolved to attack the Covenanters assembled there and Sir George Ogilvy of Banff and Sir John Gordon of Haddo, the first accused, were appointed joint commanders. An attempt was made to justify the proposed attack by means of a band of association subscribed by the gentlemen involved, which declared that their 'engadgement was for the mantenance of the King's prerogative, next for the duty, service and honour and safetye of Huntly and his familye, and for their own mutuall preservatione'. The Covenanting party was surprised on 14th May, shots were exchanged and they eventually fled in confusion. Gordon of Rothiemay speaks of the Gordons firing 'a salvo of their musketts along the street which they seconded with three or four shott of their fielde pieces,' but he denies there was any pursuit by the attackers. Only two gentlemen, he claims, fell on the Covenanting side, one Alexander Forbes, servant to Forbes of Torquhan, and James Stalker, servant to Lord Fraser, the death of the latter being the subject of the present charge. There is certainly nothing in the account of the incident given by Gordon of Rothiemay or Spalding to suggest that Stalker was taken two miles from the village and killed while he was a prisoner. Indeed it is recorded that two Covenanting prisoners were released by the Gordons.

The case made little progress before the Justiciary Court, and eventually the Justice Depute sought the advice of the Privy Council on the question of relevancy. After hearing the Justice Depute, and considering the process, their advice was that the process be remitted for advising to the King and Parliament, and this course was followed. Both Fraser and Haddo remained active in the political struggles of the day. Fraser was a leading figure among the Covenanters. He was one of the Parliamentary Commissioners appointed in July 1644 for proceedings against rebels. In 1645 he was one of the Committee of Estates and in 1649 was appointed a member of the Committee for the defence of the Kingdom. The first accused, Haddo, remained active on the opposite side. For his services to the King he was created baronet in 1642 and he joined Huntly when he rose for the King in 1644, as a result of which both were excommunicated. He was eventually taken by Argyll on 8th May 1644 after attempting to defend his house, and warded in Edinburgh. His last appearance in the present case was on 14th June 1644 when he was brought from ward. The pursuers however failed to appear and there was no further procedure. By that time his fate as a rebel must have been determined. He was eventually condemned to death for various acts of treason (but not including Stalker's death, though murder under trust was treason by 1587 cap. 51) by a Commission of Parliament which included the Justice Clerk and the two Justice Deputes, in July 1644 (*APS* VI(i).161, 171(b).293. Cf. Hume II.507). See Gordon of Rothiemay, *Scots Affairs* (Spalding Club) II.215, 256, 259; III.199, 200, 246; Spalding, *History of the Troubles* I.133-4.

(165) [17 November 1641.]

Sla[*uchter*]. *Stalkeris* contra *Gordoun of Haddo.* [*Protest*].

Anent the criminall letters direct at the instance of John Stalker of Eister Dryla[1] as father, Andro, Lord Fraser, as maister,[2] with the brither sisteris and remanent kyn and freindis, of umquhile Mr James Stalker, aganis John Gordoun of Haddo,[3] and John Gordoun his servand, chairgeing thame to find cautione actit in the buikis of adjornall for thair personall compeirance befoir his Majesteis Justice and his deputtis this day and place to have underlyne the law for the slauchter[4] of the said umquhile Mr James Stalker, committit in maner and at the tyme specifeit in the saidis criminall letters.[5]

Compeirit the said day, in presence of me, nottare publict and clerke depute in the office of Justiciarie, and of the witnessis underwrittin, in that pairt of the said tolbuithe of Edinburgh quhair the Justice Generall and his deputtis ordinarlie sittis, haldis and keipis thair Justice courtis, the said John Stalker of Drylaw, persewer of the saidis criminall letters, and producet the samyn deulie execute and indorsat upone the said Johnne Gordoun of Haddo and Johnne Gordoun, his servand, and offerrit himselff reddie in persuite of the defenderis foirsaidis for the slauchter of the said umquhile Mr James Stalker his sone; Bot becaus this day being the day appoyntit be his Majestie and Estaitis of Parliament for ryding and finischeing of the present parliament and affairis of this kingdome agitat thairintill,[6] and that the Justice Generall nor nane of the Justice deputtis ar present for keiping of this Justice court be occasione of the said Parliament and ryding thairof and of thair attendance thairintill, askit instrumentis of the

1 At Davidson's Mains in W Edinburgh.

2 See legal note 1.

3 Haddo was a common name in Aberdeenshire. Gordon's relations with Lord Fraser at this time are illustrated in *APS* V.504a, 579a, 660a.

4 See legal note 2.

5 This summary does not specify the date or locus. The text however makes it clear that the incident occurred at Turriff and arose from the so-called Trot of Turriff on 14th May 1639. See Prefatory Note above.

6 The court did not sit on the day of the riding of Parliament (see next case).

productione of the said criminall letters dewlie execute and indorsate as said is, and protestit for releiff of his cautioneris fund for reportting of the samyne, as also that he may have new letters and chairges direct against the saidis defenderis for thair tryell and puneischement of the slauchter abonewrittin to sic lauchtfull day as sall be assignit to him be the Justice Generall and his deputtis to that effect; Quhilkis premissis war done within the said laighe tolbuithe of Edinburgh in the southe end thairof, quhair the Justice ordinarlie sittis for administratione of justice, to all his Majesteis leidges, betwix the houris of ellevin and twelff befoir none, day, yeir and monethe foirsaid, in presence of me John Bannatyne [nottare publict] and clerk depute in the office of Justiciarie, as also in presence of John Bannatyne, younger, George Bannatyne, his brother, my sones, James Douglas, John Hamiltoun, and James Kynneir, the thrie ordiner officeris of Justiciarie, witnessis specially desyret and requyret to all and sindrie the premissis.

Instrument. John Gordoun of Haddo.

The samyn day, in presence of me nottare publict and clerke depute foirsaid and witnessis underwrittin, compeirit *ut supra* John Gordoun of Haddo and John Gordoun his servand, quha and ather of thame exponit and declairit that thai war chairget be vertew of criminall letters reaset at the instance of Andro, Lord Fraser, as maister, John Stalker of Eister Drylaw, as father, withe the brither sisters and remanent kyn and freandis, of umquhile Mr James Stalker, sone to the said John Stalker of Eister Drylaw to find cautione actit in the buikis of Adjornall for thair personall compeirance befoir his Majesteis Justice and his deputtis this day and place in the hour of caus to underly the law for alledget airt and pairt of the slauchter of the said umquhile Mr James Stalker, in forme and maner and at the speciall tyme set down in the saidis criminall letters, for obedience of the quhilk chairge gevin to thame at that tyme be James Grahame, messinger, and eschewing of the danger of horneing and cleiring of thair innocencie of the alledget slauchter abonewrittin, thay not onlie fand William Seatoun of Schithin cautione for thair compeirance this day to the effect foirsaid, bot also for thair said cautioneris releiff and tryell of his and his servandis innocencie of the saidis alledget crymes, compeirit and willinglie offerit thameselffis reddie to underly thair lauchfull tryell as altogidder innocent of the said alledget slauchter; and in respect nane of the Justice deputtis was present to hald the said Justice court and to proceid in thair lauchfull tryell, as said is askit instrumentis of thair entrie and compeirance, and protestit for releiff of the said William Seatoun of Schethin, thair cautioner, and that na letters sould be direct aganis thame for the said alledget slauchter in any tyme cuming. This was done with the laighe tolbuithe of Edinburgh in the south end thairof quhair the Justice ordinarlie sittis for administratione of justice, betwix ellevin and twelff houris befoir noone, day, yeir and monethe foirsaid, in presence of me notare publict and clerk depute in the office of Justiciarie, John and George Bannatynes, my sones, James Douglas, John Hamiltoun and James Kynneir, ordiner officeris in the said office of Justiciarie, witnessis speciallie requyret and desyret to all and sindrie the premissis.

(193) [16 March 1642: Robertoun J.D.]

Sla[uchter]. Continewit to the xix of Merche instant. Stalker contra *Haddo.*

Intran.—Johnne Gordoun of Haddo; Johnne Gordoun his servand.

Dilaittit of airt and pairt of the slauchter of umquhill Mr James Stalker, servitour for the tyme to Andro Lord Fraser, and sone to Johnne Stalker of Eister Dryla, committit upoun the fourteine day of Maii imvic threttie nyne yeiris.

Persewaris.—Johnne Stalker of Eister Dryla, as father, William Scott, brother in law[1] to the defunct, Sir Thomas Hoip of Craighall, knycht barronet, his Majesteis Advocat, for his Hienes intreis.

Prelocutouris in defence.—Mr Johnne Gilmour, Mr William Forbes[2] and James Gibsone.[3]

The laird of Haddo and his said servand takis instrumentis of thair entrie and protestis for thair cautioneris releiff.

My Lord Advocat declaires that he insistis allanerlie at this time againes the said laird of Haddo for the cryme lybellit.

The said Johnne Gordoun, servand to the laird, with Mr Johnne Gilmour, advocat, his prelocutour, declairit that he is now servand to the laird of Haddo and was servand to him the tyme of the alledgit slauchter lybellit, and quha is **(194)** sone to James Gordoun of Tillelt, quha was sumond to this persuitt as airt and pairt of the slauchter lybellit, and is past fra be his Majesteis Advocat at the leist nocht insistit againes, compeired this day and askit instrumentis of his compeirance and protestit for releiff of his cautioner and that the Judge may ordeane his expenssis to be refoundit to him for keiping of this dayis dyet as also that na letters be direct againes him for the cryme foirsaid in any tyme cumming.

My Lord Advocat protestit in the contrair, as also takis instrumentis of the reiding of the dittay togidder with the defunctis testament producit for instructing thairof.[4]

The pannell takis instrumentis that nane compeired bot Johnne Stalker of Eister Dryla, father to the defunct, William Scott his brother in law, with my Lord Advocat, as persewaris.

[1st Defence.] It is alledgit [I] be Johnne Gordoun of Haddo now upoun pannell and his prelocutouris foirsaidis, denying alwayis the sumondis and slauchter libellit, that thair can be na proces grantit upoun this dittay becaus the slauchter being confest to haife beine comittit in oppin hostilitie the tyme of the lait unhappie troubilles, quhairin it is acknawledgit that thair war numberis of men upoun the feildis on both sydis, and that four hundreth of the name of Gordoun and thair complices war accumpaniet, togidder with quhom the laird of Haddo is alledgit to haife beine, the said slauchter gif any was committit

1 See legal note 3.

2 Admitted advocate 12 June 1634, *Lyon's List*, p. 74.

3 Admitted advocate 6th February 1627, *Lyon's List*, p. 80.

4 This testament was in Lord Fraser's possession on 10th September 1641 (*APS* V.660). It is not recorded in the Edinburgh Register of Testaments.

fallis under the Act of Pacificatioun and Oblivioun,[1] quhairby it is declairit that in respect the lait commotiounis and trubillis, by the mercie of God and the Kingis wisdome and cair, ar turned to ane quyet calme and confortabill peice, that such things as haith fallin furth in these tumultuous tymis quhillas all war silent quhither prejudiciall to his Majesteis honnour etc. or to the perticular intreis of the subject, quhich to examine in als strict court of Justice might prove ane hinderence to ane perfyt peice, sall be buried in perpetuall oblivioun etc., and that all actis of hostilitie, quhither betwix the King and his subjectis or betwix subject and subject, falling out by the occasioun of the lait trubilles preceiding the conclusioun of the treatie etc., that the same and quhosoevir haith ensewit thairupoun etc. sall in no tyme heireftir be callit in questioun nor recentit as ane wrong, nationall or personall, quhatsoevir be the qualitie of the persone or personis or of quhatsoevir kynd of degree, civill or criminall, the injurie is supposit to be, and that no mentioun be maid thairof in judgment or outwith bot held and reputtit as tho never any sic thing had beine thocht or wrocht, dischargeing all Judges etc. to ceit proces or execuit sentence or onywayis molest the leidges in tyme cumming. Lykeas the Kingis Majestie *in verbo principis* promised to caus the act be trewlie observit be all the leidges, as the said act at mair lenth beires, in respect quhairof no sic letters aucht to haife beine direct at the instance of the Kingis Majesteis Advocat, the pairteis intreist, nor can the Justice Generall or his deputtis proceid or grant proces thairupoun. Lykeas the pannell craives that my Lord Advocat may concur with him in his exceptioun foundit upoun the said Act of Oblivioun.

It is answerit be my Lord Advocat that the exceptioun, swa far as it is foundit
(195) upoun the persewaris grant that thair was twa contrair cumpanies in the feildis, [is] contrair to the lybell, quhilk beires that the defunct was attending the committe of that pairt of the cuntrie, quhilk committe albeit befoir the articles of pacificatioun at Berwick or sensyne declairit be speciall Act of Parliament to haife beine Lauchfull, Parliament 2 Act 29,[2] and that the name of Gordoun gathered thameselffis to the number of fyve hundreth and tymouslie, in the morning be twylight, surprysit the committe quha war compellit for saiftie of thair lives to flee; And the defunct being servand for the tyme to my Lord Fraser on of the committe, haifeing fled af the town of Turreff, on the quhilk the assault was maid, be the space of twa mylles, was takin prissoner and keipit and detenit prissoner be the spaice of twa or thrie houris, induring that tyme was under the mercie and power of the apprehender; And as to that pairt of the exceptioun proponit upoun the Act of Oblivioun it is answerit that the samyn is not nor cannot be extendit to this cryme of murthour lybellit, becaus albeit the Act might comprehend all actis of hostilitie committit be non covenanteris againes the covenanteris, *vel e contra*, yit it cannot comprehend this murthour lybellit, becaus it is a cryme of the natur that gif the persewaris and assailyieris at that tyme had beine under ane martiall governament of generall or crowneris it was punischabill be law as murthour, except it had beine done be the speciall warrand of generall or crowner, for, albeit in actis of hostilitie all violence be lauchfull in the conflict, yit all crymes committit eftir the ending of the conflict

[1] See legal note 4.
[2] See legal note 4.

fallis under the punischment of the law, and it is not lauchfull eftir any persone is takin prissoner and keipit and detenit and under the mercie and power of the takeris to kill and slay them; And as the pannell, gif ane woman, had beine takin upoun the uther syde and brocht within his power could not haife been stuperat and violat be him, bot he being maried wold haife beine guiltie of the cryme of adulterie,[1] nochtwithstanding of this Act of Oblivioun, so meikill the moir haifeing the defunct within his power and mercie, and killing him with cald bluid, he is lyabill to the punischment of murthour committit under trust quhilk [be] the Act of Parliament [15]87 is tressonabill cap. 29,[2] becaus be the commoun law and law of all natiounis a prissoner being takin and under the mercie and power of the taker is *equiparat carcerato et existenti in publica custodia* and swa is under the protectioun of that soverane power to quhilk the takeris and apprehenderis ar subject, quhois protectioun is violat gif any violence be usit againes the pairtie incarcerat bot be ordour of Justice. Nixt the said Act of Oblivioun beires ane speciall exceptioun beiring the samyn nawayis to be extendit to murthereris etc. and utheris exprest in the Act; Lykeas in the propositionis and articles given in by the Commissioneris of Scotland eftir the Erle of Loudoun, now Lord Chancellour, his returne from the Parliament of Scotland this article following is secund in number beiring that, leist malefactouris quho committit murthour or the lyk crymis craive the benefeit of the said Act of Oblivioun (for quhom it is nawayis intendit), that thair wold be ane exceptioun from the said Act of all legall persuitt intentit or to be intentit within the spaice of ane yeir eftir the dait of the treatie againes the malefactouris exprest thairin, and speciallie againes murtheris. To the quhilk article this answer is maid be the Inglisch Commissioneris for his Majestie that the said secund article is condiscendit unto, quhilkis articles and answeris ar joyntlie with the said Act of Oblivioun ratified in parliament; And trew it is that the cryme lybellit is murthour of the qualitie above exprest and the letters are intentit upoun the nyntene of November 1641[3] quhilk was within twa dayis of the ryseing of the Parliament; And thairfoir the pannell can nawayis cleith himselff with the said Act of Oblivioun and his Majesteis Advocat cannot concur for his defence againes **(196)** the law, bot hes just and necessar caus to persew the pannell for his dew punischment.

[2nd defence.] [II] The pannell as of befoir denyis that he committit or gave any command, or was airt and pairt, or was presentt at the slauchter lybellit, bot declaires, as the trewth is, that he was a myll from the plaice of the alledgit slauchter the tyme of the alledgit committing thairof,[4] and yit adheris to the defence as being maist relevant notwithstanding of the answer.

And [I] as to the first pairt thairof, beiring that the Act of oblivioun cannot comprehend the alledgit murthour lybellit,[5] becaus it is of that natur that gif the persewaris and assailyeeris had beine under martiall governament it was puncischabill except it had beine done be warrand of generall or crowner, for

[1] Rape would have been a more apt analogy.
[2] This is an error for cap. 51.
[3] This must be an error as the case was in court on 17th November.
[4] See legal note 5.
[5] It appears to have been accepted by counsel for the panel that murder was libelled.

albeit violence in the conflict be lauchfull yit crymis committit eftir ar punischabill, to this it is answerit that now and in this plaice it is not propper to disputt in the generall *quatenus* actis of violence or uther injuries ar lauchfull or unlauchfull, as being committit the tyme of any conflict or *ex post facto* and immediatlie thaireftir, seing, thankis to God, all these troubilles being endit, all actis of hostilitie in generall done the tyme thairof and *in tuitu* and by occasioun of the samyn ar without any sic exceptioun takin away and appoyntit to be buried in oblivioun, and it war of moist daingerous consequence gif now it sould be lauchfull to call in questioun sic thingis as war done the tyme of these troubilles and in hostilitie quhither ather pairteis did keip thameselffis within preceis reules of militarie discipline or not, for then quhatevir hes beine done in the Kingis houssis, cities or feildis *citra modum* and reule of discipline againes men, unmaried weomen and utherwayis, or quhatevir tumultis or convocationis war maid, or gif any of the Kingis leidges war apprehendit spuilyeit or robbit without lauchfull and preceis ordour, [there] sould be all now rangitt up and brocht in questioun, quhairby the Act of Oblivioun sould be elusarie and the cleir intentioun thairof prejudgit, quhilk is that no such actis and deidis done the tyme of these trubilles and *in tuitu* of the commotiounis and differences than in the kingdome sould not be called in questioun, quhither prejudiciall to the Kings auctoritie and honnour or to the lawis and liberteis of kirk and kingdome, or to the perticular intreist of the subject; And yit to cleir that the deid lybellit can nawayis interpret to be ane murthour in any sort as is alledgit in the lybell and throughout the haill reply, it is cleir by the law of the Majesty that *murdrum dicitur quod nullo vidente vel sciente clam perpetratur praeter solum interfectorem etc.,*[1] and be Mr Johnne Skeine *De Verborum Significatione*[2] upoun the word *murdrum* affirmes that murthour is quhen any man, be ane propensit malice, lyis in waitt for ane uther man, and according to his malicious intent slayis him, and that it is committit willinglie and wittinglie[3] be ane, quha of set purpois, lyis quyetlie in waitt for that effect, quhilk being·propperlie murthour, different from simpill slauchter, merites only the paines of tressone and utheris dew thairto. Nather is all homicid *ex proposito* or *deliberatum* to be callit murthour, for then thair sould be skairs any difference in criminall dittayis betwix simpill slauchter and murthour, and gif so then also all slauchter upoun foirthocht fellony micht be callit murthour,[4] quhilk is agains all law and the lawis of this kingdome; And, albeit *homicidium ex infidiis* may be interpret to be propper murthour, that kynd of homicid is cleirlie defynit to be *quando aliquis expectat alium positus in loco qui ab illo provideri veresimiliter non poterat animo eum occidenti illumque ex improviso venientem aggreditur et interfecit,* quhilk cannot quadrat **(197)** with the caice lybellit, this slauchter being committit *ut supra* in oppin hostilitie in the feildis in oppin view; And, albeit it had beine committit in the qualitie lybellit eftir the defunct was disarmit and in the mercie of his apprehender, that cannot mak the slauchter murthour bot the moist it can be it is *homicidium simplex dolosum* in tumult, and as man [*may*] be vehementlie

1 IV.v.3, Cooper edition 253.

2 See legal note 6.

3 For contemporary discussions of 'willingly' and 'wittingly' see above *LA* v *Irvine of Lenturk* 1635, I. pp. 247-9 and *Crichton of Frendrach* v *Lady Rothiemay*, I. p. 277-285.

4 As it was by Mackenzie, I.XI.i.

presumit *calore iracundiae,* speciallie seing thair could no sic foir purpois be in the pannell to kill this defunct, seing it is confest be the lybell he askit quhat he was and swa could not knaw him; And as it can nawayis be interpret to be murthour so nather slauchter in trust or assuirance (betwix the twa thair is great difference), becaus it is not nor cannot be alledgit that he randerit himselff upoun assuirance from the pannell of saiftie and it is cleir by the Act of Parliament in *anno* [15]87 cap. 51 that that mainer of slauchter is only tressonabill, quhair it is done under trust, creddit, assuirance and power of the slayer, swa that unles it war lybellit and provin that the man slayer had given assuirance to the pairtie takin in his power, that act millitattis not againes him, and be that same act the difference betwix murthour and slauchter in that kynd is also cleir, the twa being set down *disjunctive* and *a separata.* Lykeas the lybell itselff cleires that the defunct was nawayis under assuirance of the slayer, seing it affirmes that the pannell, eftir he was takin, demandit his name, and eftir heiring the defunctis answer, being ane naikit man, he is alledgit to haife given command to pistoll and dispatch him quhilk is the cleir contraire to assuirance and trust. Farder it is not propper to disputt quhither the slauchter was done be auctoritie of generall or crowner, in quhilk caice it is acknawledgit that the slauchter might be lauchfullie and ordourlie done, for gif it war propper, then the pannell wold retort the answer in respect of the lybell itselff beiring that they war fyve hundreth men convenit with displayit ensignes, banneris and towking [*beating or 'tucking*]' of drummis, and that the pannell was ane speciall leader, quha is alledgit to haif committit or haif given command to committ the slauchter, and swa the persewar be the lybell acknawledgis quhat he requyris be the reply to be necessar to the lauchfulnes of slauchter or uther actis of hostilitie. Bot heir, in respect of the Act of Oblivioun, these questionis ar altogidder unnecessar, and that cannot bot comprehend the deid lybellit nochtwithstanding of the circumstances alledgit to aggravat the samyn, albeit they war trew, as they are altogidder fals.

Item, to the instance adducit anent the violating of ane woman, gif any sic thing had beine committit, it merites no answer being no act of hostilitie or any such act as by any sens could be thocht to be comprehendit within the Act of Oblivioun, seing thairby not only the woman is injured, bot the committer violatts his faith and conjugall deutie to his awin wyff and wrongs the intreist of the uther husband, and all this not *intuitu* of the quarrellis of the tymis bot from his inordinat lust, quhilk non could defend or excuis, haifeing no cohaesioun or respect to the differences or commoun troubilles of the tyme; bot it is not our caice, nather is the defender obleist to disputt the same.

As to the Act of Parliament [15]87 it is answerit alreddie. *Item,* quhair it is alledgit that ane prissoner being takin and under the mercie and power of the taker it is *equiparat carcerato* being under the protectioun of that soverane power to quhilk the takeris ar subject: First the pannell denyis the similitud, and a pairtie takin cannot be thocht to be in the caice of a persone in waird unles assuirance be given him and it be declairit to him that he is to be usit as ane prissoner, bot in this caice no sic thing can be alledgit, nather can the defunct be said to be ane prissoner seing it is evident be the lybell that eftir he was apprehendit it is acknawledgit that without any considerabill intervall of tyme and befoir he **(198)** come af the feildis and befoir he was put in the credit or keiping of any he was killed, and that soverane power, to the quhilk both pairteis war subject, haif ordanit that and all uther such deidis to be buried for the ressonis *ut supra*; And it is knawin that the verrie tyme of the committing of the slauchter thair was utheris killed on both sydis viz. on Gordoun in Strabogie upoun the pairt of the Gordounis, and on Alexander Forbes servitor to the laird of Tachone on the uther syde, quha being all killed at on tyme and in the same plaice it cannot bot be thocht that the slauchter of the defunct, gif it was committit eftir taking, behoved to be upoun suddane passioun and wraith aryseing from the slauchter of the uther.

And quhairas it is alledgit that the Act of Oblivioun hes ane speciall exceptioun beiring the samyn nawayis to be extendit to murthereris, and adduces the secund article given in be the Commissioneris of Scotland to the Inglisch commissioneris and thair answer thairto, quhilkis ar joyntlie with the Act of Oblivioun ratified in Parliament,[1] and subsumis that the cryme lybellit is murthour of the qualitie mentionat in the Actis, and that this lybell was intentit within twa dayis eftir the riseing of the Parliament, it is answerit, the exceptioun of the Act of Oblivioun cannot militat againes the pannell, *Primo* becaus the slauchter lybellit can nawayis be interpret ane murthour for the ressonis *ut supra*; *Secundo*, albeit it might be of that qualitie, yit the exceptioun cannot be meanit of sic deidis, murtheris, robries as fell out by occasioun of the troubilles be way of hostilitie, bot is cleirlie to be meanit of thiftis, robreis, murtheris etc. committit utherwayis and in uther caices amongs privat pairteis and not be way of publict hostilitie, for utherwayis quhatsumevir guidis haith beine spulyeit, reft, robbit or plunderit be ather pairtie from uther the tyme and by occasioun of the troubilles, the reiveris, roberis and plundereris might be all callit in questioun thairfoir nochtwithstanding of the Act, quhilk war to frustrat the intentioun thairof and tend to the disquyetnes of the cuntrie.

It is triplyit be his Majesteis Advocat [*Primo*] that the pannellis denyell of his being bot a myll from the plaice of the alledgit slauchter, that is contrair to the lybell, and contrair the defunctis testament producit and red, quhilk beiris that the defunct being takin and disairmed and craiveing mercie of the pannell the laird of Haddo was absolutlie refuissit of all mercie and command given to dispatch him.[2] *Secundo* he cannot be hard to deny, in respect of the exceptioun proponit in the Act of Oblivioun, and as the proponer of ane exceptioun upoun ane remissioun *confitetur crimen*, swa also quha proponis *super generali abolitione*; And quhair it is alledgit that this is not the plaice to disputt anent the comprehensioun of the Act, it is answerit that it is the only and propper plaice to disputt quhat crymis can possibillie comprehend it and quhat not, under the generall wordis of the law. Lykeas the pannell and his procuratouris hes grantit ane exceptioun upoun the poynt of adulterie and thairfoir ressoning *a minori negative ad majus* gif the les be not includit the greater cannot; And as to the answer maid to that pairt of the reply concerning the attrocitie and haynousnes of the murthour (quhilk *suppositive* gif the cumpany assailyeing had beine *sub disciplina martiali* war still punischabill) that this is not the plaice to disputt *quid factum sit citra modum disciplinae militaris*, it is answerit *si citra*

[1] See legal note 4.

[2] How in these circumstances the deceased could survive to prepare a testament and to describe the incident in his testament is not disclosed. See legal note 7.

modum not punischabill, bot *si ultra* as this is; And quhair it is alledgit that the cryme lybellit is not murthour, opponis the plaicis citit be the pannell, and speciallie *in legibus Malcolmi* 2di. cap. 15,[1] quhilk the proponer callit *Regiam Majestatem* albeit the buikis of *Regiam Majestatem* follow eftir the lawis of Malcolme the secund, quhilk plaice beires that *publicum murdrum locum habet in interfectis per felloniam*; And gif the proponer found his cotatioun upoun the 4 buik of the *Majestie* cap. 5, intitulat *de homicidio*, quhilk beires *quod duo sunt genera homicidii unum quod dicitur murdrum*, it is answerit that that plaice condiscendis allanerlie upoun ane perticular spaice of murdrum, viz. *murdrum privatum quod nullo vidente vel sciente clam perpetratur,* and swa it is not pertinentlie alledgit to eleid the reply, and that it is so the uther cotatioun maid be the pannell out of Skineus upoun the word *murdrum*, quhilk distinguisches *murdrum inter privatum et publicum*, and defynis *murdrum publicum* as it is defynit be Malcolme the secund viz. *quod habeat locum in interfectis per felloniam*; And quhair it is alledgit that murthour only hes plaice *interfecto per infidias*, this cannot be affirmit nather be law nor ressone, bot is contrair to plaices adducit be the pannell *ut supra*; And to alledge that the murthour lybellit is only *homicidium dolosum*, that war to mak murthour and homicid all one *quia omne homicidium est dolosum*, bot of the law *homicidium animo determinato commissum* with the qualities mentionat in the lybell, upoun the defunct takin prissoner disermit asking mercie and refuissit, is the hiest plaice of murthour *et accedit proxime* to that murthour quhilk be the Act of Parliament [15]87 [cap. 51] is declairit tressonabill, albeit this be not so persewit in this lybell; And quhair the defender preissis to excuis *ab animo deliberato* out of the wordis of the lybell that the pannell knew him not till he declairit quhais servand he was, that is no excuis, bot first *tacite* implyis *animum deliberatum* againes all the servandis of my Lord Fraseris, becaus so sone as the pannell knew be his answer that he was my Lord Fraser servand, he answerit that he was one quhom he was seiking and commandit to dispatch him; And quahir it is denyit that he was ane prissoner and that the defunct did not rander himselff upoun promeis of saiftie, he was not in that conditioun as he might seik quarteris being takin in oppin feildis againes his will, and the trust was the greater upoun his pairt that he did not resist and tyed [*bound*] the pannel in Christianitie and honnour rather to haife spaired him; And quhair it is alledgit that he was killed and dispatcht *immediate et calore iracundiae* it is answerit that he was prissoner be the spaice of twa houres and above befoir he was killed, quhilk sall be cleired to the assys; And gif *sub calore iracundiae* it was not accidentallie bot *sub ratione vindicti* upoun the nameing of his maister.

And as to the answer maid to the cryme of adulterie repeits the former answer.

And quhair it is alledgit upoun the wordis of the lybell that the pannell is callit ane cheiff leader, that exeames him not fra the merciles creweltie againes a prissoner, except he war abill to verefie that he was chosen generall or crowner; And, quhair it is denyit that the similitud holdis betwix ane prissoner and ane

[1] Skene, *Auld Lawes*, p. 4; *APS* I.737, cap. 2.

incarcerat, it is answerit that the samyn must hold becaus they ar both captives and depryvit of thair liberteis and the definitioun quadrats to both.

And quhair it is alledgit that this murthour cannot be challengit becaus the Act of Oblivioun is maid by the auctoritie of the Soverane power to the quhilk both pairteis war subject, and hes ordanit all such crymis to be buried, that is *manifesta petitio principii quia illud est* "*το κρινομενον*;[1] And quhair it is answerit againes the perticular exceptioun specifeit in the Act of Oblivioun quhilk exceptis murthour *per expressum*, that the said exceptioun cannot includ the cryme lybellit becaus not murthour, repeits the former answer that it is murthour, and that in the hiest degrie; And, quhair it is alledgit that the exceptioun is only meanit of murthour committit utherwayis and in uther caices nor quhilk ar committit be way of publict hostilitie, it is answerit that the exceptioun is of murtheris generallie and that in respect of the haynousnes crewaltie and attrocitie of the cryme *cum terminis distinctis ab homicidio*; **(200)** And quhair it is alledgit that the spuilyeers of guidis or plundereris might be also exceptit gif this war not the meaning of the Act, it is answerit that all roberis or volneris ar includit in the exceptioun and not spuilyeeris and plundereris, and the exceptioun must be takin according to the trew propp333rietie of the wordis contenit thairin, quhilk according to thair awin severall natures and qualities ar both to be meanit and judgit.

The pannell befoir answer to the triply addis to his duply the particularis following, omittit to be answerit to some pairties of the reply, viz.: [*Primo*] quhairas the persewar in the first pairt of his reply denis that thair war twa contrair cumpanies in the feildis, bot that the defunct was attending the committe of that pairt of the cuntrie, and affirmes that the name of Gordoun surprysit the committe quha war compellit to flie for saiftie and that the defunct fled af the town of Turreff twa myllis, and was takin or detenit prissoner twa or thrie houres and during that tyme was under the mercie and power of the apprehender; it is answerit that the pannell at that tyme knew no such committe, and he is glad that all committeis haldin at that tyme ar now at lenth ratified be King and Parliament and will not disputt quhither or no then in law he was subject to that committee. *Secundo* it cannot be instructit that thair was then any meiting of ane committe, bot the trewth is that the cuntrie being devydit, pairteis drew to sydis and was in airmes, ane againes uther, at that tyme and be the spaice of many dayis befoir, during the quhilk tyme thair was onsettis and skirmisches on both handis. *Tertio* the defunct cannot be thocht to haife beine had as prissoner or keipit be him twa or thrie houris, nor under his mercie, assuirance or power during that haill tyme, for the ressonis contenit in the uther memberis of the duply and is cleir contrair to the lybell itselff and to the defunctis alledgit testament quhilk was producit bot now abstractit be the persewar, beiring that eftir he was disairmed, and quhen Haddo was informed quhat he was, he said he was on of thes quhom he was seiking and then command was given to pistoll and dispatch him, quhilk cleirlie evinces ane acknawledgment that he was no tyme in the assuirance or mercie of Haddo bot that he could get no mercie at his handis, and thairfoir he can nawayis be reputt as prissoner, nor can the slauchter be interpret murthour ather *ex infidiis* or *proditorie* quhilk is only the

[1] That which is being judged = the point at issue.

murthour propperlie to infer the paine thairof different from the paine of simpill homicid.

Item, quhairas the persewar alledgit in fortificatioun of the exceptioun contenit in the Act of Oblivioun the secund propositioun given in be the Scottis commissioneris *ut supra*, answeris that propositioun is condiscendit to according to the provisioun addit to the Act of Oblivioun and cleirlie evinces that the exceptioun cannot quadrat with this caice, seing it is expres againes thiftis, reiffes, hearschippes, oppressiounis, depredatiounis and murthour to be persewit within ane yeir eftir the treattie, and cannot be interpreit of oppressionis and uther deides done upoun the occasiounis of the presentt disturbances *ut supra*. *Item* quhair the Kingis Advocat denyis his concurs to the defence as being againes the Act of Oblivioun and exceptioun thairincontenit, answeris the defence is foundit upoun the Act and the exceptioun in the Act militatis not againes the same, and thairfoir the Kingis Advocat sould not refuis his concurs, and the pannell takis instrumentis of his Lordschips refuissall.

[*Answers to the prosecutor's Triplies.*] [*Item, Primo*] it is answerit to the triply and first member thairof, that the defunctis testament cannot be respectit and can prove nothing againes the defender, being a declaratioun emittit be the **(201)** pairtie his enemie for the tyme, and yit it nawayis proves quhat is lybellit bot contrarie viz. that mercie was refuissit him eftir he was takin and apprehendit and disairmed and does not condiscend upoun the tyme during quhilk he was in the apprehenderis power, and swa it is cleir that he was never in his mercie assuirance nor can be reputt as prissoner, seing ordour was given presentlie to dispatch him, and it does not condiscend quha gave the ordour, and the trewth is that Haddo was not the giver of it. *Secundo* quhair it is alledgit that the pannell cannot be hard to deny in respect of the exceptioun foundit upoun the Act of Oblivioun no moir then gif he proponit ane exceptioun upoun ane remissioun, in quhilk caice he behoved *confiteri crimen*, answeris the difference is manifest, becaus the pairtie quho takis himselff to ane remissioun does it upoun ane acknawledgment of the cryme, quhairas the Act of Oblivioun excludis the persewaris intreis prohibeitis proces to be intendit and discharges the judge to proceid upoun the crymis includit thairin quhither the defenderies be guiltie or innocent.

Item, quhair it is answerit that this is the only propper plaice to disputt quhat crymis ar comprehendit within the generall wordis of the law, it is answerit that it is certanlie propper to disputt quhairfoir crymis befoir and eftir the troubilles sould not be comprehendit within the Act, as also that the Act sould not be extendit to sic personis as ar contenit in the exceptioun, bot seing the generall wordis of the Act cairies all crymis or injuries of quhatsumevir kynd, or qualitie committit the tyme and upoun occasioun of the troubilles, it is certane that the qualitie of the cryme contenit in the generall law sould not be disputtit and far les uther circumstances as quither or no the pairteis conteine thaimselffis within or transgres the ordour of militarie discipline; Nather does the defender grant the caice of adulterie adducit, bot ressonis only be way of suppositioun; Nor is the argument *a minori ad majus* from adulterie to murthour relevant, becaus thair is nothing moir or les to be excludit out of the generall law bot such perticularis as ar expreslie mentionat in the exceptioun, and gif *argumentum a minori* war in this plaice guid, then from adulterie it might be ressonit to deidis done againes the Kings auctoritie or uther pointis of tressone againes the King, quhilkis nevertheles gif any was ar all buried in oblivioun be the said Act.

Item: the pannell neides not answer to that pairt of the triply, quhairby the persewar takis advantage of the word *citra*, for the defender sall hald it as deleit being a mistaking and use the word *ultra. Item;* quhair the persewar alledgis ane uther mistak affirming that the defender calles leges Malcolmi, Regiam Majestatem, the defender acknawledgit ever the difference and the plaice alledgit be him was that quhilk he producit in judgment out of the 4 buik of the *Majestie*;[1] and quhairas it is alledgit that be the law of Malcolm 2 cap. 15 it beires that *publicum murdrum habet locum in interfectis per felloniam*, and that the plaice in the *Majestie de homicidio* condiscendis only upoun ane spaice of *murdrum viz. privatum* and swa alledgit not pertinentlie adducit, and answeris the lyk plaice out of Skineous[2] that *publicum murdrum* is defynit to be *quod habet locum in interfectis per felloniam*, and that thair is no law or ressone to affirme that murthour hes only plaice *in interfecto per incidias* [*sic*], it is answerit that the definitioun of murthour alledgit be the persewar is not guid nor provin be the plaices adducit, for thes plaices does not define murthour *ut supra*, for than quhosevir sould kill *per felloniam* sould be a murtherer, and the word fellonie cannot be taken so lairdglie [*widely*] to infer murthour as *homicidium deliberatum,* and *murdrum* sould be thocht to be ane of that same, becaus it is cleir that *fellonia* and *dolus* in effect ar one and that same as appeires by Skineus *ad verbum fellonia;* And it is cleir be the statut of Alexander the secund cap. 2°, quhair it is said *si aliquis de furto homicidio seu consimilibus felloniis* swa that the word is generall; and quhair it is said in the law of King William[3] that *publicum murdrum locum habet in interfectis per felloniam*, that is ather to be interpret in a generall sens of *publicum homicidium dolosum* or *publicum homicidium* in the perticular caice of *infidiie* or *proditioni*, and it war againes all ressone and the constant prattick to affirme that *homicidium animo deliberato commissum* not being expreslie lybellit *ex infidiis et proditorie*; nather can the deid lybellit be thocht murthour upoun the qualities mentionat in the triply, becaus he was prissoner and askit mercie, nor becaus of the answer mentionat in the lybell and testament that he was one quhom the defender was seiking, being my Lord Fraseris servand, quhilk *tacite* implyis *animum deliberatum* againes all his servandis, becaus albeit he had *animum deliberatum* againes all, then on the uther syd yit that evinceth nothing againes the defender to mak him a murtherer, and it is certaine that thair is moir requyrit to mak murthour so propperlie termed as it is takin in the Act [15]87 or in the exceptioun of this Act, for it man be ather *ex infidiis* or *proditorie*, and heir thair is no sic thing lybellit that assuirance was given or that the deid was committit *ex infidiis* or *proditorie*, quhilk presupponis *nullam precedentem inimicitiam et nullam intervenientem rixam*; and albeit the defunct had trustit his taker yit *nihil ad rem* except his taker had given him assurance; And albeit *sub ratione vindicte* yit no murthour seing *vindicta* and *iracundia* makis *homicidium simplex;* nor could the defunct be callit the pannellis

[1] IV.V.2, Cooper's edition, p. 253.
[2] See p. 493 above.
[3] This has not been traced in *APS* I.369-384, or in Skene's *Auld Lawes.* Cf. *Auld Lawes*, p. 4.

prissoner; and yit the dissimilitud betwix ane pairtie takin in the feildis imediatlie killed, and ane prissoner killed, is moist cleir, and thair is no *petitio principii* in the caice alledgit.

Item, the exceptioun in the Act is of murthereris generallie, as of robberis, of personis committeris of these haynous deidis *extra casum* of the publict troubilles, and deidis done in that caice can no mor be exceptit then oppressiounis, reiffis and spuilyeis, and thair is no difference betwix reiff and spuilyie persewit criminallie, and it is certaine that oppressionis done be occasioun of the troubilles cannot now be persewit and yit the word oppressioun is perticularlie set down in the foirsaid secund propositioun the meaning quhairof must be *ut supra*; And the defender takis instrumentis that the wordis of the exceptioun ar acknowledgit be the persewar sould be takin in the trew proprietie and thairupoun the defender subsumis that the word murtherer sould not be impropperlie extendit ather to infer a cryme againes the defender or to limit the generall Act of Oblivioun, quhilk generall Act sould rather be extendit *quia favores sunt ampliandi.*

Item, the defender takis instrumentis upoun the reproductioun of the testament and of the wordis thairof beiring that the defunct, according to his memorie and judgment, that he was killed be Johnne Gordoun, his servand, and does not *positive* affirme anything ather of Haddo or of his servand namit Johnne Gordoun than bot this Johnne Gordoun now past fra, swa that the testament cleires nothing bot uncertantie.

The Justice continewis this dyet with his interloquitouris upoun the alledgances foirsaidis and answeris maid thairto to Saturday nixt the nyntene day of Merche instant, and ordanit cautioun to be fund be the pannell for his compeirance that day under the paine three thousand merkis money. For obedience of the quhilk ordinance anent the finding of the said cautioun compeirit Mr Alexander Seattoun of Tilry and become actit and obleist for the said Johnne Gordoun of Haddo his entrie and compeirance befoir the Justice and his deputtis in the tolbuith of Edinburgh the said nynteine day of Merche instant under the paine foirsaid.

The personis of assys sumond to this day wairnit *apud acta* to the said nynteine day ilk persone under the paine of thrie hundreth merkis.

(208) [19 March 1642: James Robertoun J.D.]
[Libelled as murder. Continued to 24 June 1642.]

(230) [24 June 1642: Colvill and Robertoun JJ.D.]

Persewaris.—Andro Lord Fraser, as maister; Johnne Stalker, as father.

Prelocutouris in persute.—The laird of Innerleyth, younger; the laird of Inglistoun; James Windrahame of Wowstoun; William Douglas of Goger; Mr Thomas Young of Lany; Sir Thomas Hoip, his Majesties Advocat, for his Hienes intreis.

Prelocutouris in defence.—The Erle of Home; My Lord Gordoun; my Lord Seatoun; the laird of Dincrub; Sir George Hamiltoun of Blaikburne; Sir Frances Sinclair; Mr John Gilmour advocat.[1]

[Continued to 25 June 1642.]

(231) [25 June 1642: Colvile and Robertoun JJ.D.]

Sla[*uchter*]. *Continewit to the first of Julii nixtocum.*

Intran.—John Gordoun of Haddo.

Dilaittit of the murthour of umquhile Mr James Stalker.

Perseweris.—John Stalker of Dryla as father; My Lord Fraser as maister; and Sir Thomas Hope his Majesteis Advocat.

Prelocutouris in defence.—Mr. John Gilmour.

The pannell takis instrumentis of his entrie and protestis for his cautioneris releiff.

My Lord Advocat desyret the witnessis to be callit upone, quha war summond be the Lordis letters to this day, to the effect the qualitie of the cryme may be knawin quither it be murthour or not, quhilk is necesser to be knawin befoir the exceptione quhilk is foundit upone the Act of Oblivione be discussit.

It is answerit be Mr John Gilmour, for the pannell, that thair can be na witnessis ressavit till the lybell be fund relevant, and the exceptiones alreddie proponit, bothe aganis the relevancie and peremptour of the haill caus, foundit upone the Act of Oblivione be first discussit, for the exceptiones ar foundit *in jure;* and be the nottour circumstances, baithe contenit in the lybell and mentionat in the exceptiones, it will appeir to the Judge, albeit the lybell war relevant as it is not, that the alledget slauchter is not any sic murthour as [is] contenit in the exceptione of the Act of Oblivione; and it is ane unhard noveltie to crave witnessis *in statu cause quo nunc est*, and the ceiting of the witnessis hes noe more warrand nor the ceitting of ane assyse, nather of quhich can be callid or ressavid befoir the discussing of the alledgeance.

It is answerit be my Lord Advocat that the cryme contenit in the lybell is directlie crewall murthour and soe dissignet, in slaying of ane prissoner with cald bluid and quha was under trust of the pannell eftir he was tane, and the pannell be proponeing of the peremptour exceptione foundit upone the Act of Oblivione is presumet of the law to grant the lybell in the same caice as he did propone ane exceptione upone his remissione; and now, be the pannellis objectione maid aganis the exceptione[2] of the witnessis, he grantis that the onlie dispute will be upone the qualitie of the murthour gif it fall within the Act of Oblivione or not, and thairfoir thair is ane absolute necessitie that the qualitie of the murthour be first tryet.

[1] There is no explanation of the sudden appearance here of these new prelocutors, who again appear on 6th July.

[2] This must be a slip for 'accepting'.

It is answerit for the pannell quither murthour or not murthour is the questione quhairupone the dispute hes bene alreddie maid, quhilk the pannell he repeittis, and soe to affirme it heir in this place murthour is *contraversum pro confesso*; and the defenders exceptione foundit upone the Act of Oblivione and aganis the receptione of the witnessis is no acknawledgement of any murthour one the pannellis pairt, bot contrariewayis the exceptione upone the Act of Oblivione importtis ane denyell that it is any sic slauchter as may import murthour mentionat in the exceptione contenit in the Act, quhilk is sufficientlie cleirit be the lybell and former dispute quhilk the pannell referris to the Justice; bot howsoevir thais exceptiones ar alwayis understuid *posito non dato* and in the estait of the proces as now it is to admit precognitiones is aganis law and custome befoir discussing of the defences foundit aganis the relevancie of the lybell and peremptouris.

The Kingis Advocat takis instrumentis of the pannellis answer, and is content of thair awin consentis that the exceptione, quhilk be the defenderis awin grant is proponit aganis slauchter, be fund relevant and proven, and thairfoir desyres that the lybell aganis crewall murthour be put to the knawledge of ane assyse.[1]

It is answerit for the pannell thair is no new exceptione proponit bot a repetitione of the former aganis the receptione of the witnessis, quhilk the pannell referris to the Judge. Lykas the pannell takis instrumentis of my Lord Advocattis declaratioun that he is content that the exceptioun foundit upone the Act of Oblivioun be fund relevant and provin, whilk exceptioun is proponet against no uther slauchter than this slauchter lybellit, quhairof the pannell being frie, na witnessis can be ressavet for preveing of the alledget murthour quhilk is affirmet to be the qualitie of this slauchter off the quhilk he is frie; bot quhidder it be slauchter or murthour it is nocht propper heir to dispute becaus it was dispute of befoir; and the pannell disassentis expreslie frome ony precognitioun cravet as being a matter that may tend to the disturbance of the publict peace and is against all law and custome as said is.[2]

The Justice continewis the dyet to Fryday nixt, being the first of Julii, and ordanis the pannell to find cautioun for his re-entrie that day under the pane of sax thousand merkis. Lykas for obedience thairof compeirit George Gordoun of Tilliefowdie and become cautioun for the pannell his re-entrie that day to underly the law for the said allegit cryme under the pane foirsaid.

(232) [1 July 1642: Colvile and Robertoun JJ.D.]

Sla[uchter]. Continewit to the saxt of Julii instant.

Intran.—Johne Gordoun of Haddo.

Dilaitit of airt and pairt of the murthour and slauchter of umquhile Mr James Stalker sone to Johnne Stalker of Eister Drylaw committit upone the xiiii day of Maii 1639.

[1] In other words the L.A. admitted that the Act of Oblivion was a complete defence to a charge of slaughter.

[2] See legal note 8.

Persewaris.—John Stalker as father; my Lord Advocat.

Prelocutouris for the pannell.—Mr John Gilmour advocat.

The Justice continewis this dayis dyet anent the tryell of the allegit murthour and slauchter lybell it, with the alledgeances and answeris maid be aither pairtie, alsweill persewaris as defenderis in the said cuas, to the saxt day of Julii instant, that in the meane tyme he mycht be advyset with the Lordis of his Majesteis Secreit Counsall anent the pronunceing of his interloquitour thairintill,[1] and ordanit the pannell to find cautioun for his re-entrie that day under the pane of sax thousand merks money.

Compeirit Thomas Gairne of Cannophill and become cautioun for the said Johnne Gordoun of Haddo his compeirance befoir the Justice and Justice deputtis, the said saxt day Julii instant, to the effect and under the pane foirsaid; Lykas the said laird of Haddo obleist him for his saidis cautioneris releiff.

(233) [6 July 1642: Colvile and Robertoun JJ.D.]

Sla[*uchter*] *Stalker* contra *Gordoun of Haddo. Continewit to the nixt Parliament in Junii* 1644.

Intran.—Johnne Gordoun of Haddo.

Dilaittit of airt and pairt of the murthour and slauchter of umquhile Mr James Stalker, sone to John Stalker of Eister Drylaw, committit in the moneth of Maii 1639 yeiris.

Persewaris.—Andro Loird Fraser, as maister to the defunct; John Stalker of Eister Drylaw as father; Thomas Stalker as brother, William Scott in Deane brother in law; the laird of Innerleyth younger, with the uther persewaris insert in the act 24 Junii 1642; Sir Thomas Hope etc. his Majesteis Advocat.

Prelocutouris in defence.—The Erle of Home; the Lord Gordoun; the Lord Seatoun; the laird of Dincrub; Sir George Hammiltoun etc.; Sir Frances Sinclair; Mr John Gilmour, advocat.

The pannell takis instrumentis of his entrie and protestis for his cautioneris releiff.

Continewit to the xiiii day of Junii 1644.

The Act of Counsell underwrittin was producet to his Majesteis Justice quhairof the tennour followis:—

At Edinburgh the fyft day of Julii 1642[2] the Lordis of Previe Counsall haveing hard the Justice depute,[3] and thairwithall haveing sene the proces led befoir the

[1] I.e. a reference to the Privy Council on the question of relevancy.

[2] *RPC*[2] VII.288. Their lordships had already intervened on 14 February and 17 March 1642 to suspend captions against the panel to enable him to appear in the Justice court.

[3] See legal note 9.

Justice deputtis at the instance of his Majesteis Advocat and Johne Stalker aganis the laird of Haddo, for the alledget murthour committit be the said laird of Haddo upone umquhile Mr James Stalker, sone to the said John, thay doe advyse the Justice and his deputis to remit the advyseing of this proces to his Majestie and the Estaittis of the nixt Parliament. *Extractum de libris actorum Secreti Consilii S.D.N. regis per me Archibaldum Prymrois etc.: Sic subscribitur,* Arch. Primrose, *Clericus S. Consilii.*

Efter productioun and reiding of the whilk Act of Counsall the Justice continewis this dyet to the fourtene day of Junii 1644 yeiris upone the first Tysday, quhairof the nixt Parliament is sett and affixt and ordanit the said Johnne Gordoun of Haddo to find cautioun for his personall compeirance befoir his Majesteis Justice generall and Justice deputtis within the tolbuth of Edinburgh the said fourtene day of Junii, in the hour of caus in anno foirsaid, to underly the law for the cryme abonewrittin under the pane of sax thouseand merkis money. For obedience quhairof compeirit judiciallie Alexander Innes of Coxtoun, quha, be his aith declairing himselff to be past twentie twa yeiris of age, become actit and obleist as cautioner for the said Johne Gordoun of Haddo to enter and present the said John Gordoun of Haddo befoir his Majesteis Justice Generall and Justice deputtis the saidis day and place in the hour of caus to underly the law for the cryme abone expremit under the said pane of sax thouseand merkis money; Quhairupone ather pairtie *hinc inde* askit actis and instrumentis. Lykas the said laird of Haddo being personallie present become actit and obleist to releve his said cautioner of his cautionerie abone writtin and of all pane and penaltie to be incurit be his said cautioner thairthrou etc.

(380) [14 June 1644: Colvile and Robertoun JJ.D.]

Protestatioun. Alexander Innes of Coxtoun anent his releif of his cautionerie for John Gordoun of Haddo.

Compeirit Mr William Forbes, advocat, as procuratour for Alexander Innes of Cokstoun, quha exponit and declairit that upone the saxt day of Julii 1642 yeiris John Gordoun of Haddo, being than criminallie persewit befoir his Majesteis Justice at the instance of John Stalker of Dryla, and his Majesteis Advocat, for his Hienes intreis, for the crewall murthour and slauchter of umquhile Mr James Stalker, sone to the said John Stalker of Dryla, the mater was that day contenowit be his Majesteis Justice to this xiiii day of Junii instant; Lykas at the said laird of Haddo his requeist and desyre for obedience of his Majesteis Justice ordinance, the said Alexander Innes of Cokstoun become than cautione actit in the buikis of adjornall for the said John Gordoun of Haddo his entrie and compeirance this day and place in the hour of caus to underly the law for the said alledget murthour under the payne of sax thousand merkis, as the actis of adjornall maid thairupone beiris; And, in respect nather the said John Stalker nor his Majesteis Advocat compeiris this day to insist in the said laird of Haddo persuit, and that the said laird of Haddo is presentlie in waird within the tolbuithe of Edinburgh reddie to be brocht furthe thairof and to be enterit one pannell incaice of any persewer to insist against him for the cryme foirsaid, the said Mr William Forbes, as procuratour foirsaid, askit instrumentis thairupone, and protestit for releiff of Alexander Innes of Cokstoun, his cautioner, of his former cautionerie and releif of the payment of the soume and penaltie abonespecifeit, and that he may be fred of all payment thairof.[1]

Legal Notes

1. Another example of a master pursuing for injury to his servant is *Wellwood* v *Reid* 1640 above p. 387.

2. Without knowing the precise terms of the original criminal letters it is impossible to know whether murder was libelled or only slaughter. Slaughter is alleged in the summaries of 17th November 1641 and 16th March 1642; murder in those of 19th March and 28th June and in the Privy Council extract narrated in the entry for 6th July 1642. The panel's plea that he was exempted by the Act of Oblivion of 1640 was met by the Lord Advocate's reply that the Act contained an exception of murder and so the issue of slaughter or murder was introduced. It is difficult to believe that the Lord Advocate would have been allowed to allege murder unless it had been libelled. In the entry for 16th March 1642 however the defence appears to admit that it was libelled. As a final element of confusion, the entries of 1st and 6th July 1642 allege both murder and slaughter.

3. This is a unique example of a brother-in-law as pursuer. Hume does not seem to have recognised the competency of this (II.122).

4. That an Act of Oblivion was contemplated is clear from *APS* V.341b, 344a, 345b, and the Lord Advocate did not dispute that it had been passed. It has however been omitted from all the standard editions of the statutes because all the proceedings of the Parliaments of 1640 and 1641 were rescinded by the Rescissory Act 1661 cap. 15 (cap. 126 in *APS* VII.86). The reference to Parl 2 cap. 29 cannot be traced and was unknown to or ignored by Mackenzie (*Observations*, 1687, p. 386) and Hume (II.507). The pacification of Berwick was on 18th June 1639 (Hume Brown, *History of Scotland*, II.314) and in the *Acts of the 2nd Plt. of Charles I*, 1641 (a rare publication in the Advocates' Library) in 'Rescinded Acts' c.18.1. the Articles of Treaty were ratified including the provisions 'concerning an Act of Ratification and Oblivion' (pp. 68, 79, 85).

5. This is one of the few cases where alibi was pled and as usual the Lord Advocate replied that this was contrary to the libel and so not open to proof. See also *Davidson* v *Anderson* 1641, above p. 409.

6. This is the first case in the volume where reference was made to *Regiam Majestatem*; Skene's *De Verborum Significatione*; and Skene's *Auld Lawes*.

7. There have been other references in these volumes to admissions in the deceased's testaments favourable to the panels being founded on (above I.21).

8. If murder was libelled there was no reason why the case should not have gone to the jury, but the Justices seem to have found the point difficult, and eventually referred the matter to the Privy Council. See below, 1 July 1642.

9. The Justice depute evidently appeared in person before the Privy Council and made submissions on the case.

10. No conclusion was ever reached in the case. See Prefatory Note above p. 484.

(165) [18 November 1641: Colvile and Robertoun JJ.D.]

[*Mutilatioun and Thift*]. *Jardane* contra *Edmestoun and Rois*.

Intran.—Frances Edmonstoun in Wolmet,[2] Alexander Rose thair.

Dilaittit of airt and pairt of the mutilatione of George Gerdane in Wolmet of his rycht hand;[3] as also for airt and pairt of the thiftious steilling and away-taking be way of maisterfull thift and stouthereiff of twa clokis of Inglische

[1] See legal note 10.

[2] Woolmet is E of Liberton in Midlothian and S of Portobello; on several occasions the clerk has spelled it as 'Wowmett'.

[3] See legal note 1.

cloithe and ane stand of claithes of Inglische claithe, perteneing to the said George Jerdane, togidder with twentie pundis of reddie money, all being within his kist standing within his dwelling hous in Wolmet, committit in the letter end of October 1641 yeiris.

Perseweris.—George Jerdane in Wolmet, Sir Thomas Hope of Craighall, knycht, his Majesteis Advocat.

Prelocutouris for the pannell.—Mr Thomas Nicolsone, younger.

The Justice with consent of ayther pairteis contenowis this dyet to Weddinsday nixt 24 instantis, and ordanit the pannellis cautioneris to stand obleist for thair entrie that day under the paynes contenit in the former act of adjornall anent thair entrie this day.

The persones summond upone this assyse war wairnit *apud acta* to compeir the said day ilk persone under the payne of 200 merkis.

(167) [24 November 1641: Robertoun J.D.]

Intran.—Frances Edmeistoun in Chirrahall.[1]

Dilaittit of airt and pairt of the mutilatioun of George Jerdane in Wolmet of his rycht hand, and remanent crymes contenit in the letters.

Perseweris.—George Jardane in Wolmet; Sir Thomas Hope of Craighall, his Majesteis Advocat, for his Hienes intreis.

The Justice for causis moveing him contenowis this dyet to this day aucht dayis, the first of December nixt, and ordanit the pannell to find cautione alsweill for his awin entrie that day as of John Edmeistoun in Wolmet, his father,[2] and of Alexander Rose thair; for obedience of the quhilk ordinance compeirit John Park, servand to Sir Archibauld Douglas of Quhittinghame, knycht, and become cautione for the entrie of the saidis John Edmonstoun, Frances Edmonstoun, his sone, and Alexander Rose in Wolmet, the said first day of December nixt, befoir his Majesteis Justice and his deputtis in the tolbuithe of Edinburgh in the hour of caus and underly the law for the crymes contenit in the saidis letters and under the paynes contenit in the Actis of Parliament.

(170) [1 December 1641: Colville J.D.]

Intran.—Frances Edmistoun, sone to John Edmistoune in Wollmet.

Dilaittit of the hurting, wounding and mutilatioun of George Jarden in Wollmit of his richt hand; as also for airt and pairt with the said John Edmistoun, his father, and Alexander Rose in Wollmitt for cuming to the said George Jarden his dwelling hous in Wollmett, breking up of his kist and steilling and awaytaking fuirth thairof of twa cloakis of and ane stand of cloathes of Inglisch cloath, with twentie pundis or thairby of reddie money being thairintill,

[1] Probably Sheriffhall, a little SE of Woolmet.

[2] As later appears, the father was charged as the principal in the theft.

pertening to the said George, committit under night in the letter end of October 1640.

Persewar.—George Jarden.

[Continued till 2nd December 1641.]

(171) [2 December 1641: Colville J.D.]

Compeirit the said Frances Edmistoun, with the said Mr Thomas Nicolsone, Captane William Douglas, and Hew Tod, wrytter, his prelocutouris[1] and producit ane Act of the Lordis of Secreit Counsall off the dait the first day of December instant commanding the Justice to desert this criminall dyett for the reassonis thairincontenit, of the quhilk Act of Counsall followis:—

At Edinbrucht the first day of December 1641 yeiris, anent our Soverane Lordis letters raisit at the instance of Frances Edmistoun, servitour to Captain William Douglas, making mentioun that quhair he being scriver [*paymaster*] to the said Captains cumpanie at Newcastell [about Martinmas 1640 he was sent to round up deserters, and in particular the complainer, and] the said wound (gif any be) was given in execution of his office, the said George was a runnaway and refractarie to the orders of war and Committe of Estaitis for the quhilk he deservit to dee. [The Lords, after hearing parties and several witnesses find] that the said George Jardane wes a runnaway, and that the persewer [in the application to them] had commissioun to apprehend him and cairy him back, and that any wound he received wes in opposeing the said commissioun, and so he procured the same deservedlie.[2] [They therefore directed the Justice to desert the diet, but to reserve to the said George any lawful action he may have against the said Frances for loss sustained in his goods.[3]] [See *ad longum* in *RPC*[2] VII.158.]

Eftir productioun and reiding of the quhilk Act of Counsall the Justice, for obedience of the command mentionat thairintill, desertit the foirsaid criminall dyet; quhairupoun the said Captaine William Douglas askit actis and instrumentis and protestit for releiffe of the said Johnne Edmistoun, Frances Edmistoun, his sone, and Alexander Rose, defenderis, thair cautioneris.

LEGAL NOTES

1. This is a case of justifiable wounding by a soldier attempting in the course of military duty to apprehend a deserter, viz. the complainer. Hume does not mention it, but it is noticed by Pitmedden (I.86, II.181) who cites it in the context that mutilation in circumstances where 'one is obliged to obey' lawful orders, as a soldier or messenger executing a caption, is excusable. The proceedings before the Privy Council are another example of a pre-trial there. The precise procedure adopted is not clear but from the reference to the panel having initiated the process there it was probably on a grant of letters precognition (see also *Oswald* v *Rutherford* 1636, above p. 328).

2. This is one of the few cases, like *Paton* v *Wilson* 1641 (above p. 458) where the panel's solicitor is recorded as appearing with counsel as prelocutors.

3. The Privy Council took a surprisingly lenient view of the charge of theft of both cloth and money by continuing it for civil pursuit presumably because the panel's father was said to have been primarily responsible.

[1] See legal note 2.
[2] See legal note 1.
[3] See legal note 3.

(166) [18 November 1641: Colvile and Robertoun JJ.D.]

Demembratioun. James Roger and utheris. Protestatioun of Assysouris.

Compeirit the samyn xviii day of November 1641 judiciallie Williame Lawsone in Treanch, and Williame Layng in Tilliemair, and declairet that thay and ather of thame war summond be William Symsone, messinger, to compeir befoir his Majesteis Justice and his deputis yisterday the xvii of November instant in the tolbuth of Edinburgh to pas upone the assyse of James Roger in Bogiesyde,[1] Robert Wrycht in Calzeoch of Clat, and Alexander Robsone in Tuilyement [Tillyminet], as thay that war dilaittit of airt and pairt of the amputatioun and dismembring of James Barrie, servitour to Thomas Davidsone in Badievyn, of the thombe of his rycht hand and remanent crymes specifeit in the criminall letters direct thairanent; And in respect that thair was na judge present yisterday becaus of the ryding of the Parliament and swa na court was keipit[2] thay compeirit this day and place and tuik instrumentis of thair entrie and compeirance to the keiping of the said Justice court; And thairfoir protestit that thai be nocht callit or convenit upone the said assyse in ony tyme cuming , and gif thay sall happin to be callit or convenit as witnessis to depone anent the said James Barrie his hurting and dismembring at ony tyme heireftir[3] protestis for thair expenssis alsweill for cuming to the keiping of yisterdayis dyet as for thair citatioun and keiping of ony dyet heireftir, quhilk protestatioun the Justice admittit.[4]

LEGAL NOTES

1. Another case illustrating that the Court did not sit on the day of the riding of Parliament.

2. The persons protesting here had been cited as jurors. The terms of their protest however shows they anticipated they might also be called as witnesses—a further indication that some of the jurors at least were expected to know something of the facts.

3. There is no explanation of why the case did not proceed, but presumably the pursuers were absent.

(166) [19 November 1641: Colvile and Robertoun JJ.D.]

For useing of false weightis. Donald Foullar and Alexander Hay. Protestatioun.

Compeirit Donald Foullar, merchand burges of Innernes, quha with Alexander Hay, indweller in Leyth, his prelocutour,[5] exponet and declairet that he was chairget be vertew of criminall letters direct at the instance of Sir Thomas Hope of Craighall, knycht barronet, Advocat to our Soverane Lord, for his Hienes intreis, and of James Rois of Markinche, proveist of Innernes, his Lordschipis informer,[6] to find cautioun for his personall compeirance befoir the Justice Generall and Justice deputtis this day and place in the hour of caus to underly the law for alledget contravening of the Actis of Parliament[7] in the

[1] E of Rhynie and S of Huntly, Aberdeenshire; Clatt is 2½ miles E of Rhynie; Tillyminet is near Gartly; all are in the same district.

[2] See legal note 1.

[3] See legal note 2.

[4] See legal note 3.

[5] See legal note 1.

[6] See legal note 2.

[7] [1425 c. 57, 1426 c. 69, 1457 c. 73, 1491 c. 33, 1503 c. 96, 1587 c. 115, 1607 c. 2, 1621 c. 17.]

alledget useing of ane fals stane weght [nocht] allowit be the lawis of this kingdome, and remanent allegit crymes specifeit in the saidis criminall letters as the samyn in the selff proportis;[1] For obedience of the quhilk charge gevin to the said Donald be the officer executour thairof and tryell of his innocencie of the saidis allegit crymes, he nocht only fand Angus Makfersone, burges of Innernes, cautioun for his entrie and compeirance this day and place to underly the law for the saidis allegit crymes, bot also, for the said cautioneris releif and cleiring of his awin innocencie of the allegit crymes contenit in the saidis criminall letters, he compeirit this day and willinglie offerit himselff reddie to underly the law for the samyn as altogidder frie and innocent thairof; And thairfoir in respect na pairtie persewar compeirit this day and place to insist in his persute for the saidis alledget crymes, quhairof he affirmet himselff to be altogidder innocent, askit instrumentis thairupoun, And protestit for releif of the said Angus McFersone, burges of Innernes, his cautioner foirsaid as also that na letters nor charges sould be direct or execute agains the said Donald Fouller for the alledget crymes abonewrittin at the instance of ony pairtie in tyme cuming, and farder that in caice of the raiseing of ony letters agains the said Donald for the alledget crymes abonespecifeit at ony tyme heireftir that the pairtie at quhais instance the saidis letters sall be raiset and direct sall befoir the outgeving thairof find sufficient cautioun and souertie to the Justice Clerk[2] and his deputis actit in the buikis of adjornall for refounding to the said Donald Foullar of sic expensis and charges sustenit be him in travelling fra his awin hous within the burgh of Innernes to this burgh of Edinburgh and attending upone the keiping of this dyet, he having stayit and maid his residence for the tryell of his innocencie of the former allegit crymes within this burght of Edinburgh thir sax oulkis [weeks] bygane to this present day, and that the said expensis sall be modifeit be the Justice and accoirding to thair liquidatioun, upone the quhilkis all and sindrie the premises the said Donald Foullar askit instrumentis.

Legal Notes

1. The panel's procurator is described simply as an indweller in Leith, and may not have been a solicitor, but, if as is likely, Fowler was a Gaelic speaker, he would need an interpreter.

2. The prosecution here is by Criminal Letters though at the instance of the Lord Advocate. James Ross, provost of Inverness, is named as informer. In his capacity as provost he was bound by statute to take steps to enforce the Act 1621 cap. 17 on standard weights and measures.

The accused appeared for trial but there was no appearance for the prosecutor and no explanation for his absence. The accused protested that it be a condition of any further proceedings against him for the alleged offence that the party pursuing find caution for refunding the expenses he had sustained in connection with the present proceedings. There was no liability on the Lord Advocate to pay such expenses. No claim indeed was competent here against either Lord Advocate or informer. The Act 1579 cap. 78 exempted the Lord Advocate from the penalties imposed as a result of rash prosecutions. These were to be paid by his informer, but only where the party accused was acquitted or past from. The Act 1587 cap. 88 providing for expenses of the party maliciously charged only applied where the accused was found innocent.

3. For the earlier history of this case and further details of the charge see *Records of Inverness* (New Spalding Club II.176).

[1] See legal note 3.

[2] Sir John Hamilton of Orbiston, appointed in 1636 (see above p. 328).

(167) [24 November 1641: Robertoun J.D.]

[*Adulterie and incest* *Kirko* contra *Maxwell* *Past fra*]

Intran.—John Kirko in Sundaywall;[1] Harbert Maxwell of Tinwall.[2]

Dilaittit of the cryme of adulterie and incest, committit be the said John Kirko with Margaret Edger, dochter lauchfull to umquhile [ ] Edger of Inglistoun in Glencairne, as also with Elspeth Edger, lauchfull sister to the said Margaret Edger, being baithe gottin of ane father and borne of ane mothair, quha and ather of thame hes borne bairnes to the said Johnne Kirko in the said incestuous copulatione; And the said Harbert Maxwell for the cryme of adulterie committit be him with Helene Hanna, the spous of Thomas Scot in Drumfreis for the tyme, with quhom he hes cohabitat and keipit cumpanie thir sevin yeiris bygane and [quha] hes borne to him childring in that adulterous copulatione.[3]

Perseweris.—Sir Thomas Hope of Craighall, knycht, his Majesteis Advocat;[4] Mr George Blak minister at Dinscoir.[5]

Prelocutouris for the pannell, viz. John Kirko, Mr Rodger Mowat advocat.

The said Mr George Blak, as informer to his Majesties Advocat, producet the criminall letters dewlie excute and indorsate upone the saidis John Kirko of Sundaywall, Harbert Maxwell callit of Tindell [Tinwald], and lykwayis upone John Lyndsay in Lagane, for the cryme of adulterie committit be him with thrie severall wemen *viz.* Bessie Roddin, Bessie Millikin, and John[et] McQualt, quha and ilk ane of thame hes bornes bairnes to him in the said adulterous copulatione, askit instrumentis upone the productione thairof, and protestit for his cautioneris releiff.

The saidis John Kirko of Sundaywall askit instrumentis of his compeirance and protestit for releiff of Andro Kirko of Glaisteris, his cautioner, and thairwith declairit that the said Mr George convenit him for the alledget crymes contenit in the letters befoir the Committie of Estaittis of Parliament,[6] befoir quhom the said Mr George succumbit in the probatioun, and thairthrow he was assoilyeit be the said Committie of the saidis alledget crymes and can nawayis in that respect be persewit criminallie for the samyn befoir his Majesties Justice.[7]

Thaireftir the said Mr George Blak past *simpliciter* fra that pairt of the saidis criminall letters aganis the said John Kirko, and declairit that he wald not persew the samyne at any tyme heireftir befoir his Majesties Justice, but prejudice alwayis of his persuit of the said John Kirko befoir the Lordis of Secreit Counsall as accordis of the law, quhairupone the said John Kirko askit instrumentis.[8]

1 Sundaywell 3½ miles W of Dunscore.
2 Tinwall 4 miles NW of Dumfries.
3 See legal note 1.
4 Although the L.A. was the first pursuer this was a prosecution on criminal letters not on indictment; see previous case for another example. For distinction see Hume II.153-155.
5 In *Fasti* II.272 as Blake; the parish is now Dunscore. See legal note 2. According to the *Fasti* he demitted the charge before 12 March 1640.
6 Not in *APS*.
7 See legal note 2.
8 See legal note 3.

The said Mr George Blak declairit that he passes fra the persuite of the said Harbert Maxwell of Tinwell for the crymes set down in the letters direct aganis him, quhairupone the said Harbert Maxwell askit instrumentis, and protestit for releiff of John Maxwell of Drumcowtrane his cautioner and that he sould not be callit nor persewit for the said alledget cryme in any tyme cuming.

Adulterye. John Lyndsay. Fugitive.

The samyn day the said John Lyndsay in Lagane, being oftymes callit upone to have compeirit befoir his Majesteis Justice and his deputtis this day and place to have underlyne the law for the filthie cryme of adulterie committit be him with the saidis Bessie Roddin, Bessie Mullikin and Jonet Makquolt, as he that was lauchfullie chairget be vertew of the saidis criminall letters to have fund cautione for his personall compeirance befoir his Majesties Justice and his deputtis this day and place to have underlyne the law for the crymes foirsaidis, oftymes callit lauchfull tyme of day biddin and nocht compeirand, the Justice thairfoir be the mouthe of John Hamiltoun, dempster of court, decernit, adjudget and declairet the said John Lyndsay to be fugitive fra his Majesteis lawis and all his moveable guidis to be escheit to his Hienes use as fugitive for the cryme foirsaid.

LEGAL NOTES

1. This is another of the rare examples where two separate and unconnected parties were prosecuted together.

2. The panel Kirko's defence that he had already been acquitted by the Committee of Estates of Parliament—whose competency to judge is by no means clear—and the pursuers' reaction suggests that a plea of *autrefois acquit* would have been sustained as in the cases reported above (i.83, 91, 308).

3. The whole prosecution appears to have been instigated by the minister, who having failed to establish his allegations before the Committee of Estates, had convened the panels before the Justice Court, led no evidence at all against them, and passed from his pursuit of them. This is one of the few cases in these volumes of an informer intervening (see above i.30, 76, 239). If ever there was a case appropriate for the imposition on the reverend prosecutor of a penalty and liability for expenses competent in cases of malicious prosecution (Act 1579 c. 78 and 1587 c. 88), this was it.

(169) [26 November 1641: Robertoun J.D.]

Fire raiseing and stouthrieff. Frendraucht. Captaine James Gordoun. Desertit.

The quhilk day William Creichtoun, sone to James Crichtoun of Frendraucht, being ofttymes callit as cautioner and souertie for reporting our Soverane Lordis letters dewlie execute and indorsate and persewing thairof, purchest at the instance of the said James Creichtoun of Frendraucht and Sir Thomas Hope of Craighall, knycht barronet, Advocat to our Soverane Lord, for his Hienes intreis, aganis George Marqueis of Huntlie, Lord Gordoun etc., as cautioner and souertie for Captane James Gordoun, portioner of Urquhart,[1] *alias* callit James the sojour [*soldier*], to have enterit and presentit him befoir his Majesteis

[1] 4 miles E of Elgin.

Justice and his deputtis this day and place in the hour of caus to have underlyne the law for alledget airt and pairt of the treassonable reaseing of fyre, burneing and distroying of dyverse houssis and coirnes, steilling, reiveing and awaytaking be way of maisterfull thift and stouthreiff off dyverse horse, nolt, scheip, guidis, geir, insycht and plenischeing perteneing to the said James Creichtoun of Frendraucht and his tennentis dwelland upone his landis of Crombie[1] etc., as he that become souertie for repoirting and persuite of the saidis letters this day and place aganis the said Captane James Gordoun conforme to the act of adjornall set down thairanent lawfull tyme of day biddin; And the said James Creichtoun of Frendraucht nor na utheris in his name compeirand to produce the samyn nor to insist in the said Captane James Gordoun his persuite for the crymes foirsaidis thairincontenit, thairfoir the Justice be the mouthe of James Douglas, dempster of court, decernit and adjudget the said Williame Creichtoun, sone to the said James Creichtoun of Frendraucht, as cautioner foirsaid to be unlawit and amerciat in the paynes contenit in the Actis of Parliament, *viz.* for not reporting of the saidis letters dewlie execute and indorsate upone the said Captane James Gordoun and the said George Marqueis of Huntlie, his cautioner, in the payne and unlaw of two hundrethe merkis money.[2]

Fire reaseing.

Compeirit the samyn day the said Captane James Gordoun, portioner of Urquhart, *alias* callit James the sojour, with James Gibsone, advocat, his prelocutour, quha exponit and declairit that for obedience of the chairge gevin to him and to George Marqueis of Huntlie, his cautioner, for his entrie and compeirance befoir his Majesteis Justice and his deputtis this day and place to underly the law for alledget airt and pairt of the treassonable reassing of fyre, burneing and distroyeing of certane houssis and cornes and remanent crymes contenit in the criminal letters direct aganis him at the instance of James Creichtoun of Frendraucht, and the tennentis and occupyeris of his landis of Crombie, Cowbairdie, Coirnehauche,[3] and utheris mentionat thairintill, quhairof he affirmes himselff to be altogidder innocent, the said Captane James Gordoun, for cleiring of his innocencie thairof and for the said George Marqueis of Huntlie his releiff of his cautionerie abonewrittin, compeirit this day and place and offerit himselff reddie to underly the law for the saidis alledget crymes; And in respect na pairtie persewer compeirit to produce the saidis letters against him nor to insist in his persuit, being oft tymes callit upone to that effect, he askit instrumentis thairupone, and protestit for releiff of the said George Marqueis of Huntlie, his cautioner, and that na letters nor chairges sould be direct or gevin out aganis him at the instance of any pairtie for the alledget crymes abonespecifeit in any tyme cumming.

LEGAL NOTES

1. This is an echo of the burning of Frendraught Tower on 8th October 1630 (see above p. 350). The course taken by the present case suggests that the Crichtons had tired of the

[1] 2 miles W of Aberchirder, Banffshire. See legal note 1.
[2] See legal note 2.
[3] Cobairdy is 4 miles NE of Huntly, Corniehaugh 5 miles NNE.

pursuit or found the Marquis of Huntly too formidable an adversary. For a full account of this mysterious occurrence see John Hill Burton, *Narratives from Criminal Trials in Scotland*, 1852, I.202-235; and this volume pp.

2. From 1535 c. 35 (on a narrative of the abuses occasioned by persons issuing and then withdrawing criminal letters) the Clerk of Justiciary or his deputes were obliged to take security from parties purchasing Criminal Letters that they would return these to the Clerk duly executed and endorsed under the pains specified in the letters. The customary penalties however were found insufficient to prevent abuse and were increased by the Act 1593 c. 170, made to apply also to non-compearance before the Justice and to depend on the rank of the party. There was apparently doubt (McKenzie, *Observations* p. 278 under 1593 c. 166: Hume II.265) as to whether 'the party' referred to the prosecutor or the panel. The course taken here, namely to fine the pursuer's cautioner 200 merks—the sum specified in the Act for an unlanded gentleman, shows the Justice favouring the former interpretation and modifying the penalty prescribed in the Act—though the Act expressly precludes such modification. The fine appropriate to the status of the private pursuer here should have been at least 1000 merks.

(172) [8 December 1641: Colvil J.D.]

Menzies contra *Stewart and utheris. Rapt. Continewit to the xv day of Merche nixt.*

Intran.—Donald Stewart in Glengowlantie.[1]

Dilaitit of the violent rapt and ravischeing of Katharene Menzeis, onlie laufull dochter to Alexander Menzies in Gairnetullie,[1] committit in the monethe of August last.

Persewers.—Alexander Menzeis of Gairnetullie, as father to the said Katherene Menzeis, Sir Thomas Hope of Craighall, knycht barronet, his Majesteis Advocat, or his Hienes intreis.

The persewer producet the letters with the executiones thairof, quhairby the said Donald Stewart, now upone pannell, Neill Stewart, his brother, John Stewart, also his brother, John Stewart in Glengowlantyne, Ewin McQueane in Drumquharrie,[1] James Stewart in Bunrannache,[2] Duncane McGregour, servitour to John Stewart of Innerchannochan,[3] Fyndla McFarlane in the Hauche of Gairnetullie, Cristiane Nikgilliequhone, his spous, and Anna Nikgilliequhone, hir sister,[4] war upone the xxvi day of November last denuncet rebellis and put to the horne and registrat thairat in the schireffis buikis of the schirefdome of Pearthe for not finding of cautione actit in the buikis of adjornall to have compeirit befoir his Majesteis Justice and his deputtis this day and place to have underlyne the law for rapt and ravescheing of the said Katharene Menzeis, committit in maner and at the tyme specifeit in the saidis letters,[5] upone the productione quhairof the said Alexander Menzeis, persewer, askit instrumentis, and protestit for releiff of John Loutfut, tailyeour, burges of Edinburgh, his cautioner; Quhilk protestatione the Justice admittit.

[1] Glengoulandie is on the road from Kenmore to the River Tummel and Grandtully is 2½ miles E of Aberfeldy, all in Perthshire. Drumcharry is 2 miles NW of Kenmore.

[2] Bunrannoch is at the E end of Loch Rannoch. The other place mentioned may be inverchadden close to Kinloch Rannoch.

[3] He was forfeited for adhering to Montrose in 1645 when his estate is described as both Auchannachin and Innerchannochan (*APS* VI(i).317, 322). The place has not been located but is mentioned in *Argyll* v *Stewart of Ladywell* 1641 above p. 423.

[4] See legal note 1.

[5] One assumes that the locus, which is not mentioned in the record, was properly specified in the indictment.

The pannell takis instrumentis of his entrie and protestis in respect of his compeirance for releiff of Alexander Menzeis of Comrie, his cautioner; And as concerning the horneing producet aganis him beirand him to be denuncet upone the xxvi day of November last for not finding of the said cautione, the samyn is null in the selff in respect that upone the aucht day of the said monethe of November lastbypast, he, for obedience of the said chairge, fand the said Alexander Menzeis of Comrie cautione for his compeirance this day and place to the effect foirsaid, quhilk is be the space of auchtene dayis preceiding the pretendit denunceatione producet; For the quhilk cautioneris releiff and tryell of his awin innocencie of the rapt and ravischeing lybellit, offerit himselff reddie to defend in the said mater as innocent of the samyn, and thairupone askit instrumentis.

Continewit to the xv° of Merche nixtocum.

The Justice in respect na intimatione was maid of his finding of the said cautione to the officer executor of the saidis letters to the effect ane assyse mycht have bene summond be him this day for the pannellis tryell, and that na assyse is summond to that effect,[1] continowis this dyet and the pannellis tryell of the cryme foirsaid to the fyftene day of Mairche nixtocum, and ordanit the said Donald Stewart, now upone the pannell, to find new cautione for his re-entrie and compeirance befoir his Majesteis Justice the said day to the effect foirsaid under the payne of fyve hundrethe merkis money; For obedience of the quhilkis ordinance compeirit Robert Murray, sone to David Murray of Buth,[2] and become cautione for the entrie of the said Donald Stewart befoir his Majesteis Justice the saidis day and place to the effect and under the payne foirsaid.

Amerciat.

The quhilkis day Alexander Menzeis of Comrie, being oft tymes callit as cautioner and souertie for Neill Stewart, brother to the said Donald Stewart in Glengowlantie, to have enterit and presenttit him befoir his Majesteis Justice and his deputtis this day and place to have underlyne the law for airt and pairt of the rapt and ravischeing of the said Katharene Menzeis, dochter lawfull to the said Alexander Menzeis in Gairnetullie as he that became cautioner actit in the buikis of adjornal to have enterit him for that effect, lawfull tyme of day biddin and nocht compeirand, the Justice thairfoir, be the mouthe of John Hamiltoun, dempster of court, decernit and adjudget the said Alexander Menzeis of Comrie, as cautioner foirsaid, to be unlawit and amerciat in the paynes contenit in the Actis of Parliament, *viz.* for not entrie of the said Neill Stewart in the payne of ane hundrethe merkis, and siclyk that the said Neill Stewart for his not compeirance sall be denuncet his Majesteis rebell and put to his Hienes horne and all his moveable guidis to be escheit and inbrocht to his Majesteis use as fugitive fra his Hienes lawis for the said cryme.

The samyn day Johnne Stewart in Gathe,[3] brother to the said Donald, John

1 See legal note 2.

2 This, which is rendered Bithny at p. 513 may be Buchanty in Glenalmond, NE of Crieff.

3 This Garth is just S of Glengowlandie.

Stewart in Glengowlantie, Ewin McQueane in Drumquharrie, James Stewart in Bownerannache, Duncane McGregour servand to John Stewart of Innerchannochan, Fyndla McFarlane in the Hauche of Gairnetullie, Cristiane Nikgillivie, his spous, and Anna McGillievie, hir sister, being oft tymes callit to have compeirit befoir his Majesteis Justice and his deputtis this day and place to have underlyne the law for airt and pairt of the rapt and ravischeing of the said Katharene Menzeis, dochter to Alexander Menzies in Gernetullie, as thay that war lauchtfullie chairget be William Fergussone messinger, to that effect, lauchtfull tyme of day biddin and not compeirand, the Justice thairfoir be the mouthe of John Hamiltoun, dempster of court, decernit and declairit thame and ilk ane of thame to be outlawis and fugitives fra his Hienes lawis for the cryme foirsaid, quhairupone the said Alexander Menzeis in Gairnetullie, as father to the said Katharene Menzeis, askit actis and instrumentis.

(119) [15 March, 1642: Robertoun J.D.]

Desertit. Rapt. Menzeis contra *Stewart and utheris.*

The quhilk day anent the actioun and caus contenit in the criminall letters raisit at the instance of Alexander Meinzeis in Gairintullie as father to Katharine Meinzeis, his only lauchtfull dochter, and Sir Thomas Hoip of Craighall, knycht barronet, his Majesteis Advocat, for his Hienes intreis, againes Donald Stewart in Glengowlantie and remanent defenderis mentionat thairintill, chairgeing thame to haife fund cautioun for thair personall compeirance befoir his Majesteis Justice and his deputtis in the tolbuith of Edinburgh the aucht day of December lastbypast in the hour of caus to haife underlyne the law for alledgit airt and pairt of the rapt and revisching of the said Katherine Meinzeis committit in the moneth of August 1641 as the saidis criminall letters proportis, upoun the quhilk aucht day of December the said Alexander Meinzeis in Gairintullie, as father to the said Katherine, and his Majesteis Advocat for his Hienes intreis, compeirand personallie as persewaris of the saidis letters, quha producit the samyn deulie execuit and indorsat upoun the said Donald Stewart and haill remanent defenderis mentionat thairintill beirand the said Donald Stewart, Neill Stewart his brother, Johnne Stewart also his brother, Johnne Stewart in Glengowlantie, Ewin McQueine in Drumquharrie, James Stewart in Bunranache, Duncane McGregour, servitour to Johnne Stewart of Innerchannochan, Findla McFerlane in the Hauch of Gerintullie, Christian Nikgilliquhone, his spous, and Anna Nikgilliquhone, hir sister, to be upoun the twentie saxt of November im fourtie ane denuncit rebellis and put to the horne and registrat thairat in the schireffis buikis of the schirefdome of Perth for not finding of cautioun to haif compeirit befoir his Majesteis Justice and his deputtis the aucht day of December last to haife underlyne the law for the alledgit cryme abonwrittin on the ane pairt; Lykeas on the uther pairt the said Donald Stewart in Glengowlantie compeirand also personallie the said aucht day of December last in presence of his Majesteis Justice, and being enterit upoun pannell, askit instrumentis of his compeirance and offerit himselff to the tryell of the law for the alledgit cryme abonespecifeit, and in respect thairof protestit for releiff of Alexander Meinzeis of Comrie his cautioner; And as concerning the horning producit that day againes him, beirand him to be denuncit upoun the said twentie saxt day of November last for not finding of the said cautioun, it was than alledgit that the said horning was null in the selff, in respect that he upoun the aucht day of the said moneth of November last of befoir for obedience of the said chairge fand the said Alexander Meinzeis of Comrie cautioun for his compeirance that day and plaice to the effect foirsaid; For the quhilk cautioneris releiff and tryell of his awin innocencie of the alledgit rapt and revisching abonwrittin he than offerrit himselff reddie to defend in the said matter as innocent thairof; Eftir the proponing of the quhilk alledgance of the nullatie of this horning abonwrittin the Justice in respect thairof and verefficatioun of the samyn as also be ressone na intimatioun was maid to the officer executour of the saidis letters of the finding of the said cautioun and that thairfoir na assyse was sumond be him to that day, continewit the said dyet and the said Donald Stewart his tryell for the cryme foirsaid to the fyfteine day of Merche than following and now instant; Lykeas cautioun was fund be the said Donald for his re-entrie and compeirance this day and plaice befoir his Majesteis Justice to underly the law for the alledgit cryme abonespecifeit under the paine of fyve hundreth merkis as the act of adjornall maid thairupoun in the selff proportis; For the quhilk cautioneries releiff, *viz*, Robert Murray, sone to David Murray of Bithny, the said Donald Stewart in Glengowlantie, compeirand personallie in presence of his Majesteis Justice this day and plaice and enterand himselff upoun pannell, nocht only offerrit himselff to the tryell upoun pannell, nocht only offerrit himselff to the tryell of the law for the alledgit cryme abonementionat, bot also for cleiring of his innocencie thairof producit ane testimoniall writtin and subscryvit be Mr Johnne Cunisone, minister at Dull, quhairof the tennour followis:—

Upoun the aucht day of Merche imvic fourtie twa yeiris Donald Stewart, lauchtfull sone to John Stewart of Overlarisch, and Katherine Meinzeis, lauchtfull dochter to Alexander Meinzeis in Tomtewin,[1] both within the paroche of Dull, war lauchtfullie maried in the kirk of Weyme, with consent of the said Alexander Meinzeis, hir father, be Mr Johnne Cunisone minister at Dull, eftir lauchtfull proclamatiounis, befoir these witnessis Sir Alexander Meinzeis of that ilk, knycht, Duncane Meinzeis, fiear thairof, William, Thomas, Robert and George Meinzeissis, sones lauchtfull to the said Sir Alexander, Johnne Stewart foirsaid of Overlarische, John Stewart, brother sone to the laird of Appen, Findla Dow in Weyme, and Johnne Stewart *alias* McCondochie VcRobert in Glengowlantie, with sindrie utheris: In witnessing quhairof I Mr Johnne Cunisone, minister foirsaid, haife writtin and subscryvit this testimoniall with my hand at Dull the twelt day of Merche imvic fourtie twa yeiris, *sic subscribitur* Mr Johnne Cunisone, minister at Dull.

Upoun the productioun of the quhilk testimoniall of the dait tennour and contentis abonwrittin, the said Donald Stewart in Glengowlantie, defender foirsaid, askit actis and instrumentis; And in respect thairof and that the said Alexander Meinzeis now his father in law (quhais dochter is lauchtfullie maried with him in presence of the witnessis foirsaidis be the said Mr Johnne Cunisone, minister, conforme to his former testimoniall) nawayis compeires to prosequeitt

[1] Tomtagewan is 2 miles NE of Aberfeldy.

and follow fuirth the saidis criminall letters, bot be his consent hes ratified his dochteris mariadge abone-specifeit, protestit that the saidis criminall letters sould be desertit *simpliciter* and that na criminall letters sould be direct againes him at the instance of quhatsumevir pairtie in any tyme cumming.

The Justice, in respect of the said testimoniall producit, desertis the letters abonespecifeit and this dayis dyet appoyntit thairto, quhairupoun the said Donald Stewart askit actis and instrumentis.

LEGAL NOTES

1. This is an unusual case in which eight men and two women were charged with rape of the same girl, the compearing accused being presumably the principal and the others art and part. The marriage of the complainer to the principal accused with the consent of her father, makes a 'happy ending,' in virtue of which the father, by failing to appear at the trial diet, abandons the charge. It will be observed that though the alleged crime took place in August 1641, the marriage only occurred on 8th March 1642, a week before the second diet. Presumably because of the terms of the minister's certificate the Justice, in deserting the diet, refrained from exacting any penalty from the pursuer.

2. The case emphasises that to avoid being put to the horn for not finding caution *judicio sisti* (see Hume II.154) it was necessary not only to find caution but to intimate this to the messenger at arms who served the criminal letters. See Mackenzie, *Criminals*, II.xxi.7; Hume II.154.

(181) [7 January 1642: Colville and Robertoun JJ.D.]

Mutilation. [*George Norie*]. *Acquit.*

Intran.—George Norie, merchand burges of Edinburgh.[1]

Dilaittit of the hurting, wounding, and mutilatioun of David Tailyeour, citiner [*citizen*] of Lundoun, of the thomb of his left hand, comittit in the moneth of Merche 1640 within the brught of Edinburgh, upoun the north syde thairof, at the heid of the cloise callit Mr. Thomas Craiges Cloise.[2]

Persewaris.—David Tailyeour, citiner of Lundoun; and Sir Thomas Hoip of Craighall, knycht barronet, his Majesties Advocat for his Hienes intreis.

Prelocutour in defence.—Mr. Thomas Nicolsone, younger, advocat.

The persewar producit the criminall letters deulie execuit and indorsat, askit instrumentis thairupoun, and protestit for his cautioneris releiffe.

The pannell takis instrumentis of his entrie and protestis for his cautioneris releiffe.

The Justice with consent of ather pairtie continewis this dyet to Wednisday nixt, *duodecimo* instantis, and ordanit cautioun to be fund be the pannell for his entrie that day to underly the law for the cryme foirsaid, under the paines contenit in the actis of Parliament; quha for obedience thairof fand Johnne Merschell, merchand burges of Edinburgh, cautioun for his entrie to the effect and under the paine foirsaid.

The witnessis, togidder with the personis of assyse, sumond to that day and wairnit *apud acta* to compeir upoun Wednisday nixt, ilk persone under the paine of twa hundreth merkis.

[1] He had been admitted a burgess on 22nd September 1641.

[2] There were two closes of that name, both to the north of St. Giles on ground now occupied by the City Chambers. The more famous was named after the author of the *Jus Feudale*, a former J.D.; see *Old Edinburgh Club* xii, 27.31, *APS* 1695 cap. 77, IX.475.

(182) [12 January 1642: Colvile and Robertoun JJ.D.]

Mutilation. Acquit.

Intran.—George Norie, merchand burges of Edinburgh.

Dilaittit of the hurting, wounding, and mutilatione of David Tailyeour, citiner of Lundoun, of the thombe of his left hand committit in the monethe of Merche 1640 within the brughe of Edinburgh, upone the northe syde thairof, at the head of the close callit Mr. Thomas Craigis Close.

Perseweris.—David Tailyeour, citiner of Lundoun, Sir Thomas Hop, his Majesties advocat.

Prelocutour in defence.—Mr. Thomas Nicolsone, younger.

The pannell takis instrumentis of his entrie and protestit for his cautioneris relieff.

My Lord Advocat declairis that he insistis aganis this pannell *pro mutilato saltem pro vulnerato*, and for verificatione of that pairt of the mutilatione, producet ane testificat under the chirurgeanes handis, beirand that the deacones and maisteris being convenit and haveing viseit and cognossit the twa woundis gevin to David Tailyeour, persewer, the ane wound in the end of the thrid joynt of the index or foirmost finger, the uther in the thombe neir, the connextione or the end of the secound arkteir [articulation?] of the thombe, boithe being in his left hand, hes fund be the said testificate that the tendones and ligamentis ar cute, and sua he is maid altogidder mutilat and unhable of actione of his said thombe, quhilk thai declaire to be of verritie be the subscriptione of James Rig, David Douglas, Andro Brown and John Scot, subscryvit at Edinburgh the ellevint of Januare, writtin be thair clerke and seillid be thair seill.

It is alledget be Mr. Thomas Nicolsone as prelocutour for the pannell, that the pannell aucht to be assoilzeit fra the persuite lybellit, becaus it is offerit to be provein that the pannell being convenit be the persewer for the alledget mutilatione or wounding of him the tyme lybellit, and that befoir the bailleis of Edinburgh, and haveing bene put in prissone be the bailleis, the pannell was dismissit out of prissone at the intreatie of the persewer, and that same day the persewer and defender now upone pannell did drink togidder and war freindit, at the least the day thaireftir.

Secundo, the testificat producet cannot be respectit to instruct that the persewer is mutilat, because the samyn is bot ane naikit assertione of private men, quhilk cannot bind a cryme upone the pannellis bak unles the samyn war under thair handis upone oathe and conscience, at the least unles thai war present at the bar to declair the samyn upone oathe, speciallie in respect ane of the subscryveris thairof hes declairit the samyn day that he could not sweir the persewer was mutilat.[1]

Thridlie, the pannell aucht to be assoilzeit fra mutilatione or vulneratione becaus it is offerit to be proven be witnessis present at the bar that the persewer did give himselff the wound lybellit, in sua far as it is offerrit to be proven that

[1] See legal note 1, second para.

the persewer going down Mr Thomas Craigis Close was drawing his awin sword (quhich most be presumet was to have struckin the pannell quhom he had boxit befoir), and in the drawing of his sword to [i.e. too] haistilie he gave himselff the said straik; lyaks immediatlie upone the doing thairof, befoir evir the persewer had done any thing with his sword or any thing done to him, Captane Thomas Fischer being in the close occasionallie [i.e. by chance] for the tyme tuik the perseweris sword frome him and impeidit any occasionall mishap that mycht have followit.

It is anserit be my Lord Advocat that the first alledgeance is nawayis relevant except it war alledget that the persewer had expreslie remittit the criminall persute; *secundo* the mutilatione was not than competent it no[t] being persewable *nisi post annum et diem*; *tertio* it is not probable bot be aithe of pairtie: And as to the secund alledgeance, oppones the testificat producet *per collegium chirurgerum*, writtin be thair clerk and subscryvit be four of thair number, and no necessitie of oathe in everie particular testificat, thay being sworne be thair calling: And as to the thrid it is contrair to the lybell beiring that the pannall woundit the defender, of the quhilk wound he is mutilat, quhilk lyble and treuth thairof is onlie tryable be ane assyse, and the contrair or negative of the lybell, of the quhilk nature the thrid alledgeance is, cannot be provein be witnessis, in prejudice of the constant forme of procedouris *in criminallis*, be referring the samyn to the tryell of ane assyse.

It is replyit be Mr. Thomas Nicolsone as prelocutour for the pannell, that the first alledgeance is relevant notwithstanding of the first member of the anser, becaus the defence beiris that thai drank togidder and war aggreit, quhilk importis a passing fra any actione, notwithstanding the secund member of the anser, becaus albeit the persewer could not persew mutilatione within yeir and day, yit within yeir and day the persewer may agrie for ane wound quhilk mycht be mutilatione eftir yeir and day; and notwithstanding of the thrid member of the anser becaus the alledgeance is *facti* and thairfoir is probable be witnessis.

The secund defence is relevant notwithstanding of the secund anser maid thairto unles the chirurgeanes war present at the bar.

The thrid defence is most relevant notwithstanding of the anser maid thairto and beiris na such negative as my Lord Advocat alledges bot beiris a positive that the persewer woundit himselff.[1]

Assisa.—Williame Bowman, tailyeour burges of Edinburgh; Patrik Gibsone, merchand burges thair; Alexander Blair, tailyeour burges thair; George Nicoll, cuik, indweller thair; George Sword, wrycht; James Wrycht, smyth; John Cleghorne, litster; John Ramsay, merchand; Samvell Guthrie, litster; Thomas Steane, hatmaker; Johnne Weir of Boigsyde; Thomas Weir of Kirk toun; John Glen, merchand; James Wylie, merchand; James Forrester, weiver.

My Lord Advocat takis instrumentis of the sweiring of the persones of assyse, and protestis for wilfull errour gif thai acquit the pannell of the crymes lybellit in respect of the chirurgeanes testimoniall producet, notwithstanding of the alledgeances maid be the pannell in the contrair.

[1] See legal note 1.

The pannell and his procuratour protestis in the contrair gif the assyse fyle him of the said cryme in respect of the alledgeances foirsaidis, and replyis maid to the persewers anseris abonewrittin.

The persewer for cleiring to the assyse of the pannellis guiltienes of the hurting wounding and mutilatione of him in maner abonespecifeit producet Captane Thomas Fischer as witnes for verefiecatione thairof.

Compeirit the said Captane Thomas Fischer, quha being solemlie sworne be the Justice judiciallie in presence of the pairtie and assyseouris, deponit that the day of the tuilzie [tussle] betwix this persewer and the defender, heiring thairof saw not quha war the first onsetteris, bot following ather of thame down Mr. Thomas Craigis close, he saw David Tailyeour persewer following George Norie, defender, the said George haveing his sword drawit in his hand, bot gripit and hald in be William Bowman, tailyeour, ane of the persones of assyse, and saw the said David Tailyeour, persewer, lying one his bak, quha be ressone of the staynes [steepness] of the close, had fallin haveing his sword halff drawin out and his left hand bleiding, quhilk sword being bloodie the deponer tuik frome him and keipit the samyn the space of a monthe thaireftir; and farder knawis not.[1]

Quhilkis persones of assyse, being ressavit, sworne, and admittit, removet altogidder furth of court to the assyse hous quhair, be pluralitie of voittis, thai electit and choyset the said William Bowman, chancellour, thaireftir ressonet and voittit upone the poyntis of the said dittay, and being ryplie and at lenth advyset thairwith, and with the verificatione and probatione producet be the persewer for cleiring of the said dittay and crymes foirsaidis contenit thairintill, re-enterit agane in court, quhair thai all in ane voce be the repoirt and declaratione of the said William Bowman, chancellour, fand, pronuncet, and declairit the said George Norie to be clenget, innocent, and acquit of the hurting wounding and mutilatione of the said David Tailyeour of the thombe of his left hand, in respect the hurt and wound ressavit be him thairupone hes proceidit frome himselff be his furious drawing of his sword and bluid fund thairupone in following and persewing of the said David Norie at the tyme specifeit in his dittay,[2] quhairupone the said George Norie askit actis and instrumentis.

The samyn day the said George Norie desyret lawburrows of the said David Tailyeour seing he dreadis him bodilie herme, and at commandement of the Justice be his great oath hes sworne that he dreadis the said David Tailyeour bodilie herme, as said is.

The Justice in respect of the said George Noreis aithe, ordanit the said David Tailyeour to find cautione to the said George for his indemnitie in his persone and guidis, under the payne of twa hundrethe merkis;[3] for obedience of the quhilk ordinance compeirit judicially Samivel Bridisdane, citiner of Lundone, quha become actit and obleist as souertie and lawburrows for the said David Tailyeour, that the said George Norie sould be harmeles and skeathles of him in his persone landis and guidis, and on nawayis is to be molestit nor trublit be him thairin, nor be na utheris of his causeing, sending, hounding out, comand, resset, assistance and ratihabitione quhom he may stope or late, directlie or

[1] See legal note 2.
[2] See legal note 3.
[3] See legal note 4.

indirectlie in tyme cumming, utherwayis nor be ordour of law and justice, under the payne of twa hundrethe merkis money; quhairupone the said George Norie askit actis and instrumentis.

Legal Notes

1. It is unfortunate that the Justices depute did not give their decision on the interesting legal questions argued *in limine*, but apparently they were not pressed to do so, and counsels' efforts must have been designed only to influence and impress the jurymen who were present. The defence's first point was that the parties had settled their dispute, to which it seems an adequate answer that the right to prosecute was never given up. The Lord Advocate's contention that a year and a day had not passed at the time of the reconciliation, which was essential before a prosecution could be commenced for mutilation (see *Haliburton* 1640, above p. 389), was met by the plea that a discharge could be granted at any time. His further point that oath of the party was required was answered by an appeal to the general doctrine that any question of fact could be proved in any way.

The second defence submission was that a certificate by doctors was not competent evidence, unless (a) on soul and conscience, and (b) they appeared to swear to it, and by modern standards this was unanswerable. The Lord Advocate however maintained that the medical profession was in a privileged position, and it appears to have been so held in *Crawford* v *Scott* 1631 (above vol. I, 166, 168) and *Cheyne* v *Mowat* 1642 (see p. 463), and in any event the nature of the wound here was a small matter.

The third point, which was eventually sustained by the jury, was that the wound was not given by the accused, but was self-inflicted. Even at this late date the Crown objected to this as contrary to the libel, to which Mr Nicholson replied unconvincingly that he was proponing a positive proposition not a negative one. The verdict marks the end of the old doctrine that the defence could not allege any fact contrary to the libel.

2. The crown called only one witness who did not see the 'onset', and today the case would never have been allowed to go to the jury. This is another illustration of the practice of including witnesses in the jury. The principal eye-witness indeed became foreman of the jury. The complainer himself did not give evidence at all. He had probably returned to London. The doctrine that a single testifying witness was insufficient was traced back by Hume only to 1705. The principle can have had no place at this period, when the functions of witness and juror were not distinguished. Hume II.383.

3. It is interesting that the jury gave the ground of their decision, i.e. that the wound was self-inflicted, thereby sustaining the special defence. This is the first instance traced of this special defence.

4. It is unusual to find a protest by the panel for error against the assize if they convicted (but for another example of such a protest see Currour v Fraser, 1641, above, p. 455). It is rare too for an acquittal to be followed by lawburrows found by the prosecution.

[2 February 1642: Colvile and Robertoun JJ.D.]

Force [*Alexander Gylour*] *Convict and Baneist*

Intran.—Alexander Gylour, servand in the Base[1] and clymer of the craig thairof.

Dilaittit of the filthie cryme of forceing and violent abuseing of Jonet Boussie, dochter to George Boussie, scheiphird to Alexander Smyth, dwelland within the barronie of Wauchtoun,[2] ane young virgane nocht past ten yeiris of adge, be forgaddering with hir upone the sevintene day of Junii jmvjc and fourtie yeiris at a place callit the ganging myre within the maynes of Wauchtoun, as schoe was addressing hirselff to the scheiring of certane girse [grass] within the said myre,

[1] The Bass Rock, East Lothian.
[2] 3 miles south of North Berwick.

and thair violentlie forceing and defloreing of the said Jonet Boussie agains hir will and consent, schoe in respect of hir young yeiris not being of abilitie to resist him, and thairby violentlie for satisfeing of his filthie lust ryveing of hir secreat pairtis to the effusione of hir blood and danger of hir lyffe.

Persewere.—Mr. John Oliphant, substitute to his Majesteis Advocate, quha producet the dittay abonewrittin for the cryme foirsaid,[1] togidder with the roll of the persones of assyse summond to this day for the pannellis tryell of the said cryme.

Assisa.—James Smyth in Knowis; Mathow Schireff in Houstoun; John Faw in Knowmylne; James Myller of Goullabank; John Butter in Beanestoun mylne; William Smyth in Brounrig; Alexander Wilsone in East Fortoun; William Wert thair; James Kirkwoid in Skugall chancellour; George Sandielandis of Gilliswallis; Patrik Quhyt in Myresyde; Richard Schireff in Houstoun; James Fall in Tuniegaame; Niniane Dudgeone in Gilmertoun.[2]

The persewer producet the depositione of the said Jonet Boussie, the defoircet virgane, with the declaratione of the mydwyffis judgement anent the violent rapt and renting of hir secreat pairtis, togidder with the judgement and assertione of Doctour Sibbet and Doctour Scot, Doctouris of Phisick, concerneing the said rapt, and the said mydwyfis testimonie thairupone, for verificatione of the schamefull and violent abuse of the said young virgane be the pannell in maner specifeit in his dittay; and protestit in respect of the productione thairof for wilfull errour in caice the assyse sould acquit.[3]

Quhilkis persones of assyse being ressavit, sworne, and admittit, eftir accusatione of the said Alexander Gylour be dittay of the schamefull and abhominable rapt, forceing, and abuising of the said Jonet Boussie in maner and at the tyme specifeit thairintill and verefiecatione thairof be the depositiones and declarationes producet be his Majesteis advocat for cleiring thairof the samyne they removet altogidder furth of court to the assyse hous quhair thai electit and choyset the said James Kirkwoid in chancellour of the said assyse, and thaireftir ressonet and voittit upone the poynttis of the said dittay and haill circumstances thairof, and being ryplie and at lenthe advyset thairwith, togidder with the depositione and declarationes producet be his Majesteis advocat for vereficatione thairof, re-enterit agane in court quhair thai all in ane voce, be the mouthe of the said James Kirkwoid, chancellour, fand pronuncet and declairit the said Alexander Gylour to be fyllit, culpable, and convict of the violent and schamefull forceing of the said Jonet Boussie ane young virgane not past ten yeiris of aidge renting and ryveing of hir in hir secreat pairtis to the effusione of hir blood in great quantitie, with this declaratione that thai could not fine nor affirme that the said Alexander Gylour had sic carnell copulatione with the sic young lase as ane man hes with ane woman in respect of hir young yeiris and

[1] See legal note 1. Oliphant was admitted advocate in 1625. He is referred to in *Lyon's List*, p. 167, as 'Kings Solicitor'.

[2] These places are all between North Berwick and the Haddington-Dunbar road, and near the locus, except that Gilliswalls has not been identified.

[3] See legal note 2.

minoritie abone writtin,[1] quhairupone the advocat as persewer askit instrumentis.[2]

The Justice contenowis the pronunceatione of dome upone the former convictione untill the tyme he be advyset with the Lordis of his Majesteis Privie Counsall thairanent, and in the meanetyme ordanit him to be returnet and to remane in waird quhill the pronunceatione thairof.[3]

LEGAL NOTES

1. This is one of the few cases taken on indictment in this volume.

2. Hume (II.406) rightly criticises this conviction on the ground that, not only was no evidence led before the assize, but no evidence was produced to them taken under the authority of the Justice depute. The Lord Advocate relied entirely on written depositions by the victim, the midwife and the doctors. This was quite contrary to any reading of 1587 cap. 91, though this Act, as pointed out above (p. 487), seems to have been disregarded as a matter of course. But the most significant point in the case is that—of the testimonies produced—obviously no one but the victim could have identified the panel, and in the absence of any confession there was thus by modern standards no corroboration on the most essential matter. The inference is either that corroboration was not considered necessary or, if it was, that the jurors were entitled to supply it from their own knowledge.

3. The accused, if really guilty, was fortunate to escape the highest penalty, which was probably not exacted here because of the paucity of the evidence. Next day the Privy Council (VII.[2] 192) ordered him (wrongly designed John Gylour) to be scourged, branded on the cheek, and banished. Hume (I.302) mentions three earlier cases where the death sentence was pronounced in similar circumstances and Mackenzie, I.xvi, 1 and 8, considered the crime capital.

[3 June 1642: Colvill and Robertoun JJ.D.]

Murder. Hunter contra *Mure. Continewit to the tent of Junii.*

Intran.—James Muir, tailyeor in Birsto;[4] Margaret Fleyming, his spouse; James Bischope, burges of Edinburgh.

Dilaittit of airt and pairt of the crewell murthour of umquhill Robert Hunter, indweller in Birsto, at the leist committit be the personis on pannel be thair hounding out of Johnne Muir, tailyeour, indweller in Edinburgh, and of the speciall caussing of the said James Muir and Margaret Fleyming, his spous, and of the said James Bischope, quha was murdreist be the said Johnne Muir off thair speciall caussing, sending out, as said is, upoun the secund day of Merche last 1642, be way of hamesuckin within his awin dwelling hous in Birsto, in forme and mainer specifeit in the criminall letters direct againes thaim thairanent.[5]

Persewaris.—Euphane Speid, the relict; Thomas Hunter, eldest sone; Alexander Hunter in Westhousses, as brother to the defunct; Sir Thomas Hoip of Craighall, knycht barronet, his Majesteis Advocat, for his hieneis intreis.

Prelocutouris in defence.—Mr. Thomas Nicolsone; Mr. James Baird, advocatis.

[1] i.e. this was not a completed rape.

[2] An extract of the conviction in slightly different terms in *RPC*[2] VII.531.

[3] See legal note 3.

[4] Bristo then a village on the south boundary of the city, now well within it and between the Old College and the Royal Infirmary.

[5] See legal note 1.

The persewaris producit the criminall letters deulie execuit and indorsat upoun the haill defenderis insert thairintill, and namlie [*specially*] upoun Johnne Muir, tailyeour, indweller in Edinburgh, principall committer of the said crewell murthour of the said umquhill Robert Hunter, quhairby he being lawfullie chairgit be William Mowatt, messinger, to haif fund cautioun actit in the buikis of Adjornall for his personall compeirance befoir his Majesteis Justice and Justice Deputtis this day and plaice to haife underlyne the law for the said crewall murthour, quhilk chairge was execuit be the said William Mowatt, messinger, upoun the sevint day of Merche last 1642, the said Johnne Muir for his disobedience in not finding of the said cautioun was, upoun the fourteine day of the said moneth of Merche, deulie and ordourlie denuncit rebell and put to the horne be James Grahame, messinger, be vertew of the saidis criminall letters, and registrat at the said process of horneing upoun the fyfteine day of the samyn Merche, conforme to the Act of Parliament; upoun the productioun quhairof the persewaris askit instrumentis and protestit for thair cautioneris releiff.

The pannell takis instrumentis of thair entrie and compeirance and protestis for thair cautioneris releiff, as also takis instrumentis of the not compeirance of Johnne Muir, committer of the said slauchter, quha thairby and be his absence hes takin the cryme upoun him.

The samyn day the said Johnne Muir, tailyeour in Edinburgh, as principal actour and committer of the slauchter and murthour of umquhill Robert Hunter, eftir productioun of the criminall letters abonwrittin, being oft tymis callit to haif compeirit befoir his Majesteis Justice Generall and Justice deputtis this day and plaice to haif underlyne the law for the slauchter abonwrittin, lawfull tyme of day biddin and not compeirand, the Justice thairfoir be the mouth of John Hamiltoun, dempster of court, decernit and adjudgit the said John Muir tailyeour in Edinburgh for his absence and not compeirance to be declairit outlaw and fugitive fra our soverane lordis lawis, and all his moveabill guidis to be escheit and inbrocht to his Majesteis use, as fugitive thairfra, for the cryme foirsaid; quhairupoun the persewaris askit instrumentis.

The personis on pannell offerris thaimselffis reddie to abyd the tryell of the law for the crymis lybellit agains thaim as altogidder innocent thairof and disassentis *simpliciter* to all farder continuatioun, and thairupoun askit instrumentis.

The Justice continewis this dyet to Fryday nixt, the tent of Junii instant, and ordanis the pannell to find cautioun for thair re-entrie that day, ilk persone under the paine of twa hundreth merkis. For obedience quhairof compeirit Robert Jacksone, maltman, at the wast port of Edinburgh, quha became cautioun for the entrie of the said James Muir and Margaret Fleyming his spous; And siclyk compeirit David Newlandis merchand and Hew Kennedie, skynner, quha become cautioun conjunctlie and severallie for the said James Bischope, skynner, that they and ilk ane of thaim sall compeir befoir his Majesteis Justice and Justice deputtis the said day and plaice to the effect and under the paines foirsaid, quhairupoun the persewaris askit instrumentis.

The personis of assyse togidder with the witnesses summond to this day, ar wairnit *apud acta* to compeir the said tent day of Junii instant, ilk persone under the paine of twa hundreth merkis.

[10 June 1642: Colvill and Robertoun JJ.D.]

Intran.—eodem die.—James Muir, tailyeour in Birsto; James Bischop, skinner burges of Edinburgh; Margaret Fleyming, spous to the said James Muir.

Dilaittit of airt and pairt and being in cumpany with Johnne Muir, tailyeour, indweller in Edinburgh at the slauchter of umquhile Robert Hunter in Birsto.

Persewaris.—Euphane Speid, the relict; Thomas Hunter, eldest sone; Sir Thomas Hoip *etc.* his Majesties Advocat.

Prelocutouris in defence.—Mr. James Baird; Mr. Thomas Nicolsone.

The pannell takis instrumentis of thair entrie and protestis for thair cautioneris releiff.

The persewaris producit the witnesses following viz. Robert Muir indweller in Innerask,[1] Johnne Riddell, indweller in Edinburgh, Johnne Or, warkman in Edinburgh, Andro Walker, warkman thair, Johnne Aytoun, warkman thair, Johnne Pattoun, theiker [thatcher] in Pleisance, James Ferrie, indweller in Edinburgh, James Halyburtoun, cordiner in Birsto, Robert Ralstoun, notter in Edinburgh, James Pithie in Sanct Mairie Wynd, Robert Blaikie in Wasthousses, Johnne Muir, scholemaister at the wast port of Edinburgh, David Gibsone, procuratour befoir the commissaris of Edinburgh, Thomas Tait in the Potteraw, George Young, meilmaker thair, and desyret that thai micht be ressavet, sworne, and examinat for clearing to the assyse of the fact and deid lybellit in the dittay anent the pannellis guiltines thairof.

To the quhilk the pannell and thair procuratouris answerit that unto the tyme the dittay be fund relevant and remittit be the Justice to the knawledge of ane assyse, na witnesses can be ressavit, bot the said dittay being fund relevant and referrit to ane assyse the probatioun be witnesses and thair declaratioun most be maid judiciallie in presens of the judge pairtie and assysouris conforme to the Act of Parliament [1587 cap. 91].

The Justice continewis the dyet anent the tryell of the slauchter lybellit to Tysday nixt, the xiiii day of Junii instant, and ordanit the witnesses abone nominat to be examinat in this matter to be present the morne in the counsall hous, and thair to mak and set doun thair several depositiones accoirding to the interrogatouris to be prononet and producet thairintill be the persewaris, and thairfoir ordanit the pannellis to find cautioun for thair re-entrie and compeirance the said xiiii of Junii instant to underly the law for the cryme foirsaid under the panes contenit in the Actis of Parliament, to the ressaveing and admissioun of the quhilkis witnesses, the pannell with thair prelocutouris consentit, upone conditioun that thai may haif witnesses summond to the said day for proveing of sic exceptiones and alledgeances as sall be proponit in this caus for cleiring of thair innocencie of the cryme lybellit, to the quhilk the persewaris with his Majesteis Advocat condiscendit [agreed], quhairupone the pannell askit instrumentis.

The pannell and thair prelocutouris desyret that at the examinatioun of the witnesses foirsaidis thay may be present to heir and understand of thair declara-

[1] Inveresk.

tioun and depositiones to be maid be thame in the premisses. The persewaris craves the lyk that thay or sic utheris as sall be nominat be thame may be also present at the examinatioun of the witnesses.

The Justice ordanis ather pairtie, alsweill persewaris as defenderis, to nominat ane to be present for ather of thame to heir the saidis witnesses depositiones; accoirding to the quhilk Mr. Johnne Oliphant was nominat be the persewaris, lykas Robert Fleming, mercheand, lait bailzie of Edinburgh, was nominat be the defenderis to be present at the saidis witnesses exmination.

The Justice, as of befoir, continewis this dyet to Tysday nixt, and ordanit cautioun to be fund be the pannell for thair re-entrie that day to the effect and under the panes foirsaidis, quha for obedience fand Robert Jaksone cautioun for the said James Mure and also David Newlandis, merchand, and Hew Kennydie, skynner, cautioneris conjunctlie and severallie for the said James Bischope thair re-entrie the said 14 of Junii nixt to the effect and under the panes foirsaidis, quhairupone ather pairtie *hinc inde* askit actis and instrumentis.

(223) [14 June 1642: Colvill and Robertoun JJ.D.]

Sla[uchter]. Edinburgh. Tertio Itineris xv^{im} dierum.

Intran.—James Muir in Birsto; Margaret Fleyming, his spous; James Bischop, skynner burges of Edinburgh.

Dilaittit of airt and pairt of the slauchter of umquhill Robert Hunter in Birsto, comittit be way of hamesuckin within his awin dwelling hous thair upoun the secund day of Merche last 1642.

Persewaris.—Euphane Speid, the relict; Thomas Hunter, eldest sone; Sir Thomas Hoip etc. his Majesteis Advocat.

Prelocutouris in defence.—Mr. James Baird; Mr. Thomas Nicolsone.

The pannell takis instrumentis of thair entrie, as also that the witnesses ressavit the last dyet of this proces ar examinat, and offeris thaimselffis to the tryell of the law for the alledgit cryme lybellit as altogidder innocent thairof, and craives that the lybell may be discussit presentlie anent the relevancie thairof, and that the samyn being fund relevant may be remittit to the knawledge of ane assyse, speciallie in respect that the witnesses ressavit the last dyet ar examinat alreddie, quhilk is extraordinar and aucht to haif beine done in presence of the pannell and assyse.[1]

My Lord Advocat takis instrumentis of the examinatioun of the witnesses, and craives that he may haif ane competent day assignit to him for examinatioun of mae [more] witnesses.

To the quhilk the pannell and thair procuratouris altogidder disassentis, inrespect the witnesses ar examinat alreddie, quhilkis witnesses sould haif beine examinat in presence of the pannell and assyse the last dyet of the procese, at quhilk tyme, gif the samyn had beine done and the witnesses ressavit and examinat in presence of the assyse, my lord Advocat could haif craivet no delay, and thairfoir now haifeing gottin thaim extraordinarlie examinat, na mae witnesses can be

[1] See legal note 2.

ressavit or examinat, bot the dittay with the probatioun thairof aucht to be referrit to the knawledge of ane assyse without farder continuatioun.

The Justice [*sic*] continewis the tryell of this matter to ane fyfteine dayis wairning, and ordanit the pannell to find cautioun for thair re-entrie and compeirance being within the cuntrie, within the said spaice of fyfteine dayis being chairgit to that effect, and upoun lx dayis wairning incaice they or any of thaim be furth of the cuntrie for the tyme, to underly the law for airt and pairt of the **(224)** slauchter of the said umquhill Robert Hunter, to the quhilk continuatioun and finding of the said cautioun the pannell altogidder dissassentit; nevertheles for obedience of the said Justice ordinance compeirit Robert Jacksone, maltman at the west port of Edinburgh, and become actit and oblesit as cautioner and souertie for the said James Muir and Margaret Fleyming, his spouse, and siclyk compeirit David Newlandis, merchand burges of Edinburgh, and become actit and obleist as cautioner and souertie for the said James Bischop, that they sall compeir befoir his Majesteis Justice and his deputtis the thrid day of the nixt Justice air of the Sherefdome of Edinburgh quhairin they dwell, or soner, quhan or quhair it sall pleis our soverane Lord or pairtie grevit upoun fyfteine dayis wairning, they being within this kingdome for the tyme, and incaice of thair being fuirth thairof upoun lx dayis wairning, to underly the law for airt and pairt of the slauchter of the said umquhill Robert Hunter under the paines contenit in the Actis of Parliament, with this provisioun alwayis that incaice of thair being furth of the cuntrie, as said is, na letters to be direct agains thame befoir Mertimes nixt and that upoun thrie monethis wairning to be given to thame for thair compeirance as said is.

LEGAL NOTES

1. Apart from the notorious case of Muir of Auchendrayne (1611) this is the first case noted of incitement to murder. It was overlooked by Hume in treating of this topic (I.267, 278-9).

2. It was futile for the panels to complain of the examination of the witnesses outwith the presence of the assize, as being contrary to 1587 cap. 91 (p. 523), for they had expressly consented to this (p. 522), but they were entitled to object to the leading of further evidence to which they had not consented. The practice of disregarding the statute was of long standing, and Hume (II.405) is wrong in thinking that *Crichton of Frendraught* v *Lady Rothiemay*, 1636, above i.280, is the first example, and in any event, there the defence expressly consented. The first instance in these (printed) volumes is *Lord Advocate* v *Gourlay*, 1626, above i.49, 52, where the only objection taken was not to the deposition procedure in general, but to the facts that the witness was a *socius criminis* and that the deposition was privately taken and not before the Presbytery.

[7 June 1642: Robertoun J.D.]

Sla[*uchter*]. *Burnes* contra *Moreisone. Continewit to the morne. Convict et decollat.*

Intran.—Johnne Moreisoune in Cambus;[1] Robert, David, and Patrik Moreisounis, his thrie sones.

Dilaittit of airt and pairt of the crewall murther and slauchter of umquhill James Burne in Cambus, within the sherefdome of Clekmannane, comittit upoun

[1] Just west of Alloa; the panels' names are given as 'Moreis' in *RPC*2 VII.237. It later appears the father was charged as principal.

the aucht day of Apryll lastbypast, 1642, upoun the arrabill landis of Cambus occupyit be the said umquhill James Burne in mainer specifeit in thair dittay.[1]

Persewaris.—Marioun Chrystie, the relict; Issobell Burne, laufull dochter; Johnne Thomas, and Robert Burnes, as brether; James Burne, as brother sone to the defunct; Sir Thomas Hoip of Craighall, knycht barronet, his Majesteis Advocat, for his Hienes intreis.

Prelocutouris in defence.—Mr. James Baird, Mr. Johnne Nisbett,[2] advocattis.

The persewaris producit the letters deulie execuit and indorsat, togidder with ane Act of Counsall quhairby Johnne Dow in Allaway[3], Robert Moreis in Newbigging, and Patrik Moreis in the town of Tulliebodie, upoun the twentie sevint day of Apryll last, become actit and obleist in the saidis buikis of Secreit Counsall[4] as cautioneris and souerteis, conjunctlie and severallie, for the saidis Robert, David, and Patrik Moreisounis, sones to the said Johnne Moreisoune in Cambus, to enter and presentt thame befoir his Majesties Justice and his deputtis this day and plaice or ony uther day quhairunto they salbe lawfullie wairnit, to underly the law for the slauchter abonespecifeit, ilk ane of thame under the paine of fyve hundreth merkis; upoun the production quhairof they askit instrumentis and protestit for releiff of Robert Burne, tailyeour burges of Edinburgh, thair cautioner.

The pannell takis instrumentis of thair entrie and protestit for thair cautioneris releiff, and thaireftir alledgit that na proces can be led againes thaim at the leist againes the saidis Robert, David, and Patrik Moreisonis, sones to the said Johnne Moreisoune, inrespect they war not lawfullie chairgit, nor na chairge was given to thame to compeir this day and plaice to underly thair lawfull tryell for the said alledgit cryme, nor yit was thair any coppie of thair dittay given to thame for that effect, and thairfoir craivit of my Lord Justice to haif ane competent day assignit to thame to anser to the said dittay, and they in the meane tyme to haif inspectioun thairof.[5]

The Justice continewis the tryell of the said Robert, David, and Patrik Moreisones for the cryme foirsaid to ane fyfteine dayis wairning, and ordanit cautioun to be fund be thaim for thair compeirance within that spaice quhenevir they sould be chairgit, ather personallie or at thair fatheris dwelling hous in Cambus, and be oppin proclamatioun at the mercatt croces of Stirling and Clekmannane, to compeir befoir his Majesties Justice to underly the law for the cryme foirsaid, ilk ane of thaim under the paine of fyve hundreth merkis money, for obedience quhairof compeirit Johnne Howstane, burges of Stirling, Johnne Moreisoune, couper thair, Johnne Dow in Allaway, Robert Moreisoune in Newbigging, and Patrik Moreisoune in the town of Tullibodie, quha become

1 Further details are given below (p. 528).

2 Though admitted advocate in 1633, this is the first appearance in these records of the future Sir John Nisbet of Dirleton, Lord Advocate and judge after the Restoration and author of the *Doubts and Questions* published in 1698. (*Lyon's List*, p. 165.)

3 Alloa.

4 No record of this in surviving *RPC* but it is recorded that the panels at their own request were transported from Stirling to Edinburgh for trial (*RPC*[2] VII.237).

5 See legal note 1.

actit and obleist as cautioneris conjunctlie and severallie for the saidis Robert, David, and Patrik Moreisonis, sones to the said Johnne Moreisoune, to enter and presentt thaim befoir his Majesties Justice and his deputtis in the tolbuith of Edinburgh at quhat tyme or how soone it sall happin thaim to be chargit in mainer foirsaid, upoun fyfteine dayis wairning, and underly the law for the said alledgit cryme ilk ane of thaim under the said paine of fyve hundreth merkis.

Thaireftir, the said dittay being red, and the said Johnne Moreisone in Cambus being accusit be vertew thairof for airt and pairt of the slauchter abonespecifeit, it is alledgit be the said Mr. Johnne Nisbett, as procuratour for the thrie sones, that he takis instrumentis of the reiding thairof, and that it is acknawledgit be the dittay that the stroak with the quhinger was gevin be nane of the thrie sones, nawayis acknawledging that the said stroak was given be the father.

To the quhilk it is anserit be my Lord Advocat that, except Johne Moreisoune, the father, now upoun pannell, and his procuratouris confess the stroak with the quhinger to be given be himselff allanerlie and not be ony of the sones, the dittay standis relevant bayth agains him and his sones.

It is duplyit for the pannell that he opponis the dittay beiring the said acknawledgment, and that it is a great inconsequence for the pannell that unles he as father tak upoun him the cryme, that the dittay quhilk cleires the sones in sua far as concernis the stroak with the quhinger, sould conclud ather him or his sones to be airt and pairt of the slauchter, quhilk mycht haif beine committit be ane uther, lykeas the pannell condiscendis upoun James Hendersone, the defunctis sone in law, to be the giver of the said stroak.

To the quhilk it is anserit be the persewaris that the alledgance foirsaid aucht to be repellit inrespect of the dittay.[1]

It is craived be the procuratouris for the father, now upoun pannell, that they may haif ane sight of the dittay and ane competent tyme grantit to thaim to advyse thairwith in regaird that he hes not so meikill seine the same or any coppie thairof, it neiver being hard in any judicatorie that ane man sould be put to anser anent any thing, meikill mair upoun his lyff, without inspectioun of his claime or dittay, quhilk was never refuisit, nor can be refuisit to any.

It is anserit thairto be the persewaris that, in respect the pannell was takin with hoatt bluid, thaireftir committit to prissone, quhairin he hes remanit this moneth bygaine, during the quhilk tyme he might haif had recourse to the clerk for obteaning sicht of the dittay or ane coppie thairof.[2]

It was urgit for the pannell that, seing he never saw the dittay nor was summond to anser thairto, that he aucht both to be summond and get ane coppie of his dittay, seing it was never hard that any pairtie was put to the knawledge of ane assyse without ane sight of the dittay; and quhair it is alledgit be my Lord Advocat that he was takin with hoatt bluid, he cannot be said to be taine with hoatt bluid because he denyis the cryme, nather is it provin as yit that he did the samyn; and quhair it is alledgit that he is takin out of prissone it is anserit that his imprissonment is not a declaratour of his guiltines and cannot prejudge him of the benefeit of the law quhilk is undenyit to any subject.

[1] See legal note 2.
[2] See legal note 3.

The Justice continewis the dyet to the morne, and ordanit the pannell to haif ane sicht of the dittay in the meane tyme, with this provisioun, that he be content that the witnessis to be producit be the persewaris for cleiring to the assyse of the pannellis guiltines of the cryme lybellit, to be ressavit and examinat.[1]

Thaireftir the witnessis following viz. James Kirk in Allaway, John Andersone in Blakgrynge, Johnne Artcher in Powhous, Robert Campbell, maltman, in Stirling, and Robert Howstane, baxter thair, being callit upoun war, of consent of pairtie, ressavit, sworne, and admittit, and ordanit be the Justice to compeir eftirnoone to be examinat, and continewis as of befoir the dyett to the morne ordaining the pannell to be taine bak to waird in the meane tyme.

The personis of assyse wairnit *apud acta* ilk persone inder the paine of twa hundreth merkis.

(216) [8 June 1642: Colvill and Robertoun JJ.D.]

Sla[*uchter*]. *Burnes* contra *John Moriesoun in Cambus. Convict. et decollat.*

Intran.—eodem octavo Junii—Johnne Moreisoune in Cambus.

Dilaittit of airt and pairt of the slauchter of umquhill James Burne in Cambus committit upoun the aucht of Apryll lastbypast.

Persewaris.—Marioun Chrystie, the relict; Issobell Burne as dochter; Johnne Burne, Thomas and Robert Burnes, brether to the defunct; James Burne brother sone; Sir Thomas Hoip of Craighall knycht, etc.

Prelocutouris in defence.—Mr. John Nisbett, Mr. James Baird, advocattis.

The pannell being demandit be the Justice gif he had cum to ane remorse of conscience for the slauchter of umquhill James Burne, committit in mainer specifeit in his dittay, and earnestlie desyrit to cum to ane cleir confessioun thairof,[2] he with great repentance confessit and declairit judiciallie that he tuik the foirsaid slauchter upoun himselff, and that he gaive the said stroak with the quhinger to umquhill James Burne himselff and crap [crept] to him upoun his kneis, the said James Burne being lying upoun his youngest sone for the tyme,[3] affirmeing with great attestatioun that as he sould anser to God at the latter day of judgement that his thrie sones war altogidder frie of the said slauchter, bot that he himselff was the only man that gave the said stroak to the said James Burne, quhairof he deceissit, and craivit God mercie thairfoir, and the relict dochter and remanent freindis persewaris for the same, and earnestlie prayit thaim nawayis to persew his thrie sones for that slauchter, they being altogidder innocent thairof, as he sould anser to God.

1 See legal note 4.

2 Evidently the evidence of the previous day had been convincing. The Justice Depute was apparently satisfied of the panel's guilt, and was not inhibited from saying so in calling on him to plead.

3 See legal note 5.

The Justice, in respect of the pannellis confessioun and declaratioun abone-writtin, ordanit the pannell to be put to the knawledge of ane assyse for the said cryme.[1]

Compeirit thaireftir Mr. Johnne Nisbett as procuratour for Robert, David, and Patrik Moreisonis, sones to the said Johnne Moreisoune now upoun pannell, and in thair namis askit instrumentis of thair fatheris former confessioun and declaratioun maid be him, and protestit that in regaird of the thrie sones innocencie they may be fred from all criminall persuitt for the said slauchter in any tyme cumming.

My Lord Advocat askit instrumentis and protestit in the contrair.

Assisa.—Johnne Archbald in Kirkfald of Tillibodie; William Cowstane in Ferritoun; Johnne Gallaway in Menstrie; Malcolme Alexander in Gairnell of Menstrie; Archbald Rewll in Athray [Airthrey]; William Chrystisone, elder, at the brig of Stirling, chancellour; Patrik Wright in Logie; David Jamesone in Tillibodie; Johne Rany, smyth thair; William Ker, thair; Alexander Ramsay in Ferritoun; Johnne Younger, thair; Robert Miller in Mainer; Johnne Alexander in Mainernewk; James Hendersone at the brig of Innerallane.

The Advocat takis instrumentis of the sweiring of the assyse and protestit for wilfull errour in caice they acquit.

Quhilkis persones of assyse being ressavit, sworne and admittit, eftir accusatioun of the said Johnne Moreisoune be dittay for the cruell slauchter and murther of the said umquhill James Burne in Cambus be cumming with his thrie sones viz. Robert, David, and Patrik Moreisonis upoun the aucht day of Apryll last bypast, being boddin [equipped] with quhingeris, battounis, and utheris wappones invasive, to the grund and landis of Cambus neir to the brig of Tillibodie, quhair the said James Burne with James Hendersone, his sone in law, war in sober and quyet mainer for the tyme teilling and labouring the land occupyit and possest be the said James, and thair invaddit and persewit him for his slauchter [i.e., with the intention of], gave him ane cruell and deidlie stroak in the foirheid with ane battoune, quhairwith he fell down to the grund upoun his faice and was not abill to ryse agane, and thaireftir the said Johnne Moreisoune, the father, come to the said umquhill James Burne being lying upoun his faice as said is, gave him ane deidlie stroak with ane drawin quhinger in the back throw his bodie to the effusion of his bluid, off the quhilkis stroakis and deidlie woundis the saidis James Burne, presentlie deceissit, committit upoun set purpoise, provisioun, and foirthocht fellonie, as at lenth is contenit in his said dittay. The saidis personis of assyse thaireftir removit altogidder furth of court to ane secreit pairt within the said tolbuith quhair they be pluralitie of voittis electit and chuisit the said William Chrystisone in chancellour, thaireftir ressonit and voittit upoun the said pointis of the said dittay and being ryplie and at lenth advysit thairwith, togidder with the judiciall confessioun and declaratioun maid be the said Johnne Moreisoune, quha tuik the cryme upoun him, and that the stroak with the quhinger was given be him to the said umquhill James Burne quhairof he decissit,[2] they re-enterit againe in court quhair they all in ane voice be the repoirt and

[1] See legal note 6.
[2] See legal note 7.

declaratioun maid be the said chancellour, fand, pronuncit, and declairit the said Johnne Moreisoune in Cambus to be fyllit culpabill and convict of the slauchter abonwrittin of the said umquhill James Burne. For the quhilk caus the Justice, be the mouth of Patrik Barrie, dempster of court, decernit and adjudgit the said Johne Moreisoune to be taine to the Castelhill of Edinburgh upoun Fryday nixt, the tent day of this instant, and thair betwix twa and thrie eftirnoone, his heid to be strukin from his bodie, and all his moveabil guidis to be escheit and inbrocht to his Majesties use for the said cruell slauchter, quhilk was pronuncit for dome.[1]

LEGAL NOTES

1. It was improper that the panels should not have received a copy of the criminal letters, but they also complained (p. 525) that they were never charged to compear. If that was so, it is odd that the pursuers are narrated to have produced the letters duly executed and that security had been found for the panels' compearance. While the sons were granted an adjournment, the trial procecded against the father (p. 525), and it was not until later that he protested that he also had not received a copy.

2. This is the second case in these two (printed) volumes where a third party was blamed, though naturally the Lord Advocate replied that this was contrary to the libel (p. 526). The first was *Paton* v *Wilson* 1641 above p. 458.

3. The Crown seem to have expected the father to have applied for a copy of the letters himself, which seems absurd even if he was in prison (see p. 526).

4. The father was only allowed a sight of the letters on condition that he consented to an immediate examination of the witnesses (p. 527). This was harsh. No jury had been empanelled, and there was no time for him to consider the charge before the evidence was led.

5. The facts are so obscurely stated (p. 527) that it is impossible to tell whether they would have justified a plea of provocation. The sentence, however, does not suggest that provocation was involved.

6. This is another case where, despite a judicial plea of guilty, the panel was put to an assize (p. 528).

7. The conviction seems to have proceeded on the confession, and not on the evidence led the afternoon before. The depositions do not seem to have been read (p. 527).

8. There is no record of any further proceedings against the three sons, so evidently the father expiated the alleged guilt of the family.

(220) [9 June 1642: Colvill and Robertoun JJ.D.]

[*Demembration*]. *Alexander* contra *Young*. *Past fra.*

Intran.—The samyn day David Young, eldest lauchfull sone to David Young of Kirktoun.

Dilaittit of the cruell and malicious pluffing [blowing] out, with ane pluff and ane hard clay bullett being thairintill, of Andro Alexander, lauchfull sone to Andro Alexander in Kirkcaldie, of his left eye (his rycht eye being of befoir lost and tint in the pox), and thairby dismembering him of his said left eye, being the only eye quhairwith he had sicht, and sua making him altogidder blind, committit in the moneth of Julii 1641.

Persewaris.—Andro Alexander, as father to the said Andro Alexander younger, his sone; Andro Alexander, younger.

The persewaris producit the letters deulie execuit and indorsat upoun the said David Young, sone to the said David Young of Kirktoun, defender, askit instrumentis thairupoun, and protestit for thair cautioneris releiff.

[1] See legal note 8.

The pannell askit instrumentis of his entrie and offerit himself reddie to underly the law for the cryme abonwrittin, specifeit in the letters, as altogidder innocent thairof, and protestit for his cautioneris releiff.

The persewaris thaireftir being demandit be my Lord Justice gif thay wold insist in the persuitt of the said David Young, younger, for the cryme abone-specifeit, the said Andro Alexander, younger, and the said Andro Alexander, his father and administratour to him for his intreis, for anser thairto declairit that they and ather of thaim with ane consent and assent past *simpliciter* fra the persuitt of the said David Young, sone to the said David Young of Kirktoun, *jure lite et cause* for the said alledgit cryme, and fra all actioun ather civill or criminall competent to thaim against him for the samyn; quhairupoun the said **(221)** David Young askit actis and instrumentis, and protestit as of befoir for releiff of William Nairne in Bandarg, his cautioner, and that na letters nor chairges sould be direct or execuit agains him at the instance of the said Andro Alexander or his said father for the said alledgit cryme in any tyme cumming, quhilk protestatioun anent the said cautioneris releiff the Justice admittit.

LEGAL NOTE

Pitmedden's comment on the case (I.23) is that no decision followed on it because 'the parents transacted for their children, in respect they were but young boys at the school, and the crime was considered as done *ex lascivia et non ex dolo*'. As Sir Alexander was not admitted advocate till 1661 (*Lyon's List*, 189) he can hardly have remembered the case, but must be reporting the general understanding of the Parliament House. It is not clear whether the injury was accidental or reckless. Another case where this seems doubtful is *Black*, 1646 (*RPC*2 VIII.50) where the defender was disposed of on finding assythment and caution for a remission.

(225) [16 June 1642: Colvile J.D.]

[*Plough-breaking*]. *Gray and his tennentis* contra *George Broun*. [*Protests*].

Compeirit judiciallie George Brown in Phillopstoun, quha exponet and declairet that he was chairget be vertew of criminall letters raiset at the instance of Sir William Gray of Pittindrum, knycht, heritour of the landis of Kilpont,[1] George Lyne, James Reid, John Dik, George Scharpe, and Johne Hodge, tennentis to the said Sir William of the saidis landis of Kilpont, to find cautioun for his personall compeirance befoir his Majesteis Justice and his deputis this day and place in the hour of caus to underly the law for allegit airt and pairt of the allegit cuming with his complices upone the aucht day of Apryle last bypast, under silence and clud of nycht, to the grund and landis of Kilpont and maynes thairof, occupyit and lauboret be the said Sir William his tennentis to his use, quhair thair war foure plewis pertening to thame with the pleuch graith [gear] thairof lying upone the grund of the saidis landis, left be thame the day befoir thairupone to the morne thaireftir, to haif bene yokit upnoe the morne thaireftir, and thair expres against the tennour of the 82 Act of the ellevint Parliament of our Soverane Lordis darrest father King James the saxt of blissed memorie;[2] beirand that quhatsumevir persone or persones cuttis and distroyis

[1] Philipstoun is 4 miles E of Linlithgow and Kilpunt 1 mile ESE of Broxburn.
[2] 1587 cap. 83 in Glendook.

ony plewis or pleuch graith in tyme teilling [tilling] sall be puneisched thairfoir to death as thevis, the said George Brown with his complices insert in the saidis letters maist maliciouslie brak, cuttit, and distroyet the saidis foure pleuches with thair haill pleuch graith pertening thairto, and maid the samyn altogidder unproffitable for laubouring the saidis landis; lykas it is allegit in the saidis criminall letters that upone the day preceiding, being the sevint day of the said moneth of Apryle last bypast, the said George Brown sould have cum to the ground of the saidis landis with his complices, quhair the said George Lyne was teilling with his pleuche for the tyme, and that he and his complices maist proudlie and maliciouslie boistit the said George, thraitnet him, and avowit to cutt and distroy his said pleuch and promeist that the samyn pleuche, with all the rest of the pleuches pertening to the said Sir William Gray or his tennentis, sould nocht teill the saidis landis, bot that they sould lay the samyn waist and mak the saidis landis altogidder unproffitable to him and his saidis tennentis, accoirding to the quhilkis vowis and thraitningis sua maid be the said Geoge and his complices at that tyme, thay sould have cum under silence and clud of nycht about twelff houris at evin to the ground of the saidis landis, upone the said sevint day of Apryle last, and thair violentlie and maliciouslie sould have brokin the said George Lyne his said pleuche and haill pleuch graithe thairof, and thaireftir threw and caist the samyn in ane deip stank [pool] neirby, contravening thairby the tennour of his Majesteis Actis of Parliament and incurring the panes and puneischment abone writtin mentionat thairintill, as at lenth is contenit in the saidis criminall letters. Off the quhilkis crymes abonewrittin the said George Brown, as he was maist frie and innocent, sua he for cleiring of the samyn, immediatlie eftir the geving to him of the said charge for his finding of cautioun to underly the law for the cryme foirsaid, compeirit and willinglie offerit him selff reddie to underly the law for the cryme foirsaid as innocent of the samyn, disassenting *simpliciter* to all maner of continuatioun; and in respect the said Sir Williame Gray, nor nane of the foirnamet persones his tennentis, persewaris insert in the saidis criminall letters, nawayis compeiris this day and place befoir his Majesteis Justice to insist in the said George Brown his persute for the alledget crymes abonewrittin, quhairof he affirmet him selff to be altogidder innocent, being oft tymes callit upone to that effect and nocht compeirand as said is, the said George Brown askit instrumentis of his awin personall compeirance and offer abonewrittin, and protestit for releif of James Kay in Abercoirne, his cautioner, for his entrie and compeirance this day and place to the effect abonespecifeit, as also that na letters sall be direct aganis the said George him selff for alledget crymes abone expressit at the instance of quhatsumevir pairtie persewar in ony tyme cuming; quhilk protestatioun anent the said cautioneris releif the Justice admittit *etc.*

The samyn day compeirit Mr. Robert Patrie, writer, and producet the criminall letters, deulie execute and indorsate, purchest be Sir William Gray of Pittindrum, knycht, heritour of the landis of Kilpont, George Lyn, James Rid, George Scharp, John Dick, and Johnne Hodge, tennentis to the said Sir William of the saidis landis of Kilpont, aganes George Brown in Philipstoun, William Small, his servand, James Gray in Strabrok, and [ ] Gray his sone, be vertew quhairof the saidis James Gray, [ ] Gray, his sone, and William Small, ar denuncit rebellis and put to the horne and registrat thairat, for not finding of cautioun to haife compeirit befoir his Majesteis Justice and his deputtis this day and plaice to haif underlyne the law for cutting and destroying of certane of the said Sir William Gray and his tennentis pleughes and pleugh graith in the moneth of Apryll last, than lyand upoun the grund of the saidis landis in tyme of teilling, contrair the tennour of the Actis of Parliament, upoun the productioun of the quhilk horning againes the persones foirsaidis the said Mr. Robert Petrie, as cautioner foirsaid, askit actis and instrumentis and protestit that he mycht be fred of his cautionrie.

LEGAL NOTE

This is the first case noted of plough-breaking, which by 1587 cap. 83 was a capital offence as a statutory theft. In *Douglas of Drumlanrig* v *Scotts*, 1616 (*Pitcairn* III.382, 389) the panels were hanged under this Act for injuring sheep. It was an extension of 1581 cap. 110. In modern practice, such offences would be prosecuted summarily as malicious damage to property. See Hume I.124-125.

Prefatory note to Appointment of Lord Kerse as Justice General

On 18 November 1641 the King at Holyroodhouse appointed Sir Thomas Hope of Kerse, second son of the Lord Advocate, for one year and more during his pleasure, to the office of Justice-General of Scotland, vacant *per remotionem vel dimissionem D. Willelmi Elphinstoun novissimi justiciarii generalis,* with an annual fee of £200 sterling (a large sum in those days) out of the fines and escheats of justice courts and justice ayres. The Commission here printed is of 14 January 1642, and is reproduced in abstract in the Great Seal Register (*RMS* IX.1032, 1037). Scot of Scotstarvet's comment (*Staggering State* 159) is that he was appointed 'Justice General but by what good right I know not.'

The appointment of his predecessor, Elphinstone, is not in that register, nor recorded in the Books of Adjournal, though he sat on several occasions between July 1636 and March 1639 (above, i.276, 287, 294, 299, and see *APS* V.247, 249, 593). Brunton and Haig state he was an Ordinary Lord of Session before he became Justice-General (296). David Scot of Scotstarvet (*Staggering State*, 159) says that he retired to England for political reasons and died there 'in a hard condition as may be supposed, the King being unable to help him'.

Kerse served for an even shorter time. Having been born in 1605 he died on 23 August 1643 (*Lyon*, 105). The following was his first case, taken immediately after he had presented his commission. Pleading before him was his father, to whom he had formerly acted as advocate-depute (above, i.278). The only exception from his jurisdiction was that of the Marquis of Argyll.

(250) [7 July 1642: Colvile and Robertoun JJ.D.]

Sir Thomas Hoip of Cars, knycht, his gift as Justice Generall of Scotland.

The samyn day compeirit judiciallie the right honorabill Sir Thomas Hope of Carse, knycht, Justice Generall to our Soverane Lord, and producet his Majesties gift grantit to him under his Hienes great seall, of the dait the 14 day of Januare 1642, quhairof the tennour followis:—Carolus, Dei gratia Magne Britannie Francie et Hibernie Rex fideique defensor, Omnibus probis hominibus suis ad quos presentes litere pervenerint salutem, Sciatis quandoquidem nos non ita pridem per literas nostras patentes sub nostro sigillo de data decimo octavo die mensis Novembris ultimo elapso providimus et promovimus predilectum nostrum dominum Thomam Hop de Kerse, militem unum senatorum nostri collegii Justicie, ad munus et officium Justiciarii nostri Generalis infra hoc antiquum et nativum regnum nostrum Scotie, et nos statuentes stabilire dictam

(251) supremam curiam Justiciarie in omnibus libertatibus privilegiis et prerogativis eidem pertinentibus quequidem ob gravitatem muneris ingentes sumptus et non vulgarem curam et industriam ex parte dicti domini Thome Hope postulavit, ac nos benigne volentes annuum addere prefato domino Thome Hope ad subeundum munus fidei sue a nobis demandatum in fideli executione eiusdem, idcirco de novo fecimus et constituimus, tenoreque presentium facimus et constituimus, memoratum dominum Thomam Hope durante omnibus sue vite diebus Justiciarium nostrum Generalem, infra dictum antiquum regnum nostrum Scotie, ac dedimus et disposuimus, tenoreque presentium damus et disponimus, dicto domino Thome Hope antedictum officium cum omni cognitione jurisdictione honoribus privilegiis emolumentis commoditatibus et casualitatibus eidem spectantibus, cum potestate ei per se ipsum eiusque deputatos ab eo constituendos, pro quibus respondere tenebitur Justiciarie curias apud burgum nostrum de Edinburgum vel quecunque alia loca Justicie administrande nostris subditis commodissima et maxime idonia tenendi et affigendi, idque in omnibus causis criminalibus et civilibus[1] ad jurisdictionem Justiciarii nostri generalis per leges et praxim dicti nostri regni spectantibus, et similiter itinera Justiciarie secundum actum parliamenti anno domini millesimo quingentesimo octuagesimo septimo [cap. 82] aliaque acta eatenus confecta tenendi et affigendi omnesque literas et precepta necessaria ad hunc effectum dirigendi ac utendi et exercendi omnem potestatem et jurisdictionem Justiciario nostro generali per leges et praxim dicti nostri regni competentem, et nos pro exercendo et obeundo dicto loco et officio dedimus et concessimus, tenoreque presentium damus et concedimus, memorato domino Thome Hope totum et integrum annuum feodum et salarium ducentarum librarum monete sterline sibi persolvendum e paratissimis nostris redditibus et casualitatibus per comissionarios nostri thesaurarii computorum nostrorum rotulatori collectori novarumque nostrarum augmentationum thesaurarii aliosque receptores nostrorum redituum pro tempore, ad duos anni terminos festa videlicet purificationis beate Marie virginis et domini Petri[2] ad vincula respective insipien primum terminum solutionis ad festum purificationis beate Marie Virginis proxime sequentem, et ita deinceps annuatim et terminatim durante omnibus vite diebus dicti domini Thome; ac volumus et ordinamus dictos commissionarios nostri thesaurarii computorum nostrorum rotulatorii colectorii et novarum nostrarum augmentationum thesaurarii presentes et pro tempore existentes bene et gratanter per solvere memorato domino Thome Hope dictum annuum salarium et feodum annuatim et terminatim ut predicitur durante omnibus sue vite diebus; declaratur omni modo, prout nos per presentes declaramus, quod neque prior donatio concessi dicto domino Thome Hope neque presens hec nostra donatio antedicta officii Justiciarii nostri generalis quovismodo prejudicio erit hereditario juri Justiciarie pertinenti ad predilectum nostrum consanguineum et consiliarium Archibaldum, Marchionem de Argyle etc., infra vicecomitatum nostrum de Argyle et insulas, neque extendetur ad bondas contentas in ejus infeofamento earundum secundum eius jura et infeofamenta sibi desuper confecta et in

[1] This shows that the Lord Justice General had civil jurisdiction as well as criminal, e.g. assythments.

[2] 2 February and 29 June.

parliamento nostro ratificata, et similiter quod nullatenus prejudicio erit donationibus sub nostro secreto sigillo concessis dilectis nostris Magistro Alexandro Colvile et Magistro Jacobo Robertoune, quibus constituti sumt nostri deputati in dicto officio Justiciarie, et similiter quod memoratus dominus Thomas Hope non ulterius immediate precipiet et levabit mulctas et amerciamenta dicte curie nisi in quantum allocabitur ei per commissionarios nostri thesaurarii predicti et reliquos commissionarios nostri scaccarii, idque in satisfactionem sibi dicti annui salarii ducentarum librarum monete sterline sibi ordinati modo et durante spatio antedicto. Mandamus etiam omnibus nostris subditis ut honore afficeant et pareant dicto domino Thome Hope tanquam nostro Justiciario generali, et ut surgant et illi assistant et concurrant in omnibus administrationem Justicie et legum et actorum nostri parliamenti executionem tangere valentibus. In cuius rei testimonium presentibus magnum sigillum nostrum apponi precipimus apud maneriam nostram de Windsore decimo quarto die mensis Januarii anno domini millesimo sexcentesimo quadragesimo secundo et anno regni nostri decimo octavo per signaturam manu S.D.N. regis suprascriptam.

(252) Eftir productione and publict reading of the patent and gift abonewrittin the said Sir Thomas Hope of Kerse, knycht, Justice Generall abonewrittin, in presence of the saidis Justice deputtis gave his aithe *de fideli administratione* in the said office, and thairupone askit instrumentis and actis of court.

[7 July 1642: Hope of Carse J.C.;[1] Colvile and Robertoun JJ.D.]

Adultery and murder. [*Margaret Cuningham*]. *Convict. et decollat.*

Intran.—Margaret Cuninghame.

Dilaittit for contraveneing the Actis of Parliament[2] in committing of the filthie cryme of adulterie with Robert Innes, ane mareit man, in the quhilk filthie copulatione, in the monethe of October lastbypast, ane bairne was borne and brocht furthe be hir within the dwelling hous of Robert Law, wrycht burges of Edinburgh, to the said Robert Innes, confessit be hir to be of verritie, as also be the said Robert Innes himselff, ane mareit man,[3] quha maid his publict repentance as ane adulterer for the same in the eister kirk of Edinburgh,[4] incurring thairthrow the payne and puneischement of daithe specifeit in the said Act of Parliament; and siclyke for the crewall and unnaturall murthour of the said young infant chyld immediatlie eftir hir beiring thairof at the tyme foirsaid, incurring thairthrow lykwayis the said payne and puneischement of daithe for murdouring of the said young newborne infant.

[1] See legal note 1.
[2] See Hume I.454. The Acts were 1551 cap. 20, 1563 cap. 74 and 1581 cap. 105.
[3] See legal note 2.
[4] See J. Cameron Lees, *St. Giles*, Edinburgh (1889) p. 237.

Persewer.—Sir Thomas Hope of Craighall, knycht barronet, his Majesties Advocat for his Hienes intres.[1]

My Lord Advocat followis furthe the persuit of this dittay baithe for the adulterie and murthour joyntlie but [without] prejudice of the Act anent adulterie and payne thairin contenit quhair ane bairne is borne in adulterie.

The Justice findis the dittay relevant and ordanit the samyn to pas to the knawledge of ane assyse alsweill for the adulterie as murthour *conjunctim.*

Assisa.—John Bawdrie, smith burgess of Edinburgh; Andro Borthwick, pewderar thair; John Bawdie, pewderer thair; Thomas Inblische, pewderar thair; Jas. Campbell, merchand thair, chanceller; Thomas Armestrang, merchant burgess of Edinburgh; Jas. Melrois, merchand thair; Archd. Graham, merchant thair; Rot. Kirk, merchand thair; Andro Beattie, tailor thair; Andro Duncan, tailor thair; George Ker, tailor thair; George Norie, merchand thair; David Duncan, merchand thair.

My Lord Advocat takis instrumentis of the sweiring of the assyse, and of the judiciall confessione and declaratione maid be the pannall of the adulterie **(253)** lybellit, and for verificatione of the murthour of the chyld eftir beiring thairof,[2] repeittis the judiciall declaratione of the witnessis following, *viz.* of Mr. William Colvine, ane of the ministeris of Edinburgh, Mr. Archibald Skeldick, minister,[3] John Pearsone, ane of the bailleis of Edinburgh, Mr. Patrik Hendersone, reader thair, George Wachope, merchand burges thair, quha being sworne, declairit and affirmit that the pannell eftir hir delyverie of the adulterous chyld and murthour thairof, being brocht up to the tolbuithe of Edinburgh in ane wand [*wicker*] bed, and examinat baithe anent the beiring of the adulterous chyld and murthour of the samyn, schoe confessit[2] and declairit in thair presence and audience hir murthouring of the said chyld immediatlie eftir hir beiring and delyverie thairof,[4] and in respect of the premissis his Lordschip protestit for wilfull errour aganis the persones of assyse incaice thai acquit.

The pannell declairis that schoe confessit to the witnessis that the chyld was murthourit be hir eftir the beiring thairof, as is contenit in the dittay, quhairupone my Lord Advocat askit instrumentis.

Quhilkis persones of assyse . . . removet altogidder furthe of court to the assyse hous . . . fand pronuncet and declairit all in ane voce the said Margaret Cuninghame (conforme to hir awin judiciall confessione of hir adulterie committit be hir with the said Robert Innes and beiring of the said chyld gottin be him with hir thairintill, as also of hir awin declaratione maid be hir with great tearis of repentance that the samyn chyld was murthourit be hir to conceill and suppres hir said adulterie) to be fyllit and culpable and convict of the said cryme of adulterie committit be hir in maner foirsaid, as also of the murthour of the

1 See legal note 3.

2 She pled guilty to the adultery but not to the murder and no evidence was accordingly led to the former. The evidence on the charge of murder was of the panel's extra judicial admission during her examinations by a committee including two ministers and a bailie, while she was in custody in the Tolbooth.

3 Neither of these ministers appears thus in the *Fasti.* William Colvine may be William Colville, minister of Cramond and, after 1639, of Trinity.

4 See legal note 4.

said infant chyld borne be hir thairintill. For the quhilk caus the Justice, be the mouthe of Patrik Barrie, dempster of court, decernit and ordanit the said Margaret Cuninghame to be tane to the marcate croce of Edinburgh and thair hir head to be strukin fra hir bodie;[1] and all hir moveable goodis to be escheit to his Majesteis use as convict of the said cryme.

Amerciat

The samyn day Peter Wat, merchand in Edinburgh, Thomas Duncane, brewer thair, William Moffet, merchand thair, Thomas Gledstanes, merchand thair, George Archibald, tailyeour thair, Andro Steane, merchand thair, and Andro Cromie, merchand thair, being ofttymes callit to have compeirit befoir his Majesteis Justice and his deputtis this day and place in the hour of caus to have past upone the assyse of [the said] Margaret Cuninghame, dilaitit of the cryme of adulterie committit be hir with Robert Innes ane mareit man, and for the crewall murthour of the said adulterous chyld immediatlie eftir hir beiring thairof, in maner and at the tyme specifeit in hir dittay, as thai that war lauchfullie sumond be Johnne Hamiltoun Justice officer, being all personallie apprehendit [*cited*] to the effect foirsaid, lauchfull tyme of day biddin and not compeirand; the Justice thairfoir, be the mouth of James Douglas,[2] dempster of court, decernit and adjudget the foirsmentionat persones assyseouris for thair absence and not compeirance to be unlawit and amerciat ilk ane of thame under the payne of ane hundrethe merkis.

Legal Notes

1. Immediately after presenting his commission the new Lord Justice-General, Hope of Kerse, took his first trial, and his father, to whom he had formerly acted as advocate depute prosecuted before him.
2. The confession of the paramour, which would now be incompetent as made outwith the presence of the accused, was libelled (p. 534), but apparently not founded on by the L.A. or the assize.
3. The panel had no legal defender though on two capital charges on indictment.
4. A confession made by the panel to ministers and others in prison, when she was in such a condition as to have to be carried before them in her bed, says little for the standards of fairness of the time. But confessions to Church Court in such cases were admitted in evidence (see *L.A.* v *McCraithe* (1626) above i.47). At the trial, however, she admitted having made the confession.
5. The severity of the sentence was, of course, due to the additional charge of murder of the child. Adultery by itself was punished by banishment, as in *John McCarrell,* 1639, above p. 379.

Prefatory Note to L.A. v *Walker and others*

The previous history of the case is as follows. On 13th November 1641 the deceased's brother, John Drummie in Kirkside (of Montrose) supplicated the Estates of Parliament, on the narrative that his brother-in-law Robert Walker had committed adultery with Margaret Graham and been ordained by the Kirk Session to cease association with her, that the panels resolved to put the deceased (Robert Walker's wife) to death because she had found this out, and that they did so. Parliament was moved to grant a commission for the apprehension of the panels, and for their examination before the magistrates of Montrose, 'and for torturing thame to mak thame confess, and being found guiltie to put thame to death that the

[1] See legal note 5.

[2] It was unusual to have two Dempsters on duty on the same trial—Patrick Barrie originally, and here James Douglas.

land may be purgeit of sin' (*APS* V.706). The specification of the *modus* was quite different to that in the present indictment, in that in the former she was said to have been strangled in bed with 'ane cord or curch, and thairefter caried to the croes of Morphie (i.e. the cruives of Morphie, which is on the North Esk river, the boundary with Kincardineshire) and shott hir in thair'. The panels, it was alleged, had been examined by the laird (Sir David Graham) and the magistrates, and 'were found to varie in thair declaratiounes, so that it is presumed and thought be the haill countrie that they ar guiltie'. This supplication was granted so far as apprehension and examination by the magistrates was concerned, who were to report to the Privy Council (*Ibid.* V.396), but not as to torture for which they probably had no facilities.

The *Register of the Privy Council* then takes up the story (*RPC*2 VII.244), and narrates that as they till remain obstinate, notwithstanding the great presumptions of their guilt, it is expedient to bring them to trial before the Justice. Their Lordships directed the magistrates of Montrose to transport them to Dundee, whence they were to be passed to Cupar, whence to Burntisland, and finally to the bailies of Leith, who were to enter them in the tolbooth of Edinburgh within six hours. There is no evidence that they were ever tortured. The depositions of the panels, confessing the crime, which were put to the assize by the Lord Advocate must have been taken in Edinburgh.

[15 July 1642: Colvile and Robertoun JJ.D.]

Murder. Convict and hangit for the murthour of Issobell Drymmie.

Intran.—Robert Walker in Charletoun[1]; Margaret Grahame thair; David Grahame, hir brother, thair.

Dilaitit of airt and pairt of the crewall murthour of umquhile Issobell Drymmie, spous to the said Robert Walker, committit under silence and cluid of nycht in the moneth of [ ] lastbypast, be hounding out[2] of the said David Grahame be ather of the saidis Robert Walker and Margaret Grahame, to the committing of the said horrible murthour, in sua far as the said Issobell Drymmie being sent out of hir awin hous be the saidis Robert Walker, hir husband, under nycht to ane nychtbouris hous for ane pynt of aill, schoe was schamefullie and crewallie strangled and murthourit be the said David
(236) Grahame, quha was sent and houndit out be the said Robert Walker, hir husband, and Margaret Grahame to the committing thairof, quhilk murthour being sua committit, the said David Grahame with the said Margaret Grahame, his sister come to the said Robert Walkers hous and declairit to him that the dead [*deed*] was done, quhairat the said Robert rejoyset and immediatlie thaireftir tuik furthe the said Issobell hir plaid, hir pittiecoit and aprone, and past with the said David Grahame to the place quhair the said Issobell was lying dead and pat hir said pittiecote over hir head and knat [*knotted*] the samyn with hir aprone about hir, and wrappit hir within hir awin plaid; and thaireftir the said Robert with the said David Grahame careid hir to the mylne lead [*lade*] of Kinaver;[3] threw the quhilk lead the said Robert hir husband traillit hir to ane salmond crove [*cruive*], and tuik hir up in his armes and laid the said dead corps within the crove with hir plaid over hir; and thairby mast crewallie murthourit the said Issobell, quhilk the saidis Robert Walker, David Grahame, and Margaret Grahame confessit to be of verritie be thair depositiones.[4]

1 Just N of Montrose.
2 See legal note 1.
3 Kinnaber Mill is on the North Esk, north of Charleton.
4 See legal note 2.

Persewer.—Sir Thomas Hope of Craighall knycht, his Majesteis Advocat, for his Hines intreis.[1]

The persewer producet the dittay with the pannellis depositiones for verificatione thairof, beirand the murthour abovewrittin to be committit be the persones foirsaidis and ilk ane of thame, as also that the said Robert had lyne in adulterie by [*away from*] his wyfe with the said Margaret Grahame ane halfe yeir of befoir; and becaus he and schoe war dilaittit to the sessione of the kirk of Montrose for the said adulterie, thay thairupone consavit the daithe and destructione of the said Issobell his spouse for reveilling the said adulterie, and thaireftir pat the said murthour in executione in maner foirsaid; and upone the productione thairof askit instrumentis.[2]

Assisa.—James Dikie in Charletoun; George Dikie thair; Alexander Grahame, burges of Montrose; John Hird thair; David Buchannane thair, chancellour; William Couttis thair; George Brown thair; Robert Duncane thair; William Ker thair; James Mudie thair; Williame Jamesone thair; Johnne Deanes thair; William Caird thair; Alexander Arnet thair; David Carnagie thair.

[The assize retired] reasonet and voittit upone the poynttis of the said dittay, and upone the haill poynttis of the depositiones now producet for verification thairof. [Verdict: all three guilty of art and part. Sentenced to be hanged at the castle of Edinburgh.]

LEGAL NOTES

1. It is remarkable that about this time there should be two cases of murder involving 'hounding out' or inciting a co-accused to commit murder. See *Hunter* v *Muir* 1642 above p. 520.

2. In relation to the first two panels Hume (I.281) treats this case as one of accession after the fact which he considered a powerful circumstance in support of a charge of art and part 'as it strengthens a train of facts which go on the whole to prove participation of the enterprise, and indeed to presume a promise of that assistance which is afterwards given'. The prior plan and incitement of the third panel by the first two is specifically libelled, and the case is no exception to the principle that accession after the fact *per se* does not amount to art and part guilt of the crime libelled.

3. This is another prosecution on indictment which is comparatively rare in these volumes.

4. The indictment refers to the panels' confessions. Notwithstanding their 'obstinacy', referred to by the Privy Council, however, they appear to have been unrepresented and appear neither to have admitted their guilt or the verity of their depositions before the assize. The only evidence produced by the prosecutor was the depositions. Corroboration of such confessions —short of a formal plea of guilty—which would be essential in modern practice was apparently considered unnecessary. (Cf. *Sinclair* v *Clark* 1962 J.C. 57 per Lord Justice Clerk Thomson at p.62.)

(260) [20 September 1642: Colvile J.D.]

Contravening banishment. Thomas McKie. Continewit to Thurisday nixt the 22 *instantis.*

Intran.—Thomas McKie, sumtyme schireff clerk of Wigtown.

Dilaitit of the contemptuous contravening of ane act and sentence of banischment, pronuncet and gevin out aganis him in ane court of Justiciarie, haldin

[1] See legal note 3.
[2] See legal note 4.

within the tolbuth of Edinburgh be Mr. Alexander Colvile, his Majesteis Justice depute, upone the xvi day of Januar 1636[1] yeiris, quhairby and for the counterfuteing, fenzeing, forgeing, and devyseing of ane fals acquittance or discharge of the sowme of ane thouseand pundis money, with certane byrune annuellis thairof, addettit to umquhile Johne, Lord Hereis, conforme to ane obligatioun maid to him be umquhile Archibald McKie of Myretoun Hereis, quhilk fals discharge was deulie and lauchfullie improven befoir the Lordis of Sessioun, and conforme to thair Lordschips decreit daitit the tent day of December 1635 yearis[2] fund and declairet to be fals and fenzeit, and the said Thomas remittit to his Majesteis Justice to be puneist for the said falset; and, he being put to ane assyse for the said falset and convict thairof befoir his Majesteis Justice the said 16 day of Januar 1636, the dome and sentence of banischment was pronuncet aganis him upone the secund day of Februare thaireftir 1636, ordaning him nocht only to be declairet infamous sua to be repute and estamat, and to have lost his office and incapable of ony publict charge thaireftir, bot also adjudget to be baneischet furth of this kingdome of Scotland during all the dayis of his lyftyme, and nocht to returne bak agane within the samyn at onytyme thaireftir under the pane of deid. Quhilk dome being imbracet be him, and conforme thairto haveing past af this kingdome, he hes maist contemptiouslie returnet bak agane within the samyn, and hes remanet **(261)** thairintill doing his effairis within the schirefdome of Wigtown and stewartrie of Kirkculdbrycht and utheris pairtis, as gif na sic sentence had bene gevin out against him, incurring thairthrow the said pane and puneischment of daith as at lenth is contenit in his said dittay.

Persewar.—Sir Thomas Hoip of Craighall, knycht barronet, his Majesteis advocat.

Prelocutouris in defence.—Mr. Samuel Gray, John Dunlope, advocatis.

My Lord Advocat producet the extract of ane act of the Lordis of Secreit Counsall[3] commanding him to persew the pannell for the cryme foirsaid, off the quhilk act the tennour followis:—

Apud Edinburgh 23 Junii 1642 the Lordis of Secreit Counsall ordanis and commandis Sir Thomas Hoip of Craighall, his Majesteis Advocat, to persew criminallie to the death Thomas McKie, prisoner in the tolbuth of Edinburgh, for contravening his act of banischment, quhairby he was banischet the kingdome for falset, and nocht to have returnet agane within the samyn under the pane of deid, for doing quhairof thir presentis sall be to the said Lord Advocat ane warrand: *Extractum de libris actorum Secreti Counsilii S.D.N. regis per me Archibaldum Prymrois clericum eiusdem sub meis signo et subscriptione manualibus: sic subscribitur* Arch. Prymrose *Clericus S. Consilii* etc.; upone the productioun and reiding of the quhilk act of Counsall my Lord Advocat askit instrumentis.

[1] See above i.259, 262.

[2] This is not booked in any of the three volumes of the Acts and Decreets covering that date, viz. vols. 462, 463, 465.

[3] *RPC*[2] VII.280. These proceedings had their origin in 1641 in a supplication from the Presbytery of Wigton to the General Assembly asking for McKie's arrest. When the matter was brought before Parliament by the General Assembly his arrest was ordered. *APS* V.323.

My Lord Advocat askit instrumentis of the reiding of the dittay.

It is allegit be Mr. Samuell Gray,[1] as prelocutour for the pannell, that na process can be led this day aganis him, becaus the coppie of the dittay and the principall dittay producet ar disconforme, as also that he is nocht citet upone xv dayis as he aucht to have bene, and thairfoir desyres ane autentik coppie of his dittay and ane convenient tyme to be grantit to him to anser thairto, and that he may use his dilligence to seik his remissioun quhilk was superscryvet be his Majesteis sacreid hand, and was producet be him in excheker to have bene exped, quhilk was the speciall ground and caus of his returneing to this kingdome, being ane sufficient warrand for his returne; and craves in lyk maner delay may be grantit in this persute to the effect he may supplicat the Counsall for obtening warrand to serch out and delyverie bak to him of his said remissioun, and to mak chose of sic advocatis for his defence as understandis the estait of this cause *ab initio*.[2]

It is anserit be my Lord Advocat that the alledgeance aucht to be repellit, in respect of the coppie delyverit to the pannell, quhilk aggreis *in substantialibus* with the principall dittay, and that thair was na necessitie of geving to him of ony thairof, he being in waird and committit thairto for contravening his act of baneischment; nather can ony delay be grantit to him to seik for his pretendit remissioun, quhairupone he intendis to found his alledgeance for returneing hame agane, being expres contrair the tennour of his act of baneischment; nather can the pannell have ony continuatioun grantit for cheising of advocattis seing thair is twa compeirand this day for him.

The Advocat takis instrumentis of the pannellis judiciall confessioun maid be him this day, quha declaires that he was out of the cuntrie the space of ane half yeir eftir the pronunceing of his dome of banischment and that he hes returnet bak agane thairto without licence.

It is duplyit be the pannell and his prelocutouris that seing it is constant be the memberis of Excheker that thair was ane remissioun judiciallie to the Lordis of Excheker retenit and nevir gevin up agane, thairfoir humlie craves my Lord Justice to grant to thame ane calling day alsweill for supplicatting the Counsall as for seiking out of the said remissioun.

The Justice continewis this dyet to Thurisday nixt, and ordanis the pannell to be tane bak agane to waird; the persones summond to this day upone his assyse ar wairnet *apud acta* to compeir the said day, ilk persone under the pane of twa hundreth merkis etc.

(262) [22 September 1642: Colvile J.D.]

His Majesteis advocat contra *Thomas McKie.*

Intran.—Thomas McKie, schireff clerk of Wigtoun.

Dilaittit of his contemptuous contraveneing of ane act of banischement quhairby he being convict be ane assyse upone the saxtene day of Januare 1636

[1] Admitted advocate 1624, *Lyon's List* 90.

[2] No counsel had appeared for him in the original prosecution (above I.259, 262).

yeiris, in ane court of Justiciarie than haldin within the tolbuithe of Edinburgh be Mr. Alexander Colvile of Blaire, Justice depute, for the counterfuteing feinzeing and devyseing of ane false dischairge of the soume of ane thousand pundis money with certane byrune annuelrentis thairof addettit be umquhile Archibald McKie of Myrtoun Hereis to umquhile John Lord Hereis, conforme to ane obligatione maid to the said Johnne Lord Hereis thairanent, quhilk discharg was improven befoir the lordis of sessione and fund and declairit be thair lordschippis to be false and feinzeit; and upone the said convictione the said Thomas McKie, for the falset abonespecifeit, the dome and sentence of banischement was pronuncet agains him, ordaneing him to be declairit infamous and adjudget to be baneist furthe of this kingdome dureing all the dayis of his lyftyme and nocht to have returnit bak agane at any tyme thaireftir under the payne of dead; quhilk dome being acceptit and imbracet be the said Thomas, and hie haveing actit him selff in the buikis of adjornall upone the secund day of Februar thaireftir 1636 to pas af this kingdome with all expeditione and nawayis to have returnet bak agane within the samyn under the said payne of dead, the said Thomas notwithstanding thairof hes returnet bak agane to this kingdome and remanit thairintill in dyverse pairtis within the schirefdome of Wigtown and stewartrie of Kirkculdbrycht in plane contempt of the said act of baneischement and incurring thairthrow the said payne and puneischement of deathe mentionat in the said act.

Persewer.—Sir Thomas Hope of Craighall, knycht, his Majesteis advocat, for his Hienes intreis.

Prelocutouris in defence.—Mr. Samuell Gray, Johnne Dunlope advocatis.

My Lord Advocat producet ane supliecatione gevin in to the Lordis of Secreit Counsall be Thomas McKie now upone pannell with thair Lordschippis delyverance on the bak thairof, daittit the xxi of September instant,[1] subscryvit be my Lord Chancellour J.P.D., off the quhilk suppliecatione the tennour followis:—

My honorabill and verie good Lordis of Secreit Counsall unto your Lordschippis meanis and schawis I, your Lordschippis poore servitour and oratour, Thomas McKie, sumtyme schiref clerk of Wigtown, that quhair the unhappie misfortune quhilk befell me *anno* 1636 I was alreddie puneisched and sentenced conforme to ane Act of Counsall, quhairby I sustenet great schame and skeathe, and payit to his Majesteis thesaurar at the tyme fyve thousand merkis, quhilk hes consumet all my meanis by and attour uther extraordiner advantages takin be my creditouris in my adversitie, my poore estaite quhairupone my wyff and small bairnes sould have bene educat being morgadget upone ane claus irretant, and within the fourtie dayis grantit be the Counsall to me for setling of my affairis at hame eftir my convictione befoir I was haldin to remove out of the cuntrey, I obeyit the act of banischement, quhilk it pleaset the Kingis Majestie out of his mercie and grace to grant to me ane remissione, superscryvet withe his hand, quhairwith I returnet at the end of halff ane yeir, and the samyn being producet in Excheker it was detenit and keipit thair frome me, albeit I purchaschet the samyn upone my verie great chairges as I am able

[1] Not in *RPC*.

to qualifie bothe the purchesing and productione in Exchekquer of the said remissione be testificattis subscryvit be the Erle of Traquair, Sir John Hay, and Sir James Galloway with many utheris famous witnessis that will depone and declair thair aithes thairupone; and sensyne quhan some evill willeris procuret commissione against me to baneisch me af the cuntrey and to wraik and undoe my estait it pleaset the Lordis of his Majesteis Secreit Counsall be thair warrand and act of the dait the first of October 1639[1] to allow my remaneing in the cuntrey for setling my affairis to the first day of Maii nixt thaireftir 1640, at quhilk tyme trubles and warris be sea and land war soe great and dangerous that all passage was impeidit and all within the cuntrey keipit in, and dureing the space according to the committie, thair ordinance, within the schirefdome of Wigtown quhair I leivet, I furneischit souldieris and airmes and payit all dewteis incumbent to me and for troup and baggage horse according to my estait and thair impositione, so that I was fund helpfull and necessare to remane, lykas I have testificattis in wryt subscryvit thairupone to verefie the samyn; and in all the foirsaid tyme I have bene extreamelie puneisched bothe in my bodie and meanis, and hes lyin in miserable captivitie since August 1641[2] quhairin I doe still remane; and now I ame of new ceittit and indytit at my Lord Advocattis instance befoir the Justice Generall to be put to deathe for alledget contraveneing of the act of convictione, quhairby I was ordanit to tak baneischement upone me and be put to daithe iff evir I returnet bak agane to this kingdome; and yisterday the twentie of this instant 1642 I was pannellit upone my lyfe for alledget contraveneing of the said act, and upone certane defences proponit be my advocattis (for the tyme) that my Lord Justice Generall sould not be sudden to proceid against me for my lyfe, I being so soir puneisched alreddie, the samyn was continuit to the xxii of this instant and na langer, quhairfoir and upone the quhilk exigence my only recourse is to your Lordshippis for mercie and compassione as your Lordschippis, quha now in this poynt representis his Majestie, utherwayis my lyfe is lyklie gone: Heirfoire I humlie beseik your Lordshippis for Godis caus to commiserate my poore and hard estait and of my poore wyfe and childrene, and to grant me mercie that thair be na farder proces befoir the Justice against me in the mater lybellit in regaird of the schame, skeathe, and meserable puneischement I have sufferit alreddie, to the ruine and distructione of my poore meanis wyfe and bairnes; and that I am yit content as of befoir to tak baneischement upone me and nevir to returne under the payne of deathe conforme to the first act, and granting me ane competent tyme for my removeing out of the cuntrye or to tak sutche uther course anent the premissis as your Lordschippis sall think for saveing of my lyfe quhairof I stand in danger, at least quhill his Majesteis will and pleasour be farder knawine.

And your Lordschippis anser followis thair Lordschippis delyverance upone the bak of the said supliecatioun:—

At Edinburgh xxi Septemberis 1642, the Lordis of Privie Counsall ordanis the Justice Generall and the deputtis to proceid aganis Thomas McKie conforme to the law of the kingdome: *sic subscribitur* Loudoun Cancellarius J.P.D.[3]

[1] Not in *RPC*.
[2] See *APS* V.323.
[3] Not in *RPC*.

The said Thomas McGie and his prelocutouris takis instrumentis of the dittay producet and reiding thairof being persewit allanerly at the instance of my Lord Advocat without any informer or any pairtie pretendand intreis as greivet and prejudget be the cryme of falset contenit in his dittay; nather is he convenit for any uther fact or cryme committit be him since the dome and sentence of convictione was pronuncet aganis him, nor since his returneing to this kingdome; quhilk being premittit it is alledget be Mr. Samuell Gray, his **(264)** prelocutour, that the conclusione of the dittay cannot be sustenit aganis this pannell for his alledget contraventione of his said act of baneischement contenit thairintill, nather can he be put to the tryell of ane assyse thairfoir, becaus it is offerit to be proven for the pannell that the tyme of his returneing and entrie to this cuntrey, he had his Majesteis Remissione for the crymes of falset contenit in the dittay, and sua was *in tuto* and *optima fide* to returne to his awin native cuntrey he haveing his Majesteis gracious warrand dispensand with the factis and payne of daithe contenit in his dome, the quhilk Remissione was producet be the pannell and presenttit judiciallie to the Lordis of his Majesteis, Excheker immediatlie eftir his returneing to this kingdome quhair the said Remissione as yit remanis; at the least the clerkis of Excheker aucht to be comptable for the samyn as being the pannellis propper evident, producet out of his awin hand as ane evident importing lyfe or daithe, and sua the pannellis Remissione being sua producet the least that can be grantit in equitie and justice seing the pannell is content to verefie by the clerkis of Excheker, memberis of that court and be my Lord Advocat, persewer, thair declarationes, that the samyn Remissione was judiciallie exhebeit, red, and considderit; and farder to cleir the granting of the said Remissione be his Majestie, the pannell heir produces ane testificat under [the hand of] Sr James Galloway, Maister of Requeistis to his Majestie, testifeing upone his conscience that his Majestie out of his grace and goodnes past the said Remissione, and for verifiecatione of the productione thairof befoir the Lordis of Excheker produces the testificate of Sir Johnne Hay, than Clerk of Register and officer of estait, quhairby he declairis that he saw and red the samyn and that the samyn was producet in Excheker and red publictlie, and that he had it in his handis, as also produces ane missive letter direct be my Lord Traquair, Thesaurer for the tyme, to Sir Patrik McGie, quhairby he declairis that he saw the said Remissione producet in Excheker, and that the samyn is in the handis of Mr. Patrik Brown, presenter of the said signatour; and sua the productione of the said Remissione being soe cleirlie verefiet be the testificattis producet, and to be farder cleirit be the memberis of the Court of Excheker thair aithes, and be utheris famous witnessis, the pannell, proponeing this exceptione first dilatorie, craves ane competent day to be assignit to him for recoverie of his awin propper evident, quhilk concernis him soe neir as his lyfe speciallie seing he hes payit 5000 merkis to my lord Traquair Thesaurar for the tyme, for his Remissione and his lordschippis assistance in the expeiding thairof, and to Captane Walter Stewart 500 merkis as agent and solicitor betwix his lordschip and the pannell, with ane thousand pundis farder to Sir James Galloway for passing the said Remissione under his Majesteis sacreid hand, by and attour his great and exterordiner chairges surpassing twentie thousand merkis and extreame puneischement induret be the pannell by his miserable captivitie and lying in waird this yeir and ane halfe bygane or thairby; and thairfoir, befoir any farder procedour be in the this proces, the pannell humlie craves ane competent day to be grantit to him for recovery of his Remissione, and that Mr. Patrik Brown and utheris memberis of that court may be examinat upone oathe gif thai saw the said Remissione producet in Excheker and had the samyn in thair handis, quhilk exceptione is proponit be the pannell dilatorie.

It is anserit be my Lord Advocat that the said alledgeance in sua far as it is proponit dilatorie, aucht to be repellit in respect of the delyverance of the Lordis of Seceit Counsall, gevin upone the pannellis awin suppliecatione craveing a delay foundit upone thir selff same groundis, contenit in the said **(265)** dilatour exceptione, ordaneing the Justice notwithstanding thairof to proceid conforme to the lawis of this kingdome.

It is duplyet for the pairt of the pannell that the Lordis of Secreit Counsall thair delyverance excluidis not the pannell frome his lauchfull defenssis competent to him of the law ather dilatour or peremptour, bot gives allanerlie warrand to my Lord Justice to proceid aganis the pannell according to the lawis of the kingdome; bot sua it is that be all law and be the lawis of this kingdome, dilatouris most be first proponit, speciallie sieing this dilatour is foundit upone wreit and testificattis producet and the aithes and depositiones of the Members of Excheker quha ar all in town, and in civile materis of litle moment termes and dyetis will be assignit to persewers and defenderis for proveing of thair lybellis, replyis, exceptiones, duplyes etc. *multo magis* in this cace *ubi agitur de capite et in criminalibus.*

It is replyit be my Lord Advocat that the delyverance of the Lordis of Secreit Counsall excluidis the exceptione proponit dilatorie, becaus it is ane anser to the pannellis petitione quhairin he cravet ane delay upone thir same groundis quhilkis ar proponit in the exceptione uset dilatorie; and, quhair the petitione cravet a delay and the Lordis ordanis justice to proceid, it is ane denyell of the petitione for delay; and the similitud adducet in civill judicatoreis hes na affinitie with the criminall, quhairin according to the lawis of the kingdome thair was nevir, nor cannot be, ane day assignit to prove ane alledgeance ather peremptour or dilatour conforme to the lawis or practique of this realme the exceptione not being fund relevant and thairfor noe delay can be grantit for proveing of the dilatour.[1]

It is quadruplyet for the pannell that the alledgeance standis relevant notwithstanding of my Lord Advocat anser foundit upone the Counsallis warrand ordaneing the Justice to proceid according to the lawis of the kingdome becaus the Lordis of Secreit Counsall hes gevin ordour to my Lord Justice according to the lawis of the kingdome to judge, and sua it is that be the lawis of the kingdome dilatouris, speciallie this dilatour proponit, is ressavable *in hoc indicio*; and, quhairas my Lord Advocat wald seame to tak advantage of the ingeveing of the pannellis suppliecatione to the Lordis of Secreit Counsall and delyverance thairof ordaneing the Justice to goe one conforme to the lawis of the kingdome, anseris that it sould not be respectit, nor dois not prejudge the pannell of his exceptione, alsweill dilatour as peremptour, speciallie *in hoc indicio*, quhair the cace sua standis, and the Remissione was producet publictlie and

[1] I.e. the L.A. argued that the alleged remission was not a relevant defence at all.

judiciallie in Excheker, quhilk aucht not nor sould not in law insnair the pannell producer thairof, being his awin propper evident, bot that evin ane competent tyme most be grantit for proveing and taking of the oathes of the haveris of the Remissione and upone thair haveing thairof.

The Justice be interloquitour ordanis the pannell to propone thair alledgeances peremptorie if thai any have.[1]

The pannell for obedience to my Lord Justice ordinance now repeittis thair former exceptiones first proponit dilatorie, and now propones the samyn peremptorie, and repeittis the samyn with the haill memberis thairof and testificattis producet, and protestis that utheris famous witnessis quhom the pannell sall condischend upone may be examinat upone the haveing of the Remissione or sieing of the samyn judiciallie producet in Excheker.

It is anserit be my Lord Advocat that he takis instrumentis upone the proponeing of the pannellis alledgeance, in sua far as it beiris that the pannell, for obedience of the act of adjornall, removet furthe of the cuntrey, quhilk is the first pairt of the assumptione specifeit in his dittay; and quhair he alledges warrand for his returneing and the Remissione past be his Majesteis hand, it is anserit that the signeing of the Remissione be his Majestie could not be ane warrand to the pannell for his returne except the Remissione had bene past, componit, and exped the seillis, and the act of adjornall excluidis him obsolutlie frome returneing under the payne of deathe quhilk laid upone him ane necessitie not to returne at all, bot he mycht have sent the Remissione heir to have bene past and to have abiddin and stayit thair at his place of baneischement till he had gottin knawledge that the said Remissione was compleitlie past. *Secundo* the pannell most condischend upone the dait or tyme of his returne and quhan he presenttit his Remissione to the Excheker, and quhat anser the samyn gat fra the Lordis of Excheker, for gif it was stoppit or refuiset in respect of the haynousnes of the cryme and of the purchessing of the Remissioun fra his Majesteis obreptitiously, the pannall was *in pessima fide*, haveing returnit upone the pretence of this warrand, quhilk was no warrand to him for the ressone foirsaid, yit immediatlie eftir the refuisall he sould have returnit to his baneishment; and my Lord Advocat takis instrumentis of that pairt of the letter producet be the pannell, subscryvit be the Erle of Traquair, quhilk beiris that the Remissione was stoppit in Excheker.

Tertio as the exceptione is nocht relevant sua it is nocht verefiet, for nothing can verifie a Remissione gevin be the Kingis Majestie under his awin hand bot the signatour suprascrivit, quhilk is not producet, nather is it knawin or condischendit upone quhat was the tennour of the Remissione and quhat war the conditiones thairof.

Quarto albeit it war producet yit being stoppit or refuiset be the Excheker, quhilk is testifeit be my Lord Traquhairis letter thairfoir, and in respect thairof the alledgeance proponit peremptorie be the pannell aucht to be repellit, speciallie seing it is lybellit in the dittay that the pannell remanit within the cuntrey be the space of four yeiris and abone, and the pannell condischending upone the dait of his ingeveing and presenting his Remissione to the Excheker

[1] A dilatory defence was a preliminary one, or, as it would now be called, an objection to the relevancy, as opposed to a peremptory defence, which was a defence on the merits.

and his [?their] Lordschippis refuissall thairof, it will be constant that his four yeiris being within the cuntrey ar all eftir the refuissall or stop of his Remissione in Excheker; Lykas in respect of the notorietie of the refuissall of the said pretendit Remissione be the Lordis of Excheker and the notorietie of the pannellis falset and prejudice quhilk the kingdome sustenit and mycht susteane be his remaneing within the cuntrey the parliament gave warrand to the Erle of Galloway to tak and apprehend the pannell quha did apprehend him and bring him to waird quhair he hes remanet sensyne.[1]

It is duplyet for the pannell to the first member of the perseweris reply (that the Remissione was na warrand to the pannell to returne to this cuntrey, it not being componet past and exped throw the seallis), that the samyn Remissione grantit be his Majestie and superscryvet signatour was ane sufficient warrand to him to returne to this cuntrey and to abyde, pas, and repas, albeit evin not exped or presenttit to the Excheker, for the passing, componeing, and expeiding thairof in Excheker is onlie *in hunc effectum* for the compositione and nawayis to enervat [*weaken*] or tak away the force of the Remissione, quhilk **(267)** being anes grantit to the pannell was sufficient and wald be (gif it ware lying in judgement) presentlie sufficient to liberat the pannell *a pena mortis*, quhilk is the certificatione of the act of banischement and conclusione of the dittay, and the maist that can be inflicted upone the pannell is that same selff puneischement formerlie inflicted speciallie seing the pannell hes done his exact dilligence in presenting the samyn to the Excheker *et per illum non stetit* that the samyn was not exped, bot aucht to be reproducet to him as his awin propper evident for his defence, the uphalding or abstracting quhairof being nawayis the pannellis dead [deed]; and the pannell hes done the equivalent as gif the samyn had bene componit and exped since he hes producet my Lord Traquhair his letter, beiring the foirsaid Remissione to be producet, to quhome the fyve thousand merkis abonementionat was delyverit as for the compositione thairof, and for his assistance, quhilk the pannell uses *in hunc effectum* to verefie the productione of the said Remissione in the Excheker; and quhairas it is replyit that the pannell mycht have remanit at the place of his baneischement quhill his Remissione had bene exped, yit his returneing being warranted be his Majesteis superscryvit signatour is sufficient, albeit he had bene onlie beirer of ane missive for saiftie of his awin lyfe, let be ane formall signatour, quhilk is trewlie testefiet to have bene superscryvit be his Majestie[2] be Sir James Galloway, his Majesteis Maister of Requeistis for this kingdome, quhilk is producet and heir repeittit, and utherwayis verefiet be Sir Johnne Hay his certificat producet and utherwayis to be verefiet be the clerkis and memberis of Excheker and uther famous witnessis *omni exceptione majores*.

Secundo to the secund member of my Lord Advocattis reply it is anserit that the pannell hes no necessitie to condischend upone the dait of his returne or presentting his Remissione to the Excheker, seing it is notour that the samyn was trewlie producet and wald be sufficient in the selff to defend the pannell *a pena mortis* gif it war heir extant in judgement as it aucht to be, and it is sufficient that the samyn is grantit befoir the tyme lybellit or in the tyme lybellit of the pannellis

[1] See *APS*, 5 Aug. 1641, V.323a, 335a.
[2] See legal note.

abode or returneing to this cuntrey, and the pannell hes no necessitie to condischend quhat anser the samyn gat past or not past being anes judiciallie exhebeit and producet; and gif neid beis it is offerit to be proven that Sir John Hay, than Clerk of Register, tuik up the said Remissione becaus he thocht the samyn was prejudiciall to him as Clerk of Register, and quha had the benefeit of presenting ane clerk to the Registratione of Seassingis and Revertiones in Galloway, to the quhilk clerkschip the pannell was provydit dureing his lyftyme, in respect the said Remissione not onlie dispenssit with the factis of falset lybellit contenit in the act of banischement, bot also a restoiring of the pannell to his former office and fame and to establische him to his former keiping of the Register of Seassingis, to the quhilk place Sir Johnne Hay had provydit Thomas Stewart, now clerk and keiper of the said register; and quhairas my Lord Advocat takis instrumentis upone the wordis of my Lord Traquairis missive beiring the said commissione [*sic*] to have bene stoppit in Excheker, the pannell declairis that he uses the samyn allanerlie in sua far as it proves the productione of the said Remissione in Excheker, and the alledget stopping thairof was nothing else bot ane halting and delay of geveing anser and no absolute refuissall at all, and albeit not past yit the samyn as superscryvit be his Majestie is sufficient to liberat the pannell *a pena mortis*; Lykas the pannellis miserable captive in waird **(268)** neir by the haill space of the tyme lybellit, and for uther great and weightie materis of the kingdome, and that seldome the tyme lybellit or of befoir thair was any sitting Excheker to give anser to the pannellis suppliecatione, quhilkis only impeidit the pannell in expeiding the said Remissione and presentting it throw the Register and Seillis.

To the thrid member of my Lord Advocattis reply, that the Remissione is not producet and sua not verefeit, the pannell for anser thairto repeitis his former anseris and testificattis producet, beiring that the samyn was producet judicially in Excheker quhilk aucht nawayis to be a snair to the pannell and to bring him in hazaird of his lyfe speciallie (as is affirmit) it being abstractit be ane member thairof in maner and for the caussis abonespecifeit.

To the fourt and last article it is anserit *ut supra* that the alledget stopping of the pannellis signatour and Remissione was naways ane absolute refuissal bot ane halting and delay for ane tyme, quhilk was not the pannellis fault, he being incarcerat the maist pairt of the space and tyme lybellit; And as for the pannellis alledget abyding within the cuntrey dureing the space of four yeiris bygane thair is allanerlie twa lybellit, nather can the samyn be respectit, becaus as the pannellis entrie in the cuntrey was lauchfull, sua was his abode thairin also lauchfull, he haveing his Majesteis Remissione *ut supra*; And, for the alledget prejudice that the kingdome hes sustenit throw the pannellis remaneing within the cuntrey, the persewer nawayis condischendis nor lybellis upone any new cryme committit be the pannell the tyme of his remaneing within the cuntrey, nor yit since his act of banischement. Finallie the pannell did na wrang in abyding within the cuntrey becaus his Majestie had formerlie gevin him libertie be the Remissione abone expressit, to returne thairto, lykas the Lordis of Secreit Counsall be thair act daitit the first of October 1639[1] upone ane suppliecatione gevin in be the pannell to thair lordschippis, allowis the suppliecant

[1] Not in *RPC*.

to remane within the cuntrey for setling of his effairis till the first day of Maii thaireftir, notwithstanding of the act of baneischement, quhairwith thair lordschips dispenssis, quhilk space is ane pairt of the tyme lybellit, the quhilk allowance of the Lordis of Secreit Counsall grantit to the pannell to remane within the cuntrey dureing the said space is not only sufficient to liberat him for that space bot lykwayis sufficient to liberat him for his alledget contraveneing his act of banischement, and quhilk Act of Counsall in effect is ane passing fra the said act of banischement and tollerating of the pannell to remane still within the cuntrey quhair he hes byddin this yeir and ane halff bygane in miserable captivitie within the wairdhous of Edinburgh throw the suggestione and instigatione of his unfreandis; And as for the pannellis alledget remaneing in the cuntrey since Maii 1640 the pannell cannot be thocht to have contravenit the act, becaus that yeir was the tyme of the trubles and thair was nothing bot warris in all sydis, baithe by sea and land, as is mair nor nottour to the haill cuntrey, soe that thair was no passage for the pannell to remove himselff out of the cuntrey being gairdit and hedget in with garisones in all sydis; lykas dureing the tyme of his abode within the cuntrey he buire burding, according to his estait and rank, in the publict effairis of the kingdome, and payit his tent and twentie penny and furneist souldieris and bagadge horse and uther personall service nycht and day, quhilk is verefeit be productione of twa tickettis, ane be Lewtennent Colonell Williame Stewart, daitit the fyft of August 1640, ane uther **(269)** be Alexander Gordoun of Achleane, daitit the auchtene of August 1640, and ane thrid be John Murdoche, proveist of Wigtown, daitit the threttene of August 1640; lykas the pannell was evir willing to subscryve the Covenant as twa suppliecationes and twa references thairin heirwith producet beiris, and sua he was a steidable member to the commone wealthe be his abyding within the cuntrey; And as for the pannellis remaneing in the cuntrey he can be in na worse caice nor thease quha war none Covenanteris and oppin ennemeis to the publict, quha abyde still within the cuntrey, and quhais factis and transgressiones ar past over and forgevin be the last parliament; And his yeir and ane halffis imprissonement may satisfie for any pretendit eschaip, gif any sall be fund being warrantit be his Majesteis Remissione *ut supra*; And, as for the tyme he hes remanit within the cuntrey since August 1641 to this tyme, that cannot be imput to him as ane transgressione of the act, becaus he hes bene keipit still in waird and brocht in be ordour and warrandis purchessit be his unfreandis and thair misinformationes alledget aganis him.

My Lord Advocat takis instrumentis of the Act of Counsall producet daitit primo Octobris 1639, geveing licence to the pannell to remane within the cuntrey to the first of Maii thaireftir, and alledges that this purges not the pannellis remaneing in the cuntrey till the dait of the said Act of Counsall and eftir the first of Maii, to the quhilk his licence restrictit him, he haveing remanit as ane contravener of the act of banischement; and albeit fra that tyme the cuntrey was in trubles yit that cannot liberat him of the payne of the act of adjornall throw his remaneing within the cuntrey; And, as to his subscryveing of the Covenant and payment of the tent and twentie penny and furneischeing horse and wadges for sojouris, it is anserit thair is nothing producet for verefieing the subscryveing of the Covenant bot only ane testificatione of the committie fra the presbetrie of Wigtown subscryvit be the clerk thairof, beiring him to be admittit to subscryve the covenant; and the beiring of his proportionable pairt of the chairges that tyme of the trubles cannot liberat him fra the payne of the act of banischement, becaus thease dewteis war payable further of his landis quhilk his wyfe, albeit he had bene furthe of the cuntrey, wald have been lyable unto; And as to the last poynt *a simili* foundit upone the Act of Oblivione[1] it is anserit that the pannellis cryme is not comprehendit under that act, and the act cannot be extendit *ne quidem a majoritate rationis* gif it war in that cace as it is not, lykas the pannell can found nothing upone the Act of Oblivione, becaus, befoir the dait thairof, the Parliament gave ordour for taking of him as ane notorious committer of falset, be vertew quhairof he was apprehendit and committit to waird within the tolbuithe of Edinburgh, quhairin he was wairdit lang befoir the Act of Oblivione, and still remanit wairdit thairintill quhill the Act of Oblivione was maid; Lykas the Lordis of Secreit Counsall, quha is the best interpriteris of the Act of Oblivione, be thair act of the dait the last day of Junii last bypast hes gevin ordour to his Majesteis Advocat to persew the pannell to the daithe for the cryme foirsaid contenit in his dittay.[2]

The pannell repeittis his former defenssis, and addis thairto that be the lait Parliament all penall statuttis is remittit and dischairget *et mors est maxima pena omni penarum.*

(270) My Lord Advocat anseris that the cryme contenit in the dittay foundit upone the act of banischement is not contenit in the penall statuttis, and the penall statuttis ar onlie pecuniall bot not capitall.

It is farder anserit be the pannell to that pairt of my Lord Advocattis former anser, anent the pannellis taking and committing to waird be directione of the Parliament, that [with] the alledget warrand gevin for his apprehensione and committing to waird be ordinance of the Parliament, thair is nothing producet be the persewer to verifie the samyn, nather is thair any new recent fact or cryme committit be the pannell dureing his abod within the cuntrey, bot allanerlie for the alledget contraveneing of the act of banischement quhilk is tane away be his Majesteis Remissione *ut supra.*

The Justice contenowis this dyet to the morne and ordanit the pannell to be tane bak to waird thairin to remane. In the meane tyme the persones of assyse wairnet *apud acta* ilk persone under the payne of thrie hundrethe merkis.

(70) [23 September 1642: Colvill J.D.]

Continewit to the xvi November.

Intran.—Thomas Makgie.[3]

Dilaittit of the crymes foirsaid specifeit in his former dittay.

Persewer.—Sir Thomas Hope of Craighall, knycht barronet, his Majesteis advocat, for his Hienes intreis.

1 According to this report the Act of Oblivion 1641 6 (for which see above p. 488, 502) was not formally pled by the defence until the L.A. put the idea into their heads (see next paragraph).
2 The order narrated above (p. 539) was dated 23 June.
3 Evidently at this date Mackie and Makgie were alternative spellings of the same name.

Prelocutouris in defence.—Mr. Samuel Gray; John Dunlope advocattis.

The Justice continowis his interloquitour upone the alledgeances forsaidis, contenit in the proces and anseris maid be his Majesteis Advocat thairto, to the saxtene day of November nixtocum, and ordanit the pannell to be returnet bak to waird in the meane tyme upone the quhilk continowatione the pannell askit instrumentis.

My Lord Advocat disassentit thairto and protestit in the contrair.

[16 November 1642 no entry]

LEGAL NOTE

This case is so diffuse that it is difficult to discern the real reason why the L.A. objected to the plea that a Royal remission for the original offence of 1636 of forging a discharge (see above i.259, 262) was a bar to a death sentence for breach of banishment. The *Privy Council Register* has nothing relevant apart from authorising the King's Advocate to prosecute (*RPC*2 VII.280), nor has Hume. Mackenzie (II.xxviii.3 where he gives the wrong date) thought the objections were (1) that the panel returned to the country before any remission was granted, and (2) that even at the diet of trial it had not yet 'passed the seals'. The first was technical in the extreme. Although the facts are far from clear, it appears that the panel had obtained a Signature superscribed by the King (see p. 543), and presented it to Exchequer as a warrant for a remission under the Great Seal, but that normal procedure was blocked in the Exchequer office, allegedly by persons acting maliciously and that the completed remission had never been issued. The royal writ itself did not constitute an effective remission until it had passed the Exchequer and the Great Seal. The function of the Exchequer was to advise on the propriety of the proposed remission, and to fix assythement when appropriate. At this stage representations could be made by interested parties, and on cause shown the remission might be stopped and a report made to the Crown. The Lord Advocate's contention was that the remission had been so stopped (p. 545). The defence denied this (p. 546-7) but neither side produced any formal minute on the matter. The Justice-Depute refused to decide anything, and the case disappears from the Books of Adjournal on 23 September 1642 when the panel was still warded.

His efforts, however, were eventually successful, Parliament on 11 May 1648 ratified an act of the Committee of Estates setting McKie (or McGhie, as he was alternatively styled), at liberty but how long he had languished in prison is not clear (*APS* VI.(ii) 123). On 2 July 1648 he seems to have got a Crown grant of a 40s. land in Penningham parish, Wigtownshire (*RMS* IX.1988).

A later case on the same topic is *Irvine* v *Bell* 7 June, 1644.

(274) [11 November 1642: Robertoun J.D.]

Murder under trust. Creichtoun contra *Urquhartis and utheris. Declared fugitive.*

The samyn day compeirit judiciallie Patrik Rankeine,[1] servitour to Mr. James Baird, advocat, and producit the criminall letters, deulie execuit and indorsat, purchest at the instance of James Creichtoun of Frendraucht, as father, Deame Elizabeth Gordoun, as mother, James Creichtoun, younger of Frendraucht, George, Frances, Elizabeth, Issobell, Marie, Heleine, and Margaret Creichtounis, as brether and sisteris, with the remanent kyn and freindis of umquhill William Creichtoun, secund lauchfull sone to the said Laird of Frendraucht, elder, and his Majesteis Advocat for his Hienes intreis, aganis Walter Urquhart of Crombie, James Urquhart of Auldcraig, Patrik

[1] Admitted advocate 1631. *Lyon's List,* p. 170.

Meldrum, sumtyme of Iden;[1] and Adame Gordoun, servand to the said Walter Urquhart, quhairby the foirnamit personis defenderis being chargit to find cautioun actit in the buikis of adjornall for thair personall compeirance befoir his Majesteis Justice and his deputtis this day and plaice to haif underlyne the law for the tressonabill, barbarous, and cruell murthour under trust and freindschip of the said umquhill William Creichtoun, secund sone to the said Laird of Frendraucht elder; and for thair dissobedience of the said charge war deulie and ordourlie denuncit rebellis and put to his Hienes horne and registrat thairat; in name and behalff of the persewaris specifeit in the saidis criminall letters askit actis and instrumentis, and protestit for releiff of George Baxter, servitour to the said Laird of Frendraucht of his cautionerie for repoirting of the samyn; Lykeas the saidis Walter Urquhart of Crombie, James Urquhart of Auldcraig, his brother germane, Patrik Meldrum, sumtyme of Iden, and Adame Gordoun, defenderis foirsaidis, committeris of the said treassonabill murthour, being oft tymis callit to haif compeirit judiciallie befoir his Majesteis Justice and his deputtis this day and plaice to haif underlyne the law for the samyn as they that war lauchtfullie chargit be vertew of the saidis criminall letters to that effect, lauchtfull tyme of day biddin and not compeirand, thairfoir the Justice, be the mouth of James Douglas, dempster of court, decernit and adjudgit and declairit the foirnamit four defenderis and ilk ane of thame to be outlawis and fugitives fra our soverane Lordis lawis, and all thair moveabill guidis to be escheit and inbrocht to his Hienes use as fugitives thairfra for the treassonabill and haynous murthour abonwrittin; Quhairupoun the said Patrik Rankeine also askit actis and instrumentis.

LEGAL NOTE

There is no specification of locus or date, but three of the accused lived near Frendraught, and since two were on the Roll of Delinquents for 1641, presumably the date was earlier (*RPC*2 VII.510-511).

(276) [22 November 1642: Robertoun J.D.]

Forbes of Bythe v *Darganoch. House-breaking. Unlaw.*

The quhilk day Robert Ker, servitour to James, Lord Carnagie, being oft-tymes callit as cautioner and souertie for reporting the criminall letters dewlie execute and indorsate and persewing thairof, purchest at the instance of John Forbes, sone to umquhile John Forbes of Bythe, to tak souertie of William Dalgarnok of Garneistown, Patrick Dalgarnok of Towie[2] of Clat, his brother, and Arthour Dalgarnok, sone to the said William, that thai sould compeir befoir his Majesteis Justice and his deputtis this day and place in the hour of caus and underly the law for breking up of ane loft chalmer within the place of Bythe in the monethe of Apryle 1629 yeiris, and breking up of ane chairtour kist

[1] Old Crombie is 2 miles SW of Aberchirder in Banffshire. Old Craig is near Daviot, Aberdeenshire, 5 miles NW of Old Meldrum. Eden is at the NW corner of Aberdeenshire, 3 miles south of Macduff. Frendraught is 6 miles east of Huntly.

[2] Byth is 4 miles west of New Pitsligo in NW Aberdeenshire. Gairniston is 3½ miles NNE of Turriff. Towie of Clatt is 2 miles E of Rhynie.

thair standing thairintill, steilling and away taking of the haill [writs] perteneing to the said John Forbes of Bythe of his landis and baronie of Byth, Fintrie and Towie Forbes, and remanent crymes contenit in the saidis letters, lawfull tyme of day biddin and nocht produceand the saidis letters deulie execute and indorsate; The Justice thairfoir, be the mouthe of John Hammyltown, dempstar of court, decernit and adjudget the said Robert Ker as cautioner foirsaid to be unlawit and amerciat in the panes contenit in the Actis of Parliament,[1] viz. for nocht repoirting the saidis letters deulie execute and indorsate upone ilk ane of the saidis thre defenderis in the pane of . . .

LEGAL NOTE

The Privy Council made provision on 28 February 1643 for the safe appearance of Patrick Dalgarno of Towie before the J.D. on 1st March 1643 (*RPC*[2] VII.401).

[1] I.e. 1535 cap. 35; 1579 cap. 78; Hume II.127

THE STAIR SOCIETY

Instituted in 1934 to encourage the Study of the History of Scots Law

---

CONSTITUTION

1. The Society shall be called 'The Stair Society'.

2. The object of the Society shall be to encourage the study and advance the knowledge of the history of Scots Law especially by the publication of original documents, and by the reprinting and editing of works of sufficient rarity or importance.

3. Membership of the Society shall be constituted by payment of the annual subscription, and shall cease if this be in arrear for one year.

4. The amount of the annual subscriptions shall be fixed by the Council from time to time, and shall be payable in advance on 1st January in each year.

5. The management of the affairs and funds of the Society shall be vested in a Council consisting of the President, Vice-President, a Chairman, a Vice-Chairman and not more than ten ordinary elected members.

6. The President, Vice-President, Chairman and Vice-Chairman shall be elected annually at the Annual General Meeting, to hold office for the following calendar year, and shall be eligible for re-election. Those elected at the Inaugural Meeting shall hold office until 31st December, 1935.

7. The ordinary members of Council elected at the Inaugural Meeting shall hold office from that date. At every Annual General Meeting thereafter the Society shall elect members to fill any vacancies on the Council that may have occurred, or that may be due to occur at the end of the year, members so elected to hold office from the ensuing 1st of January. The original members of Council shall hold office until 31st December, 1939, and, at the Annual General Meeting to be held in November 1939, all of these members, except two (selected by agreement or by lot), shall be eligible for re-election. The two so selected shall retire as at 31st December following, and shall not be eligible for re-election for one year. Thereafter, at each Annual General Meeting two of the ordinary members of Council shall retire as at 31st December following, and shall not be eligible for re-election for one year. The two members to retire annually shall be those who have the longest continous period of service and, as among those of equal service, shall be selected by agreement or by lot.

8. In addition to the elected members, the Council shall have power to co-opt as additional members of Council any member of the Society who, in their opinion, may be fitted to render special service in promoting the work of the Society. Such co-opted members shall hold office for such period, not exceeding five years, as the Council may in each case determine. At no time shall the co-opted members of Council exceed three in number.

9. The Society at the Inaugural Meeting, and thereafter at the Annual General Meeting, shall appoint a Literary Director or Directors, a Secretary and a Treasurer, and such other officers as may from time to time be deemed necessary, who shall be subject to the direction of the Council in the performance of their duties, and who shall receive such remuneration as the Council may determine. Those so appointed shall not be members of Council, but may be invited to attend any meeting of Council.

10. Any casual vacancies in the offices of President, Vice-President, Chairman, Vice-Chairman or elected members of the Council, or among the officers of the Society, may be filled up by the Council, appointments so made to be for the period till the 31st of December following the next Annual General Meeting.

11. In any year in which a volume is published each member who has paid his subscription for that year shall be entitled to receive one copy.

12. The Annual General Meeting shall be held between 1st November and 31st March at such time and place as may be fixed by the Council. If the Meeting is not held until after 31st December in any year, office-bearers and members of Council then due to retire shall remain in office until the Meeting is held. The Council may also at any time call a Special General Meeting of the Society, and shall do so on a requisition from not less than ten members, which shall specify the object for which the Meeting is to be called. Seven days' notice shall be given of all General Meetings.

13. The Constitution of the Society as contained in these Rules may be amended at any General Meeting on twenty-one days' notice of the proposed amendments being given to the Secretary and included in the Agenda circulated for the Meeting.

PUBLICATIONS OF THE STAIR SOCIETY

1. An Introductory Survey of the Sources and Literature of Scots Law. By various authors. With an introduction by The Rt. Hon. Lord Macmillan, P.C., LL.D., Lord of Appeal in Ordinary. 1936.

1*a*. An Index to Volume No. 1, compiled by James Cowie Brown, M.A., LL.B., Ph.D., was issued in 1939.

2. Acta Curiae Admirallatus Scotiae, 6th September 1957—11th March 1561-2. Edited by Thomas Callander Wade, M.A., LL.B., Solicitor, Falkirk. 1937.

3. Hope's Major Practicks, 1608-1633. Edited by The Rt. Hon. James Avon Clyde, LL.D., formerly Lord Justice-General of Scotland and Lord President of the Court of Session. Vol. 1. With portrait. 1937.

4. Hope's Major Practicks, 1608-1633. Edited by the Rt. Hon. James Avon Clyde, LL.D., formerly Lord Justice-General of Scotland and Lord President of the Court of Session. Vol. II. 1938.

5. Baron David Hume's Lectures, 1786-1822. Edited and annotated by G. Campbell H. Paton, M.A., LL.B., Solicitor, and Assistant to Professor of Law in the University of Glasgow. Vol. I. With portrait. 1939.

6. Lord Hermand's Consistorial Decisions, 1684-1777. Edited by F. P. Walton, K.C. (Quebec), LL.D., Hon. Fellow, Lincoln College, Oxford, formerly Director, Royal School of Law, Cairo. With Biographical Sketch of Lord Hermand by James Fergusson. With portrait. 1940.

7. St. Andrews Formulare, 1514-1546. Text transcribed and edited by Gordon Donaldson, M.A., Ph.D., and C. Macrae, M.A., D.Phil. Vol. I. 1942.

8. Acta Dominorum Concilii, 26th March 1501—27th January 1502-3. Transcribed by J. A. Crawford, M.A., LL.B., Advocate. Edited with an Introduction by The Rt. Hon. James Avon Clyde, LL.D., formerly Lord Justice-General of Scotland and Lord President of the Court of Session. 1943.

9. St. Andrews Formulare, 1514-1546. Edited by Gordon Donaldson, M.A., Ph.D., with Prefatory Note by David Baird Smith, C.B.E., LL.D. Vol. II. 1944.

10. The Register of Brieves, 1286-1386, as contained in the Ayr MS., the Bute MS., and Quoniam Attachiamenta. Edited by The Rt. Hon. Lord Cooper, LL.D., Lord Justice-Clerk. Thomas Thomson's Memorial on Old Extent. Edited by J. D. Mackie, C.B.E., M.C., M.A., Professor of Scottish History and Literature in the University of Glasgow. 1946.

11. REGIAM MAJESTATEM AND QUONIAM ATTACHIAMENTA, based on the text of Sir John Skene. Edited and translated with Introduction and Notes by The Rt. Hon. Lord Cooper, LL.D., 1947.
12. THE JUSTICIARY RECORDS OF ARGYLL AND THE ISLES, 1664-1705. Transcribed and edited, with an Introduction, by John Cameron, M.A., LL.B., Ph.D. 1949.
13. BARON DAVID HUME'S LECTURES, 1786-1822. Edited and annotated by G. Campbell H. Paton, M.A., LL.B., Solicitor. Vol. II. 1949.
14. ACTA DOMINORUM CONCILII ET SESSIONIS, 1532-1533. Edited by Ian H. Shearer, M.A., LL.B., Advocate. 1951.
15. BARON DAVID HUME'S LECTURES, 1786-1822. Edited and annotated by G. Campbell H. Paton, M.A., LL.B., Advocate and Lecturer in the History of Scots Law in the University of Glasgow. Vol. III. 1952.
16. SELECTED JUSTICIARY CASES, 1624-1650. Edited and annotated by Stair A. Gillon, B.A., LL.B., Advocate. 1953.
17. BARON DAVID HUME'S LECTURES, 1786-1822. Edited and annotated by G. Campbell H. Paton, M.A., LL.B., Advocate and Lecturer in the History of Scots Law in the University of Glasgow. Vol. IV. 1955.
18. BARON DAVID HUME'S LECTURES, 1786-1822. Edited and annotated by G. Campbell H. Paton, M.A., LL.B., Advocate and Lecturer in the History of Scots Law in the University of Glasgow. Vol. V. 1957.
19. BARON DAVID HUME'S LECTURES, 1786-1822. Edited and annotated by G. Campbell H. Paton, M.A., LL.B., Advocate and Lecturer in the History of Scots Law in the University of Glasgow. Vol. VI. 1958.
20. AN INTRODUCTION TO SCOTTISH LEGAL HISTORY. By various authors. With an Introduction by the Rt. Hon. Lord Normand, P.C., LL.D., Lord of Appeal in Ordinary, 1947-53. 1958.
21. THE PRACTICKS OF SIR JAMES BALFOUR OF PITTENDREICH. Edited by Peter G. B. McNeill, M.A., LL.B., Ph.D., Advocate. Vol. I. 1962.
22. THE PRACTICKS OF SIR JAMES BALFOUR OF PITTENDREICH. Edited by Peter G. B. McNeill, M.A., LL.B., Ph.D., Advocate. Vol. II. 1963.
23. THE ORIGINS AND DEVELOPMENT OF THE JURY IN SCOTLAND. By Ian D. Willock, M.A., LL.B., Advocate and Professor of Jurisprudence in the University of St. Andrews. 1966.
24. WILLIAM HAY'S LECTURES ON MARRIAGE. Transcribed, translated and edited by The Rt. Rev. Monsignor John C. Barry, M.A. (Cantab.), D.C.L. (Rome), Rector of St. Andrew's College, Drygrange, Melrose; Consultor to the Pontifical Commission for the Revision of the Code of Canon Law. 1967.
25. THE JUSTICIARY RECORDS OF ARGYLL AND THE ISLES, 1664-1742. Edited by John Imrie. Vol. II. 1969.
26. MISCELLANY ONE. By various authors. With a Preface by The Rt. Hon. Lord Clyde, LL.D., Lord Justice General and Lord President of the Court of Session. 1971.